T0369538

# AMERICA'S IRRESISTIBLE ATTRACTION

## BEYOND THE GREEN CARD

JOHN S. DINGA

ISBN: 978-1-4269-6123-6 (sc)
ISBN: 978-1-4269-6124-3 (hc)
ISBN: 978-1-4269-6125-0 (e)

Library of Congress Control Number: 2011904288

*Trafford rev. 04/01/2011*

 www.trafford.com

**North America & international**
toll-free: 1 888 232 4444 (USA & Canada)
phone: 250 383 6864 ♦ fax: 812 355 4082

# Introduction

America continues to attract like a magnet. But first, it is important to disabuse oneself of the false notion that American government will be Father Christmas, providing everything for free. In America there is no free lunch and so we learn to earn our keep!

The United States is not a utopia and living here is not quite the nirvana once imagined from back home but the imperfections have not stopped people from doing everything possible to get along. The melting pot lingo may no longer be abuzz the way it used to be, but the idea lives on in spite of the many hurdles along the way. Short term visitors, permanent residents and those that have gained citizenship can contribute in important ways. Whereas under other skies dissidents are treated as *deviants*, here in America they are considered *different* and given First Amendment protection for articulating their concerns. The rise from relative obscurity of Scott Brown of Massachusetts to become a US senator, of Arnold Schwarzenegger to become the governor of California and finally of Barack Obama to the presidency of the US are powerful messages to the world that, in spite of the many hurdles the system actually works to bring out the best in its people. The particular election cycle that led to Barack Obama becoming America's 44th president was very enriching. Once naturalized, citizens have the right to get involved with the politics of choosing who represents them at local, state and national levels, and be voted themselves if they show leadership qualities!

Family members and friends back at home do turn to resident immigrants for help in overcoming visa requirements. Some ask for direct financial assistance to make the life at home a little more livable and home remittances make up a good chunk of the home country's outlays. Successful immigrants might even invite leaders of the opposition and ruling parties back at home to come and witness American democracy in action. A stay here in the US, no matter how brief, especially during crucial elections, can help politicians see and explore plenty of opportunities to help straighten up things back at home. Nothing is better than the vast market place of ideas during election campaigns, opinion polls and other activities that enable citizens and those seeking power to gauge each others' needs. Such visits can help narrow the huge gaps that often exist between rival parties who indeed might have a lot in common yet resort to gun battles and other unorthodox means to get to power.

In spite of its many recent problems, American democracy remains a beacon for many in the world. Individuals rise to personal challenges and through team work, are able to go beyond personal needs to those of the community, the nation and the world beyond. When Barack Obama won the 2008 presidential election, one of the first calls he received was from his GOP rival John McCain, and then he appointed archrival, Senator Hillary Clinton his Secretary of State. President Obama has since used his predecessors –Bill Clinton, George Bush, and Jimmy Carter - in various missions around the world. What could be better than transplanting such practices to Egypt, Ivory Coast, Iran, Pakistan, Zimbabwe, Haiti and others where former presidents hardly exist?

But people need to know that living in America has its challenges – challenges not often imagined when the desire to immigrate pushes them to cross deserts, oceans and unfriendly skies. America makes quite an effort to provide for everybody but it is certainly not a bed of roses the way people often imagine before arriving here. Only by eating the pudding do we quite come to terms with its taste, isn't it? An important lesson that America teaches its citizens and citizens of other nations is choice, competition and freedom of the press. In science as in arts, in music as in dance, in politics as in economics, competition underpins and improves the quality of what people do. It is the antithesis of monopoly which often stymies quality improvement and subjects people to stagnation and substandard life. From the top, leaders learn to accede to elective office by submitting themselves to the rigors of election campaigns. Once they win by healthy competition they are more likely to encourage healthy competition in all spheres of life that impact the lives of the citizens – at school, at work, on playgrounds, at campsites, market places and others. Hardworking people who are prepared to put aside all past glories - big academic diplomas from home or previous important positions - and get involved with the very basics do succeed. Attending school enhances job prospects but even without it there are opportunities that provide on-the-job training. Some people choose to make a living by panhandling, others by collecting bottles and selling them to recycling plants and still others by karaoke, the only drawback being their inability to afford health insurance for the rainy day. To live in America without health insurance is reckless. For those who want the big bucks, Hollywood, sports, the music industry and Wall Street are the places to go. The incestuous staffing of public or private enterprises with persons drawn largely from the blood lines of those at the helm is doubly tragic for nationhood – not only are well deserving and meritorious congeners left out of the show, often mediocrity goes unpunished for fear of hurting village ancestors dead and alive. Getting the job of one's dream is one thing; keeping it is a different ball game altogether.

# 1.

## The Dollar Speaks.

Yes indeed, money talks – especially the US dollar - and people have to listen, if they choose to live in the United States, support a family and have some fun too. The only problem is that the dollar itself doesn't listen. And that's a big problem because while it can make ordinary mortals rise to the skies, it is equally responsible for some catastrophic downfalls, often including death.

Getting the Green Card after those long years of patient waiting may appear like the end of a very long journey until the new immigrant lands in the US only to discover that, like a toddler initiating the early steps in life, the real odyssey lies ahead. Welcome to America and to the rat race to get an education, find a job, find a place to live and earn one's keep. Oh, yes there are lots of bills to be paid – mortgage, car, health insurance, including mental health, groceries, winter outfit from foot to head, and more. With time there will arise the need to look back at those dear ones left behind – the extended family, friends, local community and probably the government.

At some point one of my favorite items on the CBS networks was the wisdom dished out by former South African president and Nobel laureate, Nelson Rolilahlah Mandela. Nelson Mandela accomplished many things, such as signing into law the 1995 Truth and Reconciliation Commission, a humane alternative to the Nuremberg-type trials put in place elsewhere; but his greatest influence may be for something he did not actually do – run for a second term of office as his country's president. On a continent where presidents rule until they become senile and effete and run out of ideas, Nelson Mandela is a rare bird indeed. But I have scarcely ever had the privilege to listen to President Mandela's words of wisdom to the end because money-making commercials quickly push them off the TV. Nothing could better bring home how much our society is dictated to by the powerful force of the dollar. At the lower end of the economic ladder people work for the dollar but higher up, the dollar works for people. Quite a system!

Our love affair with money virtually trumps and silences everything else, including people with great ideas. Because of the power of the dollar, radio talk hosts have more clout over our air waves than politicians. Nelson Mandela is hardly alone. In America's competitive corporate world, a medical doctor has been heard telling a colleague that money speaks, in reference to how money power is used to put people and events in their places, using oversight organs to monitor how the dollar was earned and spent in hospitals and healthcare institutions. During Chinese leader, Jiang Zemin's visit to the US some time in 1979, President Bill Clinton made some clumsy effort to tax him with human rights in his native China. The august visitor simply said "duly noted" and expected President Clinton to leave matters at that. But Clinton apparently failed to get the hint, following which Jiang Zemin gathered courage, wit and a dose of Einsteinian inspiration and declared: *"relative democracy"* and *"relative human rights"*. The US president could do no more, considering America's economic interests in China - Boeing aircrafts, Westinghouse reactors and big loans, among others.

Alaska's governor and John McCain's running mate for the 2008 presidential election, Sarah Palin, made headline news when it was revealed that the Republican National Committee had spent a whopping $150,000 for her wardrobe during a major financial crisis. And to show how much the dollar had come to dominate our lives, a CBS reporter asked the winners of a $207,000,000 jackpot in one of the nation's many lotteries what they intended to do the next day.

"Going back to work of course" answered one of them. The reporter was stunned, wondering why anybody with such a bonanza would want to work again. To put an end to her bewilderment, the lucky winner added, "I love my work" and this was received with a string of *aahs* and *oohs*. In the darkest sky, there are almost always some bright spots. Things may have become tough or bad but one can take comfort in knowing that parts of the US society still believes in conventional values, including the dignity of work. The winner's good fortune did not deter him from continuing along the path of service to society. Or was he following the money?

How many Americans in a similar situation would consider returning to work which is often considered drudgery? Ask the average American these days if they love their jobs and the answer is invariably "it pays the bills". TGIF greetings are slowly but surely passing into the category of worn out clichés reminiscent of a distant past. It could not be otherwise when people thank God for the Friday only to rush from their first or second shift regular jobs to their weekend jobs, often lasting the entire grave yard shift. Wasn't TGIF supposed to be uttered in yearning for week end rest and the chance to be with family and friends and do other things than work?

For many people jobs are simply a matter of survival. The job market poses enormous and sometimes unexpected challenges to US citizens and immigrants alike. Jobs that were once considered substandard, dirty, smelling or dangerous are being sought after by everyone today. Slaughter houses, sewage plants and prisons are receiving more than their fair share of applicants. Donning thick leather gloves, a desperate job seeker is hired at one of many "labor ready" facilities and sent to try his luck at any of a number of trash collecting units, hauling sodden carpets, moldy mattresses, or nail-studded lumber into a truck. Squeezing shut his nostrils, he goes through a mound of garbage, home to rats, spiders, and even raccoons. To pay the bills a young stylish woman of 30 dutifully applies herself at working in a poultry plant at Tyson's Food Inc. where she cuts diseased or damaged flesh off chicken carcasses, a much less glamorous or desirable job and salary than in the heydays.

Her roommate, a former gymnastics trainer for the well-to-do, finds herself as a prison guard at a women's prison. Long term joblessness has hit the labor market like an epidemic, causing desperation in many homes. Skilled workers and the more educated ones have taken up all available openings in restaurants and offices, leaving unskilled workers, teenagers, school dropouts, high school graduates and recent immigrants to take care of the rest. Unemployment rates, the barometer used to measure the health of the US economy, have remained above 9% for some time in spite of President Obama's massive economic stimulus measures, and they were an important determinant of the outcome of midterm elections in 2010.

With such stiff competition employers don't have to pay too much for salaries to lure workers. Employers who once rejected applicants for failing to make eye contact during interviews - considering such gestures as evasiveness, dishonesty or disinterest - soon found out that there were cultural undertones associated with some of such nonverbal communications, a majority of them in the cheap labor pool, related to respect for authority or seniority among Asians, Africans and even among the Navajos of the US. Ahmad Darvesh, a doctor from Afghanistan found employment at a cash register in Wal-mart at Lynn while his colleague Mariya Bratslavekiy from Russia was happily employed as a phlebotomist for a private healthcare facility next door in Somerville. A two-star general from the same country worked for Wackenhut as a security guard at $11 per hour in the next town over. Former Iraqi translator and interpreter for the US military and now a jobless immigrant, Ihsan Yaqoob could not even find a job to enable him keep "up from the bootstraps" as an article of faith. Here was a man who could very well stay in his native Iraq and get usefully employed in the tourist industry, preparing and serving barbecued fish and showing his country's important historic sites to visitors and vacationers – the holy cities of Najaf and Karballah, Biblical sites like Ur, the birth place of Abraham, Babylon where Old Testament residents gained fame for trying to build a tower to reach the sky, the confluence of the Tigris and Euphrates, where the Garden of Eden once stood, Mosul with tombs of many Old Testament prophets or places in nearby Turkey where Noah erected his tent on Mount Ararat. But the Iraq war had turned things upside down and would take time to put right.

As for Alhaji M. Magida, he was hopeful of finding a job but hope became quite elusive with time. These persons worked for the money. These were tough choices and low level employment close to unemployment, what some at the Migration Policy Institute in Washington D. C. called "brain waste". An Albanian judge, Robert Gjoni did dishwashing, valve assembly and security guard work. Jean-Pierre Kitembo a French professor of Congolese nationality worked as a cashier in a parking garage. These were considered lucky by the thousands still roaming the streets and flooding the temp agencies and employment centers. If they ever thought that theirs was the lot of immigrants, Americans too were caught up in the bind. Accountants waiting tables or doctors driving taxi cabs are no longer news as people give up looking for work and join the ranks of the unemployed or continue to be underemployed, managing two or more part-time jobs that offer far fewer hours per week to conveniently pay the bills. For the lowly paying jobs, employees ask for nothing more than many hours of work to catch up with their bill payments. That is a commodity employers have had to ration out. It is not rare to find employers who consider an employee experienced or educated beyond utility simply because they cannot offer a salary commensurate with the qualification or skills presented.

Although age discrimination in employment is unlawful, the interviewing process places a lot of older employees in an obvious disadvantage in these lean years. Because younger persons are prepared to accept lower pay, they are often favored even if inexperienced and erratic some times, but employers surely prefer those likely to be with them for a while. Thus by day, Xia Huang is a PhD student in molecular biology while by night he changes to Joe Wong the entertainer in an art project. His girl friend, Moon began as a babysitter for a few families but soon put to use the Asian reputation for being good in mathematics, tutoring algebra and pre-algebra for kids in the neighborhood where she babysat. Word soon got around and Moon became a commodity in demand. The twenty-year-old had a flair for the subject which she put to good use. Girls who had turned their backs to the subject became interested as Moon demystified here and there, making mince meat of a once awe-inspiring topic like the distributive property: $X(a+b+c+d) = aX+bX+cX+dX$, calling the once mysterious unknown X, a given number of crunchy Nestle Butterfinger candy bars given by a family to trick-or-treaters, a, b, c, d, during the Halloween evening. Even the dumbest kid became interested and energized! Yes, there is money to be made in America and those with the brains actually go at it with plenty of gusto.

Competition for jobs on the US market is very stiff for nationals as well as immigrants. Anyone who considers the above cases as very low pay or substandard for the employees must think again. For the most recent immigrants, the best way to survive in America is to put aside all notions of a previous life and start from scratch. As conventional wisdom puts it, to make a good long jump, one must take several steps backwards. Yet many persons forsake this conventional wisdom to their detriment. Immigrants entering the United States with big academic qualifications soon find out that their paper qualifications serve merely as passports into jobs; performing those jobs requires a lot more. Just as passports are put away in the safe storage once inside the US, diplomas too are kept aside after a job offer. Work ethics here in the US are often quite different from what obtains elsewhere and for those who had been used to getting paid for eight hours at work instead of eight hours of work, often multitasking to accomplish in the same time span what might require more time by other arrangement, it can be quite shocking and stressful.

Investors put a lot of their money into businesses and expect good returns as employees navigate the twists and turns of the work place, coping with written and unwritten instructions for diverse persons, some very prone to sexual and other harassments. Kow-towing to the customer poses a special challenge. It is often difficult to know just what the right thing to do is and even American citizens have found themselves caught off-guard. Juan Williams, for example, a seasoned journalist and news analyst working for both the National Public Radio and Fox News found himself caught in such a no-win situation when he lost his NPR job simply for saying that whenever he saw persons wearing Muslim garbs on airplanes, he felt nervous and worried. Poor thing, his source of daily bread straddled two worlds – the world of NPR supposedly invested in objective news and the world of Fox News where opinionated news would be the norm. Sarah Palin could not help wondering aloud why NPR would defend the First Amendment yet fire an employee for using it, a prelude to public outcry demanding curtailment of the funding NPR receives as a corporation for public broadcasting.

It is all so different from what was predicted by our twentieth century scholars that advanced technology would liberate people from the drudgery of work and usher in an unprecedented era of leisure. A certain Professor Julian Huxley predicted less time at work, businessman Walter Gifford was sure every man would have the chance to do whatever he'd like with plenty of time to cultivate the art of living, and sociologist Henry Fairchild was sure factories would turn out more goods than we would know how to dispose of wisely, and so forth. But it did not happen! The predictions were all off the mark. There has been explosive growth all right but it would appear that people have taken their productivity gains in the form of money instead of time. Society chose money over time!

Globalization and the new technology have brought a lot of pressure, a 24/7 economy where the line between home and work is blurred. Overworked, overstretched and overscheduled human beings have become too stressed out. Things have not been made any easier by the recent financial meltdown with loss of jobs, loss of homes and a string of health problems. The womenfolk have not been spared as some rightly return home to a "second shift" job involving preparing supper, cleaning the house, washing clothes, picking up kids from daily activities, helping with homework and more. Long hours of work without proper rest or recreation surely take a toll on family life.

Is it fair to oblige well trained professionals – doctors, nurses, lawyers, journalists – from other countries to go back to school and learn English and recertify? Should they accept such low pay or should they not? Do the job offers match their expectations or self esteem? Probably not. Yet, the truth is that daily realities of living in America and paying bills – groceries, utilities, rents, mortgages, entertainment and others - impose their demands on everybody and when those realities come calling, there is little room for rationalizing what employment one accepts. The tug-of-war between what obtained before at home and what was to follow here in America ultimately tips in favor of the latter. It may be unfair to require recertification or an ESL course of study but it seems a prudent thing to do if one intends to bridge the gap between what one knows and what is required of a new position. Imagine how embarrassing it is to be unable to open a capped container and take out one's pills simply because the instruction for doing so is in a language one cannot understand. To be able to vote one needs to read and understand the various options in a typical ballot initiative. Those facing litigation need at least to be able to say the elements of their Miranda rights (I refuse to answer on grounds that I may self incriminate) rather than remain mute. What good is looking for employment here in America equipped only with knowledge of an outmoded technology such as the once famous Aschheim –Zondek test (testing for pregnancy by injecting a woman's urine into African clawed frogs) or its ancient Egyptian equivalent of sprinkling the woman's pee on wheat or barley seeds to stimulate sprouting when these had since been superseded by state-of-the-art technologies for detecting HCG?

The National Bureau of Economic Research said the recession which began in 2007 ended in 2009 but most persons interviewed said nothing had changed; the hardship was still palpable. Former president Bill Clinton, whose Global Initiative forum focused mainly on linking corporate donors to non-profits, said he had decided to turn his attention to the domestic situation where the biggest problem remained the mismatch of skills; jobs being created did not have qualified people applying for them. This posed a special problem for those who chose the quick fix of dropping out of high school to earn the buck. According to him the way forward would be job-specific training to cut down the five million unemployed persons hanging around.

Getting employment is just one thing; keeping it is another ball game altogether. Coming from other countries most immigrants are faced with basics such as acquiring knowledge of the English language for purposes of communication. Most jobs require it and promotion is almost always predicated on performance which is a reflection of how well one has mastered the art. Those who have felt the frustrations of being at the receiving end of a telephone conversation know why communication skills feature so prominently in certain jobs. Almost all career counselors lay emphasis on literacy as the one factor that can influence IQ and an employee's earning potential. Along with computer skills, competence in language use can make all the difference between getting employed and being left out of the work force.

While some persons, drawing inspiration from an earlier life at home, may opt for self employment such as driving, it soon becomes clear that even in this activity, one needs language skills as well. For indeed how does a driver (taxi man, delivery guy), whose native language is not English, react when confronted with a road sign like NO TURNING ON RED at an intersection? Should he stop the car, turn and proceed or proceed and then stop? Complicating such a quandary may be unhelpful promptings from cars hooting from behind or someone jaywalking ahead with ears hooked to electronic gadgetry. Before 1973 it was quite simple; at a red light cars came to a stop and proceeded only after the green light came on. But in that year, faced with the Middle East oil crisis, the nation went into serious soul searching. Wasn't it so wasteful having a car running for several minutes on the spot while waiting for the green light to come on? The US Congress decided to legalize turning at a red light – to cut down fuel use in cars idling unnecessarily. That was during Gerald Ford's presidency and it was one of many measures to cope with the oil embargo that affected the nation's supplies. Other measures involved strategic reserves, mandated fuel efficiency standard for cars placed at 27 miles per gallon.

What should a driver do when an orange-yellow school bus stops ahead – stop or just pass (overtake) carefully and drive on? Suppose the school bus stopped in the opposite, on-coming traffic, should the driver stop or just proceed? And if one came from countries where vehicles have the right of way and pedestrians are educated to "look left, look right, and look left again" before crossing, to drive in some of our cities where pedestrians impulsively bring traffic to a standstill, not necessarily at zebra crossings, what is the right thing to do? Hitting pedestrians on the road is a painful experience; getting hit from the back is equally painful.

On the other hand what do passengers in a crowded city train make of an announcement like "The doors on the left will open only" made by a new hire, clearly an immigrant, judging from his accent? And suppose one were an enterprising driver from one of those countries where self employment obliges one to just get a motor cycle, jump on it and begin to transport passengers back and forth, helmet or no helmet, would it be OK to venture into that line of activity here in Uncle Sam's land? If so, when and if confronted by a state trooper, should one just slip a few dollar bills into the hands of such an officer and move on as is the practice back at home?

If one were to accept employment as a news reporter (journalist) in one of the many news media that abound, how does one cope with previous notions brought from experiences under other skies, where the rules are different? Many third world countries have press censorship, leaving the newsmen and women very little latitude in what they can report or write about. Coming from such countries to practice out here is like getting out of prison to lead a free life. In other countries news is something that has already happened and the task of a reporter is simply to relay it as faithfully as possible to the public. Here in America, it is that and much more. As a matter of fact, news often involves reporting even that which has not yet happened. Bizarre but true. "Breaking news" has pushed American journalism to extremes of extrapolation, speculation and anticipation. It is typical to see titles like "Former State Senator Dianne Wilkerson to plead guilty in her corruption trial" where the element of news is still to take place at some future time. Elsewhere, news involving a top government official or matters before a court are considered *sub judice* and not subject to any reporting until disposed of, violations being subject to punitive sanctions. A Zimbabwean journalist who speculated about His Excellency Robert Mugabe's impending marriage found himself on the wrong side of the law just like his Cameroonian counterpart who wrote making an informed guess about the state of health of the president, but here in America, the news men are virtually in competition with investigators and the courts to "get there" first, a practice that carries with it some hidden dangers.

Freedom of the press is good but it also has its downside especially in the wrong hands. Smart journalists know that they are part of a team, with editors playing a pivotal role in news dissemination. No matter how smart a journalist is, the editor must never be sidelined or ignored because it is this individual who takes the barometer of the social, political and economic setting into which the news is released and so is better placed to gauge the impact of news. A sense of self-righteousness can do a lot of harm to an otherwise brilliant career. Julian Assange, a typical bright news man originally from Australia, miscalculated or failed to calculate before using his whistle blowing website, *WikiLeaks*, a stateless news organ committed to freedom of speech, to disseminate potentially explosive classified information from US government files. He arrogated to himself the role of sole arbiter, judge and custodian of the truth but failed to consider the outcome of his decision to spill secrets, the consequences of which an entire planet must now cope with. His became known as IED (Internet Explosive Device) and it rattled many countries, friends as well as foes of the United States (those who fear America, respect it, scorn it, need it) and earned for him a status no different from that of Anwar al-Awlaki. At a time when the US already enjoys the unenviable title of number one exporter of contempt, such action only made matters worse. And those hailing him as their hero, naively assuming that only the government employee who had direct access to the classified information would face prosecution, fail to take into consideration the joint venture theory used by law enforcement to prosecute all those involved with committing a particular crime. In a country where one man's hero might just as well be another's villain, some newspapers took upon themselves to run a competition for "man-of –the-year" title. President Barack Obama virtually trailed Julian Assange, followed by the Chilean miners rescued from their 69 days ordeal. Could Julian Assange be emulating Dr Daniel Ellsberg, the man accused of conspiracy and theft of Pentagon papers at the time of the Vietnam War, put on trial and who has become a hero today? How far should a journalist go in using the First Amendment freedom of speech and free flow of information? Is this part of investigative journalism really? So many questions but so few answers!

On the eve of the ninth anniversary of the September 11 bombing of New York City's WTC by terrorists, news outlets carried the story of the suspension of the threatened Qu'ran burning by pastor Terry Jones, following a deal struck with Imam Mohammad Musri, president of the Islamic Society of Central Florida on behalf of Imam Feisal Abdul Rauf and those behind the construction of a mosque near Ground Zero in NYC. The obscure priest from Gainesville, Florida had announced that he would be burning the Muslim holy book to protest against the planned construction of the Ground Zero mosque. But Imam Faisal and Imam Mohammad Musri denied that there was such a deal! News outlets carried the story and in no time at all, the entire world was holding its breath, concerned about the event (Qu'ran burning) and its possible consequences.

What was going to happen? What could have motivated the obscure pastor Terry Jones to come up with such a stunt? Had he weighed the magnitude of the consequences of his actions at all? It was bad enough that opposing camps were pitched for and against the proposed mosque. Surely that was not the type of legacy 9/11 was supposed to leave behind! The aftermath of the tragic 9/11 was that, for hours and days and months later, all sorts of people joined together to help and to comfort. In lower Manhattan a variety of people of all faiths and ethnicities came together to help, embodying the very essence of community and outreach – rescue workers, neighbors, friends, strangers, everybody. The watchword was resilience. Together with important American sacrifices such as the coalition that rescued Kuwait from Saddam Hussein's invasion in 1991, the humanitarian response to the tsunami that hit Indonesia after 2005, the post 9/11 solidarity of Americans was a legacy worth preserving. Why would any one American erase this good memory? Why would any sane persons give Muslims the pretext to remember only that American laws permit Americans to burn the Islamic holy book without consequence?

And then there is the ethical consideration involving confidentiality of news sources. It somewhat trivializes the solemn duty of the court and makes it harder to find a jury of one's peers that can deal with a matter without prior bias. How many persons are prepared, like Judith Miller, to go to jail rather than reveal the source of a news item? Obviously persons practicing journalism need to be aware of such delicate issues before accepting employment requiring their application in Uncle Sam's land. The aggressive search for news certainly has its downside but a lot of it is good for society. Thanks to collaboration between the police and other investigative forces, crimes are easily solved. That is what happened when a pair of snipers went on the rampage in Washington D. C. over a three week stretch in October 2001, killing many innocent persons in the process.

America is also called the lottery society for a good reason. Oregon has held lotteries, the winners promised access to affordable health insurance. Since there are more persons in need of insurance than there are policies to go around, a lottery makes sense. In New York City, the average sale price of a house or apartment is $700,000 and up, falling out of the reach of most families. Smart government policies give people access to affordable housing but the slots are so few that access is decided by lottery. Demand far exceeds supply, according to NYC officials. Over the past decade the tantalizingly attractive (Diversity Lottery) immigrant visas that magnetize people to the US were given out by a type of lottery, involving a tangled mess of red tape and a huge backlog, delays of from five to eighteen years – to get the green card. Only a relatively lucky few ever get it – 50,000 out of 1.5 million applicants worldwide.

It is quite natural for feuding parties at home to find themselves working on the same team once here in the US and even enjoying it. Carrying such a spirit back home can be a rewarding experience for the home country, the US and the world at large. Somalis often gather at the Butterfly Coffee near the mosque in Boston discussing and debating which idea is the best, even if they never quite agree on one, for their poor and war ravaged country. Albanians meet at Select Café, sampling espresso and cappuccino and reminiscing about social, political and economic unrest back home. Haitians congregate at Bon Appétit, their home-away-from-home, mulling over their island nation's problems and the Irish are known to find solace at The Banshee, one of dozens of pubs where they sit to talk about the deep recession in Ireland that has created a new wave of immigrants. Around the Intercontinental, cultures commingle to stir the senses – succulent sushi with rare tequilas, salsa music overlooking the Boston Harbor, Rumba dance with rum potions, and Provencal cuisine at ultramodern guest rooms overlooking the water front.

## *Paying Cash for Sin.*

The new Catholic Church of the twenty-first century was facing a public scandal of monumental proportions that shook the foundation of the institution. It was shameful, heart-breaking, maddening, and disastrous all at once. Newspaper reports assailed Christians all over - a report here, a conviction there. The idea of Catholic priests sexually molesting children and adolescents, most of them boys, was at first considered a tragic anomaly. By 2002 the floodgates had opened and suddenly there were crimes everywhere as news media brought the stories to light. Worst of all, the bishops who supervised the priests seemed like accomplices, transferring abusers from church to church without warning their new pastors or parishioners and all too often the offenses simply began again! Cardinal Bernard Law of Boston came under fire for his role in protecting the priests who preyed upon innocent children. He took cover in his transfer to Rome where he became archbishop emeritus of Boston and archpriest of the Basilica di Santa Maria Maggiore and, with others of his rank, took part in electing former archbishop of Munich, Joseph Ratzinger to become the new pope, Benedict XVI. The latter also came under fire for similar acts of negligence in his former diocese. As all roads led to Rome, so did the many protests against predatory Catholic priests.

Cardinal Sean O'Malley took over from the embattled Cardinal Bernard Law who was heavily criticized for protecting the errant priests. Together with other clergy, he prostrated himself in front of the altar at the Cathedral of the Holy Cross to ask for forgiveness from the sins of the scandal. There was public outcry and the need for female priests was resuscitated and reechoed. The Church paid millions of dollars in legal settlements to victims, their lawyers and their families, payments that could not undo the damage done. There was a great distrust of bishops as "shepherds" and a crisis of confidence ensued. Financial contributions fell and *ad hoc* groups formed and pressed for change. The days of unquestioning lay deference to the hierarchy were virtually over. The laity determined to assert itself as "the church".

At first cases of abuse seemed isolated and unrelated in Louisiana, Rhode Island, New Jersey, Texas, Washington State and Pennsylvania. Father James Porter, a priest in Fall River, Massachusetts, had apparently molested kids early in his career, but the complaints were handled quietly by the local bishop via repeated transfers to new assignments. Porter quit the priesthood in 1974, married and moved to Minnesota where he continued to molest children, including his own. Lawyers and TV reporters in Massachusetts, working with some of the victims, unraveled the sad story by 1992 (by then Porter's crime was outside the statute of limitations).He was arrested, brought back to Massachusetts, tried and imprisoned in a psychiatric facility where he died in 2004. The diocese paid each of his Fall River victims $100,000.

That set the precedent for monetary compensations for sin. Converting those early sins into dollar payments was to prove a big mistake, first, by blurring the narrow line separating church and state and secondly, opening the floodgates for more demands for such monetary settlements here and there. Cases cropped up in the US, Ireland, Munich and elsewhere. Suddenly forty-year-olds began to recall that they had been molested as kids by some priest. As if those were not enough, the pope's personal preacher wrote and ventured to compare the attacks on the Catholic Church to anti-Semitic attacks on Jews, in the process incurring the wrath of Jewish groups, especially those under the delusion of owning the copyright to the Holocaust. Hell broke loose. Self-righteous ranting flew all over the place with the ADL boss leading the way in reaction to the pope's pastor reading a letter from his Jewish friend during Good Friday service. He had stepped onto a no-go zone and was soon to face the ire of those whose radars scout around for anti-Semitism, real and imagined.

The Archbishop of Canterbury, Rowan Williams, did not help matters when he too joined the fray by bluntly lambasting the Catholic Church under Pope Benedict XVI, saying the abuse scandal was a colossal trauma to Ireland and added that the Catholic Church in Ireland was losing all credibility because of its poor handling of the crisis. The blame game was in high gear. Even though he did not mention Pope Benedict XVI directly, there was little doubt he was paying back the Pope in his own coin. The pope's earlier overture to dissatisfied Anglicans to convert to Roman Catholicism did not sit well with the Archbishop of Canterbury. Between the Anglican church and the Vatican there is a schism dating as far back as the 16th century when King Henry VIII decided to annul his marriage to Catherine of Aragon. The laity, those on the sidelines, those who yesterday genuflected before their priests to make confessions – everybody rose up to throw the proverbial stone at priests and the pope, totally oblivious of Christ's own teaching in the matter - "Judge not". How times change!

Both the Catholic Church and the Anglican Church are going through difficult times. Rowan Williams is apparently frustrated over the pope's lack of sympathy for the Anglican church especially as the church is losing disaffected persons who quit because they can't cope with Anglican ordination of female priests or the schism over America's Episcopalian church's decision to ordain gay and lesbian bishops. Williams had pleaded for patience and understanding to work out something but so far got no support from Africa, Asia and

Latin America. The Archbishop saw the Pope as opportunistic in trying to take advantage of Anglican woes. Meanwhile Pope Benedict XVI continued to go about serenely with his papal duties, stating that the church needed to do penance for its sins, a view sharply in contrast to those held by senior church people who emphasized defending the church and the pope from orchestrated campaigns by hostile news media.

Some time ago the Boston Globe brought Father John Geoghan to the notice of the public. His crimes involved preadolescent boys, often from troubled families. He too benefitted from transfers whenever complaints were lodged and he continued to be labeled "dedicated". He was exposed, defrocked, convicted of a minor offense, (more serious charges, including the molestation of James Costello for years, were pending), sent to jail and while there, he was strangled in his cell in 2003 – a sordid end to a sordid story. Church officials agreed to pay $55 million to his victims, $28 million of that amount to the lawyers. Thanks to the power of the dollar, those gargantuan amounts that changed hands, most parts of our nation has since enjoyed peaceful sleep as strident calls for retribution dwindled.

The cardinals, church bishops and pope heaved a sigh of relief as they waited for the next salvo when another set of persons in their middle ages would come forth and clamor for reparations for sex abuses they had suffered in childhood. Church attendance suffered a tremendous decline as well as the sacrament of baptism. Parents lost hope in the priests, preferring to keep their kids away from the predators. But they also faced a dilemma; at death, children that were not baptized could neither go to heaven nor to hell. They would be placed in limbo. What an option! Later when more revelations came up in connection with abuses elsewhere, Pope Benedict XVI wrote a letter apologizing directly to the victims and expressing remorse for the "sinful acts committed by the clergy", an irate followership did not buy it. The reaction was mixed with the majority of affected persons and their families unleashing the harsh criticism on the pope and even calling on him to step down. On top of the Irish government's scathing report, critics accused the church and the police of collusion in covering up sexual abuse by priests in Dublin, the continued reassignment of a priest shown by a local psychiatrist to be dangerous to work with children. The pope said abusers "must answer for it before Almighty God and before properly constituted tribunals", and urged them to pray for forgiveness, yet that did not satisfy many. Offended Irish natives, especially some women who attended mass at South Boston's Gate of Heaven parish were unrestrained in their judgment of the pope, calling on him to resign for putting the church organization before the welfare of children. But the pope is never removed from office by the wishes of ordinary mortals. That role belongs to God, doesn't it?

Visiting the UK, Pope Benedict XVI met with Queen Elizabeth II, the titular head of the Church of England in a gesture of mutual respect and reconciliation, preached compassion but also warned against aggressive secularism even as he expressed shock about the degree of perversion in the priesthood.

Many young people are known to go into the seminary with the purest of hearts and noblest of intentions, to devote their lives to God. The first thing they learn has to do with textual criticism where they look at the existing papyruses and scrolls and learn about the recension of the texts – tortuous, often controversial historical path from Hebrew, Greek, and Latin versions of the books of the Bible, together with all Apocryphal books that got rejected, right up to the King James version and all their later English translations. It turns out that that is not what was taught at Sunday school.

Out of the chaos many Catholics hoped something good would come out, especially the adoption of a change so that priests could be allowed to get married. What could be better than jettisoning an antiquated version of Catholicism that made unmarried priests counselors of married persons? The feeling was that by allowing marriage to its priests, the church would have moved in the right direction to halt or at least curb the incidence of child abuse. But such a proposition presupposed that priests had a heterosexual orientation, an idea not quite borne out by the facts; the fact that most of the child victims were boys pointed in the direction of gays (homosexuality). Also, information from the Justice Department seemed to point in the direction that two thirds of convicted child molesters or offenders were or had been married, which cast doubt on matrimony as the magic solution.

## *Sex and the Dollar*

Meanwhile the men of God were clearly not amused when society appeared to be adulating top radio late night show host, Dave Letterman and cinema producer Roman Polanski over their own shameful sexual exploits that had come to light. One had had sex with a thirteen-year-old girl and was a fugitive from justice for thirty years until his arrest at a Swiss airport; the other had come forward of his own accord - prompted by an alleged CBS colleague's sinister attempt to blackmail him - and owned up and apologized for his relationships with female colleagues inside his office in the Ed Sullivan Theater, which ***Entertainment Tonight*** famously called his "love nest". How could society show so much indulgence for these but not the priests? How could society reduce the very same act of sin to entertainment on one hand while asking for the heads of sinners on the other? It did not take long for answers to spring forth from every corner. Unmoved, one citizen reminded the clergy that he could not recall Polanski the film director vowing piety or celibacy or establishing centuries-old trust with congregants. Another conceded that child abuse is abominable, made no defense for Polanski but insisted to point out that it was the breaking of their vows and breach of trust that made the clergy's sexual abuse of minors particularly abhorrent.

All seemed to agree that Christianity teaches that everybody is a sinner, so when members of the clergy condemned lay persons for behavior that other clergy had been complicit in covering up, they ought to expect to reap the disdain they had sown instead of ranting against it, which confirmed their being in denial of the despicable acts. An answer given fortuitously by another defender of the entertainment gurus was that priests are held to a much higher moral standard by the society. Still, none could explain why the same act was condemned as a sin in one context and celebrated as entertainment in another. The other lame excuse offered was that no one voted for the men of entertainment to uphold the law and that no one had been hurt by their acts, even though poking fun at people and their behaviors could be considered social control in the same manner as the acts of priests. In a world that glorifies sex and at a time when sex impacted so many lives, sex abuse threw the Catholic Church in turmoil but the hierarchy tried hard to downplay it. *The Church demonizes homosexuality as a matter of doctrine and banishes women in the priesthood. This places priests in a homophilic world stress, certainly irrepressible urges that can be indulged in only by the exploitation of the vulnerable and the available – objects of desires which in most cases are boys, prepubescent or adolescent.*

But how did the tradition of celibacy all begin? It started as an ascetic discipline – hermits, desert monks, virgins – born partly of mysticism and of ancient ritual purity codes, and partly of neoplatonic contempt for the physical world that had nothing to do with the gospels. Renunciation of sexual expression by men fitted nicely with a patriarchal denigration of women. Even though it contradicted the clear example of Jesus, it did define the church of "the Fathers". Non-virginal women such as Eve the temptress of Adam were seen as the sources of sin.

Then came the middle Ages and the Second Lateran Council of 1139. At that time celibacy was made mandatory for all Roman Catholic clergy in a reform designed to brace clerical laxity as well as remove inheritance issues from the administration of church property. But the requirement for celibacy was so extreme that it had to be mystified as a sacrificial opening to a special intimacy with God. According to Pope Paul VI, "It is not opportune to debate publicly this topic which requires the greatest prudence and is so important." Yet it was equally another Church Council that had initiated and put in place the clerical discipline of celibacy. What a contradiction! How then could Pope Paul VI say another Church Council was not qualified even to discuss it? It laid bare the blatant power play for all to see. Catholics finally knew or at least had reason to suspect that celibacy was being maintained as a requirement of the priesthood because of internal church politics, not because of any spiritual or religious motive. God was not the issue; the Pope was. That sent men streaming out of the priesthood and stirring in those who remained a profound identity crisis. Priestly celibacy in a world full of sex is quite a challenge and the setting of too high a standard (exclusivity with Jesus) was bound to be problematic in a world where marriage was virtually experimental with couples practicing partner swapping like atoms in a molecular reaction.

And so the Council did not take up the issue of priestly celibacy and Pope Paul VI sought to settle it with his 1967 encyclical, *Sacerdotalis caelibatus* which was no good. The entire church was now plunged into a culture of dishonesty. For the sake of mere appearance of the hierarchy's authority, sexual proscriptions have been officially upheld, even while the hierarchy itself looked the other way when those proscriptions have been massively repudiated. Catholic laity ignores the birth control mandate; priests find ways around the celibacy rule, in meaningful relationships with secret lovers or in exploitative relationships with the vulnerable and criminal acts with minors. And so lies, denials, arrogance, selfishness, cowardice – such are the ways in which the priests currently live in spite of their outward virtues.

Dave Letterman's apology – a kind of public relations stunt to his confused audience and staff with his usual rambling jokes - appeared to have opened Pandora's Box instead of laying the matter to rest. While he cut short the blackmailer's scheme which aimed at extorting $2 million from him, he unleashed a tabloid frenzy and the nation was treated to all sorts of salacious gossips and stories of love affairs of celebrities, reminiscent of "Mad Men" of the sixties. (In a deal reached with NY prosecutors for attempted larceny, Dave Letterman's blackmailer was apparently given the option of serving six months in jail or doing one thousand hours of community service and giving up his right of appeal). Many questions went unanswered. Did the "Late Show" host preside over a work place where sex with the boss was commonplace? Were promotions of female workers carried out in a healthy manner? If the sex was consensual as claimed, was it not mixed with who had the power? In a world where some brave women type with one hand, keeping the boss off with the other hand in his misuse of gender-based power, the public was left with imaginations of what latitude women had navigating promotions, salary increases and other benefits under such bosses in an America where gender equality was supposed to be a given. Was it true that his job as a comic meant that Dave Letterman should not care what happened off screen, that his celebrity status made his work place dalliances inevitable? Was it true that women had thrown themselves at him because that's what they did to powerful men and powerful men are usually too powerless to resist? Difficult to say, faced with the sepulchral silence on the part of the women involved.

The Letterman saga had hardly died down when ace golfer, Tiger Woods had an accident in his driveway, necessitating a few stitches at a nearby hospital, thanks to his wife's timely intervention to pull him out of his damaged Cadillac Escalade which had hit a fire hydrant and a nearby tree outside his Orlando, Florida home. But Woods's accident was pushed aside and a can of worms opened as salacious gossips spun around the man's domestic activities. Where, for example, was he going at that unholy hour of the night? Was he involved in some sort of domestic violence? He did not make things easy for himself when he refused to let the police interview him about the accident, claiming privacy issues. Before long, the billionaire golfer and uber-perfect Tiger – wealth estimated to be beyond the dreams of the Sultan of Brunei, billion dollar smile, fitness level outside of Jack Lalane league - was linked to an ever growing list of extramarital affairs involving blond mistresses. Human imagination went wild and Internet blogs had a field day. Big business for the tabloids meant headache for the sponsors of golf! The matter would not die down even as the once quiet and reserved Paragon of gentlemanliness assumed the proportion of a typical Shakespearean tragic figure. The accident involving the world's number one golfer and Associated Press's nominee for "Athlete of the decade" suddenly paled as the focus shifted to infidelity to his Swedish model wife, trysts with high class socialites, porn stars, and Perkins waitresses, prompting one cynic to say that honesty is not always the best policy. It also became clear that in the era of Internet, athletes in general and those enjoying celebrity statuses with extravagant salaries especially have a price to pay – their privacy.

Golf without Tiger Woods was unimaginable. Businesses that had endorsed him began to develop the flu even as Nike Inc's boss Phil Knight conceded that sex scandals surrounding the great Tiger Woods were part of the game in signing endorsement deals with athletes; nevertheless there was palpable concern in other businesses, notably sponsors like Accenture PLC, Procter and Gamble's Gillette, AT&T Inc., Trojan, Pacific Bulletproof, T-Mobile, Holiday Inn and lots of others that had made it possible for the star athlete to find himself in the billionaire league. So great was the pressure that Tiger Woods took a leave of absence from the PGA to focus attention on repairing his damaged image and, in his own words, being a better husband, father and person. His loss of the number one spot to a certain Lee Westwood followed quickly on the heels of his divorce. Americans are very good at overcoming their tragedies and rising to great heights. It took the tragedy of Chappaquiddick for the late Edward Moore Kennedy to become a great Senator; Tiger woods might be heading in that same direction even if he suffers financial hits here and there as a result of reduced endorsements.

According to *The Associated Press*, David Beckham, another sports icon and legendary soccer star was suing *In Touch* for publishing a story that he had sex with prostitutes, even naming a certain 26-year old high class call girl as having told *In Touch* that she had slept with the soccer legend five times in 2007. How this new scandal developed, only time would tell.

Roman Polanski, the film maker arrested and detained in Switzerland for sleeping with a minor thirty years ago, found a fervent and vociferous defender – France's Culture minister, Frederic Mitterand. It turned out that *Monsieur le Ministre de la Culture* only ended up stirring a hornet's nest. Only a few days later and thanks to research by a certain Mademoiselle Marine Le Pen, a relation of France's ultra-right National Front Party parliamentarian Jean-Marie Le Pen, the world learnt that Frederic Mitterand had been a promoter of sex tourism in Bangkok brothels in South-East Asia. Mlle. Le Pen brought to light the culture minister's 2005 autobiography, *La*

*Mauvaise Vie* which had not attracted much attention when first published. Birds of similar plumage surely do hang out together, don't they? How would President Sarkozy react to this, with the nation's eyes and ears riveted on the impending case involving him and former Prime Minister de Villepin? How would third world citizens react to this, coming as it did from those who set the agendas for their impoverished nations? What was civilized society coming to and what was this weird symbiosis between celebrities caught in bad behavior and the tabloids showering them with publicity simply because only the rising ratings mattered?

What a culture of celebrity worship! Our society elevates ordinary mortals to incredibly high pedestals and as soon as they begin to lose their luster, adulation turns into scornful censure as they are dropped like rotten eggs. Edward Kennedy, John Edwards, Eliot Spitzer, Dave Letterman, Mark Sanford, Newt Gingrich, Bill Clinton, Tiger Woods, Sarah Palin and the list continues. Society even picked quarrels with Hillary Clinton for standing by her man when he was wrapped with the Monica Lewinsky scandal. Society's ambivalence does not quite help the citizens either. A twisted relationship between presidential candidate, John Edwards and his campaign aid, Andrew Young brought to light the darkest instincts inspired by the dollar. The latter was said to have been persuaded to publicly accept paternity for a child the candidate had fathered out of wedlock with his mistress. After a period of hiding the bills underwritten by the presidential candidate who first denied any relationship whatsoever with the mistress in question, the enabler came out of hiding, disgusted with the breach of contract and got back at John Edwards, armed with damning voicemails, text messages and e-mails for his own publication! What a sleaze! What an obsession for the White House! Infidelity to a cancer-stricken spouse, poor sales pitch to the American people as keeper of morality and conscience, hopes of being picked as Obama's running mate, belated confessions to the affair and fatherhood ...all these put the American voter in a nightmarish state of what could have happened. The National Enquirer of December 2007 published these details but most of the other press organs were still ignorant of it. Although

Ken Gormley's *The Death of American Virtue: Clinton versus Kenneth Starr* dwells mainly on a former US president and his tribulation with the system, it could very well cover cases like the above as well.

Once upon a time scandals were a rarity. These days, thanks to the tabloids, they have become a staple. In the days of Confidential, scandals were really something; with the onset of reality television, Us Weekly, National enquirer and the celebrity culture as a whole, American ambivalence – publicly we loathe scandals but privately we love them – there has been a proliferation of scandals in all news media. They seem to help the careers of some celebrities too. How can powerful persons become so powerless when confronted by affairs with mistresses? How could Governor Mark Sanford of South Carolina and a rising star in the GOP risk so much to go for a week's tryst in Buenos Aires?

Thanks to the American press, Sarah Palin and her family are ever in the limelight, the media coverage giving her as much attention as America's first family. The former Alaska governor's daughter, Bristol, the man with whom she had a child out of wedlock, Levi, and Sarah Palin herself became Alaska's most well known family indeed, commanding in the process a type of Romeo and Juliet aura. Levi was said to be seeking Sarah Palin's former job as mayor of Wasilla in Alaska. "Sarah Palin's appeal lies in her very polarizing figure – people love her or hate her – and as a politician she demonstrates a rare flair for going after the bottom dollar" declared Anna David, journalist and editor of the book *"Reality Matters: 19 Writers Come Clean About the Shows We Can't Stop Watching"*. Unlike Swaziland, Spain or the UK, the US does not have any royalty, but she surely has politicians and movie stars and as one observer put it, "we have a parade of sinning, confessing adulterers, cognitive dissonance of beautifully coiffed, Ivy League men and women rooting around in the dirt". As another astute observer remarked, to conceive a child out of wedlock as her ultraconservative mom ran for vice president of the United States placed the Palin daughter and her family just where they belonged in American society – on top of the news where top dollars also belong.

Following on the heels of the 9/11/2001 catastrophe involving the crash of civilian airplanes on NYC's twin towers and the Pentagon, various letters laced with deadly anthrax were dispatched by post to persons in the US, especially to Senator Tom Daschle and his staff in the US Congress. There were a number of deaths and quite a few persons fell ill from inhaling the deadly anthrax. Who had sent them and why? The FBI went to work and in no time at all Dr Steven Hatfield, a researcher was designated as a person of interest. Imagine the embarrassment and tribulation that that gentleman was put through before being let go with an out-of-court settlement of $5.8 million. Meanwhile the attention of the FBI had shifted to another person of interest, a researcher like Dr Steven Hatfield, working on anthrax too. His name was Bruce Irvin. Bruce Irvin was the only bioterrorism suspect responsible for the attacks using the anthrax strain that killed five persons and rendered others sick. Using DNA taken from the bodies of persons killed in the attack, the FBI was able to trace the specific strain (Ames type) of germ to an Army Lab and specifically to Bruce Irvin. The correlation between the DNA of the letters of the two sources left no doubt about the provenance of the toxin. As the FBI zeroed in on him the scientist committed suicide and died. Going by what historians tell us, such things do recur.

The way the 2008 nomination of the Democratic candidate for president was going, with Hillary Clinton running neck to neck with Barack Obama, at one point it looked like the nation was going to turn to some type of lottery to decide between the two rivals to avoid the unpleasant scenario of having super delegates decide. People called on Hillary to step aside and make way for Obama but the lady candidate held her ground tenaciously, vowing to fight to the finish. Victory looked so tantalizingly close at hand. The gap between the prochoice (young, unmarried women) and prolife (married women) narrowed significantly as both sides actually saw one of their kind on the threshold of making history. With respect to her prochoice and prolife supporters, candidate Hillary Clinton found herself confronted by an unusual catch-22 situation: when abortion is illegal as the prolife lobby would want it, women die;

when legal as clamored for by the prochoice, babies die. There was talk of turning to the super delegates to decide and indeed some of them were beginning to make their choices; yet most persons felt uncomfortable that our democracy should be going along that road. Eventually Hillary Clinton bowed out and endorsed Senator Obama, to the relief of many, while disaffected persons simply switched to the John McCain camp in disgust.

Since a candidate for elective office cannot possibly shake every hand, television has virtually become the biggest megaphone, getting the lion's share of money for advertisements and political campaigns. It is estimated that to win an election to the House of Representatives it costs about $1.4 million while to become a senator one needs to spend upwards of $8 million. Spurred on by a Supreme Court decision to allow corporations and unions to spend unlimited amounts on political activity that calls for the election or defeat of candidates, a slew of groups affiliated with the GOP pumped millions into contested races across America. According to the Center for Responsive Politics, conservatives like the US Chamber of Commerce spent $121 million, dramatically outpacing the $79 million by liberal organizations like Planned Parenthood. Many polls showed that the Democrats had a significant advantage over the GOP in nearly three dozen races categorized as tossups; the candidates had more money in the bank than their GOP opponents. But of course the greater war chest or name recognition does not always win. Thus in 2006 Americans swept the Democrats into power in spite of the GOP outspending them by $100 million. The tide of discontent with George W. Bush did the trick. In the midterm elections of 2010, quite a few wealthy candidates fared poorly even after spending well above $500,000 of their own money in running for elective office. Persons like former Hewlett-Parker chairperson Carly Fiorina, former e-Bay CEO, Meg Whitman and cofounder of World Wrestling Entertainment, Linda McMahon joined the league of persons like Ross Perot, Steve Forbes and William Randolph Hearst who spent big and lost big, prompting Arizona State university's political science professor Jennifer Steen to say that raising $100,000 in increments of $100 assures a candidate 1000 votes whereas writing a $100,000 check in self-financing guarantees only one vote. Of all the statistics mentioned, 9.6% kept recurring as the most potent weapon against President Obama's administration; persons who lost their jobs turned the president's 2008 campaign theme from *"yes we can"* to *"No you won't"* and dubbed his healthcare legislation *"Obamacare"*.

America needs to look back from time to time at the contributions of persons like the famous Justice Louis Brandeis who left his mark on the judicial landscape, a man who showed how to balance loyalty to enduring verities with the demands for flexibility in assuring the nation's future. A Harvard graduate born of Jewish parents and raised in Louisville, Kentucky, Louis Bandeis was a Boston-based lawyer who became a very influential Supreme Court judge, leaving his mark on free speech and privacy matters as well as laying the foundation stone for many of our current liberties. According to attorney Brandeis, lawyers should not only do well, they should do some good (public interest work) too and avoid turning law firms into commercial commodities. In retrospect, paying attention to his 1914 book, *"Other People's Money and How Bankers Use It"* which cautioned against industrial conglomerates and their unchecked growth, leading to financial collapse and human misery, might have averted America's recent financial meltdown.

By a 5-4 decision early in 2010, the US Supreme Court granted corporations complete autonomy to spend at will to support or oppose political candidates, a decision that was greeted with mixed feelings by Americans, including President Barack Obama during his State of the Union speech. While expressing his deference to separation of powers, President Obama was unequivocal in expressing the damage such a ruling would have on politics in America. Was it really a triumph for the First Amendment as some contended? Did the ruling in *Citizens United versus Federal Election Commission* actually sweep away what some persons called "a caste system in which some groups of citizens can freely engage in vigorous, unfettered political speech while others face criminal penalties for doing the same thing"? Even Justice Stevens of the Supreme Court dissented, arguing that the Court was legislating in place of Congress and that the decision overturned a one- hundred-year law!

President Obama expressed his worries about the ruling which he saw as giving the green light to a new stampede of special interest monies in politics, a major victory for big oil, Wall Street banks, health insurance and other powerful companies. His concerns and declaration, considered a real chutzpah, stated that it could open the floodgates to special interests, adding "I don't think American elections should be bankrolled by America's most powerful interests." Together with the 2% of the US population the president wished to tax, but was opposed by his opponents, it made for a very difficult time for the ordinary citizen. An argument such as "the rich take care of the rest of the population by creating jobs" virtually puts the rich in the nonprofit category, leaving an undue burden on the middle class. The Supreme Court decision overturned two precedents and a 2002 McCain –Feingold Act, sweeping away restrictions on corporate spending during election campaigns, restrictions seen in many quarters as censorship. Justice Anthony Kennedy said the government had no right to dictate where a person might get his/her information or what distrusted source he/she might not hear, a practice which he equated to using censorship to control thought, a thing he found unlawful.

The New York Times was quick to react by excoriating what it termed a disastrous decision that would thrust politics back to the robber-baron era of the 19th century, freeing corporations to deploy their vast treasuries to overwhelm elections and intimidate elected officials into doing their bidding. But others argued that the decision extended to all corporations the same First Amendment freedoms that media corporations took for granted. Analyzing the decision, a Times article headlined "Lobbies' New Power: Cross Us and Our Cash Will Bury You." It did not take long for a Washington Post/ABC News poll to show that 80% of all Americans (Democrats, Republicans, independents) were against the controversial 5-4 SCOTUS decision of the Supreme Court, supporting Senator John McCain's prophetic prediction on CBS program, *Face the Nation* that Americans would turn against it.

Other citizens used more acerbic language in denouncing what they called a despicable decision that put career politicians in a bind, sandwiched between service to citizens and kowtowing to corporate interests. Some saw such a ruling as a dangerous move towards "government of the corporations by the corporations for the corporations", corporations having been virtually equated to human beings. Some said it was undisguised hypocrisy or condescension, by which voters were considered mindless dolts or even automatons, unable to speak up or vote their consciences. There were palpable fears that equating corporations (creatures of the law) to human beings and doing away with the limit on campaign spending, the justices unfairly drowned out the very people who make up the nation and whom the Constitution was supposed to protect. Others saw the decision as coming to terms with a fact – that we have virtually become corporations since corporations run our lives, feed us, shelter us, nurture us, fail us etc. Thus the Supreme Court was seen to have restored the rights of corporations to be proactive in the electoral process. No wonder retired Supreme Court Judge, Sandra Day O'Connor went campaigning for civic education in schools, committed to educate young people about the selection of state judges through merit appointments rather than public elections, a process that can undermine the independence of the courts. Big spending in judicial campaigns sends to voters an unintended message that justice is for sale.

Visiting French patriot and public man, Alexis de Tocqueville noted among other lessons, that the pre-democracy period in America was characterized by a few wealthy persons uniting to fight against the common folk. His writings highlighted the rise of individualism and the pervasive influence of commerce on character. Among other things the French patriot would be taking home the best lessons of the American Revolution to help his countrymen find their way in a modern political wilderness. He and fellow European John Stuart Mill congratulated and praised the United States for overcoming those evils in governance such as class interests by which small minorities wielded powers of legislation, opposing both general interest and general opinion of the community on a tacit compact among the various knots of men who profited by abuses to stand by one another in resisting reform. How could the justices, living through the painful lessons inflicted by corporate America – leaders of a few dozen industries resisting healthcare reform, climate change legislation, financial control legislation, military budget - turn on its head this sacred practice that had guided the nation for so long? Why would they seek to resurrect practices that had since been jettisoned?

Clearly a sort of reform is badly needed for both representation and the financing in politics. Because of the practice of Gerrymandering, it is estimated that 400 out of the 435 Congressional districts in the US House of Representatives can become safe, virtually excluding candidates of the opposing party ever winning there! That is unacceptable as it will usher irresponsible politics and foster overrepresentation of the base of each party as well as enhance the power of money and the incumbent. The consequence of developments like these is that the primary, rather than the general election will become decisive and even in the primary itself, where the dollar really speaks loudly, only wealthy candidates or those capable of raising money can be chosen. And since money is in the hands of the corporations, banks, law firms....

In his 2008 run for the presidency, Barack Obama the candidate became the first candidate in modern era to reject public financing, thus freeing himself to amass a staggering $745 million in campaign contributions, some from lawyers, lobbyists, donors connected to the healthcare industry, investment commercial banking, real estate interests, Hollywood and TV industries. Other level headed thinking advised moderation, stating that campaigns do lose in spite of fortunes spent on advertizing over television, radio, and newspapers. Obviously smart voters need not fear much, especially if they think for themselves. The big problem lies with persons who exhibit herd mentality. In 1958, John Kenneth Galbraith published "*The Affluent Society*" in which he argued that big business had grown more powerful than the laws of supply and demand, since corporate advertizing could generate the demand needed to keep production high. But in the very 1958, Ford Motors Company pulled the plug on *Edsel*, its model car that American drivers refused to buy in spite of all the fanfare and commercials that went with it. Corporate advertizing is not always irresistible if one also considers the story of New Coke. The big question remained whether big companies would take the Supreme Court bait and how customers would react to it.

Smart women backed by mathematical knowledge work at selling commercial air time for television stations. They gauge when television viewership is highest and charge advertisers accordingly. It is interesting how advertizing has evolved over the years. First there was the news, with snippets here and there to advertize a product, during which the newscaster took a little break. With time the snippets came to occupy more space and time, often sharing the broadcast 50/50. At this rate it is possible to foresee a future in which news becomes a mere footnote in adverting slots! As a matter of fact it is happening already in sports. An angry Bostonian gave the disproportionate space allotted to advertisements as one reason he did not bother to view the 2011 Super Bowl where the game itself was a mere 30 minutes out of the total duration of 3 hours 48 minutes. During the 2007 Super Bowl the cost of a television slot of thirty seconds was $2.7 million and climbing. In 2010, as the New Orleans Saints faced the Indianapolis Colts, it had risen to $3 million dollars and revenue from television commercials was estimated at $70 billion, all based on the revenue potential of any show. The more people watching a show, the more its revenue potential as calculated by researchers like Nielsen. A candidate for an upcoming gubernatorial election chose to launch his campaign at that time, paying a fifteen seconds TV slot for a mouth-watering sum. Good bargain. The very impressive New Orleans victory, coming five years after Hurricane Katrina devastated their state, was a doubly sweet one. Greetings like "Hi" or "How are you" quickly gave way to "Who dat?" the unofficial slogan of the Saints, their new way of saying hello. Along with the celebration of *Mardi Gras* – colorful, celebratory and bead-filled carnival carried out on Tuesday - there were lots of excitement with a new drink called hand grenade – a concoction of alcohol, such as half a liter of rum served in a container shaped like a battle field assault weapon

Cases like the 1995 trial of O. J. Simpson proved that a courtroom murder case can be a "TV gold mine." The setting was California. Governor Wilson, staggering under a huge budget deficit during that trial, was advised to avail himself of such a gold mine. Americans spend huge amounts of money on advertisements. This is the best and quickest way to take ideas and products to consumers. People use all sorts of devices to display their ads – yard signs, Internet ads, radio slots, TV slots, trolley banners, bumper stickers, and more. Michael Moore's film *"Capitalism: A Love Story"* says it all. During the 2008 primaries and caucuses, the major political parties paid for advertisement slots on television, in weblogs and road side placards to convey their messages. Senator Barack Obama was said to have surpassed all other contenders in fundraising and spending, thanks to innovative use of the Internet to reach out to his supporters. The power of the dollar surely paves the way for US politics.

The downside of the quest for more and more wealth does not always correlate positively with good health, a key element in measuring the standard of living of a people. Obviously one cannot enjoy wealth if one is sick or even dead. Health in the US is far behind health in other developed countries. First of all life expectancy at birth in the US is 78.1 years, far behind Japan's 82.2, Canada's 81.2, France's 80.9, Italy's 80.2, Germany's 79.3 or South Korea's 78.7 years. In the US the infant mortality rate is 6.3 per 1,000 live births compared with Singapore's 2.3, Japan's 2.8, Hong Kong's 2.9, or France's 3.3.

Politics was costing too much money and campaign fundraising was changing the face of politics. Hopefully the new trends in dispensing up-to-the-minute political news and discussions through MySpace, Face book, YouTube and other websites would enable poor candidates enjoy a level playing field in 2008, the year of the young voters. In Natick, Massachusetts, customers became rather rare at luxury stores like Tiffany and Co., Nordstrom, Burberry and others, thanks to a consumption explosion and an unprecedented economic meltdown which had taken quite a toll already. A customer, when shown a checkered bag encrusted with black marine motifs at $2,350, just smiled, thanked the sales agent and walked on content with her Target sample costing a modest $16. The sales agent tried desperately but failed to impress her with the possibility of putting her cell phone in a pocket of the expensive bag. Shoppers, including the status seekers, were simply browsing, not buying at all. Louis Vuitton continued to fill magazines with all sorts of models but the customers were not just buying. Retail sales had hit an all time low from Black Friday right up to Christmas and stores across the country were threatened with closure. Falling back on hand-me-downs became quite trendy again in families that would have scorned the idea not too long ago.

Concurrently the word from the pulpit at that time was that church attendance had risen significantly and priests - the only white collar workers who actually wore white collars - expressed undisguised euphoria as they rhapsodized over the pleasant change they were witnessing. What could be more natural than returning to the houses of worship what Wal-Mart, supermarkets and corporate America had snatched from them over the years? In addition to his earlier call for more empathy among Americans, President-elect Barack Obama sent a Christmas message asking them to revive the good old spirit and help one another. And expanding on Obama's call, our local priest added that in cold, rainy, snowy or generally inclement weather, it would be wonderful if drivers, as compassionate citizens imbued with empathy, could remember that they were in the shelter of a vehicle while pedestrians were not, and so express extra generosity about giving the folks on foot the right of way. Of course there were always some who claimed to be compassionate yet, as one of Boston's citizens noted, could not find compassion if it were put in their bowl of soup.

At difficult times like these the older generation has a really difficult time convincing the youths that countable things (houses, cars, money) may not often count in life whereas those things that actually count (character, heroism, honesty, stoicism, honor, altruism, bravery) are not countable at all. The lure of the dollar is formidable! People pursue opportunities to make the buck in activities that generate more benefits than costs and those short on cash simply borrow. Thus people pursue education to the extent that future benefits (earnings) exceed costs (tuition, lost wages) even if they have to go into debt to achieve this. The first time I heard of an attorney charging $80 per hour for his services, I cringed. Yet that was peanuts compared to $700 per hour or the heavy contingency fees charged by some divorce attorneys for hard and fast work or their clients' expense of as much as $10 million for a divorce settlement seven months into a marriage that did not work out, especially in romance circles where womenfolk tend to follow their hearts rather than their heads. And then there was a nineteen year old man charging $4,000 an hour! Oh la la! Oh la la! It sounded crazy. Well, that happened to be the going rate for a young man incredibly involved with computers, mountain hiking and other outdoor activities to bother about things like drugs, gangs and crime which preoccupied his peers. The boy was in his own league, the next generation of Bill Gates, one might say. An uncle had indulged him in every conceivable piece of computer equipment, including state-of-the-art CPU, monitors, the latest in color ink jet, laser printers and lots more that could enable him retrieve lost data from old model hard drives and convert the data into ASCII text for reading on any new model computer. Of course such an amount again pales into insignificance when compared with the reported hourly wage of $15,100 for CEOs of giants such as Wal-Mart. Or the type of money made by celebrities of Hollywood and the television world. When the Los Angeles Times asked whether Paula Abdul was worth $20 million, many readers wondered aloud if the former judge of *American Idol* was negotiating for a salary raise to or of $20 million with producers of the program. Then Americans learned from a Hollywood reporter that Paula's exit was immediately followed by a $45 million per annum deal between *American Idol* and Simon Cowell one of the hosts. Actor Charlie Sheen of *Two and a Half Men* on CBS was reported to net $2 million per episode and Bristol Palin was supposed to be on a speaker's circuit for $15,000 to $30,000 per appearance.

American culture apparently needs more judges and critics of the Simon Cowell type, especially in music, dressing, dance and other forms of art and is quite prepared to pay top dollars for them. *American Idol* is that necessary lightning rod that gives insight into the music business, shapes consumer taste and prepares potential artists and asks consumers to consider the entire music industry from all angles. Pop stardom is not a right; it is earned. When a consumer culture is not particularly evaluative critics become quite necessary. Ingenuity and improvisation are all in the mix with creativity and a business sense. Reality shows are said to be a first line of defense against mediocrity, evaluating an artist's work before it enters the market place. They enable consumers to be choosy and to develop critical thinking instead of a herd mentality. Yet businesses are always ever on the lookout for ways and means of stimulating consumption by stirring shopping, such as tax holiday weekends in the Bay State where people can buy things without paying the required sales tax!

Thanks to America's huge appetite for entertainment, and a corresponding willingness to underwrite it, entertainment business is booming in the US. From the lone singer at train stations in major cities, playing drums or guitars for whatever donations passengers put in their upturned hats, to persons making cross country tours singly or as a band, there is money to be made. An enterprising friend of mine once conjured the idea of taking on a big corporation by going to one of Reverend Al Sharpton's press conferences, presenting him with any number of grievances, weeping profusely on camera while the Reverend put on his most furious look and consoled him, so that a jury would be moved to make a substantial award of many millions for pain and suffering. How's that for getting rich through ingenuity and creative thinking? The case of a Japanese Jacuzzi (a type of mafia) boss who, not only got access to the US, but succeeded in dribbling the FBI and some of our most prestigious medical institutions into placing him on the top of the waiting list for a liver transplant remains in a class of its own. In all, the tab as reported by CBS's 60 minutes was a six-figure amount. The US dollar speaks very loudly. Meanwhile, China and Russia are still playing their love-hate relationship with capitalism, not quite embracing it and not totally repudiating it either as both have some of their richest guys in prison or about to get incarcerated – Russia's Mikhail Khodorkovsky and China's Huang Guangyu. China's break neck growth naturally carries along with it some casualties, especially since 2008 when it plunged by 9%, prompting Premier Wen Jiabao to say that China must urgently reverse the sliding growth.

One method of assessing America's cultural values is to observe the way people are punished for wrongdoing. In America those who run afoul of the system are punished by fines (take away their money) or by incarceration (take away their freedom).The dollar has become such a powerful tool that people use it to hit hard at those they wish to sanction. Courts use it and so do individuals and corporate bodies. During a Grand Slam tournament of the US Open in New York, Serena Williams was fined $10,000 for unsportsmanlike conduct when she lost a game to rival Kim Clijsters and proceeded to speak to the line judge using profanity-laced tirades and even smashing her tennis racket. That was nothing compared to what another sports person, Dallas Cowboys rookie, Dez Bryant, paid for a silly faux pas. By some tradition of the NFL, rookies are required to perform some menial chores for veteran teammates. By refusing to carry shoulder pads, wide receiver Dez Bryant found himself sponsoring a dinner for his team mates at a Dallas steak house for a tab of $54,000! The alternative would be to wash dishes for a month. The ACLU, by prosecuting organizations and persons involved with hate crimes, succeeded in procuring substantial cost awards that virtually put some of those organizations out of business.

Writing about the situation in Cameroon, a country twice cited by Transparency International as planet earth's most corrupt nation and featuring for many years on the IMF's highly indebted countries list, an American journalist made the following remarks : "The first impression one gets on landing at the international airport in Douala is that city roads are bumpy, full of potholes and very poorly maintained; railway and airline services are mediocre or nonexistent, small time savers have quite a task getting access to their savings in the banks". The overall impression was that the collectivity was poor whereas on those very roads one could see expensive luxury model cars like SUVs and Mercedeses, posh villas in reserved residential areas of the city and other paraphernalia of wealth, all property of tycoons who made a fetish of "celebrating their milliards" stashed away in Swiss banks or in attics of their houses. The same could be said of California, considered the world's eighth wealthiest economy. While governor Arnold Schwarzenegger struggled to balance his budget, the state of California is home to some of America's wealthiest citizens – Hollywood actors and actresses and corporate giants in the Silicon Valley. What a world!

English soccer celebrity, David Beckham, drafted to bring the game's fame and money-making to California via the Galaxy, was reputed to be so at home at the Ritz that he spoke derisively about the so-called decrepitude staff and service at our Sheraton here in Braintree, Massachusetts, calling it "the worst Sheraton in America" and even referring to its clientele as "cubicle dwellers from Syracuse in dandruff-speckled sports coats" (Grant Wahl's *The Beckham Experiment*). Such customer arrogance exploits the notion of the customer being invariably right thus placing customer service personnel in an unfavorable situation. It prompted some persons to vow to fight back, introducing CustomerHallofShame.com to check some of such excesses.

Just as William Shakespeare once created a shrewd attorney, Portia, to use all of her legal ruses and rescue a defaulting debtor from the fangs of an irate Shylock, determined to take a pound of flesh for an over due loan, today's attorney will have to come to the assistance of a former wife whose aggrieved husband is asking for his kidney back or one million five hundred dollars in lieu, as part of a divorce settlement. Blood may be thicker than water for some family members but for others money is by far thicker than blood. Angered by his wife's philandering escapades with other men after benefitting from a kidney donated by him in his zeal and commitment to do anything to seal their marriage, Romero expressed justified ire and felt the only way to seek redress was to make Margo pay dearly for her folly of embarrassing, insulting, hurting and humiliating him.

How did he find out about his wife's marital infidelities? Romero was good at putting bits and pieces together to arrive at important conclusions. First, he had come home one day and noticed that Margo was not at home – a rare happening indeed. Where was she? Frustrated but not yet irritated, he had buried his head in a newspaper. And then his wife returned, head bowed low and hands busy extracting hat pins. She had gone straight to the mirror to inspect herself, smiling self-consciously, all this while not realizing that her husband was home reading. She smiled, her fingers fluttering around the thick swirls of hair that had come loose with her hat. Her face was visibly flushed when she turned round to face her husband who had sneaked up from behind her. Margo felt like a deer caught in the headlights of an oncoming vehicle. Her husband had taken due note that one of the tiny muslin-covered buttons on the back of Margo's bodice had been fastened into the wrong buttonhole. Romero knew that Sonita, the house help was a very fastidious woman who could not have allowed such a lapse – a tiny betraying detail of a great betrayal. He took his wife's face between his hands and looked at her. He thought her lips had a softened, bruised look as well. Suddenly he did not want to touch her! He let go of her face, rubbed his hands down the side of his trousers as if wiping off contagion from the terrible swine flu.

"Is it Charlie?" he asked simply. She hesitated, fumbled for words, tried to concoct a lie about having gone to see Charlie's wife but Romero slapped her hard on the cheek and snapped "Don't. Don't trouble to lie to me. I spend my life among sexually reckless persons, the suckers and their kind." He hit her again around the lips, mashing them against the teeth and shouted in rapid succession, "*You have been kissed. You have been undressed. Someone has fucked you!*" as he pointed to the ill-fitting button. Trembling, she had said tentatively "No, not him. No one you know" as she moved back from him. But she knew she was lying. Charlie had done this to her! Incredibly she felt like Gustave Flaubert's Emma or the Emma of Jane Austen on the other side of the English Channel. In fact she felt rotten inside.

But Romero himself was no saint. The man who had uttered very harsh words against Boston's Catholic bishops during the much publicized sex abuse scandals was using his anger to cover up his own philandering. Romero's anger had shot at him in a rather strange way and he had rushed furiously out of his house and gone straight to his own mistress. Dana who lived in the next town over was just dressing to go out. He simply unbuttoned Dana's jacket impatiently, threw it on the bed, undressed her, and kissed her with unprecedented urgency. Dana submitted to rather than participated in the ensuing, untender coupling, after which she simply asked him "What was that all about?" Marital infidelity had since provided business savvy persons with a way of making money. Did those couples know so? Ashleymadison.com is one website whose authors claim that they did not invent infidelity but simply perfected it to help those who already reached the decision to cheat on their spouses, offering them discreet, secure password-protected methods. And they seem to be doing very well, thanks to their knack for wooing clientele. Prices are kept relatively low, enabling them make up for loss in unit price by greatly increasing the volume of their sales – a proven method in vogue in the sale of goods and services such as phone plans, coffee, taxi fare, and more. Craigslist.com is another website that helps couples to meet. Using an innovative formula and targeting T-riders of Boston's MBTA, it came up with TRIST score (Train romance Index Score Total) dividing the total number of missed connections by the average daily ridership for a particular station or T-line and multiplying by 10,000 the quotient so derived. In this way Park Street station came on top as the place to meet a mate, Kenmore square last and Downtown Crossing, Kendall/MIT, Central Square and other places some where in the middle.

That was not the Romero Dana had known at all. It was someone else. Where did the love go? Not too long ago, when they had just met, Romero was the typical laidback type, a real lover who took his time. Dana remembered one night in particular when they socialized leisurely in Downtown Boston, after an evening dinner together. Romero had leaned towards her and said, "You are so good." She in turn had replied "You too are so good." And then he had added, "For the record I definitely want to sleep with you" to which she had simply replied "You do?" The man she considered Mr. Right Now, and who doubled as Mr. Right for Margo, did not bother to answer her question but he knew he had taken an important step to get even with his wife. The next step would be to regain the kidney he had donated to her in her moment of great need. Could his ex-wife survive without taking cover under the wings of an attorney? Only time would tell.

Meanwhile poor Margo went around carrying the stigma and burden of Charlie in her head as well as a body in need of all sorts of surgery. She had an approach-avoidance conflict with respect to everybody and everything Charlie that she met and she needed surgery for her ovaries which she dreaded very much. A string of Charlies gave her sleepless nights. Boston is notoriously littered with all sorts of Charlies and so the task of running away or avoiding them proved daunting for her. She had had it with "pasa doble" an antic of Cuban origin involving a love triangle with her at the center. She knew its dangers from the way it ruined a glamorous marriage in the UK, pushing Diana the queen of hearts to her death in a Paris tunnel. She tried deleting the man's name from her cell phone memory and computer, got rid of T-shirts, toothbrushes, coffee mugs, other clothing, residual gifts - everything. But his name lingered on in her mind. She wanted everything reminiscent of Charlie out of her psyche. For six months she seemed to be succeeding in stamping out the name from around her - no more what Charlie said or liked or did. It had been a terrible mistake.

But Mayor Menino's Boston did not help her in this giant effort to eradicate Charlie from her life. Some of her many friends came to take her out to have some fun and cheer up. Innocuously they had planned a treat for her and of all places, they had chosen to have lunch at one of Boston's best - the iconic Charlie Sandwich Shoppe in the South End. They realized their error too late to do anything about it. One week later Margo's cousin and his family invited her to meet them at Charlie Hotel in Cambridge. "How about some place else?" the miserable Margo suggested very timidly, trying not to be ungrateful. The well meaning family then came up with Charlie Kitchen, just across the street. Would that be okay? She reluctantly acceded, not wanting to be a pain in the neck of well meaning relatives. To get there, Margo needed to get a train ticket.

For some reason the MBTA had switched from the old system of payment by tokens to paying by Charlie cards which functioned just like ordinary credit cards. After the meeting with her cousin's family, she decided to call on an old friend only to find out that she had moved to a new apartment somewhere in Charlestown. Her friends took her on a drive, passing through many interesting places, crossing the Charles River, only to end at the Chestnut Hill Mall where her two friends ended up going for ice cream at Charley's, a short drive past the Charles River. Another friend took her to the Red Sox game and stopped at a small café on Charles Street, next to where her dental appointment would be the next day – at Charles River Park. She screamed out "Give me a break, Boston! There are so many other names! Why the obsession with Charlie, Charley or Charles? What cruel marketing genius came up with all these names any way? Why was Boston such a Charles City? Did she really need all those reminders? She was glad to be able to say "No thanks" to any e-mails emanating from match.com, especially e-mails with username Chuck, Charles or any combination of these although her neighbor next door was one fanatic who promptly responded to MSPCA's designation of Charlie as the most popular pet name by changing their lovely Amigo to Charlie.

Truth be told, Romero, like his wife, was a victim of one of America's elusive quests – the soul mate. The idea draws inspiration from some obscure Greek mythology, propounded by Plato in his *Symposium* and passed on down the line that at one point in the beginning all humans did not look the way they do today. Instead they were hermaphrodites with two heads, four legs and four arms – a perfect melding of two people joined together, seamlessly united into one being. Since each had the perfect partner sewn into the very fabric of their being, each was happy. But in their happiness they neglected the gods, so Zeus punished mankind by tearing them apart, forcing them to spend the rest of their lives in search of that vanished half – the soul mate. Love is the singular fantasy of human intimacy that one plus one will some day, Zeus willing, equal one.

Love of course will soon be a thing of the past if the trend in the art of choosing discovered by researchers in India holds true and stands the test of time. Principal investigator, Sheena Iyengar compared Indian couples who married for love and those brought together through arranged marriages, using an index of happiness. At the start of the study those who married for love scored relatively higher than those brought together by parental arrangement. Ten to twenty years down the road, the same couples were surveyed again and it turned out that the situation had radically reversed with those in the arranged marriage category scoring much higher on the marital bliss scale than those who had married for love! The conclusion was inescapable that love marriages start out hot and then cool off with time whereas arranged ones start out cold and heat up later. The other inescapable conclusion was that marriage should be handed over to the family which should be trusted to make the right decisions.

Sam Yoon, a youthful Vietnamese American had teamed up with candidate Flaherty to oust Tom Menino from the post of mayor in impending elections. The first round had led to the elimination of Yoon and McCrae. Menino had ruled Boston for sixteen years and was gunning for an unprecedented fifth term of office, the kind of thing characteristic of third world democracies but then again the man's popularity remained unchallenged until the last weeks of the campaign when some unfortunate deletion of e-mails led to a call for investigations. The rivals, who had since made transparency in governance their watch word, had got a last minute godsend. People like Margo campaigned for Flaherty with all her energy, hoping that his victory would change the face of Boston for the better. But Menino had name recognition and quite a heavy war chest. Going by what the Metro newspaper said, his campaign budget was around $1.7 million and growing. Why did the incumbent mayor so much want a fifth term of office? And if he was so assured of reelection why would he spend such a colossal sum on his campaign? How could he raise funds with such facility? Had his sixteen years as mayor made him addicted to power, hence the drive to break spending record to retain that power?

Any way, Charlie was only part of Margo's problem. Her other obsession was to remain young and beautiful. What is it that makes a woman beautiful? There might be many things but she knew her breasts certainly occupied the pride of place. The shape of a woman - her torso, narrow waistline, wide hips, skin tone, full lips and hair, all count for a lot in any woman's attractiveness. Therefore it is the ovaries, and more specifically the estrogen they produce that makes a woman. Without ovaries Margo knew she would gain weight, especially around the midsection, her skin would lose elasticity, her lips would lose their fullness and color and hair would be thin. Ever since 1959 when John Howard Griffin, a white journalist darkened his skin and traveled through the southern United States to experience what it meant to be black, America knew that to be black was virtually a curse. His publication, **Black Like Me** proved it all beyond reasonable doubt. Hair and skin are very essential to the idea of beauty and attractiveness, especially to a woman. They are arousing and primal in their appeal. Inside each inch of skin are numerous sweat glands, hair, blood vessels, nerve endings through which a woman shivers, shudders, sweats, quivers, blushes. Subjecting the ovary to a surgical removal -an operation the experts call oophorectomy - has serious consequences for a woman. Removing the woman's ovaries means taking away her hormones and a thing called her libido. Did Margo have to forgo her ovaries? It was a tough choice between feeling desirability (libido) and being desired by men. Should she opt to be desired or feel desire? Margo needed her ovaries for the latter and her breasts for the former in the short run; later the doctor could take charge and do whatever needed to be done, but first she needed to live, Charlie or no Charlie, husband or no husband. Breast and ovarian cancers continue to be the average woman's nightmare.

That would be pushing matters into that gray area where doctors feel ill at ease. Ever since 1984 when Yale physician and ethicist Jay Katz had an epiphany and proceeded to write *The Silent World of Doctor and Patient*, patients have been involved in making important decisions about their lives, especially in serious matters like breast removal in case of cancer. Patients have a choice to make and that is important. The old school where doctors virtually played God, opposes this, arguing that the doctor knows better but according to the new thinking, doctors work for the patients and so must not override them in such matters. So like most modern patients, Margo would have to ask a lot of questions, look up information on the Internet and seek a second opinion before deciding. After all it was her body, as the saying goes, and it was she who must sign the informed consent before any doctor could go ahead with her surgery.

American society, awash as it is in sex - variously credited to Elvis, Helen Gurley Brown, the birth control pill, and now the Internet and Viagra - places a lot of stress on the individual, especially a woman wanting to be loved. Viagra in particular has contributed enormously in shaping how society thinks and talks about sex, love and how the twosome are linked. First released about 1998, the drug has helped millions of men revive sex lives diminished by age or disease. It has also made sexual dysfunction a very hot topic in public discussions, with commercials coyly targeting prime time television to bring erectile dysfunction its maximum impact on the audience. Even though Viagra has some proven benefits, commercial interest tends to make our sex lives seem like something that can and should be fixed with the drug! The little blue pill from Pfizer Company, known as male enhancement medication, works by blocking an enzyme found in the lungs and penis and is responsible for regulating blood flow. It has virtually become a "quick fix" for some interests.

Sex is all pervasive in America, explaining almost everything human beings do and think about, especially at the beginning of a relationship. It is a full time preoccupation in some circles - hookers love it as much as cougars, making a living on their backs as much as on their asses. People worry when they can have sex, how good they can make it, who can give it to them, where and so forth. Sex accounts for a lot of people's feelings at work and in the homes – worries, lust, obsession, fears, boredom, desires, and heartaches. It is the dynamo that drives society forward, responsible for get-togethers and splits. Sex has its own lingo and new ones continue to crop up to the chagrin of lovers of English who feel that such anti-literate short-cuts pervert, corrupt and degrade the language. The latest are puns involving *"sexting"*, a harmless word that began around 2005 and soon became the abhorrent *sextension*(braided pubic hair), *sextortion* (blackmail resulting from leaked sext messages), *sextracurricular*(cheating on a professor) to *sextermination* (a type of bed room violence ending in one's complete and utter *sextinction*).

Love triangles involving husband and wife or boyfriend and girlfriend and a third party provide materials for movies, novels, television programs and cash flow, keeping lawyers and doctors in business as well as professionals in the entertainment industry. The oldest profession changes names from time to time in response to social and legal pressures but remains basically the same. One day it is called "erotic services" the next day it is renamed "adult services" even as the main actors remain unchanged. The Internet has added a new dimension to it. These days, by simple use of the mouse, it is possible to use one's e-mail or websites like Craigslist.com to advertize one's wares and entice customers into prostitution rings. But there is a catch. The police or students of criminal justice can easily trace and catch criminals simply by looking up the correspondences of a crime victim. That is how Philip Markoff, the famous Craigslist killer was traced, arrested and detained before he committed suicide and died in his cell.

Yet we know that anxiety about our sexual partners does not necessarily need medication to fix it. Some persons definitely think that it is OK to want to amp their performance to abnormal levels. Taking advantage of these human attitudes, those with Internet connections have been unduly bombarded with commercials, unsolicited mails, invariably spam, playing off all sorts of desires and worries, for profit motives. Belatedly some persons came to realize that sex can be affected by things like domestic quarrels over who takes out the garbage to the local dumpster, lack of trust in a partner, bread winning, loss of job and other issues involving power dynamics that have nothing whatsoever to do with taking medication. But the pharmaceutical industry is not relenting in driving men and women to seek the elusive success, stigmatizing women over their supposed low wattage desire, a commodity that has no measuring yardstick as yet. Money, marketing – what a pair!

Will Viagra follow the path of the birth control pill, now in its fiftieth year? The drug known as the morning after pill came into being with lots of drumbeats from every quarter – advocates hoped it would eradicate world-wide poverty. It was blamed for ushering the sexual revolution. Thanks to the pill, poor women would use direct action by refusing to supply the market with children to be exploited and used as slaves. Those lofty goals turned sour when one of the pioneer promoters turned around and colluded with people seeking population control for dubious reasons - racial purity. The promoters of contraceptives eyed the slums, jungles and most ignorant of peoples. The idea of nation-wide sterilization for dysgenic types in the population was off putting. Still the pill for some women was the solution to infertility and for others assisted reproduction. There were religious, social and political forces at play. Overpopulation was a problem that called for a solution but by taking the pill women might become promiscuous. Both turned out to be unfounded fears. In the developing world the poor did not even embrace the drug. Black women in particular were suspicious of those trying to control their child bearing. In post-war America a new battle ground emerged – women equality toppled the monolithic figures of society such as the Catholic Church. As a matter of fact the Vatican under Pope Paul VI came close to accepting the pill in the early 1960s but in the end reneged as the pope sided with continued church opposition.

For most Americans, the lure of the dollar continues to be unstoppable here at home and abroad, making money our most valuable commodity and the main yardstick for measuring success. Everywhere in the world the dollar is accepted for business, some times given pride of place over local currency, as in Nigeria. I have had problems using my Canadian dollars in convenience stores in New England, yet in Canada as in the rest of the world, the US dollar sells hot. Faced with a nose dive in her tourism following a currency appreciation, Australian officials knew just where to turn to for rescue – our mogul queen Oprah Winfrey. And Oprah did not disappoint them. For a tab said to be in the neighborhood of $5 million and a temporary renaming of the famous Sydney Opera House after her, she brought along her entire armada for a week long recording in the sub-continent. Cheering Australians could use her Midas' touch at such difficult times.

Of all the parameters that our society can use to measure worth, the dollar stands tall over everything else. Those that fall to pariah status quickly rise to become martyrs thanks to their knack for earning the buck. (It is a rare Pat Tillman that abandons a lucrative $3.6 million contract with his team to enlist in the military). Supreme Court Judge Brandeis appealed to lawyers to not only do well but do some good also. Did that message go through? Prophet Mohammed's powerful message that a person's true wealth is the good he or she does in the world does not quite resonate with them. Nor does Jesus's powerful message to give unto Caesar what is Caesar's. Yet these very persons claim to be the followers of Mohammed or Christ and are some times prepared to kill in their names. How absurd! "American susceptibility to appeals aimed at their guts rather than their brains", lamented Charles Pierce, author of *Idiot America: How Stupidity Became a Virtue in the Land of the Free*, "reached unparalleled levels in recent years. We lived through an unprecedented decade of richly empowered hooey".

Even at these times of a tough economic meltdown, Cyberspace has opened up totally new vistas unimaginable only a few years ago. Ever so often I am assailed by electronic mail requests from wealthy widows-turned-benefactresses from Nigeria, South Africa, Burkina Faso and elsewhere, cajoling me to give them my bank account number so that they can transfer and put into it as much as $20 million, paving the way for me to enjoy heaven right here on good old earth. So much money just for the asking! The US, like many wealthy nations, is falling prey to cybercrime from Nigeria's ambitious and daring online swindlers, euphemistically called the yahoo-yahoo boys. Fleecing money from gullible Americans is big business among this group of scammers who cajole and entrap their clients (*maga*) using ingenuity and irresistible ruses. With just a laptop computer, scammers send out thousands of e-mails requesting the transfer of millions of dollars, often said to be the fortune left behind by a deceased husband, uncle or the country's heavyweights. All that is needed would be a processing fee for some paper work or insurance. The hydra-headed monster comes in many faces – unsolicited checks or offers of credit lines, SOS by loved ones supposedly locked up in prisons and in need of bailout which can be routed through well placed bogus attorneys and many more. The FBI-backed Internet Crime Complaint Center estimates that scam reports - those notorious Nigerian letters - have risen by 33% over one year and in the infamous Nigerian cases, the most popular of which is dubbed 419 (named for a section of that country's criminal code), the US loses millions of dollars yearly. Successful operations are celebrated openly in the streets of Lagos with singing of *my maga dong pay/shout alleluia* or pop songs like *YAHOOZEE* or even oldies like *cha cha cha* to glamorize the feat.

Here at home a proliferation of financial and economic wizards of all plumages litters our landscape, some without even a modicum of Economics or Finance 101, yet eagerly and zestfully frittering away the nest eggs of clients prepared to part with their lives' savings. Todd Schaffer, a certain young man in our Commonwealth, was arraigned by Attorney-General, Martha Coakley for a string of crimes including insurance fraud, larceny and attempted larceny. The man had made twenty-one fake injury claims for the same broken tooth, pocketing a total of $36,000 in the process. Having bitten into a piece of plastic in his salad at a restaurant in October of 2002, he claimed from the owners of the eatery for the cost of his treatment. But he did not stop at that; the man went ahead and filed similar claims against 21 other restaurants, using information from the legitimate claim. Even on the other side of the law, the story was not different. America woke up to the death by suicide of one of her long serving citizens, a sheriff of Middlesex County in Massachusetts. Unable to cope with the fall out of alleged ethics violations and investigations into improper campaign contributions and pension abuse, the man signed into a hotel in nearby Maine and then shot himself. It is alleged that he was preparing to take advantage of a loophole in the state's law that allowed him to earn both his pension and his salary.

Reality television has a way of converting society's villains into millionaires almost overnight. Ongoing projects or projects planned for some not too distant future would push disgraced Michael Vicks, Atlanta Falcons quarterback, convicted and jailed for abuse, torture and execution of dogs from his dog-fighting ring, into a celebrity once again; Nadya Suleiman the controversial Californian "Octomom" who delivered eight children via *in vitro* fertilization and artificial insemination, former Illinois governor Rod Blagojevich who became notorious for trying to sell President Barack Obama's vacant seat in the Illinois senate and many more. Those who thought jerks and assholes were out of the equation might need to revisit their theories especially if they learn what happens to a big chunk of Medicare disbursements. A serious downside to increasing virtualization of business and business operations is that various corporate bodies and even governments are losing money. A case in point here in the US is Medicare and in the UK, tax services. Probes have brought to light a multimillion dollar ($60 billion per year cost to the US) scam involving Medicare. Scammers and others involved with healthcare fraud take advantage of a law that places one month delay in settling bills from companies that supply Medicare patients with products after claim submission. The very short time limit makes it difficult to spot fraudulent claims. But even as such bogus claims reach a crisis proportion, creative and innovative ways are being devised to red flag them. Similar scams in Britain have been discovered in Barclays and, similar to the situation here, the government is losing a lot of money.

As a nation Americans want to get along (cooperate) and at the same time get ahead (compete). Most adults would like to describe themselves as middle class - a reassuring term that connotes being in the same league - but at the same time they wish to be considered "just folks". Money has become an important way of keeping score in Uncle Sam's land of immigrants. Wealth denotes everything – expertise, hard work, intellect and in some cases, God's special favor bestowed on religionists. Ever since the church turned to consultants and learned that their major problem was the failure to embrace a marketing orientation in an environment that had become market-driven, the men of God took the cue and adapted quickly. Prosperity gospel quickly gained ground even if it was at odds with the other message the Bible preached about the camel's much easier passage through a needle's eye than the rich entering the kingdom of God. Today things have changed for the better. To get money is to have access to the credit card. Once upon a time debt had a social stigma. Not any more. Americans live on credit. The credit industry, as one researcher found out, sees bankrupt families as lucrative targets for high-yield lending – 96 percent of those polled were offered new credit in the first year after they declared bankruptcy. And data mining is apparently big business!

Consumers are quite prepared to take lenders upon their many "unbeatable" offers even though cheap credit dissociates wants from real needs, distances the thrill of ownership from the kill joy vexation of having to pay for it. Customers have to pay through the nose for those incredible "bargains" using their credit ratings, health, freedom and entire futures. Those who went for the so-called "no money down, low interest loans" soon discovered too late that it was not they who owned the homes in which they lived, but the banks through foreclosures. The "buy now, pay later" mentality has hurt many a dream. And it did not take long for the pillars of life to start falling – jobs, workplaces, bank accounts, home foreclosures-pushing people to take comfort elsewhere. But where? How the Mighty usually fall! Former bosses and even coworkers are notorious for acting as if unemployment were a contagion, considering that they too practice the savage existence of survival - barbaric traits that mercilessly crushed others along the way, making a mockery of our civilization.

Sports began as a form of entertainment but have since become big money in the US. Children's sports are not spared, thanks to parental involvement. Americans are obsessed with youth sports and this is hurting the kids. It is not the mere presence of adults that distorts youth sports; impulsively turning the children's affair into a *de facto* professional league is the problem. Some call it the adultification of youth sports. Among its many attendant problems are the soaring rates of injury when big money entertainment networks usurp children's games. How did the idea begin and why is it being promoted? Why would any sane adult subject a toddler to honing his swing in the dead middle of winter? Besides the physical, psychological and emotional injuries that may result, there is burnout, cheating, family dysfunction, eating disorders, drug abuse and even legal wrangling. How sad that children should witness out-of-control parents, yelling at the coach and officials, other children or at each other! How sad that parents willfully indulge children in lie telling simply to get fame, publicity and riches!

Parental boasting about children's performances is slowly running out of control. Most parents who brag inordinately about their children's performance discover belatedly that there are few sympathetic ears when things go wrong, as they invariably do. Of course parental support is a wonderful thing for children's endeavors. The problem begins when parents use their children's triumphs as a way of bolstering their own self-esteem. In the process they risk undercutting their children's sense of personal accomplishment. And there is the danger that such children may come to feel that they are failures if they do not hit the home run. What to make of 17-year-old Miley Cyrus remains to be seen as she is slowly asserting her own independence. Drafted by Disney channel and branded and boxed virtually as a durable good, the young lady became the embodiment of Hannah Montana franchise, all the frills creating claustrophobic feelings in her and prompting her to seek to be herself. Although the youthful kid was said to have been baptized in a southern Baptist church as a kind of spiritual insurance against big city life, the demands of television and fame pushed her, during the Teen Choice Awards, to dance on an ice cream cart and against a pole the way strippers do, in the process igniting controversy and much concern among parents, especially those who came along with their daughters. Perceived as her family's breadwinner, the young woman claims she wants to take care of her parents, especially her mother whom she credits with sacrificing a lot in her upbringing.

Even more damaging was the news reported of a wife-swapping Colorado family that got a six year old son involved in a diabolical scheme, a real hoax which got the nation riveted on the TV sets for hours wondering what would happen to a child trapped in a helium balloon thousands of feet above the ground and flying across Colorado. Some likened it to child abuse, others to an extreme case of narcissism where the ego drives reckless behavior, and still others to prostitution, just for a publicity stunt and a marketability scheme to make money. The child's parents eventually came clean, confessed and apologized for the whole thing but a harsh backlash had been unleashed and an anxious nation cried out and got deterrent sanctions meted out for the family's bad behavior – jail time for both parents, a fine of $42,000 for the hoax and stunt that cost the state much in rescue efforts and prohibition to make money of the scheme.

Major League Baseball was going through what some had aptly called the steroid era as players in large numbers were caught taking illegal, performance-enhancing substances in a mad quest for statistics, fame, record-breaking, bigger contracts and more money. Cheating became the order of the day even as players knew that steroid taking is a disgrace to the fans, families and the game. Did a particular player take steroids to enhance performance at sports or was it to correct an underlying testosterone deficiency discovered by a PCP? Manny Ramirez, Dodger's star, formerly of the Red Sox, was suspended from Major League Baseball for fifty games, after testing positive for a banned substance, his being HCG, a female fertility drug. Other household names like Barry Bonds, Alex Rodriguez, Sammy Sosa, and Mark McGuire had suffered similar fates. All those sports icons were guilty of breaking rule #1 on Professor Finch's list – do not do anything you would hate to see on the front page of the local newspaper.

But of course players and sportsmen and women were hardly alone in doing drugs for performance enhancement. In 2002 a news item appeared as headline on major world papers. A surgeon in one of Boston's prestigious hospitals had anesthetized a patient on an operating table, sliced him open and then walked out on him, just to go and cash a check. What was so special about that check? Nothing really. The only unusual thing turned out to be that the surgeon was under the influence of methamphetamine, a raging addiction that rendered him "insane" and in financial straits. That act earned him ten years of imprisonment and a malpractice insurance settlement of $1.2 million, partly up-front payment and the rest in annuities.

A bill to allow patients the use of marijuana under certain circumstances came up for consideration. Why marijuana is illegal in the first place remains unclear given that powerful drugs like morphine, Demerol, valium, and oxycontin are legal and routinely given to patients. The notion of positive role model was turned on its head as players cheated, broke the rules and got a bad reputation and bad health. When will this murky climate be sanitized? Will big money push practitioners to go the way of the National Rifle Association and turn a blind eye to society's tribulations? Will sports promoters consider introducing a test along the lines of glycohemoglobin (HbA[1]C) used to monitor compliance with diabetes treatment and control? In this way smart sportsmen and women who test negative when indeed they consume performance enhancing drugs can be fished out, named, shamed and possibly sanctioned as well.

Americans wistfully waited for President Barack Obama to change Washington D. C. but few believed he could. The corrupting power of the dollar is just too much. With a culture dominated by overly ambitious money-grubbing Washington hot shots called lobbyists, the new president had an uphill task ahead of him. Over the past decades lobbying exploded to become Washington's biggest business. Money became be-all and end-all electoral politics guided by campaign consultants, pollsters, media management and permanent campaigning. The number of back-slapping, cigar-chomping influence peddlers was sobering. Serious entrepreneurs cropped up who realized that money could be made in Washington by helping others get what they wanted from the federal government. Some called it "earmarks", others "sweetheart deals" and still others "pork barrel projects". All that its practitioners did was build a firm and get their clients endless millions in earmarks which members of Congress sent to their constituencies. Apparently it is a lucrative business in which one simply bribes lawmakers and their staff, lavishes Congress with campaign contributions for access and good will. These are legal since there is no *quid pro quo*. Campaign lobbyists would come to roost in Washington, spending time with members of the House and Senate who in turn spent a quarter or even a third of their time soliciting campaign contributions, a practice that prompted Leon Panetta, President Obama's new appointee as CIA Director to say "legalized bribery has become a part of the culture". Members of Congress rarely legislate; they just follow the money, spending their time dialing for dollars. Things got so bad, the new CIA Director could not help lamenting over the quality of persons now running for Congress, where it is all about winning, no longer about governing.

The 2008 race to the White House was one with a lot of difference indeed. Choosing between the GOP candidate John McCain and his Democratic Party opponent, Barack Obama introduced quite a wrestle of wills at many levels, not the least of which was the family. As if it was not difficult enough to have different neighbors supporting rival candidates, within the family there were cases of husbands supporting one candidate while wives went for the opponent. In one typical case, a wife wrote checks in support of her GOP candidate, carrying his bumper sticker on her car as her husband did the exact opposite for the rival candidate. When it came to shared spaces like the front lawn, it was a bit tricky and the cordial and courteous camaraderie often ruffled, one partner almost needing a defibrillator to stay alive. This was resolved by not placing any campaign sticker on the lawn at all. And then as a result of the fuel crisis when car pooling and other economic measures became imperative, necessitating the grounding of one car, the husband found himself driving his wife's car with all the GOP paraphernalia on it. How awkward! Some called him a closet Republican but he was a Democrat at heart. The man considered buying dark sunglasses to conceal the fact that he was actually behind the wheels of a car bearing oddities for the candidate he was campaigning against. That was not all. Soon the couple's six-year son voiced his support for candidate Barack Obama and that nearly turned the tide, shaking the delicate tolerance and blowing the top up. On election morning however, husband and wife went out the door, called their son and told him they were going to the polls to cancel each other's vote. And so it was. Without perhaps realizing it, that couple had passed on a wonderful message to their son, their neighbors and the entire voting block that it is possible to be married and to support rival candidates in two opposing parties and still maintain serenity. To appreciate its importance, one needed only turn the radio or television to find out what was happening in far away Kenya where husbands were murdering wives, schoolmates killing schoolmates and neighbors raping neighbors, following Kenya's famous free and fair elections which necessitated former UN Secretary-general Kofi Annan's rushing in to broker peace between government and opposition parties.

Victorious Obama received that magical election night telephone call from his rival, conceding defeat and graciously wishing him the best. It was awesome. The president-elect moved quickly to put in place his working team, receiving former rival Hillary Rodham Clinton and conferring with her as well as Senator John McCain in a show of commitment to reach across the aisle in tackling the thorny economic and other problems confronting the nation. Senator Barack Obama was very gracious in victory and people admired him for that. That was a powerful message for politicians in parts of the world where winner-take-all continued to be the norm.

Nevertheless, as a country America had set a bad example for its citizens and we all had to pay the price for our addiction to the unrestrained binge of borrowing. Fortunately China's national policy of encouraging savings came quite handy to meet our needs. Of course there would be a stiff price to pay; sitting at the same table to negotiate, creditor and debtor could never have the same clout. American consumers struggled but failed to cope with their debts. The nation was in debt to the tune of many trillions of dollars. Things were falling apart and the US economy was no longer holding. Everybody was in debt. This was often shown by statistics such as the number of mortgages in default or unemployment claims filed. Cash-strapped communities were throwing caution and ethics to the wind in their frantic efforts to balance the books. Pressed for tax dollars to make up loopholes in their budget, for example, elected officials in Oakland, California were prepared to consider circumventing a Federal law against the growing and consumption of cannabis. Suddenly everyone was talking about medical marijuana and avoiding the ethics of allowing the drug. As the next midterm elections approached, Proposition 19 featured prominently as a ballot issue whereby California's citizens would vote to legalize the so-called recreational marijuana, sending shock waves down to Mexico, Nicaragua and Colombia where drug lords and crime syndicates waged wars to supply consumers in the US! More graphically, on a certain Tuesday, a Taunton mother, Carlene Balderama, shot and killed herself just two hours before her home was due for foreclosure auction. How did so many families borrow so much that any setback (a lost job, an illness, an upward adjustment in mortgage rate) was bound to be ruinous?

The easy answer is that consumers had been assaulted by offers from companies eager to lend them money. Students just graduating from school often found themselves beginning their working life with credit card debts! A foreclosure epidemic seemed to have hit the US. Some blamed it on avaricious homeowners who believed that real estate prices would rise for ever, making the American dream – *you can be anything you want to be; in America anyone can make it* - tantalizingly close. Greed too was a factor. So also were undue optimism and the impulse to purchase from home-shopping shows. The popular belief was that the American dream would be incomplete without a home to go with it. Unrelenting commercials urged people to go from renting to owning. Good old financial planners who had spent their time advising clients how to invest (mutual funds, annuities, stocks, and bonds) suddenly found themselves in the embarrassing situation of no longer teaching about maximizing gains but minimizing loss, thanks to the recession, the Bernard Madoffs, and public skepticism. How to convince these good people to have faith in the financial market remained a big challenge. Financial advisors and money experts of all sorts of coloration would appear before a client with million dollar cliché-cum-sales pitches such as "What do you really want? What are you striving for? Do you want to earn $1,000,000 when you are thirty? Do you want to retire a millionaire?" Lots of mouth-watering propositions indeed. Such financial goals did put many on the road to madness and elusive happiness.

Were the actors playing by the rules at all? In the past, banks and credit card issuers made money by lending to people who could repay. Consumers relied on sound advice from financial institutions about what they could afford and so assumed that no one would lend them more money than they could pay back. But with time the credit card business evolved, relying on the fees (penalties) paid by borrowers with fitful repayment histories. This proved by far more lucrative than lending to creditworthy borrowers who could repay easily and regularly. Boom! Then came the securitization and collateralization of mortgages, a process involving packaging them together, cutting them up in tradable securities, and selling them off to many entities along the line so that at any one point in time it was difficult to determine who the real creditor was. CMO (collateralized mortgage obligations) were developed by First Boston Corporation in the early 1980s to help Freddie Mac finance mortgages. The incentive to ensure that borrowers could repay was reduced! Mortgage brokers went wild! They were just speculators, a euphemism for gamblers. It became clear that banks contributed to worsening the housing crisis by improperly processing foreclosures, prompting Shaun Donovan, secretary of the Department Housing and Urban Development in the Obama Administration to declare that the Administration would respond with the full force of the law wherever problems were discovered.

In retrospect, it seems like the mortgage meltdown could indeed have been prevented. The alarming rate of proliferation of subprime mortgages in the US banking system was reported to Alan Greenspan, the Federal Reserve Chairman at the time but he apparently ignored it and failed to crack down on the practice. Similar recommendations from the GAO (General Accounting Office) and a task force from the Clinton Administration fell on deaf ears. Citigroup, HSBC and similar banks went on underwriting the subprime loans with relish. Belated proposals to empower the Federal Reserve gave the impression that the institution lacked the power in the first place. But Alan Greenspan did not lack the power; what he lacked was the will to implement useful regulatory measures. After September 11, 2001, easy money policy and banking deregulation were at the root of the meltdown as real estate lobbyists went to work, shaping government policy by opposing regulation. House ownership was parroted as a boon to low income neighborhoods, social and economic mobility with lenders increasingly funding mortgages for amounts perilously close to or greater than the value of the underlying properties, all in pursuit of lavish fees and greater profits.

It would task the Harvard PhD enormously to unmask the smart guys. Financial institutions which ran the risk that overwhelmed customers could declare bankruptcy, turned to the Federal government to enact laws making it harder for borrowers to escape their debts. The Federal Reserve Board belatedly tightened lending rules to curb the worst home-lending abuses by requiring mortgage lenders to document borrowers' incomes and verify that they could repay any loans – a self-interest practice which the bankers had forsaken along the way.

But Alan Greenspan acted too late! He and Bob Rubin, Treasury Secretary and the brain behind Bill Clinton's economic wonders as well as Larry Summers who succeeded him could have done better for the economy if they had not become apostles of a certain Washington Consensus-based American model that harped too much on the efficiency of markets and free trade during those Clinton years and beyond. It is true that Adam Smith had spoken eloquently about his belief in the notion that markets are efficient, produce optimum welfare and should therefore be left alone to work their magic, free of government intervention which chokes and distorts, unlike the unseen but efficiently operating hand. But was Adam Smith necessarily right? At the time his theory was propounded, the British navy ruled the seas and Britain could and did dictate trade conditions to any of her colonies throughout the Empire as well as to her rivals. As a matter of fact, in addition to Adam Smith (*The Wealth of Nations*) there was also David Ricardo (*On the Principles of Political Economy and Taxation*) who could never allow England to outsource her textile mills to Portugal, no matter the sugar-coated talk of reciprocal trade and manufacture, a doctrine of simple free trade with limited insights valid in 1817, the very serious flaw American negotiators made in their deals with China, parroting it around as a win-win situation when indeed adversarial would have been the ideal! And then there were the newer generation of experts and apostles in the field – John Maynard Keynes (the market can remain irrational longer than we remain solvent), George Soros, master market player and the reality of market perception, efficient market expectation.

Moving manufacturing facilities to China was done as a panacea to reducing costs of production in addition to getting a larger market but has that been borne out? How smart was the move to leave behind skilled labor, capital and technology only to go and be confronted with an abundance of unskilled labor in China? Faced with the superabundance of unskilled labor upon landing in China, the next option was to train them of course. Corporate training and transfer of technology was crucial to make any head way. The initial manufacturing facilities became de facto university laboratories! And so the pursuit of profits brought US citizens into some complex and unforeseeable realities. The dual personality of a typical US citizen-cum-CEO came out when faced with job loss to his country of origin on one hand and his fiduciary responsibility to his shareholders to maximize profits on the other. Under such circumstances, rallying to the flag the way his predecessors would have done forty or fifty years earlier was out of the question.

Alan Greenspan, Bob Rubin and Larry Summers embraced and championed the idea of an efficient market and free trade with deregulation and made believe that it was responsible for the prosperity during the Clinton years. Efficient market hypothesis (EMH) became virtually a religion, an extension of Reaganomics, extolling the magic of the market, a religion that ruled thinking about financial and other matters till the crisis of 2008. The Federal Reserve Chairman (*The Age of Turbulence*) actually wondered "Why inhibit the pollinating bees of Wall Street?" in subscribing to the idea that deregulation would engender financial innovation that would reduce risk, increase productivity of capital and promote greater prosperity. The man's faith was unshakable that markets would police themselves, so any restrictions on fund investment behavior would curtail risk taking. Such views naturally opposed government regulation or anything done "by the book".

Even then that provided only part of the answer. Distinguished Ivy League professors who had trumpeted the dawn of a new era of stability scrambled to explain how exactly the worst financial crisis since the Great Depression of 1929 had ambushed their entire profession.

In a period of soul-searching commentators began to speak in terms of the arrival of a "Minsky moment" or a "Minsky meltdown" as some insiders called it. Hyman Minsky was an obscure macroeconomist who died over ten years ago, unknown to many, but lately his name began to emerge from the shadows as perhaps the most prescient thinker regarding what the world was going through. He was an expert in the subfield of finance and crisis – an unfashionable subfield - and probably saw what was coming and even predicted the kind of meltdown hammering the global economy. Great Nobel Prize winning economists belatedly considered incorporating his insights and his books were once more in print and selling briskly. Minsky's star was only rising then as economists searched for a fix for the world economic meltdown! The man believed in capitalism but he also believed that it had a genetic weakness, arguing that modern finance was far from the stabilizing force that mainstream economists portrayed; rather, it was a system that created only the illusion of stability while simultaneously creating the conditions for an inevitable and dramatic collapse. According to him the system contained the seeds of its own destruction. "Instability" Minsky wrote, "is an inherent and inescapable flaw of capitalism". How prophetic!

Economics has often been subjected to powerful orthodoxies, such as the one born after World War II (neoclassical synthesis) preached the belief in a self-regulating, self-stabilizing free market, thanks to a few selectively absorbed insights from John Maynard Keynes, the great economist of the 1930s who wrote extensively about the way capitalism might fail to maintain full employment. Most economists still believed that free market capitalism was the fundamentally stable basis for an economy, though thanks to Keynes, some of them now acknowledge that the government might, under certain circumstances, play a role in keeping the economy on an even keel. Did we not see Henry Paulson and Ben Bernanke injecting lots of money into the economy? Also, President Obama has written to the Wall Street Journal indicating that he had taken measures to clear the way for business growth. Among other things he said he was mandating a government-wide review of those rules already on the books to remove outdated regulations that stifle job creation and make the US economy less competitive. Hopefully such measures as well as the appointment of a former corporate executive as his new Chief of Staff should counter the perception that his administration is insensitive to business interests.

Minksy, like Paul Samuelson who became the public face of the new establishment in Washington D. C., studied at Harvard University with the legendary Austrian economist Joseph Schumpeter and future Nobel laureate, Wassily Leontief. But Minsky was made of a different cloth; unlike his colleagues who were obsessed with mathematical models, he pursued research on poverty, hardly a hot topic in economics. Yet that kept him busy even if not a mainstream culture. In addition to poverty he delved into finance, a relatively important topic even if it had no place in the theories formulated by Samuelson. Minsky asked the simple but disturbing question: "Can it (Great Depression) happen again?" Drawing from Keynesian lessons (that government could step in and micromanage the economy and smooth out the business cycle and keep on an even keel), he stayed away from what he called "bastard economics", concentrating instead on drawing his own far darker lessons from Keynes' land mark writings which dealt not only with employment but also with money and banking. He emphasized that capitalism was by its very nature unstable and prone to collapse, that far from producing that magical equilibrium, capitalism would do the very opposite – it would lurch over a cliff. That bore the stamp of his advisor, Schumpeter, the Austrian economist famous for "creative destruction". Minsky spent more time thinking about destruction than creation and came away formulating an interesting theory: not only is capitalism prone to collapse, it was precisely its periods of economic stability that would set the stage for monumental crises. He called his idea "Financial Instability Hypothesis".

According to this hypothesis, in the wake of a depression, financial institutions and businesses are extraordinarily conservative. With the borrowers and lenders who fuel the economy all steering clear of high risk deals, things go very smoothly – loans almost always paid on time, businesses generally succeed, and everyone does well. The success however, inevitably encourages borrowers and lenders to take on more risk in the reasonable hope of making more money. Success breeds disregard of the possibility of failure. And so people forget that failure is a possibility, hence the "euphoric economy" develops eventually, fueled by the rise of far riskier (speculative) borrowers whose incomes would cover interest payments but not the principal and the Ponzi borrowers whose incomes could cover neither, and could only pay their bills by borrowing still further.

Talking of the business of medicine, or more appropriately, the way medicine had been converted into a business, the CEO of a medical foundation once said, "money talks" when Medicare and three other insurers decided to go tough and hit hospitals where it hurt the most – their wallets. In an innovative program to curb the high incidence of injury and infection resulting from carelessness on the part of healthcare delivery personnel, the insurers took the decision to place hand-washing spies all around, set surgical sponges that sounded an alarm if left in the body of a patient and room sterilizers that promised to wipe out bacteria lurking in bedrails. Topping the DO NOT PAY list established by Medicare were infections. Hospitals would not be reimbursed for breaches, especially when such errors added up between $10,000 and $100,000 to the cost of a patient's hospital stay. Some study showed that pneumonia, a blood-borne infection caught in hospitals, killed 48,000 patients and cost $8.1 billion in 2006. That was an awful lot of money and loss. As a matter of fact sepsis (blood infections acquired at surgery) was responsible for 20% of the deaths. Of recent MRSA (methycillin-resistant *Staphylococcus aureus*) has been very much in the news because it made our hospitals virtually dangerous places to visit!

Incredibly suicide became an increasingly popular response to indebtedness. Consumer bankruptcy attorneys frequently attested that their clients showed up at their offices with cyanide or guns in their cars in case they got no help. Can death be an effective remedy for debt? To save his honor, a Japanese may choose to take his own life. Under similar circumstances, an American would turn to his insurance company. Those Caribbean vacations, closets full of designer clothes, adjustable rate mortgages and more killers had turned the American dream into a nightmare. People kept wondering why God or some abstract economic climate caused the credit crunch. It was certainly not God that did it; it was human beings masked as financial institutions. Some of them had faced trials and gone to jail but most of them were still out there in the corner offices getting fat on the blood and tears of debtors. A few had committed suicide but the heavyweights were very much around. Suicide seemed to have become the way out for some of the baby boomer generation with unrealistic life expectations, leaving some to wonder whether organizing candlelight vigils for such deaths did not have the unintended consequence of sending out the wrong message. The regulatory bodies had gone to sleep or so it seemed. What on earth happened to the SEC? How was it possible for Angelo Mozilo, former Countrywide Financial CEO to get away with the fraudulent practices the Federal Regulators were belatedly charging him – falsely leading investors to believe the mortgage giant had avoided subprime lending mistakes even as Countrywide continued to issue riskier and riskier loans?

How did Alan Stanford succeed to use his Stanford group to fraudulently place his investors and clients' CDs in jeopardy? What will happen to the economies of Antigua, Venezuela, Caiman Island, and all other third world countries where those fraudulent schemes were operated? How can third world countries be blamed for stashing away their stolen wealth in Swiss banks when thousands of

Americans did the same, using the UBS to shield them from paying taxes to Uncle Sam? How could Bernard Madoff get away with $50 billion dollars worth of people's lives' savings?(Testifying before a Congressional committee, a whistleblower actually said that he had alerted the SEC about Bernie Madoff but not one person listened to him!). It would appear that taking advantage of regulatory agencies turning a blind eye to such misdeeds, the perpetrators cooked up a scheme by which they obtained money from new investors to pay off earlier ones until the scheme collapsed as there were no longer new investors signing up. This operation was eponymously named after Charles Ponzi who devised the scheme around 1920, promising investors 50% returns on their investments in just 45 days! People from humble roots who sought to get rich quickly were the usual victims of this type of scheme. Persons bent on getting easy money are usually so gullible, they hardly stop to think or verify the tantalizing "secret ways" to wealth.

It is still very troubling though that for many persons, the recent financial meltdown simply descended like an epidemic with no warnings at all. "Not quite," insisted one expert, stating that we all saw this coming long ago and there is no use pretending about it. He traced the root cause of the problem to the early 1980s when Ronald Reagan came to the helm and Americans began to gamble and win and think magically. New American homes quadrupled in prices and Dow-Jones industrials jumped from 803 in 1982 to upwards of 14,000 around 2007. The share of household incomes spent on debt servicing mortgage and other customer debts rose by 35%. At around 1982 an ordinary household could save 11% of its disposable income but in 2007 this had dropped to barely 1%. Until the late 1980s only the state of Nevada and New Jersey had casinos for gambling; these days at least twelve states do and in 48 others there is some sort of legalized betting practiced. As one observer put it, it is as if we had Christmas and Mardi Gras all year round. The size of the average home increased by 50% and Americans lived literally and figuratively large, gaining as much as twenty-five pounds of weight yearly. Today's ubiquitous obesity comes as no surprise at all, the rate having risen from 11% in 1970 to the present 33%. Society is paying the price for our uncontrolled profligacy. Take the airlines, for example. With the average weight gain over the years, obesity poses a problem for air travel as passengers encroach upon the space and convenience of those seated next to them. The inability to bring down arm rests that separate the seats on an aircraft is a problem. So also is the inability to fasten seat belts. For many travelers such indices of obesity take away the joy of traveling. For the airlines, this surely hurts the pocketbook.

So if these things were seen as far back as that, what happened? Well, Americans simply ignored them. That is the simple answer. Some people just shrugged them off. What else could be expected from a steadily declining household income, the ballooning of the values of houses and 401(k) s? The dotcom boom and its power as well as its new economy brought about magical thinking. Americans clearly lived like the jolly grasshopper which had fun while the dutiful ant was busy preparing for winter. We all lived in Alice's wonderland in spite of the gut feelings we had that all was not well. This type of lifestyle is also called the impostor syndrome – a deep feeling of unease clad in an exoskeleton of ostentation the way top executives of AIG and other investment banking goliaths felt even as tax payers' dollars were doled out to them. More than one American thought that arrogant, ignorant and greedy would be a more befitting interpretation of AIG than American International Group.

Clearly it seems as if we have all lived in this dreamy world for the three decades from the 1980s till the 2000s, the spirit of an awesome winning streak in a gambling casino, a winning that went on and on and on, until we finally reached this dead end. Delayed gratification took a back seat in our scheme of things as chain stores mesmerized us with their products at super cheap rates. 9/11, like the Iraq war, felt more like a bump on an otherwise smooth drive of overspending and overleveraging. The number of holidays multiplied, each coming with its own mercantilist underpinning –Christmas and those jingle bells, thanksgiving, mothers' day, fathers' day, Halloween, Valentine's Day and others.

Deep down, Americans knew that this was unsustainable! Nobody raised a finger, not even our many economic wizards who were content to pontificate that unfettered capitalism and the withering away of some of our enterprises and industries was a healthy and necessary part of a vibrant, self-correcting economy. In retrospect, authors like Ken Gormley place the decline at around the time Robert Fiske began investigating former President William Jefferson Clinton over some land deal in Arkansas. He found no wrongdoing on the part of the Clintons but the GOP was not satisfied; Kenneth Star was appointed as independent counsel to take over. Ken Starr, who liked to be considered a modern day Atticus Finch, also found insufficient evidence and was about to shut down the investigation when a certain Linda Tripp appeared on the horizon with a juicy story involving a tape of conversations between Monica Lewinsky and the former president. Things changed overnight. Urged on by the climate of witch hunting that reigned at the time, Ken Starr's investigation changed course and began pursuing this godsend with lots of gusto. Even then that line too led to a cul-de-sac because the US Senate in 2001 acquitted Bill Clinton of perjury charges. But by then the damage had been done; the seeds of the nation's blue states and red states had been sown, reflecting America's divided political landscape.

Yet in placing the nation's economic problems squarely at the doorsteps of the Democrats and their president, the Republican Party appeared to be oblivious of a fact that Bill Clinton left office in 2001, leaving behind $236 billion surplus which President George W. Bush, a Republican walloped in eight years, thanks to his two wars – Iraq and *Operation ANACONDA* launched to capture Osama bin laden dead or alive by massive bombardment of his hideouts in the Tora Bora mountains of Afghanistan –subsequently passing on the deficit of $1.2 trillion to President Barack Obama in 2009. Surely the American people had not suddenly developed amnesia! Or had they?

Actually as far back as 1979 Jimmy Carter did raise a finger but the nation failed to listen to him, probably because he spoke from the nadir of his presidency and of the Democratic Party as well. For indeed President Jimmy Carter's address, dubbed *"malaise"*, was a bold statement of conservative ideals. Imagine what could have happened to this nation if Democratic defeatism was not hailed to the exclusion of a more rational assessment of Mr. Carter's message. Jimmy Carter did not confront what he saw as a sense of public alienation, spawned by inflation, an oil crisis, withdrawal from Vietnam and the Iranian revolution. As the man saw it, the way forward lay in conservation, energy independence, and acceptance of the fact that the US could no longer bend the world to its will. President Carter warned against the temptation of "the path that leads to fragmentation and self-interest. Down that road lies a mistaken idea of freedom, the right to grasp for ourselves some advantage over others." The former president clearly pointed out that on the contrary "All traditions of our past, all the lessons of our heritages, all the promises of our future, point to another path, the path of common purpose and the restoration of American values." Unfortunately obsession with the greatness of America did not allow this powerful message to sink into the national psyche.

At that time the debate before the US Senate to apply the normal gas requirements for cars was not received kindly at all, especially by operators of America's favorite car – the SUV. The standard, known as CAFÉ (Corporate Average Fuel Economy) sought to raise fuel efficiency of vehicles from 13 to 27 miles per gallon. Opposition killed the bill and gas consumption and fuel imports rose. Naturally America found itself in the crisis simply as a result of a willingness to sacrifice for cheap oil both hard won freedom and the fortunes and lives of their children. As national security continued to be defined in terms of protecting the source of cheap oil, its source or who controlled it, yearly petroleum imports rose to $400 billion and with them the trade deficit.

Even till this day and in spite of the painful lessons we are living through, some experts still rely on gambling away the nation's limited resources by staking state budgets on the fortune of gambling, an activity that depends so heavily on the poor who can least afford it. Thousands of dollars go into boosting advertising for scratch tickets, a most dubious means of raising taxes. The tickets are cheap, plentiful and have virtually become today's crack cocaine found in almost every convenience store around the corner and those who buy the most are the poor blue collar workers with a quixotic dream to make it rich very quickly. Treasurers easily get carried away by the lure of the lottery and they go asking the legislature to make available budgetary provisions for advertising to reach out to casual middle class players, convinced that this will provide the state with a means of raising awareness about big jackpot games. Unfortunately it does not always work out that way. The big bucks spent on advertising in newspapers, television, or websites, and aimed at persons who do not usually buy the scratch tickets, do not often pay dividends. Only the blue collar workers are involved with this most addictive game which can wallop over 70% of the advertising budget. Did JFK not state categorically that if a free society cannot help the many who are poor, it cannot save the few who are rich? How can a state lean so heavily on the backs of those who can least afford it? State authorities are even going further to contemplate slot machines which are as addictive as the scratch tickets. Isn't this a form of regressive taxation that is also unreliable? Why opt for it? The push for casinos for the Wampanoag came back on Governor Deval Patrick's agenda again.

Gambling as a way of raising revenue is very debatable. Proponents of casinos and slot machines seem to be getting support from the top at the highest level of the State government, where law makers are worried about worsening budgetary situation and increasing unemployment. Gambling, according to them, is an economic life line that will bring in jobs. They eye Foxwoods and Mohegan but wonder where to implant another without protests from local residents. Opponents warn that expanded gambling will suck money out of the economy and introduce unwelcome traffic and the evils of addiction, indebtedness and crimes. Some have alleged that the evil of addiction is such that can keep parents away from their kids left in a parked car all day long! Studies have been carried out which consistently showed that crime and family strife always go up in the larger regional economy after casino gambling is introduced, making attorneys who often double as shrinks, the only persons unnecessarily excited about this as a means to shore up their sagging client load. It is not enough to win a state license; approval from a host community's residents is equally important. How these opposing views play out in the months ahead will determine which way Governor Deval Patrick and President Barack Obama's policies go.

Of the virtues of our Founding Fathers (sobriety, hard work, practical ingenuity, commonsense and fair play) we have combined also our wilder, faster and looser side (impatience, self-invented gamblers) that made possible and continues to make possible the American dream of riches for the plucking with little or no supervision, turning a blind eye to the prudence of saving and building and instead extolling the fantastic but crazy idea that anybody, given enough luck and liberty, can make a fortune overnight. That is what brought the present painful crisis on us. We must now make the painful but necessary shift from an unfettered individual zeal for the individual getting and spending to a rediscovery of our common good. That is the enormous challenge facing President Obama and the US leadership.

Instead of committing suicide, others turned to American ingenuity and appeared to be doing just fine. There were proposals for Mutual Fund swap to help absorb some of the heavy losses in stocks by offering something else. Peer-to-peer (P2P) lending grew as banks failed to meet the needs of the small enterprises. There was also trade by barter which some had already begun to practice. And as the banks collapsed, the sale of mattresses soared, reflecting the need for alternative places to store hard earned dollars. Wasn't that where it all began in the first place? Some have suggested getting rid of banks altogether since banks were the root cause of the nation's problems. Mattresses would do just fine to store money. As for jobs, that is a hard one. Systemic flaws, risky banking and poor corporate investment contributed to the mess, making money to stop flowing and putting people out of work. If, as one of our countrymen has so kindly suggested, money is reclassified as an "endangered species" a lot of good can come of it. Like all other endangered species, money will then require special treatment, deserve government protection and assistance until such a time that jobs start multiplying again as such endangered species are wont to do in captivity, before being returned to the wild. Isn't that awesome? Why all the fuss about a government option when that is the sure way forward?

When oil prices shot up, it became too much for workers at a dental office in Arlington, Washington, some of whom began to ride their ponies to work, thus actually cutting down to one horse power in energy consumption. American ingenuity came on display all over, especially in job creation. Faced with an unrelenting slowdown that had hit conventional retail stores, shrewd business persons turned their entrepreneurial wizardry in many new directions. In my city where one man's trash is another man's treasure, thrift stores became very popular. People who lost their jobs and could not immediately land alternative glamour jobs could be seen picking all sorts of trash for clothing and other items of interest.

Hard times usually call for adaptation of life styles and one way of doing so is through green thinking - reusing instead of sending off to landfills. Gone are the days when men sported expensive watches and women a different handbag for every occasion, thus helping makers of leather goods to cope with the economic crisis. Even though job uncertainty due to the economic slump prompted some men to cut back on spending, women in large numbers continued to take steps to cheer themselves up with all sorts of treat. Hand-me-downs were gathered, washed, bleached and put to use once more, for about one quarter of the cost it would take to purchase a brand new equivalent in retail stores. (Many still went to retail stores but only to procure those special items of clothing needed for a job interview). There were some discarded items still bearing $300 price tags on them and it was not unusual to come across brand names like Ann Taylor, Ralph Laurent, Prada, or Louis Vuitton. Yard sales, flea markets, auctions and thrift shops became quite trendy again. Thanks to yard sales and other give-aways, those with an appetite for acquiring up-to-date, state-of-the-art items made it possible for others to own hand-me-downs or discarded stuff still in good condition. Operators spent days sorting, pricing and tagging pre-owned goods like antiques, books, strollers, toys, purses, shoes, military uniforms, items recovered from grandma's basement or attic, donations and many more. One operator befittingly called her store *The Hodge Podge*. In general most of the items were from women who easily discarded what they considered old-fashioned, unlike men who wore theirs till they disintegrated.

Surely the economic crisis had its good side too. It brought out a lot of creative potential in people. Many persons abandoned their personal cars for mass transit, thanks to increased fuel cost, the problem of slow crawling traffic at rush hour and expensive parking fees in the metropolis. Thanks to the Internet and to websites like Craigslit.com, many families living in the city and working in the suburbs were able to link up with those doing the reverse commute into the city; in this way, their home garages could be rented for a modest amount by those unable to afford the municipal rates. What could be better than making some money for a car garage that would otherwise remain unused during the 8-hour shift that the owner was away? Economists have a name for such a scheme. It is called a win-win situation.

On a bigger scale websites cropped up with all sorts of green jobs. Greening the world identified tons of new and emerging occupations, including energy auditors who measure the energy efficiencies of buildings, carbon traders who deal in carbon credits, chief sustainability officers to oversee a company's environmental policies. Green-collar jobs entered popular lexicon as President Obama's economic stimulus money sent searchlights around for shovel-ready projects, hands-on category responsible for weatherization and boosting energy efficiency in offices and homes. Companies were created to use patented microorganisms to convert biomass into ethanol fuel or specializing in solar installations. Applicants were advised to start anywhere – certified electricians, plumbers, any craft of their choice and to visit Clean Energy Centers in each city or town where they would be assisted to fit into existing processes involving creation or implementation of green products and services or design processes incorporating recycling, reuse or remanufacturing. How exciting!

Meanwhile some disturbing but inescapable questions were being asked, such as "What went wrong with the Harvard MBA?" Why would three prominent Harvard graduates of Business Administration find themselves in so much hot water? It was puzzling that Jeffrey Skilling, a convicted felon, deposed as CEO of ENRON Corporation was serving 24years in prison for fraud; that Stan O'Neal was ousted by Merrill Lynch and Co. after failing to know about the mortgage risks that led to the biggest write down in the company's history: that Jeffrey Peek was struggling to sell CITI Group Inc's assets after the leading company's shares dropped 73% in twelve months. Here was a bank that, through fraud and misconduct, made life difficult for Larry Hagman, fondly remembered as the actor who played the part of the villainous J. R. Ewing in "Dallas," the 1980s TV series. Where was the appeal of elite education and schools as a whole? No wonder some began to speak derisively about continuing with college education. Why go to college when one could get rich without a college degree? Naturally the nation depends on its experts to guide thinking and action on many issues where knowledge is limited. This imposes enormous responsibilities on the experts to know what they are talking about. The present crop of Harvard graduates is not alone in shouldering responsibilities for America's plight. Robert McNamara, one time Secretary of State under Presidents John F. Kennedy and Lyndon Johnson, was a product of the Harvard Business School, a whiz kid and mastermind of World War II logistics who went on to become CEO of Ford Motor Company at age 44. As key protagonist of the Domino Theory and Vietnam War, he belatedly admitted that the war had been a mistake, a burden he carried right to his grave and today is remembered as the smart guy whose errors and arrogance led to hundreds of thousands of deaths.

The MBA, whether from Harvard, Babson or any number of elite institutions around the nation, was a requirement for progress up the corporate ladder, equipping their owners to meet the challenges of an ever changing global environment, a tool for change of careers, acquisition of soft skills such as staff motivation or the change of management to number crunching so as to find an outlet in accounting or corporate finance. Such a qualification would provide individuals with confidence and knowledge to compete in the larger world beyond, imbibing them with principles of how to manage others, beginning with a mastery of self, assessment of strengths and weaknesses, and an acceptance of the basic fact that we are all humans - vulnerable and imperfect. The Harvard business school was founded in 1908 to teach business leaders how to make decent profit by doing decent business. This was the reality until 1970 when University of Chicago's Milton Friedman began to sound a different note, with making money for shareholders or final risk takers a priority. Shareholder sovereignty became the dominant doctrine. But it was debatable whether shareholders had more at stake than other stake holders, especially when seen in the light that they could divest themselves of risks more easily than the others.

With respect to the economic and financial meltdown, our financial experts continued to advise that over the long haul, short term swings were not going to affect long term output and that stocks would outperform bonds which in turn would outperform cash. For purposes of investment diversified portfolios were recommended. They said the market was cyclical and drew attention to the bull market of 1999 – 2000. Markets tend to repeat themselves, the experts agreed. Good advise, except that there was a déjà vu ring to it, coming as we faced the terrible economic crunch. The big boys had thrown everything in limbo. Elizabeth Warren, an expert in bankruptcy and consumer finances nominated by President Obama to oversee the Congressional Oversight Panel charged with keeping tabs on the $700 billion bailout of the financial sector, an outfit formally designated Troubled Assets Relief Program (TARP), had some very revealing remarks to make concerning the treasury's lack of documentation and the contradictory account of what it intended to accomplish under the economic stimulus plan.

Her findings did not bring about peaceful sleep for the tax payer at all because they revealed a culture clash in which the policy of public participation with a goal to allocate benefits and pain as fairly as possible went diametrically opposite to Wall Street's (insider) culture built on self interest institutions maximizing their benefits without a lot of outside interference. That explained the clash seen in the AIG affair. How could such a goal be realized with taxpayer subsidy? The insiders (investment bankers and other financial institutions) could not possibly eat their cake and have it too. The repeated bailouts or calls for bail out were a singular illustration of Albert Einstein's definition of insanity –doing the same thing over and over and expecting a different outcome. While their arrangement worked well for them, the need for outsider money to fund it did not sit well with the taxpayers.

It might come as a surprise to many but apparently Governor Arnold Schwarzenegger of California did not accept a salary for his services, nor did Phil Bredsen of Tennessee. Governor Jon Corzine of New Jersey was said to accept only $1 per year just like New York City's mayor Michael Bloomberg. Actually the mayor said he got even less than that after tax was deducted! Lately the three giants of General Motors, Ford and Chrysler proposed to put themselves on a salary of $1 per year too in their pleas for the US Congress to bail their companies out of the financial crunch threatening their operations. Who could have believed that the big giants – General Motors, Ford and Chrysler – would put aside their private jet planes, take ordinary automobiles like regular mortals and come to Washington D. C., cap in hand and on bended knees, begging members of the US Congress to bail them out financially? And they did! Who could have foreseen that Ford's stocks would take a nose dive and slump down to $2? Who could ever foresee those moguls accepting to work for $1 per year or no pay at all?

If the Boston Globe's Parade magazine is to be believed, the wealthiest Americans would be found among the singers, actors and actresses of the entertainment industry in Hollywood and those in the sporting arena, like Tiger Woods. These Americans make money in the millions of dollars per year whereas mortals like math teachers, governors ( Sarah Palin of Alaska, former Illinois governor, Rod Blagojevich), mayors and the heroic Captain Chesley Sullenberger who epitomized the nation's bravery, patriotism, intellect and efficiency all at once, were mere thousandaires. What is one hundred thousand compared with three to five millions? Our system of values is incomprehensibly skewed with Wall Street oil traders making between $1 million and $2 million per year whereas brain surgeons and topnotch scientists are trailing far behind them at around $600,000. Understanding airline industries and their way of life has always been rocket science for me all along; the matter of low pay is only one out of many paradoxes. Cruising at 400 miles per hour and 4000 feet above planet earth, flight attendants have no problems going about serving coffee and Chateaubriand to passengers, as the aircraft ploughs through potentially dangerous clouds, but once on the tarmac and cruising leisurely at ten miles per hour, the very flight attendants must be seated and buckled up.

Piloting US Airways flight 1549, Captain Chesley "Sully" Sullenberger III, took off from New York's LaGuardia airport on Thursday January 15, 2009, bound for Charlotte, North Carolina. In just two minutes after being airborne, his aircraft flew into a herd of geese which knocked off both engines instantly and the plane began to lose altitude. The exchange between Captain Sullenberger and air traffic control was amazing for its revelation of the character of a trained, experienced and smart professional. Cool, calm and very much in control, the former air force pilot took charge of the plane, maneuvered it skillfully and bravely, and force landed it on the Hudson River, barely missing the George Washington bridge and in the process saving the lives of all the crew and passengers on board. President-elect Barack Obama could not have got a more befitting icon to show off to Americans and the world at large, what his presidency envisaged for the years ahead. But the captain's salary paled in comparison to his heroic achievement. How could the much tooted free market of supply and demand allow such disparities? Detractors were quick to say that the captain did only his job, nothing but his job, especially when, a few months later, another pilot and his assistant overshot the airport of their destination by one hour, having been absorbed in something other than piloting their aircraft and minding passenger safety.

# 2.

## From Nowhere to the White House?
## (Yes we can).

*Rosa sat so that Martin could walk.*
*Martin walked so that Barack could run.*
*Barack ran so that our children can fly.*

These lines appeared in newsrooms and the front pages of many newspapers following Senator Barack Obama's spectacular victory over Senator John McCain in the 2008 race to become America's 44th president. It was an event without precedent and pregnant with meaning. Who could forget Rosa Parks, the small, fearless black woman who refused to surrender her seat to a white passenger and to sit in the back of a bus in Montgomery, Alabama thereby precipitating the momentous civil rights movement? And who could forget Martin Luther King Jr., the charismatic civil rights leader who courageously led the civil rights march to the US capitol, extolled the idea of judging persons by the content of their character rather than the color of their skin, energized by his dream to see America united some day - but alas! - slain by James Earl Ray? Indeed Senator Barack Obama the rising star was surely following in the foot steps of those great pioneers and carrying on the relay baton.

Clearly the paternalism of the white slave master of the pre-civil war period is over and no one can deny it. An unsung hero like the celebrated Morris Dees, founder of the Southern Poverty Law Center of Alabama, can rejoice that his life's work did not go in vain, in righting the wrongs of a divided society, from an early childhood of offering drinking water to blacks serving in his parents' cotton fields, to litigating against hate crimes perpetrated against the very blacks, stopping the forced sterilization of black teenage girls and many more.

*Southern slave masters had a totally different view than their northern counterparts. March, a visiting nineteen-year-old chaplain from the North was so touched by the attention Grace, a slave girl showed to incapacitated Mrs. Clement that he remarked on the relationship of affection and trust between master and slave to his host who had developed the science of Niggerology. Clement laughed and said that the only way to keep the slaves honest was not to trust them and proceeded to give incidents that led to such a conclusion, citing all sorts of vices – laziness, deceit, debauchery, theft and more – to which slaves would fall once trust were bestowed on them. The northern visitor argued without success that it was perhaps the condition of enslavement rather than any inherent nature that accounted for the slave's lack of honor, drawing attention to the fact that the heart is crimson in whites as well as blacks and that wickedness may dwell equally in either.*

*To this the southern slave owner brought down his hand on the table in fury and protested that he had not spoken of wickedness, arguing that one does not speak of wickedness in a child of four or five, a child who has not attained the age of reason. To him the child knows not the distinction between falsehood and honesty, does not think of the future or of consequence but only of the desire of the moment and how to satisfy it. So it was with the Africans, he concluded, pontificating that they too were like children, morally speaking, and that it was incumbent on the whites to guide and guard them until their race matured.*

*For taking a hog and feeding his children, Zeke was thrown in an underground prison for three days by slave master Mr. Canning. Horrified by such cruelty, March the visiting chaplain asked for an explanation from the slave. The slave said he was not guilty of stealing; his master said he was.*

*Asked to explain why he was not guilty, Zeke said his task consisted of feeding the corn to the mules. Both corn and mules belonged to the master. They were his property. Similarly he had fed the hog to his children. Both hog and his children were his master's property as well. He saw no difference at all. The infuriated master did not buy it. He blasted that some Negroes thought emancipation meant to be liberated from toil, which had been the lot of all children of Adam and Eve from the moment they were cast out of the famous garden of Eden.(March* by Geraldine Brooks*).*

These words describe the kaleidoscope of a historical past that merges imperceptibly into present times, what James Baldwin called *These Yet To Be United States,* a period that has been beautifully captured in poetry big and small, in prose, in legal lore, in history, in cinema and other documentaries. In addition to the above lines, the following from a refrain from my own childhood came to mind, when local magicians thrilled parents and children with *American wonder* as they performed and entertained with legerdemain :

*Come and see, American wonder,*
*Come and see, American wonder.*

They brought to mind also *Voice of America's* signature tunes as that radio network woke millions of people from the night slumber for another new day:

*Yankee Doodle went to town*
*Riding on a pony,*
*Stuck a feather in his cap*
*And called it macaroni*

*Yankee Doodle keep it up,*
*Yankee Doodle dandy.*
*Mind the music and the step,*
*And with the girls be handy.*

Bizarre as it may sound today, there were moments in this country when a woman, as well as the baby in her womb, would be considered property of the slave owner and there were moments when a black man was assessed to be only seven-eighths of a man.

The edict of 1808 which was largely ignored by plantation owners invested in slave labor was an important act of Congress:

> *Be it enacted, by the Senate and the House of Representatives of the United States of America in Congress assembled, that from and after the first day of January 1808, it shall not be lawful to import into the United States from any of the kingdoms of Africa any Negro with the intent to be Sold or to be held to service or labor…*

How could such an edict be implemented when there was still so much work to be done, work needing "the strength and the sinews of the African world"? Jamestown in Virginia, the point at which Europeans first landed in America as well as the entry point of slaves from the Atlantic trade was doing brisk business with chattel cargo destined for the Tobacco Farms, especially King Tobacco (the jovial weed to which Europe was very addicted) that trumped cotton, peanut, hog and sugar to sweeten England's tea and all other activity involving land and in need of muscle, brawn and sweat from chattel. Chattel was bought with cash or even battered with sacks of corn, beans or oatmeal and smoked or salted meat from European merchants.

Henry David Thoreau in a July 4, 1854 address entitled "Slavery in Massachusetts" denounced the shameful episode of slavery and the unholy zeal with which officials of the Commonwealth enforced the provisions of the Fugitive Slave Law: "The whole military force of the state is at the service of a Mr. Suttle, a slaveholder from Virginia, to enable him to catch a man whom he calls his property; but not a soldier is offered to save a citizen of Massachusetts from being kidnapped." That's how bad it was.

Way before that there was the case of 23-year old Thomas Sims, a runaway slave from Georgia who was captured and sent back into slavery by authorities in Boston, Massachusetts, supposedly in compliance with the Fugitive Slave Law of 1850, a controversial North-South Compromise. That was before the Civil War. Shameful! Where was Boston's pride of having played an instrumental role in the antislavery movement? Why capture a free man in the North and send him back to slavery in the South? It was a wake up call for abolitionists, legal experts, authors, academics, religious leaders and African-Americans in Boston to pass from theoreticians into fully invested militants that ignited the nationalist movement.

Around 1850 California was admitted into the Union as a free state, upsetting the fragile balance of 15 free and 15 slave states in existence. The proslavery South which was already whispering "secession" demanded something as a compromise for a free California; hence the 1850 Compromise toughened the Fugitive Slave Law that denied suspected fugitives both jury and the right to testify in their own defense. In the state of Massachusetts the judge's hands were tied as he refused to rule the law as unconstitutional and instead issued a certificate attesting that Thomas Sims was indeed the property of James Porter of Georgia. At that time escapee slaves as well as their helpers were at great risk. Thousands of southern slaves were guided to freedom by "conductors" along the underground rail road - a clandestine network of escape routes that left Boston, snaked through Concord, Lincoln, and found their way north to New Hampshire, Vermont and into the forests of Canada. And some of the conductors were supporters of the new Republican Party who hated the Fugitive Slave Act. Some fugitive slaves even escaped to England. What an irony that innocent blacks were forced to flee to England to seek asylum in monarchy from the injustices and cruelty of a republic!

The wake up call galvanized Boston's literary fraternity to work – Emerson, Thoreau, Melville, Hawthorne and many others turned their energies and the power of their pens to give voice to the antislavery movement and tell the world about the shameful acts. Harriet Beecher Stowe produced **Uncle Tom's Cabin**, one of the greatest literary influences of the antislavery attitude.

How the times had changed! Racial problems still persisted of course and were very vexing. In the 1960s the nation turned to the powerful tool of the civil rights movement; now the movement has lost steam and there is palpable need for new tools. What did the civil rights movement do? Through the courts and government agencies, legal prohibitions were enforced against discrimination. Private businesses and universities fashioned out diversity policies based on the civil rights principles and private individuals went for color blindness in race relations and condemned discrimination and bias. All of these measures helped curb *de facto* discrimination that was fed by the wide spread belief of blacks being inferior to whites. The civil rights movement, via legislation, succeeded wonderfully to curb racial discrimination inside theaters, restaurants, hotels, and other public places. Discrimination in employment decreased too but it still persists and calls for a different type of tool. Public figures guilty of uttering overtly bigoted statements suffer widespread condemnation and often loss of jobs. There is no doubt that racial animus is at an all time low, the most spectacular barometer being the wonderful team that worked to get Barack Obama elected as America's first black president.

President Obama underwent the momentous event of taking the oath of office at the US Capital and appeared in front of a large crowd massed on the Mall - structures where slaves were once held in pens, ready for auction on an open market; structures whose foundations were laid by slaves. Seventy years ago, Marian Anderson was denied the possibility of staging a concert in the Constitution Hall by the Daughters of the American Revolution, claiming it was a "whites only" hall, even as that talented black singer had as her champion, first lady Eleanor Roosevelt, the very first lady who punctured the myth of black inferiority, letting herself flown by the father of black aviation against all the secret service fuss. The "concert that awakened America" was eventually staged outdoors at the Lincoln Memorial in front of a crowd ten times larger than the original venue could accommodate. How times have changed! Like Marian Anderson, Nina Simone, a music prodigy, also known as the high priestess of soul or the black woman tutored by Muriel Mazzanovich, whom she fondly called her "white mama," was denied admission into the Curtis Institute of Music in Philadelphia because of her color, only to be given a posthumous doctorate in 2003, fifty years later, by the very institution, anxious to make amends for past racism. Thurgood Marshall did not stop at rejection; he took the college to court that refused him admission, and won. What a long journey!

Eight former US presidents once held black persons as personal property - Thomas Jefferson, James Madison, James Monroe, Andrew Jackson, John Tyler, William Henry Harrison, James Polk and Zachary Taylor. And from the White House, President Abraham Lincoln, also from Illinois like Barack Obama today, signed the famous Emancipation Proclamation that freed the slaves, in the process writing down the following, "If slavery is not wrong, nothing is wrong." It finally gave meaning to the founding ideal of the government that all men are created equal.

Even though slavery came to an end following a bloody civil war, it gave rise to the beginning of another painful chapter for black America. Douglas A. Blackman ( *Slavery by Another Name – the Reenslavement of Black Americans from Civil War to World War II*), details the rise and flourishing of African-American involuntary servitude, long after the passage of the 13th Amendment to the U. S. Constitution (prohibition of slavery and involuntary servitude), the 14th Amendment (guaranteeing the right of citizenship and due process of the law to all born or naturalized US citizens), and the 15th Amendment (enfranchisement of the blacks).

But why all of this? White planters and industrialists in the Southern United States faced a dilemma following the loss of slave labor as a result of the above amendments. Agriculture and the emerging mining and smelting industries required large numbers of workers. Planters, coal mine operators and industrial employers found it repugnant negotiating labor contracts with former slaves or paying them wages for their labors. So the opponents of Reconstruction and black citizenship launched attacks on African-American economic and political rights. One shrewd way to do so was to exploit a provision of the 13th Amendment allowing the use of unfree labor "as a punishment for crimes of which the party shall have been convicted". It was a subterfuge that involved mine owners, planters, sheriffs, magistrates, legislators, other local officials and large corporations. By convicting African-Americans of minor crimes and trumped-up charges (vagrancy, riding freight trains, disturbing the peace, petty theft, nonpayment of an alleged debt), fines imposed by the courts were magnified and levied far beyond the ability of the convicted to pay. The convict would then be sentenced to hard labor, and his or her contract sold to a farmer or commercial concern. Thus States, municipalities and those individuals managing the buying and selling of contracts were guaranteed plenty of capital, cheap labor and a powerful tool for the social control of African-Americans. That was the birth of the series of obnoxious laws called Jim Crow and the period of black political and economic disenfranchisement.

The end of the civil war and abolition of slavery also posed the thorny problem for southern whites, of how to prevent the newly freed African Americans from contaminating the white race and debasing white politics. Jim Crow laws provided the ideal answer to both of these. Through violence and legal chicanery Southern States managed to nullify the rights blacks had won, inscribe Jim Crow into legal and political structures for many generations – segregation of rail roads, rail road cars, allocation by local school boards of fewer tax dollars to black schools than to whites. Also, white farmers preferred black farm hands to whites because they could get more work out for less pay, unions excluded black workers and companies refused to hire them. The Ku Klux Klan, with the complicity of law enforcement officials, lynched black men and women. Farmers used peonage to hold blacks down in their plantations. It was a dark period that aptly introduced "America's original sin" into popular lingo.

Thanks to Jeffersonian democracy and other enactments, those monumental problems were faced and overcome by Americans of African origin - the tenacity of Rosa Parks, Martin Luther King Jr. and countless unsung heroes along the way. Barack Obama was hardly the first African American to run for the White House. Before him there had been Julian Bond, Shirley Chisholm, the Reverend Jesse Jackson and the Reverend Al Sharpton. Senator Obama simply took the relay to a higher height and left his historical mark on the landscape. As a matter of fact Collin Powell might well have been the first black US president if he had not declined to run at a time when the White House was virtually his for the asking.

At one point, Condoleezza Rice was considered the most likely opponent for Democratic candidate Hillary Rodham Clinton, well before Obama appeared on the horizon. US history has undergone quite some momentous changes of late. Only thirty years ago, who could have imagined a White conservative Republican from Texas appointing a black Alabama woman, PhD and former Provost of Stanford University as his secretary of State? Race and gender gaps are slowly closing and that is good for the nation. Gone are the days when women had difficulty getting legal access to "male only" jobs and gone are the times when blacks were confined to society's backwaters. Today New Hampshire is toying with rewording her Constitution to introduce gender neutral word for men in (*All men are created equal*) even if such a change brings along problems in grammar and syntax; the female gender must not just be assumed, it should be seen to be included.

America is a pace setter in many ways. Yesterday it was Irish Americans that fought their way from one type of discrimination onto power, paving the way for other minorities. It is easy to forget that the Irish too had a rough ride along almost a similar path. Remember the rough journey from Smith to John F. Kennedy? In those early days "Catholic Christians turned Romeward as naturally as the needle seeks the North" even if it brought them some problems. Immigration into the United States of America was massive between 1820 and 1840. It slowed down around the time of the Civil Wars and resumed around 1880. The major group was Irish immigrants fleeing the potato blight due to a deadly fungal infection that caused crop failure and famine. Governor Al Smith of New York, son of Irish immigrants and first Catholic to run as presidential candidate of a major political party was humiliated and defeated in the 1928 election. Of course the Irish did not give up; nor did the Catholics.

By 1960 there was a changed climate for American Catholics. A young senator from Massachusetts sought nomination. John Fitzgerald Kennedy and his family skillfully maneuvered public opinion, reinforcing the idea that excluding Catholics from the White House was unacceptable bigotry. The West Virginia primary in May of that year was a turning point. JFK's support was solid but because the State had a miniscule Catholic population, his campaign presented it as a decisive test. JFK handily defeated Minnesota's Hubert Humphrey and the candidate proceeded to deal a severe blow to the religious issue in an address to the Greater Houston Ministerial Association in September. "I am not the Catholic candidate for President. I am the Democratic Party's candidate for president, who also happens to be a Catholic. I do not speak for my church in public matters, and the church does not speak for me," he thundered. Memorable words indeed!

Whereas fellow Irishman James Michael Curley embraced the politics of loyalty and deference to his origins, his neighborhood, ethnic group, class or level of attentiveness to his constituents, Kennedy looked instead at where he wanted to go. To Curley and his supporters, forgetting where one came from was a cardinal sin in politics and he did everything possible to exchange government programs for votes, almost as a *quid pro quo*. Kennedy embraced and lived the American dream. Much later Bill Clinton won the presidency by a slightly different twist of the same message – building a bridge to the future. Barack Obama, a product of racial miscegenation, rejects the politics of racial or gender identity, sexual orientation or victimhood, preoccupying himself solely with the creation of a new American society that gives everyone the opportunity to be themselves without fear of losing their pride or dignity simply because of physical makeup. Only Barack Obama's unique background and qualities can bring together all the ingredients for this consistent, unrelenting commitment to the change through inclusiveness and bipartisanship. He clearly called it "our chance to answer that call, our moment, our time to put our people back to work and open doors of opportunity for our kids, restore prosperity and promote the cause of peace." Those whose agenda consists of appropriating to themselves the first black president will naturally feel disappointed but true Americans with a liberal bent see something positive and advantageous in this new development in the life of the nation.

It is possible, as Jack Penn once put it, to make stepping stones out of stumbling blocks. Obama did it in 2008 just like J. F. Kennedy before him. The 2008 race to the White House ended in Obama's victory. Hillary Clinton, my candidate, had fought hard and tenaciously for the Democratic Party nomination but lost and ended up endorsing Barack Obama as the presidential nominee. 2008 was simply not her year in spite of her gallant fight, the support of her husband, the wonderful Bill Clinton who had coaxed, charmed and wooed the American electorate in 1992 with the catch phrase "*buy one, get one for free*" his slogan alluding to his conviction that he and his wife Hillary were both presidential material. With all of Bill's weight behind her and the formidable support of female voters and die hard Clinton admirers, the former first lady still could not make it. That spoke a lot about how formidable an opponent Barack Obama had become and what a team he had put in place for his own campaign. "*Yes we can*" was proving to be too powerful a force to knock out. Indeed by winning the Iowa caucus early in the game, Senator Barack Obama had given a clear and unambiguous message – that an overwhelmingly white electorate was finally prepared to vote an African American for US president.

John McCain the GOP rival and father of three daughters said he owed Hillary Clinton a debt for inspiring millions of women to believe that there was no opportunity beyond their reach. Barack Obama, himself a father of two daughters, praised Hillary Clinton who "had made history for doing what no woman had done before". Only 95-year-old Juliet R. Bernstein had given up hope of seeing a woman president in the US. She wondered if McCain's or Obama's daughters would be able to walk through the glass door that had been closed to women for so long. The 1870 enfranchisement of black men (15th Amendment to the US Constitution) followed fifty years later, in 1920, by that of women ( the 19th Amendment ) seemed to have ordained the order of things to come. Could Barack Obama's 2008 victory simply be following this natural order of things?

Against the background of an unprecedented economic and financial meltdown, John McCain and Barack Obama ran the 2008 race to the White House to remedy what George W. Bush had put to ruins over the eight previous years. While Senator Obama of Illinois, the Democrat, proposed an economic salvation plan consisting of sharing wealth by freezing any additional taxes for the middle class and taxing only America's wealthy 5%, his rival came up with a war plan called creating wealth, which effectively meant that he would not put any extra burden on the class that supposedly created jobs and generated incomes. Senator McCain painted Senator Obama as a *Socialist*, for proposing a Robin Hood type of economics that would rob the rich to pay the poor. Americans, ever so ready to pick the latest label, jumped uproariously on the McCain bandwagon and began to denigrate the S-word as well as the idea of spreading the wealth. Overnight, a certain Joe the Plumber (real name, Joe Wuzelbachier) became the poster kid and war horse for the McCain campaign. Senator John McCain proclaimed the man as a typical All-American Joe, in the manner of Joe Palooka or Joe Six-pack, and claimed that Joe the plumber had wanted to buy over a plumbing business but could not afford it, a claim which turned out to be untrue, but the man willingly obliged to join the Arizona Senator's campaign bandwagon in Ohio. And fighting tooth and nail to narrow the wide gap that separated his campaign from Senator Obama's, John McCain went into overdrive, strenuously tying Senator Barack Obama at every turn to ACORN, the Reverend Jeremiah Wright or to the terrorist, Bill Ayers. What a tactic! And yet the opinion polls failed to respond. When he continued to harp on "*the fundamentals of our economy are sound*" a bogus idea laid bare by the September 15 collapse of the financial market, it was clear to American voters that John McCain was indeed out of touch with reality. Those seven words proved disastrous for John McCain's presidential dreams. Things were not helped when, in some of his rallies, the mention of Senator Obama's name was greeted with boos and calls like "Terrorist" or "Kill him" by people in the audience.

It was difficult not to develop goose flesh upon hearing such utterances and instinctively images of the assassinations of JFK, RFK, and MLK flashed through many minds. Even Ronald Reagan's fate reemerged. Would the US be plunged into another political assassination and spend the decades ahead probing its actors and, if so, to what end? After so many decades our theoreticians had not come close to concluding the Kennedy assassination or putting a halt to its many theories such as the conspiracy to commit and then to cover up the assassination of one of America's most loved presidents. Till today there are innuendoes, more theories, speculations, reports backed by all sorts of ballistics analyses calculated to nullify the Warren Commission's report on the matter. Fantasies galore and every conceivable concoction can be found that the CIA or the mob or persons other than Lee Harvey Oswald did it. Absurd but thrilling all the same.

In America conspiracy theories exist for anything and everything. Curiously it is not always the low class peasants but the well educated middle class that spawn such theories. But why? In his book *"Voodoo Histories: The Role of Conspiracy Theories in Shaping Modern History"* British author David Aaronovitch says such theories take root among the casualties of political, social and economic change, with factions eager to claim responsibility for success or lay blame for failures at the feet of a collection of scapegoats. Who would want to kill Obama and why? To lose the presidential race was bad enough to contemplate; but to lose such a nice man to an assassin's bullet was unsettling. The entertainment industry, ever more interested in making a buck than anything else, was more than happy to promote such oddities from persons with herd mentality or IQ far down south. "Would the White House still be known as White House after Obama got elected president?" some wanted to know. How incredible that Barack Obama should occupy the sacred White house!

But by voting overwhelmingly for Senator Obama, Americans in their immense majority made their views known. Well before the January 20 swearing in, hordes of America's corporations and financial institutions had been making pilgrimages to Washington D. C. to ask for financial bailout for their enterprises. Ironic isn't it? Some of the very forces which had hitherto decried the welfare state and asked for the free market to be really free of government influence, were shamelessly lining up and asking for government intervention to save them from drowning. They had put aside their mantra of "letting the market decide who wins or who loses." Was it a loss of memory or could the S-word have been rehabilitated so soon? Reaganomics had virtually become a thing of the past. How times change!

The 2008 election cycle provided incredible challenges for both political parties, especially for Barack Obama the first serious black American to run for the White House. Among the many challenges was the idea of consistency of the candidate's message. To the American electorate a politician running for office is either consistent or hypocritical. Some Americans assert that far from being a liability, hypocrisy is an essential part of democratic politics. During the 18ᵗʰ and 19ᵗʰ Centuries, anxiety was fixed on religion and the fear that atheists would inveigle their way into politics by going through the motions of public piety. Such concerns had morphed into a generalized anxiety about political honesty in general. If politicians poured out platitudes to get elected, how could one trust them to do what they promised, once in office? But politicians are what we make of them. We vote them into office because they proclaim tax cuts which we hear as good music to the ears but when they get into office we too want things done –a road constructed here, a bridge built over there, this project here, that other one there – making it impossible to realize them without tax increases! The populist Tea Party complicates matters when its members advocate small government, market forces and lower taxes as if these were arbitrary concepts unconnected to the people's wishes. No sane individual goes out to create a big government; governments are the products of the task at hand. Obviously if it could take ten police officers to keep the peace in a municipality, we would not be asking for twenty, another name for big government, which is taboo in the ears of those who love small governments. It requires a big government apparatus to police the southern border that is gateway for illegal immigrants. And refusing to pay taxes goes directly against one of JFK's momentous pronouncements on the yardstick for measuring patriotism – *"ask not what your country can do for you; ask instead what you can do for your country"*. The challenges faced by BP's catastrophic operations on the Gulf of Mexico and its resulting spillage of contaminant made many persons to realize that it requires a strong government intervention to make things happen. Nobody chanted small government any longer because the magnitude of the problem was obvious.

Accusing opponents of hypocrisy is a powerful campaign tool, especially a flagrant hypocrisy that can bring down a candidacy. Yet effective leadership is about good judgment, foresight, and the ability to adapt to whatever the world might throw at a candidate. Why exactly should any sane person prefer hypocrisy? If we fear that a hypocrite will turn out to be a flip-flopper who won't stick to any position once it ceases to be convenient, then we must look at what is so inherently desirable about being consistent. The opposite of hypocrisy in this case is consistency, isn't it? A hypocrite who tailors his or her public face to suit the needs of the moment is an adaptable person - a crucial trait in political leadership. Politicians who are consistent end up doing one of two things –maintaining consistency by constantly changing what is believed to suit changing political requirements or having a belief that is simple enough to run through everything said. If we don't want our politicians to change their minds, we must ensure that their minds are uncluttered by anything requiring them to rethink. An uncluttered mind is occasionally an aid to clear thinking and effective decision-making. But isn't it naïve to see this as the supreme qualification for leadership? "The spread of secondary and latterly of tertiary education", said the astute Peter Medawar "has created a large population of people, often with well developed literary and scholarly tastes, who have been educated far beyond their capacity to undertake analytical thought". How realistic can this be in a constantly changing world where events clamor for attention? Senator Barack Obama professed consistency and held Senator Hillary Clinton down for several months on the charge that she had voted to authorize President George Bush's invasion of Iraq; Hillary Clinton defended herself by saying that if she had known then what was known at the time of their campaign, she would not have voted for that war. George W. Bush had tricked the US Congress into believing that Saddam Hussein had weapons of mass destruction, worked in concert with Osama bin Laden, and so was a threat to both his people and the free world.

President George Bush, like Prime Minister Tony Blair of Britain, grounded his convictions about Saddam Hussein on his deep gut feelings and religion and like the prime minster, sustained his convictions only by ignoring evidence produced to show that Saddam Hussein was no partner to Al-Qaeda and had no weapons of mass destruction. Neither leader was considered a hypocrite; both held the course on Iraq with near perfect consistency. Thus the vote for consistency brought America into the Iraqi imbroglio.

The blind use of flip-flop label to disqualify candidates for elective office is most unfortunate indeed. The American electorate still has to learn that it is OK for a leader to change his/her mind about a policy choice provided she or he is convinced that new, credible circumstances have come to light to influence a decision. As a matter of fact many of our past leaders were known to have flip-flopped. The senior George Bush is remembered for his famous speech "*Watch my lips; no new taxes*" and yet upon taking office his first act was to increase taxes. President Jimmy Carter tried unsuccessfully to convince fellow Americans to cut down their consumption of fuel with its consequent dependence on the volatile region of the Middle East for supplies. When Americans would not hearken to his plea, he turned around and declared that any interference with the sea lanes in the Gulf region would be met with an American response, a strange application of the Monroe doctrine but it stood and today the US is embroiled in a ceaseless war in the Gulf. President Richard Milhous Nixon was known for his opposition to China's admission to the United Nations but he was the first US president to make an official trip to Beijing and to open the way for all the diplomatic hoopla that followed. Thomas Jefferson was one principled politician who hated power-grabbing with all of his gut instincts, yet he settled for the Louisiana Purchase from the French, a decision and an investment in America's future that made the nation stronger and better too. Supporting that purchase turned out to be one of the best presidential decisions ever.

George W. Bush Sr. had led Saddam Hussein to believe that the US had no interest at all in his territorial dispute with Kuwait but only five months later he turned around to amass a force of half a million to tell the Iraqi leader otherwise. At one point Russian leader Mikhail Gorbachev threatened to resign but eventually stayed on. Former British Prime Minister, Margaret Thatcher, on her part, threatened to stay in power but turned around and resigned. And it is a known fact that the great Abraham Lincoln told the Southern States of the Union that he would not abolish slavery. Guess what he did when he became president of the US!!!!!!!!!!!!! In 2004 Americans used the flip-flopping label to disqualify candidate John Kerry from being elected, not giving much weight to what had led to his change of heart about Vietnam. And yet what America needs at any time is good leadership from men and women of vision who take bold decisions to make the Union better and by extension the world beyond.

In retrospect the lesson President George Bush and Vice-President Dick Cheney taught Americans is never ever to deviate from a chosen course of action, even if it points to catastrophe. That Americans preferred this type of leadership in 2004 to what was often derogatorily called the flip-flopping of Senator John Kerry was ridiculous. Use of the blanket label "hypocrite" to designate everyone, including those who change their position according to changing circumstances is most unfortunate. The flip-flop (gotcha) is often used by some candidates as a negative factor in painting their rivals. This places enormous responsibility on the voters to decide properly. As an incumbent President, George W. Bush used it against Massachusetts Senator John Kerry, a decorated war veteran who had first voted for the war in Iraq but then voted against the bill for funding its execution. By highlighting such a gaffe, George Bush who had never fought in any of America's wars, projected his rival as an undecided candidate not to be trusted with leadership. And Americans went along with that and let him win! Clearly we all must now share responsibility for Iraq.

As George Bush's Administration edged obdurately closer to war with Iraq, it badly needed a *casus belli* (smoking gun). The president sought at all costs to connect the elusive dots between Osama bin Laden and Saddam Hussein. And yet in authorizing the president to use force against nations determined to have aided the terrorist attacks of September 11, 2001, Congress had clearly specified that the resolution should fulfill the requirements of the War Powers Act. It had specifically placed a premium on establishing an Iraqi connection. There was none, yet the president took America to war, giving a very wrong message to the world with disastrous consequences. It was clear that President George W. Bush was not a historian and that those advising him did not have history as their forte. Otherwise a simple look at their notes would have told them that the US got Iranian Prime Minister Mohammad Mossadegh out of office simply by using the CIA in Operation Ajax. Manuel Noriega of Panama was equally dethroned with little bloodshed. Even President Nyerere of Tanzania was able to liberate the people of Uganda by removing General Idi Amin Dada from Office with a neat surgical operation. How could President George W. Bush plunge the nation into eight years of an unwinnable bloody war? And in his memoir he speaks of a clear conscience? How clear can a conscience be when linked to mythical weapons of mass destruction (WMD) and justifications punctuated by contempt for torture in Guantanamo?

It came as no surprise that when it was suggested to Vladimir Putin to seek a political solution to Chechnya, the Russian president sent word back to George Bush saying "Why don't you meet Osama bin Laden, invite him to Brussels or the White House and engage in talks?" The man whose inner soul President Bush claimed to see went ahead to add that what he wanted the most from America was just what he had given America after 9/11 – complete support. Clearly such attitude contributed to strengthening our own president's resolve.

Yet George Bush's own flip-flopping was legendary. He first voted against nation building in Afghanistan and Iraq but later on went for it; he praised the 9/11 report even though he had opposed the formation of the commission that produced it; he began negotiating with North Korea even though he had first promised not to. All politicians do the flip-flop thing really. And Senator Barack Obama was not quite free of the stain. He who was originally for public funding of campaigns turned his back to it and opted for private funding, when he saw his fortune improve with massive support, discombobulating many in the process and causing others to wonder whether such a flip-flopper could be trusted with the White House. And people legitimately asked whether Senator Barack Obama was so rich because of his many supporters or whether he had so many supporters because he was rich. Nice question.

Fingers were also pointed at Senator Barack Obama as being a hypocrite supposedly because he had been so prepared to ask for Don Imus's head but proved reluctant to do the same for Rev. Jeremiah Wright. Seen in that perspective, the senator had a credibility issue on his hands, not a double standard one, implying that as a trans-racial candidate he should have disowned Rev Wright with as much conviction as he did Don Imus. Critics asked if it was more acceptable for a Black man (Rev. Wright) to promote racial violence than for a White man (Don Imus) to utter racial epithets. Those side issues only served to compound the main preoccupations. Americans wanted an experienced candidate, which Barack Obama was not. But he offered hope which the electorate wanted after the gloomy Bush years. It would be nice to get hope and experience, the entities that had endeared Franklin Delano Roosevelt to the American people. FDR continues to be the standard by which US presidents are measured, the man who produced a unique bond between himself and the people, a true believer in democracy - the capacity of ordinary Americans exercising their collective judgment to address the ills that affect their society. In that political landscape of 2008, Barack Obama came closest to those ideals, promising hope, experience and in the process raising morale too.

Could the US president change the world? Leslie H. Gelb, a foreign policy expert thought it was possible. And the rest of the suffering world still under oppression believed so too. Two hundred years ago, the framers of the US Constitution set up a government with a system of checks and balances, so that no branch could ever dominate. As a result the president shared power with Congress on domestic, economic and foreign policy issues. However, over time and with great debate, the president became the dominant decision maker on war, peace and foreign affairs. Thus on November 4, 2008, as in other years, voters had the monumental task of electing that person who would likely decide how and when the Iraq war should end, whether to enlarge war efforts in Afghanistan, whether the US should negotiate with or attack Iran (would Ahmadinejad become the new Saddam Hussein?), start global trade talks while protecting domestic jobs, combat global warming without creating undue stress and strain on the economy. He would determine how to deter an empowered Russia from using its military superiority across its borders as it had done a while earlier in Georgia.

Congress had virtually abdicated its constitutional right and responsibility to declare war, the last time it exercised that right being during World War II. Since then presidents had sent US troops to combat zones – Korea, Vietnam, the Gulf, and Afghanistan – strictly on their own authority. Congress still had the legal authority to overrule the Chief Executive and cut off funds for those wars but it had used that power rather sparingly – Nixon's request for money at the end of the Vietnam War, Reagan's aid program to the anti-communist contras in Nicaragua. But Congress did not stop or alter Bill Clinton's unpopular order to send troops to Bosnia and to bomb Serbia over Kosovo. Most recently Congress voted funds to enable George Bush pursue the Iraq war in spite of vocally mounted criticisms.

In their remarkable work, *America and the World*, Zbigniew Brzezinski, a Democrat and foreign policy adviser to world leaders for over 50 years and Brent Scowcroft, a Republican and National Security expert, discuss pressing foreign policy challenges, world-wide crisis of confidence in US leadership, consultation with allies, not acting unilaterally, conveying credibly that the era of American self-indulgence is over, and recognizing global interdependence. They indicate the need to state categorically that the world needs America and that no one benefits from America's political and financial troubles, not even those nations who wish the US ill. The US need not act like a bull in a China shop however, and need not be the global decider. Pointing to the way forward, the authors say a US president needs to revive bipartisanship at home, appoint respected people from the other party to top national security posts, end military involvement in Iraq, avoid over-militarizing Afghanistan, energetically push the Israeli-Palestinian peace process and engage with China in a way that acknowledges that nation's new global importance. There is no doubt that President Obama paid close attention to those words of wisdom as he formed his working team.

If people get the government they deserve, it places a special burden on the electorate to pick their leaders very carefully. It poses a special challenge on elections too. What are elections for? Should they be media circuses? Should they be auction sales where candidates sell themselves to the highest bidders? Should elections not be moral contracts between those who wish to lead and those consenting to be led? What then should the voters do – whisper or debate the main issues? If politicians were angels, would any nation need smart voters? What can the ordinary citizen do to become a better voter? Can the herd mentality be overcome? Some observer has stated that one should pick the next president as if one's child's life depended on it. This may be slightly hyped but it surely drives home the importance of this civic duty. First of all, in a multicultural society like the US, it is important to know what matters to the individual - national health care versus national security; global warming or the make-up of the Supreme Court; what qualities count most in a leader – empathy, decisiveness, intelligence, integrity, candor, competence, eloquence, civility. To whom should a president turn for advice? What should be a citizen's top priority? What principle should one stand by even if it puts the presidency at risk?

It is wise to consider what friends and family think of a particular candidate and to find out what different news outlets say about such a candidate. It is naïve to get all of one's news from just one source since news organs can be biased occasionally. Regularly checking television channels, different news papers, local and international tabloids, seems to be the way forward. Engaging in healthy debates around the dinner table and in beer houses, but nothing to bring about a civil war, is good for politics. Some voters have expressed the feelings that politicians lack respect for them, especially in the way they and their operatives around Washington D. C. carry out slime campaigns trying to win over what they consider easy-to-manipulate voters. It is useful to call to mind Eleanor Roosevelt's useful guidelines - that great minds debate ideas and events whereas small mediocre minds focus on people! But of course respect has to be earned! This can only be done when voters stand on firm grounds. But do they? When the Republican Party lost control of both houses of Congress in 2008, America seemed to have weighed eight years under George W. Bush and the GOP. But to give President Obama and the Democrats a shellacking in 2010 and give back the House to the very GOP was a bit difficult to rationalize.

On April 6, 1968, in the nation's capital, a certain Oscar King shot at passing cars during the violence that broke out all over America following the assassination of the Reverend Martin Luther King Jr., causing wounds that have lingered till today. Oscar King hit at least one car, a car in which his own sister was riding and the bullet killed her. That was a tragedy and it triggered a paroxysm of destruction across America! There had been riots before but nothing close to the 1968 riots in scope. Those riots had a lasting impact on America. The momentum of the civil rights movement was disrupted and white support for it undermined. Cities were hollowed out as the exodus of whites to suburbia was accelerated and forces opposed to government initiatives on behalf of society's poor were opposed. A conservative backlash among suburban white voters frightened and repulsed by the violence discredited President Lyndon Johnson's Great Society programs for the poor.

After those riots, middle class whites fled, followed by middle class blacks, to say nothing of jobs, commerce and hope. Rebuilding efforts never gained much traction and those left behind were consigned to violent purgatories of crime, poverty and drugs. Burglaries, robberies and murders soared. The Broken Window theory was born and became a handy tool for officials of law enforcement. The Democrats' traditional ruling coalition had begun to fall apart several years earlier when their embrace of the civil rights movement had cost them the South of the US.

The summer of 1968 was the most tumultuous year of the twentieth century, when Richard Nixon and Hubert Humphrey hired advertising agencies to package them almost like marketable products and sell them to the American people. That was the age of television when the image, not the man, mattered. Today, forty years down the road, the means of communication have expanded exponentially to include the Internet but human nature remains very much the same. The main question remains what the buyers need to know as they navigate their way through the political market place. Analytic tools sufficiently sophisticated enable the tailoring of political messages to subgroups, targeting groups down to congressional districts and precincts where there are undecided and swing voters. News media provide the informed citizen the right tools to make a good decision. As Andrew Mwenda, founder and managing editor of *The Independent* said when threatened by Uganda's black mambas, journalists encourage debate and equip the citizens with information to make educated choices. Facing sure death from the pistol of a military intelligence officer, who said he could make Mwenda disappear without a trace, the journalist who had courageously declared Yowero Museveni a worse coward than Idi Amin, stood his ground and maintained those words – the very words that had made Walter Cronkite a celebrity in America. And how true!

In 2008 it was a great idea to watch our candidates give their views during important debates that formed part of the overall campaign. The debates brought out their intelligence, character, spontaneity and other useful traits that guided and helped voters in assessing their temperament for leadership. Some candidates are better on radio than on television which shows things like boredom, poor dressing habits, bad language or bad makeup. Thanks to the television, potential voters can watch candidates and assess their body language during important debates. Body language can help or hurt a candidate in such debates. Negative emotions, dishonesty, resentment and other socially unacceptable traits are easy to spot in such situations. Some persons can make strenuous efforts to disguise them but they almost always leak out unexpectedly. Viewers easily get turned off by a candidate's bad behavior, such as constantly looking at his/her watch. Intelligent candidates who have a mastery of the facts are easy to pick from a televised debate. During the 2000 presidential race, even though the Supreme Court contributed to the election of George Bush, those debates, especially the second, contributed to Al Gore's loss of voters. The Vice-President's head shaking and eye rolling when President George Bush was speaking had adverse effects that neutralized the many good points contained in his presentation. It was instructive to watch how the candidates performed under pressure. It was important to know whether one's favorite candidate was thinking on his/her feet or using canned texts. Did the candidate decree for questions to be filed in ahead of time? Was the candidate humorous and able to deflect an unpleasant situation gracefully without appearing mean spirited?

This proved to be a very strong point for Senator Barack Obama during the debates with rival John McCain, a trait he shares with his good friend, Deval Patrick who won reelection in Massachusetts because of his gubernatorial comportment, where others fell victim to negative campaigns, lies, calumny and language that incited hatred. Was the candidate witty? Did the candidate have the facts or only showmanship? Voters did take note of the fact that Hillary Clinton and Barack Obama answered the moderator's questions without looking at each other at all, the tension reflecting their mutual opposition and unwillingness to acknowledge each other led to pressure being mounted on Hillary to bow out of the race and endorse Barack Obama.

Running for the 2008 election to the White House, Senator Barack Obama did something unusual to ignite civic engagement among America's youth. This was palpable from coast to coast. It had not always been so. The last four decades of the twentieth century had seen a drastic decline in youth involvement in civic life from 60% to 28%, a rise in apathy that coincided with an increase in incivism. When the national tragedy of 9/11/2001 struck, the civic seismometer across the US showed a sharp spike as community mindedness increased. America's flag could be seen almost everywhere on the national landscape. The last time such an event had taken place was Pearl Harbor.

The increase in youth participation in civic life was seen in the climbing election turn out that characterized the 2008 presidential nominating contests in primaries and caucuses and the very extraordinary candidacy of Senator Barack Obama, the Illinois senator. But the very civic renaissance and revitalization of US democracy were also under threat and could be aborted if backroom dealings by political insiders or the so-called super delegates were ever called into play. Professor Robert D. Putnam, Public Policy expert at Harvard University's J. F. Kennedy School of Government warned so. Who should be blamed if we ended up electing the wrong person into the White House again? The question hung in the air. Karl Rove, the architect of George Bush's election was eclipsed by the hordes of youthful voters and their neighbors and coworkers who felt the need to do something radically different. Those who had refrained from earlier voting saw the folly of their action. The Obama wonder came powerfully into play. New Hampshire pollsters shook their heads and wondered how they had got it so wrong. Believers of the Bradley effect were tongue tight. Hillary Clinton and John McCain who had trailed in the polls won their respective parties' contests in the primary. Unexpected outcomes kept pollsters wondering who the heck had picked up the telephones and talked to them. The Obama train was just gaining momentum.

The indirect vote system may soon be a thing of the past as moves towards eliminating the Electoral College gain momentum. It is clear that Americans do not like the idea of the person they pick for president losing the final tally the way Al Gore lost to George W. Bush in 2000, simply as a result of this influence of the Electoral College. The framers of the Electoral College were great people who did not trust the average voter in such crucial matters but times have changed. Massachusetts and New York must now follow the lead of states like Illinois, New Jersey, Hawaii, Maryland and Washington to usher in such a welcome change, so that the nightmare of George Bush's victory over Al Gore in 2000 becomes history. As a matter of fact, just as I finished writing these lines, Governor Deval Patrick of Massachusetts did just that by signing into law the National Popular Vote bill that allows the Commonwealth to give all twelve electoral votes to that presidential candidate receiving the most votes nationally.

There were many obstacles to overcome, among them the delicate issue of race and religion. The Reverend Jeremiah Wright, Obama's minister and friend became the other center of attraction, following his rants at the pulpit which many considered hurtful rather than helpful to Senator Obama's campaign. The priest's remarks brought race into the center stage, a distraction candidate Obama would have loved to avoid. As pastor of the Trinity United Church of Christ in Chicago, Reverend Wright had married the Obamas, baptized their two girls and, it was said that he even consulted with the candidate before the decision to run for the presidency. Senator Obama described the pastor as an old uncle who sometimes would say things that he didn't agree with, things that were inflammatory and appalling, all statements that had been the subject of controversy and ones that he vehemently condemned. Supporters welcomed the candidate's unambiguous stance.

Senator Obama did the right thing to condemn inflammatory and appalling language that created controversy and shifted attention from the things that mattered for his campaign. But then again, were those not the utterances that the West brandished when trying to explain the fact that Islam's literal interpretation of the Qur'an and lack of creative criticism are responsible for the great disparity between its followers and followers of the Bible? Church and State may stand separate on paper but church and politics are not too far apart. Nowhere in the democratic world than here in the US are a candidate's religious views more of an influencing factor to millions of voters.

Senator Barack Obama had a photograph of himself taken at some point wearing a traditional Somali garb, causing Muslims to suspect that there was no fate worse than being labeled a Muslim. Without specifically mentioning Senator Obama's middle name as was done by those stoking the fear fire then, Senator John McCain expressed his discomfort at the prospect of a Muslim president; Obama's campaign team made frantic and strident efforts to distance the candidate from the Islamic faith of his late father. Religious fear-mongering was apparently acceptable, even encouraged in America. And yet there were hopes that the 2008 election would mark the beginning of color-blind and gender-blind politics in America, paving the way, hopefully, for religion-blind politics later but then religion kept coming to the fore. It was difficult to understand why Americans would treat a mere name as if it were an inheritable trait. The candidate's middle name became a handy tool in the hands of his opponents and detractors alike.

But what is in a name, really? Don't parents all over the world name their kids after their choice mentors, idols and the like? What difference does society make between its Hitlers and Einsteins, its Solzhenitsyns and Brezhnevs, whose similarities outweigh dissimilarities? Unlike France which practices assimilation, America is a melting pot that absorbs everything exotic. France strenuously retains French names as nontranslatable yet is quite at ease changing Peter to *Pierre*, Klein to *Petit*, Mzee to *LeGrand*, Drinkwater to *Boileau*, Salvatore to *Seigneur*, Toogood to *Toutbon* and, to make the British really angry, Falklands to *Malvinas*. That is the Hexagon's choice. But this is America! It is true that candidate Obama's father was Hussein, a Muslim and that he had named his son Hussein as well. But that was only a personal choice, like any other choice, subject to change. The proof is that Barack Obama eventually grew up as a Christian. Christians, like Jews, have switched religion to Islam as their fancies carried them. So what was the cachexia all about, as if Hussein Obama's accession to the White House would usher in World War III?

In addition to religion, racism and sexism featured prominently. The 15th Amendment to the US Constitution gave black men the right to vote and the 19th Amendment gave women the same right. And in 1984, Geraldine Ferraro became the very first woman to be nominated as Vice Presidential running mate. Quite a slow progression indeed! In that year six out of ten persons were pleased to have a female VP on the Democratic ticket; in 2008 nine out of ten said they liked to see a woman president. Slowly but surely change was in the air. The long journey for womenfolk was finally nearing its end and a level playing field was in sight about ninety years after women got the vote and title IX (they can do or be anything they want). Women make up a majority of college students and the work force, even if the average woman still makes just 77 cents for every dollar made by a man. Three women had been confirmed as Supreme Court justices and 2008 brought a woman tantalizingly close to becoming US president. Three women have occupied the highest cabinet position – Secretary of State.

But are women happy with their lot? Not yet. The sky is the limit and going by newspaper articles that spice newsstands around, some are claiming "the end of men" while others prefer to christen the current financial meltdown a "he-cession". The profile of a rich, successful yet incredibly lonely working woman is still a reality of the times as can be seen in movies and magazines.

It is undeniable that racism and sexism were issues in the 2008 primaries, especially as the two minority groups made a showing at primaries. It is also clear that the nation as a whole considered racism a greater evil than sexism and so decided to turn against it by allowing Senator Barack Obama to take a shot at the White House. But Obama may not end racism and its attendant evils in American society and it is obvious that the civil rights movement is no longer an adequate tool to address the injustices caused by entrenched racism over the years.

What tools other than civil rights can the nation use to eliminate the last vestiges of discrimination in America? Racial injustices, bias and bigotry may have reduced in frequency but racial segregation and the disadvantages associated with living in isolated, economically depressed and crime-ridden neighborhoods remain the legacy of past racism, not current discrimination. Of course racism is still a problem because we still cope with persons who distrust or belittle others based on stereotypes and racial tensions, and hatred and contempt continue to trouble social interactions in schools and at work places. Inequality remains a big problem, giving the impression that there are two Americas – a black poor one and a more affluent multiracial one. Many of the nation's poor blacks live isolated lives in inner cities with little or no contact with mainstream American society or conventional job market. In such a set up fathers unable to support their families simply walk away and abandon them, and young single mothers, overwhelmed by the challenges of single parenthood, give up education and hope of any upward mobility. The ghetto has developed its own language called Ebonics, a language that can be off-putting for employers who abound in mainstream America. Thus deprived of employment opportunities, residents in the ghettos readily and easily turn to full-fledged crime – peddling of crack cocaine, carrying out turf wars and others.

Campaigning for the 2008 presidential election, candidate Barack Obama drew attention to black fathers who abandoned their responsibilities of parenting the children they bring into the world, acting like boys instead of men and in the process, weakening the family. Reverend Jesse Jackson picked quarrels with that stance, chastising Obama for ignoring the structural impediments to quality fathering faced by black men. He felt that emphasis should not only be on the personal and moral responsibilities of black males, but also the collective moral responsibilities of government and public policy. Any remedy that failed to target the decline of inner city neighborhoods and the attendant ills missed the point. Therefore, the argument went, if the Obama administration wished to do anything palpable and make headway, it must tackle head-on the problems of the urban poor – job creation, more effective schools, better public infrastructure, and a revamped criminal justice system. It was only in tackling such problems that the nation could be able to turn the corner and its back to a shameful racist past and then break the cycle of poverty and dysfunctional behavior. The millions of people currently a drain on national resources (jails, public assistance) would hopefully, be converted into productive forces that contribute to the economy and civic culture.

Most of today's generation of African–Americans cannot imagine the deprivation, oppression, and humiliation that their ancestors suffered a few decades ago, being forcibly brought to America as slaves, legally defined as chattel and treated as less than human. It took a bloody civil war to secure emancipation but the Jim Crow laws enacted thereafter codified the inferior social position of blacks. State-sponsored racial discrimination was reinforced by private vigilantism – white mobs and organized racist groups such as the Ku Klux Klan terrorized blacks throughout the American South and the first race riots were sparked by racist whites in Northern cities like Chicago, Obama's adopted home.

Even far into the 2008 election cycle, there were Americans swearing to God and to their great grandparents that they could not and would not vote for Barack Obama because he was a Muslim, a black man, a terrorist, not "one of us" and a whole gamut of reasons. Four days away from Election Day, *Focus on the Family Action* weighed in with "If Barack Obama is elected president, America will descend into a fiery hell spiral, hastening the end of the world as we know it." The group added that a Democratic victory the following week would inevitably lead to terrorist strikes on four American cities, Russia rolling into Eastern Europe, Israel getting hit by a nuclear bomb, Americans only being allowed to get gay-married, and the end of the Boy Scouts – a real Armageddon scenario indeed. What a prophecy! All of such fear mongering calculated to make Barack Obama, the Democratic candidate, unelectable! Against such macabre predictions were young men and women, black and white, working hand in hand to realize a dream – Martin Luther King Jr's 1963 dream that some day, America would witness "little black boys and girls joining hands with little white boys and girls as brothers and sisters." The dream was more than realized – big white boys and girls indeed joined with big black boys and girls as well as the men and women of what was once a divided nation. It could not have been otherwise; blacks and whites have always been intimately intertwined whether as slave and slave masters or mistresses and lovers at various moments. The products are visible on our freeways, schools, neighborhoods, beaches, parks, shopping malls and workplaces.

The current disparity in arrests and incarceration of blacks can be addressed by providing employment opportunities to lure young people away from crack cocaine and their turf wars. That is part of the policy being applied in far away Afghanistan to lure the Taliban away from insurgency. Crime is a constant threat especially for people who have virtually no hope of finding honest work at a decent wage. Is it racism that makes many work forces disproportionately white? This is a debatable point but there is no doubt that given the dynamics of the job market, where most jobs are filled through social networking and a growing number of jobs require objective technical skills as well as the "soft skills" (charm, good demeanor, a determined can-do attitude), dropping out of school prematurely and living in the isolation of the inner city presents a definite hurdle for most blacks. Role models too are needed to teach the attitude appropriate for the work force. These values can be taught and they ought to be taught if there are blacks prepared to forego their lifestyles and embrace them. But to be honest, breaking gang affiliations is not an easy task and the war on drugs has become a quagmire, prompting some to advocate the decriminalization of some drugs or putting forth the Boston Miracle – breaking gang affiliations and patterns of criminal behavior by offering potential criminals the choice between finishing school and finding employment or tough criminal sentences if they don't.

Sexism in America is rather subtle. The news media and general public have zero tolerance for racism whereas for sexism, they just laugh it off or ignore it with expressions like *"Iron my shirt, shine my shoes"*. Many said that Hillary Clinton reminded them of their mothers, a clear indication of latent sexism, misogyny or down right myopia. Governor Sarah Palin of Alaska, self-proclaimed hockey-mom or pit-bull with lipstick, drafted in as Senator John McCain's running mate in a strategic move to woo disaffected Hillary supporters, created some fireworks but was unable to turn the tide against the Democrats. Was the press unfair to her as some alleged? That point remained debatable for a long time. But there was no doubt that the youthful and glamorous Alaska governor had brought some of the harsh criticisms on herself. Her outlandish claims concerning the bridge to nowhere, the metaphor presenting her as a hockey mom( pit bull with lipstick) and other unnecessary attacks on Senator Barack Obama's association with Bill Ayers did not help the GOP cause at all. Nor did she impress the American electorate with her answers to Katie Couric's questions on CBS concerning her Foreign Service experience or which newspapers, if any, that she read. If she had to be the womenfolk's compensation for losing the smart and tenacious Hillary Clinton, she had to show a lot more than she did. Fortunately for the society at large, the beauty of democracy lies in the fact that ultimately the individual voter, left inside the voting booth, can toy with conscience, learning, life's experiences and the totality of all those campaign messages – the hateful, the altruistic, the belligerent, the soothing, the "not one of us" versus the inclusive call for common action – to decide into which box that ballot paper should go. 2008 proved beyond doubt that when challenged, the majority of men and women can stand up and be counted.

Obama the candidate needed all the support he could get. Intolerance was surely in the eyes of the beholder, wasn't it? Far more significant about Colin Powell's endorsement of Senator Barack Obama the Democrat was what the decorated general said about Senator John McCain, running mate Governor Sarah Palin, and the Republican Party as a whole. Among other things, Colin Powell said, *"I'm also troubled by, not what Senator McCain says, but what members of the [Republican] Party say – such things as 'Well, you know that Mr. Obama is a Muslim'. The correct answer is 'He's not a Muslim, he is a Christian, and he's always been a Christian.' But the really right answer is 'What if he is?' Is there something wrong in being a Muslim in this country? The answer is 'No, that's not America'.*

Coming from a person with gravitas, the person still surrounded by an aura of Powellmania, whose salesmanship former president George W. Bush used to befuddle the UN and pitch his case for the Iraq war, people listened very attentively. Upon endorsing the Illinois Senator, Colin Powell called him a transformational figure and stressed that that was what the US needed at that moment of its history. A transformational personality would be less likely to be a visionary than one who could recognize and adapt to new realities, be free of binding ideological preconceptions and possess the pragmatic flexibility to face facts and to acknowledge when established practices had lost their effectiveness. He would try new ways of doing things.

Echoing President Lincoln's view that the dogmas of the quiet past being inadequate to the stormy present, thinking anew, disenthralling ourselves to save our country, Colin Powell said new realities demanded new approaches. Even the incumbent President George W. Bush had been obliged to cast aside his faith in pristine free markets and his contempt for international institutions to embrace the new realities in Iraq and on the economic front at home. His successor to the White House must therefore be someone who could change the Federal government's way of regulating capitalism and coordinating economic decision-making with other countries. Examples of such transformational figures in history were easy to cite. Richard Nixon's name readily came to mind. President Nixon will always be remembered for altering the Cold War balance of power when he put aside his previous biases and opened up to Mao Zedong's China. President Lyndon Johnson did the same thing when he set aside past prejudices and signed into law the Civil Rights Act and the Voting Act, thus transforming a previously segregated society. Thanks to the Founding Fathers this country was made great from the word go.

Barack Obama's accession to the presidency was like receiving a poisoned gift and it did not take long for the stark realities to face the new president. His nomination of Sonia Sotomayor, the first Latina woman to the Supreme Court to replace retiring Justice David Souter, raised the usual criticisms from the Republicans, ever so ready to find blemishes in anything put forward by the Democrats. It was hoped that the GOP and Democrats in the Senate would quickly confirm her appointment. Republican Senator Arlen Specter's carpet crossing to the Democratic Party followed by Minnesota's Al Franken's victory over Norm Coleman, the Republican, brought the Democrats tantalizingly close to the magical 60 votes needed for a filibuster-proof Senate majority for the job.(A filibuster is a tactical maneuver to delay, derail and possibly kill a bill).

Anxious to find fault with the nominee, Newt Gingrich had gone into her past and picked out a statement she had made some time ago about a Latina being better able to make a judgment than a white male, thanks to the fact that race and gender had informed her life experience and shaped her world view. Rather than see the positive aspect of her declaration, critics, in addition to screwing up the pronunciation of her foreign name the way Americans are wont to do, were quick to label it reverse racism. The critics, mostly white males, failed to come to terms with one fact – that hitherto, their own race and gender had shaped world view. Indeed isn't it true that given her unique background as a Hispanic, the fact that she had been forced by her experience to see the factors that feature in our decision-making, she might reach a better conclusion than a white male?

In a climate of simmering resentment that people were being urged to study the alien's language instead of the other way around, such reactions were understandable. That issue so far was the only bump on an otherwise smooth ride on Sotomayor's way to the bench of the Supreme Court. When Sonia Sotomayor first made the statement about her being better qualified than an ordinary white guy for handling certain situations, nobody paid special attention to it. In a country like the US and at a time when employability depended so much on the resume and job interview, it was quite conceivable that the lady was selling her skills in the competitive job market. Everybody did it. Revisiting such a declaration later to unearth those remarks and use them out of context as a calculated roadblock to her confirmation was ironic, disingenuous and even counterproductive because employers still paid top dollars for employees who brought a vast wealth of experience to their jobs.

In the course of her confirmation hearings, the nominee was made to virtually renege on her previous declaration and to state that she would apply the law strictly as it was(a local tabloid had this headline: *Sotomayor Vows Fidelity to the Law as hearings Start*), this to pacify her detractors and the fringe that sought to block her appointment. Some thought the entire hearing process tended to trivialize the law and make it look less vibrant and less than an entity with a remarkable blend of real world facts and abstract principles. It took away the nuance and thought characteristic of lawyering and made the art look like a mere mechanical exercise completely at odds with the notion of a living Constitution intended to depict the law as a tool for social reform.

In so doing, the nominee brought to light the old debate about the law as it ought to be versus the law as it was. What is natural law and who are the men and women of law? Europeans call them advocates, Americans know them as attorneys but the world knows that they are simply lawyers. Some are considered with some justification, as descendants of ancient sophists - a society of men bred up from their youth in the art of proving by words multiplied for the purpose, that white is black and black white, according to how they are paid. (Jonathan Swift: *Gulliver's Travels*).

Sonia Sotomayor's nomination reflected President Obama's centrist policies. The left rejoiced at the choice of the Puerto Rican lady while the right snarled at what they considered the triumph of identity politics over merit, forgetting that she was an Ivy League graduate, even if she was Latina. Republicans had the difficult choice of continuing with baseless critiques and alienating their progressive minority supporters in following that course.

Also, at around that very time, the Supreme Court ruled 5- 4(along the usual conservative –liberal lines) in favor of white firefighters who had appealed against a Connecticut court decision with Sonia Sotomayor on board, cancelling a fire fighters' examination which was judged biased because there were no minority (colored) candidates. In reversing the lower court's decision, the Supreme Court argued that there was no evidence produced to show that a disservice had occurred or that a minority had been cheated in the particular exam or that nonwhite firefighters had been illegally denied promotion on the basis of race. In the eyes of the Supreme Court, New Haven Connecticut had violated Federal Civil Rights Law by throwing out the results of the promotion examination after it yielded too many qualified white applicants but no acceptable black candidate. Some called it reverse discrimination. This came to many as no surprise because Justice John Roberts, himself a minority, was known for his lack of sympathy for minority issues. How that ruling would affect Sonia Sotomayor's impending confirmation remained to be seen.

Was that a severe blow to the candidate's chances? And bigger than even Sonia Sotomayor was the question of how the ruling would affect promotion policies for employers nationwide, many of whom had been operating under Affirmative Action programs designed decades earlier to promote racial diversity in the work place as well as redress some of the wrongs of the past.

There was a catch-22 situation here. If a strong case was to be made about the fire department not hiring minorities, such a case would be strengthened with educated and certified blacks in search of work, otherwise the case was not water tight. On the other hand if minorities preferred to stay out of school where the skills and diplomas for such jobs are obtained, it made no sense complaining of being discriminated against or even instituting litigation to fight it. As a matter of fact, in throwing out the lower court's judgment in the case of discrimination against minorities, the Supreme Court pointedly argued that there was obviously no minority candidate in the first place.

All the same Sonia Sotomayor was eventually sworn in by Chief Justice John Roberts. Puerto Rico's *Primera Hora* declared: "At last, Sonia!" sending the four million inhabitants of that American territory into a frenzy of great expectations and ending one heck of a job interview! In a world where girl power is still slowly emerging, where many societies still suppress women through terrible and culturally acceptable measures like genital mutilation, sex slavery, forced marriage, female subservience, honor killings and other atrocities, there was room to celebrate this one victory for womankind. The GOP reaction to every Obama act so far remained a resounding no, a typical partisan roadblock. The party would have to answer whether it was so morally objectionable to be guided by empathy when making a court ruling or voting on legislation in Congress, especially voting into law a bill to control the possession of hand guns or texting while driving. Most persons shied away from the logical option of voting to make legislation that would preempt rather than cure the disasters that went with such acts for which legislation was required.

A small but not insignificant detail remained. Should voting not be done on the same day for everybody? Proponents and supporters of BeAbsentee.org said no. And they proposed a number of excuses for voting on a day other than Election Day (first Tuesday in November) – some cast their votes months in advance of that day, either in person or by mail or at designated early-voting places as absentees. Over the years the number of votes so cast had soared from 4 million in 1980 to 27 million during the 2004 election. That number was sure to keep growing as the list of excuses grew in response to requests to make voting more convenient - a lot of people were too busy, some had better things to do on election day, they didn't have to stand in line, it might rain or snow on election day, people might fall ill or be caught in traffic, it is so much easier to cast a ballot from the convenience of one's couch by mailing it, and so on. And the system seemed to accommodate each of those excuses offered by able-bodied but lazy persons who would rather stay away from the polls.

And they seemed to be succeeding too. Oregon had done away with polling places entirely; 100% of its elections were conducted by mail. Following closely was Washington State with more than 70%. Ohio jumped on the bandwagon for the first time recently, inviting residents to vote as early as September 30 and even letting some register and cast the ballot on the same day if they showed up by October 6.

There is naturally a price to pay for this new trend. In this era of "have-it-your-way" convenience, where it seems unreasonable to expect voters to wait till November 4 to cast their votes for president, senator or city councilor, these voters cast their ballots without the benefit of all the information, analyses and discussions that bloom in profusion during the last few weeks of an election campaign – the debates, the endorsements, voter guides, candidates' speeches, heightened media attention etc. They miss the focus that Election Day gives to the process of democratic decision-making and the important lessons in civics are muddled or lost. Does it make sense for jurors to be allowed to render a verdict before hearing from the final witnesses and closing arguments? Does it make sense for theater critics to skip the final act of a play in order to write their reviews? It is almost certain that the last word is yet to be said on this trend and the quality of future generations of voters will need to be improved since voters have the enormous responsibility of choosing the right candidate for elective office.

Thanks to the vast majority of educated, enlightened and committed voters, this country can avoid some of the pitfalls that end up getting the wrong persons into the White House or Congress. A good citizen with knowledge of civics takes time to assess the candidates running for office as well as their strengths and weaknesses before deciding. If the US had to depend on its unenlightened and biased voters - of which there are many - it could spell disaster. It is not difficult to spot prejudiced voters from their utterances. Some of Senator Barack Obama's staunchest opponents claimed that they could not vote for him because they did not know him, adding that they felt Sarah Palin was their choice because they knew her better. And yet, of the two, Barack Obama had been on the campaign trail for nearly two years, had published two important works which spoke a lot about himself, his upbringing, his religious background and his vision. How could any American not know him yet profess to know Sarah Palin, the Alaska governor, a virtually unknown quantity brought to the lime light from relative obscurity just because Senator John McCain went scouting for someone to help him swing over disaffected Hillary Clinton supporters who had been angered by her bowing to Senator Barack Obama as front runner on the Democratic ticket? When people make statements such as "he is not one of us" it betrays the bigotry and myopia that guides them in their voting pattern. Such statements negate the noble idea of a melting pot that derives strength from America's diversity. Who exactly would be considered "*us*"? And how could this possibly help sell democracy abroad in Iran, Iraq, Afghanistan, Pakistan, Rwanda and the rest of the world where George Bush had been crusading with a messianic zeal to spread the word? Those were very disturbing utterances and served only to cast a cloud over our belief in a colorblind society. But the good America had come too far to let a good dream die. Even though the smart Hillary Clinton bowed out, America was more than compensated by an even smarter Barack Obama!

Listening to those varied voter reactions and having jumped onto the Obama bandwagon following Hillary Clinton's bowing out, my mind went back to a distant past. With a dose of wishful thinking, I recalled an event I lived through during the troubled sixties when I was doing a twelve-month clinical internship in Mercy Hospital, Springfield in Western Massachusetts. It was a requirement by the ASCP (American Society for Clinical Pathology) for my certification in medical technology. For one year at that hospital I was required to rotate through phlebotomy, clinical chemistry, hematology, blood banking, coagulation, histopathology and toxicology. John Volpe was the governor of Massachusetts and Senator Robert Francis Kennedy had just been assassinated by a certain Sirhan Sirhan, following his spectacular victory in a California race for the White House, on the heels of Martin Luther King's assassination. His brother, Edward Moore Kennedy was struggling to cope with the fallout of his imbroglio involving the death of MaryJo Kopechne at Chappaquiddick. The unwinnable Vietnam War raged on. Each day I carried out all the necessary quality control operations to ensure a problem-free day and to attend to outpatient and inpatient cases as instructed, beginning with phlebotomy.

There was little or no problem dealing with pediatric cases other than enlisting the cooperation of parents to help with very apprehensive and unpredictable kids who dreaded the needle. As for the geriatric ones, well, one could count on a dose of good luck because those elderly persons were often dehydrated and difficult to collect blood from. Of the in-betweens, there was a particularly difficult Mrs. Kczkczinski whose case was complicated by her volatile temperament, her obesity and excessive adiposity, so that the collection of blood from her arm was a real Calvary. There was also the patient's very difficult and unfriendly attitude to cope with. Mrs. Kczkczinski hated students in general and when the student happened also to be black, it posed a special problem.

That was my plight on a certain morning as my supervisors, Dr Rini and Sister Dianne took their seats behind the curtain and monitored my professional performance on a videotape equipment. Would I be able to find Mrs. K's vein hidden in the massive adiposity of her antecubital fossa? Would my needle cooperate? Well, I gathered as much courage as possible, went in, made the sign of the cross and greeted Mrs.K. I told her - gesturing with thumb and index fingers clenched - that I needed just a little amount of her blood for some tests. Would it be OK to collect it? In a rather resigned manner and without a smile, the patient stretched out her left arm to me and turned her face to the wall. Simply looking at her arm I could tell from all the blue marks how much extravasation of blood had taken place from previous blood draws. Nervous and trembling, I opened my wares, took out the tourniquet, tied it around her arm and felt for her vessels. There was neither a visible vein nor a palpable one. I was stuck. What was I to do? I reflected for a while and then recalled that in one of his clinical lessons, Dr Rini had suggested to try a "blind probe" in such circumstances – simply do a good alcohol wipe, tie the tourniquet, insert the needle and try to play around till luck smiled and it entered a vessel with good caliber. I did just that and lo! I saw blood rush out and, quickly I inserted the vacutainer tubes one after another till I had drawn all the blood needed. And then I withdrew the needle, cleaned up the wound, applied sterile gauze and a band aid. And I was done. When I thanked Mrs. K, she opened wide frog eyes and simply asked in disbelief "Is that all?" I must have surprised her.

But the real surprise was not in what had gone before; it was in what followed later. From that day on, whenever anyone came by to draw blood from her, Mrs. Kczkczinski invariably pleaded if they would "please send that black boy". It might sound like some amount of wishful thinking but it was my gut feeling that Americans in general, and the most bigoted in particular, would some day come to value Senator Barack Obama the way that patient valued me, the student intern. All that America needed to do was give the Illinois senator a chance.

Is it not possible for persons of divided loyalties to cohabit happily? Absolutely! Husband/wife, son/daughter, father/son, brother/sister and all sorts of rivalries exist in sports (Patriots versus Jets or Red

Sox versus Yankees), religion, politics and more. Divided houses are not uncommon where the upstairs houses Republicans and the downstairs Democrats, or vice versa, where one spouse swears by the First Amendment while the other does so by the second. It is not unusual on the morning of an important election, for an American husband who is a Democrat and his wife a Republican to go hand-in-hand out of their house, greet their children and tell them "We're off to the polls to cancel out each other's vote." It is hard but doable and their love never diminishes simply because they belong to two different political parties. Warring over political differences is so wasteful of energy and time.

Senator Barack Obama's spectacular victory sent messages around the world. There is no doubt about that. Places like Africa from where the new president traces his roots, will most likely be impacted by his victory. A society cannot hope to move ahead if it makes no provision for healthy competition at all levels and in all areas of human endeavor. Kenya had just gone through a presidential election that turned out to be rigged and bloody, prompting former UN Secretary-General, Kofi Anan to rush to the rescue and work out some sort of a power-sharing arrangement pompously called an African solution to an African problem. Unfortunately that solution endorsed a very dangerous precedent that in future, an unpopular head of state could organize elections, lose, refuse to give up power, and stay put, using the nation's resources still at his command, and then expect this magic solution. As a matter of fact strongman Robert Gabriel Mugabe of Zimbabwe did precisely that even as his country slid into a recession with inflation estimated at several thousand percents. How anyone could buy a loaf of bread for currency in the billions, only Mugabe (Bachelor of Science in violence) and his mentor, former South African president, Thabo Mbeki (Bachelor of Science in silence) in their infinite wisdom could understand.

On March 30, 2008 the people of Zimbabwe went to the polls to elect their parliamentarians and a new Head of State, against a backdrop of economic woes characterized by an inflation of 100,000%, a loaf of bread selling for $12.000, 000! Just imagine stretching a $100,000,000 note for a purchase of bread and asking for change! In a sane world one would expect incumbent president Robert Mugabe to be vomited by the impoverished and oppressed peoples of Zimbabwe. As a matter of fact it all passed off very peacefully and predictions were that Opposition leader Morgan Tsvangrai would boot out the man who had ruled Zimbabwe for 28 years and brought the economy to its knees. But between casting of ballots and declaring of results there were gymnastics involving the doctoring of ballot results from the field, a typical African phenomenon seen in Cameroon, Kenya, Zimbabwe and most of what had been aptly called tropical or AK-47 democracies. All the euphoria of Opposition supporters began to evaporate as time went by with no results forth coming. There was talk of behind the scenes dealing between MDC (Movement for Democratic Change) and ZANU-PF party but apparently it was all wishful thinking. Mugabe was in no mood to relinquish power. The sepulchral silence was to give the incumbent strongman time to hone his rigging machinery! One week later, the entire world heard that the MDC had won 99 seats in parliament against ZANU-PF's 97. But the crucial issue of the presidency remained taboo and no one heard from the Chairman of the Election Commission even as members of Mugabe's ruling party went into a conclave and decided that Mugabe should present himself for a run off election against the MDC. Still no official vote count of the much tooted peaceful elections! Where was the neutrality of the Electoral Commission if Mugabe's party, the ZANU-PF could keep its task of declaring the results of the presidential election on hold, while it entered into a conclave? It soon became clear that the long delay in declaring the results of Zimbabwe's presidential and parliamentary elections that had taken place over one month earlier was predicated on the arrival of Chinese arms for strongman Mugabe's thugs to use against protesting citizens, especially of the Opposition MDC of Morgan Tsvangirai!

Robert Mugabe's painful antics eventually drove Zimbabwe thirty-nine odd steps into the doldrums, necessitating aid from outside. The man became so dependent on the $8.5 billion outside aid that he avoided the risky move of sabotaging the power-sharing deal he had struck with Prime Minister, Morgan Tsvangirai. Zimbabwe's economy needed that much money to revamp it but western donors were too wary of the man, conditioning any such assistance on the release of political prisoners; the man's thugs and cronies were desperate to stay in power but they were even more desperate for the foreign cash, making Human rights groups such as Amnesty International to play the vital role of acting as the international community. President Mugabe –cynical, narcissistic and defiant all at once - was reported by some journalists who interviewed him to actually shed tears when feelings of betrayal and nostalgia of the good life with the British royal family or memories of cricket crossed his mind.

Taking the oath of office with his hand placed on the Bible, singing the Star - Spangled Banner together, accommodating former rivals and even appointing some into his cabinet were powerful signals that Barack Obama, the new American president sent around the world, that it is possible to work across the political divide and serve the motherland. If world leaders could learn from President-elect Obama's socializing with defeated rival John McCain and appointing members of the GOP in his administration, political tension would go down several notches. Hillary Clinton's maiden visit to Japan, Indonesia, South Korea were pointers in this very positive direction.

## *Presidential Pet, Bo and the Pet Industry.*

President Obama was awaited to deliver on his promise, made during the election campaign, to give his two lovely daughters a puppy. He could not renege because he had made this promise in front of millions of Americans. So Malia and Sasha were in the great expectations mood. Their realistic parents took their time to do it right, preparing their move to the White House as well as searching for the proper puppy. The entire nation waited to see the promise come true.

Would the dog be for the girls only or for their father as well? Would the girls do better than boys to take care of the dog? The Obamas have no boy in their family. In fact the last time a son lived in the White House was around the 1960s when John F. Kennedy was the tenant. Since then it has been only girls – Lyndon Johnson, Richard Nixon, Bill Clinton, Georg W. Bush and now Barack Obama. Did US presidents always have dogs? The out-gone president George Walker Bush had Barney and a Miss Beazley. President Dwight Eisenhower (Ike) had Heidi, President Nixon had Checkers and Lyndon Baines Johnson had Him and Her, both known as LBJ. Does this mean - as some have suggested - that a president without a dog is considered a communist? Who started this fad any way? Beyond the few seconds of photo-ups (ear scratching) that a president makes with his dog as he alights from Air Force One, what else does he do with it? I can bet my last dollar that the real caretakers (or *caregivers* to use the more appropriate designation) would be elsewhere in the background. This is like during the Victorian times when children were fed, scrubbed, and presented to the parents for four or so minutes at the end of the day. Dog duty is probably the same in the White House.

And what kind of dogs do presidents like? Surely no scary dogs would be allowed unless somebody wished to scare the poor fellows of the secret service or future invitees to the White House. Would a pit bull, a Rottweiler, a Doberman, German shepherd or some yappy little Chihuahua do? Or would it be a Labradoodle (a Labrador poodle hybrid popular among allergy sufferers like Malia) or a Golden Retriever? Who would walk the dog on a rainy day or a winter night? And what about the dog poop? How about vet bills?

Whatever the case, the way the Obamas chose their dog surely created ripples across the nation and beyond. Whichever breed the first family settled on would certainly start the so-called "101 Dalmatians" effect - a sudden burst of popularity resulting from a movie or celebrity putting the spotlight on a particular breed of dog. Breeders capitalize on this and create market-driven puppy mills that produce dogs like cash crops rather than loving pets. So far Obama's Midas' touch had been a godsend to many persons, especially in his native Hawaii. Mass production of dog breeds is common among the Amish and Mennonite communities, where it is common to find commercial dog breeders who are less than humane with their dogs, prompting officials to raid their premises as was the case in Sparta, Tennessee some time ago. The pet industry in America is supposed to be recession-resistant and to be taken seriously indeed although in Massachusetts, Wonderland's Greyhound Park for dog racing was shut down as a result of a voter-approved ban, bringing to a halt the source of livelihood for about 85 employees as well as the associated expanded gambling that would allow slot machines.

One hundred years ago, a certain Thorstein Veblen, an economist, lampooned the house pet in these terms: the ultimate emblem of conspicuous consumption, an 'item of expense with no industrial purpose'. If that man were on the scene today to see for himself how things have changed! The $43 billion pet industry in general and dogs in particular are in high demand. Every effort is deployed to convert wild wolves, foxes, and even minks into domestic animals for human companionship. Animals are genetically selected for behavior, especially domesticated behavior that can be regulated through a complex combination of molecules such as hormones, or neurons and neuron receptors. People are breeding dogs to look a certain way. Mutations are studied meticulously and those that induce a change in color, coat, and degree of perkiness of the ears are a premium. Collaboration with followers and disciples of scientists like Dmitri Konstantinovich in far away Novosibirsk in Russia or geneticist, Dmitri Belyaev, the fox domesticator makes possible so many great things as *Canis lupus* is turned into *Canis familiaris*.

Over the years the archetype of a stylish American woman strolling outdoors with her dog on a leash changed imperceptibly to a dog sitting in front of the fireplace in the living room and then to a dog in the bed room, curling next to a sick child or pet owner who does not hesitate to call her his or her "baby". Quite a leap! It is easy to trace this development leading to the dog's enhanced family status over the last century. Changing times have brought about fragmented social networks – people living alone, increased rate of divorce, more childlessness, increased distance between once closely knit family members, much less community involvement in the lives of people. Researchers speculate that a lonelier society may be more willing to see human qualities in pets. American society can be quite lonely indeed. Pets in general and dogs in particular easily fill the gap created by the loss of a social support system. Once upon a time a Labrador retriever was brought by its owner to a gas station for companionship while she worked. The smart pet soon became a sensation, jumping from car to car as employees went about assisting customers who stopped to fill their tanks. It did not take long for the owner of the business to fashion out a uniform for the pet like for other workers, given the extra fillip brought to the business. Dogs have been trained to do a good number of chores where human beings are either absent or wanting. They sniff dangerous drugs for the police, bombs for the military and are able to smell the breath of diabetics and tell when the blood sugar level is dangerously high.

The elevation of status for pets calls for some responsibility on the part of owners. Here Americans are not wanting at all. Expense on pet food, expenses on all sorts of expertise (veterinary dermatologists, professional dog groomers, pet food nutritionists, marketers, legal gurus, spa operators, pet insurers, Christmas gifts for pets, pet names) run into the billions of dollars. Yesterday a sick cat could quite easily be euthanized to put her out of her misery; today the cat owner is more likely going to help it get a kidney transplant. The demand for natural pet chow is high, so is that for pedicures and manicures. The society for the prevention of cruelty to animals (SPCA) is a big organization committed to doing for pets every conceivable thing that is done for human beings, including erecting the best hospitals equipped with ultramodern, state-of-the-art instruments and pet custody battles are fought in courtrooms as never before whenever divorce tears a couple apart. The movie, *Hotel for Dogs* is reputed to have netted a huge profit and $250,000 of the proceeds from ticket sales were directed to animal shelters and breed-rescue groups. Spending $3000 for flat screen television sets for dogs is not far-fetched because owners know that their pets love to watch movies. It is a sheer exercise in futility drawing attention to the fact that people are dying of starvation in Africa or elsewhere in the world of natural disasters because many a wealthy pet owner would rather take their companion to an upscale pet hotel with luxury suites. Materialistic? Over-the-top? That is quite debatable indeed. As I finished these lines, Michael Vick, an NFL star player was sentenced to 23 months in prison for running a dog fighting operation and word got on the air that Americans had launched an airline specifically for pets. Pet Airline would make an inaugural flight from New York to California and back, the recession notwithstanding. Together with luxury hotels for pets, dog beds, specially designed spas, and services like pet sitting, pet walking and pet grooming, our four-legged VIPs can rise up and be counted.

Other less romantic pets abound even if their story is not as exciting as that of man's best friend. The case of an Orlando, Florida killer whale, Tilly, which ended up dragging its trainer, Dawn Brancheau under water and killing her in front of horrified spectators whose thrill and applause turned into a mournful silence in the SeaWorld, falls in a category of its own. Chimpanzees, birds and snakes have been used as pets. So also have monkeys. As a matter of fact the capuchin is a small South American species of monkey that has been as valuable as man's best friend. It is smart, very agile, has manual dexterity and can be trained to do an incredible amount of work for its owner. Persons with muscular dystrophy, multiple sclerosis, Lou Gehrig's disease, or quadriplegics who suffered car accidents resulting in serious spinal cord injury owe their lives to the capuchin which assists with such tasks as picking up a dropped telephone, switching the light on and off, opening bottles, playing CDs, working the microwave, feeding the severely disabled and most importantly, providing companionship. All that is needed is some good training which the clever, curious creature picks up quite quickly. Lots of persons with the above diseases owe their lives to these smart, live-in creatures. It is no exaggeration that people have had a harder time adopting one of these than adopting a human child, the package going as far as $50,000 some times. One day a Cambridge, Massachusetts woman woke up to find a four-foot long snake in her room – a Colombian red tail boa- after she left her window open all night. Animal Control was able to take the serpent to the MSPCA, Boston Animal Care and Adoption Center where it would remain waiting either for the rightful owner to show up or for a foster parent to adopt it. Another woman, also a pet owner brought

Boston's Redline subway train to a halt between Andrew station and JFK/Umass because of a missing boa that was supposed to have been wrapped around her neck. In addition to aging vehicles, signal failures and switching difficulties, authorities of the MBTA now add a missing snake as cause for train delays. The missing slippery pet, named Penelope had got its owner quite distraught after she searched her purse and found nothing, the serpent having slithered between the legs of fellow passengers into thin air. Riders and employees of the T helped in the search to no avail. The MBTA allows guide dogs on the train. But snakes? This was a new one in the long chain of American rights which only they could determine whether it pleased their fellow citizens or not.

In the Commonwealth of Massachusetts, a certain Gary Blumenthal, six feet five inches tall, promised to dress like a giraffe when next presenting his budget for persons with disabilities under his organization. He had learned a painful lesson that animals received far more sympathetic hearing from legislators and the governor than human beings. Many other advocates agreed, especially those who spoke for battered women, immigrants, and other disadvantaged groups threatened with budget cuts. A gaffe by some overzealous individuals saying that animals at the Franklin Park and Stone zoos would be euthanized following budget cuts led to much braying, saber rattling and passionate recriminations and a quick reversal of the cuts by Governor Deval Patrick. How's that? The MSPCA routinely takes care of abandoned pets or those surrendered by their owners. Our four legged friends could not ask for more. Some pet owners are asking for tax relief. HAPPY (Humanity and Pets Partnered Through the Years) Act is said to have introduced a bill to allow pet owners deduct the cost of food, veterinary care and other pet-related expenses from their income taxes, up to $3500 a year.

But most of the pet money is in private reserves, out of the reach of any governor. In 2007 a hotel icon, Leona Helmsley left $12 million in her will for her dog, Trouble, an amount considered dog food when compared with the $60 million inherited by a German shepherd named Gunther III from its owner, Countess Karlotta Libenstein. Recently an anonymous donor left $8 million to the

Wombat Awareness Organization (WAO) to take care of wombats. What on earth are wombats? Apparently these are chubby, nocturnal marsupial natives of Australia.

It is only a matter of time before people begin to ask for time off from work for pet bereavement and mourning with the possibility of organized collection for the event. Persons have bequeathed colossal amounts of money in their wills to their pets. These expenses reflect not only postwar prosperity but also how much hunger for communion has pushed us as a society to go from the utilitarian model of animal-human interaction to "humanization", making domestic animals junior members of the family rather than beasts. President Obama actually told George Stephanopoulos of the ABC news how much it had been tougher finding the right fit of puppy than a Secretary of Commerce for his cabinet nominee. We lean on our pets for the support once provided by humans who are no longer in our lives.

And finally, during the Easter weekend of 2009, the Obama girls were all smiles as their father proudly presented them with the puppy promised long ago – a Portuguese water dog (PWD) reportedly a gift from the late Senator Ted Kennedy of the Kennedy dynasty. The pet, named Bo, met one of the important conditions imposed by the new president's family – it had to be hypoallergenic.

## *Michelle Obama – First black first lady.*

America has had all sorts of first ladies but Michelle Obama is the very first black first lady on record. What does this mean for her as an individual and for the black race in general? These days it is fashionable to hear people say they never thought they would be able to see a black president in their life times. At 44, Michelle Obama is the youngest first lady since Jacqueline Kennedy and together with the former first lady and Princess Diana she is ranked among the world's most elegant and well-respected ladies. Many expect her to usher in a glamorous era in Washington, some already calling it Bamelot.

Among her primary tasks will be that of knocking down a number of stereotypes about black women and black culture in general. Michelle Obama has the monumental task to change also the way African-Americans see themselves, their lives and their possibilities. It is a terrible responsibility. In addition to being classy, which she already is, she has to fight to eliminate the stereotype of black women that has been around for ages – angry, hotheaded, foaming-at-the-mouth drug addicts, always ready with a quick one-liner and a roll of the eyes.

Fortunately for her, much of her work is already done and so does not need speaking to spread the message that she is both an academic and a professional, the product of Ivy League education (Princeton, Harvard), one of America's best. She has spent time in boardrooms and topnotch law firms. Such universal appeal is an important tool in her hands because she can hold her own in any setting around the world, including the supposed challenge for a beauty contest emanating from Carla Bruni, France's first lady. While President Obama is a keynote speaker at many graduation ceremonies around the nation, his wife too is doing the same at other campuses. It was fantastic to watch husband and wife pitch camp for the city of Chicago for the 2016 Olympics even if they eventually lost to Rio de Janeiro. That was wonderful.

With her good education Michele Obama is well equipped to calibrate her remarks for any audience, especially black audiences. It is indeed gratifying to see the number of educated women engaged in traditionally, male-dominated activities such as driving city buses, trains, piloting aircraft, heading corporate offices and more. These days as many women as men are software engineers, accountants, lawyers, judges, and doctors. She ought to stop considering herself as the "little black girl from the south side of Chicago" and if the news media try to portray her as a domineering, angry black woman or a fist thumping terrorist as some cartoonists are wont to do, she is advised to respond with a smile and wear pearls and J. Crew cardigans. She has already proved her taste in fashion designs for herself and her girls. That daring, election-night red-speckled dress, designed by Narciso Rodriguez was smart. That genuine, chic, relaxed and affectionate performance with her husband on "60 Minutes" was a winner.

The easy warmth between the presidential couple will surely send a powerful message to the black community and make Bill Cosby especially proud. Nearly 50% of all African-American women are single and there are woefully few public examples of solid stable black marriages. Michelle is creating a protective cordon around her daughters, Malia and Sasha, just as the Carters did for Amy and the Clintons for Chelsea. Parenting is a problem among black families. Michelle will need to avoid taking such controversial stance as being "Mom –in-Chief" in these days with wars between the stay-at-home and working women. Most African-American families cannot survive without two incomes and for single moms, it means working two jobs, leaving little time to stay with the children. Having been a working mom herself, she knows how to juggle that portfolio.

Beyond these personal issues, she will have to tackle some meaty ones as well. Hillary Clinton took on healthcare issues with disastrous consequences. Laura Bush chose noncontroversial interests like literacy. So far Michelle has indicated her interest in military families and the struggles of working parents. Will she focus on the black community? Will that be too parochial? Her personal appearance is quite an asset. Fortunately she did her homework over the years to develop and retain that neat, sleek appearance. The tall lean appearance of an athlete will send a powerful message home to those of womenfolk who have virtually given up on the way they look. The alarmingly high rate of hypertension and obesity among African-American women and children is a matter for concern, the culture of sedentary life being part of the problem. Sedentary life (too much time spent in front of the television, playing video games, surfing the web) should be fought at all costs and excuses like the fear of messing up one's carefully done hair does not quite help matters.

Once upon a time if one needed information, one went to the library; for concert or cinema tickets one went to the box office and to meet someone, one dressed up and went to the bar or the club. These days technology has changed all that and wiped out any reason to go anywhere, hence kids grow chubby, waiting for things to be brought to them, hence businesses of all types are more than willing to oblige, arguing that if Mohammed won't come to the mountain, then the mountain ought to go to Mohammed. In some quarters it is the convention to blame the computer or the television for all the ills associated with getting fat, extremely fat and lazy and dependent.

Too often the overweight problem has been seen only in the context of fast foods and oversized helpings but evidence also points to the medicinal side effects of some drugs, especially the liberal use of psychiatric drugs to treat emotional problems like depression or anxiety. Thanks to James Gottstein, a smart Alaskan attorney, the world now knows that drugs like zyprexa, used to treat schizophrenia and bipolar disorders, can cause unwanted obesity in patients, yet its manufacturers carefully concealed this fact. Understandably, some parents are resentful of any moves taken to monitor their children at school, citing defense of liberty, respect and privacy matters as of more importance to the Federal government than such intrusions into people's lives, and fretting over the natural outcome of prosperity culture, of excess glory of capitalism. Yes, fat prejudice and the assault on one's honor have permeated society and any suggestion, no matter how mild that a person is fat, heavyset, or has an hourglass figure meets with resentment. One does not need rocket science to know that civilized society places a much higher premium on growing up than growing out. Of the many female shapes out there – rectangular, equilateral triangle on its head or base, hourglass – it seems the hourglass and rectangular shapes receive the greatest amount of disdain, adipose tissue having infiltrated and spoiled the nice curves. Yet such views show how ignorant some persons are of the role of government in matters of public health. We heard that before. Under conditions of uncertainty, when things are not easily controlled by knowledge, people turn to magic, witchcraft, cultural taboos and, as in the present case, defense of liberty and privacy. In this world of freedom of expression, people are not lacking to mount a defense for fast foods, accused of ensnaring kids. The unanswered question is "But where are the parents?"

Michelle Obama needs to be strong and firm in taking some initiatives such as the problem of obesity and weight control. There is nothing wrong with screening children early in life, availing them of facilities that combine belly dancing classes with mental relaxation to strengthen and shape the body, do figure of eight movements (complete rotation of the hip to enhance curves) and many more – marshal arts, jujitsu, tai chi, tae kwon do, kick boxing - to forestall problematic body images later in life. It is a well known fact that childhood obesity predisposes to a number of health problems such as heart disease, type 2 diabetes, asthma, sleep apnea, precocious menstruation, and social discrimination. The psychological stress of social stigma can result in low self esteem which in turn can hamper academic pursuits and normal social functioning.

People have played ping-pong games with the debate of nature (genes) versus nurture (lifestyle) and often come out with the wrong conclusions. Genes have been with us for thousands of years and we can do little about them but we surely alter our environment and can change our lifestyles or worldviews like quitting smoking or fighting obesity. How often have we watched helplessly as people, entrenched in the belief that a husband or Allah is in control, trivialize or even spurn preventive medicine (vaccination) or other dangerous lifestyles? There is no doubt that people are very bad judges when it comes to deciding what gives happiness and lasting satisfaction, often settling for ephemeral pleasures derived from money, a new car or the move to California, New York or Boston.

If Michelle Obama is going to be sidetracked by those complaining that America is the land of the free, where nothing in the Constitution authorizes the federal government to take charge of the way American children eat and play, nothing will be done. Parents who reason this way end up missing a forest of good will simply to rail against an atypical tree. Fortunately, for every parent that reasons this way, there are three dying to get government intervention to put things right. How can a problem be treated if the preliminary diagnosis is not made, if the necessary measurements (weight, height, BMI) are not determined? One thing about physical fitness is certain – start early in life rather than later, when it has become nearly impossible to bend down and lace one's shoes or clip toenails, because the stomach has become too large and the back too stiff to allow such agility, possible only with adorable James Bond type of girls like Halle Berry strolling along on stilettos.

At the extreme of obesity is a human being weighing 450 pounds, sitting with legs wide apart and a sagging stomach in between, a person wearing size XXXL T-shirt, size 65 slacks and lying on an operating table for doctors to carry out the most modern surgery available for weight reduction – a procedure called Roux-en-Y gastric bypass which consists of clipping the stomach to reduce its size from quarts to ounces. To be able to reach such a mountain of a patient and carry out the surgery, the surgeon may need to climb on two wooden stools piled up together! It is a last resort for those unable or unwilling to control their appetite for food, especially persons who navigate the way to school or work by passing through neighborhoods with franchises for Taco Bell, Burger King, McDonalds, Kim Toys, Dunkin' Donuts, pizzerias, steak houses, IHOP (international house of pancakes) and many more. In addition to road side posters, fast foods spend billions of dollars in marketing and advertisements on television, the Internet and social media sites, targeting children, some as young as two years of age. The US Center for Disease Control and Prevention estimates that two thirds of American adults and fifteen percent of children are overweight and obese. That's quite a load to carry around and still feel comfortable in a country which places a high premium on being slim because fatness is tantamount to failure and so society sneers with simple looks or the unspoken question "How can you afford to look like that?" nudging people towards the irresistible allure of get-thin-quick. Thirty years ago the cubicle at work was quite spacious but over the years and with America's steadily increasing girth, it has shrunk and become inadequate, so much so that one observer could not help quipping "the cubicle is inversely proportional to the size of its occupant". Overcoming this by opting to work from home is good but that too may predispose to sedentary life and more weight gain.

The invitation extended to Somerville's mayor Joseph Curtatone to come and speak at a nation-wide program devoted to combating childhood obesity was most welcome indeed. The Argenziano Elementary School in Somerville, Massachusetts is experimenting with novelties that other towns need to emulate. By a wise selection of names like smart spinach, x-ray vision carrots, cool cucumbers, brave beans and others for their vegetable-of-the-month names, authorities help the kids make the connection between vegetables and nutrition values as they move away from junk foods.

A responsible government cannot avoid taking what New York Times called "a sweeping initiative aimed at revamping the way American children eat and play –reshaping school lunches, playgrounds and even medical checkups - with the goal of eliminating childhood obesity. Children in third world countries may suffer from under nutrition but when it comes to combining physical exertion for better shape, they are unbeatable. Michelle Obama needs to be strong and firm in taking some initiatives such as the problem of obesity. Her husband has been blamed for everything under the skies; neglecting this area of national life can hardly go unnoticed. In recognition of her campaign so far against childhood obesity in the US, her dignity and loyalty to a president faced with a tumultuous political year, readers of Boston's Metro newspaper chose her as their favorite and inspirational personality of the year 2010.

And talking about hair, there is plenty of homework to do about black hair and its management in a world where, for too long, white skin color and white hairdo rather than good grades in calculus or mathematics have been used as the yardstick for measuring success or tools for tearing through racial barriers, entry and acceptability into mainstream. It is high time myopic notions like "blonds have more fun" be relegated to a distant past, giving young dynamic black women a chance on a level playing field, especially when it is so well known that beauty lies practically in the eyes of its beholder. What could be nobler than shredding this myth in our world of many opportunities?

Youthful actress America Ferrera from Honduras, appearing on Vanity Fair's Hollywood cover, said *"that's not just Hollywood, that's fashion, that's marketers, that's advertisers, that's business. And there are still people who have that incredibly narrow-minded perspective and they're only hampering themselves. They should learn to make money off all other people in the world who aren't white...That's people following trends rather than setting them.*" The black community needs leadership in this area too. Won't it be nice if Michelle Obama could put together a team of persons with good credentials to tackle the problem of black hairdo? Oprah Winfrey, Halle Berry, Beyonce, Tyra and so many names immediately come to mind. There is a growing industry, worth $12 billion as of now, that caters for black beauty. Its origin is traceable to a certain Madame C. J. Walker, black American millionaire, who started it all one hundred years ago – turning black hair, considered bad or not behaving, into straight, shining hair that behaves properly. Since that time, black women all over have each undertaken this awfully painful odyssey - as some are wont to call it - to attain the good, behaving hair that enables them gain acceptability at work, at school and in society at large. Indeed black women with straight, silky hair continue to be given preferential treatment over their sisters with wooly hair in very much the same way it was during slavery! Need that be so?

Mothers are not helping matters when they complain of how tough it is to comb their daughters' hair, initiating these little ones into the Barbie doll and salon fad very early in life. Little black girls are born into this world and initiated with such things as the Barbie dolls introduced by Mattel, with corresponding kits that highlight the long, straight silky or wavy hair. A mild protest by mothers who consider this a reinforcement of white standards of beauty did not have the desired impact. Afro, braids or dolls depicting the hair black girls are born with are not yet in the works. Black kids are born with hair that is slowly eclipsed by this artificial one being promoted by a toy conglomerate like Mattel. Thanks to hair that once belonged to some Somali or Ethiopian, many black women with hair problems can simply graft it on and find their way in modern society. To attain any degree of satisfaction with their natural hair, the biggest problem is the two hour stay at beauty salons to undergo a painful experience involving the treatment of hair with cream that contains many products, among them sodium hydroxide which is very corrosive. It is pathetic to watch a woman swoon in pain and grab the swivel chair on which she sits as the beautician or stylist sections her non-behaving wooly hair and applies this cream to tame it. Such harsh treatments have done wonders for women who lost hair to dandruff – infected patchy spots of scalp that look like dried up cornfields after a harvest. Surely there must be some alternative to such Calvary to obtain acceptable hair. With good leadership, some of the billions of dollars in the industry can be redirected to funding research for a better formula for black women.

Interestingly, as the size and architecture of the female hairdo grew in complexity and makeup, those of the male diminished progressively. From those good old Afros of the sixties, all we have today are increasing degrees of short hair with a weird penchant for the billiard ball head, giving the impression of preference for baldness even among the young. This style, which under other skies represents bereavement, is quite trendy in America.

With good leadership, able and willing to turn to research, an appropriate answer can be found. Understandably this is not easy at a time when skepticism reigns supreme in some of our research efforts, where attack on scientific progress has become routine and the phenomenon of denial a handy weapon. Out of fear, parents and activists in denial have openly rejected vaccination as a means of protecting children against some of mankind's ravages, proposing alternative medicine, prayer and other combinations. The truth is that we either believe in the evidence that can be tested, verified, and repeated or we don't and continue to remain in darkness while the world moves on. Evolution, global warming, swine flu, and genetically modified crops - the list is long of those things linked in the minds of opponents. But all it takes is a judicious weighing of the benefits against the theoretical harm especially in areas where synthetic biology has the potential to deliver breathtaking answers for the world's problems as well as reduce the planet to what Britain's Prince Charles calls a "grey goo". Parents have refused to let their children be vaccinated against the flu and measles, polio, the H1N1 virus and other communicable scourges with the bogus, unproven allegation that these cause autism. If these diseases have started gaining ground in places like northern Nigeria and the United

Kingdom, it goes to show what greater risks parents take when they choose not to vaccinate their children.

Science has made enormous progress, some of the main actors being unsung black heroes. Today Hela cells are used all over the world for research purposes – discovery of the Jonas Salk vaccine used in immunizing against poliomyelitis, discoveries in chemotherapy, gene mapping, drug development for herpes, leukemia, Parkinson's disease and many more. But how many people know that Hela cells were extracted in 1950 from a cervical cancer by biopsy from Henrietta Lacks, a mother of five? Henrietta had since died but her cells live on, multiplying in Petri dishes across the world, generating both knowledge and wealth even as the source is kept in relative obscurity, reminiscent of the famous Tuskegee experiment on African-American syphilitics, valued for the knowledge they gave while being allowed to die of their infections in the presence of penicillin.

Last but not the least is Michelle's skin color – brown. In an era where beauty has been consistently defined on television and magazines as having a fair skin complexion, long straight hair, Michelle will be gracing the cover of Vogue and other magazines – the ultimate affirmation of beauty. Self-esteem among African-American peoples must reflect the diversity of colors. Cappuccino is good and so is *café-au-lait* or ebony. People of African ancestry need to regain their self-esteem and stop poisoning their bodies with skin-lightening hydroquinone and other toxic substances.

It is only a matter of time before Michelle Obama finds her place among trend setting American female authors, especially those who have gone through three main phases in their works – a feminine phase of imitating and accommodating male standards, a feminist phase protesting against injustices suffered by women and finally a female phase drawing on women's own experiences for the source of an autonomous art. Through these phases stand many giants, some of the most amazing being Harper Lee (To Kill a Mocking Bird), Harriet Beecher Stowe (Uncle Tom's Cabin) and one might add Lorraine Hansberry (A Raisin in the Sun).

# 3.

*The Challenges Ahead – I.*

January 20, 2009 was a red letter day for President-elect Barack Obama. Beyond the pomp and pageantry of his inaugural, what was going to happen next? How did the man feel when faced with taking the oath of office to become the most powerful president on planet earth? Was he ready for the challenge? How did he feel when he took a look at his graying predecessor preparing to retire to any of his many estates – Crawford Texas, Greenwich, CT, Kennebunkport, ME or Jupiter Island, Florida? Whatever the case, Barack Obama was one man who would need a much larger dose of good luck and empathy in the years ahead. Toni Morrison the Nobel laureate said the problem lay not with Obama but with his many supporters; democracy had never been a one-man show.

So far he had moved cautiously and well, trying as much as possible to avoid any *faux pas*. Going by his early pronouncements, one could be optimistic that he would strike the right chords at the right time. Already he had thought hard and made the important pronouncement that there would be only one president at a time, especially during the lame duck period. And he was right. However, without a leader to follow or a mission to embrace, the average citizen fell back upon the most basic of human responses – self-preservation. With the economic crunch, Americans considered mainly themselves, their jobs, their retirement, their families, and their future. Top on the list would be the economic wellbeing of fellow Americans. Hopefully as soon as he took over, President Obama would wave that magic wand to begin to improve on the economic plight of US citizens. The nation, and indeed the entire world, had been holding its breath, given the magnitude of the problem that had touched every continent. Of course the wars in Iraq and Afghanistan -a giant fiscal dessicator to some, a gluttonous enzyme to others - would have to be brought to and end so that funding be redirected to more useful ends at home.

America's one time popularity in the world had been squandered by his predecessor's post-9/11 belligerence and unilateralism. He had alienated allies and engendered wide-spread anti-Americanism. The rest of the world finds fault with a US that does not recognize the International Criminal Court (ICC), still maintains the death sentence, does not have public health and does not have gun control. Hopefully, Barack Obama would reverse the negative trends and repair all the damage that had been done to America's reputation overseas. The world knew this. That explained the euphoria with which his election to the White House was greeted.

The US citizen would be expected to help the new president set his priorities right. From his home constituency of Illinois, would President Obama help to sanitize the murky political waters, starting with helping governor Rod Blagojevich disentangle himself from the mess associated with his alleged attempt to sell the President-elect's vacant seat to the highest bidder? Would he also help the citizens of Washington D.C. realize their own dream of getting appropriate representation, starting with the use of *No Taxation Without Representation* on the number plate of the presidential limousine and if possible on Air Force One? Would he examine and do something for retailers whose plight had been well documented by the National Retail Association - reduced sales and a looming closure of about 8000 stores nationwide due to poor sales that started way back on Black Friday and went on till Christmas and beyond? Business people had been obliged to offer discounts to attract a reluctant clientele and pay workers on their payrolls. It was a feat to stay in business under the prevailing financial crunch.

Rising healthcare and insurance costs would be next on the president-elect's agenda, perhaps the most important of his domestic policies. Among the many major issues Barack Obama would be putting his task force to address on taking office, would be the galloping healthcare costs and lack of insurance coverage for large chunks of the US population. The fact of US citizens crossing the border into Canada to procure their prescription medications was a clear indictment of the healthcare delivery here at home. To do a good job, the task force would have to take a few steps back in time and study how the present mess had come about.

First, some puzzling observations. An interventional cardiologist opened a patient's clogged coronary artery by inserting a flexible tube with a tiny balloon at its tip - a procedure called angioplasty. The cost, for example, would be $1700 at the Metro-West Medical Center in Framingham, Massachusetts whereas the same procedure by the same cardiologist at the Brigham and Women's Hospital in Boston would cost $2,450, a whopping 44% more! Why such a gross disparity? Would that be an exception or the rule? Hip replacement surgery at Mount Auburn Hospital was $24,535 but at BWH, the same surgery would cost $31,970! An ankle MRI was $1,100 at Children's hospital but only $490 at the Boston Medical Center; a chest x-ray was $75 at Anna Jacques Hospital but $160 at MGH. Two days of patient care for pneumonia at Winchester Hospital would cost $5,309 but at the BWH it would cost $9,000. Breathtaking! But why?

It did not make sense. Or did it? The answer lay in a well kept secret by which insurance companies paid more for procedures carried out at a handful of hospitals – Massachusetts General Hospital (MGH), Brigham and Women's Hospital (BWH), Children's Hospital, Sturdy Memorial Hospital in Attleboro– than they would for other hospitals. Private insurance data obtained by a team of investigative journalists of the Boston Globe proved to be quite revealing indeed. Three elite hospitals - MGH, BWH, and Children's Hospital all of Boston - and a few others were found to be paid on the average, 15% to 60% more than their rivals by the main Insurance Companies (Blue Cross Blue Shield of Massachusetts, Harvard Pilgrim Health

Care Plan, and Tufts Health Plan). The gap was wider still for individual procedures. Such payment pattern was found to be partly responsible for the galloping health care costs and raised questions as to why certain hospitals and doctors received premium pay for care that was no better than those of competitors. It was an eye opener. Until recently the growing pay gap could not be publicly scrutinized, thanks to the fact that contracts between insurers and hospitals included confidentiality statements. The spotlight team of journalists found scores of such disparities for routine procedures with no obvious difference in quality.

It turned out that over the past decades, hospitals had pushed up those charges to boost income from insurance companies as a way of offsetting budget cuts imposed by the Federal Government. The wide disparities reflected deregulation and lax government oversight so that hospitals with the most clout extracted big increases from insurers while everyone else fell behind. Health insurance premiums paid by the average Massachusetts family had jumped up 78% (about $1800) since 2000. Such hefty increases went to provide for the installation of the latest technologies in hospitals as well as boost salaries for the physicians employed there, thus undermining the less powerful hospitals which ended up losing personnel to the big ones that paid more. That was surely not a level playing field and understandably some hospitals cried foul, arguing that the heavyweights ought to lose their nonprofit status and therefore pay taxes, that they could not use their nonprofit status to make profit and build more capacity. It was another eye opener!

The high bargaining clout of hospitals resulted from powerful brand names and elite reputation (MGH, BWH, and Children's Hospital) as well as from geographical isolation (Sturdy Memorial Hospital in Attleboro). Partners' Health Care was formed in 1994 to fight back against the stinginess and lopsided power of insurance companies which had brought many hospitals to their knees. By bringing together MGH and BWH in Boston, Partners' became what some called the "800-pound gorilla" of Massachusetts healthcare, and was able to bend insurers to its will. In 2000, executives of Tufts Health Plan insurance dared to refuse Partners' demand for a substantial rate increase. Partners' reacted by declaring that it would no longer accept Tufts insurance at its hospitals. Within days thousands of Tufts customers threatened to change insurance rather than lose the right to be treated at those two famous hospitals. Tufts gave in to Partners' demands. Quite a strategy indeed! Disciples of deregulation called it the invisible hand or "market forces". It was obvious that people did not shop around and that's why insurance was so high. Pay rates for different caregivers varied and were kept a secret due to nondisclosure agreements about such confidential data. Thus much was awaited of a new Congress and a new US president.

The fear of lawsuits had also contributed enormously to driving up costs as doctors turned to more testing, some very costly tests and high risk procedures – the so-called *defensive medicine-* to stay on the safe side. As medicine went hi-tech, a lurking danger of too many tests being ordered and a corresponding soaring cost of bills to pay would ensue. The Diagnostic imaging industries (X-rays, CT scans, MRI) that enable doctors to "see" our bones, blood vessels, nerves, muscles and soft tissues was the fastest growing area in medicine, estimated at $100 billion a year. Such tests usually reveal astounding details and life saving information but there is almost always the tendency to overkill. What about the effect of over exposure to radiation? How about false positive results (problems that do not exist) or incidental findings (clinically harmless abnormalities)? Should every ache be subjected to a scan? Should we see cancer in every problem of the head? Why did doctors order so many tests? Were they really necessary? Working under pressure and spending less and less time with a patient, ordering more images got the doctor quick answers. For the doctor afraid of malpractice suits, more tests reduced the risk of being sued. TV Ads like *I'm Jim Sakalove. I solve problems. When doctors make mistakes I make them pay. Call me at 1-800-CALLJIM* said it all. They hung like the proverbial sword of Damocles over practicing physicians. Like in other areas of human endeavor, fallibility in medicine has about three components –ignorance for which science does not yet give a clue or gives just a limited understanding, ineptitude where knowledge is available but user fails to apply it and a third component called necessary fallibility. A better science can overcome ignorance and training and technology can take care of ineptitude but there is not much that can be done about necessary fallibility even if all the attorneys ganged up to close shop for doctors. For those who owned diagnostic equipment it was good business. Patient expectations too mattered. More and more patients were demanding "the best" – sophisticated, state-of-the-art technologies such as CTs or MRIs and this tied the doctor's hands. Thus tests would be ordered to reassure the patients of the normalcy of their conditions. Aggressive research into the causes of disease and over diagnosis brought advantages like long life but also a good number of side effects like unnecessarily high rate of PSA and bladder as Gilbert Welch, Lisa Schwartz and Steve Woloshin (*Over Diagnosis: Making People Sick in the Pursuit of Health*) point out.

Medicine has been undergoing a radical change from what obtained a few decades ago as a result of increased gadgetry and associated noise, stress, pain and many more. As far back as possible hospitals demanded peace and quiet from the surrounding communities, often by erecting signboards like *QUIET, HOSPITAL ZONE*. From ancient times right through the days of Florence Nightingale, the emphasis has always been on the "quiet art" in patient care.

Then it all changed as technology came on board. No longer were hospitals characterized by the smell of antiseptics, the cool climate-controlled air around, the bright lights striking on linoleum and reflecting on persons and objects. Noises of all types added to the mix which did not make it easier for peaceful sleep or quick recovery. Squeaking gurneys, banging doors, ringing telephones, varied banters from doctors and nurses, TV noises, overhead PA systems, pagers, compounded the beeps, buzzes, whirrs and whooshes from heart monitors, ventilators, defibrillators and other machinery. High-tech healing came with quite a price tag and inconveniences for the sick. For some patients the added noises interfered with or prolonged the healing process; for others it raised blood pressures, stress levels and brought about pain, all at a time when they are most vulnerable. Noise affects the healthcare staff as well. Hopefully the healthcare bill recently signed into law by President Barack Obama would contain guidelines for noise control through improved acoustics in the rooms and hallways and paneling that absorbs instead of bounces off sounds.

More gadgetry has also attracted an increased number of supplementary personnel in the hospitals – administrators, assistants, technicians, engineers, housekeeping staff and more. Teaching hospitals added all sorts of junior staff in training, each needing all the care of apprenticeship prior to getting the hang of it - a very difficult balancing act, giving patients the very best of cure but also giving novices the experience of the art. Insiders know that learning and teaching the younger ones must be stolen, taken as a kind of eminent domain even if patients' right to the very best must trump all else – conventional ethics, litigations, public demands of perfection without practice.

For over one hundred years X-rays helped doctors to observe the inner workings of the human body. These days a new generation of imaging devices probes even deeper. Is a chest pain due to heart problems or indigestion? With MRI the answer is both fast and accurate with high resolution images, detailed view of heart muscle with the possibility of pointing out blood vessels that are 90% blocked. Standard tests (nuclear scans) use radioactive dyes. Computed Tomography (CT) angiography is also rapid and produces multiple X-rays of the heart. MRI uses magnetic and radio waves, hence there is no risk of radiation exposure. Other MRI scanners pick up ischemic strokes (blood clots).

The legal climate here in the US and other western countries poses special challenges for the medical profession. Wrongful birth law suits oblige physicians to pay the parents of kids born with birth defects that could have been identified or predicted during pregnancy. The logic is that some people should never have been born. And so the courts stop just short of saying that some persons should not be alive. Most often plaintiffs of wrongful law suits are the disabled children themselves.

During the 2008 race for the White House, Senator Barack Obama said Americans had a choice to make in matters of health insurance while his rival, Senator John McCain promised to give each person a $5000 insurance credit to go and shop for their policy wherever they chose. Obama seemed to be leaning towards the employer-based healthcare insurance policy. Which option would offer the American citizen a better alternative? Only time would tell.

The United States Chamber of Commerce which does not usually support Democrats thought that adopting Obama's plan could lead to the unraveling of the employer-based healthcare system. What exactly did this mean? What did Americans need the most – continuing with or ending the employer-based health insurance system? How were they going to stop the skyrocketing premiums, lack of portability and wide spread ignorance in pricing and over consumption of health services? More fundamentally, how did the present mess come about in the first place, with 90% of private health care plans in the US being obtained through employers? That was an aberration when compared with automobile, homeownership or life insurance policies which were not so linked to any employment. How did things become so entangled?

During World War II a federal government wage control measure was put in place, barring employers from raising their workers' salaries but nothing was said about fringe benefits. Firms competing for top rate employees began offering medical insurance to sweeten employment offers. Much sweeter still was the idea that employers could deduct such benefits as business expenses and employees did not have to report them as taxable income. Aha! Irresistible!

During ancient times doctors, whose practices were quite modest and often rudimentary, did not make much money but in a modern society where consumption counts for so much, Americans had virtually enslaved themselves to capitalist greed. Of course there was not enough money to go round to begin with. When Hippocrates entered the scene, the entire landscape changed over night. It soon dawned on society at large that the longer people were kept alive, the longer they could pay for medical services and so energies were directed at keeping people alive for as long as possible. But human ingenuity did not end there; it was taken one step further. Over the years it became clear that waiting for people to fall sick was wasteful; it would be so much more profitable to bill people regularly even if they were not sick. That would bring in more money and more quickly too. And so the insurance industry was born. On a regular monthly basis insurance companies bill perfectly healthy human beings colossal amounts of money. Since society had decided that insurance was necessary to stay alive, everyone was happy to get insurance except the poor and the sick, who had never been happy in the first place. The United States is the one nation on planet earth with the highest healthcare costs without necessarily enjoying the best care. Doctors' bills are recklessly run up even where cheaper alternatives would do. Insurance companies are more than happy to see the soaring costs and doctors do not help matters with their propensity to go for all and every new gadget or pill.

Having agreed that insurance was the way forward, the next question was how to pay for it. Here disagreement was total. Many would like the government to pay but could not make the claim too loudly for fear of tax increases that would naturally follow. Some said it would drive the private insurers out of business. Others suggested private insurance companies but again, one was faced with companies whose preoccupation was not necessarily to offer service to the citizens. Should public (government-sponsored) insurance compete with private ones as President Obama suggested? The answer was blowing in the wind...

Believers in Reaganomics usually develop an allergic reaction whenever government is mooted in any business undertaking. President Barack Obama visited the American heartland and took his case directly to the people, and to the meeting of the American Medical association in Chicago, trying to make them see that healthcare reform was long overdue because the system in place was just not sustainable and a threat to the economy, a ticking time bomb for the Federal budget. Curiously, prevaricators and naysayers later claimed that *Obamacare*, or government takeover as they derogatorily referred to it, was all done in secrecy! The president likened the healthcare system to the struggling General Motors which had filed for bankruptcy protection in May, warning that if the system was not fixed, it might have to go the way of GM, paying more, getting less and going broke. A typical government takeover would be like what obtains at our VA hospitals, a far cry from the affordable care the president was proposing, which in addition to providing individual choice of private insurance, also guarantees protection against abuses like denial of coverage for pre-existing conditions.

The US healthcare industry cost about $2.5 trillion a year, yet left 46 million Americans uninsured according to most estimates. The president's idea of some sort of public system as a part of any meaningful plan to revamp healthcare was vociferously opposed by entrenched interest groups, notably the GOP, private insurers and the American Medical Association. Private business remained very uncomfortable with the idea of government involvement, especially the appointment of a czar of some kind to oversee their operations as well as the capping of executive pay at five hundred thousand dollars. Government participation is invariably equated to socialism and the death of competition. Yet so many 800 pound gorillas had contributed to bringing our once vibrant economy to its knees. Any solution that continued to encourage the maintenance of such gorillas through takeovers, mergers, and other unhealthy practices would bring the nation back to square one. The national landscape was dominated by 800 pound gorillas like CVS and Walgreen, the smaller pharmacies having been swallowed up by takeovers and mergers. The market's invisible hand was also wreaking havoc in many wallets and pocketbooks. Ordinarily if my PCP prescribed one dose of vitamin D per week for twelve weeks, I should be given all twelve pills in one bottle. But with the way things stood, I was obliged to make three separate pilgrimages to the pharmacy to be given a refill of four pills each time. How else would the animators of such a system make more money from refills and the corresponding co-pays of each visit? Two years after I underwent a surgical procedure that was promptly taken care of by my insurers, I received another bill in the mail for payments mentioning the same procedure! But why? Not only did the time lapse raise a red flag, the very bill finding its way into my mailbox was quite unsettling indeed. In lean years one learns to fight for one's fiscal rights. A threat to phone one of those *call for action* programs or hand over the matter to my attorneys and other forces I envisaged to mobilize and lo and behold, I realized that not only con artists do havoc to the US economy, but insurance companies and their many agents too. The powerful hands of fraud were reaching out to me for a duplicate settlement of the earlier bill! I shudder to imagine what happens to persons who do not sleep with one eye open as our ancestors advised or bother to learn the English language, let alone read between the lines.

So fierce was the opposition to a public option that the town hall meetings became battle grounds for those hell-bent on torpedoing the move. Scare tactics of all kinds emerged and disinformation was spread with relish. Populist multimillionaires spread ignorance like viruses on the Internet, where information was supposed to be let free. It was ironic that being smart became stigmatized whereas stupidity or idiocy was celebrated in stead of being pitied or laughed at. Some alluded to death panels by which the president's plan would pull the plug on grandmas and seniors and hasten their premature death – euthanasia at the hands of those entrusted to handle the new healthcare delivery system President Obama sought to put in place. The Republicans portrayed the Democrats as anti-business, a perception President Obama sought to dispel. Among those making such strident calls was a certain Betsy McCoy, a lady with little or no gravitas but very comfortable with spreading such myths, just like she had reportedly done once before in 1995 to torpedo President Bill Clinton's healthcare plan.

Most of the aberrations were traceable to the Reagan presidency when the Fairness Doctrine was abolished. Adopted in 1949, the doctrine required licensed broadcasters to air all sides of any debate on controversial issues. But upon taking office and with the feverish climate of deregulation, President Ronald Reagan revoked that useful tool, resulting in the upsurge of talk radios and the demise of counterbalancing perspectives. Those who dominate the mass media today virtually control public opinion, even in scientific matters. Loud-mouthed individuals selected to pitch the common issues won the day, forcing those that know to play only second fiddle. Things were not helped when true dedicated scientists restricted themselves to esoteric journals for communicating among themselves, leaving out the vast public.

In America today there are two currents – one that considers the American people as intelligent, rational individuals capable of identifying lies and the other that treats the people as ignorant animals ruled by fear and greed. It came as no surprise that voices were raised to ask for a revival of the Fairness Doctrine, especially following studies carried out by the Center for American Progress which showed that the nation's radio airwaves were dominated (91%) by conservative talk - a staggering imbalance in news and radio programming

President Obama remained unrelenting in his campaign, going from state to state to sell his plan directly to those who had voted for him. In town hall and AARP (American Association for Retired People) meetings, he spoke reassuringly, drawing analogies here and parallels there, to try to win over the skeptics. The man must have made a good study of Rudyard Kipling's poem *If.* Distractions multiplied about his not being born on US soil and therefore not fit to be president, a myth concocted and spread around by the O'Reillys, Coulters, Dobbses, and Limbaughs. President Obama was hardly one year in office when he began to lose the support of the easily-distracted left at the same time that he incurred the white hot rage of the hate-filled right. At such difficult and scary economic times Americans seemed to be easily led by unscrupulous demagogues in politics, business and the media, people who profited from out-attacking and blaming each other instead of challenging those powerful and greedy persons who caused the economic problem in the first place. Their schemes failed to deter the president. "If the US postal service can compete with private undertakings like FEDEX and UPS that bring mail service to our homes, is it not good for business?" Obama asked. People roundly condemned government involvement, yet they were quite happy with Medicare and Medicaid and FEDEX. Weren't those government plans as well? And the opinion polls rose and fell. President Obama could take comfort from history, knowing that President Roosevelt who gave this country its social security was called a socialist, and John Kennedy and Lyndon Johnson were accused of government takeover when they passed Medicare into law. It is the American way of life to be suspicious of the government until such a time that the government does something that is seen to be helpful.

It just didn't make sense that Republicans could not find common ground on which to agree with Democrats. As a matter of fact the reigning climate was reminiscent of a time past when Theodore Roosevelt got so disgusted with the anti-federalist attitude of the conservatives that he bolted from the Republican party and ran for president as a candidate of the Bull Moose Party, a progressive party with sound policy positions drawn from both left and right. In 1796 the original political parties were federalist and anti-federalist, all white and all males; over the years, they evolved into the twentieth century's Democratic and Republican parties. The conservative movement's "slash the liberals to pieces" or "take no prisoners" attitude of today and apocalyptic stance on healthcare reforms proposed by President Obama and the general tendency to spew hate around was manifestly self destructive. Getting bogged down in dogmatic fixity and obstructionism did not appear to be the way forward at all. If government involvement was such a bad idea, how could it be good for bailouts? For over forty years the healthcare issue remained in limbo, each generation barely toying with it and passing it on to the next. Why couldn't today's leaders take the bull by the horns and do something about it? That was President Obama's main challenge.

As President Obama addressed the healthcare issue, Partners Health care, the largest healthcare provider in Massachusetts, was in a silent expansion and unbridled competition, a process aimed at edging out Beverly Hospital which had served the outpatient population of the North shore of Massachusetts over the years. The labels, socialism or Europeanization of America, were used by the likes of Karl Rove to scare off proponents of such schemes. Did it occur to them that the GDP in the US was growing faster than that in Europe but high US indebtedness virtually drowned this? Did they realize that wealth distribution in Europe was much more even than in the US where the bottom 20% was getting poorer and poorer, the middle 40% barely breaking even, while most of the wealth remained concentrated in the top 2%? Of course such concerns were hardly ever mooted loudly, especially when private companies needed government subsidies to stay afloat.

To make healthcare affordable enough for everyone, the country needed to spend less, which meant that someone had to earn less – doctors, insurance companies and the manufacturers of all those gadgets. How that could be done without some sort of public insurance remained to be seen when doctors and insurance company lobbyists called time out. With so much financial worry in the air, the fantastic Red Sox victory of 7-0 over the New York Yankees was not adequately feted. Nor was the spectacular 2-0 victory over Spain for the World Cup games in South Africa, nor those of the two Williams sisters who sailed through a sea of Russian rivals – Elena Vesnina, Anna Ivanovic, Elena Dementieva, Maria Sharapova – at the Wimbledon to emerge champions in 2009. It is no exaggeration to state that there was probably more joy on the streets of our Commonwealth when Harvard came from behind, executed two touchdowns and beat Yale 29-29 that memorable year of 1968.

For a while the IRS actually resisted the idea of top companies offering insurance to attract top quality employees but eventually the US Congress enshrined the tax-exempt status of employer-based insurance into law, resulting in a radical shift in the way Americans paid for medical care. Tens of millions of Americans were soon signing up for medical insurance through their employments. As tax rates rose, so did the incentive to keep expanding health benefits. Health insurance was no longer reserved for major expenditures like surgery, hospitalizations and other necessities. Could Americans ever consider using their car insurance for such things as oil changes and car tune ups? Most certainly not! Yet here they were having their medical insurance pay for yearly physical examinations, prescriptions of name brand drugs instead of generics, emergency consultations for sore throats and other routine medical services.

Any wonder then why healthcare costs soared so much? Delinking medical insurance from employment seemed the logical way forward as Senator John McCain proposed with his $5000 tax credit. In this way employees would then focus on shopping around for the best bargains and help bring down costs. But how many Americans were employed and could therefore benefit this way? And what would happen to the unemployed whose numbers kept climbing? How should the US Congress fix that thorny problem? What should the president do with the problematic "welfare queens" who deliver babies to collect checks from welfare instead of struggling, as in the past, to make ends meet? And how should Congress handle the thorny problem of other welfare queens who elect to commit abortions? Who would underwrite the abortions? Would the president take a look at the successful experiment at insuring everybody underway in the Commonwealth of Massachusetts with a view to expanding it nationally? It was indeed gratifying that 77-year-old Senator Edward Kennedy of Massachusetts, the man knighted by England's Queen Elizabeth II, championed the cause for giving all Americans access to quality healthcare, a capping event in his long career in public service and especially in the US Congress.

In spite of his tribulations with malignant glioma (a fast-growing tumor of the brain), the senator had toiled aggressively and indefatigably on legislation for this noble cause. At his death his widow said it was his life's crusade, along with human rights, fighting for the poor, for education, for equality and peace, all emanations from the beatitudes and the Sermon on the Mount. In addition to healthcare, the liberal lion of the US Senate had risen above tragedy and controversy and fought for key legislations on immigration, gender equality, education, and the rights of workers. President Obama's coalition of healthcare groups – doctors, hospitals, drug manufacturers, insurers, laborers – had so far agreed on cutting down costs by $2 trillion over the next decade. Such moves were expected to favorably influence the US Congress to adopt the much awaited healthcare reform bill before 2009 ran out. But that did not happen!

Immigration issues were supposed to be confronted head-on by the new Congress and president. The resolution of many internal problems, including healthcare reform, would be made easier once that thorny matter were laid to rest. On the surface it was easy to prescribe deportation for illegal immigrants as many had proposed but this was easier said than done, just as it was for enemy combatants at Guantanamo. Our politicians, be they GOP or Democrats or independents, realized that they just didn't have that magic bullet to cure the problem. They all suffered from the same disease – wanting to make omelet, yet afraid of breaking the egg or, to use a different metaphor, longing to go to heaven yet afraid of dying. It was not a piece of cake to propose legislation to deport all those persons, some of whom were important voters being courted for the elections to come. The courts would wade into the dance as would civil rights activists. Already Americans had witnessed what a single US citizen could do to frustrate the deportation process.

Many moons ago it was fashionable to hail America as a melting pot of immigrants but recently, as governor Deval Patrick of Massachusetts conceded, the idea of embracing new comers has virtually gone out of fashion. Increased immigration had led to reduced hospitality and xenophobia, especially in the border states of Florida, Texas, Arizona and California. Experts said those states were being bankrupted by the cost of services to illegal immigrants, prompting certain persons to suggest charging $1 toll per head at border crossings to beef up patrols. In spite of the many uplifting accounts of the lives of immigrants in the US and how they positively impact the nation as a whole, demonization continued to be the war cry from many quarters (Steve Everett's *From Every End of the Earth*).Faced with the unemployment nightmare, many persons asked the president to enforce immigration laws by expelling all illegal immigrants from the US, taxing all US companies and corporations for all jobs held in other countries that provided them with cheap labor. Some pushed for a Federal government crackdown on immigrants, restricting the right of asylum seekers to work and levying $130 for each asylum application (how applicants could pay if they did not work was not clear). The ICE (Immigration and Customs Enforcement) carried out occasional raids aimed at sweeping and deporting the illegal immigrants. Such a practice had the drawback that the raids tended to disproportionately affect working immigrants with children while leaving unscathed the harsher criminal elements. Some had proposed a cut in welfare benefits to illegal immigrants and to cut aliens off welfare and health benefits as a whole. Compassion aside, the threat to public health and safety that might come from the sick and destitute could be considerable!

There were sad cases of young persons who did very well in high school, but found the door to college shut because of their irregular immigration status. In one pathetic case a kid who had passed the high school with flying colors, got a hefty loan for college enrolment, hoping to work and pay back. But without a social security number he lost his job, and with it the possibility of repaying his loan. Broke, unemployed and with the threat of deportation looming over him, such a kid was a candidate for the type of disaster that often strikes our society. In that particular case, the error apparently emanated from his parents who had been living in the United States as illegal immigrants. It was such cases that gave advocates of strict immigration controls their strongest weapon – that such students should not take spaces away from US citizens. Outsourcing of jobs to other countries could be one nice way to stem the tide of immigration into the US but outsourcing has been demonized for causing unemployment here at home. What a Catch-22!

Misinformation played a big part in the crusade. Not too long ago a Pennsylvania jury acquitted two men standing trial for the beating death of a Mexican immigrant, one of the many illegal immigrants in the country. The all-white, native born jury could not accept the premise that the defendants' prejudices had led to the heinous crime of murder. With the H1N1 (swine flu) on our hands and indications that it originated from Mexico, conservative talk show host Jay Severine made the insensitive remark that Mexicans were flu carriers and Lou Dobbs of the CNN news did not help matters by his consistent use of the expression "criminal illegal aliens", given that overstaying one's visa is a civil, not criminal offense. Lou Dobbs used the CNN platform to incite fear and hate, making a real mockery of the "most trusted name in news" and helping to tumble the very high rating CNN had enjoyed for so long. Also, Michael Savage reportedly had as his fondest and most sacred wish the clapping in irons of all persons who looked like illegal immigrants and dropping them into the San Francisco Bay.

September 11, 2001 was a watershed in this country's perception of immigrants. Rightly or wrongly all evil deeds have been placed at the doorsteps of immigrants. Things were not helped when persons began to canton themselves into isolated neighborhoods of Irish, Germans, Polish, Haitians, Russians or Cape Verdeans, keeping very much to themselves, speaking their own native dialects and eating their own foods. That certainly was a far cry from the melting pot of the past when immigrants conformed, studied English, took jobs, entered the army and fought for their new country. Today's idea of a path to citizenship through the Dream Act - military service or college enrolment - echoes some of those ideals that were allowed to die but will Congress vote for the Dream Act?.

When Arizona finally took the bull by the horns and decided to pass an anti-illegal immigration law, it unleashed nation-wide protests, starting with President Barack Obama at the White House, who described the move as "misguided" and added that it threatened to undermine the basic notion of fairness that we as Americans cherish so much, as well as the trust between the police and their communities so crucial to keeping us safe. Other protesters thought it would encourage racial profiling and widespread harassment of Hispanics and persons of brown skin. The new law, seen as a useful tool for the police, gave them the OK to arrest, detain and deport people suspected of immigration violation. Those who believed that illegal immigrants cost Americans their jobs or depressed wages - remember the Arab and his camel? - were quite delighted with the law and gladly chanted for whoever cared to listen, the idea that they could not afford the cost of illegal immigration, would rather see about theirs first – feed the hungry, house the homeless, employ the jobless, treat the sick, educate their children. Not usually heard in such protests were the brains underpinning corporate America, those who actually encouraged clandestine immigration as a way of getting cheap labor across the porous border between Mexico and us. Unfortunately many Americans saw immigrants only through prisms of criminal acts –trashing of yards, stealing and using identities, ruining credits and taking away jobs, especially the unrestrained propensity to accept low paying jobs as a result of their lack of bargaining clout.

Arizona's law ended up creating a divide as wide as or even wider than that state's prominent geologic feature –the Grand Canyon. The persistent problem in Mexico – lawlessness, drugs, smuggling, gun running – coupled with the tantalizingly attractive salaries across the border, where immigrants could earn $5 to $8 per hour compared with a paltry $5 per day back home - had led to an outpouring of all sorts of immigrants into Arizona and Governor Jan Brewer found herself compelled to act, signing a tough law that placed restrictions on the hiring of illegal immigrants. (The unstoppable governor also signed into law a bill limiting ethnic education classes, including public school programs like African-American and Native American studies or any kind of ethnic solidarity). The only problem was how the police were going to identify the illegals. What would they be looking for when arresting without warrants – people who did not look white, sound white or conform to a certain idea of how Americans should look like? Would it be people with an accent? That was a tough sell! In a meeting with US Attorney-General, Eric Holder, a group of police chiefs expressed disquiet about the law, arguing that it would strain police ties to the community, sap up limited law enforcement resources and even lead to increased crime.

First lady Michelle Obama and visiting first lady from Mexico were confronted by a seven-year-old girl who asked to know if they were going to deport her parents who had no legal papers. That was a powerful message underpinning the dilemma faced by a president who was massively voted into office by Latinos, now on the receiving end, a president whose hands were tied by what states do or do not do. Arizona's law gave sleepless nights to more than one American. Persons involved with sham marriages must have been sweating in their pants as FBI agents went around picking all sorts of suspects. Politicians must be toying with the moral dilemma of seeking the votes of persons whom the rest of the electorate would want arrested and deported. Under federal law, punishment comes in many forms, the commonest being deportation, especially for those whose *fiancé visas* had since expired. Marriage to an American had served as the common path to immigration and naturalization for many but there were abuses by persons seeking to make a quick buck, naively rushing into things without assessing all of their contours.

Are the kids of illegal immigrants illegal or legal? For well over a century the rule was simple - any person born within the country's borders is an American citizen. But times have changed and the debate, once an academic matter, has become a political hot potato, an important component of the fight against illegal immigration.

Many saw immigration in very simplistic terms, especially those who continued to live in the past, conjuring the good old days when they immigrated into the United States by conforming to the laws, becoming Americans, learning English and fighting some of America's many wars. Seen in such a light, today's immigration is simply an inundation across the Mexican border, of persons anxious to take advantage of an egotistical society of spoiled kids too good for dish washing, persons who refuse to become citizens and pay their dues to Uncle Sam. But visiting Mexican president Felipe Calderon, in challenging Arizona's crackdown on illegal immigrants, highlighted some of the serious problems which Americans create for his country – the insatiable appetite for illegal drugs and the flow of large amounts of arms to fuel the drug wars of the crime syndicates in the border areas between Mexico and the US. Would Americans cut their consumption of marijuana to help solve the problem? Not too many hands went up!

The Mexican president remained convinced that his country's problem could be curtailed if Americans would just curb their appetite for marijuana. He specifically expressed concern about California's Proposition 19, the ballot initiative known as recreational marijuana bill and aimed at legalizing this dangerous product just for pleasure. Trade between the two countries was estimated at more than $1 billion a day. Of course Mexico was not the only southern neighbor involved with the drug trade and illegal immigrants, including human trade, inundating the US. Nicaragua and Colombia have similar problems. The mayor of Cancun, Gregorio Sanchez, running for governor of the Caribbean state of Qunitana Roo, a popular and beautiful tourist haven was arrested for money laundering and drug related crimes. Simultaneously, in Kingston, Jamaica, another tourist island, police and soldiers exchanged gun fire with armed supporters of Christopher "Dudus" Coke, Coke another fugitive drug lord wanted in the US on charges of cocaine trafficking and gun running.

In the mean time there were rejectionist reactions from all over America, especially Boston and Los Angeles. In Massachusetts, the cradle of our democracy, a city councilor threatened to give Arizona the type of treatment once given to Apartheid South Africa – divest by withdrawing financial backing from businesses in the economy out there. Others advised city employees not to travel to Arizona. This was kind of tenuous given that South Africa is an entire nation whereas the companies being targeted were mere entities in the state of Arizona.

And sports? The new law against illegal immigrants placed MLB Commissioner, Bud Selig between the proverbial hard rock and the deep blue sea. Voicing his opinion would lead to alienating a part of his MLB fan base whereas keeping silent would also incur the ire of his professional players, some of whom had already spoken out against the Arizona law and even threatened to boycott the All-Star game if the law remained in effect. It was like a business in which the owner was caught between a vocal segment of his employees on one hand and his customers on the other, baseball being the nation's main pastime. Pressure seemed to be mounted on baseball players so that MLB should do what the NFL did to Arizona in 1993 –pull out of the Super Bowl in Phoenix - when that state voted to reject a Martin Luther King Jr. holiday. It is believed that by doing the same with the All Star Game of 2011, the players shall have helped to correct an injustice – the Arizona Immigration law that empowers the police to demand documentation from anyone suspected of being an illegal immigrant. Meanwhile respectable pollsters like Gallup, New York Times/CBS, Pew and other organizations seemed to point to the fact that about 59% of Americans approved of the Arizona law even if it was not perfect, and conceded that there was nothing wrong with the police asking some questions if it seemed like someone was here illegally. They conceded that boycotts would hurt the metropolitan area of the state but did not believe that western civilization would come to an end as a result. Passionate reactions on either side pointed to one important fact – that Washington should wake up, initiate a serious debate on the issue and eventually take some hard decisions on immigration.

Bashing of undocumented immigrants by elected officials or their supporters usually fails to recognize the fact that the immigrants who have now become voters may have their family members in out-of-status situations, still in need of regularization, and radio and television officials who delight in using such offensive words fail to recognize that the US is a nation of immigrants. Not even Native Americans or their descendants ever utter as much vitriol against illegal immigrants. The question keeps cropping up "What if Native Americans had laws like Arizona's?" The historians among us are usually quick to draw attention to the fact that we are all just an occupying army, the country having been built on the blood, sweat, tears and lives of people of color – black, brown, red, yellow. They contend that it is all nice and good to advocate obeying the country's laws but wonder why we ourselves never led by example or cared for laws before. Since none is indigenous to this country, who then is competent to judge and who should be allowed to stay? First we swore by the Pilgrim Fathers and then by the Founding Fathers as the reality on the ground changed. What will it be in the future?

Quick to answer are those who feel that such laws, if ever they existed, would not stop the English colonizers with their superior fire power. In those days it was a question of "might makes right". Federal law actually exists in matters of immigration but as it was not being applied, Arizona was seen by some to be doing the Federal government's job. Today America is waging a war in Iraq and Afghanistan, displacing an untold number of nationals, some of whom will unavoidably find themselves here as immigrants. Yesterday it was Vietnamese immigrants flooding in after the bloody war in South-East Asia which started with the humiliating and calamitous defeat of the French at Dien Bien Phu (Valley of death), the ensnaring of America into the debacles at QuangTri, Danang, Hue, Quang Ngae, Qui Nhon and Saigon that ended with a the division of Vietnam into two at a Geneva Conference table –a strange war which Americans called Vietnam war but Vietnamese called it American war or French war, complex issues related to geopolitics, movement of communism and the Domino theory of the fall of South-east Asia. Such artificial dividing lines, whether between the Koreas, Lebanese or Iraqis, create enormous problems for citizens of the host country and contribute to the immigration problem.

And isn't everyone in America looking for the good life? The tendency to resent the intrusion of the outsider into the domain of the chosen (select?) one is innate in all of us but diminishes as we grow older, faster in some, slower in others. I recall my resentment when a new baby came along to take away some of the attention that I considered my due or when I raised tantrums because children in the neighborhood stopped by and were treated to my mother's food. But it didn't take long for me to come to terms with the fact that those other kids were offering my mother services which I could not offer – splitting firewood, fetching water several kilometers away and more. In time Americans suffering from this entitlement complex will also come to terms with such realities. No matter how it all began, what is important is that each society has to move forward, not backward in time and one way of doing so is to restructure the society so as to accommodate the needs of its occupants and new ones to follow. South Africa overcame apartheid and convicted Britons banished to Australia as well as that island nation's aborigines did forge a society that today has become a number one tourist destination. Through the INS, America is doing the same with its yearly diversity Lottery visas.

But the solution to the immigration problem need not be political. Some ordinary citizens, comedian George Lopez among them, think that illegal immigration and the joblessness problem can be solved without resorting to politicians simply by putting aside the mentality of entitlement common among US-born citizens, their inability or unwillingness to make their own beds, take their garbage to the dumpster, wait tables at restaurants, do their own laundry, raise their kids and take on low level, low income jobs instead of complaining about other people taking these jobs. Some have even suggested that welfare checks from funds generated by hard-working citizens, should go with the low level, low paying jobs instead of sending them out to those who just sit idly back, relax and do nothing but wait for them.

Joseph Carens, a political scientist sees the problem from a slightly different angle. He evokes the issue of morality and suggests waiving any punitive action against illegal immigrants who have lived here for five to seven years. In matters of murder, burglary and parking violations, he argues, we are generally agreed that punishment should be meted out in decreasing order of egregiousness. But when it comes to illegal immigration, consensus breaks down with supporters highlighting the fact that immigrants are simply doing what any of us would do – seeking better lives, often driven by intolerable poverty. Opponents on the other hand, emphasize that illegal immigration is not only a punishable crime, it deprives Americans of employment. Deportation - embodied in Arizona's recent law - is seen as the logical lenient punishment. Yet the debate rages on with proponents of crackdown pitted against those advocating easing up a bit. Joseph Carens would recommend letting the illegals stay on moral grounds. According to him, states have the prerogative to deport illegal immigrants up to a point but after newcomers have established lives and ties in the US, they have virtually acquired the right to stay, which is a moral claim to a place in the society where they've settled. Past a certain lapse of time, deportation as being advocated by some persons is no longer tenable; it is not sending people home but uprooting them from home. In his forthcoming book *"Immigrants and the Right to Stay"* Joseph Carens suggests a time frame of five to seven years and dismisses the idea of a penalty by comparing this to the statute of limitation which imposes no penalties at all. This should provide law makers some food for thought and much peaceful sleep to persons like Zeituni Onyongo,

President Obama's Kenyan aunt who, according to WBZ news, had lived illegally in the US for years, drawing welfare checks from funds she never ever contributed to for her upkeep. But Onyongo argued that the US is obligated to help her and that she deserved everything, including US citizenship. The news broadcast stopped short of drawing Obama into the discussion, leaving the field clear for all sorts of speculations from wagging tongues - why the president could be so aloof and indifferent to the plight of his own paternal aunt if she was a worthy case and whether he had played a part in having her deportation order rescinded.

Exaggerated reaction to persons who look different varies from people to people. Parents who adopt children from far away lands have been heard expressing sorrow for having uprooted the children from their birth culture. Kids, especially those in grade schools, are notorious for taunting with all sorts of insensitive remarks, making fun of the new comers, pulling back their eyes and uttering despicable slurs. Some ignorant and hysteric adults even yell out "go back to your country" applying the same paint brush for everybody perceived to have come from the country of their bias. An incredible amount of self-loathing is created in impressionable young children by such racial taunting. In some situations, internalized racism has been so ingrained that people virtually take it as an act of faith. Education for example, has been so associated with whites that America's black kids tell their peers without blinking "you're trying to be white" just because they are making an effort to get an education. This is a very sad and bizarre development, coming after black emancipation and in spite of the achievement gap between whites and blacks as measured by test scores and dropout rate.

Older immigrants are better able to cope with taunts than younger ones who sometimes resort to physical violence in self defense. In his early days, Sylvester Sidonlook was quite upset each time he was confronted with persons who taunted him by asking to know whether he had bought his sneakers and shirts in New York when he first landed in America, the insinuation being that where he came from, people went about nude or lived up in trees. He was almost always ill prepared to handle such provocations. And then he met Kindon Massangano who had moved from Swaziland, the country shaped like a postage stamp south of Mozambique to Kamuzu Banda's Malawi before migrating to the US. Kindon was cool and level-headed in his approach to such idiocy. He would answer such annoying questions in the affirmative, adding with relish and some amount of drama that in his country, his father lived in a big tree, his mother in a modestly big tree, his brothers and sisters in smaller trees…and then, after a brief pause, he would add with lots of gusto, that the American ambassador's tree was a tiny one, like this (illustrating with thumb apposed to index finger). That elicited the required response: "*Wait a minute*," his listeners would interject, "*but that's absurd. What do you mean the US ambassador's tree…?*" But of course it was absurd, not just for the US ambassador dwelling in a tree but every other person with whom he carried out his ambassadorial duties.

As for Blaise Ntimbantunganya, he was not particularly enamored of polygamy, but when his American buddies continued to nag and heap indignities at him, poking fun at the supposedly primitive practice of marrying multiple wives, he decided to stand his ground at one point and draw his tormentors' attention to the fact that in America, men marry a wife, divorce her, marry another, divorce her again and so forth, so that at the end of the day or on judgment day, the serial monogamist does not stand on a higher moral ground than those he treats with such contempt.

Even more so than Kindon and Ntimbantunganya was Jean Baptiste, another friend from Kigali. He was seething with anger at the constant provocation and the allegation that Africans originally brought human immunodeficiency virus into the world. He conceded that his country men interacted with monkeys - spoke with them, lived with them, ate with them and generally shared the tropical forest with them. And like Kindon, he went on to put the finishing touch by describing how that simple coexistence had been completely upset by Americans who came to his country, went into the very forest and went as far as making love to those very monkeys and chimpanzees, thereby contracting the terrible AIDS virus and passing it on to the rest of humanity. Who could beat that? Kindon had developed a real art of self defense and was using it with relish. He justified some of his excesses by saying that he liked to give his white friends just what they loved to hear and in the process he would add spicing here and there to make it really good. It made him feel good too. As a member of the local tourism board Jean Baptiste said he would escort visitors to many sites, help them with local lore and, as always, give himself the liberty of putting finishing touches where appropriate. He would narrate gleefully and with a weird sense of humor about life back in his village pointing to where, according to him, his ancestors had cooked and eaten the ancestors of his visitors!

Did those fellows cross the line? Not quite. As little children growing up in their home communities, of course they did notice things even if they could not explain. Human interaction with chimpanzees is a heavy topic, encompassing sociology, anthropology, paleontology, law, folk tales, religion, evolution, development, international relations and more. Just as incarcerated prisoners in South Africa and mine workers separated from spouses turned to homosexuality to assuage an urgent biological need, so also do animals in the wild or in captivity turn to other species to remedy powerful biological needs. Intriguing experiments have been designed and carried out all over the world in an effort to probe into man's presumed proximity to the apes. Blood collected in the field have been brought into laboratories and mixed up with all sorts of antibodies to see how surface antigens bring cells together or repel them. Research has sequenced chimpanzee genome to provide a window and new insights into the difference between humans and primates - our closest cousins - to confirm or dispel the myth that human and chimpanzees differ by a mere 1%. It is quite intriguing to explore why and how human beings and chimpanzees have 99% internal similarity (genes, proteins, sperms) yet, paradoxically they look and behave so differently from the outside. Unless and until human beings get close enough to these wild cousins of ours, there is no other way to carry out such findings.

Certain facts can be gleaned right by sight but others require profound investigations in the field and in the laboratory in Europe,

Russia, US, Cuba, Kenya, Nepal, Indonesia and other places. Even though they diverged from a common evolutionary ancestor over 25 million years ago, monkeys have tails but not the apes (chimpanzees, humans, gorillas, bonobos, gibbons, orangutans). Human beings who denigrate others by calling them monkeys are only showing their own dose of ignorance. All human beings, unlike chimpanzees, possess a big brain, the ability to assume a supine posture, the characteristic of a long opposable thumb that can rotate toward the palm allowing for many skills and feet with shorter and more rigid digits that enable our bipedal upright walk.

Animals captured and reared in captivity have tremendously enriched human knowledge. The work done may be perverted and unethical sometimes. In nature a horse can mate with a donkey and produce a mule, the most popular type of hybrid species known to man. What is less common is a male lion mating with a tigress to produce a product called a liger. The only setback is that like the mule, the liger is a dead end because it is infertile, cannot produce sperms and therefore cannot bring forth young ones! The defect seems to lie with some chromosomal aberration. Portmanteau is the conventional custom by which such hybrids are named, first with the father species, followed by the mother. Thus liger is derived from lion and tiger. Other hybrids are zorses, zonkeys, tigons, beefalos, pumapards, and humanzees or chimans. TIGERS (The Institute for Greatly endangered and Rare Species) situated in Myrtle Beach, South Carolina is a place worth visiting.

Mention of humanzee (chimpanzee –human hybrid) brings to mind the name of late Russian scientist, Illya Ivanovich Ivanov whose work in Pasteur Institute in France and Guinea Conakry raised goose flesh and repulsion in many circles as it involved human beings and chimpanzees. Breeding such a hybrid was expected to put an end to the speculation in evolution circles that we all have a common ancestor. Where else but the American Association for the Advancement of Atheism could the scientist turn to for assistance with such a project? There were Darwinian proselytes of evolution as well as opponents belonging to Creationism, for radically different reasons. Inseminating female chimpanzees with human sperm was the plan in the Canary Island, in Cuba's Quinta Palatino, in New Guinea or Guinea Conakry, especially if it could be done behind flummoxed assisting African staff. Inseminating hospitalized ignorant African women with sperm obtained from chimpanzees – the notion of informed consent being moot - was also in the works. The belief in some circles that orangutans were more closely related to the "yellow races," gorillas to the blacks and chimpanzees to whites made the pairing of apes with their proper human race for reproductive purposes a desirable objective. Slices of chimpanzee scrotums were grafted on to human scrotums, a procedure known as vasoligation. At the last minute a local governor in Guinea Conakry refused to go along with Ivanov's quixotic quest, following which the man turned to his home, Soviet Union to seek permission to inseminate women there with ape sperm. This time he went for volunteers and actually got one but unfortunately Tarzan, the orangutan died of brain hemorrhage before sperm could be obtained from it. The scientist was arrested, imprisoned in Kazakhstan from where he died, putting an end to his quest. There is no doubt that others are following in his footsteps to attain the goal of ensuring the perpetuation of endangered species some where in the world.

But human-animal interactions in tropical forests were not all weird or perverted. Indeed much good came of the studies of committed scientists all over the world as they put in painstaking effort to study our hairy cousins in their natural habitats in Franceville, Gabon, Kisangani in DRC, Brazzaville Congo, Equatorial Guinea, Yaounde, Cameroon, Kinyara, Uganda, Kenya, Tanzania and other places. Plenty of PhD theses came from studies in those natural habitats and thanks to the many explorations out there, the world knows quite a lot about polioviruses, Ebola virus, simian immunodeficiency virus (SIV) and human immunodeficiency virus (HIV). Natives as well as curious visitors entered those rich forests to pry into their secrets, hunt and butcher animals for food or capture them for pets or simply study their make-up to find out what could help unravel the new epidemics wreaking havoc on human populations all over the world. Chimpanzees prey on Cercopithecus monkeys for food and are in turn bush meat for human consumption. After close contact with those cousins in the wild, human beings eventually moved to the metropolis, carrying along the germs that they had shared in relative tranquility and symbiosis over the years. In the urban areas there is sex and there are needles. Sudden exposure to thousands of new hosts led to new challenges and adaptations, some with catastrophic results. The first study materials were feces and urine tossed at new comers and intruders by apprehensive and suspicious chimpanzees. As confidence grew it became possible to obtain blood, saliva and other body fluids and tissues by more invasive methods to study diseases and gain more insights into how the animals coped with the diseases. HIV infects humans and specifically targets a population of white cells called CD4, destroying them and by so doing, weakening human response to attack by common germs. AIDS is simply the disease inflicted on human beings as a result of this depletion of CD4 below a count of 200 per micro liter of blood.

The world is what it is and the way we see it often depends on the prism through which we view it. Thus when ever we think of *The Heart of Darkness* (compliments Joseph Conrad) the mind invariably goes to the Congolese jungle being exploited by King Leopold of Belgium and savages with whom contact brought degradation for whites. Yet the flip side of this darkness refers to the innermost aspect of white exploiters of other people in the Dark Continent.

If one were tempted to berate these immigrants for their excesses, it was only natural to recall that from far back in time, either during slavery or colonialism, the Christian democratic white man and owner of slaves felt no compunction defining the black man as an animal, whose nature was virtually fixed in his protoplasm by his African genes, a man assigned to human limbo, so to speak, not by act of his master but because of the constitutional inferiority of his jungle ancestors. Far fetched? These are the type of words used by a police officer to describe a respected African American scholar when he ran into difficulties with a white police officer responding to a 911 call at his home in 2008. Yes, the black skin of the Negro has consistently been identified with impurity, ugliness, sin, evil, immorality, darkness and you name it. It is not in the interest of the bigoted white parent to explain to kids that color has nothing to do with cleanliness. As they grow up little white kids romanticize about exotic black persons. Driving a nice car in a good neighborhood is enough to have the police stop you if you are black! It is a humiliating experience that underscores the furor and violent opposition to Arizona's current immigration law.

That is not all. In the year of our lord 2010, a third year law student associated in some way with the Harvard Law Review actually wrote and circulated e-mails in which she suggested that on the average, African Americans are genetically predisposed to be less intelligent than whites. Stephanie Grace's e-mail might have been intended for private consumption but nothing that goes into cyberspace and all sorts of blogs, including abovethelaw.com, can be truly private any longer. Poor girl, if she had known! She ended up unleashing a racial controversy that got all sorts of people up in arms over the issue. Reading through the entire saga brought to mind some conventional wisdom often ignored: *Is it necessary to comment upon something you know nothing about? Which is better, to keep quiet and let people think you are a fool or to open your own mouth and confirm it?* Stephanie Grace knew in her heart of hearts that she was stirring a hornet's nest when she made her move, especially when she pleaded with her correspondents not to pull a Larry Summers on her ( an obvious allusion to the painful remarks made by former Harvard President Larry Summers about the inferiority of women in mathematics, and the consequence). As a student who had majored in sociology before coming to Harvard Law School and as someone aspiring to clerkship under a judge where she would be putting those views of hers into important legal documents and judgments, she must have known the fact that ideas of genetic inferiority underpinned slavery in America as well as genocide in Europe and elsewhere.

Naturally in matters of this type the usual divide was seen with some whites supporting her without regard to the damage done by her action. Frantic efforts were made to hide her identity even though it had already become public in Gawker, Jezebel, Abovethelaw.com and other websites. No doubt Ms. Stephanie Grace had fallen victim to what some have rightly called White People's Code by which mistakes like hers in class or at work are treated simply as mistakes whereas a nonwhite in a similar situation would have been considered not smart and her presence in Harvard seen mainly as a reflection of Affirmative Action. Such things – the looks, the sounds, the feelings, the raised eye brows and inferences put pressure on nonwhites to prove that "they belong here" whereas the white student with sheltered upbringing hardly has to worry about such pressures.

Harvard too contributes to such a problem through its academic emphasis on logical consistency over actual justice, hyper-intellectualized academic environment where students feel they can say just anything as long as they can give it some coating of logic and rationality. Did she make a consistent, rational and logical argument? Of course not! And how about social justice and the disparate treatment of non-whites in America's justice system? It would be interesting to see where on her scale of intelligence Ms. Grace Stephanie would place the handsome, blue-eyed white boy who found his way into Harvard University using forged documents and plagiarized material. It would be nice to see her reaction if and when she learned of recent findings that whites and blacks trail Hispanics as far as life expectancy at birth is concerned, that many moons ago the Harvard Law Review had Barack Obama, a black man at its head or that among the world's most intelligent persons is a certain Wole Sonyinka of Nigeria.

In a way there was a *déjà vu* ring to all of this. As far back as 1925 a War College report said that blacks did not have either the courage or the intelligence to be pilots, and like Ms. Grace, one general went ahead to state that the Negro type did not have proper reflexes to make a first-rate fighter pilot. And then the Tuskegee program came into being – an experiment designed to prove that America's Negroes did not have the capability to fly. Of course the plan back-fired big time! Did the young woman ever hear of the Tuskegee airmen at all? Here was a group of determined African Americans who, against all odds of the time, went ahead to help defeat Nazi Germany in world war II and to end Jim Crow segregation at home in America, proving to all doubting Thomases that they too were equal to the task in patriotically defending the national interest. The enemy respected them and even gave them a special name – *Schwarze Vogelmenschen* (black birdmen). First lady Eleanor Roosevelt, a woman as white as any other American of the day, let herself be flown by Chief Charles Anderson, father of black aviation, against all secret service naysayers. Did President Harry Truman not decide to integrate the formerly segregated Armed Forces? American actor and Hollywood's superstar, George Clooney, on a visit to Sudan, opened his hands and allowed an elderly woman to bless him with spittle from the mouth. How would Ms Stephanie Grace react to these?

It is said that she had been awarded a clerkship under a judge. If this is true, in that capacity she would wield a lot of power indeed, interpreting the law, helping to craft decisions that impact specific litigants involved in cases as well as wide swaths of the US population. She would handle civil rights and race issues. Should the judge under whom she would be working not know that Stephanie Grace believes that black people may be genetically inferior? If the judge is going to rely on her to interpret and apply the law should he not be aware of such views?

Apologists for her action were many and varied, including those who thought that in an academic setting there should be freedom to raise whatever one wishes and to do so without offending anyone. But in the real world ideas have consequences. Thus part of the consequence of raising controversial idiotic arguments is that people become annoyed, angry and offended. Who is prepared to stand up and be counted among those who also believe that people have no right to be offended, that people have a right to demand that others accept without emotion whatever ridiculous or hateful argument is put forth? Her leaked incendiary e-mail certainly ticked off Martha Minow, dean of the Harvard Law School who condemned it and went ahead to meet with BLSA (Black Law Students Association). Déjà vu? The famous student had no qualms writing what she did even though she knew she was dabbling in an area (biology) outside of her academic jurisdiction (law).The fact that today's *Homo sapiens americanus* has an African origin – with classless, raceless, cave-dwelling hairiness that concealed differences in color, if any, apparently does not exist for her. Her freedom of speech simply trumped it all! No wonder Mark Twain's allegory, *Huckleberry Finn*, clearly brings out our national dilemma of all time – how can anyone be truly free in a country as violent and as stupid as ours?

One of the immigrant students reacted to the ridicule that African leaders tend to stay in power eternally – Hosni Mubarak's reign in Egypt, Omar Bongo's rulership of Gabon, Colonel Muamar Kadaffi's of Libya, His Excellency Mr. Mugabe's of Zimbabwe, Abdoulaye Wade's in Senegal, Ben Ali's in Tunisia and many more, - by also drawing attention to the fact that in 1966, the city of Chicago was headed by a certain mayor Daly and forty years down the road, the very mayor Daly remained at the helm in Chicago with just the possibility that Rahm Emanuel was to leave serving as White House Chief of Staff and run for mayor of that city. "Oh, no" protested one listener. "It is not the same Daly. The present mayor is Daly the son" he went on to explain. "O. K., a dynasty then? Like the Kennedy dynasty? Or the Bush dynasty?" the unimpressed, unperturbed immigrant went on, citing more and more cases of Americans who also stayed long in power. Mayor Bloomberg of New York City and Menino of Boston were others. Didn't the pot always call the kettle black? Besides, how about the Korean dynasty that the world knows from Kim Il Sung, through Kim Jung Il and now heading unstoppably towards Kim Jung Un the four-star general recently designated by his aging father? The lively exchanges went on like this until it got to the stalemate between defeated Ivorian strongman, Laurent Gbagbo and his rival Alassane Ouattara, holed up inside a hotel in Abidjan and backed by the entire regional ( ECOWAS), continental (EU) and world body (UN peace keeping force) when the immigrants became crestfallen, knowing that the regional grouping which threatened to get Gbagbo out by force if possible was just a paper tiger when it came to such matters, or to use another metaphor, none of its leaders could venture to throw the first stone.

Mohammed, a Muslim student from Yemen had been used to jaywalking like everybody else, taking advantage of the aspiration of every American to be colorless or faceless and blending in, but then after the terrible terrorist strike of September 2001, it all changed.

Ethnicity shot to the forefront and in his own words, telling someone he was a Muslim was like telling them that he had a loaded gun in his pocket, making them turn pale from Islamophobia. That was not all. The Yemenite, probably hiding behind the invincibility of youth, would go on to greet people and assuage their angst in a very peculiar way, saying *"Don't worry, you are cool, you are all right. I left the bombs in the back of the car."*

Those young immigrants finally discovered a practical application of their nursery school wisdom – burn me once, shame on you; burn me twice, shame on me. Their messages were simple and clear - when people deliberately refuse to live by the golden rule, they must prepare for some of its ugly consequences. Good fighters do not only give punches, they also receive some. Nobody doubts the fact that our friends and families and coworkers are our comfort zones where we feel a lot at ease and often let down our guards. But if the people around us become bigoted and take delight in poking unsavory, hurtful and embarrassing fun at us in the name of joking, we need to fight back to regain our self-respect. Those students might not be graduates of the SPLC's (Southern Poverty Law Center's) pet projects but they surely had their own way of speaking up and standing against bigotry and intolerance even if they failed to consider the possibility of physical violence. They certainly took a calculated risk. Not many people would venture into such territory without first assessing their vulnerability and convincing themselves that they had taken the necessary self-defense lessons and turned into bullet-proof ninjas, capable of defining and defending their boundaries, not only verbally but physically as well. The Constitution guarantees freedom of speech but surely not anarchy, which unfettered freedom seems to breed. Should one really say it just because the First Amendment guarantees the freedom to do so? How different would anyone be from a mere robot?

However, those newly minted US citizens were smart enough to quickly concede that their new home was by far better than the ones they had left behind, emphasizing that they merely wished to make a clear distinction between a few rotten apples and the rest of the harvest. Certainly not all Americans are bigoted or intolerant or hateful or vindictive against immigrants or those perceived to be different from them. Such a prompt concession would forestall the possibility of detractors and fomenters of trouble turning to their popular war cry "if you don't like it here, why not just go back to your country?" As a matter of fact, much was made of the peaceful coexistence of so many persons from diverse and often rival cultures around the world – India's low and high casts mixing so freely, Rwanda's Hutus and Tutsis living peacefully as if there was never a 1994, Somalis, Chinese, Japanese, Koreans and many more past and present archrivals. Where else can an immigrant rise to the lofty position of governor of the State of California, a large and wealthy state? Where else can the courts order the powerful governor of such a state to cut down the prison population by 40,000 before a given dateline or else? Where else can former presidents live peacefully, go about their daily activities unmolested and even take active part in some high profile civic duties the way Jimmy Carter, Bill Clinton, the senior and junior Bushes were doing? Where else can a taxi driver send you a $5 bill in the mail, being the refund for an unintended overcharge for a fare? Only in America.

Sidonlook compared such a gesture to one of his own experiences in downtown Nairobi, Kenya. A taxi driver had taken him from somewhere on Kenyatta Avenue, gone round and round, up to Grosvenor hotel and back again, supposedly looking for 680 Hotel. He had then dropped him past Mama Ngina Avenue, taken a hefty sum of shillings for the ride only for him to discover that the taxi man had dropped him at a point directly opposite where he had picked him earlier! Was the taxi man a stranger to the city of Nairobi or had he just taken advantage of a stranger in town? Difficult to say but it was clear that the net distance traveled was zero. No wonder some had dubbed the city "*Nairobbery*".

Denying healthcare to immigrants would be a very dangerous and counterproductive proposition especially given the magnitude of the swine flu which the CDC and WHO had clearly called an epidemic, taking a toll on all continents and threatening the US population at large. At summer camps kids were sent home immediately counselors detected any flu-like symptoms. Little kids, known to catch germs like magnets, needed extra watchful parents, vaccinations, good coaching on how to cough or sneeze into their sleeves rather than their hands, a sure way to spread germs. They needed to be kept well hydrated with water and Emergen-C, and drummed into their heads the desirability of turning away from those who sneeze or cough into their faces and absolutely avoiding breathing in such potentially infections sprays directed at them.

Officials of Wal-Mart Stores Inc. even went into serious discussions with health officials about the possibility of placing vaccination sites at its many stores for the H1N1 inoculation campaign in view of the widespread nature of the epidemic. To stem the spread of the flu, innovative thinking was called for. Preventive measures, including hand sanitizers as well as the Macbeth effect –guilt-ridden, obsessive hand washing - were being popularized. Dry hands resulting from such extra efforts were a small price to pay to stay safe. Boston's Archdiocese gave instructions to its many parishes to stop offering shared wine at communions, to bow instead of shaking hands as a sign of peace. In some offices state employees went the extra step of putting on gloves before handling courier of any kind and masks became commonplace at airports. A total ban on hand shakes, considered a surefire germ spreader, was suggested. This would pose serious problems for the business executives, salesmen and the job seekers among us, groomed to consider the handshake as a perfect barometer for measuring the suitability of potential business partners.

This centuries-old handshake reportedly began in the middle ages. Two men, meeting one another for the first time, shook hands to establish that neither of them carried a weapon. The practice has persisted in the business world as a quick, unobtrusive way of sizing up someone (firm honest grip or sweaty, flabby shake?). In this age of swine flu spread, the practice pits politeness against commonsense. Graduating students in at least one of our universities were advised to cut down on handshakes, especially when receiving their diplomas at commencement ceremonies. The WHO had also advocated elbow bump in place of the potentially dangerous handshake and many Americans were already giving each other the clenched fist greeting considered equally good. People devised ways of pressing elevator buttons with their elbows instead of fingers and made strenuous efforts to balance on their two feet rather than lean on anything or persons inside the subway. Over-crowding and delays in Boston's T during rush hours, train derailments or signal failures were surely going to create nightmares for authorities of healthcare in view of persons with scratches or sore throats.

Conservative radio host Michael Savage, in spite of his record in promoting hate and hate crimes among right-wing extremists here at home, scapegoating and bashing immigrants as disease-carriers, especially the swine flu, vowed to go to court against the UK simply because Home Secretary Jacqui Smith produced a "name and shame" list of persons, he included, banned as visitors to the UK. Obviously language like the one he used with such relish did not make people welcome in a society where propriety is valued. According to the SPLC (Southern Poverty Law Center) report, killers inspired by the hate movement in America, aided and abetted the unhinged rhetoric on talk radio, cable television and the likes of Rush Limbaugh, Glenn Beck, Michael Savage and others. Incredibly, US Representative, Paul Broun of Georgia suggested that President Obama might establish a Gestapo-like security force in America, quickly explaining to the Associated Press "I'm not comparing Obama to Adolf Hitler. What I'm saying is there is the potential." What kind of mind would compare a highly popular, democratically elected American president to the most evil human being of all time remains for Americans to decide.

By some logic 1.3 million Californians were out of work while 1.3 million undocumented aliens settled in that state. But then those undocumented aliens were also 1.3 million consumers helping to create work! Do such statistics make of immigration a bane or a boon? How accurate do the statistics reflect the realities in the nation? Take a random sampling of ten persons at a local hangout like the Dunkin Donut. Right off the bat they may give the impression that immigrants have taken their jobs but a closer examination soon reveals that only about two or three of them fall into this category, the rest simply being persons who would rather hang on to food stamps or other welfare doles than try to earn a buck through hard work. Here was a state like California whose economy is usually rated eighth in the world, yet governor Schwarzenegger has trouble balancing his budget. The situation is reminiscent of many third world countries where the collectivity (roads, banks,) is poor yet individuals display unbelievable wealth (luxury cars, private aircraft, breathtaking homes). The Hollywood world with extremely wealthy actors and actresses makes California's story quite eerie indeed. A study by Alexis de Tocqueville Institution, a nonprofit, showed that the ten states with fewest immigrants had on the average, the highest unemployment rates. Does that add up to popular expectation?

Of course xenophobia has no interest in scientific studies. A certain Governor Wilson once made headlines calling for Constitutional Amendment barring citizenship for children of illegal immigrants born in the US, adding that America could no longer let compassion overrule reason. Much applause accompanied his remarks since votes invariably went where emotions went. The slaughter of thirteen innocent citizens by a 41-year-old Vietnamese immigrant at the American Civic Association in Binghamton, New York did not endear immigrants to the rest of the population. What could have motivated someone, who had been a beneficiary of TOEFL (Test of English as a foreign Language) training offered at the center, to commit such a heinous crime was not clear. How the man came in possession of a heavy caliber automatic pistol was the price society must pay for its lax gun laws. Putting an end to the American Dream for all those other immigrants was really tragic.

Ever heard of legal rights for illegal immigrants? Well, they exist or can be created at short notice. At a time when the issue of illegal immigration reached a boiling point in US politics, a certain Robert Hildreth, native of New Bedford in Massachusetts, who had worked for the International Monetary Fund (IMF) in Bolivia, South America and made himself a millionaire trading in bonds in Latin America, became very upset to learn that Immigration officials had rounded up five hundred illegal immigrants in a New Bedford factory, shackled and flown them to Houston, Texas for deportation. He vowed to fight for the immigrants and swung into action right away. First, he provided emergency aid, rent and food and then got involved with the legal issues, mobilizing upwards of one hundred lawyers, *pro bono* defenders of the immigrants, paying bail for 40 of the detainees, spending over $200,000 of his own personal money. Finally he cofounded the National Immigrant Bond Fund to serve the entire country. Robert Hildreth confessed that he considered it a campaign, a war to protect the America he knew and cherished, a life-long thing he cared about, convinced that the main difference between the United States and Japan, China or any of the other developed nations is that the US accepts immigrants whereas the others do not, that the US is a winner whereas the others are losers, a claim boosted by Angela Merkel's declaration around that time that multiculturalism in Germany had failed. Robert Hildreth was emphatic that no one could beat an immigrant nation. Flying back to New Bedford with one of the released detainees, he realized that a booking error had been made and the guy who had traveled to Houston in shackles was now put in first class! Only in America was such a thing possible, he contended. Whatever the case, no one was better placed than the new US president to know that part of America's genius had always been the ability to absorb newcomers and to forge a national identity out of the disparate lot that arrive the shores of the United States. It was only after Barack Obama became a popularly elected US president that the picturesque Slovenian city of Piran made the timid effort of electing a black mayor – Ghanaian-born Dr. Peter Bossman, a member of the Social Democrat, a leading party in the center left government. So also did Poland.

In spite of the importance of immigration, President Obama and Congress were under tremendous pressure to do something about the economy first. So great was the pressure that in providing the TARP(Troubled Assets Relief Program) funds for companies, Congress wrote the 2008 economic stimulus package and inserted into it language that provided for limiting H-1B visas for highly educated workers from other countries. Such a job protection policy for US workers may be good in the short run but its long term effect will very likely be counterproductive as it will affect international students, universities, businesses, and the moral standing of the US which the Obama Administration set out to reclaim. Many experts are convinced that the creators of the next generation of Microsoft, Google, and Infosys may well be found among those being shut out of the US by such a policy. Even the provision for the quicker-to-get EB5 Visas for persons able and willing to invest their monies in US businesses cannot fill the lacuna created by the H-1B bottleneck.

Not only that, the nation needs to produce that breed of individuals who will, in future, contribute to quiet diplomacy in solving some of today's intractable problems opposing the Christian West to the Islamic East. Thanks to such low key, quiet diplomacy, it was possible to make contact with persons like President Abdelaziz Bouteflika of Algeria to reach and workout a cease fire with Mohammed Abdelaziz, the leader of Polisario people fighting Morocco to gain their independence over Western Sahara; President Mathieu Kerekou of Benin to reach the isolated Colonel Muamar Qaddafi of Libya and his number two, Dr. Omar al-Montasser and work out a little miracle that made him release the persons responsible for planting a bomb on a US plane that exploded over Lockerbie in Scotland and to open up that country's nuclear weapons facilities for inspection by the IAEA (International Atomic Energy Commission) which then paved the way for reestablishment of diplomacy with the West. Similar contacts were made with Sudan's leader el-Bashir and the fighters of Somalia. None of these contacts would have been possible if West did not meet East at a personal and intimate level (Mark Siljander, *A Deadly Misunderstanding*). As a matter of fact, even without resolving his country's long standing disputes with Morocco, Muhammad Abdelaziz went on to become an outspoken critic of terrorism.

It is true that many Americans remain very skeptical of current moves by peace-loving Muslims to erect a mosque near Ground Zero, when viewed against the background of those who had danced on the streets when New York City's World Trade Center was brought down by terrorists using hijacked aircraft in 2001. Understandably some have called for reconciliation only after the payment of adequate compensations to either Uncle Sam or the families of those traumatized as a result of that incident.

Will the construction of the proposed Islamic Center and mosque near Ground Zero, ostensibly to build bridges show a way forward for reconciliation? New York City's Landmarks Preservation Commission unanimously voted to OK it but a storm began to brew as ignorance, bigotry, ethnocentrism, sophistry and politics remained formidable obstacles still to overcome. Critics call it Ground Zero mosque, especially those who see Islam as the malevolent force that brought down the twin towers of the WTC in the first place. They liken the whole exercise to survivors of the Holocaust erecting a monument in honor of Hitler or a Japanese Cultural Center being erected at Pearl Harbor! How the prospect of a rising minaret instills fear in the hearts of ordinary mortals! No wonder Switzerland voted to ban the minaret. But Muslim roots are said to predate the twin towers of New York. In late 19th Century, a part of lower Manhattan was called little Syria, inhabited by Arab immigrants, Christians and Muslims from the Ottoman Empire. President Obama first took an unequivocal stance for the project but in view of the harsh criticism from some members of his party, he began to back track.

Whichever way one looks at it, placing the mosque near Ground Zero will certainly reopen old wounds just as surely as denying its construction is bound to defeat the original reason for founding the American nation – religious freedom. It is chilling to imagine that this whole enterprise might have been engineered by al-Qaeda, the Taliban or their agents here in the US to foment trouble, divide the nation and make fun of the world's superpower. Far fetched? Only time will tell. Others wonder whether it is permissible to build a synagogue and Jewish center in the holy city of Mecca or in Sudan, warning, rightly or wrongly, that the proposed center will probably be taken over by radical Islamists using their world-wide, centuries-old strategy.

Imam Feisal Abdul Rauf and his wife Daisy Khan are Muslim leaders often fantasized about by the right wing as "modernists" or moderates who openly condemn Al-Qaeda's death cult and its adherents, the very peaceful Muslims our own Sarah Palin asked to "refudiate" plans to build the mosque. Imam Rauf, a Sunni from Kuwait, has written extensively, saying American democracy is an embodiment of Islam's ideal society. And western experts are actually advocating that leaders like him be sought out and empowered to fight extremism. The big question is whether we of the Land of the free and home of the brave should not distinguish between fighting terrorism and fighting Islam as a whole. Should all African-Americans, for example, be condemned as criminals simply because one of them robbed a bank? Should all French people be thrown out of the US just because someone ate soggy French fries? Should Muslim Americans be shut out completely or should they be part of the discussions? What better way to quell the hardliners for good? And should New York take on this issue alone without input from the Federal government the way Arizona went about illegal immigration? Governor David Paterson suggested moving it farther away from the trade center out of respect for the feelings of those opposed to it whereas New York City's mayor, Michael Bloomberg came out in support, calling it a test of the separation of church and state. Is it really impossible to have peace between Muslims and Judeo-Christians? Aren't we reacting in the same allergic manner as those in the East who hastily pronounced a fatwa (death sentence) on Carla Bruni, France's first lady, just for coming out in solidarity with Iranian woman, Sakineh Mohammadi Ashtiani, sentenced to die by stoning for alleged adultery?

Under the circumstances what is the right thing to do? Should the west resort to the kind of tit for tat publicity stunt prescribed by little known pastor Terry Jones from Gainesville, Florida with his Qu'ran burning crusade or should it occupy the moral high ground and teach by example, putting to good use low key quiet diplomacy as advocated by US Congressman, Mark Siljander in his quest to bridge the East-West divide by highlighting what the people of the great faith traditions share– the same core beliefs, common values and ideals like compassion, solidarity, respect for life and kindness towards others? How can the stabbing of a Muslim taxi driver in New York City, the burning of the Qu'ran or demonizing of children with Muslim names represent the teaching of Jesus? Where did mainstream America go? How can we, as a great nation, restrain the primitive instinct of making declarations like "All terrorists are Muslim" or "All Muslims are terrorists" which we all know are untrue? Surely our own Timothy McVeigh was not a Muslim; nor was Harry Reid and of course we live with lots of peace-loving Muslims in our towns and cities. Surprisingly, throughout his travels in the East (Bahrain, Qatar, and United Arab Emirates) Imam Rauf found a very low key reaction to the whole thing compared to what obtains here in the West, as pan-Arab news media like Asharq Alawsat and the rest think it is less an affront to Islam as a whole. And how will all of this affect Christians who journey to Muslim lands for work or proselytization?

There is no doubt that it takes a special type of courage to bring about reconciliation across such a divide, a very rare type of courage indeed, and in backing such a project, President Obama demonstrated just such courage. It happened before and might just happen once more. Today, Jenin, a West Bank town once known as the "city of suicide bombers" enjoys a degree of peace and tranquility, thanks to a rare courage shown by a Palestinian father who donated the organs of his twelve-year son Ahmed Ismael Khatib - shot dead by Israeli soldiers who mistook his toy gun for a real one - to Israeli Jews, Arabs, Druzes. The father's lofty ideal was to promote peace, convinced that saving lives is much more important than religion of any kind. Even strong-willed Israeli premier, Ariel Sharon was so moved by the gesture that he offered his apologies to the family. The 2005 documentary *"The Heart of Jenin"* made by German film maker, Marcus Vetter who braved it into Jenin – another aspect of rare courage -is a testimony of this wonderful feat which also succeeded to bring back to life a West Bank cinema abandoned since 1967, the year of the first intifada. Today kids in Jenin spend their time indoors instead of on the streets. And Palestinian community organizer, Ayed Morrar, dubbed "Gandhi" in *Budrus,* the film on nonviolent protests is another illuminating example of courage.

It is difficult at this time to predict how this whole drama will end. But Americans need to take a few steps back and recall a few facts – that one big difference between the US and most of the world is the existence of a Bill of rights here and that the US is made up of a diverse population remarkably held together in such a way that the rest of the world admires us. Whether it was the unwillingness or inability to come to terms with the fact of an obscure individual with a weird name becoming US president and thereby personifying the American dream is not quite clear but microphones picked up some aspiring but frustrated leader at a social event lamenting the "Kenyan anti-colonial mentality", a clear allusion to President Obama. This nation which is far from perfect actually attracts like a magnet.

Finally House speaker, Nancy Pelosi brought to Congress the deliberations and final product of the Obama healthcare reform. The fear of health monopoly had led Congress to urge for collaboration in handling such a delicate matter. The overhaul proposal encouraged hospitals and doctors to join forces and create networks or better coordination of patient care. However, large provider groups carried the risk of using their market strength to raise prices and reap higher profits. The oft cited model was that of Mayo Clinic in Minnesota which reputedly provided efficient care – linked computers and standardized treatments. But as with Partners, linking Massachusetts General Hospital, Brigham and Women's, Children's Hospital and 4000 physician network of community affiliates, such conglomerates stand accused of using their enormous clout to dictate prices and marginalize competitors. In a study carried out on the issue of mergers, it was found that the wave of hospital mergers took prices up by 5% to 40% in some cases, even as people argued that provider groups usually forced insurers to pay more. Clearly consolidation was seen to be bad for business in spite of the counter argument that patients paid more for inefficiency and variance of care. How competition could be carried out among providers and costs controlled remained to be seen.

As a way forward, the idea of creating a strong government-backed insurance option to set payment rates was then tabled to force insurers to compete. A more radical idea was for government to set universal rates the way many industrialized nations do. None of those options was seen to have the political chance of surviving. The Federal Trade Commission is supposed to back anti-competitive provider mergers.

Ultimately the proposed bill embodied the requirement that employers offer insurance to employees or face penalties; it provided fines for Americans who failed to purchase coverage and subsidy to help those of low income to do so. Insurance companies would face new prohibitions against charging more for older people or denying coverage to persons with preexisting health conditions. The price tag stood at $1 trillion over a ten year period and covered 95% of Americans. Unresolved as yet was the thorny problem of using tax payer money to pay for abortions and healthcare for illegal immigrants. A modified government insurance (the famous public option) was to be provided for states to opt in or out of it. Why the lawmakers singled out abortion - out of all the other controversial items to be covered, such as gender reassignment surgery for those desiring a sex change or multiple births from in vitro fertilization - was not clear.

The Obama Administration would have to address the recession which had swallowed the nation's economy. The FAA, FCC, CDC, EPA, FDA, SEC and the rest were supposed to sanitize the landscape but had failed to do so. How could all those organizations fail? Why did so many things fall apart? In retrospect, part of the answer lay in Fed Chairman, Alan Greenspan's idea of turning a blind eye to the very efficient market forces, of not 'playing by the books' and so letting deregulation take its course. Government regulation would have required putting in place appropriate infrastructure and government procurement as well as providing special tax incentives to ensure a true laissez-fair rather than a free-for-all capitalism and influencing public policies to preempt people being falsely lured into "buying snake oil." Facing members of Congress in October 2008 the former Federal Reserve boss actually admitted that the economic crisis had put him in a state of shocked disbelief, revealing a flaw in a life time of economic thinking. Experts like Clyde Prestowitz (*The Betrayal of American Prosperity*) saw a misreading or misapplication of a rigid economic orthodoxy across the political and social spectrum, making bankers and policy makers to cherry pick those parts they found congenial to their choicest risks, discouraging whistle blowing and scholarship that warned of disasters and influential trend setters consorting with financial risk takers.

That Bernard Madoff could live comfortably in Palm Beach Florida and concoct a Ponzi scheme - an arrangement that robbed Peter to pay Paul - to defraud investors of $50 billion and wipe out entire retirement savings told just the tip of a very large iceberg. Some estimates had it that Bernard Madoff enjoyed $22 manicures, $40 shaves and a $7 million penthouse. Nothing could be done to satisfy all of the man's bitter victims, especially those investors he was alleged to have bilked over the years, some of whom were thirsting for his blood or asking for him to be stoned to death for the lives ruined. The Elie Wiesel Foundation for Humanity, Yeshiva University of New York, Zsa Zsa Gabor, Larry King, Steven Spielberg and a charitable foundation dedicated to Jewish causes were said to be some of the big losers lamenting over their nest eggs. And yet a certain whistleblower by the name of Harry Markopoulos claimed that he had been royally ignored by the SEC when he approached, alerted and persuaded the organization that there was something wrong with Bernie Madoff's investment returns. Why had no one at the SEC listened to him? Obviously they were following the gospel according to the Federal Reserve Chairman of the time.

And gone was America's love affair with large, fuel-guzzling cars. Was a recession a good or bad thing? Economists who are the experts in this matter were divided. While nobody liked the loss of jobs and massive unemployment that went with it, some saw a silver lining. They said real estate and stocks were cheaper, and going back to school was ideal at that time. This they termed opportunity cost since wages were stagnant and nothing would be lost by returning to school except that getting school loans at that time with no certainty of a job after graduation posed the problem of repayment when the time came. According to this view, people enjoyed better health because they smoked less, drank less, took fewer drugs and were more likely to attend to the elderly and the kids. This was not difficult to explain. As people were out of work, there were fewer car accidents, less congested traffic, a drop in manufacturing and corresponding drop in pollution and pulmonary infections. One small step for all those who took the bus, the trolleys, the subway trains and other aspects of mass transit, translated into one giant leap for planet earth. By taking these alternative routes, they surely prolong the life of our atmosphere which is being polluted by numerous private cars belching out carbon dioxide and other noxious gases that contribute to acid rain, smog, heart disease, respiratory problems and more. Some said a true recession would be two consecutive quarters of negative GDP growth and an unemployment rate around 8.2% as in the 1970s.

The St. Patrick's(Irish Heritage) Day festivities of 2008 were rendered cold by a declaration from Martin Feldstein, President of the National Bureau of Economic Research, a Harvard professor and leading expert on economic trends, that the situation was bad and getting worse, after citing a record of bankruptcies, job losses and a housing crisis. The professor's research bureau was apparently the official judge of a recession. The nation had already had two consecutive quarters of economic retrenchment. Bear Stearns, one of the world's largest and most celebrated investment banks was at imminent collapse if J. P. Morgan Chase did not come in to bail it out. Would President George W. Bush saddle America with a recession in addition to everything else? Bill Gates tried to buy over Yahoo but the deal flopped partly because Google campaigned against it. Perhaps it was good that way. The last time Yahoo tried a similar deal with Netscape, it ended in a deadlock over what the name of the new company should be. *"Netanyahu"* was first mooted but quickly dropped, following rumors that Israeli Premier Benjamin Netanyahu would sue over the use of his name. Microsoft gave Yahoo an ultimatum to accept the offer or suffer a hostile take-over! Soon AOL too waded into the bid and calls went out to media mogul Rupert Murdoch to intervene. It was interesting how the financial crisis affected companies differently – while Google Inc. was hiring new employees, Yahoo Inc. was instead firing.

The magic word "bailout" took on center stage, starting with a historic bail out of the private sector to the tune of over $700 billion as Treasury Secretary Henry Paulson, Federal Reserve Chairman, Ben Bernanke and President George W. Bush conferred to restore confidence in stock and credit markets, and reduce the jittery reaction of taxpayers.

The crisis which began in the nation's housing bust, quickly spread to stock and credit markets, pushing the global financial system to the brink of collapse. All of this came at the end of an extraordinary week that saw the failure of the investment firm, Lehman Brothers Holdings, Inc., government take over of insurance giant, American Insurance Group (AIG) Inc. for $85 billion and a run on money market funds reminiscent of the bank runs during the 1929 Depression. Fannie Mae and Freddie Mac had taken on too much risk in their operations because of an implicit guarantee by the government to back their debts. Some economists worried that by insulating people and businesses from risky behavior, they were being encouraged to take on more risky behavior in future. Could the US afford to give such a guarantee to the entire financial system? Of course not! Would Morgan Stanley consider a take over by Wachovia Corporation or selling to China Investment Corporation? Judge James Peck decided after midnight that Lehman Brothers could sell its investment banking and trading business to Barclays Bank (British).

Wall Street always claimed that government interference impeded markets, arguing against regulatory agencies and failing to see the free-for-all that would result in the absence of regulation. Over and over one heard how government was not good at running things, how government should be kept away from management of such things even though government remained the major shareholder! Political campaign contributions and lobbying became such a prominent feature of the rich and crowded Wall Street-Washington corridor, earning another name for the US – Goldman Sachsony. Surely regulation makes markets better – more accountability, more transparency. But the question remained, why major investment houses were allowed to buy billions of dollars of complex securities backed by unsustainable mortgages. An enterprising employee of Wachovia bank became expert at the financing of commercial properties through the infamous process by which debts were minced and turned into bonds to be bought and sold by Wall Street traders. Residents in complexes like Stuyvesant Town housing who had waited for years after winning the special lottery that gave them access to those facilities became hooked to the scheme. Loan delinquency rose from less than 1% to around 8.5% in 2008. Bear Stearns and the financial markets turned into a Wild West and cowboy capitalism populated with firms that expected somebody - government, taxpayers – to clean up. Fannie Mae and Freddie Mac, two mortgage giants were in a mess after the Federal government encouraged them to buy more than $400 billion in sub-prime mortgage loans between 2004 and 2006. All those so-called NINJA (no income, no jobs, and no assets) mortgages completely eclipsed the animal instincts in economics. Americans had turned John Maynard Keynes' lessons upside down. Belatedly former Federal Reserve Chairman Alan Greenspan admitted that he had been wrong.

Give two or three Americans their favorite beers –Budweiser, Sam Adams, Schlitz, any – and may be a pizza to go with and then watch and listen to them tear Europe apart. Poor Europeans - they suffer from Euroclerosis, low growth, high unemployment, high tax, inflexible anti-entrepreneur welfare states and so on and so on. Yet most of these persons, together with their bankers and economists, are virtually clueless about Europe or Asia. All they know is American success as a result of good old ingenuity, pioneering spirit, rugged individualism and the operation of the free market. For them success is achieved in spite of rather than because of government intervention. Frankly very few persons know or bother to know that their business interests are aligned with the interests of either the state or federal government. The simple truth is that corporations are chartered by the government. By so doing benefits such as shareholders' limited liability losses are conferred on them; in this way individual shareholders do not bear the burden of losses alone if ever they occurred. The new powerful speaker of the House of Representatives, John Boehner actually shed tears, overwhelmed by emotions over reminiscences of his rise from janitorial duties and waiting tables to his present lofty position where he virtually calls the shots and leads the crusade to undo President Obama's healthcare reform legislation.

No wonder livid customers asked for heads to roll on Wall Street as a result of the depravity of American capitalism, people selling mortgage investments without telling the buyers that the securities were made with help from a client who was betting on them to fail! Regulators accused Goldman Sachs, Bear Stearns and the rest of fraud. This was one giant of a broken promise indeed. Retirement benefits like healthcare and pension had come to symbolize the American Dream, especially with pledges by corporations to their employees. But it all went up in smoke, including death benefit payments to widowed persons. Bounced checks flew all over the place. But why? Why were businesses forced onto bankruptcy courts following the rip offs? How could obligations to widowed persons be erased, forcing some to put pride in their pockets and go picking and selling empty cans of drinks and other castoffs to recycling companies for token payments?

Early in the game companies had encouraged employee savings by promising subsidies only to turn around and rescind the agreement, with Congress looking the other way! As a matter of fact Congress did not just look the other way; Congress actually passed legislation empowering bankruptcy courts to protect the corporate frauds, leaving employees in the cold. Scrapping the health insurance promised to persons who retired earlier was a severe blow. The defined-benefits plans were jettisoned for defined-contributions in the form of 401(k) s into which employees put a fixed sum of money for their retirement. With life expectancy on the rise, there was the risk of returning to the situation one hundred years earlier when individuals assumed all the risks for their retirement. What a setback!

In El Paso, Texas, classroom teacher George Padilla lamented over the wrong message conveyed to the kids he had dutifully taught over the years, inculcating into them the fact that screwing up is punishable, that if they did not put in the effort and get passing grades, he would not pass them and to top it all, that in the real world people would be fired if they didn't do well on their jobs. The AIG drama contradicted most of that wisdom, especially when executives of failed companies were being rewarded with exorbitant bonuses instead of being fired. How those miscreants should be bailed out with taxpayers' money without any conditions remained an enigma to many. But the feeling was quite strong that somewhere along the road, Barack Obama, the new US president ought to impose some sort of a ceiling on executive pay and exorbitant bonuses, especially for those companies benefitting from the blank check called bailout, if not immediately, then at least as soon as they recovered. TARP must not be abused.

Americans became very angry and furious for having been used, duped, lied to, betrayed, ripped off, conned, humiliated, scammed, cheated, plundered, crooked, screwed over, hosed, and dishonored. The list was long. Some were angry over Guantanamo, Abu Ghraib and Iraq; others over water boarding or the so-called enhanced interrogation, torture, eavesdropping, the suspension of habeas corpus, and other acts classified as war crimes or crimes against humanity. So angry were Americans that they were prepared to take out their anger on the wrong targets, including Hillary Clinton whose infectious laughter during the 2008 campaigns they derided, spurned and refused to endorse, in this way turning on its head an old mantra that laughter is the best medicine. Some Americans tended to judge women running for office by their looks, their laughs or their mannerisms rather than the content of their brains, yet in office it is mainly the brains that would be needed to get the nation out of economic and other entanglements.

Politicians invariably contribute to the mess when they treat voters the way they do. There is mutual distrust between voters and Congress as one sees from the many ads that litter the landscape when Democrats, Republicans and independents work overtime to outdo each other. From one ad one comes away with the impression that the election of one candidate over another would lead to the unraveling of the American Constitution. Another ad portrays political rivals as persons hiding entire families of illegal immigrants inside their sports coats, just waiting to leap out on election night and engage American kids in wild sex, underpaid jobs, gay marriages and other crazy things. The conclusion is inescapable that it is far easier to concoct bucketfuls of questionable "facts" and toss them at easy-to-manipulate voters than come up with a legitimate case thoughtfully put together.

Others were apoplectic over those who had ruled and raped the financial system. Some wished to see George Bush, Dick Cheney, Donald Rumsfeld and others brought to some bar of justice somewhere soon. George W. Bush and Dick Cheney had surely taught America's current and future generations one enduring and inescapable lesson – to be great one does not have to be good. But any such trial risked splitting the country in the nastiest kind of division. Putting an ex-president on trial would have a costly price tag in social cohesion and domestic peace. President Barack Obama had his plate so full that it was doubtful if he would want to be associated with such a dangerous scheme at such a moment so early in his mandate or even tolerate it during his watch. Enlisting the assistance of his two immediate predecessors for the Haitian relief could not have been possible if Obama had followed that vindictive agenda and put George Bush on trial. That is a fact. Some expressed the view that it was necessary to exorcise the demon of torture and to do so, they recommended a commission of inquiry, not to criminally indict the CIA officers or midlevel officials who acted under authority granted by the previous Commander-in-Chief. Such inquiry, it was hoped, would be to demonstrate that American democracy was capable of correcting its worst errors. How popular a move would it be for a president to criticize his predecessor? The question hung in the air.

Under the existing climate would it be a wise undertaking? Should President Obama do it just to pay Dick Cheney in his own coin for continuing to run his mouth over the way the new administration was operating? As Vice President under George Bush, Dick Cheney avoided the press with a religious devotion. Why was he now so openly criticizing the new president's policies on torture? Was he irked by Obama's refusal to continue the use of fear and torture as tools of governance or placing the country on a permanent war footing? The former vice president claimed that he had no fear of losing an election and no post he was vying for, not even Rush

Limbaugh's unofficial post as of head of the GOP or the quixotic campaign to see Obama fail. So what motivated him to take on an incumbent president only a few months into his presidency? Did he want to replace Michael Steel the new GOP boss who was said to be planning to give the party a hip-hop makeover? Wasn't that a distraction from the things that mattered, such as the effort to get the economy going again? If he sincerely wanted a debate on national security with the new president, why take him by ambush at a time when the nation expected him to be concentrating on writing his memoires? How could he so soon have lost sight of the fact that for eight long years he lived in a very big glass house with plenty of closets full of skeletons? The leakage of the identity of a CIA agent had not yet been put to rest; Americans knew that Skipper Libby had been sent to jail only for obstruction of justice, the substantive matter still in abeyance.

Was Dick Cheney aware of America's two visions – America the great and America the good – each with its downside? Surely he and President George Bush had done everything during their eight year mandate to uphold the first image of a great swaggering America; now President Obama was on the way to reestablishing the good image of the nation, including its good name and moral authority in the world. America needed such a balance. Wasn't that why the people had voted for Obama against the GOP machine? Wasn't that why Obama's overall rating at the polls continued to be high in spite of attempts by detractors to sully his efforts? How could aspiring Vice-President Sarah Palin oppose leading America in a way that could make our allies admire and adversaries respect us? What point was there satirizing President Obama in her speech to the Tea Party (limited government, free market, low taxes) convention? Can US voters value laughter over heavy national security issues? Warmongers were clamoring for the man to go tough on Iran where practiced restraint was called for regarding that nation's repressive approach to dissidents protesting their rigged presidential election. Continuing to see America only in terms of weakness was a misplaced priority. President Obama's rescinding of some of George Bush's acts while in office – lifting the ban on stem cell research, making public the classified documents on torture by CIA operatives, decision to close down the Guantanamo prison, facilitating financial remittances by Cuban exiles to their homeland – had received approval, even if some diehard Bush supporters deemed them inappropriate.

It was with a lot of relief that many Americans learned of the lifting of the ban on stem cell research. Too many people had waited in vain for an organ transplant in their last days on planet earth, all because the organs were not just there. Tissue engineering is at the frontiers of science and scientists spend sleepless nights studying how organs develop from cells and tissues. It is the hope that before long, organs can be grown from scratch to replace old or diseased ones. Progress in this area of research has been taking place quite quickly. Not too long ago, newspapers carried pictures of the famous ear grown in a Petri dish and subsequently implanted on the back of a mouse. Naturally people longed for a similar miracle in humans but how soon? Scientists are regularly presenting papers about their work on heart valves, lengths of blood vessels, segments of intestines and others grown in the laboratory. Soon bioengineered livers will be at the fingertips of our scientists so that those in end stage liver failure won't die waiting for a transplant that never came.

Guantanamo, like Abu Ghraib, had dragged America's moral standing into mud and needed redeeming. President Obama certainly did the right thing when he opted to close down Guantanamo, even though the mechanics of doing so would require time, planning and plenty of resources. The presence of a US prison on Cuban soil did not make sense in the first place. How had this come about? Built in 1903 on a land area of 45 square miles which Cuba leased to the US – on condition of US withdrawal after taking control of the island in the Spanish American war –Guantanamo is the oldest overseas American naval base. It was used mainly as a "coaling" station for the US fleet patrolling the Caribbean but had since become redundant with the switch to oil. Its main purpose had since been to serve as American determination to show up Fidel Castro, an irritant to Castro who publicly decried it as a symbol of America's imperialist tendencies, boasting that he never cashed the checks sent to him for rents. But the question remained: "Why not just turn it over as a good will gesture to Fidel's brother, Raoul, the new Cuban leader?" After all the US turned over the Panama Canal to Panamanians and the world did not come to an end. What good was there continuing to keep Guantanamo?

When giants like AIG received bailout monies to the tune of $165 million and turned around to finance the bonus payments for their executives instead of the much tooted "shovel ready" projects, people thought the insurance companies had crossed the line. One argument put forth to justify the bailout was that AIG had to respect the contractual agreement with its employees, lest America be seen as condoning lawlessness. "Not so fast", went a counter argument, which warned that bonuses were supposed to be compensation for good work, not mediocrity that brought the company to its knees and in need of a bail out. The blame game was on and in high gear. The argument that bonuses were intended for "retention" of key employees was countered by asking where such employees would otherwise go, given the market situation characterized by the recession. A very furious member of Congress recommended the Japanese prescription, that the executives responsible for the mess come before the American people, apologize and then go out and do one of two things – commit suicide or resign. Taking one's life under such circumstances creates more problems than it solves. Surely it cuts down the agony and suffering of one individual but leaves a burdensome legacy for family, friends and the nation.

Watching the giant CEOs go cap in hand in front of the US Congress for a bailout, I could not help feeling some degree of guilt for fellow Americans whom I had despised by the road side as they too asked for spare change – a quarter here, a dollar there. Weren't they too doing the American thing? Panhandling is panhandling, whether to sustain an ostentatious life style in corporate offices or eke out a living in the shelter or by the road side. America could not spite one and embrace the other. *Vous avez parlé si clairement sur la necessité de faire l'aumône,* Victor Hugo once declared, *que j'ai presque envie de mendier.* (You have spoken so lucidly about the need for giving alms that I am almost inclined to begging). America will continue to live with penury and excessive wealth, starvation and hyper-alimentation for a long time to come. It is quite a challenge distinguishing the fake from the real or the professional from the occasional, especially as scammers and con artists could switch from one to the other with relative ease. A certain shrewd John Ruffing once told me that he had devised the method of showing preparedness to give away five dollars, ten dollars or whatever panhandlers asked for, but first he demanded an identity card as collateral till such a time that they came to pay back the money borrowed. At that point, the scammers and other fakes usually made themselves known by their subsequent utterances – outburst of profanities. Yet there are elusive ones such as the twenty-three-year old who put up quite an elaborate scheme to bilk sympathizers and unsuspecting persons out of thousands of dollars, portraying herself as a cancer victim –shaved head, shaved eye brows, plucked eye lashes, starved look and a bogus charity website.

It is clear that overwhelming greed had contributed to the nation's recession. Bernard Madoff, whose serenity equaled that of a typical James Bond nemesis, and the faceless AIG executives could rightly be blamed for the nation's collective miseries. Psychotherapists had diagnosed this as a sickness, people suffering from addictive dysfunction pretty much like gambling, alcoholism or drug abuse. They had chased runaway materialism, especially here in America where the economy was virtually a deity. Such persons felt that a healthy economy was one that was always growing. Greed apparently filled up the gap where something else should have been. For such persons, developing a stronger sense of community was not important, not sought after or encouraged; only a quick fix solution such as "I will be really happy and successful if I can earn so much money" and then carried to extreme "I'm prepared to put my life at risk, even commit criminal acts." Bernard Madoff received 150 years of imprisonment on the 29th day of June 2009 probably a joke compared to Imelda Marcos's 1,824 years. Whether it brings closure to those he had robbed is another matter altogether.

The great depression of 1929 ended when President Franklin Delano Roosevelt's New Deal and the Industrial Revolution merged to satisfy production needs of the second World War, a combination of need and circumstance that unified this great country and transformed it from an agricultural to an industrial economy, ultimately affecting the fortunes of the middle class.

2008 and 2009 found the nation in very bad shape, a situation similar to 1929, this time from both a national and world economy, requiring an understanding of global thinking and participation in order to lead to global prosperity. Sacrifices, a change of national attitude and some degree of patience were called for. But then those who had the power to act continued to look in the rear-view mirror instead of looking also ahead and extrapolating to see what opening up to the Asian tigers could actually mean! To understand the crisis of 2008 one needs to take several steps back in time, probably as far back as 2001 and the preceding Clinton presidency when wooing China into the WTO looked like an exciting proposition. President Clinton and his team saw globalization as almost synonymous to Americanization and negotiators sought not only to get China into the World Trade Organization but also to grant it the status of most favored nation. Was there room for free trade or a market-oriented economy or any iota of reciprocity in the negotiations? What about the authoritarian rule? What sort of cooperation could states applying neo-mercantilism hope to share with one with state-guided strategies? Was there a provision for the US to gain free access to Chinese markets? Was it really necessary to bring the Chinese into the community of nations, place them on the road to democracy and make them more like us? Were American negotiators narcotized?

And yet the dramatic shifts taking place called for extrapolation into the future and a degree of circumspection. Many factors were at play in conditioning the economy. The decade that led up to 1980 saw FEDEX revolutionizing package and cargo delivery using overnight air express service in the US, a development that expanded to Asia and Europe. UPS joined in the competition and soon it was possible to pick a parcel from one point on the globe and deliver it on the opposite side of it in just 48 hours or less. That was not all. The Internet followed soon after. A pet project of the Defense Advanced Research Project Agency (DARPA) and the national Science Foundation (NSF), the Internet remained for a long time a plaything of geeks and a tool for persons carrying out research in elite university institutions until the browser entered the scene in 1995. And then it all changed - communication, business, organization, social life, and many more. Globalization entered popular vocabulary.

If there was a job that could be done or sent digitally anywhere in the world, a maximum of two seconds was required to accomplish it! Round the clock factories churned out optical fiber cables to fill in the trenches being dug in the streets of our cities and towns. Orders for switches, routers and all sorts of high tech gear rose as start-ups sprang up, in the words of one observer, like weeds after rainfall – Cisco, Google, Amazon.com and many others. The digitized jobs were carried along the optical fiber cables at the speed of light, bringing London, Rio, Singapore, Bangalore, Shanghai and other places virtually next door for businesses like accounting, designing software, analyzing brain scans and many more, including biotechnology and nanotechnology. Global production and supply chains became the order of the day. Countries in south-east Asia with export-led economic policies turned into low cost centers of production. Nothing could be more tantalizing for American businesses with maximization of profits through cost cutting. Why pay an American $20 per hour for a job that could cost just one quarter of that in India? And so air express delivery and the Internet ushered in the new phenomena of off shoring and outsourcing by moving production overseas and providing local services to Call Centers far, far away.

Americans quickly adopted the e-mail and websites for every taste and purpose, introducing along with them enormous demands for massive expansion of the Internet. The Asian tigers, Chinese dragons and Indian elephants were born, all copying Japan in one way or another by export-led growth even as Americans remained clueless about those nations' successes, harping on the needlessness of semiconductors and speaking disparagingly of Japan's Lost Decade, yet that country's auto companies continued to expand, "eating Detroit's lunch" and producing all of America's computer games, silicon, tools, chemicals and other items on which US production lines depended. It was an expensive joke but a well placed American official actually said the Japanese would sell us Toyotas and we would sell them poetry, prompting a chairperson of the Ford Motor Company to lament during a Congressional testimony:"I wish someone would tell me that manufacturing is not un-American".

Suffering from the onslaught of Japanese semiconductors, in 1992 Motorola looked for a means to reduce costs. Lured by the Chinese population of over one billion potential consumers, Motorola became one of the first US companies to move and establish a plant in Tianjin, paving the way for others to follow. In India where manufacturing was not a priority as in other east Asian countries, the large reservoir of educated, highly skilled, low paid professionals went for instant communication at Bangalore, New Delhi, Bombay and other cities ideal for outsourcing of Call Centers, office operations and businesses that could be digitized. China became the world's new workshop for global manufacturing and export of inexpensive goods with giants like Wal-Mart Inc. outsourcing there to the tune of $9 billion and as India became the location of choice for off shoring of services. All of these developments led to loss of jobs in the US, a loss aggravated by the vigorous promotion of domestic consumption as the engine of growth which went on to further promote more imports from Asian countries. Should American prosperity be built on borrowing and spending or on saving? Where were the benefits of the larger Chinese consumer market to offset the losses? Where were the exports to China to reduce trade imbalance and deficits? What good was a strong dollar if it stymied exports? The answers were blowing in the wind.

America was going through bad times. Homelessness, another hydra-headed face of the financial crunch, was on the rise. In a boom (good economy) housing costs usually go up and low rent apartments decrease in number or disappear altogether. In either case it is not good for the poor who are then left out. In a bust (bad economy), there is double trouble due to job losses and home foreclosures. The poor are hardest hit and at risk. This calls for Americans to embrace the spirit of St. Francis of Assisi and show a great interest in the poorest of the poor, show compassion and companionship by volunteering their time, their services and other resources to come to the aid of the estimated 700,000 homeless of America even if some Americans feel that there should be no free lunch since they themselves work hard for every mouthful. Such persons are often overheard shouting out "Get a job" or similar sneers directed at the destitute.

Skid row - human misery and debasement – had cropped up all over. Homeless and street people camped in parks, doorways, commons, libraries and burial grounds; their presence usually provoked mixed reactions of fear, excitement, fascination and curiosity among sociologists, anthropologists, psychologists, journalists, the clergy, and the common folk. Prince William, the future king of England spent a night out in the open, not as a stunt, but to highlight the plight of the homeless. Homeless people lead a life of mystery, misery, poverty and want. They can be seen gathering at Harvard Square for a free meal at a church or soup kitchen. Some carry out panhandling and in four hours can make $11.25 which they stash in a sleeping bag where they keep snacks salvaged from dumpsters. Boston has every conceivable panhandler in the hub, the most noticeable being an elderly drummer at Downtown Crossing who entertains with an intricate display of thud and clangor and a young man aged around twenty-five who pitches at a strategic corner of South Station for maximum exposure to the volume of humanity that goes by everyday, displaying his amateurish sign "Traveling Broke". He doesn't do much traveling since he is a daily sight squatting virtually on the same spot.

Most homeless persons keep their families and probably friends in the dark about their condition, having probably burned their bridges some where along the line, especially those who were born wealthy but got into their current state through alcoholism, drugs or gambling. Do they take a shower at all? The answer would be no, going by their physical appearance – a wandering individual with or without a cardboard bearing some crudely written message, a disheveled, windblown hair, an occasional smile displaying hair-splitting smile with rotten teeth. Do they brush their teeth or comb their hair? Good questions. And should homelessness be a society's problem or and individual's? For a capitalist society noted for the uneven distribution of wealth, there is nothing strange about destitution and homelessness even though this runs against the country's standing in the world. The amount of compassion shown to destitute persons struck by earthquake in Haiti or tsunami in the far east makes it difficult to understand that here at home minds can be so closed to equally destitute people. Or can it? Faced with some of such situations most people race through the age old philosophy that the world is a delicate balance between good and evil and so by performing just a simple kind act, it is possible to tip the balance in the direction of good.

Some uplifting stories do come out from among the homeless and destitute. One picked up a lost wallet with a good amount of dollar bills in it and for the next few hours he toyed with a wrestle of wills – whether to hand it in or use the money to procure Christmas presents for his kids. His sense of moral values won out and he took the wallet to the police from where its owner was traced. Out of gratitude and an equally high moral sense, the owner sought and got in touch with the homeless person, expressed appreciation for his acts and handed him some token of appreciation. Some how the story got to the local news media and the following days, Americans flooded that man with gifts in cash and kind. So overwhelmed was he that he eventually redirected some of the gifts to the shelter for the homeless where he lived. Another was picked from the gutter by a videographer and taken straight to a radio studio where he was offered a job as a type of disk jokey, and a house to live in! It is incredible how much good will exists in spite of all the gloom.

On the other hand, individual choices at various times in life cannot and should not be visited upon the whole society. Surely when people fail to find a sibling, a parent or even a friend for moments of such abject poverty and want, it reflects more on those individuals than on the society as a whole. The choices people make in life have consequences, including their estrangement from family and friends. Yes, indeed, some persons burn their bridges and feel ashamed to take back what they had regurgitated. But by far the biggest challenge for Americans is telling the real from the fakes.

The paradoxical coexistence of homelessness and empty homes in the capitalist landscape may be puzzling at first but it soon becomes clear that the economic meltdown brought about job losses which in turn resulted in unemployment and mortgage delinquency, forerunners of home foreclosures. Newspapers are usually full of statistics of homelessness in the land of the free and home of the brave –number and percentages that rise and fall, but little is mentioned concretely about the epidemiology of the scourge. Random giving to an occasional panhandler by the road side is good, but surely not good enough. One innovative idea mooted around is that municipal authorities ought to make it possible for a special type of parking meter to be set up specifically for collections destined to serve the homeless and help curb panhandling as a whole. But that is going to be a tough sell. The number of persons turning to panhandling, especially young, able-bodied individuals, is sobering. Resumes that portray persons as going from CEOs to panhandling and on to the job market must be quite common these days. President Barack Obama is on record as hailing the volunteers that make life a little easier for needy citizens; hopefully he will bring the full support of his office to this novel idea.

Some have suggested falling back on the good old formula of kindness which seems to have gone out the window. But how can we show kindness without making eye contact as a prelude to recognizing and acknowledging fellow citizens, before a handshake or small talk? Once upon a time it was the practice to reach out to a favorite teacher, tutor or mentor and pay tribute for the positive influences they had on us or the role they once played to change our lives. It used to be the practice to let someone in a hurry cut in the line in front of us. Imagine what a difference five minutes saved can make for such a person who might otherwise miss a flight, bus or a train. Going up or down an escalator is an ideal place to study the character of the persons in our environment. As in the parking lot it is easy to spot those in hurry, the laid back type, the considerate, the compassionate, those with altruistic genes, those who couldn't give a hoot about the next person the quick tempered and more.

Once upon a time it was fashionable to offer a little apology for stepping on someone's toes, acknowledging a job well done, especially by an employee or coworker, devoting some time to help a neighbor with raking leaves, changing a flat tire or plowing away snow or ice from sidewalks or driveways, especially where a property owner would be liable for prosecution if people fell and got hurt on their unplowed pathways. It used to be the practice to open the door at the approach of the mail man, acknowledge him/her and appreciate his/her services. It used to be the tradition to donate items of clothing to the Salvation Army. Items like eye glasses, bicycles, tricycles, cell phones, laptops and toys which are no longer in use but still occupying useful space in our limited apartment can change the lives of underprivileged children far on the other side of the world. Wealthy persons have created endowment funds for the benefit of schools, Boy Scout movements, the Red Cross, religious organizations and many other agencies that benefit from a 501 (c) (3) status. How nice to drop a quarter or two into a parking meter where someone's allotted time is about to expire! How nice to put one's money into a bank (trust funds) and instruct that the interests earned be channeled to benefit the organization of one's choice while the capital is retained in the account. Persons whose children have grown up and left the nest can elect to volunteer their time instead. Those who fly frequently and have accumulated unused flyer miles can donate these as well. It looks like our world can still be made a better place to live.

In matters of charity, the US is ranked fifth, way behind Australia, New Zealand, Canada, and Ireland. Those who have studied the matter say the reasons for such lagging in generosity and volunteering can be found in overwork that leaves less time and energy for such endeavors. Americans work longer hours and retire much later in life than the others. The beauty of giving to charity is that the donor benefits from tax breaks. The government encourages such an approach because it is a way of carrying out social policy by trying to use the tax code to promote positive and responsible behavior on the part of citizens. Wasn't it a bad idea to let hitch hiking die a natural death? Consider those wonderful volunteer women in Palo Alto, California who give of their time to watch the dangerous railroad crossing that had become the scene for a cluster of suicides for four teenage girls. What monetary value can society place on one extra life saved? There are so many ways to enrich lives and make the world a better place once more, starting with such modest attempts at wherever one finds oneself. Isn't it true, Kai Schmidt Saultau, German volunteer to the University of Buea, Cameroon, even if one runs into problems shining the light on local untouchables, their mediocrity and allergic reactions?

Perhaps Toni Morrison had this in mind when she alluded to people expecting Obama to provide all the answers. Obama could never solve all of America's problems alone. That is where a twelve-year-old boy came in. The young man, who shall remain nameless, was driving with his parents when, at some point, their car came between a Mercedes car on the right and a homeless person on the left. Both caught the boy's attention at the same time. Bingo! If in a world of HAVES and HAVENOTS, the HAVES could just half their fortune, the HAVENOTS would be able to eat too. The boy began pestering his parents with all sorts of questions. Could the Mercedes rider not help the homeless person? Why ride Mercedes cars when more modest cars like Toyotas could save money that would provide a roof over the poor? It is true that the Toyota Company was having a difficult time with gas pedals getting stuck to the floor and causing the cars to accelerate, even without the driver's control. *Still…* If people could just cut down on their lifestyles, so much money would be saved and made available to America's needy. He went on and on and on until his mother, out of exasperation, asked him what he intended to do about it. Without blinking the boy suggested that his parents should sell off their sumptuous mansion and help the homeless. And that is exactly what the couple did several months down the road. They sold their home and moved to a more modest house, passing on the rest of the proceeds to charity for the benefit of the homeless. What a way to uplift the spirits of an Obama besieged by the GOP and even members of his own Democratic Party!

Studies by two British scientists, Kate Pickett and Richard Wilkinson, had shown that with striking consistency, the severity of social decay in different countries reflected a key difference among them – not the number of poor or the depth of their poverty but the size of the gap between the poorest and the richest. Their study showed that the US topped the chart among developed countries for some social ailments – drug use, obesity, violence, mental illness, teen pregnancy, illiteracy and others. Quite an indictment of the richest nation on planet earth!

Other studies showed that there was a compassion boom, the amount of compassion in the nation having increased significantly, leading to increased bonding and people helping others to overcome the difficult times. Whether it was President Obama or the economic crisis, the effect was the same. A Parade magazine poll showed that Americans were working to improve their communities and the world at large. Public service was no longer a mere phrase or school requirement. People out of work were actually volunteering to stay connected to their communities, honing their job skills, supporting the causes they believed in at local or national levels, all a reflection of the strong belief that one person's action could improve the world and make a difference.

How did they do this? Many persons worked hard and taught their children the importance of activism, imparted lessons, and led by examples such as talking to the kids about important issues and causes, discussing their own charitable contributions or efforts, taking the kids to meetings or places where they volunteered, urging kids to follow role models, encouraging them to donate to causes of their choice. One father took his eight-year old daughter to a facility where the child just held the hand of a 95-year-old. Those at the end of life and out of public view do appreciate such human touch of affection! Simple altruism can make the world much better. Non-profit organizations that use the talents and resources of local universities to address local environmental problems are good examples of relaying what Mahatma Ghandi left with us – being the change that we want to see in others, starting from our own back yards, giving back to the communities that made us what we are today, make us feel better about ourselves, meet our moral obligations, fulfill a sense of duty.

## *Billionaires to the rescue?*

There are other innovative ideas. If a US billionaire could spend $35 million for a second trip to space in a Russian Soyuz capsule, it seems a nod in the direction of homeless people would not be too much to ask for in the name of compassion. As a matter of fact, Ralph Nader, the legendary consumer protection advocate and twice candidate for the presidency, thought the super-rich could and would save America. At 75 and embracing his new career of novelist, Nader said seventeen elderly, progressive and super-rich but demoralized Americans who decided that they did not want to leave the country the way it was (just grumbling and playing golf), were going to, in one year, turn around both big business and Washington D. C. (Ralph Nader's book *Only the Super Rich Can Save Us* is worth reading). With determination like that of William Henry Gates Sr.'s it is possible that President Obama might just get what he needs, short of taxing the wealthy 2% of Americans, to get America going again. The senior Bill Gates is convinced that those who have made their fortunes through society's input can and ought to give back something to the society, a view at variance with some of his peers determined to bequeath everything only to their kids, convinced that they owe the society nothing at all. Mexican tycoon, Carlos Slim Helu might have displaced Bill Gates and Warren Buffett from the number one and two slots in Forbes' ranking of the world's billionaires but America still commands the lion's share of this category of the super rich, including our own Michael Bloomberg of New York. China may have come forward as the one nation other than the US with the largest number of billionaires but she still lags behind what a determined US team can do to reverse the tide. Face book's Mark Zuckerman and his partner Dustin Moskovitz are joining the Warren Buffet and Bill Gates bandwagon and answering the clarion call to give away at least half of their fortunes to philanthropy. One can be modestly optimistic.

It will require quite some effort for the senior and junior Bill Gates, Buffets and other billionaires to bring on board all those who believe in a different creed as far as their wealth is concerned. Some have challenged why the rich should share their wealth, especially legitimately earned wealth, to help an overspending government balance its deficit. The school of thought which invests solely in the creed of fast growth, increase in quarterly earnings to raise the value of a company's stock and the notion that a CEO's core responsibility is to shareholders certainly misses the important lesson that from the Great Depression of 1929, corporations must be thoughtful institutions that consider the impact of their actions on all forms of stakeholders - employees, customers, suppliers, the community in which they are embedded and indeed the larger society and the government.

Some experts believe that a good chunk of our homelessness results from persons leaving their home states and flocking in to States like Massachusetts or California to take advantage of the better healthcare and health insurance systems in place. To get treatment for something like gender reassignment surgery (a sex change operation), apparently Massachusetts insurance would cover such things whereas elsewhere, there would be no such coverage. It is ironic, isn't it, that people leave their decent homes and come to endure a state of homelessness simply to benefit from healthcare facilities? The chronically homeless are better taken care of by Medicaid and given permanent living quarters which improve their wellbeing and are far less expensive for Medicaid than spending money on institutional care (hospitalization, shelters, detox facilities, jails). A policy of "housing first" is thought to be compassionate and economically more sensible.

29% of America's borrowers (not necessarily subprime mortgages) proved to be badly delinquent and 6% had already lost their homes to foreclosure. What on earth happened? Why were the subprime loans called the liars' loan? How did lying become an epidemic affecting so much of the US economy? Well, it turns out that 88% of borrowers were allowed to state their incomes instead of being asked to produce documents like pay stubs, W-2 or similar more credible proof of income. The lending industry called this type of stated income loans "liar's loans" because most persons lied to get them. A study examined 100 such loans in 2006 and found that 90 of them actually over-stated their real income to get the loans, inflating the real figure by as much as 50%. Thus people earning $3000 a month were given loans based on a supposed income of $4500! It did not take long to have the disastrous consequence of such blatant lying to be reflected on the subprime mortgage crisis. No wonder the breakdown of social norm that became a world-wide crisis!

The US economy generally had little tolerance for lying. In economic terms lying is inefficient, expensive, and increases costs. It is generally agreed that one hallmark difference between first and third world economies is the relative absence of lying in the former - a generalization disproved by Mohammad Yunus, who first introduced microfinance loans in his native Bangladesh and went on to earn the Nobel Prize for economics in 2006. Capitalism evolved in the direction of more trust, more transparency and less self-serving behavior, said a columnist for Forbes magazine in 2002. Such evolution did not take place because capitalists were naturally good people; instead it took place because the benefits of trust (being trusting and trustworthy) were potentially immense and because a successful market system taught people to recognize such benefits.

That was then. Like an epidemic, lying spread to all aspects of American life. It became the staple of sports men and women who take performance enhancing drugs and then lie about doing so. A good number of our superheroes shone because they took banned substances like steroids to enhance their performance, prompting one angry fan to say that they must now use their tainted millions wisely to enlist the help of public relations gurus who alone can coach them how to untangle the web of lies they have woven around them. Thanks to the power of television, the nation could actually live a typical liar telling Katie Couric of CBS an emphatic no one day only to turn around, admit and apologize the next day. Lying became the spice of politics as seen in the actions that led to the impeachment of Illinois governor Blagojevich. Senator Roland Burris who took up the vacant seat left when Barack Obama became US president did so by telling a number tall truths which came to light slowly. The number of Obama nominees who later withdrew for one reason or another testifies to the way lie telling had impacted life in America.

People failed to pay their taxes and lied about that until they got appointed to top positions of responsibility and then under the vetting spotlight of Congress, were forced to withdraw.

As housing prices fell 6.7%, foreclosure filings rose 23%. The subprime crisis exposed a financial house of cards built on too much borrowing and too little regulation. A credit freeze reflected that lending institutions had lost trust in each other. For eleven consecutive months there were job losses, leading to an unemployment rate of 6.7%, a fifteen year high. And retail sales in November were the weakest ever seen in thirty-five years. Dow-Jones fell more than 4500 points during the year. Surely the old market oligarchies were still doing business as usual but something was changing. New ways of seeing things were being presented to a burgeoning democracy through blogs.

Joseph Schumpeter, a great Austrian economist saw recession the way a naturalist sees forest fires, and called it capitalism's "creative destruction" at its most ferocious. During such lean times more adaptable companies and new industries push aside the less fit ones. Naturalists echoed the same idea when they asserted that forest fires were periodic purges that burned off dead wood and made room for new growth. But other economists challenged this view, contending that even in times of boom there was room for creative destruction, citing the turmoil in the airlines, music and newspaper industries during the past few years.

But economists generally agree that recessions do right economies that have lost touch with reality - culling unhealthy companies, exposing financial gimmickry, punishing groundless optimism and the rampant speculation that feeds it, such as the fanciful Internet ventures of the 1990s and housing over the past few years. Recessions help shrink trade deficits. The US imports far more than it exports, leading to an imbalance. In a recession the dollar value drops as well as household budgets, and so we buy less from abroad, thus narrowing our deficits. Also, the drop in the value of the dollar means our external export increases and helps shrink our deficits further. But reducing the US trade imbalance and the foreign debt that finances it are a necessary evil, a painful necessity.

At the time of the UK show, the aircraft industry came under what some aptly called "cloudy skies". As the cost of gas continued to soar (it was then $147/barrel), Washington decided to reopen bidding for the $3 billion air tanker contract for the US Air force, which had been earlier awarded to Arran Aerospace in Dinan, France, against Boeing's objections. The heavy duties had become a big liability – the superjumbo Airbus A380 as well as the midsize 787 Dreamliner. As oil prices went up, orders went down. Airlines were coping by culling their fleets, dropping flights, charging for checked bags and adding surcharges on to ticket prices to offset fuel outlays. There was palpable need for efficient planes to combat rising fuel costs. And so airlines were rethinking, postponing and canceling orders for new planes. In July 2008 the EU decided to require all airlines using European airports to buy pollution credits as from 2012. Innovation usually calls for green skies. Engine makers like Rolls-Royce, General Electric, Pratt and Whitney were urged to work harder designing new technologies to cope with the rising cost of fuel. Only the Middle Eastern countries like Abu Dhabi, Qatar, and Saudi Arabia were active in the ordering of new aircraft.

America's debt continued to mount. At one point its creditors included Japan ($585.9 billion), China ($800 billion), United Kingdom ($307.4 billion), OPEC Countries ($179.8 billion), and Caribbean Banking Centers ($147.7 billion). It is ironic, isn't it, that the UK had become America's third largest creditor? After World War I, the US emerged as the major global power and the UK declined in part because the US owned so much British debt. As the 43rd president of the US, George W. Bush incurred more national debt than his 42 previous predecessors in office. What a borrowing! The total Federal debt stood at $10.6 trillion, not including the $1.7 trillion in unsecured loans taken on for Freddie Mac and Fannie Mae and another undetermined amount for bail outs of Bear Stearns, AIG and the Wall Street mortgage mess as a whole. The entire Iraq war was financed by debt, including raiding the Social Security surplus and borrowing from China. If the US were a developing country, there would have been calls for the IMF and World Bank to step in and bail it out by imposing financial discipline of some sort; this painful option was skirted simply because the dollar remained the world's reserve currency. The US can print money to pay its debts, so the likelihood of default is remote. But experts warned about the global situation, especially as the financial crisis continued to dent the huge foreign exchange of those governments that had bankrolled the Bush spending spree.

Does the US owe too much? Yes and no. By some accounting the government is spending too much but by others, not enough. By January of 2008 the US public debt stood at $7.5 trillion or 53% of the country's total economic output (also called gross domestic product or GDP). Compared with Japan's debt-to-GDP ratio of 192%, Saudi Arabia's 20%, France's 80%, UK's 69%, Canada's 72%, India's 60% and China's 18%, the picture was not as bleak as some made it to be. That is the best measure of the country's economic health. The hope was that the figure should not rise to near 90%.

Once part of the British Empire, the US now enfolds its former colonial master beneath the wings of its own Empire (those in denial prefer hegemony), furnishing the UK with American weapons and expecting it to support US policy across the world, including invasions, with loyal rhetoric and even soldiery (Kathleen Burk: *Old World, New World: Great Britain and America From the Beginning).* What a reversal of fortunes in the space of a few hundred years! Extraordinary turnabout! What a history! In 1812 the US actually dared to go to war with Britain, determined to seize Canada while Britain's back was turned, fighting Napoleon Bonaparte. "The acquisition of Canada this year," wrote Thomas Jefferson, "as far as the neighborhood of Quebec, will be a matter of marching and will give us experience for the attack of Halifax the next, and the final expulsion of England from the American continent." But it didn't work out that way. In fact, to give President James Madison a black eye, the British even raided Washington D. C. and burned the White House. During Grover Cleveland's presidency the British War Office drew up a war plan to defend Canada against US attack by attacking America. Three British army corps had to invade the US from three different directions, one to march in from Montreal, and the other two to land at Boston and New York, with support from an Indian uprising. Unbelievable as it may sound, Britain's Tony Blaire pandered to the US president on the advice of Bill Clinton and much heartache accompanied such British submission to the US. Will David Cameron join in the dance? That is the million dollar question.

So what happened that all our economists missed the brewing crisis? Some were heard asking themselves "How can we do better?" According to Drake Bennett, a dense, invisible lattice connects house prices to insurance companies, job losses to car sales, the inscrutability of financial instruments that helped to spread the poison, the sense that the rating agencies and regulatory bodies were overmatched by events, the wild gyrations of the stock market over several past months. It was hard to understand what was taking place. An entire field of experts dedicated to the studying of the behavior of markets had failed to anticipate the biggest economic collapse of our time. Did we misread Adam Smith and his original message about the wealth of nations? Did his disciples misapply the free market idea? Where did things go off the rails? Of course it was clear even in Adam Smith's time that the notion of governmental non-interference in markets was a myth, the British navy ruling the seas and virtually dictating the pace of things, including trade, in the colonies and to rivals around the world.

Experts in the field from elite institutions and economic powerhouses (Harvard, MIT, University of Chicago, Columbia University, UC Berkeley, Princeton, Yale, and Johns Hopkins) scratched their heads in disbelief. They challenged long held views such as the stability of business cycles, resilience of markets, and the power of monetary policies. Every field from academic finance to academic macroeconomics went back to the drawing board. Some persons even thought the field of economics had grown specialized, abstruse and divorced from the way real world economies actually worked. Could future meltdowns be predicted? The world waited for answers.

Economists would be playing a central role in the Obama Administration – Federal Reserve, Council of Economic Advisors,

Treasury, and Economic Recovery Advisory Board. Leading economic figures like Larry Summers and Ben Bernanke would play pivotal roles. Americans asked to know why stocks earned more than bonds. What exactly was money any way? What accounted for bubbles such as the housing or dotcom? Could psychology and behavior economics help? Why did humans fail to act as rational, self-interested beings that economic models call for in thinking about the future, in susceptibility to peer pressure, overestimating abilities and underrating the odds of bad things happening? Why did we create the subprime crisis? How were we to explain the rationality of an investor in good times and blind panic in the bad? How could we better understand modern financial insanity, the deadly sin of greed, the dynamics behind the high-tech investment follies, the craze characterized by a herd mentality, the belief that most old-time businesses were going to be replaced by the Internet? How did our rating agencies fail us?

Slowly but surely the new field of behavioral economics may provide some answers, if not for past failures, at least to show the way forward. A new approach called nudging, championed by Richard Taylor, a behavior economist, opposes the econometric crunching of numbers and instead proposes the nudging of society. By a series of elegant choices, businesses can alter client behavior in ways that conventional economics could not. One version advocates the posting of the amount of carbon dioxide emitted by a car or a plant in a factory. Another proposes a well placed icon such as a fly at an airport landing site and a third puts forth software to check emotionally–loaded language in e-mails as a measure of civility of the users. Versions of this approach are already being tried out in Michael Bloomberg's New York as well as in Massachusetts and it is hoped that the practice will gather momentum once the outcomes become apparent. By posting the number of calories in a food item – a muffin, a doughnut, a hamburger – buyers are nudged to come to terms with what they are taking into their bodies and then conduct the wrestle of wills whether to go ahead or not. Dunkin' Donut franchises provide ideal settings for this type of exercise where the aroma of coffee is known to attract consumers the way nude bodies attract mosquitoes, the magical effect being felt as both smell and taste.

Warren Buffet's legendary capacity to make wealth placed him in a special category for President Barack Obama to nominate in his dream team of the American Recovery and Reinvestment Act (ARRA) to fix the financial crunch besetting the nation yet the money czar was not one of those shortlisted at all. Why? With Warren's Midas' touch and prolific and amazing knack for making fortunes, did he not deserve a place at Obama's cabinet? The boss of Berkshire Hathaway, estimated at $62 billion net worth by Forbes magazine, was next only to his good friend Bill Gates at that time. He was said to have shown aptitude for numbers and money making well back in his high school days when he earned $175 a month for delivery of newspapers, far more than his teachers earned. By the end of his high school he was worth $5000, his business being the reselling of pinball machines, refurbishing of golf balls and others. The man, reputed for attracting and compounding business opportunities and cultivating relationships, likens himself to a wet snowball on a long hill. His guiding principle in careers, businesses and life in general, according to this view, projects him as a nucleus on to which the snow can attach and grow bigger. Warren Buffet, the oracle of Western Capitalism, was known for his optimism even in the face of the financial crunch. Talking about Geico, a subsidiary of his Berkshire Hathaway, Warren Buffet said that he and his CEO felt like two hungry mosquitoes in a nudist camp, seeing juicy targets everywhere. When the National Bureau of Economic Research announced the end of recession in June 2009, Warren Buffet differed, stating that the nation was still going to get out of it, especially when real per capita gross domestic product returned to its pre-downturn level.

And did President Obama consider drawing inspiration from Muhammad Yunus, 2006 Nobel laureate in economics and founder of the Grameen Bank who had made it possible for his reliable, enterprising but poor native Bangladeshis to benefit from micro financing? Muhammad Yunus made microcredit the rock star in the world of international aid. Moved by the precarious life of the poor in his native Joba village, adjoining the university, the American-trained economics professor at Bangladesh's university at Chittagong, decided to make available small loans from his own pockets before proceeding to found the Grameen Bank, devising an algorithm to evaluate creditworthiness to those usually ignored by traditional banks. The 98% repayment rate of the unsecured loans was quite a success story in the antipoverty program even if skeptics at MIT's Jameel Poverty Action Laboratory in Boston have carried out their own studies challenging it. Thanks to micro financing, Kwabena Darko, a poor Ghanaian had taken a microloan and started what grew to become the largest poultry farm in his country, Ghana, going from very small to creating a business that transformed his country. What an inspiration! The young man made one major decision early in life – to buy a hen instead of a rooster. Hens do lay eggs which eventually hatch into chickens; roosters do not. The millennial generation needs such basic knowledge for sustainability of the economy.

Google has become a household name, thanks to two brilliant young men, Sergey Brin and Larry Page who started off, very modestly, their entire assembly of hardware barely fitting into a two-car garage and one or two spare rooms partly occupied by a ping-pong table. The story of how the twosome met and proceeded to launch a company that grew to become an important and very influential company on planet earth is worth reading. Those persons seeking to raise children into billionaires may consider looking into their profiles and how Montessori schools, scientific parents, intense family dinner debates and other factors contributed to bringing about such Silicon Valley wizards. Today, anybody who wants to know anything simply carries out a Google search and in less than a nanosecond the answer pops up – quite an advance over the weeks or months of tedious research that would be required at libraries.

There has been a move to hone and rethink models that describe the huge interlocking wheels of the US economy, to find a way to include the human tendencies that could bring things to a grinding halt. Important as banks have been, they have not been hot for a long time; recent events made them sexy again and it is clear that they will be attracting young talents in the years ahead. The financial crisis has reshaped debates, chastening believers in the self-correcting abilities of free markets, emboldening those who saw the need for more active government intervention. The long running debate had been seesawing back and forth from one crisis to the next. How should the younger generation react to the economic crisis? As the nation sought to rebuild its economic framework, young people were going to inherit whatever was left behind, especially the continued reliance on obsolete technologies, declining educational standards (some high schools were actually designated dropout factories!) and college attendance, rising unemployment statistics and more. How should the youth consider their careers in the bleak economy? Should they continue to tie their destiny narrowly to the dollar or should they head towards an appreciation of what directly invested in the community, what was considered broadly productive civic and economic activities? Is it enough to be impatient and angry, voting out the Republicans in one cycle, voting in Obama and the Democrats the next, only to return the GOP two years down the road because they did not turn the economy around? Where does such ping-pong politics lead to? How can the electorate expect a small fix to repair the big mess accumulated over a decade? Should the GOP "coup" of the 2010 midterm elections giving Republicans control of the House of Representatives be taken literally as voter disgust with President Obama and the Democrats? I wonder. If American voters are amnesic and so forgetful of the recent past, will they be equally myopic and not see into the near future? How will they vote in 2012 when faced with voting out a president whose healthcare reform, derogatorily called *Obamacare*, gave them a safety net during the hard economic times when they lost their jobs through no fault of theirs, a safety net they got against all odds, including the GOP's uncompromising NO and threat to repeal and replace the healthcare plan?

It is interesting when two odd currents meet. Americans are sometimes so confused they fail to distinguish between principle and privilege. And yet there is a fundamental difference between supporting an abstract principle and backing a campaign that just happens to come by at a certain point in time to mesh with one's interests and run parallel for a while. What happens when principle and interest no longer run parallel but clash head-on? Only time will tell as 2012 approaches.

The task was not made easier by the nature of economics itself. Is economics a science, like the other sciences, or not? In a room full of medical doctors, for example, given the broad outlines of an illness, chances are that they can easily assess and figure out a diagnosis and eventually a treatment as well. Today medical science can implant a number of stem cell lines into the spine of an accident victim, the product of years of painstaking laboratory investigations involving animals like mice, guinea pigs and others. The same is true with ivermectine use in human and veterinary medicine for the treatment of various helminthic infections. Not so with economics, especially when PhDs and Econ 101 brains are trying it out and dribbling the nation with their art. At the heart of the financial meltdown, one hundred economists invariably came up with one hundred different theories and policies. A classical Einsteinian insanity was the result with the unproven idea of giving tax breaks to society's richest 2% alleged to be responsible for job creation and growth – increased manufacturing and increased export – and yet over and over the US economy had refused to respond, necessitating the recent injection of stimulus money to help out where tax payers' monies in Medicare and social security reserves had been dumped into dubious schemes. The John Hancock Tower, considered one of Boston skyline's defining features and a modest effort at Manhattanization, was virtually auctioned for $20 million like an ordinary item on a flea market or yard sale and next door, Harvard university- America's oldest college, like MIT, its Cambridge neighbor - was responding to the dwindling endowment funds and the recession by scaling back construction work on its much trumpeted science center.

And yet close by, the Swiss food giant, Nestlé was responding by expanding and opening a new store called Nespresso, with plenty of fanfare while the film industry was making a head way into Plymouth County with projects for TV, movie, video game and other commercial productions that could make Massachusetts a movie center like Hollywood. Other miraculous feats of engineering were going up – highway buried beneath downtown, the world's longest tunnel extending to the harbor, a quarter-mile-long cable-stayed bridge gracefully spanning the Charles river. The tangle of construction work – multi-million dollar megaprojects involving condominium towers and big name developers and other real estate boom was designed to gentrify yet keep the city's diversity. The infrastructural network so confused one of Boston's attorneys that he went asking for help from a police officer how best to get to court. "Just commit a crime" answered the humorous officer good naturedly and in camaraderie known only to Boston's residents, before guiding the man to his destination. Gone were the sprawling, empty vacant buildings with crumbling ceilings and broken windows and graffiti and towering grass, which police officers used to test their Broken Window theory in crime prevention.

Economics is a strange science, if it is a science at all, for indeed the simplicities of the science have been dwarfed by the complexities of individual and collective human behaviors. Sophisticated computer modeling, Nobel laureates and lots of deep thinking could not quite explain how to make economies grow or why they even shrink. President Obama appointed Harvard-educated architect and New York City's Housing Commissioner, Shaun Donovan as the new boss of Housing and Urban Development to "bring fresh thinking, unencumbered by old ideology and outdated ideas to resolve the housing, mortgage and economic crisis that had dragged the nation into a recession". Paraphrasing Albert Einstein, the president said "we can't keep throwing money at the problem, hoping for a different result" and felt confident that Donovan would be the right person to rekindle the American dream of owning a home for low income persons and also to dispel the idea that the mortgage crisis was due solely to greedy lenders. Obviously the way forward would be to approach the old challenge of affordable housing with new energy, new ideas and a new, efficient style of leadership.

In a world where many were lamenting the bailout idea for homeowners unable to pay their mortgages, such words were very soothing, especially for those who had actually played by the rules, getting mortgages they could afford and making timely payments.

Letting the banks fail and foreclosures to continue was surely a recipe for spiraling from a recession into a depression, which no sane person advocated, even those with self-righteous indulgence. It is true that capitalism was built on rewarding risks and could not be changed overnight but the Obama administration had an economy to save, a task far loftier than the talk of "moral hazard", risk with bailouts or encouraging future irresponsible behavior. After all, whenever we made an investment, whether in real estate or 401(k), we took a risk and hoped to make a profit which did not always turn out so. That's life. Wasn't investing in a tax-sheltered annuity in order to supplement retirement income a form of speculation involving risks as well? Must the government bailout those who chose that option? Neither pure socialism nor pure capitalism is stable in the long run; a free market system with regulation, social benefits to ease the inequities of the free market should be the aim. It was clear to all that Ronald Reagan's tax cuts (the famous supply side economics) and increased spending had been a type of Ponzi scheme that brought America to its knees.

The Great Depression of 1929 devastated classical economics and in the years following, the British economist, John Maynard Keynes came up with new ideas, including the idea that individually rational economic decisions could add up to collectively disastrous consequences, that the "stickiness" of prices and wages could lead to long term unemployment and stagnation, that the government as a result had to step in to kick start the economy. On the other hand, Milton Friedman, a critic of Keynesianism and fervent advocate of unfettered free markets solved the seeming paradox of simultaneous inflation and high unemployment by proposing the solution of sharply restricting the money supply.

In such a difficult economic climate and given the relatively diminished size of the Republican Party, new thinkers were badly needed to come to the rescue. The party of ideas had become stuck in a wilderness and was looking for a way out. The challenge was enormous to keep the identity of the party of conservatives – people preferring the past to the present – yet show the country that Obama's stubbornly high popularity rating at the polls and the wide Democratic majorities in both houses of Congress were just a temporary setback. Disciples of Milton Freedman, the towering free market economist and Whittaker Chambers, the watchdog of Communism's dangerous seductions, were in short supply. Two costly wars - Iraq and Afghanistan - meant to spread freedom had made the American public understandably suspicious and the idea of the free market was badly in need of a reappraisal. So also was the ebbing issue of gay marriage. What should be the way forward for conservatism? Could social science help out and find a solution to some of those problems long couched in the language of morality? Could the free market ideology be unshackled from unpopular corporate policies that the society was saddled with? What could be done to win back the middle class, formerly enamored of small government but now quickly and readily warming up to Obama's idea of government intervention in the economy? Of course Obama only inherited what George Bush, a Republican president had started – the $700 billion of government money meant to bail out what had failed by free market definition. People's morbid fear of government was incomprehensible when viewed in the light of the very persons turning to government for bailouts, unemployment compensation, Medicare and others.

The new thinking tried to draw the fine line between conservatives falling out of love with business and falling back in love with the free market, urging that the market needed protection from business, not government. It was no easy task, given the Republican Party's long association with big business. How could capitalism then be saved from the capitalists? Italian–born economist, Luigi Zingales of the University of Chicago and his colleagues argued convincingly that powerful companies, when given the chance, work hand-in-glove with government bureaucrats to craft laws and regulations that protect them while limiting competition and transparency, the underpinning of capitalism! And that's exactly what had happened when financial service firms carved out for themselves regulations and took risks that damaged the entire financial system, ushering the current financial crisis. And they were quick to point out that both the Bush and Obama administrations had made matters worse by catering only for the 800 pound gorillas (the big banks and automobile companies) instead of rescuing first the workers.

Even Henry Paulson, former Treasury Secretary continued to be dogged by ethical issues that had occurred during his watch, especially since it came to light that as treasury secretary and the man entrusted with solving the financial meltdown, he had continued to have dealings with AIG, his former employer. He got two waivers – one from the White House and the other from the Treasury department- on September 17, 2008, one day after the government agreed to lend AIG $85 billion! That decision to prop up the teetering financial institution was quite circumspect and calls for a probe were targeting just that conflict of interest as an example of how the free market had been stymied by the cozy relationship between big business and government officials. It came as no surprise when Senate majority leader Harry Reid persuaded the no-nonsense bankruptcy scholar and Harvard professor, Elizabeth Warren, to take on the task of chairwoman of the Congressional Oversight Panel to monitor TARP and put some order into the business. The woman who was subsequently nominated "Bostonian of the Year" was seen as a square peg in a square hole, the one needed to bring sanity into what the banks did. It was hoped that she would shine some light on subprime mortgage companies and others in the financial sector who, in the words of Boston Globe magazine's Charles Pierce, "bury their brigandage under a blizzard of sub-paragraphs and dependent clauses."

No wonder the Cash for Clunkers program became so popular. Congress quickly voted an additional $2 billion dollars to fund it. Persons with gas guzzling old cars and trucks (clunkers) were urged to exchange them for a rebate of up to $4500 and newer, more efficient cars that gave more mileage per gallon of fuel. What better way to fight climate change and environmental pollution! That at last was one way to let the ordinary Joe feel the impact of government bailout and it was hoped that the formula would be extended to the thorny issue of home foreclosures.

Other thinking focused on the plight of the family, rather than the individual, since the family is the building block of society. W.

Bradford Wilcox, a social conservative, cited the breakdown of the family as a serious problem for the nation. He remarked that kids not raised by their married biological parents were more likely to drop out of high school, be depressed, commit suicide and end up in jail or become teen mothers –all liabilities to society. He placed the blame squarely on the decline of the two-parent family, bringing about increased economic inequality and child poverty. According to him, two old taboos – divorce and single parenthood - had lost most of their force and gay marriage was only a tiny problem. Indeed in support of this the Schott Foundation that carries out research and develops policy came up with the sobering statistics of 1.2 million black male students dropping out of high school each year with nowhere to go but the prison pipe line or to face the consequence of poor education the rest of their lives.

To fix these, the thinking was that tax structures should be so configured that marriage becomes more attractive than mere cohabitation. The nation toyed with various policies, presented as carrots and sticks to influence fatherhood, focusing on unmarried and /or nonresident fathers, trying to tease, force, manipulate or nudge them into greater financial accountability (wage garnishing for child support purposes), marriage, emotional involvement with their kids – anything to reduce the incidence of single motherhood and welfare use as public assistance. Lowering the amount of benefits, requiring employment of single mothers, penalizing subsequent pregnancies by capping financial disbursements, denying benefits to teen mothers not living with their parents, denying assistance where single mothers failed to reveal the paternity of their kids and assigning the states the right to collect child support to replenish state coffers – are all methods aimed at increasing the cost of single motherhood and lifestyles of welfare queens. The new thinking envisaged easing the burden on society and the tax payer. The weight of the burdensome dynasty obsessed with the vision of "cradle-to-grave welfare state at tax payer expense" was acutely being felt and resented. Most often children brought up under such defective conditions became society's future nightmare as overindulgent parents failed to draw the line between acceptable and unacceptable behavior, thereby depriving kids of critical learning experiences in life. Overindulgence in which parents declare that everything is OK, when indeed it is not, create intractable problems for later life when kids leave the home cocoon and venture into the world beyond.

The plight of women is rather delicate. In spite of all the talk about gender equality and the large number of women in the labor force, women are still under-represented in the technical fields. One reason often offered is that women are more interested in less geeky environments (computer and Star Trek stuff) than men. Another is their reluctance to relocate where expanding companies want to deploy new hires. Under the circumstances, balancing the work force can pose some intractable problems for everybody. Women too face the problem of delivering babies and raising them, something men do only casually. The last time I visited a stay-at-home mom, I came away convinced that child raising is a full time job. Some actually call it a second shift job. For the short time of my visit, I was witness to an eight-month baby screaming to be fed, a two-year old pitching a fit for not being allowed to open the door for his dad, and a seven-year old protesting against having fish again for dinner. Poor mom! She was visibly exhausted. Taking a full time employment with that amount of domestic challenge would be suicidal; it becomes understandable why the career and promotion would suffer a setback even if staying at home is not a bed of roses.

But the cost in family life can be quite heavy especially for persons like the husband in the above family, a gentleman we shall simply call Bob. Entering the house that day Bob was welcomed by his seven-year-old. Before he had time to sit down and relax, his son asked him how much he earned per hour. Stunned, the gentleman momentarily ran out of words. Although he had always prided himself as the father of a prodigy, he hardly expected such a question from his boy. Was the boy in cahoots with his mother over some mischief? All the same he managed to compose himself and tell his son "$50". If he was surprised by the boy's question, what followed next discombobulated him. Bob Jr. rushed to his room where he had stashed away all his money gathered from various sources – birthday presents, trick-or-treat leftovers and others. Within a few minutes he was back with a handful of dollar bills which he handed over to his father. "What is it, son?" the dad inquired. Scratching his head in a rather mischievous manner, his son said that that was pay for one hour of his time so that he could spend with the family. Bob took that as a wake up call and decided to do something about balancing his work and family life. Among other things he decided to prioritize his time, waking up everyday at six o'clock, sitting down to examine his thoughts and inspiration, answering his e-mails and making a check list of what needed to be done during the day, leaving him ample quality time to spend with his family.

Complicating this picture is a study by Basic and Applied Social Psychology which seems to indicate that when wives take on husbands' last names, they tend to earn less because they are judged more dependent and less ambitious, even if more caring and kinder than those who keep their maiden names. But the most powerful argument is that men and women are not equally attracted to science or mathematical disciplines; where women display an interest, they can hardly be held back. Studies by the US Bureau of Labor Statistics show that more women are getting degrees than men, an outperformance that coincides with their increasing opportunities in the work force due to job shifts from male-dominated manufacturing in factories towards a service economy in offices.

Most Americans agree that for the US to maintain its edge, it needs to recognize and accommodate the fact of the world's interconnectedness. Bucketfuls of deep red iron ore from mines in Australia are loaded into trains which transport them to a port from where a Chinese ship carries them to Japan to be refined into steel ingots and then converted into Toyota Corolla cars in a factory. Thousands of such cars are loaded into giant ships across the Pacific Ocean to Seattle, Washington for distribution across the United States. A Norwegian passenger liner then carries some of the cars back to Australia to be used by the miners who worked the iron ore. Such a chain of operations involves so many of the world's people – Australians, Chinese, Japanese, Norwegians, Americans and probably more. Some call it the butterfly effect.

For too long history had concentrated on ledgers, letters and log book entries about the land borders of the United States, leaving unacknowledged the vast impact of the Pacific Ocean on the nation. Thanks to sea-going transportation which antedated air travel and automobiles, China provided much of the labor for the railroads that tied the country together and the Korean War was largely responsible for spawning the military-industrial complex. And there is no doubt that engineers and programmers from East Asian nations fueled the technology booms.

A similar chain of events can be traced linking people who never ever stopped to think that they were linked in so many invisible ways – globalization's reach – melting ice in the Arctic, a result of carbon emanating from pipes and smokestacks, US investment bank Lehman Brothers, a major firm toppled in the financial crisis that shook the world from Iceland to Dubai, the election of Barack Obama, a man whose life was shaped in Hawaii, Kenya and Indonesia and the US. Domestic problems in Bolivia, South America can result in the shortage of cell phone batteries because that country has the world's largest reserves of lithium which is vital to small batteries. The war in Joseph Kabila's Democratic Republic of Congo impacted our production of jets as Congo was the leading exporter of cobalt, a metal crucial to jet engines.

Walk up to any two love birds cavorting on Boston Commons or strolling along the Rose Kennedy Greenway and ask them if they know Laurent Gbagbo. Chances are they may think of some newly discovered planet or so. Try asking about Alassane Ouattara and the reaction will be an equal blank. Or they may think you are some type of jerk, disturbing their quality time together, time to talk better things like the rivalries between NE Patriots and New York Jets, NE Patriots and NY Yankees, Celtics and Lakers, Green Bay Packers and Pittsburgh Steelers. With Valentine's Day around the corner they will probably be anxious to get going on their frolicking. Follow them discreetly and watch them cross over to South Station, approach *Au Bon Pain* or enter *Pizzeria Regina* for some Italian treat. They may go up the mezzanine and enjoy some quiet moment away from the crowd. Continue to observe and they soon emerge at

Rosie's bakery for more treats –chocolate bars topped with roasted pistachios. Oh, they are awesome! But the price! Why have candies become so expensive? At this point, if you approach them and tell them Alassane Ouattara is responsible, they probably will open frog wide eyes and look at you as some sociopath. Go ahead and add that Ouattara is the man who won Ivory Coast's presidential election but was blocked from entering the presidential palace because the incumbent, Laurent Gbagbo refused to hand over, and so he got mad and used the clout at his disposal and placed an embargo on cocoa leaving the ports of his country. Ah!!!!!!!!!!! It begins to make sense! The distance between Ivory Coast and America suddenly narrows down. That's why chocolate is so expensive. Baule-speaking Ivorian farmers have been blocked from harvesting and selling their cocoa and so the world is starved of an important raw material. Ah!!!!!!!

The unsung heroes of the Congo notwithstanding, the world cannot so soon forget that it was from the uranium mine of the tiny savanna village of Shinkolobwe that the deadly cargo was obtained and dropped over Hiroshima and Nagasaki to end WWII in 1945. If quiet diplomacy were not used to cool things down between India and Pakistan, the world risked the threat of nuclear annihilation since both nations possess atomic weapons. Next door to the DRC, Kenya is a country which once derived its wealth from the tourism industry and the athletic prowess of its long distance runners. The tourist haven comprises the legendary travel destinations like Zanzibar island, Serengeti national park, Mount Kilimanjaro, Lake Victoria, the Rift Valley, Olduvai Gorge, those serenades of whooping hyenas, dawns of bubbling bird songs, softly calling lions, hippos and crocodiles partially submerged in water, leaving only eyes, ears and noses above the surface and lots of other attractions that brought in foreign currency into the region. Flower cultivation for export is also another important industry in Kenya. The East African nation could proudly add to its money-making machinery simply by using the Obama connection. America's 44th president traces his roots to Kenya and people will certainly be interested to visit and find out more about the man who made history by becoming the very first black American president. Safari business is on the way to getting a good boost and *matatu* (bush taxi) operators can smile broadly. And who knows, those enterprising Cameroonian operators of *NordCamtour* might just wake up from slumber and go for their share of the pie by rekindling the diminished Kenyan connection, opening up new vistas for the teeming mass of the unemployed..

It is often easy to argue that technology trumps the need to go overseas as most young persons prefer to see it, since most things can be found on the Internet these days. But what could be better than knowing the people who are different from us, in trying to understand their customs and beliefs and other systems unfamiliar and foreign to us? We are all passengers on the same vast planet, so it is essential to travel around and see the intricacies of humankind for oneself, to achieve the kind of wisdom necessary to be fully informed citizens and participants in the world. Authorities who frustrate travel at whatever level are not doing the world any good. Over 100 years ago, Samuel Clemens (Mark Twain) a river boat pilot on the 3000-mile Mississippi said it best: "Travel is fatal to prejudice, bigotry and narrow-mindedness". Such a message, from someone who enabled us to picture the magnificent Mississippi, from its start as a cold, tiny crystal clear stream in northern Minnesota to its warm muddy merger with the Gulf of Mexico in Venice, Louisiana, a picturesque and varied journey going through forests, prairies, swamps, towns and cities, is still true today.

Some of the most profound policy changes in recent US history had been achieved by presidents elected in times of great economic stress after voters rejected their predecessors. Franklin Delano Roosevelt (successor to Herbert Hoover) pushed through the New Deal with job programs, Social Security and regulation of the stock market during the great depression of the 1930s. Ronald Reagan, who succeeded President Jimmy Carter, introduced tax cuts, deregulation, tight monetary policies and military buildups, following a period of high inflation and stagnant growth. Reaganomics - *far from being a solution, government is the problem* - became a creed with far reaching implications in America. Doris Kearns Goodwin, a historian, states that what happens in times of crisis is that the president can mobilize the sentiment of the country in a way that goes over the natural competing interests in Congress and the smaller obstacles in the way of change. Disciples of Reaganomics who utter strident cries for governmental nonintervention fail to recognize the fact that some amount of government involvement is necessary to balance the excesses of the private sector. This is far from asking government to run people's lives as some Americans fear. Persons who blindly negotiated bad loans with banks (bought homes with no down payment from banks willing to write risky, often bogus loans) are today blaming the government, Uncle Sam and Barack Obama when things failed. But when the going was good, government was anathema. They wish to have it both ways! An angry voter assailed his congressman in a town hall meeting with "keep government hands off my Medicare" obviously ignorant of the government's role not only in creating Medicare but also keeping it going. A prominent political leader like John Boehner who will be leading the GOP in 2011, even went to the extent of announcing "If you want your healthcare to run like the post office, just turn it over to the government". What to make of those who condemn the government in one breath and lavish praises on the excellent care provided by the VA (Veterans Administration) hospitals in the next? And of course AIG, Chrysler and Bank of America are back in business and doing well, thanks to government intervention to rescue them from failing!

Former Alaskan governor and running mate for Senator John McCain in the 2008 presidential election, Sarah Palin became a popular and ubiquitous television figure as well as the face of the anti-tax Tea Party, tossing populist rhetoric here and there, shouting her lungs out about government intrusion into peoples' lives instead of standing back to let American ingenuity do its magic. It looked like organized society had lost appeal for her and her staunch admirers. To let the individual decide sounds really fantastic indeed. Ms Palin thinks government is on a spending spree, making Americans work 100 days out of the year for government before starting to work for themselves and so elected officials must be reminded that government should be working for the people rather than the people working for the government. This puts the famous JFK declaration on its head!

Voters who swore in her name must be wondering whether to go for the Kennedy message or that doled out by the flamboyant Sarah Palin. Understandably the tax payer was upset over burdensome taxation and the wanton wastes often laid bare in pork barrel projects and many other sweet deals sandwiched into important legislation to please leg-dragging senators. But to take this type of reasoning to its logical conclusion is quite worrisome indeed. The idea of government getting out of peoples' lives is a tall order, a recipe for anarchy and disaster of incalculable proportions.

To put aside organized society and its many encumbering structures so that people give unfettered expression to their freedoms simply means that Americans can cohabit the way they want, marry or not, according to their whims, produce children or not depending on their moods, abandon the children if and when it suits them. Such views make it all right for government to sit idly by and watch sister murder brother, and later colleagues at university, with mother giving tacit support by calling it an accident or pleading insanity according to her standing in society, or even denying that it ever happened. Such a state of affairs will make it possible for a son to murder his father and benefit from total denial given by a loving celebrity sister or mother. When enterprising individuals bilk spouses, companies or other organizations of large amounts of money and take off to some distant shore or tax haven to live prodigally and then to return home impoverished and ready for welfare and food stamps, that should make supporters of antigovernment and anti-tax campaigns happy. From the lens of the Tea Party, it seems OK to argue that one should not pay taxes for someone else's child to get an education or for someone who prefers to sit all day long on the couch and watch Dr. Phil, Oprah and the rest.

Education in general and civic education in particular would help fill some of the lacunae in such reasoning, but then when people drop out of school prematurely to pursue the dollar, such useful pursuits are forestalled. Ask the average American who discovered the Internet and you will get every conceivable answer – Bill Gates, Face book, Google, Microsoft, AT&T, Steve Jobs, Intel and a host of others – but not the government or better still, the partnership between the government and DARPA and the NSF. Believers in Reaganomics, who come in many colors, tend to treat government with disdain and condescension, barely tolerating anyone who comes as a messenger from the government. The most mirthful laughter is generated in an audience of such persons as soon as anyone tries to suggest government intervention of any kind. Yet they are virtually positively schizophrenic about government action. The very persons who don't believe that the government can do anything to be helpful, who perceive their government as a blundering idiotic bureaucracy that screws up everything, a power-hungry oppressor bent on controlling their lives to the finest detail, are the same persons who hail the EMH (efficient market hypothesis), express exaggerated fears of government rationing healthcare or completely taking it away. The ambivalence that says no to regulation in matters of the finance industry or healthcare but a resounding yes in matters of illegal immigration, gay marriage, medical marijuana, legalized suicide escapes proponents of such things. It is unthinkable to pay for others. No, it just cannot happen. Yet simply targeting the removal from office of all those out there in Washington without any notion of a credible alternative is no different than when young military officers organize a coup d'état, get to office and then realize that they have nothing but the AK-47 to offer the people!

While it may seem logical to concentrate on educating one's own child rather than some stranger's child, according to this logic, the truth is that there are persons who have no kids, yet pay their taxes to enable the government meet its many obligations to the citizenry. Are we not all beneficiaries of by far more than we pay to the government in taxes? As an organized society, we choose to live together and survive together, a life style quite different from earlier selfish lifestyles in the wilderness, caves and other hideouts. With organized society altruism of a higher order was inevitable. Why revert to an earlier lifestyle of the Dark Ages? After the CBO (Congressional Budget Office )put out an estimate stating that President Obama's healthcare reform bill recently passed into law, together with the House reconciliation, would cut down the federal deficit, members of the Tea Party rejected it. According to them, their commonsense trumped the education, job experience and total number of years put into studying such issues by all those in the CBO!

The contradiction inherent in Sarah Palin's clamor for small government escapes many supporters of her cherished movement. Every American wants to grow by working hard. If one takes any unit of growth – the individual, family, company, community or the country as a whole – it is inescapable that growth means multiplying the number of functional subunits involved, with economic and social ramifications. Given also our propensity to cross the line, imagine just what it will take to keep this vast expanding array to toe that proverbial line! Should President Obama make the government smaller by cutting down the number of patrol men along our 700 mile border with Mexico, the number of policemen in our crime-ridden cities, the number of firemen that respond to our numerous city fires or the forces fighting our two wars? Just where should the cut start and end?

Such thinking continued to stymie President Obama's efforts at healthcare reform and it would come as no surprise if they torpedoed those efforts to put things right only to turn around later and blame the government again. Yes indeed, the greed of the private sector plus the thoughtlessness of the public are main ingredients for our healthcare crisis. Private industry looks only at its own immediate interests. Why sane Americans would ask to entrust the funding of an essential service like health care to the private sector defies logic, knowing that it will use whatever role it is given to thwart the public goal and bend it to its own needs. Insurance companies do not make money by paying claims; they do so by denying payments to those in need. It is for this reason that most people argue that healthcare should be a matter between patients and doctors, not the patients and insurers, an argument that unfortunately fails to take cognizance that we crossed the Rubicon long ago!

How did this apply to President Barack Obama concretely? A president has more power during a crisis when elected to fix something – push through a variety of programs when he is strongest and when the fear of not backing him is greatest. Some felt that

Obama should seize the opportunity presented then to harness the price-setting power of Medicare's single payer model to increase efficiency and reduce the cost of health care and insure Social Security's long lasting solvency. For too long, Republicans had held back fixing Social Security, because they were fixated on individual accounts.

Fortunately Rahm Emanuel, the man President Obama had appointed as Chief of Staff indicated that rule #1 is never to allow a crisis go to waste, it being an opportunity to do big things. Thus the President foresaw a massive and costly economic stimulus package (at that time estimated at $850 billion) aimed at job creation. He also foresaw expanding national service programs such as AmeriCorps as well as identifying wastes and programs that did not work. Under George W. Bush, federal bureaucracy had grown tremendously due largely to outsourcing of contracts, especially national security and counterterrorism.

One of the earliest lessons new immigrants learn on landing in Uncle Sam's country was that there is no free lunch. An invitation to a free lunch, even if one's name is not Monica Lewinsky, should be treated with much trepidation, knowing that people are often wired to tape all conversations. Yet everywhere immigrants went, they were invariably confronted with free sample, free trial offer, free checking, free this, free that and to top it all, His Excellency George Walker Bush Jr. added a free $600 from Uncle Sam! Too good to be true! And when ever anything appeared too good to be true, it was logical to apply Professor Xiao-Mein's rule to it to show that it was probably not good enough. The economic stimulus package of $600 sent by the IRS to each person declaring income tax for 2007 could not be free money at all. Government could not shell out billions of dollars just to "stimulate" the economy. Or could it? Alaska's governor Sarah Palin, herself a beneficiary of a much talked about wardrobe as John McCain's running mate during the 2008 presidential election warned "Beware of accepting government largesse" as she stepped down from the governor's chair eighteen months ahead of the end of her mandate. Her book, ***Going Rogue*** also criticized the way she was saddled with a $50,000 tab for her vetting to become the vice-presidential candidate although this was contested by the McCain team. Having learned the bitter lesson of borrowing and spending, why would any sane American want to go on a spending spree then? It just didn't add up at all. There must be a Keynesian catch-22 somewhere! (As suspected, the IRS eventually demanded and got back its money from wage earners during the 2008 tax season, thanks to the yearly ritual of filing form 1040). So why was there such fuss then about the titans paying back Uncle Sam's bailout instead granting their employees fabulous bonuses?

There were palpable fears that one effect of the downturn would be to sap universities of money and weaken their ability to play a major role in the nation's development. Among America's economic blessings, research universities come on top of the list because of the role they play as centers of innovation to provide the US with an edge in fields ranging from biotechnology to fuel cells. E. Gordon Gee, President of America's largest university, Ohio State with 50,000 students and a budget of $4 billion agreed, adding "We are the economic stimulus. The future of the nation is going to be ideas-driven, so colleges are the smokestack industries of tomorrow, in need of money infusion into intellectual infrastructures such as the National Science Foundation, the national Institutes of Health - the best way to focus on support for those things that will be important to knowledge economy". And he was right.

The Obama administration placed a high premium on education but the contours of his policies were still not clear. Education in general and education of women in particular would be looked at very critically. Educated mothers, especially the stay-at-home moms, provide basic core education for their kids, communicate with them, and prepare them physically and emotionally for school. Every year schools waste millions of dollars in remedial and behavioral intervention programs for kids who come ill prepared to learn. It is a cruel irony indeed that it is the tax dollars of working mothers which go to fund such remedial programs. What a way to maintain life's equilibrium! In difficult times it is important to graduate students with the problem-solving, communication and collaboration skills so necessary in the competitive work place ahead. Law makers need to take note of this as they make the necessary painful cuts. Boston tops the nation's most intelligent cities, according to Daily Beast website survey, coming well ahead of Philadelphia and New York and is a pioneer as well as a paradox in education. Greater Boston is home to more than one hundred universities and is on top in per capita graduate degrees. The number of PhDs per square mile surely beats the rest of the country yet boys tend to lag behind girls in the education effort. Something is not right. According to some experts, for every one hundred boys that graduate from high school, there are one hundred and fifty girls, prompting some to advocate the scrapping of coeducation institutions and the reestablishment of single sex institutions to reduce the intimidating climate and enhance the performance of boys. With students reading fewer than four hundred pages a week as a result of obsession with electronic gadgets, one can only imagine what the future holds for learning. But this is a debatable proposition. Recently research data from the US Census Bureau showed that one out of every five black males between 20 and 24 years of age was neither in school nor at work, confirming the findings of the Schott Foundation report. That is a sobering statistic, especially when viewed against the background of a Federal fiscal deficit of $1.35 trillion dollars provided by the nonpartisan Congressional Budget Office –quite a big figure comparable only to big blame game going on in Congress.

Something is very wrong with education in America and it has kept concerned citizens worried. How can citizens communicate and proceed to solve common problems if they lack the necessary educational tools? As someone aptly put it, communication takes place in a context of shared, unspoken knowledge and values; in the absence of these only chaos can reign. To educate kids for the twenty-first century, there ought to be a pride of place for critical thinking, reading and comprehension, writing, the ability to ask pertinent questions and other skills. It would appear that a cabal of professorial gurus comfortably entrenched in educational departments throughout the country is bent on destroying teachers and the noble work they are doing in education, exercising intellectual monopoly in a free society, politicizing the principle of common content in the curriculum. American education cries for serious reforms in a number of areas. Those who know are unequivocal that in addition to recruiting and paying teachers commensurately, letting the real professionals with hands-on experience develop the curriculum and standards, the school year needs to be lengthened by cutting down long summer vacations that are a relic of agrarian economies and that attention should be paid to classroom discipline by promptly removing disruptive and disrespectful elements.

It is sobering that a smart-looking young woman can emerge from fame and adulation on *"American Idol"* only to enter ignominy on Fox News program where she cannot answer a question like "Which European country has Budapest as its capital?" Her answer *"I thought Europe was a country?"* or her nonplussed remark when informed that the country is Hungary *"That's a country? I've heard of Turkey. But Hungry?"* speaks volumes about the degree of ignorance, cultural illiteracy and their glamorization in modern-day America, the net result of child-centered theories of pedagogy even as television projects more and more of Jerry Shore, Niede Polizzi and others. Former Alaskan governor, Sarah Palin's escapades also took her to Fox News where she insisted on being present for the Tea Party convention from which many were distancing themselves, prompting a blogger to quip, "Hey, she chooses to appear on Fox, she chooses to speak at the tea party Convention, she knows well where she shines best without her brain being questioned". The laughter industry was having a great time. In spite of the laughter she generated along the way, the unstoppable Ms Palin used that forum to lash out at and satirize President Obama's administration's way of handling the botched airplane bomber, Umar Farouk Abdulmutallab, saying "What America needs to fight terrorists is a Commander-in-Chief, not a professor of Law", prompting one of the president's top advisers to complain bitterly about playing political football with matters of national defense. She still won the poetess's ovation all the same.

It is regrettable that fourteen year-olds should have the performance level of seven-year-olds, which some are peddling as comedy. The present emphasis on critical thinking devoid of facts is a fallacy. Those with hands-on experience agree that the education of children needs specific knowledge guidelines (core curriculum devoid of some of the electives of public schools) and challenging tests to go with them. Standardized testing (SAT, ACT) without these misses the point if it is not associated with smart programs like KIPP (Knowledge is Power Program), OLPC (One Laptop Per Child), SMART (Shaping Minds Around Reading and Technology), ROR (Reach Out and Read) which help improve reading to maximize scores on the above tests, improve long term reading prospects and kick people out of ignorance.

America needs to bridge the achievement gap between it and the rest of the world and within the US, between privileged whites and disadvantaged African-American and Hispanic children. Complicating the problem is the often conflicting views of all manner of experts. Some advocate paying kids to stay in school, an idea others consider absurd, given that education is free in the first place. How on earth do you pay a child to take something like a birthday present which is free to begin with? Psychologists are quick to draw attention to the danger of using such extrinsic motivations as financial incentives which only serve to kill the intrinsic ones – learning for its own sake. Reading has been pushed to the back burner by new technological devices! Even those pursuing sports cannot downgrade reading. It is always a pleasure to listen to the Williams sisters interviewed over radio and television networks, answering questions intelligently and expressing themselves so effortlessly. The same cannot be said of other sportsmen and women, especially those who failed to put a priority on academic work.

When President George W. Bush addressed immigrants and those out of work, asking them to study the English language in order to get good paying jobs, it sounded so logical, meaningful and convincing. Some of them set out to do just that. But with time the message turned rather hollow and some immigrants shook their heads in disbelief, wondering whether to pick quarrels with the message or the messenger. For indeed, the quality of the president's language and the message could hardly be said to convince that a better command of English was a prerequisite for better paying jobs when he was notorious for declarations such as:

*The important question is how many hands have I shaked? They misunderestimated me. I know how hard it is for you to put food on your family. I don't care what the polls say about the economy. I don't. I'm doing what I think what's wrong. I don't want nations feeling that they can bully ourselves and our allies. I want to have a ballistic defense system so that we can make the world more peaceful, and at the same time I want to reduce our nuke-ular capacities to the level commiserate with keeping the peace. We cannot let terrorists and rogue nations hold this nation hostile or hold our allies hostile. We just had some really good news out of Yugoslavia. I'm especially pleased that Mr. Milosevic has stepped down. That's one less polyslavic name for me to remember. The legislature's job is to write the law. It's the executive branch's job to interpret the law. Laura and I don't realize how bright our children is until we get an objective analysis.*

Malapropisms like these did not go unnoticed to comedians and new immigrants. When George Bernard Shaw observed that England and America were two countries divided by a common language, he had in mind one type of rivalry, an undeclared competition between the Queen's language and America's other lingo. Here was another to add to those created by rap musicians and their hip hop cousins. The president's version, with a Texas chuckle, only compounded the problem. Coming along with his "No Child Left Behind" message, this left people wondering. Of course language is power. The words we use can move people to tears or to laughter. They can inspire people to great deeds or urge them to mob action and even start a war – George Bush's crusade or *axis of evil*. Our words reflect our preoccupation with the times, our cultural values, our history, pictures of what we value the most. Surely the leadership we have, more than anything else, ought to reflect these values. Our ever present Sarah Palin is fast catching up with former president George W. Bush in dyslexia or malapropism, proudly dishing out invented words here and there, the latest being "*refudiate*" which prompted one seasoned observer to offer the spicy remark that he was in total *agreeingment* with her right to add to our "*vocapillary*" in the spirit of *Shakespearesian* word play, using creative language to underscore her *integrality*. Who can beat poetic license of this type?

Less than 24 hours after the attack on New York city's world trade center, NATO invoked article 5 of the North Atlantic Treaty declaring that the action against the WTC and the Pentagon were in fact hostilities against all 19 member states of NATO. The White House began talking about the "global war on terror". Addressing the joint Houses of Congress, President Bush talked about the world coming together to fight a new and different war. But to most of the Muslim East this looked like a very old war indeed. The West has always viewed Islam as being dedicated to the destruction of the West; the Islamic East saw the "war on terror "as one against their religion and way of life.

There was an aura of déjà vu in the Muslim world. President George W. Bush of the US did not only declare war on terrorism, he went on to make the dangerous statement "This crusade, this war on terrorism is going to take a while." That single word *"crusade"* punctuated by expressions like "axis of evil" and "either you're with us or against us" did it! It caused an uproar in the Muslim world and he was forced to backpedal as White House staff took pains to apologize for his use of the expression. Such a slip, such an innocent gaffe struck a raw nerve in the Arab world where it was seen and confirmed as the worst fear of all – global war emerging from the ashes of the WTC would be cast in the horrific but familiar terms of one religion's effort to wipe out the other – the Crusade. Crusade, derived from the French word *"croisade"* (marked by the cross) brought back old memories of the righteous battle against evil – the holy war. Crusades brought bad memories for Muslims. During the horrific killing spree called the crusades, many thousands of Muslims were raped and murdered by marauding Western armies, clothed with symbolic crosses splashed across their chests, shields and helmets. Indeed their very killing instruments (swords) were shaped like crosses. In the course of those campaigns they demanded that their prisoners convert, a process involving the confession that Jesus was nailed to a cross.

Fortunately for America, Barack Obama came on scene when he did. President Obama, according to long time presidential adviser, David Gergen of Harvard University's Kennedy School of Business, is one of the only presidents who, if he were not sitting in the Oval Office, could earn a good living as a writer, the best combination of writer-orator since JFK. Irish Nobel laureate, Seamus Heaney agrees that the man has a knack for using words as a tool. But faced with criticism that he was all talk, the new president made a tactical shift upon entering the White House, vowing less poetry and more workmanlike, in the process, following Mario Cuomo's dictum of campaigning in poetry but governing in prose. Memorable and unforgettable lines can be found all over his many speeches at home and abroad (Egypt), such as his victory speech after the 2008 Potomac primary: *We need to do more than end a war; we need to end the mindset that got us into war.* Such eloquence surely had their effect on his predecessor George W. Bush who already picked quarrels with him for overuse of the epithet "unprecedented" to describe acts like town hall meetings with Chinese students for which he Obama could not possibly claim sole author.

Part of the problem with education is that not enough emphasis is placed on the teachers themselves. Until this aspect is addressed, no amount of in-put into **Head Start, No Child Left Behind, Race to the Top** or any other type of program will deliver the goods in student performance. The older generation of teachers used to be quite blunt in confronting their lazy students: *"either you raise your standard to reach mine or I bring mine down to your level, but I'm not prepared to lower my standard".* It would appear that teachers, like parents, have been forced to drop their high expectations to cope with the times and the results are there to see. In some areas one is hard pressed to tell the difference between teacher and student, given the overall drop in standards. In the airwaves, center and epicenter have virtually been reduced to synonymy and few are losing sleep over it. There are many more – malapropism here, confused tenses there, jumbled syntax over there and so on. Fortunately President Obama's Education Secretary has recognized that the system of teacher evaluation is broken. What good is it subjecting kids to all the varieties of educational experimentation when the answer to a better future may very well lie in a good but neglected teacher? Teachers can bring life to the student, deliver just the right contemporary analogy to make sense of a murky notion in the distant past, ignite a student's passion for poetry or art, and help connect those dots that demystify seemingly incomprehensible notions in mathematics.

Each time the plight of those kids lagging behind in school work comes up, it is unavoidable to be become nostalgic for those early teachers and their little rules for spellings. "Remember, always *i* before *e* except after a *c*". Such mnemonics, even as illogical as they were in view of the so many exceptions (neither, neighbor, leisure, seize, weird,) proved to be very useful indeed. The rule "when *ing* comes to stay, *e* just flies off" helped many kids to cope with verbs transitioning from simple present tense to the progressive or continuous tenses. Such foundations were invaluable to tackling harder areas of grammar and reading in later years. Today's generation of kids deserve no less. Of course teachers can also discourage an otherwise good student from pursuing their dream. It is therefore imperative to evaluate teachers too by a variety of means, including student evaluations. If teachers are subjected to assessment by those who benefit from their output, society could have one useful tool that would serve multiple purposes, including the incentive to push for better performance.

Gone are the days of basing it all on higher education credentials or years at the job. Research needs to be directed to finding out the best ways of measuring "added value" from teacher in-put to the policy of hiring and deploying, evaluating, promoting and paying teachers, with a special premium placed on what happens inside the classroom. All of this presupposes that the other factors – family background, differences between communities, parenting methods, family stability, and socioeconomics - are taken care of by the appropriate agencies. The system of school governance giving teachers, principals and parents some of the authority usually reserved for central officials and school boards can go a long way to improve things. Reintroduction of community principles and civics lessons, stressing extracurricular events, teachers interacting with students in and outside of the classroom and teaching respect for human dignity are components long neglected in society's obsession with the rights of the individual. Only teachers with a sense of calling can facilitate academic and spiritual growth in children.

For current users of discoveries and inventions that make life easy for us, the usual reaction is "Who cares about who discovered or invented what?" Well, if nobody in today's America cares, perhaps somebody should begin to ruminate over Mitsutomo Yuasa, a Japanese historian/physicist whose 1966 theory "*The Shifting Center of Scientific Activity in the West*" stated that every 80 to 100 years, the "center" of scientific activity shifted from one country to another. During the period from 1540 to 1610 it was Italy that led and then the center moved to England (1660-1730), France (1770-1830), Germany (1810-1920) and finally the US (1920 to the present). According to Yuasa's theory, America's pivotal shift period will be 2000 to 2020. And it seems the shift is already underway. That is not all. In warning Arab Oil ministers in 1970 about shifts in the oil business, Sheik Ahmed Zaki Yamani said, "The Stone Age didn't end for lack of stones". Even though current Secretary-General of OPEC, Abdallah el-Badri of Libya can beat his chest about the proven oil reserves of 1.3 trillion barrels and market forces(new commerce, speculators, financial markets) that determine oil prices, unlike the 1973 situation which was made possible by oil companies, he still worries about the present quest for alternative energy sources because, OPEC countries, even with more sun and more wind than most of the other countries, do not have enough money to subsidize new energy sources. It seems logical to speculate that America's unchallenged global leadership of the IT (information technology) age today is not going to end for lack of information or technology. It will end probably because Americans are losing interest in careers in science, technology, engineering and mathematics. Perception is reality; in the years ahead, young persons who spend their time enjoying the goods produced by their parents may soon wake up some day to find themselves in a terrible state of want. Music piracy, identity theft, all sorts of Internet crimes point to one thing – today's generation is complacent, taking the easy way out. They are missing an important lesson – that knowledge is power but it is so only for those who have it.

During his recent visit to Asia President Barack Obama was seen to be very deferential to most leaders out there, including the Burmese military junta holding Aung San Suu Kyi under house arrest. Americans expected him to take those leaders head-on in matters of human rights abuses. Was he walking softly, as some claim, and carrying a big stick as his own way of delivering the message to mainland China? What could be the meaning of such deference to his Asian counterparts? Was it an admission of Mitsutomo Yuasa's predictions of Asia's preeminence? Was President Obama laying the ground work for accommodating what is known as Asia's century? Could he have been reacting to the US National Intelligence Council's conclusion that the world is witnessing the rise of major global players similar to the advent of a United Germany in the 19$^{th}$ century and a powerful US in the 20$^{th}$ century? Is the world's geopolitical landscape really changing? Is Obama a pacifist who favors appeasement to the detriment of national security? If so how does one explain the stepped up covert and overt military action in Afghanistan? And the quiet arms sale to Taiwan?

Also, over the past years there has been much talk about a new global order. Some foreign policy experts have begun to speak openly about America's decline and Asia's rise to preeminence. Shanghai High School kids did so well that they topped the PISA (Program for International School Assessment), the only thing lacking, according to some of the kids being how to think. Fareed Zakaria's bestseller, *"The Post-American World"*, Parag Khanna's *"The Second World: Empires and Influence in the New World Order"*, and last but surely not the least, *"The New Asian Hemisphere: The Irresistible Shift of Global Power to the East"* by former Singapore ambassador, Kishore Mahbubani, initiator of the debate on "Asian values" are quite revealing. Taking the idea one step ahead is *"When China Rules the World"* by a prominent columnist for the Guardian, Martin Jacques. Already China (GDP of $1.34 trillion over the last quarter) is virtually replacing Japan (GDP of $1.29 trillion) as the world's #2 economy, after the United States, and is ready to cement its own status as one of the world's most formidable superpowers if the trend continues for twelve months. Japan's likely slip comes as it grapples with a shrinking population, lower than expected net exports and slower capital expenditure. Japan became the world's second largest economy around 1968 after years of rapid expansion but the bubbles burst in its housing and stock markets in the 1980s and early 1990s, causing a period of stagnation. Naturally as China's economy grows the country will be become more assertive in world politics and finances and the world will accordingly expect more in combating climate change and doing more for the global economy.

But why are so many predicting America's decline? Could it be just the present economic crunch prompting the prediction of the US and UK packing off to the Superpower Retirement Home? Won't these predictions go the way previous predictions went about Japan's ascendancy – hyper-charged economy built on a real estate bubble that imploded? Such beliefs have triggered the mini-industry of books on Eastern renaissance. Almost every author is convinced that Asian nations, from Singapore to Malaysia to China is about to take the final step from rising economic power to global hegemony, all using state-controlled economic policies to dominate every industry while delivering modernity – good governance, growth and the rule of law, more appealing than the messiness of Western democracies. Can this be true? By some alarming estimates(Clyde Prestowitz *The Betrayal of American Prosperity*) China exports $46 billion worth of goods to the US, including everything from shoes, clothing, toys, automobiles, computers, photo voltaic panels for generating solar energy to advanced telecommunication gear, whereas in return America exports only $7.6 billion worth of waste paper and scrap metal, disdainfully called *millennium's dung* to highlight the painful parallel with Rome on the eve of the collapse of that ancient empire, when carts and mules laden with silks, spices, marbles, timbers entered the great city along the Ostia Road and carried back just dung. According to this view, America's annual trade deficit of $600-800 billion with China reduces her from the world's leading lender to the largest debtor nation with a corresponding dramatic reduction in bargaining leverage, a regrettable situation that can be avoided simply by changing course and halting the ironic emergence from isolationism ( no foreign entanglements) to a nation trading its productive and technological base for geopolitical and military advantage, spending ridiculously colossal amounts of money per foot soldier on the ground in Afghanistan, yet crawling behind Japan's 63.6 Mbps (Megabits per second) at a disgusting 3.9 Mbps!

Could this not be an illusion, given the many stumbling blocks each of those nations faces? What about China's demographics as influenced by the One Child policy? Isn't it conceivable that the population will age rapidly, so rapidly that in the year 2040 China will have at least 400 million seniors with little or no retirement benefits and not enough working age people to sustain it? A population that hopes to grow old before it grows rich is certainly a recipe for disaster! To the mix one must add political unrest or what the authorities prefer to call "mass incidents" which is sure to grow as income inequality goes up and environmental problems add to the stress. Already Chinese leaders are seriously contemplating relaxing the one child policy as well as the forced abortions and sterilizations, a pointer to the difficulties ahead. India is no different. What values, ideas, or histories, if any, are there to hold together the Asian nations like Europe or the United States? To become a global superpower requires economic, political and military might; it does not seem as if any of the Asian giants matches the US right now, given that during the tsunami that struck south and south-east Asia not long ago, the region's nations relied mainly on the US navy to coordinate relief efforts. German scholar and writer, Joseph Joffe has called the US today's default superpower; no one in today's world trusts any one else to play the global hegemon, which naturally falls on Washington D. C. Government controls surely have quite an impact on innovation and productivity; consequently firms and companies that thrive on innovation, like Google, are scared of investing under such climates.

But China is curiously schizophrenic when it comes to classification according to the UN system of developed or developing nations. On the one hand, China flexes its international muscles and demands to negotiate as an equal with the heavyweights or the world's dominant powers especially in matters of economics, trade, research, education, technology, armaments and space programs. With a population of more than one billion, China engages the world market with a rare tenacity and shrewdness, undervaluing the RMB and thus making her exports artificially cheap and contributing to America's trade imbalance of $270 billion. However, in matters of human rights and environmental concerns, China puts on another identity altogether – that of a developing country which might suffer great harm if held to the same standards as the others. And Germany, like the other great nations, does not quite swallow China's copycat practices, a true reflection of the lack of Intellectual Property protection laws!

It is expected that in the years ahead, business leaders will take cues from the Oval Office in choosing management styles. Out goes George W. Bush, the unilateralist, the decider; in comes Barack Obama, the consensus builder, the delegator, the community organizer and his motivational style. Management educators, strategy consultants, and business sages of all stripes will be looking for leadership clues and cues to help them steer their vessels. President Barack Obama's policies, management traits, world view, public and private partnerships, are likely to influence how American business is conducted and taught (business schools will be the natural training grounds for the next generation of CEOs) in the years ahead. The man's successful campaign style will provide a case study in organizational brilliance – clear strategy, alignment of goals and tactics, smart planning and execution. The capacity to adapt to fast-changing circumstances and the deployment of the Internet to build a distributed network of supporters and donors were two key elements. In this connection Barack Obama liked to say *"It's not about me, it's about you"* thus putting voters in the center of the political universe. The same can be done for customers of businesses so that what happens in the White House will have an impact on the business landscape. One person with an unshakeable belief in the nation's future is a first generation citizen of Plymouth, Massachusetts whose optimism is backed by ninety-two years of experience. At a time when citizens of a European country like France are up in arms against their president for raising the retirement age from 60 to 62, plenty of US citizens are doing the reverse – going from retirement back to the workforce. What can beat the amount of mentoring the senior citizens will provide the younger generation before calling it quits?

How was it in the past? What type of templates did past occupants of the Oval Office give for business? During the Wall Street crash of 1929, Herbert Hoover had an inadequate, laisser-faire posture and Franklin Roosevelt had a determined improvisation style. Bill Clinton's management style was casual during the T-shirt-and-jeans technology boom of the 1990s. Ronald Reagan, inheriting a sagging economy and reviving it, set a leadership tone, projected optimism and delegated many tasks. Dwight Eisenhower, Supreme Commander of Allied forces in Europe during World War II, was a master motivator leading troops on D-day (400,000 troops stormed the beach in Normandy while being shot at). America's 43rd president, George W. Bush had the famous quote that he was "*the decider*". A decider does not need to listen. That explains the way things were run at Wall Street institutions such as Lehman Brothers and Merrill Lynch, with the consequences shaking the financial system world wide at the time Obama acceded to the US presidency.

In addition to the citizen's many rights is the right to take part in the decision-making process. Democratizing policy making is an important and modern process. This is something citizens of third world countries still dream of. Anxious to save the economy, all that an American citizen needs to do is get a laptop, a few good ideas and go to work. Before long the highest point in the decision-making process will be responding to his/her ideas, thanks to blogging.

In 1907, faced with the imminent collapse of the financial system, America's most powerful banker, J. P. Morgan brokered a solution to the crisis behind closed doors of his personal library in New York City. The man gathered the nation's banking titans into one room, locked the door and refused to let them out until they pledged to help each other through the crisis. By hammering out a solution in secrecy, he stopped the panic in its tracks. Thus was born the conventional method of solving such thorny problems by managing threats to the nation's economy.

In 2008 the response to the Wall Street crisis started that way too, with the nation's bankers gathering in the office of the Federal Reserve for a closed door meeting at which the Treasury Secretary urged them to rescue the beleaguered Lehman brothers, powerhouse of the mortgage industry. This time the efforts failed, so Henry Paulson the Treasury Secretary turned to the US Congress for help. He asked for three quarters of a trillion dollars to buy up bad assets stating, "Trust us; we know what we are doing". But this was not 1907. The sprawling network of experts in economics and finance picked apart Secretary Paulson's plan live, in public and on blogs with plenty of vitriol. They were not just loud-mouthed hacks howling from the sidelines; among them were top academic economists such as Nobel Laureate Paul Krugman, Nouriel Roubini Tyler Cowen as well as financial industry insiders who actually knew a lot about credit default swaps, collateralized debt obligations, and lots of other esoteric instruments at the heart of the crisis.

The bail out plan benefitted from information on historical context and cutting critiques. Bloggers also offered counter proposals – direct capital injections into banks or direct purchases of mortgages. Readers began to badger their senators and representatives to oppose Paulson's plan. A few weeks later the US Congress rebuffed Paulson, sending shock waves through the financial markets. Blogs thus helped shape Washington's response to the crisis – policy makers charged with monitoring and fixing the markets. The national crisis was thus hashed out by experts in full public view. The blogs offered a crash course in economics as authoritative as any textbook and far more accessible too. Voodoo economics took a convenient back seat.

The democratization of policy-making combined technical discussion of liquidity traps, yield curves and profane putdowns, all with heckling headlines. They threw open the doors to the very messy business of everything, including declaring a recession, structuring government bailout. Thanks to a blog like *The Big Picture*, readers were able to learn that the ongoing bailout of the financial system was larger than the combined cost of the Louisiana Purchase, the

Marshall Plan, the New Deal, the Vietnam War, and the nation's space program! Everything had been converted into pie charts and graphs for all to see.

When the subprime lending crisis broke out in the summer of 2007 bloggers leapt into action, unpacking, dissecting and making sense of the gathering storm. Journalists discovered the blogs too and used them to remedy the gaps in their knowledge of obscure issues like securitization and structured investment vehicles; and many of those issues began to appear in the pages of major newspapers. It is good for a nation that its citizens and journalists read blogs like *Naked Capitalism, The Big Picture, Marginal Revolution, Global Economic Trend Analysis,* and *Calculated Risks.* Policy makers ought to pay attention to what the blogs are saying as well and bloggers have urged concerned citizens to be proactive and write to their senators about the issues. These days countries practicing press censorship by denying accreditation to journalists or their newspapers end up facilitating the proliferation of free lance practitioners as Egypt realized in the clumsy attempt to stifle Al Jazeera!

Ford Motors seemed to have done something right and did not come for a bailout, so President George Bush gave General Motors and Chrysler a total rescue plan of $1.7 billion. But US tax payers were not particularly happy with the rescue for companies that had been complacent and refused to live with the times. Yesterday GM was contemptuous and looked at Japanese companies with disdain, not giving them much of a chance to succeed in the competitive US market; the underdogs sensed this and went to work right away. Today the very Japanese companies are giving GM a stiff competition, thanks to timely innovation. Toyota may be having a bump on the road as a result of braking problems and accelerators being stuck, causing the cars to behave like runaways but this will be fixed quickly enough. Smart drivers know that a stuck gas pedal notwithstanding, simply placing the car on neutral and applying the brakes cuts off the gas and slows the car to a stop. Humbled Akio Toyoda, CEO and grandson of the founder of Toyota Motor Corporation, appeared before investigators of his company's safety crisis involving a series of vehicle recalls, promising to look into the problems.

Enterprising Americans, ever so ready to make a buck out of any crisis, took on Toyota. In California there was a probe going on in connection with a Toyota Prius accelerating to 90 miles per hour and the driver being unable to bring it under control either by applying the brakes or placing the vehicle on neutral or even shutting off the motor, even as he was level-headed and witty enough to make a 911 call to summon police assistance. Incredibly Americans were prepared to shrug off a death toll of 100,000 per year due to hospital mistakes but were outraged by a few dozen deaths resulting from Toyota's mistakes. What an ambivalence!

The story of how Toyota overtook General Motors on its own home turf has been told in many versions but one that makes the most sense to me involves highlighting two different world views, one held by authorities in Washington D. C. and the other the rest of the world. While it looked sensible and prudent to build brand new plants or convert the abandoned or failing auto -manufacturing plants into green energy industries –solar panels, wind turbines, batteries – Washington insiders and those of the dream world shuddered at the thought of protectionism and instead recommended buying the needed items from foreign producers abroad. Such a short term solution dovetails perfectly with consumer interest. Yet, the progressive developing world (China, Japan, Korea, Singapore, France, Taiwan, and others) would have chosen the alternative – offer tax breaks, free land, capital grants and government order to get started, knowing that to get to the economies of scale with large scale production some catch-up would be necessary no matter how costly it is at the start. The long term approach would also create jobs as well as reduce US deficits. Emphasizing this conventional wisdom of doing everything to catch up with those that had gone before, a Japanese vice minister in the ministry of international trade and industry (MITI), Naohiro Amaya summarized this very elegantly by saying "We did the opposite of what the Americans advised" (Clyde Prestowitz, *The Betrayal of American Prosperity*). Where America is obsessed with and prioritizes geopolitics and national security, the others favor long term strategic economic and technological development.

Like GM, Pan Am once filled our skies but today it is virtually extinct. How times have changed! At some point in the past, the popular slogan was "What's good for GM is good for the country". That was when the middle class was expanding and Americans took for granted that it would continue to expand, that GM workers would get good wages and benefits, own homes and send their kids to college and get health insurance package and secure pension plans. Founded in 1908, General Motors rose to dominate the US and global auto industries under the stewardship of pioneer CEO, Alfred Sloan, a man who pledged to "deliver a car for every purse and purpose". Instead of keeping one car for fifteen years people were urged to change them every five years.

Today things are moving in the opposite direction and it seems they have but a government paralysis. Plagued by rising oil prices, the auto giant's offerings, including Hummer and Pontiac, failed to chime with the green consciousness of customers. In an era when conventional wisdom dictates the use of smaller, cleaner and more fuel efficient cars, after recovering from bankruptcy and the $30 billion additional taxpayer funds made available for restructuring by the Obama administration, downsizing seems to be the way for GM to go.

Eventually General Motors filed for Chapter 11 (Bankruptcy). The icon of US industrial might thus went down as the biggest bankruptcy case in US history. Faced with those realities, current president and CEO, Frederick A. Henderson promised that General Motors would be leaner, greener, faster and stronger in the years ahead, thanks not only to rebuilding, but also to reinventing the company. For some GM simply became Government Motors. One can only hope that the company which gave so much mileage in status and pop culture such as David Hassel Hoff's high tech TransAm ride in "knight Rider" can deliver on its promises.

Meanwhile consumers began to do a lot of soul-searching to see what role they should play in the General Motors debacle. There were US citizens who swore that they would stick with US cars as a matter of principle and there were those who claimed that buying Detroit Iron was like throwing away good money after bad money, hence showing selective patriotism. Some toyed with questions such as: Am I better off buying a foreign-built car sold by an American company, thus enriching American management or buying an American-built car sold by a Japanese company, thereby enriching the American worker?

The plight of General Motors drove home a rather painful lesson, that never again should any organization be allowed to reach that monstrous stage of being described as "too big to fail." Current thinking is to come up with a better system of oversight that can forestall such a thing before it happens. Attention is being focused on "systemic risks and how to identify and manage them, taking note of complexities such that the collapse of one part risks collapsing the entire system. The building of larger and more complex networks drew inspiration from the so-called Metcalfe's Law (a network's value increases in proportion to the square of the number of people or devices in it). The key is to manage risks, not avoid them because it is not just possible to completely avoid them. Studies will be focused on finding out why, for example, an old and prestigious investment bank like Lehman Brothers could collapse so suddenly the way it did. What type of contingency should be built into the risk model? How should government regulators manage such complex systems? Whenever a system or an organization is described as "too big to fail" then such an organization shall have crossed the safety zone. It should not have been allowed to get there, so regulators would be required to routinely monitor the largest and most connected firms in each industry. How this plays out remains to be seen. AOL has already agreed to purchase The Huffington Post so as to create media group that will have a customer base of 117 million visitors per month in the US and 270 million globally, creating fears in some circles that such a peak, like 80% of similar acquisitions and mergers often fail. They had in mind when Time Warner bought AOL at its peak.

Government regulators telling an industry it cannot grow or innovate sounds very offensive and is tantamount to meddling in the free market but that is precisely what the Sherman anti-trust law was intended to do and had been doing until its animators went to sleep. Anti-trust laws guard against firms growing so large that they stifle competition. An anti-systemic risk law would aim at averting risk before it becomes too late. Government intervention will surely prevent markets from carrying out activities or behaviors that are self-destructive. The failure to deal with systemic risks creates a system that is both uncertain and unjust, makes an otherwise free market to be at the mercy of one firm. Such a firm, while generating immense profit by taking enormous risks, almost always ends up making everyone bear the burden, as was seen in the use of taxpayer monies for bailouts. Yet these realities were made murky or non-existent at all at that time when the efficient market theory virtually dominated thinking on Wall Street and the teaching of investment in business schools. The complexities of the market were treated as if they were handed down by God himself. Envious of science in general and particularly the unerring laws of physics, animators made strenuous efforts to give economics a mathematical flavor by all means. Econometrics developed quickly with the arrival of computers and took mathematization of economics into the fast lane, yet they all failed because of many false assumptions, especially when the human mind could not exactly be made to match particles of matter that respond to gravity and other natural forces. Consumer preferences change according to immeasurable whims such as panic.

The Obama Administration must now come to terms with the fallout of the bail out. Disillusioned citizens want their pound of flesh, especially when faced with banks paying huge bonuses to its CEOs against near zero interest payments for savings or any mention of shareholders. No wonder many persons contemplated withdrawing their savings from banks and putting them under their mattresses! New York's attorney-general, Andrew Cuomo, asked for the first eight banks to receive bailout money under the Administration's troubled assets relief program (TARP) to furnish data on their expected bonus payout for 2009. Bank of America, Bank of New York Mellon Corp., Citigroup Inc., Goldman Sachs

Group Inc., JP Morgan Chase and Co., and Morgan Stanley State Street Corp and Wells Fargo Co. probably forgot that there is no free lunch in America. Well, pay back time had arrived and tax payers surely deserved to get their dues before the bonuses and other compensations went to most highly paid bankers - the traders. It was bad enough to refuse payment of just interest to those who saved or invested their cash in the 800 pound gorillas; it would be worse that, under their noses, the banks should pay such ridiculously high bonuses to their workers. Some said it was vengeance on the part of the Obama Administration. If the distribution of pain, as some saw it, helped to even out the earlier uneven distribution of gains, so be it.

Thanks to democracy and the new information age, and thanks to the stubborn economic crisis, big ideas for financial reform that had languished for years became attractive once more and those who had considered such bold moves taboo in the past became its greatest proponents. It became common place to hear bold suggestions like taxing Wall Street instead of taxing the common folks to clean up after their reckless bankers or, instead of tolerating behemoths considered "too big to fail," why not break them up before they do more damage to the country? Instead of genuflecting before the Federal Reserve Bank, why not strip it of its secrets and cleanse it of self-interested bankers responsible for shaping Federal policy? Having used public money to bail out bankers, members of Congress became palpably terrified of voter retribution as the next elections loomed ahead. Long time friends of Wall Street began to speak fearlessly against the soft stance taken in oversight institutions like SEC.

No matter how much President Barack Obama did at the level of Washington D. C. to improve the economy and create jobs, individuals around the country, especially African Americans, have to do their own part to bring about the desired improvements in their lives. Only individual efforts can cure the complacence and indifference that tends to hold people back. And it is gratifying that some blacks are heeding the wake up call and sounding the alarms. Larry Elder's *Stupid Black Men* is one of them. Citing Kofi Anan, a black man who just ended his term as United Nations Secretary-General, Condoleezza Rice, a black woman who served as Secretary of State in the Bush Administration, a black man sitting as one of nine justices of the US Supreme Court, and a black man elected by the State of Illinois to the US Senate, the author invites blacks to look around and take note that blacks comprise 10% of the US House of Representatives, are CEOs of major companies like American Express, Time Warner and others. He then concludes by asserting that if racists were holding back blacks, they were doing a pretty bad job indeed.

Reading the momentous 1954 (*Brown vs. Board of Education*) decision, Chief Justice Earl Warren said, among other things, "*In these days it is doubtful that any child may reasonably be expected to succeed in life if he is denied the opportunity of an education …To separate black children from others of similar age and qualification solely because of their race generates a feeling of inferiority as to their status in the community…We conclude that in the field of public education the doctrine of 'separate but equal' has no place*". Obviously the strict application of that decision has done a lot of good even if more needs to be done. As for the underclass – the 20% of blacks living below the poverty level – welfare dependency, poor school standards, gang membership and violence, teenage pregnancy and drug use prevent them from joining the middle class. Economist Walter Williams notes that if by tomorrow the hearts of whites become as pure as that of Mother Teresa, these problems will not just go away. And he is right!

The question is often asked whether mainstream media are helping or hurting the black cause by harping on "leaders" like Jesse Jackson who complain that lending institutions fail to provide blacks "access to capital". Some years ago Freddie Mac released a report showing twice as many blacks had bad credit histories as whites (48% to 27%). The Washington Post reported that whites making $25000 per year or less had better credit histories than blacks earning $65000 to $75000 per year. Asian applicants had their loans granted at a higher rate than whites or blacks. Why so? Asians, especially those of Japanese, Korean and Chinese ancestry, were found to live further below their means than did other groups; therefore an Asian applicant was more likely a "creditworthy" borrower. Broadly speaking, blacks tended to have poorer credit histories and their spending habits hurt their creditworthiness. USA Today wrote, "According to Target Market, a company that tracks black consumer spending, blacks spent a significant amount of their income on depreciable products. In 2002 when the US economy nose dived, blacks spent $22.9 billion on clothes, $3.2 billion on electronics, $11.6 billion on furniture to put into homes that in many cases were rented! Favorite purchases were cars and liquors. Even though blacks made up only 10% of the US population, they accounted for 30% of the country's Scotch consumption! Detroit which was 80% black, was the world's number one market for Cognac. Lincoln was so impressed and pleased with the $46.7 billion that blacks spent on cars, he commissioned Sean "P. Diddy" Coombs, an entertainment/fashion mogul to design a limited edition navigator replete with six plasma screens, three DVD players and a Sony Play station". Very telling!

All of this prompted Hugh Price, head of the National Urban League to categorically reject the myth *"they won't lend us money because we are blacks"*. "People with bad credits are usually denied loans, end of story", he said. This then raised the following troubling question: is the ever sympathetic Los Angeles Times helping or hurting blacks when it makes the charge that lenders exploit black and minority borrowers by charging higher rates of interest? The study by the Association of Community Organizations for Reform Now (ACORN), which the writer cited, looked at the percentage of higher cost loans issued to minority communities compared with minority neighborhoods in the same metropolitan area. Residents of predominantly minority districts in the Los Angeles metropolitan area were nine times more likely to get high cost loans to refinance their homes than the residents of predominantly white communities. The article referred to a Federal Reserve study showing that across the country, blacks and Hispanics were more likely to receive the so-called sub-prime loans (higher rate of interest) than whites. The author concluded that this could not be explained simply by differences in income. Quickly it concluded "this of course reeks of racism!" There was no mention that better loan rates usually went to less risky (creditworthy) borrowers. Obviously if a study is to form the basis for policy change, the study should be credible and its conclusions valid too.

University of California at Los Angeles professor emeritus, James Q. Wilson quipped: "One needs only do three things to avoid poverty in America – finish High School, marry before having a child and, produce such a child after the age of twenty". Then he added that of the families who did so, only 8% were poor; of those who did not, 79% were poor. Sadly enough, in many black communities, pursuing academics is often equated to "acting white". Incredible but true! Today many black kids openly tease other blacks for "sounding white" and even attack those with high aspirations as "thinking you're better than somebody else". Some even extol Ebonics and equate it to a foreign language and advocate teaching it on the same footing as other foreign languages (San Bernadino Country, California)! One need not go too far to discover the origin of such fatalistic views. World history in general and US history in particular, usually embraces the 'the great man" theory of events, where the ranks of the great are invariably males of Anglo-Saxon and Scottish descent, not blacks. As late as in 2010 the French shamelessly picked a skin-colored white to act in place of a black in "*The Other Dumas*" simply as an unacceptable attempt to blur the African heritage of Alexander Dumas!

It is important to mentor, challenge and keep kids focused. Parents need to be involved in the education of their kids. Role models need to play a part in it and education must enable kids to develop confidence in themselves. Why did influential Oprah Winfrey leave America to go and open a $40 million school for poor black girls in South Africa? In her own words she was fed up visiting inner-city schools where the need to learn was not just there. Asked what they would want to be when they grew up, 24 out of a class of 30 indicated that they wished to be musicians! The Michael Jackson effect? In spite of the high rate of music piracy? But why is there such a lack of the desire to learn among America's own black kids? Soul-searching questions abound but the answers are few.

No wonder an astute observer once remarked that to hide anything from blacks, one should publish it. Debatable as such an observation may be, there is no doubt that many blacks get exploited when they end up being victims of inflated bills, often bogus insurance premiums whose fine print they cannot even read. How can schools fix the problem of high drop out rates? How can teachers teach children who fail to come to school because they hate themselves as a result of lack of parental love? A life time of hearing that "no matter how hard you work, the white man keeps you down" must surely be taking a toll. Why would such a negative influence come from parents who should be motivating? Why such a negative influence from parents who should be motivating? No doubt it is very difficult to be at the receiving end of racial prejudice, like being stopped by the police for driving a nice car or being found in a nice neighborhood, or being asked by a counter clerk if one can afford to buy an expensive item. Because of a long history of discrimination and prejudice, vices like these continue to be perceived, often when they are nonexistent. Over the years black people become so sensitive that understandably, they almost always go about with their "radars" up to gauge such treatments.

It is incredible that of all human qualities, people continue to be fixated on skin color and make so much fuss of it in determining who to interact with or to avoid, turning a blind eye to all other qualities. It is incredible that the black skin color should be so stigmatized over all others given that some of the ugliest members of the human species on planet earth are not even black.

Even in mainstream America, there are intractable problems. Experts in education, psychologists, policy makers and politicians are battling to control the center and it seems that politicians are winning out, they being the ones who pay the piper. The *No Child Left Behind Act* of 2000 illustrates this very succinctly. Those funding education have decided to impose their vision on everything, including kindergarten education. The emphasis seems to be accountability by making the kids take tests such as MCAS

(Massachusetts Comprehensive Assessment Test), SAT (Scholastic Aptitude Test), and others. Aided by neuroscientists who say that the period between birth and five years of age shows rapid brain development, these new policy bosses are pushing and fussing about with the brainy baby business, flooding the educational market with products that promise to turn the little tots into budding geniuses. The market is full of Baby Einstein materials like books, DVDs, flashcard games to help the young ones go ahead but there is palpable fear that computer competency comes with a decline in reading.

Arguing against these developments are the main actors on the field who complain that they have been sidelined in their own fief and that MCAS, for example, is a burgeoning movement to measure outcomes or what young people gain from their time in school. In the words of one upset teacher, it infringes on freedom in the classroom and is a source of students being untrained and even frightened to think on their own after years of such standardized testing. Educationists who argue this way would rather develop grit in their students than rote memory. While they accept Einsteinian ideas, they feel that downgrading Newtonian notion would be detrimental to the nation's future leaders. If Isaac Newton had just casually passed by on observing the apple fall from a tree near his Cambridge farm in England, the world would have missed an important aspect of learning. That man had grit – everybody knows that things fall; it took Newton's mental quality called grit to explain why. The falling apple is familiar to us today just as the orbit of the moon, thanks to Isaac Newton's painstaking observation over years.

Like Newton, Polish cosmographer (geographer/astronomer), Nicholas Copernicus, used the crude map made by Martin Waldseemuller to puncture the myth of a geocentric universe – earth surrounded by concentric spheres of water, air, fire, individual spheres of moon, sun, the planets, and in the outermost limit, a single sphere studded with stars...and further beyond still, a region of pure abstraction (may be God?), all circling around the Earth. That was the dogma in those early days when folks shared the philosophy that "looking up, they saw down and looking down they saw up". Scientists and theologians enthralled by the Ptolemaic theory, banded together to oppose Galileo and Copernicus. As a matter of fact Galileo was tried by the Inquisition and forced to publicly recant his views in addition to being put under house arrest. The heliocentric view of the solar system – everything circling around the sun - as we know it today was still to come. And so by simply looking down on Waldseemuller's map, Copernicus saw the skies open up. Christopher Columbus had traveled west but did not end up going off the end of the earth! That was something.

Over 500 years ago Copernicus went public with one of the most important arguments ever made in the history of ideas –that the earth did not just sit idly and immobile at the center of the universe but revolved around the sun. His theory was published in 1542 in *"On the Revolution of Heavenly Spheres"* supported by a wealth of data, including the 1507 Waldseemuller map depicting the lands discovered by Christopher Columbus and other explorers as part of a vast, previously unknown continent, far out in the western ocean and earlier thought to be part of Asia. Medieval Europe knew that the world was a sphere and that sailing far enough to the west would bring one to the east. The view of the universe by Middle East scholars and Christian theology as a set of concentric spheres was dominant during Aristotle's time. The 2500-year old model placed the earth as a solid ball of land. But it raised some basic questions that cried for answers. If that were the case, why was the earth not completely submerged by the water surrounding it?

Some scholars thought the *earth bobbed slightly off center* in the sphere of water the way an orange would in a bucket of water. But how? The answer provided again was simply that God had made it so. Wasn't it said even in the Book of Genesis? "And God said 'Let the waters under the Heavens be gathered together in one place, and let dry land appear.'" Earlier scholars had explained that God pushed the sphere of land to one side of the sphere of water, exposing one part of it to air and creating the land mass that would come to be known as Asia, Europe and Africa. "But no!" said Copernicus. It was untenable. Anybody could see that the land mass did not gradually and uniformly rise upward from the sea toward some high point some where in the middle of the known world. Nor would the depth of the abyss stop increasing from the shore of the ocean outward in such a way that no island or reef or any kind of land would be encountered by sailors on the longer voyages. Waldseemuller's map opened Copernicus's eyes to what he had been suspecting all along – the known world (Africa, Europe, Asia) on the right, a vast body of water and then far to the left, and rising majestically out of the western ocean and extending deep into the southern hemisphere, a new continent – America!

Africa and Asia having been named after women, it was only natural to name the new continent after its male discoverer – Amerigo Vespucci. Poor Christopher Columbus! If he had not restricted his explorations to the Caribbean! Vespucci had sailed south below the equator. Waldseemuller knew that it was the southness rather than the westness of the New World that was remarkable to the discovery across the Atlantic.

Most persons easily give up when faced with a difficult and demanding task. Those with grit do not; they persevere and do whatever it takes to accomplish it. Current worries about the disappearance of MCAS are probably premature. The main barometer for measuring school success over the years in the Commonwealth of Massachusetts remains in a state of flux as experts adopt national education standards proposed by the *Race to the Top* program. The success story of the Commonwealth was made possible, thanks to having both authority and responsibility to be bold and innovative, making the State, in the words of former Secretary of Education, Michael Sentence "internationally competitive"

Education that measures intelligence (Scripps National Spelling Bee, Stanford-Binet IQ Test, and SAT) is good but achievement in the real world demands more than these. Our own Thomas Edison agreed that genius is 1% inspiration and 99% perspiration. Accountability requires that schools, educators and students be held responsible for results, achievement being rewarded and failures punished, so that children get a good education and tax payers the satisfaction that their money was well spent.

Addressing the NAACP during its 100th anniversary celebration in New York, President Barack Obama was unequivocal about the importance of educating the children parents bring into the world, emphasizing that education is the best weapon against underachievement, low self esteem and many other ills. Such pronouncement would make the late W.E.B. Dubois, founder of the NAACP, feel good. So also would Bill Cosby, who made the education of children his life's crusade.

But only a few days later, the arrest of a distinguished African-American scholar inside his own home near Harvard Square in Cambridge reopened a very dark chapter in race relations, bringing back some of the ugly scenes of the past to the fore. Did they say Harvard Square? Of course to the ordinary white police officer, a black person residing there must have rung like an aberration; something had to be amiss. Statistics showed that most of the crime, in fact 52% of violent crime in Boston metropolis involved blacks. Professor Henry Louis Gates Jr. a distinguished black scholar had just returned from a trip to China and had difficulty opening the main door of his house. As he tried to force his way in through a side entrance, Ms Lucia Whalen, a vigilant neighbor thought there was a robbery going on and quickly did what a good neighbor should do - placed a 911 call to the police. In no time at all the police responded and the learned professor found himself being handcuffed by Sgt. James Crowley of the Cambridge police.

Accusations of racial profiling quickly filled the air as the two main actors gave conflicting versions of what actually happened–the point of view of the police officer not matching the view point of the professor. Tempers, egos, power play, bigotry and other emotions lurking below the surface quickly flared up. Jack Biddy, an astute observer and journalist of the Atlantic Monthly gave a very apt summary of the situation: *humiliation opens the gates of hell.* Self-righteous declarations from both protagonists and their respective supporters filled the airwaves. It did not take long for President Barack Obama to be dragged into the fray, thanks to an enterprising journalist who, inspired by First Amendment concerns and the American people's right to know, sought his opinion and got the president to say the police had "acted stupidly".

Uneasy lies the head that wears a crown. What a godsend for those in Congress seeking to take their August recess! Such a red herring was all that Republicans badly needed to stall the passage of the president's healthcare reform. The reform was opposed by members of Congress whose campaign coffers bulged with donations from insurers, drug companies and others who profit from maintaining the status quo. Obama's utterance of those two words became the rallying war cry. Freeman, a white American condemned the president for his comment yet said nothing of the journalist who had extended the microphone to him in the first place or of the American people's right to know, which must have prompted the journalist. In an era of political correctness, so much lies in the eyes of the beholder.

Of course blacks are associated in the public's eyes with a disproportionately large part of the city's crime wave. That was only statistics. Statistical tools – means, medians, variances, standard deviations and other parameters are very useful in decision-making but those who use them are usually careful to take note of random *"outliers"*. Could the learned professor not possibly be an outlier? Police sergeant Crowley did not say. Was it possible that the professor, feeling assaulted on his own turf, decided to let his ego get the better of him and not bother to acknowledge the police officer responding to the 911call? Difficult to say. Under other skies the neighbors would have played a crucial role in coming out to validate the professor's claim of being the owner of the house. What are neighbors for? But not in America where individual freedom and privacy issues trump everything else. Who would dare to meddle in a matter involving the police and someone else? Good Samaritans may find themselves on the wrong side of the law! I learned since not to get involved whenever a police officer stopped someone's car and was looking into anything. A wrong move can be costly!

If ever there was a rallying point for the party of ideas that was it. Recriminations flew about like confetti. Black Americans generally supported the professor while whites backed the police officer, with a few in-betweens. In the melee nobody bothered to ask whether a white president, like Obama's predecessor, could have equally been extended the microphone to comment on such a prosaic issue.

The main casualty of the diversion remained the very important review of the nation's healthcare bill before a Congress about to break off for August. Senators like Arlen Specter and Claire McCaskill were assaulted in the town hall meetings organized in Pennsylvania and Missouri respectively to consult with their constituents, discuss the overhaul of healthcare and possibly "shake the tree for political contributions". It would be naïve to expect the Republicans to pat President Obama on the back and say "well done" but astroturfing had turned sour as critics turned into hooligans, devising all sorts of ruses and misinformation to torpedo the president's plan, demonizing it in every conceivable language – socialist solution, Nazi plan, evil – some alleging that the president had a secret agenda to euthanize the elderly, stoking public anger against that important domestic priority.

Those nasty recriminations and remarks in the Crowley-Louis Gates imbroglio brought back an old racist joke of the Southern United States: *What do you call a black man with a PhD? A nigger.* In other words, no matter what a black man's academic or other accomplishment, to some whites, he remained an object of disparagement. Here was a distinguished professor who spent time educating students about race relations and the many evils of racial profiling, being humiliated right inside his own home by a white police officer to whom, he claimed to have adequately identified himself and the fact that he was inside his home. Here was an officer who refused to show proof of his own identity as demanded by the owner of the house and refused to offer an apology even after the police dropped the charges against the professor. Here was this very police officer demanding an apology from President Obama for his remarks. No wonder Alexander Solzhenitsyn was equally unforgiving of America, after exposing his native Russia in *The Gulag Archipelago* and migrating to the US where he expected things would be better for him. Why did the Cambridge police department hurriedly drop all charges against the professor, including the famous case of unruly behavior? What had suddenly changed in the aura of infallibility of the white police officer? And why give the public the impression that the Cambridge police department could not have even one rotten apple? If the police officer felt too important to offer the professor an apology to close the matter up, why did he think President Barack Obama was not equally too important to offer him the apology he demanded? So many questions, soy few answers.

Whatever the case, Professor Gates could count himself much luckier than Amadou Diallo, a Guinean national who received forty-one police bullets into his body under similar circumstances in New York City; Danroy Henry, a Pace University student shot and killed by a Westchester police; Oscar Grant, an unarmed black man shot and killed by a white police officer of the transit police in Oakland California, whose token sentence of two years imprisonment, spurred massive protests. The Rodney King scenario of 1991 keeps being reenacted day by day and each time the victim is invariably black while the culprit is a white police officer whose action – shoot to kill, shoot to immobilize, negligence, ineptitude or simply clumsiness - the criminal justice system could not or would not distill.

Even a black police officer, Michael Cox, was severely beaten by his own white colleagues in a bizarre "arrest gone wrong" scenario in which he was mistaken for an escaping criminal. The Police always erect a curious "Blue Wall of Silence" around themselves, close to but not quite the same as the conspiracy of silence among medical doctors, ostensibly to protect any of their members guilty of wrong doing. What they had not bargained for was a wrong done to one of theirs by a colleague - a type of friendly fire, to borrow from the military. Officer Cox had expected a simple apology from his colleagues following the period of grace which normally preceded an internal probe. He got nothing. Instead there were anonymous and threatening phone calls and a sepulchral silence from the department, until he took matters into his own hands and decided to seek redress in the courts. Those who considered Obama's election as ushering in a post-racial, color-blind America were in for a big shock.

President Obama might not solve the country's economic or health problems right away but he surely demonstrated that conflict resolution is his forte, both abroad and at home. Those who longed for the *Great America* might be disappointed in his approach but since by and large the proponents of the *Good America* were responsible for his election, the powerful hand stretched to Pyongyang and Tehran as well as that invitation to Professor Gates and Sergeant Crowley to come over to the White House for a beer were hopeful signs. Whether he treated them to Russian roulette or to beers, he certainly contributed to veering away from futile public rhetoric and refocused the nation on what mattered the most. Vice President Joe Biden eventually joined the president and the two officials for what an observer called the "Beer Summit" at the White House.

Freeing two US citizens from Pyongyang by quiet diplomacy proved that America does not always have to fire shots to obtain results. Former President, Bill Clinton's private visit to North Korea and the success in freeing 32-year-old Laura Ling and 36-year-old Euna Lee from the clutches of the reclusive Kim Jong Il, with or without the blessing of the White House was worth celebrating as part of Hillary Clinton's smart policies. The release from Myanmar prison of John Yettaw, another American sentenced to seven years for swimming to the residence of Opposition leader, Aung San Suu kyi, following Senator Jim Webb's private visit to the heavyweights in Bangkok was another proof that saber-rattling is not the only way to solve problems. That those successes took place on Barack Obama's watch was quite significant for the nation even if those who have no faith in quiet diplomacy continued to remain skeptical, unconvinced or resolutely against Obama, advocating only the use of the big stick. Why use a hydrogen bomb to do a job that can be accomplished with an AK-47? It made sense when Secretary of State Hillary Clinton addressed the council on Foreign Relations, emphasizing that the US must and had to lead in the new century where the complexities and connections of the world had yielded a new American moment, necessitating hard work and bold decisions since the world looked to the US to mobilize the shared effort needed to solve problems on a global scale. Robust international diplomacy with allies surely bore more fruit than the "go it alone" policy of yesteryears. By becoming an active participant in the international diplomatic efforts instead of staying by the sidelines, the US got tough sanctions passed by the UN against Iran.

The population of Boston could also take comfort in the firm stance taken by Boston Mayor Thomas Menino and Police Commissioner Ed Davis over another unfortunate twist of that sad drama, involving another white police officer. As if not wanting to be left out of the news and thanks to the 24 hour news cycle, the police officer, Justin Barrett, had written and distributed e-mails to his colleagues of the National Guard and even the Boston Globe, calling the Harvard scholar a "banana–eating jungle monkey" and other venomous, racist language. It was a strange twist of the proverbial kettle calling the pot black, given that both the white police officer and the black Harvard professor possess vestigial tails in their backsides in the form of fused coccyx bones. Mayor Menino was unequivocal in his denunciation, calling the police officer a cancer in the police department of Boston. By distancing themselves from such bigotry, the two leaders took the right move to assure Boston's population that the racist opinions of the officer in question had no place in the Police Department. Stripped of his gun and badge, Officer Barrett was then placed on administrative leave, pending termination hearings which should serve as a good deterrent for future gamblers of his ilk. If the police department worked so hard to earn the trust of the community in crime prevention, how could a lone rotten apple be allowed to derail such collaborative effort? A society should weep when one lone gun man enters a cafeteria and opens fire, killing four police officers. Who can say what had irked such a gunman? Who can say if he did not imperil the lives of three innocents because of the acts of one of their kind? Indeed who can say? Failing to denounce outrageous acts when they take place surely paves the way for such unfortunate retributions in the future. This chronicler wishes he were wrong.

During his suspension from the department, the police man in question quickly availed himself of an attorney and filed a federal lawsuit against the city of Boston and the commissioner, citing the violation of his rights, leading to mental illness. He alleged that the actions of Mayor Menino and the commissioner of police had ramped up a new round of international Gates-related news coverage, causing him pain, suffering, post-traumatic stress, sleeplessness, degradation among others. David Yas, publisher of *Massachusetts Lawyer Weekly* could not help wondering aloud about the irony of bringing such a law suit given that the very law was in place to combat racism and protect the oppression of minorities like Professor Gates. Police officer Barrett claimed that Mayor Menino and Commissioner Ed Davis had conspired to "to intentionally inflict emotional distress, intentionally interfere with his property rights and due process" prompting the Boston public to wonder which came first, the Menino comment or the firestorm surrounding his e-mail. Not asked but clearly implied was whether the police officer could take responsibility for his own words.

It would be a flaw to infer that all police officers are racially biased in the performance of their duties. As a matter of fact most persons are of the opinion that Professor Louis Gates could have eaten humble pie and cut a very long story short simply by respecting the police officer and letting go. But then again the professor claimed that he had done what was asked of him – show his identification. A lot of African Americans have faulted the police officer for racial profiling. Under such a charged climate it would be difficult to be objective.

As an individual, I recall a personal incident involving me and a police officer in the past. I was a learner driver at the time and, in order to speed up my learning and get a driving license, I had bought a second hand car. The regulations required that as a learner driver, I drive accompanied by a licensed driver sitting next to me with his license available for inspection. I violated all of that by going on the freeway alone. Worse, I went against a one-way street! When the police cruiser signaled me to stop, I pulled over and began to sweat profusely and made the very best effort to keep other betraying body language in check. The officer approached me, asked for my identification and, instead of my driving license or learner's permit, I deftly took out my passport. Whether he did notice any body language that could give me away, it is difficult to say. But he was awfully polite and asked why I had gone against the one-way street.

If ever there was a need for me to act fast, that was it. Which of my many personalities was I to present – a regular student on campus, my Oxfordian English, my residual French accent involving the generous use of my guttural r? I toyed with each of those ideas as the officer scrutinized me. Did he notice that I was trembling and sweating on my nose? For quite a while I had been under pressure to Americanize my English. Social campus norm expected that and the larger society around me did not hide its unease with invading British vocabulary just like the British themselves railed against creeping Americanisms, tasking the BBC for such usages as train station ( *railway station*), continuing ( *ongoing*), different to ( *different from*) and so forth. I had my sneakers on and reminded myself that they were *trainers* if the need arose, that I was going to a friend's *flat* to watch a match on the *telly*, not apartmen*t* to watch TV. I also reminded myself that I was From Cameroon (r articulated at the tip of the tongue) where we are at home with *le Français* (guttural r) as well as the Queen's language, where we keep both left and right on our highways, a product of our dual colonial heritage (good old England still keeps left on the roads whereas the *Hexagone* had since joined the rest of the world to keep right). Yes, my guttural r would do the trick to finish it up and so I felt well armed for the encounter with the trooper. But the sweating! And why did my hands choose just that occasion to tremble so much?

I was profuse with my apologies, put on my very British English tainted with some French, so that the officer knew immediately that I was alien. There was more than one good side to Cameroon's bilingual culture indeed. All along my heart kept racing, and I wondered what I would do if the officer insisted on seeing my driving license. He did not. Instead he put me through a sobriety test, asking me to count from one hundred backwards till he ordered me to stop. I did. Then he told me to recite the alphabet backwards, again stopping when he ordered me to. I did as well. Great was my relief when he asked me to go and try not to use the wrong side of the traffic again. My lucky stars! Nothing in that officer's comportment pointed to racial profiling and it would be erroneous and dishonest to jump on the bandwagon to generalize in view of that experience. Also, considering the number of times I have jaywalked in the cities of our Commonwealth and was neither caught nor fined, I think the police are not doing badly at all. Of course in matters like these it is difficult to speak for everybody.

Persons wearing weapons in holsters attended the town hall meetings, attacked the patriotism of other members and even their humanity. Experts and semi-experts of all hues roundly condemned socialism as an evil that almost always breeds poverty and corruption, urging Americans to keep it at bay. But they equally conceded that Marxism stole the birthrights of Americans, especially in the 1960s when the Federal government sidestepped the US Constitution, declared war on poverty, and promised *The Great Society*. Did America ever win that war? How could it when poverty continued to spread across the country, occupying every government agency and grounding them in debt? It was obvious that all those stories – takeovers, stimulus deals and bailouts bringing prosperity- were lies since the economy continued to implode.

"Why should healthy people subsidize the sick?" some asked, oblivious of the fact that not everyone pays tax to the government. Former Alaska governor and vice –presidential nominee, Sarah Palin contributed to stoking fears with her "Obama death panels" blog, an allegation that did not at all feature on the House version of the healthcare bill. "Death panels" was the short way of expressing inferior, government-controlled health care. But who were the hooligans disrupting the useful town hall meetings? Democrats said they were Republicans or their supporters; the party of ideas denied the charge, arguing that even democrats were disaffected by Obama's proposed reform of the healthcare. But there were faces hidden behind the mask.

It did not take long to unmask some of them. Delivering his most important address on healthcare reform to both Houses of Congress shortly after, President Obama was very heavily applauded for his propositions until a strange lone voice shouted "You lie, you lie". It was Joe Wilson, South Carolina's representative. There was much consternation that the elected representative of a people should choose to comport himself in such undignified way at a time when the whole nation was paying rapt attention to an important matter. Some felt he had insulted and disrespected not Obama the person, but the Office of President and the American people at large. Could Wilson have done so if Obama were not black? Yes and no, depending on who the microphone was extended to. The man quickly apologized but the matter did not end there – not so fast indeed, especially since he proceeded to raise funds to the tune of two million dollars, thanks to his new-found popularity. Not to be outdone was South Carolina's governor, Mark Sanford, also in the news as having disappeared for almost a week, ostensibly to go hiking the Appalachian trail but in reality the man was engaged in a tryst with an Argentine mistress in far away Buenos Aires. The one time rising star of the GOP admitted to his marital infidelities, following which his wife took steps to divorce him and turn her name into a trademark – a good, a service or product worth merchandizing.

The issue of uttering racist remarks followed by a quick apology is an American thing. Vice President Joe Biden had his share. So also did Senate majority leader Harry Reid who was being vigorously asked to step down after it came to light that during the 2008 campaign he made derogatory remarks about Barack Obama's skin color and erudition. But asking those persons to step down on such basis went against the American spirit of giving people a second chance, a spirit that made it possible for former Ku Klux Klan members to be sitting in Congress with clean guys whose youthful indulgence did not push them to such extremes.

The airwaves quickly filled with the Wilson saga, eclipsing that of the Harvard professor. Former US president Jimmy Carter was unequivocal that Wilson's outburst was simply lurking racism bubbling to the top. Painful reminders of the anarchic and violent town hall meetings came to mind. Very wisely President Obama and his advisers stayed clear of the fray and tried to distance themselves from Jimmy Carter's views or playing the race card, an action that could become a pure distraction from the very important healthcare priority. Obama stated categorically that the disagreement was over policy, not color, and even went on to cite a litany of indignities to which former President Bill Clinton was subjected as well as his wife Hillary, who barely missed the Democratic Party's nomination as candidate to become the first lady US president.

Issues of race for African-Americans, anti-Semitism for Jewish, religion for Muslim East or Christian West pose enormous challenges for any aspiring politician or professional in the US. If the politics of African-American sensitivities is thorny, that of the Jewish American is more so, especially the unwritten law against anti-Semitism. Obama knew this ahead of time and so made an effort to declare his pro-Israel stance early in the game. The disproportionate influence of Jews in America – police, US Congress, US Supreme Court, CEOs of Fortune 500 companies, major Hollywood studios, including NBC and CBS, plus comedians of Jewish descent –is a topic of hot debates.

The costly nature of anti-Semitic utterances or acts can best be illustrated by highlighting the fates of Rick Sanchez, news anchor of Cuban ancestry fired by the CNN over remarks he made concerning Jon Stewart's bigotry and the Jews running the news media ( the same type of venom Lou Dobbs was allowed to pour on Hispanics and Wolf Blitzer on Muslims), Judge Richard Goldstein, the internationally respected jurist who wrote his findings that Israel had committed war crimes in the 2009 incidents in the Gaza and a certain Ronan Tynan, an Irish immigrant who first settled in New York before being forced by circumstances to move to Massachusetts and adopt Boston as his new home. Judge Goldstein would not be able to attend his own grandson's *bar mitzvah* for fear of protesters angry at his writing that UN report.

Ronan Tynan had been embraced by New York and then scorned; he was a real victim of circumstances. Having lost a leg to amputation, Ronan worked hard and went to medical school and became a physician. But he soon discovered that his talent was in his voice, a voice that could make hearts to rise and eyes to rain. Ronan sang for New York. One day, in jest like all good Americans, he said something which someone interpreted as anti-Semitic, passed it on by word of mouth and telephone calls till New Yorkers changed from cheering Ronan to sneering him. It all happened like a dream and all the good will built over ten years just vanished into thin air. A doctor actually went as far as admitting that he would let Ronan die on the operating table if he had the chance. The New York Yankees dumped him, refusing him the possibility of stating his own side of the sad story that led up to his predicament! How sad.

It was some time ago when a realtor came to show some prospective buyers the apartment next door to Ronan's 54th East Street residence. The realtor introduced Ronan to the two ladies who happened to be Jewish. After saying hello, Ronan good naturedly warned the ladies that he often sang in his apartment and asked in a joking manner "How'd you like living next door to a loud tenor like me?" The ladies did not buy the apartment after all but shortly after the realtor came to show the apartment to another Jewish buyer. This time the realtor told Ronan, again good naturedly, not to worry because the lady and her friend were not Red Sox fans, to which Ronan said "As long as they're not those Jewish ladies."

Upon hearing this simple remark, the lady examining the apartment stopped short, stepped into the hallway and asked Ronan to explain himself. It would appear that the musician did not convince her at all. She didn't buy it, following which she simply called the Yankees and asked how they could let an anti-Semite sing "*God Bless America*". That did it! The Yankees took her version and acted upon it, refusing to cross check the veracity of the story and denying the gentleman the opportunity to clarify things or even to apologize. They claimed that it was an internal matter and so would not discuss it in public - a strange reaction from a team for whom Ronan said he sang without taking even a dime. All the same he did apologize to the Jewish lady and even promised to make a donation to her charity of choice. She apparently accepted the apology. So did the anti-Defamation League. But not the New York Yankees.

Painfully Ronan came to realize that he had made a name singing a song written by a Jewish guy who had since changed his name to something else. Ronan was judged and found guilty by someone he spoke to for seven seconds. Meanwhile his neighbor next door, another lady he had known for seven years tried in vain to convince an unbelieving New York that Ronan was a gentleman with a heart of gold, not anti-Semitic, had given her free concerts through the common wall separating them. Nothing doing! Whatever those Ashkenazi and Sephardic Jewish ancestors had planted was indeed taking root, converting what was originally a simple religion into an ethnicity; the Ashkenazi, appearing sickly but smart, with high IQs, (the theory goes that they are sickly because they are smart) are generally sensitive to anti-Semitic utterances and behaviors. Some will convert to Islam once in a while as others stick to the old religion and ethnicity, prepared to go to court over matters like someone having sex with them on false pretenses of being Jewish! Ronan learned it the hard way and just moved to Boston and hoped that the Boston Red Sox would adopt him. That would be poetic justice, wouldn't it? No wonder a fourth grader of Mexican origin in Pacoima, California, upon learning that her favorite English language teacher was Jewish, recoiled, in the words of the teacher, as if she had "suddenly transformed from Mary Poppins to a cruel, monstrous beast". The little girl had wanted to do something nice for her teacher at Christmas or her saint's day! (*SPLC's Teaching Tolerance, April 2010*). There is something called the holocaust joke. Who cracks it, when and with whom? To believe in Judaism as an ethnic culture but not in God, and yet eye the Promised Land must take quite some degree of chutzpah.

President Obama declared that it was unacceptable for the world's wealthiest nation to have more than thirty million people with no healthcare insurance and like Ted Kennedy, he called it the great unfinished business of our society, and denied that illegal immigrants would benefit from the scheme. Polls conducted around Davis and Harvard square showed that many people's grasp of the issues at stake varied from zero to not much. How many persons had actually read and could say anything meaningful about President Obama's plan? For some persons the bill of 1000 pages was so long that tackling it would require a threat of water boarding or something similar. The only persons who knew the details would be Washington's many lobbyists and a few citizens who bothered to Google the plan. But why would citizens know so little about such an important issue as the ACA (Affordable Care Act)? Apathy was clearly at work. So was fear. But by far the biggest factor was what the news media did in informing the public, dishing half-truths here, innuendos there, and lies spawned by both political parties that went unchallenged. One thing was quite clear – either many citizens already loved their representatives in Congress or were angry extremists nursing specific grievances. Neither camp would be open to persuasion, so members did not spend much time arguing the merits of the case. "If men were angels" wrote Founding Father James Madison in Federalist 51, "no government would be necessary." Neither would politicians be necessary. Unfortunately modern society is stuck with both.

But the biggest lesson politicians and their followers needed to learn is that small minds discuss people while bigger minds discuss ideas. All the insults being heaped at President Obama, especially the questioning of his legitimacy as US president, could not possibly provide an answer for the way forward. Republicans and even some democrats seemed to behave like interlopers when indeed they had so much common ground to work on - the catastrophic oily tide in the Gulf of Mexico, renewed concerns about terrorism, two lingering wars abroad and a pesky recession. Independents are better placed to change the government at any given time in the nation's history. Having broken free of the status quo by not identifying with any predefined party position that goes with a corresponding label or emphasizing a type of black versus white polarization – Republican, Democrat, Tea Party, Nut job – they recognize that the solution may well lie in the gray area.

Countering some of the criticisms in his usual level-headed way, the president tried to allay some fears and to volunteer comparisons with current practices. He said people were reacting negatively to the idea of a public plan, yet Americans had lived with FEDEX and UPS for a long time, competing with the government's postal services in bringing letters and parcels to their homes. Those who spurned the public plan simply refused to encounter any type of competition; they preferred monopolies, yet we are a capitalist nation. Professor Stephen Hawking, known for his scientific contributions and public battle with Lou Gehrig's disease, also put in a powerful contribution, stating that he would be long dead if it weren't for Britain's NHS (National Health Service) which some Americans derisively dismissed as socialized medicine or a disaster, without even knowing its merits. They even scorned France's National Health Insurance which takes care of patients also, with very little co-pay. The most absurd comparisons were made with the situation in Cuba, Vietnam, North Korea, Russia, China and other socialist and communist countries. The GOP conservatives did not stop at that. In the absence of concrete counterproposals, their supporters in the town hall sessions resorted to the newly discovered powerful tool of getting their message out through angry, disruptive, uninformed and often violent howling and screaming at the Democrats, actions completely at variance with what the Founding Fathers envisaged – thoughtful deliberations considered essential to democracy. Tom Foreman, a seasoned columnist for Boston's metro newspaper captured this type of citizen as the "looming specter of an Angry White Man, just another one of us in a room full of frustrated Tea Party types, persons who ought to be ruminating instead about how the GOP should reach out to new constituents, more folks, more diverse views while retaining core dependable conservatives."

If ever there was a case for make over, that was it. As for those Democrats who opposed even their own president, Obama had a simple message – "none of you can expect the Republicans not to go after you if you vote against this bill." The leg dragging had become incomprehensible, given that the Republicans had voted against virtually every bill put forth by the Democrats. President Obama devised an interesting metaphor to describe the situation between the Republicans and Democrats. Addressing one of his many rallies, he said "when you want to go forward you put your car in D (drive, Democrat) not in R (reverse, Republicans) and proceeded to explain that the Republicans had driven the nation's car into a ditch and abandoned it there. Now that the Democrats had pulled it out, they wanted the key back, which was unacceptable" He got a deafening applause when he asked how he could give back the key when Republicans did not know how to drive. The final vote of 220 for, and 215 against forwarding the bill to the Senate showed how wide the gulf remained in spite of all the lobbying Obama had done. What the House finally came up with was modeled after Massachusetts' pioneering healthcare plan to expand health insurance - require most Americans to obtain health insurance or pay a penalty, force most employers to provide it or face fines, offer government subsidies to help low-income people purchase plans and finally, set up a new national health insurance market similar to Massachusetts' Health Insurance Connector to help the uninsured and small businesses shop for insurance. Some hope was at last rekindled in the healthcare reform effort.

But then unbelievably, and in spite of this, the election shortly after of Scott Brown, a Republican, to fill the Kennedy vacancy, was going to torpedo the entire healthcare reform! Voters had become so angry that they were prepared to vote against their own favorite party and against the cherished plan of their long serving senator. A Kennedy legacy ruined? Away with hereditary succession! Away with back room deals and pork barrels! Barack Obama, the super candidate of 2008 was simply ignored as voters went for this unknown quantity called Scott Brown. Overnight the obscure state senator turned into a demigod, single-handedly setting the nation's agenda! The man was all about the working man in his campaign trail, railing against Washington D. C.'s focus on health instead of the economy and in the process depicting Democrats as disconnected from the problems facing truck drivers like him. Scott Brown became the 41st vote against health care legislation, leaving the Democratic Party with only 59 votes, short of that important filibuster-proof. Some revolutionary thing had taken place and people were yet to find an expression for it. How did so many right thinking people vote the wrong candidate? Or, perhaps better still, how did so many wrong thinking persons get it right?

Massachusetts had done it again! Once the hub of the universe, initiator of revolution and place from which a single shot fired could be heard round the world, Massachusetts had sparked another revolution by its decision to vote Scott Brown, a Republican to fill a gap that had been a safe constituency for the Kennedys for decades.

The messianic zeal to criticize the Democrats in general and Barack Obama in particular, no matter the facts, had become the hallmark of the GOP obstructionism. Suddenly Americans were being made to feel that it took 60 votes (no longer 51) to pass a law in Congress or approve an appointment made by the president. Hardly had Scott Brown been sworn in than he gave a press conference in which he declared that "the stimulus package did not create one new job", contradicting an analysis by the nonpartisan Congressional Budget Office which showed that the stimulus package had saved or created 600,000 to 1.6 million jobs in the third quarter of 2009. It got so bad that governor Tim Kaine could not help exclaiming about the breathtaking display of public hypocrisy with at least 116 governors, senators and representatives spending most of 2009 railing against President Obama's ARRA (American Recovery and Reinvestment Act) while at the same time requesting funds to create jobs in their districts and taking credit for projects at their ribbon cutting ceremonies. Whose interest could such prevarications serve? It was all so confusing and demoralizing.

Pioneers like the self-effacing George Washington must be squirming in their graves at the way things have turned out. Here was a patriot who served as a soldier to win the new nation's independence from Britain, brought back from his retirement in peaceful Mount Vernon to assume the highest office in the land, a patriot who, in spite of all the adulation, proceeded with much trepidation and reflection declaring, "I fear if the issue of public measures should not correspond with their sanguine expectations, they will turn the extravagant...praises which they are heaping upon me at this moment into equally extravagant ...censures." America's first politician was standing on the bridge over Assunpink Creek in Trenton, New Jersey, the spot where he had stood off the British when he uttered those memorable words on his way to Philadelphia and then to New York to take up the office of president of the United States.

In the euphoria following Scott Brown's victory over Martha Coakley, it would be foolhardy not to counsel some degree of moderation and realism, drawing inspiration either from George

Washington's words of wisdom or from what had just preceded him the year before. A simple rule of thumb, often ignored by those who get carried away by the populist rhetoric of electioneering, is to not make promises that one cannot keep. The UK's Conservative party learned this bitter lesson as angry constituents went on the rampage demonstrating outside parliament, smashing windows and throwing missiles and placards at police to vent their anger over promises not kept. Their party had made a U-turn and voted with Prime Minister Cameron to triple university tuition. Here are home the Democrats got voted out of their majority in the House of Representatives. Yesterday it was Barack Obama riding high on the crest of popularity; today it is Scott Brown and the electorate, like the major issues, remained the same. There is always a palpable push against a growing government, especially when the government is seen to control people's lives, take more and more scarce resources and put to uses that benefit politicians and interest groups, amassing debts that will burden future generations and decrease their prosperity, issuing more mandates and prohibitions that whittle away people's liberty. But then what of the other side of the coin?

Once off the campaign trail and into government, a candidate becomes faced with roads to be built, bridges in need of fixing, kids to be educated, police and fire services to pay for, the poor, the weak and the sick to be protected. The candidate can then make his or her pick as Barack Obama is experiencing today. Scott Brown campaigned on the vague but salable idea that he would lower taxes. He entered the legislature as a member of a minority party (the GOP) and with the least seniority too.

With America's ping-pong democracy, the blame game usually shifts quickly, thanks to a population short on memory but long on anger. Blame almost always follows those who wield power. It is easy to promise getting jobs for people and cutting their taxes, especially here in Massachusetts where citizens do not particularly like paying taxes. Tax dodgers or haters have since changed the name of the Commonwealth to "Taxachussets" and decided to move up north to tax-free New Hampshire and do their shopping so as to avoid paying the heavy Massachusetts tax. In Massachusetts as in the US at large, citizens demand government services – highways, libraries, and police – but want to pay little or nothing for them. They express a love-hate relationship with taxes. Going to New Hampshire involves driving, buying gas, parking, and eating lunch out there, all of which costs money. Also, consulting the facts as revealed by the Tax Foundation, Massachusetts state and local tax burden is 9.2%, 0.2 points below the national average; the personal income tax is the $29^{th}$ highest in the 50 states, and corporate tax structure is the fourth among states that have corporate income, property tax is the $8^{th}$ highest in the nation. Does "Taxachusetts" make sense then?

The citizens of Greece are today living the horrors of anti-tax life as their country's financial health remains on life support with the European Union wondering what to do about it. Some citizens have recommended calling a time out on government bashing so as to recognize and celebrate those who make it work. People like soldiers, the police, firefighters, plumbers, and others perform wonders in emergency situations. By celebrating the commonwealth of all those persons who work behind the scenes to hold our infrastructure together, often with diminishing resources, we shall have taken a step in the right direction. Some things are just supposed to work and when simple routines go wrong, there is something unsettling about that. Other things just work, not because they are supposed to but because our educated talent from scientists to technologists, engineers, mathematicians and others see to it that the simple routines actually work. They are unsung heroes and society tends to take them for granted. How many of today's generation aspire to be problem solvers?

Americans must be wondering what innovations Sarah Palin will come up with as she eyes the next presidential election, having failed to make it as the GOP vice presidential candidate in 2008 and now selling like hot cakes in the Tea Party. A CBO (congressional budget office) report, put out by trained professionals with good academic credentials and many years of job experience, after factoring in the House final reconciliation changes, indicated that the recently passed healthcare reform bill would cut down the federal deficit. But Sarah Palin's Tea Party said the CBO was wrong and that their "common sense" opinion trumped the opinion of the experts. Truth be told, most Americans wanted neither the Republican Party nor the Democratic Party; as for the vocal Tea Party, they were unsure just how to RSVP as they went ahead to tolerate the laws, policies and taxes they did not like or could not avoid. Sarah Palin had given the Tea Party an identity that was difficult to make sense of, especially when it appeared to be anti-everything, spewing negative and unwanted venom laced with outright lies about the Obama administration.

The original Tea Party was against taxation without representation but toady's party seems to be harping more on taxation with misrepresentation and plenty of half-baked ideas totally at odds or inconsistent with governance. Those high pitches venting pent-up feelings that government had too much power needed an outlet which television easily provided. People genuinely asked what good there was in canvassing for votes using misinformation. A coherent message was still wanting and it appeared that in its place supporters were filling in with vocal, racist, guitar-playing reprobates, gun-toting militia, secessionists, tax protesters, including some who demanded an end to government subsidies for Medicare, in spite of President Obama excluding 95% of them from tax increases. Can votes be cast for politicians, laws be passed and freedom thrive all based on misinformation?

The distrust of government by Americans had reached an unprecedented level. Some claimed it was due to President Obama appointing Timothy Geithner, perceived as a tax cheat, to run the treasury. Others found fault with Nancy Pelosi promising to "drain the swamp" and to "have the most open, most honest and most ethical" Congress in history but failing to deliver. Others picked quarrels with Charlie Rangel, a presumed tax cheat, being given the job of writing our tax code or Chris Dodd of Discount Countrywide Mortgages and Barney Frank, supporting Fannie Mae and Freddie Mac, two fiscal desiccators at the origin of the nation's financial woes.

People continued to see tax in terms of "my money going to things or people I disapprove of" and such anti-tax sentiments became quite high whenever the government became unpopular. Part of the problem was traceable to Ronald Reagan's election around 1980 and the introduction of the theory of supply-side economics which stipulates that lower taxes eventually lead to higher government revenues. At about the same time as Ronald Reagan's election there was a Barbara Anderson, director of CLT(citizens for limited taxes) who launched Proposition 21/2 to limit municipality's property tax revenue and its ability to raise property taxes, a complicated formula that has been subjected to amendments and modifications ever since, to render it applicable.

The truth is that whether we like them or not, taxes are a statement of what we choose to be, not what we wish we were. Difficult to understand? In my childhood I came across persons who considered cleaning city streets a sheer waste of time since the streets would get dirty again. Over the years, however, as I moved away from home, I have come to appreciate the value of making some of our money available to the government as tax money so that with it, people can be employed to keep the roads clean of the debris of our civilization – broken bottles, paper wrappings, plastics, used condoms and others. There is a terrible price to be paid for believing that we can get something for nothing, says Borosage, an enlightened observer. We look at taxes the way we look at ourselves, even if we choose to look away. It is a lesson in civics few persons bother to learn, often with unpleasant consequences such as the angry Texas taxpayer, Joseph Stack who became upset with the IRS, rambled an anti-government manifesto on his website, set his house ablaze, entered his single engine plane and crashed it on the second floor of the building housing offices of the internal revenue services in Austin, Texas, just months after Charles Ray Polk was released from prison for his own plot to blow up the Austin, TX service center of the IRS. None of this comes any closer to Timothy McVeigh's anti-government action of bombing the Federal building in Oklahoma City and killing 168 people in the process.

Presidential adviser David Axelrod did not help matters much when he told disillusioned voters that the people would never know what was in the healthcare bill until after it was passed. Incredible! What a gaffe! But that was putting the cart before the horse! No wonder the popular discontent and furor! Does democracy not require the people to know what is in the bill before rather than after it has been passed? Massachusetts voters were craving for someone outside of the traditional political structure, someone who could speak everyday bread and butter concerns in a credible way, someone courageous enough to do something about unfair credit and lending practices that had brought about the crisis. The twenty-first century economy was putting too much pressure on the middle class. President Obama's good talk was still there, his call for a broad plan of revitalization, new spirit of bipartisanship and job creation received the usual thunderous applause but beneath it all was voter cynicism and the unanswered question: Isn't that what he promised on taking office one year earlier? In all fairness to the man, he had spent the economic stimulus money, a dynamic step indeed and stopped the economic skid even if things were not yet rosy. And he did invite the Republicans to bipartisanship; it was surely not his fault that the invitation was not taken up, the GOP preferring to stick to an obstructionist agenda. He had created new jobs and saved some old ones even if 4.2 million were lost too. It could be worse! The president left no stone unturned in campaigning for incumbent Democrats in congress as well as those seeking to get in, appearing on several TV shows –Comedy Central's "Daily Show" with Jon Stewart, Discovery Channel's "Mythbusters", ABC's talk show, "The View", CBS's late night show with Dave Letterman, NBC's "Tonight Show" with Jay Leno and others.

In retrospect, around 1993, Conservative activist Bill Kristol had said that if the Republican Party did a thing to help Bill Clinton succeed in healthcare reform, it would revive the reputation of the Democratic Party as the generous protector of middle class interests, thereby threatening to relegate the Republicans to minority status. Now under a new Democratic president, the GOP was once again at it. Virginia's representative, Eric Cantor spoke of the GOP's steadfast opposition to the Democrats as a principled one after Senator Jim DeMint said in July 2010 "If we're to stop Obama on it, it will be his Waterloo. It will break him." Democrats began openly talking about the next move which would be baptized "Reconciliation," a euphemism for what in GOP terms would be called the "Nuclear Option" that would go ahead and vote with or without Republican support. Given such a charged atmosphere one could only speculate which party the electorate would choose to reward.

Where did self-reliance and self help go? Where did philanthropy go? A teacher of mine once drew a parallel between philanthropy and physical exercise, being needed the most when one is in bad shape. It makes a lot of sense. Unemployed persons and those who have lost jobs often sit and brood over their plight. A few others take to volunteering and in the process, discover new insights into expressions like "it could be worse", "the man with no shoes is better off than one without feet". One volunteer had thought his destiny was the worst possible on mother earth until he reached Mombasa, Kenya in East Africa and met a boy who actually wished that he had been born a dog rather than a boy. His reason was simple – on the streets of Mombasa dogs were fed whereas boys were waved away.

It is commonplace to hear many adults complain about the chasm between them and their kids. How much parental indulgence is acceptable for child upbringing? Should a thirteen-year old daughter be allowed to dress like a hooker on Halloween night? Parents are under tremendous pressure to provide all sorts of gadgets for their kids, some at variance with the pursuit of academic work. No serious parent enjoys seeing the half-hearted attempt at doing homework put forth by kids who wrestle with cell phones or television sets or video games and computer screens while paying lip service to their books and studies. Parents know that books are the doors to different places and times and so the serious ones urge their kids to read. The social paradox of young persons, mostly men, being hooked to video games, smart phones is taking a toll as users become addicts, replacing real friends with Internet friendships, losing sleep, missing school and work, neglecting household chores and even bodily hygiene. According to psychiatrist Jane Morris a slow epidemic is gripping the world.

Should a parent give an eleven year old a cell phone? Many parents would answer in the negative but a good number would indulge without hesitation, citing the famous leitmotif to stay connected. Staying connected from the early age of twelve and making this one's second nature can be very costly later in life. Imagine a prospective employer who is forced to interrupt the interviewing process to cope not only with a job applicant's wildly ringing cell phone but also an unhelpful and irritating conversation by the candidate seeking employment in a competitive job market. Those who oppose cell phones for such young persons are deeply aware and concerned about the distraction such a thing can cause in a child. First of all giving a child a cell phone so early in life deprives that child of many valuable learning experiences – working to save money to buy real needs, paying bills regularly as they become due and living with the consequences of nonpayment of such bills and many more. The strong urge to get a cell phone and use it often overlooks basic facts like phone bills that have to be paid. Of course when bills are not paid the phone stops working and invariably the bill is tossed at the indulgent parent, a first step toward financial irresponsibility. Cell phone use at work has reached a point where work itself seems like an afterthought.

For many young persons the world has simply become an important phone booth. Texting, twittering, surfing the Internet, taking pictures and sharing them, often pictures in the nude are some of the things that make many a reasonable parent go slowly along this road. Premature death on the highways as a result of obsession with texting while driving is almost always a thing for others to worry about until it strikes home. These days it is commonplace to find young persons careening down the freeway at 70 mph in rush hour while at the same time crunching a phone between cheek and shoulder, one hand holding a sputtering tape recorder, all part of a weird type of multitasking. Some kids ask not just for a cell phone, but one with a special design and color of their choice. Imagine what can happen during those few seconds it takes to drop a CD into a car stereo or dial a cell phone number while the eyes are off the road. And when parents accede to such outlandish demands, often the phones get lost and the next thing is to ask for an iPad, iPod, iPhone or a Blackberry and then a matching iMac. It does not stop there; sooner or later the parents will be confronted with a request for a $500,000 Mercedes-Benz SLR McLaren next. Along with the phones are associated demands like piercing body parts, beginning with the ears, nose, tongue, getting a choice tattoo, wearing Apple Bottom jeans and boots with fur so that an entire bar looks at a young woman as she goes by. The next step of dancing around a pole in a gentleman's club is not too far off. It is clear where such a life style is leading; academic pursuit is surely at the back burner.

I was stunned when for the first time I came across the theme "blacks are children who cannot help themselves." Isn't it true that *Payday Loans* trap the poor in Quicksand? Who supports the poor and who speaks for them? The Cyber News head line of December 1, 2006 stated, "Thirty-nine States still allow payday lending in some fashion, prompting liberal consumer and civil rights groups to urge a national crackdown on the practice. But then guess what!!!!!!! A prominent black leader apparently profited by acting as the spokesperson for a "predatory lender" who exploited poor and minorities by forcing sub-prime loans down the throats of unsuspecting borrowers. Why did LoanMax which specializes in high interest auto title loans hire Reverend Al Sharpton to pitch its products on TV? And why did the reverend oblige, saying, "When I am out fighting for the little guy and I need quick cash, I find comfort in knowing that LoanMax is there for me."? In another advertisement he said "There's someone in Virginia who will loan money to the people the big guys won't loan to." Incredibly, Al Sharpton's home state, New York, refused to allow LoanMax to operate in that State. Why? New York State set an interest rate cap at 16% but LoanMax's rate exceeded that. So Al Sharpton pitched a product to three other states that was illegal in his own State! How could the Reverend have missed this obvious trap and conflict of interest?

One does not need to be a rocket scientist to understand what was at stake. Banks and mortgage companies are in business to make profit and they do so by charging interests. If the interest is too low, there is no profit. If a loan is not repaid, there is no profit – indeed there will be a loss. LoanMax, for example, would loan $400 at 30% monthly interest, making $120 on a $400 for 30 days! If the average repayment were two to three months, then in 90 days the average customer would pay $360 ($120X3) for a $400 loan. If a customer took a year to pay off the debt, that would amount to spending a whopping $1440 in interest on a $400 loan! Borrowers usually paid the title recording fees, and some lenders would add $50 annual membership fee.

It got so bad that a New York Post editorial entitled "loan Shark Sharpton" slammed Reverend Al Sharpton for his practice of simultaneously criticizing those who purportedly preyed on minorities and at the same time benefitting from those very people and many New Yorkers asked: "Would you buy a used car from that guy?"

No wonder Congresswoman Stephanie Tubbs-Jones (D-OH) called predatory lending "the civil rights issue of the century." Alphonso Jackson, President George Bush's Secretary of the Department of HUD, dismissed the Jesse Jacksons, the Al Sharptons, and the Julian Bonds in these words: "They (black leaders) have created an industry. If we don't become victims, they have no income, they have no podium". Those are words from a man who had learned very useful lessons from his father, a cancer patient with almost no income, who refused to take welfare or food stamps, saying, "Never take anything you didn't earn. That's close to stealing". And so his son, Secretary Jackson stormed and attacked the idea of black victimhood: "I am not going to let the black leadership – the so-called leadership – of this country tell me that I am a victim. I believe that if you work hard, strive to do the very best, things will work out for you". America must have held its breath to see how it would work out between disgraced USDA employee and superstar of black victimhood, Shirley Sherrod, Andrew Breitbart, the blogger who quoted her 1986 speech to the NAACP out of context, lacing it with incendiary racist material thus bringing the race issue to the fore, and the White House which prematurely entered the dance without reflecting on its implications for President Obama who had studiously kept race issues at bay all along. Cried one disgusted observer: "Whites have nothing whatsoever to do with the fact that seven out of ten black children born in America are born out of wedlock. BMW (Bitch, Moan, and Whine) seems to be the identification tag of black leaders".

Even Magic Johnson found himself inexplicably in this category. Ever since the gentleman retired from the NBA and went out of prime time television, he is said to have devoted his time and energies to economic development and urban renewal in some of the most underserved areas of the US. But recently he is said to have signed on as pitchman for Jackson Hewitt's "money Now Loan", another loan shark supposedly providing instant loans to people in anticipation of their tax returns from the IRS. First of all, there is no such thing as "Instant Refund" from the IRS, says Judge Judy. The Consumer Federation of American (CFA) agrees. Only the tax preparers can advance anyone money based on their calculation of the anticipated refund. Meanwhile Jackson Hewitt is dragging H &R Block, its rival to court claiming irreparable harm from the latter's deceptive script to its agents. By pitching for Jackson Hewitt, Johnson was lending legitimacy to a product that had had a deleterious impact on the lives of the urban poor. Unscrupulous corporations tend to exploit the economic deprivation that pervades many black and brown communities of America. With the steady decline of available jobs and increasing unwillingness to provide traditional loans to persons of color, products like pay day and refund anticipation loans have gained traction in the poor neighborhoods. But instead of providing the needed assistance, these loans carry unconscionable "strings" such as 400% interest rates per annum (Jackson Hewitt's rates are said to range from 136% to 140%). Did magic Johnson know this? If not, would he then renounce the deal with Jackson Hewitt? Another wait and see.

Grainy surveillance pictures of two African American politicians – Chuck Turner and former state senator Dianne Wilkerson – showed them allegedly accepting cash from a Roxbury night club owner working in cooperation with the FBI. The case against the twosome was brought by US Attorney, Michael J. Sullivan and shook up the black political establishment with unprecedented urgency. Most observers thought it was about time too. Too much dependence on the status quo had mired the black community of Boston and the elected black leaders had been content with petty accomplishments like pulling political levers to get liquor licenses. But their constituency was in need of so much more – jobs, education, and protection against crime. Mediocrity could not continue to be accepted in lieu of significant reform. The FBI photo of Wilkerson stuffing cash into her bra pushed her long time enablers over the cliff. For too long her constituents made excuses for her violation of campaign finance and tax laws. This time, faced with the dramatic photographs and detailed bribery allegation, voters finally abandoned her, bringing her campaign to an abrupt halt.

Needless to say the practice of rallying to the defense of one's race provides the ideal weapon for proponents of racial profiling to use against everyone black, presumably because the impression is given that whenever a black commits a crime he/she takes cover under the umbrella of their race where victimhood is chanted to divert attention from individual responsibility. Massachusetts leaders must now revisit the realm of ethics and clean up their acts to protect the next generation of politicians.

And reparations for slavery? That is another thorny issue. As the Democratic candidate running for the presidency, Barack Obama said he would rather support improving schools that can help all. To offer reparations to the descendants of slaves, the Illinois Senator said no, placing him somewhat at odds with the black leadership that had been clamoring for reparations and prompting others to challenge the authenticity of his blackness. Obama felt that government should instead combat the legacy of slavery by improving schools, healthcare and the economy for all, repeating that good schools for inner city kids and jobs for people who are unemployed would do by far more in this direction. At some point two dozen members of the US Congress were sponsoring legislation to create a commission that would study reparations(payments and programs to make up for the damage done by slavery) and the NAACP supported that move. But to dismiss the suggestion made by President Obama is to miss the crux of the matter. John H. Jackson, president of the Schott Foundation that does research and develops policy says that 1.2 million black male students drop out of high school every year, some to fill the prison pipeline, others destined to face the consequence of poor education with life time job prospects, situation that does not facilitate closing the achievement gap at all.

The complexities involved in seeking redress by paying reparations to the descendants of African slaves bound and brought over to the US are many. At a time when so much of American consumption is export from China, what could be more natural than to turn to a Chinese formula for this thorny issue as well? Instead of giving people fish daily (monetary compensation for descendants of slaves) it makes sense to teach them to fish (good schools and good jobs). In a strange twist, a version of the very idea calls for present day Africans to also pay compensation in view of their ancestors' complicity in the slave trade, an outrageous idea that will only stoke the embers of smoldering prejudice between Africans and African-Americans, a tough sell indeed because Africans of today are themselves demanding compensation for the ills of colonialism that have contributed enormously to the present state of underdevelopment of the Black Continent. They too were unwilling victims of an odious scheme imposed on them! How any of these claims work out remains to be seen but dismissing President Obama's prudent approach seems to be missing the point and possibly providing a tool for people like the enigmatic Sarah Palin (*Reflections on Faith, Family and Flag*) with extremist world views and unflinching comments about race in America – that racism does not exist but is merely a misanthropic by-product of the refusal by African-Americans to shut up, toughen up and truly become American patriots, that race-based frustrations expressed by African-Americans is proof positive of dubious patriotism and questionable allegiance, that it is a ploy, a canard and a smokescreen by opponents of the new American awakening. The lady who could not help Senator John McCain win the 2008 race to the White House surely has a mouthful!

More worrying today is the idea that all the civil rights gains and progress made since slavery are slowly being eroded and reversed by the criminal justice system, a system which some have rightly called the civil rights issue of the present century. The total US population of prisoners stands at 2.4 million. If the number of persons on probation and parole is considered, the figure rises to 8 million which is nearly 3% of the total US population. That is unacceptable. The nation has apparently chosen to lock up more people for longer than any other nation in the world and of those so incarcerated, blacks and Latinos are disproportionately represented. How can this be explained? More crime? Yes, but politics plays a big role too in driving up the prison population in America since sentencing decisions made by judges and politicians are invariably tainted by politics. A majority of persons jailed for illegal drug use, for example, are blacks or Latinos, yet more than 70% of the users are indeed white Americans. The nation's conscience was pricked by a three- life- sentences parolee who went on to murder a police officer doing his duty. What were the criteria used for granting such a dangerous person parole? That seems to be the way the US is dealing with inequality and intractable social ills instead of the Great Society solutions once tooted around. It is hard power and the state of Texas plays Ground Zero in the prison boom, locking and executing more people than any other state in the union.

Yet that does not decrease the crime wave in the nation, prompting people like Judge Steven Alm of Hawaii to propose HOPE (Hawaii's Opportunity Probation with Enforcement) as a new, swift and sure tool to fight crime. Under such a scheme probation should be stricter but less harsh, faster and surer. For those on probation, random drug tests, about twice or so a week, are administered and those testing positive arrested on the spot, tried and promptly jailed for violating the conditions of their probation. Preliminary results appear to show a significant drop in crime rate as most people quit drug-related crimes and settled down to jobs.

From Europe the US is invariably seen as practicing cowboy capitalism and its associated fierce competition to innovate and stay on top or sink to the bottom. In the equally popular domain of sports, the US practices what Karl Marx would love, according to one cynic. Europe is the direct opposite of this, practicing socialism and yet her darling sport is a real Darwinian battle of survival of the fittest. Can one understand Italy and its politics without knowing a lot about soccer and the game's relationship to Prime Minister Silvio Berlusconi, the former owner of A C Milan, who converted the team's football chant into the name of his political party? See how the British adore Manchester United!

Shocked conservatives, looking at the wave of government bailouts on the US economic landscape, began warning of European-style socialism coming on board in the New World. *(Europe is generally seen as a giant welfare state while America is the land of free market opportunity where achievement reaps rewards and failure is quickly discarded).* How pockets of socialism thrive in America's vast landscape of capitalism is something few people realize. And the system works! In professional sports one would expect to find an arena of rough-and-tumble, winner-take-all but US sports are not a Darwinian battle where the fittest survive, as it were. Instead it is something close to, if not quite, a workers' paradise, a safety net impossible to fall through. The Dallas Cowboys, playing in their newest stadium with state-of-the-art facilities estimated at $1.5 billion, expect fans to dig deep into their wallets (to attend an NFL game a family of four spends about $750). Such is the money that goes into the common pool to sustain other teams.

In Europe and in big sports such as soccer, Europeans practice real free market meritocracy by rewarding success and leaving failures behind; everyone fends for himself. By contrast it is American professional sports that function as a welfare state with wealth sharing; luxury spending is taxed and passed on to the poor. The weakest teams are not allowed to fall. The NFL (National Football League) which symbolizes America abroad is a living example of a redistributive enterprise with revenue sharing provisions where massive TV revenues are put into a big pot and then handed out evenly, regardless of success. Thus the bigger teams subsidize the smaller ones that would be otherwise considered failures. Salary caps, scheduling and draft mechanisms empower the poor at the expense of the rich, all in the name of "parity" or equality. The same operates in the NBA (basketball) and even baseball. These facts are not borne out by the misnomer of a name, where the hand, not the foot, does most of the work and financial management provides a social safety net for weak teams that would otherwise suffer relegation to a lower division. The misnomer goes even further. The crowning event of the season for one of the sports is called the World Series, even as it involves only one country in the world – the US.

This contrasts with British soccer where it is every team for itself. Europe's soccer is a multibillion dollar sport with each club being a power symbol of national or regional identity and the UEFA an unfettered free market. Club owners are free to spend and sign on players as they wish, sometimes driving themselves into debt. Only the rich thrive.

In the sporting world of America however, while it is natural for any losing team like Tampa Bay or the Boston Celtics to ride from the bottom to the top, in the other America, people freely raise eye brows when companies like General Motors, Ford, and Chrysler are described as "too big to fail" and therefore need to be bailed out by the government. Citizens cried out loud to stop using tax payers' dollars to bail out multimillion dollar corporations that refused to change with the times and thus lost their markets. And so, ultimately, what some have derogatorily called the "Europeanization of America" may turn out to be the best medicine for capitalism after all. It is an aspect of Hillary Clinton's smart policy at work. If that could save GM and other auto companies and put the nation back to work, what the heck?

At some point it seemed as if President Barack Obama had inherited a poisoned gift. How did he find himself in the type of bind where he was giving Americans money to spend at a time shortly after they had learnt the painful lessons of profligate living and were doing everything to save? Every day we heard of a recession that was getting from bad to worse, tending towards a depression.

And the US Congress had just voted the Bobdignaggian amount of $787 billion economic stimulus package composed of tax cuts and spending on what was pompously called "shovel ready" projects to turn the economy around and make America the job-creating machine it once was. Having signed this into law President Obama had then to convince fellow Americans to get the money and spend. But would they? Or would they rather put their lessons to use and save the money instead? With all the talk about tax cuts for the rich who create jobs, data from Moody's Analytics Inc. appeared to show that instead of spending to create jobs, the rich saved their monies, similar to what happened under Bill Clinton, when tax cuts led to more savings. George Bush's economic stimulus package of 2008, though modest in comparison, did not do much to the economy. Former Federal Reserve boss Alan Greenspan is now advising that the Bush-era tax cuts should be allowed to expire so as to rein in the huge budget deficit (swollen to $1 trillion by stimulus spending) and stop it from crowding out private investment. Excessive consumerism with its associated corollary of borrowing stared all of us in the face and the recession with simultaneous restructuring of the auto industry delivered the most savage punch on blue-collar middle class workers. Experts said that the jobs lost in the downturn, especially in manufacturing were never going to come back, the simple reason being that companies tended to invest in labor-saving, productivity-enhancing technology here in the US as well as offshore. That did not sound too good for school dropouts and those with low qualifications.

It was interesting that in spite of the new president's popular appeal and support as well as the great effort to reach across the isle and seek a bipartisan support for a second economic stimulus package, Republicans were reluctant to support the bill. This was difficult to understand. Die hard Republicans called it liberal and socialist ideas of big government and big spending, completely at variance with the ideals of the free market. They credited the liberal legacy with the social mess into which America found itself - incalculable number of sexually and physically abused children, violence, mayhem and depravity, vile language, children going unsupervised, free to use drugs and keep the hours they choose, parents totally unfit for child raising and still being heavily subsidized by the government, millions of children living in homes without fathers, millions more with parents in prison and others. Most persons would have jumped on the bandwagon to go along with such a popular ideal to get the nation out of the recession, considering that over the eight previous years, under the watchful eyes of George W. Bush, a Republican, the nation descended into the economic crunch. How could it all so conveniently be put at the doorsteps of liberals? Or were Republicans already looking ahead to the next elections, hoping and wishing that those measures fail and be placed squarely at the doorsteps of the Democrats when the time came? Why would Rush Limbaugh express so much glee to see President Obama fail? Why did Rick Santelli rant about Tea Party in CNBC? Did Sean Hannity have nothing better to offer than negative news about the Obama administration? Where was patriotism and where was the pride of being American?

Listening to Newt Gingrich speak eloquently about the Republican party as a party of jobs, growth and prosperity for most Americans, the unenlightened easily got carried away, forgetting to ask also about the big banks, the big insurance companies, the big oil companies and the multinational corporations that conveniently moved jobs overseas to other countries to maximize their profits. It got former president Bill Clinton so incensed that he could not help asking who the last president was that gave Americans a balanced budget. Such a question needed to be asked when faced with the incessant rhetoric from the right, lambasting President Obama and Democrats in Congress about being big spenders and crazy quasi-socialists. Yes, Republicans display an aversion to socialism as a form of government that stifles innovation and intrudes into people's lives but putting such smear machinery into overdrive naively assumes and hopes that American voters suffer from amnesia, especially over the recent past.

Such attitudes did not go unnoticed. As soon as Rush Limbaugh made it known that he was interested in the purchase of the St. Louis Rams football team, there was general unease in the world of sports, unease, disgust and denunciation concretely translated by the Executive Director of the NFL Players' Association in an e-mail to the association's executive, opposing the purchase, adding that "sport in the US is at its best when it gives us reason to cheer, to unify and transcend and overcome divisions and reject discrimination and hate." Many NFL players openly said they could never bring themselves to play in his team if he succeeded in the purchase. It could not have been otherwise; the NFL, a private organization, saw right away that the prospective owner would be bad for business. Certainly as a political pundit, his inflammatory comments and especially his hurtful remarks about African American football players did not go unnoticed. Associating such a person with the NFL would be a recipe for future disasters – probes, protests, boycotts and so forth, none of which is good for profit-making business so dearly cherished by team owners. Like a rotten egg, Rush Limbaugh was quickly dropped from the list of those being considered and one observer concluded that his racist rhetoric at last was coming home to roost. How for so long society as a whole had not hit the man where it hurts most – his wallet – remained a mystery to many.

On Tuesday January 19, 2010 the people of the Commonwealth of Massachusetts went to the polls in a special election organized to select a senator to fill the seat left by the late icon of the Democratic Party, Senator Edward M. Kennedy. Earlier Martha Coakley the Attorney-General had eliminated four rivals at the primary and was now pitted against Scott Brown, a Republican underdog. In the bluest of the blue states it had simply been assumed that an unknown quantity like Brown had no chance, pitted against a Democratic candidate of such standing, a woman for that matter, who also enjoyed endorsements from Vicki Kennedy, widow of the late senator, Joe Kennedy, a nephew, governor Deval Patrick, former President Bill Clinton, incumbent president Barack Obama and many more. Martha herself had lapsed into some type of complacency during the last weeks of the campaign, sure that with name recognition and all, she could take it easy. How wrong! Scott Brown pulled the kind of trick Obama did a year earlier to become US president and neutralized all the goodwill associated with the late senator.

Hundreds of thousands of voters got fired up and defied all the odds as they went to the polls to give their support to the man who unmistakably promised to derail what the late Kennedy had called the cause of his life – universal healthcare. What a way to esteem the memory of the beloved senator!

All of the calculations failed to take note of an important variable in the equation – that over the years, angry voters of the liberal and solidly blue Commonwealth of Massachusetts tended to defy the odds and vote Republicans into office. That was not all. Angry unemployed persons as well as angry uninsured persons wanted someone they could trust, someone less likely to dribble them with the gymnastics of the issues of consequence. Something was being hidden from them, even if they could not put a finger on it and give it a name. In January 2010 it had become necessary to quickly appoint an interim replacement for the late Senator Ted Kennedy in view of the impending healthcare reform bill that required the filibuster-proof majority of Democrats. That governor Deval Patrick did as a matter of course, a thing that was once considered anathema under governor Mitt Romney, a Republican in 2004 when it became apparent that John Kerry was going to win the race to the White House. Haba! Even the blind could see this!

Three successive governors, Mitt Romney being the last of them, remained as fresh as fresh peanuts in their memories. And so voters defied the bad weather and came out in their numbers to vote for fifty-year-old Scott Brown who beat the Attorney-General 52% to 46% to occupy the coveted post, a post that the late senator had occupied unchallenged for 46 years, a post almost synonymous to Kennedy until the candidate Scott Brown reminded voters that it was really the "people's seat". Quite a powerful reminder for those with amnesia or those arrogantly oblivious of the people's suffering under the weight of a recession characterized by an unemployment of 9.5%, pains of increased taxes, pension abuse, the Wall Street bailout, exploding federal budget deficits, partisan wrangling over healthcare and plenty of what was lumped into the category of arrogance on the part of those in power. Voters had simply become fed up with the litany of malaise that dogged elected Democrats

– Governor Deval Patrick's low rating at the polls, former House Speaker, Sal DiMasi's imminent trial on federal corruption charges, former state senator Dianne Wilkerson's impending trial on bribery charge, former state senator James Marzilli accosting several women, former state senator Anthony Gallucio's imprisonment for violating the terms of his probation and fleeing from the scene of an accident, ex-speaker Thomas Finneran being disbarred for obstruction of justice; the list was long, very long indeed.

There were useful lessons to be learned, among them, the fact that prolonged single party dominance leads to stagnation. Supermajorities in state legislatures often breed political bosses and corruption. In Congress those representatives who are too confident of reelection can become politically tone deaf and complacent even if they otherwise work hard on some legislation. Nothing hurts an electorate like being taken for granted. Democratic overreach also contributed to Scott Brown, a Republican routing Martha Coakley, a Democrat in the bluest of the blue states! The election was supposed to take place in November, not January. Voters showed their distaste for such legislative sausage making, an undisguised ploy to make the playing field uneven, especially with unemployment at an all time high. Patience was running thin. Surely name recognition did not help Martha Coakley in the primary, another proof that single party dominance, with its associated arrogance, hurts. Earlier in the year Salvatore DiMasi became the third House Speaker to be indicted. In a competitive political environment such a run of corruption would be devastating to Democrats. But the party went ahead and chose DiMasi's hand-picked replacement and moved on as if noting had happened. That was not good.

In one-party states loyalty leads to advancement whereas breaking ranks on principle does not. State senator Dianne Wilkerson was caught stuffing bribery cash in her bra; her colleagues dawdled before taking steps to force her out. State senator Anthony Gallucio had to be jailed before fellow Democrats sent him packing. Did voters sense hubris in any of those moves? Probably not, prompting Senate President Therese Murray and Speaker Roberto DeLeo to arrogantly declare that when the majority is big enough to override a veto, any good governor must approach the legislature on bended knees. That was said of Deval Patrick, a Democratic governor. The absence of competition naturally led to the atrophy of political skills. Any wonder why an unknown quantity like Scott Brown should triumph over the best that the Democratic Party put forth?

Finally it happened! The healthcare reform bill passed all the hurdles and was signed into law. What a momentous event! It was an unprecedented victory that had eluded several generations of law makers. President Obama was jubilant as he declared: "Today, after almost a century of trying, after over a year of debate, after all the votes had been tallied, health insurance reform becomes law in the USA." The House had voted 219 to 212, to pass it into law and into history - a very narrow margin indeed. The health policy had been on what one observer called "life support" for one year and finally survived the main element of compromise – the ban on the use of federal funds for abortions. How then would Americans go about their abortions? The prolife, prochoice, and the in-betweens, including those opposed to shot gun weddings and those implacably against bringing forth bastard children from unplanned pregnancies, constitute a huge voting block. Persons who have seen ultrasounds of pregnancies or scientific depictions of embryonic development in books, *Scientific American* or *Life* magazines – from blood to flesh, passing through those memorable stages where fetuses float like space walkers in the unlimited universe of the womb, crooking an arm now, sucking a thumb later – carry away quite an impression as voters and must not be dismissed lightly. *Roe versus Wade* is not yet about to be overturned but the decreased decorum in the Congress speaks volumes of its emotional impact on the political landscape. Designed to revamp the $2.5 trillion US healthcare industry, the new law provides for the biggest social policy changes in decades.

But many still planned to repeal the law even as many others began to look for ways and means to alleviate the crushing burden on small companies. To Senate President, Therese Murray's plan to rein in healthcare costs by donation of $100 million, the hospital behemoth, Partners Healthcare, pledged $40 million. The fund would reduce the health insurance costs for small businesses crushed beneath skyrocketing premiums. Partners' pledge was received with much skepticism. For one thing, their pledge was considered peanuts – just one hundredth of their 2009 accumulation of cash and liquid investments of $4.1 billion. For another they were totally to blame for their high end, high priced hospitals that helped to drive up the costs in the first place, out-competing all other healthcare providers in the process and passing the costs as premiums to those insured.

It came as no surprise when one federal judge and then another ruled that the provision requiring people to buy insurance or pay a penalty was unconstitutional. The jubilation over healthcare reform was already being whittled down even if two other judges supported it. Clearly the matter was far from over and the road to the US Supreme Court looked wide open. Proponents and opponents will fight it out even if it takes years to get there. With five Republican and four Democratic appointees right now at the Supreme Court, how will it be decided if the matter went there? Can the Supreme Court vote to invalidate a federal program of this magnitude? The last time such a thing happened was in the 1930s when the Court struck down much of President Franklin Roosevelt's New Deal. In the mean time the US House of Representatives has made a repeal of the healthcare reform a top priority early in 2011. That is a tall order given that such repeal would come against a Democrat-controlled Senate ready to block such a move as well as President Obama's veto along the way. But by far the biggest hurdle would be the American population that lags behind 40 to 50 countries (Japan, France, Canada, Italy, Germany, South Korea and others) in matters like life expectancy at birth and with infant mortality far higher than Japan, Hong Kong, France and others. America's quest for more wealth at the expense of health and other values needs reappraising for one cannot enjoy wealth if one is sick or dead. Each time Republicans toss the "tax and spend" label at Democrats, the latter return the favor with "borrow and spend". More than 60% of Americans agree that the best way to alleviate indebtedness and our huge deficit is to tax America's 2% wealthy persons instead of maintaining the Bush tax cuts for everybody, convinced that capitalism's ethics cannot turn its back to the contribution of 95% of the citizens. In his state of the union address, President Obama highlighted the measures he envisaged for reducing the $1.2 trillion deficit, unemployment, and boosting competiveness of American business through investment, a language which GOP leaders interpret as euphemism for more spending.

It was quite revealing when a member of Congress admitted to a reporter that reading some of the bills or publicizing them would never lead to a vote because they were voluminous. Members of Congress do not have enough time to read through the bills they vote for, let alone publicize them. So the arguments for or against any bill may be totally unrelated to the content of the bills in question. So why do they vote? Is it just to satisfy an inner conscience as some claim or for fear of retribution from angry constituents back home? Is voting just a formality to say good-bye before retirement for those not seeking reelection? Can it be the fear of being stigmatized as the obstructionist party of NO? How on earth could anyone raise the objection that the healthcare bill was done in secret by the Democrats when President Obama went countrywide taking his case to the American heartland as other Congressmen and women debated it with their constituents in heated town hall meetings? Whichever is true, one can reasonably assume that members of Congress certainly take advantage of an American reality - public sentiment swings back and forth like a pendulum. During midterm elections in November 2010 the GOP took over control of the House of Representatives from the Democrats; just two years earlier President Obama and his party won control of both the House and the Senate. As the Republicans entered the lame duck period and prepared to use their new majority in the House to stymie the president's agenda there was talk of repealing the healthcare reform. In two weeks an incredible thing happened. President Obama's pragmatism and steadfast effort to reach out to the Republicans changed him from a write off, one-term president, in popular parlance, to something else. Some called him the *come-back kid*. The 111th Congress passed a marathon of legislations, the most remarkable being the repeal of the military's *Don't Ask, Don't Tell*. What a Christmas gift! Lame duck 2010 turned out to be a good ending for a not-so-good year for President Obama who could then confidently face 2012 and move from governing to campaign mood, having delivered on his 2008 promises. In retrospect, some of President Obama's bills survived not because they were perfect but simply because opponents had submitted nothing better for the vote than denunciations as alternatives.

# 4.

## Life on the Fast Lane

The quest to conquer new frontiers is as American as apple pie. A small kid of four or five seeks to scale Mount Everest, another to transform all the nation's homeless into happy homeowners. Indeed 13-year-old Jordan Romero achieved the feat of going up Mount Everest (29,028 ft.) with his father, and in so doing, became the youngest person ever to do so, breaking the record set by 16-year-old Nepalese, Temba Tsheri. The proud young man said he wanted to inspire children, especially the obese ones whom he considered the future of America. Spurning child labor laws and FAA regulations, another father allowed his eight-year-old son to take over air traffic control from him at the very busy JFK International airport in New York, earning for himself the ire of his employers and suspension from work. Often too young to get into the rat race and yet blessed with the American DNA of doing the impossible simply by seeing what is invisible to the average Joe, some kids work wonders, starting with parents and mentors along the way. Right now there is a growing list of volunteers for the pioneer flight to the red planet, mars in spite of the catch – an exorbitantly expensive one-way ticket!

From October 19, 1781 when the British surrendered to General George Washington at Yorktown, Virginia to end the American Revolution, there has been no looking back. Americans are on a mad rush to conquer the world around them in all domains of human endeavor. Transgender persons often submit to experimentation with their bodies, presumably to improve upon their creator's original plan. Enterprising individuals, backed by powerful attorneys and perceived as pace setters, are constantly engaging the society in a wrestle of wills over existing laws, to see how much they can get away with. The American image is personified by an individual battling against the might of society. When immigrants first come to America they often run into a head-on collision with a host of new values and lifestyles, producing a culture shock as a result of a worldview quite different from that held by peoples in other parts of the world. US culture places a high premium on money, freedom, independence, privacy, health, physical fitness and physical appearance. To gauge the importance of any of these, one only needs to take a look at what happens when an attempt is made to take them away from their owners – litigation follows swiftly. HIPAA (health insurance portability and accountability act) is a law passed by the US Congress that, among other things, guarantees the confidentiality and privacy of patient information. Divulging such information to unauthorized persons, even members of a patient's family, can attract law suits. It is common to hear Americans boasting of striking someone where it hurts the most – their pocket books.

Persons from cultures where collective family decision making is practiced may find themselves in a bind when confronted by such realities concerning their loved ones.

Matters get even more complicated and messy for persons like the Hmong from backgrounds like Laos and parts of Vietnam harboring a deep distrust for things western, apprehension about vaccination, blood tests on a little bit of blood from their finger or forearm. If a young person will not allow for a blood test to detect the presence of Hepatitis B antibodies, it can spell a bad omen. Hepatitis B virus, transmissible through infected needle pricks, at child birth or by means of other agents that break the integrity of the skin, is endemic in Laos and parts of Vietnam; persons immigrating to the US from there run a higher risk of liver cancer as a result of undetected and untreated HBV. Cultural xenophobia can thus pose a serious problem.

Litigation to seek redress is quite common. A young Asian immigrant, aware of the millions to be made, was arming herself to prosecute a physician for medical malpractice. Her doctor's prescription for contraception had not just worked at all and so she had found herself saddled with an unwanted pregnancy. That doctor must pay! But then the doctor was no push over. He too mobilized his resources and went to work. Private investigators checked into but found no unethical practices on the part of the physician. The prescriptions, the contraceptives as well as the dispensing pharmacy were all flawless. So where was the problem then?

Naturally attention shifted to the patient herself. It turned out that she had taken the medication, not by mouth as intended, but intravaginally. In her culture back at home, medicines were usually applied as close as possible to the site of the problem. Aspirins for headaches, for example, would be crushed and applied right on the head. Antibiotic ointments or creams for sores and wounds would be rubbed on the sore spots and other problem areas. So, logically, she had crushed and applied the contraceptives faithfully, where they should do their job – into the vagina. Unfortunately her common sense did not tie in with accepted practices, especially since it was clear that the pharmacist had taken pains to indicate clearly that the pills had to be taken by mouth. The court had found the doctor not guilty of any wrong doing and accordingly thrown out her claim as bogus, the poor immigrant woman finding herself at a cul-de-sac as those tantalizing millions evaporated like little confetti before her eyes. To get rich quickly takes a lot of guts.

In America the underlying belief is that human beings can and should control nature, and so daily energy is expended to this end – irrigating the land where it is dry, treating bacterial cause of disease, replacing nonfunctional kidneys, hearts or other body parts. As a matter of fact American healthcare industry views the human body simply as a machine; if it gets broken down it is simply turned over to the mechanic to fix it. What could be simpler? It is a common experience to see people jogging along city streets or working out at gymnastics centers. Low fat, low cholesterol and low calorie diets are highly prized. America does not believe that moral behavior has anything to do with infections or high blood pressure or diabetes. As a highly scientific nation, America tries not to acknowledge the reality of the supernatural, giving some immigrants the impression of ethnocentrism. At some point during their stay here, new immigrants toy with whether or not to continue to believe in the spirit world, witchcraft, shamanic healers and "evil ones". Those who go to the hospital with half-hearted belief in the healthcare delivery system pose a special challenge for providers. Applying home cultures here in America can be quite challenging and frustrating too – insisting to sleep by the bedside of a hospitalized relative, bringing one's own native doctor along to the hospital to determine if it is okay to take what the hospital's physicians prescribe, bringing home cooked meals and even medicines for a sick one, violating visiting hours and more. People in America almost generally bear their pain in silence; those from other cultures often express pain through vocal expressions such as moaning.

The immigrant begins to appreciate and empathize with Laura Bohanna (*Return to Laughter*), Chinua Achebe (*Things Fall Apart*) or Jonathan Swift (*Gulliver's Travels*) the type of difficulties at the interface of two different cultures. Of course outsiders too are often able to see things that natives ignore or do not see and this quality allows the outsider to come up with a perspective or an input that may become the life line for a struggling local undertaking if only the owner would come clean and reach a reasonable settlement with such an outsider rather than use subterfuge - "*you do not exist... people from your country can and do encounter visa problems easily... sometimes they can't reenter the US after they leave...*" - to try to dispossess him or her. Yet logic dictates that individuals, businesses, institutions and, above all, civilizations should bargain with each other so that one party's gain does not necessarily mean a loss to the other. Some times our constrained vocabularies make it difficult to carry out such lofty tasks.

Many Americans hold the view that life begins at conception and so for them abortion is synonymous to murder; others believe that it occurs much later, at the point when a fetus becomes viable, and so aborting during the first three months of pregnancy is seen as a simple medical procedure. Based on these opposing views, Americans can be roughly classified as pro-life or pro-choice. There are pockets of communities in which people's belief in God as well as the idea that he confers both health and illness, makes it difficult for them to take medicines or change their behavior to influence their illness. But mainstream America believes in the germ causation of disease and the notion that exercise and diet contribute to good health. Bridging this gap is the challenge of those charged with providing health care.

While some effort is made to accommodate other languages, especially the widely spoken ones, it is much more difficult to accommodate some cultural practices and beliefs, especially those that conflict with American beliefs and world view. The notion that everything happens for a reason obliges some people to spend time and energy to go looking for the meaning of events. It is un-American going after traditional doctors to look for the cause of childlessness, for example. The notion harbored by certain immigrants that the world is a hostile place and people are "out to get them" is totally alien. The belief that birth defects are a reflection of improper behavior in a previous life of individuals believed to be reincarnations is countered by modern scientific knowledge that errors do occur in the DNA during a cell cycle and manifest themselves in phenotypic changes of the offspring. Backed by the world view that the human body is all and all, Americans have extended life expectancy as far into the future as possible, whereas some cultures and religions consider life here on earth as a mere precursor to a better life yet to come and are willing to let go when the critical moment comes. My good friend, Ahmed thinks that it is better to suffer here on earth and enjoy a better life in the next world, than vice versa.

One of my greatest challenges and defeats – I called it my Waterloo - came in one morning during rush hour when we got trapped inside one of Boston's many MBTA buses in traffic shuttling between Wellington station and Malden on the Orange line. It was an ominous Friday the thirteenth of August! An elderly looking Chinese lady (for so I assumed) was locked in some kind of an argument with the bus driver over payment. The woman kept waving her Charlie card over and over, saying something incomprehensible as the driver struggled to make her pay for the ride, first by gentle coaxing and then later by coercing, indicating by threats that he would call 911. It went on and on as we itched to get to work. It was obvious that the Charlie card had run out of credit. But did the Chinese lady know so? What point was she trying to make really?

Anxious to get to work, yet unable to do so, passengers just sat there in disgust as the drama went on. Finally I decided to intervene, convinced that I could apply some of my well honed conflict resolution skills. Could that lady be a fare evader, the kind transit police chief Paul Macmillan routinely warned about on the PA system? She did not look it. Yet she would not budge as other passengers waited impatiently to get going and some of the irate ones had already started uttering cat calls and invectives. As a first step I had to disabuse myself of the propensity for touching – that friendly gesture which in my past would signify camaraderie but here in Boston could be misconstrued for something else and then land me in great trouble. I had been "there" before.

"*Tsao chung ha. Wo jiao John. Nee hao ma?*" (Good morning, my name is John and how are you?) I began. She just looked at me but said nothing. Was she perhaps applying her Miranda rights? (*You have the right to remain silent. Anything you say can and will be used against you in a court of law. You have the right to speak to an attorney. If you cannot afford an attorney, one will be appointed to you. Do you understand these rights as they have been read to you?*). Miranda rights originated from the 1996 police questioning of a certain Ernesto Miranda in a rape and kidnapping case in Phoenix, Arizona. Over the years the courts have slowly whittled away these rights as they turned more conservative on issues of law and order, tinkering at the edges, changing the ways police, criminal suspects and lawyers interact, so as to ease the admissibility of the confessions police wriggled out of suspects. The suspect has a right to speak to an attorney and if he or she cannot afford an attorney, one will be appointed for him/her. But there is a catch! The suspect has a right to remain silent only if she or he first tells the police that she/he is remaining silent. Tricky isn't it? How can one remain silent and at the same time tell the police about the intention to remain silent? This prompted Justice Sonia Sotomayor, President Obama's recent appointee to the Supreme Court to quip "the majority's decision turns Miranda upside down" where criminal suspects are supposed to unambiguously invoke their right to remain silent if they do not speak. A thorny issue indeed).

"*Fangxin ba, wo gen jingcha mei guangxi*" (do not worry, I am not with the police). No answer.

"*Shi zhongguoren ma?*" (Are you from China?) No answer. This was proving to be harder than I had first thought. When an elderly Haitian grandmother approached me a few weeks earlier with her repetitive "*Creole?*" I had a clue about what she wanted. But this one was proving to be rocket science for me. Unlike the French who would probably give me a kiss or a hug for my attempt at expressing myself *en français*, the Chinese lady just remained dumb. Why was she being so difficult?

"*Jiao shen me mingzi?*" (What is your name?). She seemed visibly unimpressed with my command of Chinese. Could that be it? Or did she take me for a Croatian speaking Hrvatski to her? And then something better came to my mind. I took out two dollars and handed them to her to solve the fare problem. But she shook her head vigorously and continued to wave her Charlie card. At that point the bus driver lost his mind and did something stupid as passengers joined in, some with obscenities, to berate the lady. Before we realized it the bus had slammed into an SUV ahead. The police came quickly, probably to see about the accident and possibly take care of Nguyen (pronounced NOO-EN) the difficult passenger who turned out to be not Chinese but Vietnamese! Poor me! This epiphany, that not everyone with come-to-bed eyes is Chinese, was quite humbling to me. But that again turned my attention to the other aspect of the problem: what powerful force keeps people from learning the lingua franca of everyday usage, in this case, English? Having lived in the US for ten or twenty years, it did not make sense to be unable to ask for directions, do shopping, consult the doctor or carry out other basic errands that require speaking the common language. Could it be pride? Or shame? Is it the fear of being made fun of for not speaking well? Human beings usually pride themselves for being on a higher plane than chimpanzees and other apes because we are more curious and have a language. So where is the problem with bridging the communication gap? The answer is blowing in the air...

I turned my attention to another thorny issue – healthcare. If health and healthcare are so important to Americans, how then can one explain the furor and animosity that accompanied President Barack Obama's healthcare reform legislation? I found the answer in the economics of providing them. Like taxes, healthcare costs scare the living lights out of many Americans, and insurance companies have not made things easier by skyrocketing premiums for profit motives. It is the same motives that drive Americans to vote for persons who go on the soap box and promise to cut down taxes, corporate America to outsource jobs to India, Singapore, Nigeria and the rest, where labor is relatively cheap and so profits are high. But that is looking only at one side of a complex equation. Outsourcing occurs both externally and internally. When the Commonwealth of Massachusetts sends out W2 forms to Kansas for processing, what else is that but outsourcing? But most often it is perceived only in terms to jobs leaving for oversea destinations. It is true that managers shed jobs and move operations overseas, a trendy job shift known as outsourcing. Faced with the resulting job loss here at home, career counselors advice people to respond with career change so that candidates return to school to finish their degrees or tackle new areas of study to enable them pick up new jobs on the changing job market. Surely people have enough coping with midlife crisis of divorce, remarriage, loss of jobs, loss of home, and others. Adding a return to school to the mix just makes matters a little unsettling but that seems the way to go.

Individual freedom is a powerful driving force behind most of our acts and a good chunk of our challenges is traceable to the desire to expand these freedoms over our fellow citizens and our government, opening up new frontiers. It could not be otherwise in a world where the silent voice of the past keeps urging people on:

*You see things and you say "why?"*
*but I dream things that never were*
*and I say "why not?".*

These words, invariably attributed to the late President John F. Kennedy, were really the brainchild of George Bernard Shaw. But it doesn't matter. The impact seems to be the same that Americans leave no stone unturned to explore every possible niche in their environment. The spirit of adventure and quest to conquer new frontiers of knowledge is formidable, some of it good, others not so good. This irresistible trait is quickly passed on to new generations of citizens, including immigrants.

This is quite understandable. The foundation of the nation was laid by persons fleeing religious persecution and the monarchy in England, where class system meant that family status mattered a lot. In the new world, freedom and individualism took on a higher meaning and success came to be measured by worth and one objective measure of worth is money. It is from such a backdrop that independence, hard work and the development of the land became dominant themes in peoples' lives.

In 1890, James Edgar an immigrant from Edinburgh, Scotland, came to the US and opened a department store bearing his name and situated at the site of today's George N. Covett court house in Brockton, Plymouth County in Massachusetts. The man would dress as a sea captain and then as a clown and even as George Washington, all in an effort to entertain the children of shoppers who came to his store. Bit by bit the humble tradition spread across the state and eventually the US; today, *Santa Claus* is a world-wide phenomenon. A similar story, from a modest beginning, lies behind another world-wide, money-making phenomenon - the greeting card industry. Today's New Hampshire is toying with rewording the Constitution to introduce gender neutral word for men (All *men* are created equal) even if such a change brings along problems in grammar and syntax. The thinking goes that the female gender must not just be assumed, it should be seen to be included.

In school we get lessons from teachers first and then get tested on how well we understood those lessons. Thus I broke fewer and fewer test tubes, pipettes, flasks and other laboratory glassware later in life than I did in my first year at college when I earned a prize for that feat. In real life the tests often come first, followed by the lessons as we have seen for AIDS, drugs, violent crime and many others such as an ambitious journalist dumping or leaking on the Internet a huge volume of very sensitive confidential information illegally obtained from the US government. Today kids, their parents and school authorities are caught in a web of bizarre application of the rules of the game and misinterpretation of the Constitution. Lawyers are not helping matters when, motivated by pecuniary considerations, they seek to play gymnastics with the law, interfering by tying the hands of those entrusted with the upbringing of leaders of the future. The good job being done by well balanced parents in bringing up their children is being undermined by other parents whose wickedness, stupidity, arrogance, ignorance and other negative traits make their own kids victims and problems for the society.

Early in life we learn that facts are things that do no change (the capital of the nation, the state, the height of Mount Everest) or do change repeatedly like weather, temperature, elements of the Periodic table, the school year, and so on. Between these two there is a category of facts often viewed as fixed but which change very slowly, almost imperceptibly, over our life times. Some smart guy has suggested calling them *mesofacts* since they are sandwiched in between the first two. An example is the earth's population which stood at 3 billion when I first heard about it, moved to four and right now it is around 6.8 billion. Another is continental drift – the fact that the coastal regions of South America and Africa have been drifting apart and continue to do so as we speak. Often people have moved from one part of the country and relocated to another because of prevailing economic or climatic conditions. These too change over time. Who could have foreseen the earthquakes with epicenters at Christchurch, northern Tokyo and Leogane on the west of Port-au-Prince and Curanipe, north-west of Concepcion, which shook New Zealand, Japan, Haiti and Chile recently? Or Australia's unprecedented floods? Updating our *mesofacts* is important if we have to play vital roles as mentors and leaders in our communities or countries.

Ultimately the success of a society is tied to how it rises above its many challenges. When elected representatives of the people meet in Congress and debate issues affecting those who elected them, there is room to hope that society will live long and live well. Scientists do not only publish their discoveries in respectable esoteric journals, they also Hollywoodize them to reach the largest possible audience and thanks to this fact, today we know that good old aspirin (acetylsalicylic acid if one wants to sound big and important) is a powerful agent in preventing some of our common cancers if taken in low doses over a long time.

But the good things seem to be running side by side with the bad. Today our society is drowning in the meaninglessness of a culture that tends to reward greed and guile, making it look like life is all about getting rather than giving. We are witnessing the secret or double lives of various persons and thrill seekers of all sorts who eventually come to the limelight in moments of disaster. Freedom is quite a force that pushes people on. It is very powerful and authorities have quite a task containing this thrust to push the urge to its very limit. On the eve of the important presidential election that brought Illinois Senator Barack Obama to power in the US, two radio hosts actually went on the air and told listeners that the election had been postponed and asked Democrats to cast their votes the following day, 11/05/2008. The response on the part of the Secretary of State, William Galvin, was simply "*to knock it off*". Under other skies such pranks would be greeted with dire consequences.

It is incredible what people are prepared to do in the name of defending their freedoms, especially those who had not experienced any before, people who had lived in a kind of cocoon and only upon landing here in the US did they emerge like butterflies, free to go to any height. With so much freedom, people have carried out stunts to get into the Guinness Book of Records or legerdemain to bamboozle bookkeepers saddled with the task of explaining where millions of dollars went. It is not everyday that people jump out of their single engine private planes, fake a crash and fake their deaths, yet some have conceived of such a stunt as a convenient way to convert the American dream into a nightmare for investors left in the lurch. Challenging the status quo is an American thing and nobody takes anything for granted, not even those sitting in Congress.

While President-elect Barack Obama was dutifully putting in place his dream team for the formidable task ahead and lame duck President George Bush was in the twilight of his White House years, probably working on the list of those to benefit from a presidential pardon, there arose the thorny problem of how to bail out the nation's three giant auto makers –General Motors, Ford Motors and Chrysler LLC. Plenty of sane Americans held the view that Congress should allow the titans to just sink into liquidation or bankruptcy as a result of their poor management and stewardship; many others felt strongly that those companies were too big and important to be allowed to fall. On their very first visit to Congress to put forth their case, the CEOs of the auto companies came in their usual ostentatious perks, having been ferried to Washington D. C. in their executive jets. Nothing could upset Congress and the American people more than such insensitivity to the nation's mood at the height of the credit crunch. House Speaker Nancy Pelosi barely contained her furor when she told them to go back and come more humbly and with a plan of action that could earn them a sympathetic hearing.

A fortnight later they were back and Congress put up a rescue plan of fourteen billion dollars, subject to some government oversight, translated as the appointment of an official, aptly designated *the car czar*. But the matter did not end there. Behind the scenes dealings were taking place and among other matters, the UAW (United Auto Workers) were being asked to cut down their fabulous perks. Pontificating from Congress, the elected representatives assumed that they had the upper hand until one of the aggrieved auto workers exploded in ire, demanding that members of Congress be put on a justifiable salary as well. Only with such utterances did citizens remind themselves that congressional leaders were deliberating in a very big glass house! The task of accountability is a really hot potato in an election cycle, especially when the nation's foundation is undergoing tectonic shifts from its component parts for practices that seem at variance with long held beliefs.

In addition to voting for Senator Barack Obama as the very first ever black president of the US, residents of California voted to pass Proposition 8, a constitutional amendment banning same-sex marriage and therefore retaining the conventional definition of marriage as a union between a man and a woman. In the process, they overturned an earlier State Supreme Court decision that had legalized such unions. What a dramatic illustration of citizen power! Subsequently the very California's Supreme Court dealt a stinging blow to gay marriage by voting to uphold Proposition 8, the narrow (52%) voter-approved ban on same sex marriage. What a ping-pong game in the legislative process! For the Supreme Court to reverse itself this way, it went to show the extent of people power in California's democracy. Crestfallen, citizens of that state began to seriously contemplate what future action to take, including accepting Iowa's invitation for them to come and conduct their same sex marriages across the country in Iowa.

*Berg vs. Obama* was a less publicized lawsuit, put forth around the same time, in which someone, presumably a conservative, alleged that Senator Barack Obama was not qualified to run for the presidency due to his not being a naturally born US citizen. Would he succeed or was that a storm in a teacup? Did he have the truth, the whole truth and nothing but the truth to tell the United States through the courts? What did he have that the nation had not heard before? And why not also sue the Democratic Party which had put forth the nominee, Barack Obama as its candidate? Does it make sense suing the driver of a truck for damages caused without at the same time suing the company for which he works?

Besides that particular case in court, the "birther movement" headed by a certain Orly Taitz, its self-appointed queen and aided greatly by news anchors like Lou Dobbs of the CNN, was dedicated to bringing down President Obama on grounds of his alleged not being US born. Yet the last time I checked, Hawaii had been a full fledged member of the US and that was well before Obama's birth. News organs were torn between accuracy in news reporting and presenting a balance in their coverage, especially in the economic crisis where Barack Obama's case was legitimately and factually better than Senator John McCain's. Many American sons and daughters might one day wish to become president. But an antiquated clause in the US Constitution stands on their way, a clause which prohibits any one who is not "natural born" from becoming a US president. The best they can hope for is to become a governor, like California's Arnold Schwarzenegger.

But why? Supporters of such a prohibition claim that allegiance to home countries is as embedded as DNA in naturalized Americans. Some claim that the emotional pull of one's birth place cannot be neutralized, citing the case of Russia's Alexander Soltzenitchen who retuned home after everyone thought he had become American, recent cases of Somali Americans who returned to their country and died in the unending fratricidal war raging out there and Faisal Shahzad, arrested and brought down from an aircraft as he returned home to Pakistan after planting a deadly cargo of bombs at New York City's Times Square. Such simplistic view of a complex situation fails to take into consideration that not all immigrants have an emotional pull for their places of birth; surely not those running away because of persecution or genocide. It would be erroneous to attribute such behaviors only to those immigrating into the US; at different times US citizens have also taken up citizenship in other countries such as Canada, the UK, Australia and others. During the Vietnam war plenty of draft dodgers found their way to these other places and eventually returned when the war ended.

It would appear that such concerns were apparently also felt by the Founding Fathers. Scholars trace this particular clause of the constitution to a letter dating as far back as 1787, written by John Jay to George Washington, urging the provision of a "strong check to the admission of foreigners into the administration of our government". Such prejudices persisted over the years and today even some constitutional scholars continue to argue that foreign-born people may be too "enculturated" by their nation of birth or be driven by homesickness and nostalgia into US bashing and other acts. Yet natural-born American citizens do bash the US too. Nor should such arguments apply to Obama, an uncontested and clear Hawaiian.

It was a kind of consolation for me to discover that challenging the legitimacy of the occupant of the White House is not new. Plenty of historical antecedents are on record, some with very bizarre reasons. One former president was tagged an impostor simply for getting drunk at an inaugural dance (Andrew Johnson), another because his rich dad had stolen an election (George W. Bush). As a matter of fact calling a president illegitimate goes as far back as the nineteenth century when John Tyler was called "His Accidency" for assuming office due to the death of his predecessor. Rutherford B. Hayes was labeled "His Fraudulency" for losing the popular vote in 1876. Americans picked quarrels with Thomas Jefferson for not being a legitimate American simply because of his foreign (French) ties, French cook and slave mistress. Martin Van Buren allegedly wore a woman's corset! JFK, one of America's most beloved presidents, was seen by some to be illegitimate as a result of his razor thin victory over Richard Nixon in 1960 and for some people, Lyndon B. Johnson was illegitimate for his alleged complicity in JFK's assassination in his home state of Texas. It is clear that as soon as Americans lose trust in a president they also lose reverence for the office. Who would have believed that Sarah Palin, John McCain's running mate for the 2008 presidential election would turn around and make comments in Spanish about President Barack Obama's testicles or the lack thereof? First Amendment rights surely bring out the strangest traits in us.

According to a certain CNN poll, one out of four Americans doubted that President Obama was a US citizen even though the proof existed – two Honolulu newspapers had published the announcement of his birth in Hawaii in 1961 and the Republican governor of Hawaii had also certified his birth certificate. Nothing doing! Complicating matters was the president's blackness, his "otherness" and so on for those with little tolerance for diversity and those who continued to hang on to the notion of "he is not one of us" or "a guy from nowhere" Of course bigotry and indignity of the "birther" type could never arise if the new president's father was of European origin.

Like all other nations on planet earth, America too has her own silly superstitions that no amount of scientific influence can change. Thirteen, for example, is considered to be a very bad number, so bad that many tall buildings simply do not have a thirteenth floor at all. And when thirteen falls on a Friday it is considered double disaster. Medical doctors are rarely superstitious, committed as they are to rational, logical planning and thinking. They are sensible people, usually uncomfortable if not contemptuous of the mystical. Yet there is a lurking fear of accepting call or emergency duties on Friday the thirteenth. Many would tolerate the 6th or 9th or the 14th but when it is the 13th, there is much trepidation even though there is only one British publication - the British Medical Journal - that came close to associating disaster (a 52% increase in hospital records of admissions due to traffic accidents) with Friday the 13th.

This *paraskevidekatriaphobia* (Greek for fear of Friday the 13th) has settled in the American psyche, causing mild to severe anxiety and some times a change of activity as a precaution. Taken even more seriously is superstition based on the moon (full moon, new moon, half moon), hence the century-old term *lunacy* often linked to madness. Of course these things remain superstitions until facts are brought out to contradict them. But that is not going to happen any time soon, not when a thirteen-year-old boy was struck by lightning at 1:13 in the afternoon (13:13 using the twenty-four clock) on August 13, 2010! An accident involving a Colombian plane, a Boeing 737 struck by lightning over San Andrea Island and split into three parts, killing one person and sparing 113, was a miracle that just missed August 13 by three days. For a short while, eleven appeared to be replacing thirteen as America's baleful number – the crash of hijacked civilian aircraft on NYC's world trade center on 9/11/2001 and the crash of another plane on the Bellaire high rise on the upper east side of Manhattan on 10/11/2006 – but that was only a little bump; 13 remains unbeatable.

Did someone call George W. Bush a lame duck president during the transition? *Lame?* What a label for someone who displayed a rare agility at ducking two shoes flung at him in rapid succession by Muntadhar al-Zeidi, an Iraqi journalist and symbol of the frustration and opposition to the US-led invasion and occupation of Iraq! Flanked by Iraq's premier Nouri al-Maliki and other dignitaries, George Bush was addressing an audience during his unannounced final visit to the war-torn country. The speed with which President Bush ducked those missiles made the "lame duck" label seem ridiculous. Mr. Bush made light of the matter, interpreting it as proof that democracy had finally come to Iraq. The journalist was immediately arrested and detained, but as the Stockholm syndrome set in, local lore held that he was probably jailed not so much for assaulting the US president, but for missing his target in two separate attempts.

You never know what you've got till you lose it. This ancient wisdom was brought home to our doorsteps, thanks to America's 43rd president. By transforming the world's love for America into contempt, George W. Bush had proved how much love the US once enjoyed from the rest of the world, the better to appreciate it as it had been irretrievably lost because of his reckless actions. Bush's legacy is often seen as a real inspiration to the millions who are too lazy to accomplish anything; that even they too can one day become president. In 2000 George Bush was known as the candidate you would like to have a beer with. Eight years later, the author of the *"axis of evil"* finally convinced the American people that that was probably not the best test for national leadership.

## *The Individual versus Society*

In the US there exists a sustained wrestle of wills – a battle between the individual and the society as a collectivity and nowhere is this more pronounced than in the right to smoke or to own guns. It is a fierce battle to protect the society from the nefarious effects of smoking by those unable or unwilling to quit because "they are hooked". Society uses the powerful arm of the law, persuasion, information campaigns, endless taxation and humanitarian gestures like rehabilitation facilities to try to discourage smoking. The lofty goal is to protect the greater good of the society but individuals, backed by giant corporate interests such as tobacco companies, are fighting back ferociously against what is perceived as marginalization, demonization and ostracism by the temperament of the non-smoking populace. Some even claim that the government is trying to intrude into the private lives of citizens. All of these ruses pose one serious problem for the individual smoker by taking away something very special and dear - choice. The problem with smoking is that people have learnt to smoke but failed to learn the basic etiquette that goes with it. The consequence is that they put not just their own lives on the line, but the lives of others as well, through secondhand smoking. It is sobering the number of lives that have succumbed to heart attack following years of consumption of unfiltered camel cigarettes and other brands. In addition to polluting the lungs of nonsmokers through second hand smoking, smokers also litter the environment with their unconscionable dropping of cigarette butts and packets with little or no consideration for esthetics.

Choice is a very highly valued concept in America. Individual lives are the daily manifestations of choices, some good, others bad, made in a free market of unlimited options. Americans not only have to choose a "right" mate, but to do so at the "right" time, in the right neighborhood. But choice is also quite a slippery concept because personal choices are conditioned, shaped and some times even constrained by genetic factors, family income, where we live, main cultural expectations, other social pressures and even the laws of the land. The menu is so vast, and yet ironically, people often end up saying "I had no choice." Recent studies indicate a triple rise in myopia (near sightedness) for some Americans, mainly African Americans, while the rate is doubled for others. The researchers found no apparent reason for this except that current thinking tends to incriminate lifestyles, such as more and more persons tending to subject their eyes to "near work" like peering at computer screens and small electronic devices. Additionally the studies showed that those who spent more time outdoors had much less of the condition.

While it is understandable that some members of a society may choose to show their freedom by taking their own lives in a kind of voluntary euthanasia, there is a catch doing so by smoking. Smoking affects other persons who might not so willingly wish to take their own lives. Second hand smoking victims suffer and die too at work, at home and at other places where smoke wafts freely into the limited air in the common space. Many a pediatrician has lamented the degree to which children with potentially life threatening asthma are denied the choice to live in a smoke-free home simply because parental right to smoke appears to override children's health. Unconscionable smokers have been known to blockade themselves for long in the common bathrooms of shared apartments, leaving behind a suffocating atmosphere and toxic ash in the wash basin for other users. And for some reason smokers seem to think that the problem lies in the butt of their cigarettes or cigars rather than the very offensive odors they carry along on their persons and subject others to in the shared public spaces – bathrooms, buses, libraries, crowded trains, restaurants, banks, post offices and the work place. Such persons cling to their lighted cigarettes until the bus is about to take off and then toss out the butt, carrying the more offensive smoke and smell into the vehicle, oblivious of the harm they are bringing to innocent non-smokers. The risk to persons like physicians, nurses, phlebotomists, EMTs, and CNAs who work intimately with such smokers, inhaling their nicotine breaths and other agents of halitosis, is incalculable. American smoking has successfully turned liberty into anarchy, placing the non-smoker at a disadvantage. And if smokers are so prepared to take their own lives using the cancer sticks, only the rocket scientists among us can fathom how much such smokers care for the health of fellow citizens.

I used to wonder why cigarettes are also called cancer sticks. Smoking causes cancer when substances in cigarette smoke enter living cells and cause DNA mutations, making them to grow out of control, spreading through the body, shoving aside and disrupting normal tissue. In 2006 the US Surgeon-General reported that any exposure to second hand smoking increased an individual's risk of developing heart disease and lung cancer. As a result nineteen states proceeded to ban smoking in workplaces, bars, and restaurants. Some home communities want the ban to be extended to include public parks, beaches and even private homes. Just how far the government should go in protecting nonsmokers is not quite clear yet, but communities have surely been energized. Over 90% of the 160,000 deaths that occur in a year in the US result from lung cancer caused by smoking. The CDC estimates that tobacco costs the US economy $193 billion per year yet this is inadequate according to the American Lung Association and other anti-smoking organizations. The recent decrease in the number of cigarette smokers is paying off handsomely in a corresponding decrease in the incidence of heart failure, heart attack and dangerous malignancy. But smoking remains quite a challenge!

In a typical humane approach to this problem, smokers are sent to rehabilitation facilities for a variety of cures, beginning with being told to put away everything like lighters, cigarettes, cigars, matches and pipes into a trash can, venturing into a room for a collective talk where the resident experts work them through the initial verbal steps before taking them on a one-on-one for a modest fee. They learn about the evils of smoking such as chronic circulatory problems, COPD, heart attacks, back pain, and others. Most individuals on the trying-to-quit trail feel wimpy. In spite of the well documented horrific health risks associated with smoking, which are powerful deterrents in themselves, and in spite of the fact that the US society has made it shameful to be a smoker, most smokers cannot succumb to the stigma of indignity and would rather fight than fly. Researchers at the International union against Cancers have positively established that the first 400 episodes of the show *"The Simpsons"* contained 800 references to cigarettes; such exposure of young impressionable kids to smoking by characters of the show would exert quite an impact on teen smoking.

Encouraged by the overall drop in the rate of smoking from 19.8% to 16.4% among adults, and by the drastic drop in the rate of heart attacks for those subjected to second hand smoking, the Massachusetts Department of Public Health still pushed ahead with more reforms and bans. Five years ago the Bay State banned smoking in restaurants, bars and work places; now the department is targeting cigar and hooker bars, considered the smoker's last haven, so as to drop the rate of heart attacks even further. New Jersey's State Senator

Barbara Buono is said to have introduced a bill to ban smoking at outdoor parks and beaches. There is a push to go even further and shock smokers into wakefulness of the dangers of smoking by some innovations. Ever the pace setters since 1964 when the Surgeon General of the United States put out the landmark report linking lung cancer and other diseases to smoking, authorities in the Commonwealth of Massachusetts are seriously considering a new device in the anti-smoking campaign – graphic photographs of diseased, tar-pit lungs, damaged brains, stained or rotten teeth and cancerous lips, a die hard smoker getting the poisonous fumes through an intratracheal tube subsequent to a surgery of the wind pipe, even a corpse to accompany every cigarette commercial in an honest effort to revamp the anti-smoking crusade beginning in 2012 as the multibillion dollar tobacco industry comes under FDA control. The thrust is that people have the right to smoke but they should not have the right to impose on others the health risks caused by smoking. Many employers make it a matter of policy to exclude smokers from their payroll, institute wellness programs to encourage a healthy work place and greater productivity or impose a reasonably high premium to be paid by obdurate smokers and others whose lifestyles are correlated with less productivity. Faced with budget shortfalls, some innovative thinking from health advocates has proposed a smoking tax of $1 per packet of cigarette or more to raise $9 billion for states. The International Communications Research which carried out opinion poll studies said that 60% of Americans would support such a tax. A targeted tax directed at facilities that litter the neighborhood with cigarette butts or pollute the environment with their noxious products is being contemplated elsewhere.

Banning cigarette sales in drug stores is quite odd and interesting at the same time. In theory drug stores and pharmacies are supposed to be concerned with health, yet they have been selling products that make people sick. First of all, drugstores are a rarity these days, most of them having been swallowed up by the giants like Walgreen or CVS. People usually come to the drugstore for prescriptions and advice on matters of health, just as naturally as they come to purchase those cancer sticks which pharmacists in drugstores stock up to help them compete with the giants. Gone are the days when pharmacies were just about promoting the health of their customers. These days, the larger ones carry so much other stock of merchandize that medication seems like an afterthought. The problem with the new ban is that even if any pharmacist refuses to sell to customers, the latter can simply go across the street and procure them from liquor stores, which makes of the ban a mere inconvenience rather than a deterrent. Nevertheless the ban is a good idea, a move in the right direction even if it is half-baked.

Chain smokers often experience a hacking cough, emphysema, seizures and depression, underlying a life time of cigarettes and bad nutrition, imperceptibly transforming into malignant masses in the lungs or breast and some times they pass out with a lit cigarette that ultimately sets an apartment ablaze! Where their freedoms and rights end and the rights and freedoms of others begin is a matter not always prominent in discussions. The number of women smokers who subject innocent, helpless babies in their arms to choking cigarette fumes is incredible. Can this be wickedness, arrogance, ignorance, stupidity or forgetfulness? What latitude does a nonsmoker have, emerging from a commuter train with hundreds of other passengers and following directly behind an unconscionable smoker who lights up almost immediately and spews noxious smoke, subjecting everyone else behind to suffocating air?

Resistance to quit smoking is a question of will power or the lack of it; failure is often conveniently placed at the door step of product manufacturers. An interesting case was heard in Boston's Suffolk Superior Court brought by a man whose mother reportedly died of lung cancer as a result of smoking cigarettes distributed freely to her and other African American kids in a housing project. The man's mother reportedly started receiving the free cigarettes when she was only nine years old and died forty years down the road. The lawsuit cited Lorillard Tobacco Company as enticing black children with its giveaways, a marketing strategy the plaintiff claims was illegal. This was way back in 1957 when it was illegal to give cigarettes to children and so in the eyes of the plaintiff, Lorillard broke the law.

The defense counsel for the company cited lack of evidence and the statute of limitations. Boston was all ears and eyes. It did not take long to get the outcome. A jury in the Suffolk County Superior Court of Massachusetts found Lorillard tobacco, the makers of Newport cigarettes, guilty as charged and awarded $81 million punitive and $71 million in compensatory damages to the aggrieved family. That was quite an eye opener. If Lorillard knew, perhaps it should have done what UK's biggest drug maker, GlaxoSmithKline did –out of court settlement to forestall a large jury award if the matter went to court. A payment of half a million dollars was made to the family of Avandia user, James Burford who died in 2006, allegedly because the drug company had kept hidden health risks associated with the consumption of its product.

`There is need to protect nonsmokers from the deadly fumes of their smoking congeners. A 1993 album *No Cure for Cancer* details how a regular guy, a smoker did battle with a society that seemed always to be coming after him: *"What's the law now? You can only smoke in your apartment, under a blanket, with all lights out? Is that the new rule now, huh?"* Smokers are being chased out of the home and office, to spend their time with rats at the dumpster, away from the dirty looks of civilized society, away from the lectures of friends and family and threatening spouses. All of these pressures would have worked except that most smokers are weak from being unable to quit, meek for letting others tell them that what they choose to do is not something they're supposed to do. And so they are fighting back what they perceive as "public health fascism" using for example, a Cambridge Community television program called *The Smoking Section*. It is a painful experience for a medical doctor to be faced with a heart disease patient unwilling to give up smoking. While many patients gladly cede authority to their doctors in such crucial matters, a process derogatorily called child-like regression, smokers have a harder time at it.

Smokers also demand rights and freedom! They even espouse what they see as the benefits of smoking – peaceful conviviality, development of jazz and literature and more. On their walls are displayed pictures of Frank Sinatra, Sammy Davis Jr. and Dean

Martin, all having a smoke and a laugh. Cigarette craving is irresistible for those already hooked and it is clear that minorities and the youth are hooked on menthol. The nicotine patches and gums don't just work for everybody. Nor does the practice of purchasing a whole pack of popular brands of cigarettes or cigars (Pall Mall, Marlboro, Menthol, Basic, Camel, Kool, Newport, American Spirit and Maverick, Bolivar and the many Cuban specialties around) "to just smoke one and throw the rest away." Herbal remedies reputed to cleanse the nicotine out of one's system as well as the strong jar of aromatherapy that is supposed to snap the brains out of craving do not just work. The World Health Organization has not endorsed the famous electronic cigarettes (e-cigarettes), the latest fad being trumpeted as another way to help those wishing to kick the habit.

While the non-smoking world can quote all kinds of statistics to justify banning smoking, smokers too are at work trying to prove the reverse. Need one look at the statistics of the CDC showing the demographic that smokes, and their relative socioeconomic status? Blue-collar workers are identified by the cigarettes they smoke while cigars are for the white collars, especially those with MBAs. If progressive taxation has not put smoking out of business, it looks like nothing else will. It takes a special type of will power to fight addiction and former president John F. Kennedy who signed the ban on trade with Cuba was known to have had handy plenty of Cuban cigars at his disposal when he signed the law.

By signing into law the recent historic bill on tobacco regulation, President Barack Obama took an important step in bringing order into this area. Through the FDA (Food and Drug Administration) the Federal government will have broad regulatory powers over cigarettes and cigarette products, compelling companies to more clearly and publicly acknowledge the harmful and deadly effects of the products they sell to the public, especially to minors. The bill stops short of banning cigarettes and their addictive ingredient (nicotine) altogether. 20% of Americans smoke and tobacco kills more than 440, 000 yearly through heart disease, cancer, emphysema and other ailments. This lot of heart disease is surely part of the number that brushes the teeth less than two times a day, according to a Scottish study.

Closely related to cigarettes is the problem caused by Afghanistan's poppies which provide opium, the raw material for our world's heroin. Some Afghans call it their jihad against the West for destroying their culture. It is indisputable that cocaine and heroin are responsible for fueling addiction, crime and insurgencies around the world. The street corners of almost every city in the world suffer from heroin addiction among users and many families have lost children to the addiction and its many sad sequelae. The United Nation's Office on Drugs and Crime is one authoritative source that has published details of the havoc done to the world by the growth and consumption of opium.

Competing with cancer sticks in cutting short American lives is the gun and a similar deadly scenario obtains with respect to gun ownership. The last Supreme Court decision upholding private gun ownership in spite of the spate of wanton killings in towns and cities across the US was very disquieting. From the moment American society glamorized the murderous spree of *Bonnie and Clyde* and other actors produced in Hollywood's machine as a way of entertainment in this country, guns have become an inescapable way of life. If a citizen is free to purchase guns, should another citizen not be equally free to enjoy life unmolested by the gun owner? Where should we draw the line? Why can't the ordinary citizen count on the courts for protection? When the matter pitting the District of Columbia against Heller came up to the Supreme Court, the nation held its breath as it waited for a final interpretation of the Second Amendment of the US Constitution applicable to private ownership of guns. Everyone had hoped that at last there would be some restraint on the easy access to guns following the mayhem unleashed on campuses across the nation by apparently normal Americans who went berserk and unleashed death on innocent citizens using guns easily obtained from gun stores or gun shows.

But that was not to be. By upholding the right of an individual to purchase and bear arms over the collective right of a society at the mercy of irrational gun owners, the justices have left the ordinary citizens of our society frightfully vulnerable. The nine justices of the US Supreme Court made history in their 5 – 4 momentous decision in the matter of the *District of Columbia versus Heller* on the private ownership of handguns. And yet most Americans had hoped that the justices would finally weigh in on the fact that citizens supplementing the *"well regulated militia"* of the Second Amendment as well as the potential threat –the Brits, the French - were matters of the distant past, when the militia was small. Today America is a superpower with the largest army on planet earth. What would be the justification for retaining this anachronism? To fight the government, rightly or wrongly perceived to be the biggest threat to the individual? I would gladly renounce my Second Amendment rights if it meant replacing the ballot by the bullet just as fast as I would a First Amendment that allows the mouth to take over functions originally intended for the brain. America's powerful gun lobby, underwritten by the NRA (National Rifle Association) remains very entrenched in its opposition to any and every law aimed at curbing the free flow of guns in society. The NRA's Andrew Arulanandam is on record as saying that crime can happen anywhere and so the only thing that can stop a bad person with a gun is a good person with a gun, a preposterous proposition that assumes all the victims of gun violence so far had no guns of their own! He was voicing his support for new legislation aimed at introducing guns into national parks.

The fact that there are 11,500 gun-related murders each year in the US does not mean much to those who hold such views. Contrary arguments like those offered by Daniel Webster of the Johns Hopkins Center for gun policy, that we have the equivalent of a Virginia Tech massacre everyday in the US, the main difference being that it is not just all in one place, hardly moves those with entrenched positions. In America when people get mad and have easy access to a gun, they simply use it. People get shot at over a game of dice, parking space arguments, girl friends, boy friends, and drug deals gone awry. According to RadarOnline, former Alaska governor Sarah Palin has a temporary restraining order for an 18-year-old who sent her a rather chilling message – receipt for the gun he had bought, together with a note saying that he had tried to follow the Bible but still had the devil and wickedness in him. That speaks volumes about the type of individuals who can buy and carry guns in Uncle Sam's land. Sarah Palin can consider herself lucky to know her potential assailant and even do something about it. John Lennon, rock star of the Beatles fame was less lucky as he fell, in December 1980, to the bullets fired on his back by Mark David Chapman, a real wacko, creating a surreal and horrific scene outside Dakota apartment in New York. Why did he do it?

Here we were in early 2011 and the nation got plunged again in mourning because another wacko at a shopping mall in Tucson, Arizona let loose his weapon at a meeting of Congresswoman Gabrielle Giffords and her constituents, killing six and critically wounding her on the head. Among those killed were a nine-year-old girl and a federal judge. Now that a federal judge is one of the victims of America's lax gun laws will the justices of the Supreme Court revisit *Washington D. C. versus Heller*? The private ownership of weapons would be ideal if American citizens were playing Russian roulette on a level playing field but that certainly is not the case. Slowly hyper incendiary language has replaced civil discourse in politics. And Sarah Palin's Tea Party actually equates politics to war! Americans have the right to ask what message Sarah Palin was sending out through her Political Action Committee's online website "Sarah Palin's Take Back 20" displaying scopes targeting members of Congress – even as she fights back using *blood libel*, stirring another hornet's nest in the anti-Semitic world. During campaigns for the midterm elections of November 2011, Gabrielle Giffords's Republican challenger actually appealed to his supporters, urging them to help remove her from office by joining him shoot a fully loaded M-16 rifle and Senator Harry Reid's rival alluded to the disquieting prospect of turning to the Second Amendment remedy, an undisguised threat to use the gun in case the ballot failed! Should a Congresswoman lose her life simply for supporting President Obama's healthcare reform? So if the former governor of Alaska is neither duplicitous nor hypocritical, why was that particular message abruptly removed following the shooting of the Congresswoman and six others? For someone aspiring to be president of the United States and to take over the many entanglements of this nation around the world, Sarah Palin needs to absorb a small dose of the Obama prescription – pause a little. Speaking at the McKale Memorial Center of the university of Arizona, President Obama said, "At a time when our discourse has become so sharply polarized, at a time when we are far too eager to lay the blame for all that ills the world at the feet of those who happen to think differently than we do, it is important for us to pause for a moment and make sure that we are talking with each other in a way that heals, not a way that wounds."

Prevaricators were quick to strenuously dissociate such messages – use bullets rather than ballots against rivals, reload rather than retreat - from what might have prompted 22-year old Jared Loughner, a hyper-charged political activist or a mental case, to go on his murder spree. Quite a stretch indeed! Finding no cause-and-effect relationship in those utterances would imply that the attempted assassination of Congresswoman Gabrielle Giffords as well as the Democratic losses at last November's midterm elections had nothing whatsoever to do with all the Tea Party campaigns across the nation. It would equally imply that those appeals were directed at nobody and that nobody paid attention to them. Otherwise, why accept some of the fruit but reject the others?

It is interesting to read how people are influenced by another Reagan creed. "We must reject the idea that every time a law is broken, society is guilty rather than the law breaker. It is time to restore the American precept that each individual is accountable for his actions. Acts of monstrous criminality stand on their own. They begin and end with the criminals who commit them, not collectively with all citizens of the state, not with those who listen to radio, not with maps of swing districts used by both sides of the aisle". The problem with this type of mindset is that it completely absolves a society (family, school, community, and nation) that fails in its duty to bring up civic-spirited citizens. Followed to the letter, a child who appears in school with clothing soaked in feces or wielding a gun should not in any way be blamed on lack of parental supervision and a child caught on a school bus carrying a list of enemies targeted for rough treatment such as bullying should not raise parental concern. Such logic underscores the ease with which persons of dubious character and demeanor get easy access to guns with little or no background checks. Using such logic a parole board that failed to do adequate risk assessment before releasing a person like Dominic Cinelli - a man with a history of three life sentences, who went on to murder a police officer - has no responsibility since it all falls on the murderer alone. Views of this type are only a step away from saying that individual soldiers, not the American society as a whole, bear responsibility for the killings in our many foreign campaigns. (Following the tragic gunning down of six persons gathered to hear Congresswoman Gabrielle Giffords in Tucson, Arizona, gun sales were said to have shot up by about 60%)! Logic of this type does not say where individual responsibility is taught or learned and makes the easy access to murderous guns, and publication of maps willed with literal targets and cross hairs the most natural thing in America.

Indeed to tackle the type of problems cropping up in Pakistan and Afghanistan today, America needs a leader that can stand on two legs and tell those out there that it is wrong to murder a governor for opposing execution by hanging for a woman whose only crime is being a Christian in a Muslim country and that throwing one's shoes at a foreign head of state is unacceptable. America needs a leader that can condemn the adulation of an assassin of a governor by Muslim scholars and lawyers simply because the governor upheld Common law that goes against Islamic law which gives any Muslim carte blanche to be plaintive as well as judge in his own case, and to murder in the name of religion.

It is a sobering catalog when one tries to document the number of weeping mothers and fathers of children, some as young as seven years, that have been cut down in their prime by indiscriminate use of the gun, from Boston to Chicago, passing through New York and other places in between. In Pennsylvania, just after the sad events of 9/11/2001, a gun-toting soccer mom and supporter of the NRA appeared at her daughter's soccer game with her Glock holstered on her hip. She scared the hell out of other parents and got the local sheriff quite concerned. Not long ago the very lady was found murdered by her husband in what the local press dubbed "an apparent murder-suicide." Teen violence is top of the list and experts have still to figure out why the appeal of the street and the gang is so much more powerful than the love of mothers in luring kids to sure death.

When journalists and cameramen ambush and invade the privacy of a celebrity for days on end, just like the Paparazzi did to Britain's Princess Diana, the celebrity thinks of one solution – a personal gun for protection. When an unruly young man was told to leave a birthday party because of his attitude, he used his gun to shoot the one whose party had gathered people to celebrate! Why do so many young persons have guns and carry them around? Why is black on black violence so out of control and irredeemable? And what is so special about the violence in Chicago, Florida or Dorchester in Boston? Who provides minors with guns and for what good reasons? Obviously no one would die if such persons had no guns in their reach. The notorious O'Reilly ambush aimed at getting entertainment at the expense of the citizen is supposed to be an inheritance of a practice pioneered by CBS's Mike Wallace but it places citizens at a dangerous jungle game when the courts and Congress turn a blind eye to the potential risks involved. There is need for more organizations or institutions with tax benefit status to tackle the problem of high school drop out head on. Alternatives are needed for drugs, gangs, teen motherhood. High school dropouts, whether kicked out by principals, under the supervision of parole officers or cajoled by mentors and case workers can perform remarkably well and get a future for themselves if given the appropriate prompting away from turf wars, drug dealings.

President Obama became so moved by the tragedy that he sent US Attorney-General, Eric Holder and Education Secretary, Arne Duncan to meet with school officials, students, residents and talk violence. Seeing the Reverend Jesse Jackson and Nation of Islam minister Louis Farrakhan at the funeral of a sixteen year old Chicago honor roll boy shot to death by gang members had an eerie air of déjà vu but that is the helplessness into which society had been plunged. Some day, hopefully, America will recover from the devastation caused by two disaffected dysfunctional students in Columbine High School in Jefferson County, Colorado. The two went berserk and unleashed death and destruction on their schoolmates and teachers, leaving a lot of unanswered questions: Did their parents really know them? If so how could they have failed to notice anything that would alert them to seek help for their children? Why are people so anxious to have children yet so unwilling to bring up the children to fit well into society? From where do very young children learn violence? How can a fifteen year old get the chutzpah to rape a 65 year old woman who is not a cougar? And how should society react to such a crime in a place anxious to protect its tourist industry? Does "Joint Venture Theory" - the conviction of all possible accomplices in a crime such as armed robbery - help curb crimes? Will it happen again? Isn't it true that busy parents tend to lean on greedy pharmaceutical companies to help smooth out the rocky bumps of childhood for them? Isn't it true that attorneys invariably enter a plea of insanity for every perpetrator of murder thereby giving the green light to would be perpetrators of the most egregious crimes on record? Isn't it true that today's kids are over diagnosed and overmedicated into perfection?

Of course there is some logic in the insanity plea. Only insane persons would carry out such horrific and heinous acts and since the law does not provide for death penalty for the insane, this provides a neat escape. Long term imprisonment, parole some where down the road and then back to society – *tabula rasa* – and, no need to shudder as the cycle recommences. Haven't we seen it over and over? Attorneys entertain the listening public by trying to draw that fine line between the witty, careful and scheming con man and a crazy man living in a delusional world, a man so incredibly disturbed by mental illness and insanity that his attorneys ask the court to let him go free. For such a mindset the jury of one's peers must be made of robots who just sit there and listen without reasoning. For them it is so convenient that a person with IQ in the upper stratosphere before the commission of a crime should, suddenly after the crime, register an IQ down south where one finds only persons with mental retardation. John Allen Muhammed was denied this type of plea and put to death with lethal injection for his role in the causation of agony to residents of Washington D. C. and surrounding areas over three week period in October 2002. He and his partner-in-crime Lee Boyd Malvo had randomly shot and killed thirteen persons in that stretch of time, making it a nightmare for persons leaving their houses to check their mailboxes, drop or pick up children at school, go to the shopping mall, stop and buy gas at a station or just venture out of their houses. The snipers shot indiscriminately at all ages, both genders, every profession in the nation's capital. It was a clueless murder spree. When at last captured the junior partner received life imprisonment without parole. Washington heaved a sigh of relief!

All of a sudden modern civilized society is full of persons with autism (mind blind people), especially the type called Asperger's syndrome. And those afflicted with this condition are notoriously prone to stabbing their classmates. Defense attorneys and shrinks know best about this condition. It is clear that only they can stop its over-diagnosis and propagation in the society, leaving parents the task of rising up to their task of child upbringing instead of the unnecessary overindulgence of reducing themselves to friends of their kids.

Asperger's syndrome seems to be a type of autism more common in men than in women and is said to lack the language problem of delayed speech. Affected kids are apparently very intelligent but are unable to understand instructions, are socially isolated, display repetitive behavior and obsession with certain interests. Some are said to have an impressive vocabulary (mild ones are often called little professors) but generally have difficulty with social cues like jokes, eye contact or facial expressions.

Legislators have failed to close the legal loopholes in the nation's gun laws that make it possible for serial killers, disturbed teenagers and other dangerous criminals to have access to deadly weapons and to use them freely in churches, play grounds, work places, schools, universities and even homes to cut down innocent Americans. Why did President Obama sign a law permitting firearms in national parks and wildlife refuges? Now advocates are urging a ban on all national parks – Yellow stone, Cliff of Yosemite, Statue of Liberty and others. The president of the Brady Campaign to Prevent Gun Violence, Paul Helmke, is urging President Obama and Congress to act quickly and curb guns in such majestic places. In spite of the latitude the ordinary citizen has in articulating his or her grievances, many still elect to use the gun to settle scores. The gunning down of Dr. George Tiller by Scott Roeder, an antiabortion fanatic inside a church in Wichita, Kansas where the victim was an usher, is a case in point. Not satisfied with shouting out his grievances, the perpetrator of the crime had turned to shooting down the Wichita abortion provider, ten years after a similar murder took place in New York. Dr. Tiller's clinic had been bombed in 1985 and he was shot and wounded in 1993. Two wrongs have never quite made a right but they surely do make a jerk, as Scott Roeder proved by taking the law into his hands to murder Dr. Tiller in cold blood inside a church. Judge Warren Wilbert, citing the obvious – that it was a greatly wicked thing to do, that no private individual had the right to execute judgment against Dr. Tiller, that violence breeds only more lawless violence and that we are a nation of laws - sentenced the murderer to 50 years in prison without parole. The State of Kansas and the nation as a whole could not have asked for a better deterrent for the egregious crime of taking the law into one's hands and even attempting to use the trial as a forum for getting on the soap box to give vent to one's political belief in addition to the heinous crime of first degree premeditated murder and two aggravated assaults.

The gun show loophole has become an arms bazaar, a haven that makes it possible for felons, criminals, terrorists and illegal dealers to skirt the federal laws and buy or sell guns on a cash and carry basis. Even before his trial and conviction for first degree murder and aggravated assault on members of the church, Roeder's defenders and sympathizers were already proposing the insanity plea – that panacea which has facilitated the proliferation of murderous guns and made it possible for so many insane persons to carry and use them with relish. Fortunately for society the man defiantly ignored the plea and went ahead to state that he had done it to save more innocent babies from being murdered. Implicit in his declaration was the idea that Dr. Tiller was committing an illegal act. And yet abortion is not illegal in Kansas! Nor did Roeder consider the fact that society had already provided for persons and institutions to deal with such situations, that acting in this way would render the entire gamut of law enforcement entities superfluous, including Justice Warren and the jury of his peers who presided over his trial and deliberated his fate. Our lax gun laws have noticeable consequences next door in Mexico - targeted and mistaken identity killings are commonplace and innocent bystanders die in their numbers.

Nothing could be more sobering for a nation still reeling from the mayhem unleashed by 23-year-old South Korean student, Cho Seung-Hui on fellow students at Virginia Tech University on the morning of April 16, 2007, using a Glock-19 handgun bought from Roanoke Firearms. The student had gone on the rampage, killing thirty-one students before turning the weapon on himself. Before that there had been senseless killings in Washington D. C. and Virginia around October 2002, University of Texas at Austin, Columbine High School in Colorado and others. Jim Brady has been on a wheelchair since 1981 when John Hinckley's bullet, aimed at President Ronald Reagan, missed its intended target and found its way into his head. Violent outbursts are due, at least in part to society's excessive glorification of violence in our culture and the ease of obtaining deadly weapons and even making them available to children. Recently there was the gunning down of nine persons in a home set ablaze by a man disguised as Santa Claus to perpetrate his vengeance over acrimony with an ex-wife whose family he set to wipe out at Christmas. Do they say hell hath no fury like a woman scorned? The same can be said of a man. Yet people continue to trivialize the possession of guns by everyone that can afford to buy them. At a car dealership in Missouri, people win coupons which they use to buy semiautomatic guns because, as they say, they "believe in God, guts and guns."

The furor over the so-called "crime of the millennium" has virtually died down as the murderer of Julissa Brisman and his lawyers were spared the gymnastics that usually lead to the cold case category. As expected prevaricators had started pushing the debate to the doorsteps of Craigslist.com as if that website had done anything more than provide the venue for criminal and victim to meet, the way hotels, motels and churches do. Craigslist did practically nothing to increase the risk of a woman offering herself as a stripper and provider of erotic services to a total stranger inside a hotel room! Philip Markoff, the Boston University medical student accused of slaying Julissa remained innocent until proven otherwise and his girlfriend and family were certainly standing by him even if fingerprints and all other paraphernalia connected to the crime were recovered from his room. Thanks to the powerful tool of forensic databases, crimes committed over long intervals of time, even without eye witness accounts, can be solved simply by matching evidence collected at crime scenes –letters, diaries, hard drives, foot prints, finger prints, seminal secretions from rape victims and DNA fingerprints – can be matched to names and faces of individuals who would otherwise remain a mystery to the ordinary citizen. The hands of the law are literally and figuratively long indeed, going beyond the statute of limitations.

Philip Markoff eventually made things quite easy for the prosecution, the potential jury of his peers and the American taxpayer by committing suicide inside his cell, using a crude weapon – a scalpel fashioned out of a pen – puncturing veins at the neck, wrists, arms and ankles. Under pressure from a combined team of attorneys-general in many states, Craigslist decided to censure its website to reduce the incidence of prostitution and trafficking of women for sex.

Equally dangerous and life threatening is the carrying of knives and other concealed weapons with which Americans murder each other on a daily basis. Four sociopathic teenagers, reportedly disciples of Charles Manson, the serial killer, recently burst into the home of a 42 year-old nurse in Mount Vernon, New Hampshire and stabbed her to death. What were they celebrating? Elsewhere, at a high school homecoming in California, ten persons cornered a fifteen year old girl, robbed her, beat her and raped her right outside of the ceremonial building where the dance was taking place. The assault went on for well over two hours as some of the assailants took pictures of the act with their cell phones. In Chicago, a sixteen-year –old boy was brutally beaten to death by a mob of his age mates apparently at feud with the boy's neighborhood. The incident was captured on cell phone pictures later sold to a TV station for broadcast. Who can doubt that the glamorization of such heinous crimes by news-hungry TV stations certainly contributes to the uptick of crimes in America? Boston's police commissioner Ed Davis got the wake up call when he called for a mandatory minimum jail time of ten years as a possible deterrent for young people who think and feel it is a status symbol to possess a gun. He felt that the criminal justice system needed to step in and the legislature to turn on the heat on such individuals with a propensity for gun-wielding.

Sad experiences like these are not limited to boys. The American female is no less violent than her male counterpart. Young, swan-like Phoebe Prince emigrated from Ireland, settled in the Western Massachusetts town of South Hadley, enrolled in the local high school and, like all women her age, began to attract dates as she fitted into the local culture. A group known as the untouchable mean girls soon took note of her and began to give her a hard time at harassment, first in Face book and then physically – following her, calling her names such as bitch, slut, Irish slut or whore, stalking her, intimidating her, insulting her and throwing an occasional can of soft drink at her, not because she was an Irish immigrant but simply because her peers considered the boys she dated off limits to her! All through the provocations the new girl refrained from fighting back. Finally, one day, she walked past the insults, the missiles flung at her, past the white fenced gate of her home, went into the house and went straight to the closet and hanged herself! That did not stop her assailants from hounding her or mocking her. She was bad-mouthed in school even in her death. One of the bullies gloated after Phoebe took her life saying "I don't care that she's dead". How sad! Detectives as well as news organs went about trying to solve the crime but all they came away with was information volunteered by one girl that bullies usually stalked the corridors of South-Hadley High School. The girl who volunteered the information was quickly slammed against the locker room as soon as the detectives left the school.

And so bullicide (suicide by bullying) entered the student lexicon along with cyber bullying – the use of technology to harass, humiliate or threaten fellow students as fingers take to the keyboards of laptops or cell phones to produce hateful and malicious messages to students not just within the confines of the campus or surrounding off-campus areas but to the wider world beyond, bringing about consequences ranging from a decline in academic performance to suicides. A disturbing question is: Can candle light vigils at funerals of suicide victims produce the unintended result of encouraging others to follow suit and commit suicide?

Incredibly, instead of doing something about the bullies and such a heinous crime, people blamed the victim and looked for excuses why a fifteen-year old would commit suicide. There are actually present in society parents and school officials who concede that kids are not born with bullying but learn it along the way. Some even consider it a rite of passage that toughens the kids up. Where and why did things go so wrong? Early psychologists did recognize the *Sturm und Drang* (storm and stress) that goes with adolescence and psychiatric training ought to show the way forward instead of letting this complex issue in the hands of persons ill-equipped to deal with it. Punishment was said to have been meted out to the perpetrators of the crime but it was done in such secrecy that the rest of the student body could hardly draw inspiration from the sad event. Did South Hadley authorities ever hear of the idea of a deterrent at all? What good would it serve asking the school superintendent to step down instead of calling for a deterrent sanction that should send a clear message to would-be authors of similar acts? And if a society needed a deterrent, what could be better than exposing the culprits during their arraignment and letting the stigma follow them for the rest of their lives? Yet the cowards were allowed to cover their faces as they were being ushered into the courtroom to answer for their acts.

Has modern society's quest for freedom reached the point at which anarchy reigns supreme? How can organized society be so helpless in the face of such a challenge? Why can't the judiciary help balance freedom of expression of the individual against the darker side of digital communication? Is it enough for the courts to send out the message that cyber bullying will not be tolerated? What concretely can law enforcement do to curb this malaise? Should the perpetrators of bullying as well as their parents be prosecuted? Is this the product of parental abdication or government interference with parental authority in child upbringing that has brought about this state of affairs? Some parents claim they had no idea their kids were involved in such things. Others just shrug it off and place the blame on the doorstep of an overbearing government. And what do the attorneys say other than follow the money? How can a society hope to survive by throwing out the window the practice of respect and even the Golden Rule? When Dr. William Cosby lamented that some parents let their parenting be done by video games, the Internet and television, few understood what he was talking about. We have all been caught pants down!

Through our long history of evolution we have our brutal and selfish instincts but we have also adapted to cooperate for the purpose of survival. At least findings from neuroscience say so. Society evolved by creating situations that enhanced our survival and downplayed our darker traits. Teachers and administrators of schools are supposed to put up infrastructure that guarantees these ideals. Even before the school the home is supposed to have laid the proper foundation. Can American mothers and fathers place their hands on their hearts and vouch that they have given their children the appropriate upbringing to enable them live in harmony with today's society? Haven't blind love and excessive indulgence created the monster besieging all of us today? Tolerating bullying and other antisocial behavior is recipe for later emotional and psychosocial problems – depression, anxiety disorders, addictions, bipolar disorders, schizophrenia and others. It is bad enough that some adults are working hard to validate the negative feelings children have of the older generation - hypocrites who preach one thing and do the opposite.

Today America is reeling from the fallout of the disclosure of classified documents, placing the US in an awkward, embarrassing and possibly dangerous situation vis-à-vis some of her diplomats, citizens and close allies. By leaking sensitive information to the press – The New York Times, France's Le Monde, Germany's Der Spiegel, Spain's El Pais – the whistle blowing website, *WikiLeaks* created a far reaching problem, prompting the White House to condemn the reckless and dangerous action of releasing classified diplomatic cables and Secretary of State Hillary Clinton to engage in damage control in the Middle-East, Russia and Europe. Already nominated for the 2011 Nobel Prize, *WikiLeaks'* Julian Assange is doing exactly what the Bush Administration did by revealing the identity of an undercover CIA agent in revenge for her husband's refusal to corroborate a bogus claim. There is an ugly side to unrestrained First Amendment rights, totally oblivious of the consequences and it was hardly a consolation when Hillary Clinton was told that she would be surprised to learn what a certain foreign country thought of the US. Whether Julian Assange will be proceeding to receive the Nobel Peace Prize or on extradition to Sweden to answer sex-related charges and then to the US to face charges of espionage remains to be seen but the man and his attorney are fighting to forestall both even though British authorities would have to give its consent before any such extradition. Julian Assange has expressed fears for Sweden's trial in private for rape, which he calls consensual sex. Apparently there is a price tag for going beyond admiring Swedish blonds! But the prospect of going to Guantanamo and eventually facing execution must be very harrowing! Would he do it again if he had to? Difficult to say.

Our news is replete with Tea Party rallies full of angry thugs. A fringe of our conservatives, unable to overcome despair or alienation, takes out their resentment and bitterness by boldly and explicitly clamoring for the US to be defeated in the war on terror. Hate messages are directed at some politicians, a political party, the president and some times the country as a whole. Where other countries address and treat their heads of state as Excellencies, America gladly throws taunting remarks, insults and other indignities at theirs. Free speech under the First Amendment allows them this latitude.

With the type of hyperbole Sarah Palin and former House Speaker Newt Gingrich are heaping at President Barack Obama and his administration, what else is more natural than for kids to learn or copy along? The social climate is gradually taking the feel of what we lived through just before Timothy McVeigh bombed the Federal building in Oklahoma City in 1995 – the worst act of domestic terrorism in US history. Hate groups and antigovernment extremists are multiplying in number, protesting healthcare reform, plotting to kill law enforcement officials, smashing windows in Democratic Party offices around the country. Some of their members hardly distinguish between criticizing a government policy and demonizing it, yet it is the very government that guarantees our collective freedom. Encouraged by fuel from the growing resentment over the US economy, bank and automobile company bailouts, changes in the racial demographic, they have sweepingly branded President Barack Obama's many initiatives "socialist" or even "fascist".

Curiously a culture of secrecy reigned in South Hadley and it was such a culture that enabled the perpetrators of bullying to carry on with impunity. Neither the principal nor the superintendent of schools was allowed to speak up, thanks to advice from their lawyers. The late girl's tormentors were said to have been disciplined. Just how? Some of them were said to have left South Hadley High. Were they expelled or did they leave on their own? The ethos of secrecy, of anonymity of people whispering vile things in the corridors, of people typing things on their cell phones or computers…that is the insidiousness of the weapons used against Phoebe Prince, thriving in the shadows. Secrecy was officially endorsed so that the majority of the 700 students in school –those who turned out for a vigil, to shed tears for Phoebe or to reach out to her family – could not be reassured by such official response of secrecy, a response that validated the act of bullying. People – school authorities, students, parents, everybody - had to keep their mouths shut if they knew what was good for them. They just followed the advice of their lawyers that bullies are entitled to privacy as well as to the due process of the law. Quite a strategy indeed! If such a strategy worked in the sex scandal involving Catholic priests of Boston's Archdiocese under Cardinal Bernard Law, it ought to work for South Hadley High school authorities too. Liability, but not the truth, would be the driving force. This was taking place just one year after the very school had paid for Barbara Coloroso, an international expert to come and tell them how to deal with bullying at school.

Hardly had this sad news died down than the nation woke up to the brutal shooting to death of three colleagues of the University of Alabama by a biology professor who, twenty-four years earlier, had shot and killed her own brother in Braintree, Massachusetts. At the time it happened, no detailed investigation was carried out and the matter was simply classified as an accident even as she ran away with a loaded gun and threatened people at a nearby gas station as she looked for a get away car. Was it because of parental influence or complacence on the part of the police? No wonder the popular perception that there are two kinds of justice – one for the wealthy with name recognition and one for the poor. The poor are invariably quickly arrested, subjected to the minutiae of investigation and trials while the rich are given such blanket cover as "an accident". The poor, in rehabilitation as a result of experience with crack cocaine, have their kids taken away by the state whereas hired nannies come to care for the kids of the rich. Lindsey Lohan was picked up for parole violation and a positive drug test but before midnight she had posted bail of $300,000 and was out as if nothing had happened. Detained at a Japanese airport hotel for questioning before being allowed access to the country, our Paris Hilton said she was "devastated". She was on her way to Japan a day after receiving a one-year suspended sentence for cocaine possession, the standard, slap on the wrist treatment according to one cynic, for rich white girls.

Whatever the case, society had to pay the price many years down the road when conspirators began to be haunted by their pasts. How sad! Simultaneously with the Alabama murders was another murder, still in Massachusetts, of a father by a son whose mother and an Olympic figure skater sister, were quite determined to do whatever it took, including posing a bail and challenging a state medical examiner's ruling of homicide, to defend the son whose drunken attack had precipitated his father's death. Would that too be classified as an accident? What a contrast to the uplifting story of a young woman who quit her job, studied law and, many years down the road, went on to successfully defend her loving brother wrongfully convicted of murder! Society was yet to hear the last word. As anti-incumbency anger poured forth and forced once invincible heavyweights to shy away from seeking reelection to the US Congress, and as office holders called for reopening of some of the botched investigations of the past, lots and lots of skeletons would be pulled out of many closets and brought to light. It surely puts the justice system in an uncomfortable situation when parents, especially those with name recognition or those acting in denial, rise up to support family members, turning a blind eye to their past (substance abuse, mental illness, violent crimes).

Family members in denial may and do forgive in the name of love but the criminal justice system has a much higher calling, requiring action backed by facts and evidence to protect the greater public! If a fifteen year old with very high IQ can plan, keep aside his books and instead bring a sharp knife to school with which he actually stabs a classmate several times in the back and chest, targeting the heart, lungs, and liver on which he leaves lethal wounds, how can any jury of his peers be so naïve as to accept without any supporting medical records, the plea of insanity or Asperger's syndrome from the culprit's lawyer? Denial and the instinct to pass on the buck allowed the loving family to go after the next target – those who had admitted their child into the wrong school in the first place, seeing that he suffered from autism, Asperger's and the rest. In the eyes of the loving family, everyone else was simply wrong, except their son! No wonder an eighteen year old girl can go on camera and actually state that she wanted to see what it was like to kill somebody! Thanks to the proliferation of surveillance cameras all over town, law enforcement officials have a useful ally in their indefatigable fight to sanitize the city. And those with unrestrained propensity for committing crimes know that they are taking a calculated risk. We may not yet reach George Orwell's 1984 but we are quite close as the unfortunate puncher of a Boston MBTA employee learned belatedly, after spewing racial slurs in addition to his punches on an employee who was merely doing his job. It was all caught on camera!

Violation of social norms with impunity has become very trendy indeed. Wild animals can be forgiven for displaying such vicious animal instincts, but even then, not on their kind or with such ferocity. Very disturbing is the callous indifference of onlookers. What ideological principles account for such indifference – fear of getting involved with the police, fear of becoming an unintended victim, cavalier attitude to matters involving persons of other racial hue? If violence here at home is so insurmountable where does the US find two legs to stand on in confronting the Taliban, Al Qaida and the rest? Any wonder why the Taliban and other disorganized groups in Afghanistan and the Tora Bora mountains would want to fight to the finish to keep American influence at bay? Is it possible to win the war on terror in other lands when a worse type of terror exists here at home?

Each of these behaviors poses special challenges to the nation's jurisprudence. There are two competing visions of justice – a system that allows for redemption and reevaluation of the criminal after some time and a system for strict retribution where judges and juries and parole boards have the final say. Between vengeance and justice, what should civilized citizens opt for? Those immediately affected by a murder cannot get the moral clarity to make or impose justice, hence society is called upon to use level-headed individuals to reflect and use courage and character to intervene appropriately in stead of "an eye for an eye" type of justice. Advocates of "get tough on crime" prefer strict retribution, drawing inspiration from what happened to former governor Michael Dukakis of Massachusetts and Lieutenant-governor Mark Sengel of Pennsylvania when they pardoned convicted criminals through the parole system. The power to commute a sentence lies in the hands of a governor but when that power is exercised and the pardoned individual goes out of prison only to commit more heinous crimes (murder, rape), the notion of a second chance sounds very hollow indeed. Governor Dukakis lost the presidential election of 1988 to George Bush Sr. who used the occasion to label his rival as a liberal, who was soft on crime. Belatedly the governor realized that showing leniency on Willie Norton or any other imprisoned killer was a serious mistake, no matter how full the prisons might be.(The US has only 5% of the world's population but 25% of its prisoners). No doubt Virginia governor Bob McDonnell had Willie Norton in mind when he denied clemency for Teresa Lewis who was put to death on September 23, 2010 following her death sentence of 2003 for using hired killers to eliminate her husband and stepson over insurance money.

In his final weeks in office, New Mexico's governor Bill Richardson came under pressure to give posthumous pardon to Billy the Kid, a notorious outlaw but the governor refused, saying that he would not tamper with the history of a man whose life was spent pillaging, ravaging and killing the deserving and innocent alike around 1879. Melissa Gosule was a 27 year old Boston school teacher, raped and killed in 1999 by a repeat criminal offender, a career criminal with more than seventy entries in his rap sheet, a man who was out on parole when, in 2011, he again gunned down a Woburn police officer. But why? Why again and for how much longer? An aggrieved populace sought answers. Why couldn't the judges impose a maximum deterrent sentence on such individuals with more than three felony convictions? What was the Executive Office for Public Safety doing? And the Parole Boards? How many second chances should an American be entitled to? How soon can we expect a Melissa law to clean up and overhaul the state's parole system and eliminate the holes in the habitual offender law?

But lawyers are not giving up. Just like in the case of serial killer John Allen Muhammed, up till the very last minute when Teresa Lewis was put to death by lethal injection, her attorney continued to argue that his client was insane and should not be put to death. (John Allen Muhammed and his young recruit, Lee Boyd Malvo terrorized Washing D.C and surrounding areas for three weeks in October 2002, killing as many as thirteen innocent persons before being apprehended). Many of those against the death penalty claim that the system is flawed to begin with, and that moral outrage should not degenerate into rage or bloodlust. Of course it does not stop prisoners from making demands of the system, including some outlandish ones like suing to make the state pay for a risky sex change operation or providing hair removal by electrolysis, all at taxpayer expense.

To test the system and expose the degree to which contemporary society is vulnerable to unchecked gun purchases and gun ownership, an enterprising journalist once took upon himself the following simple experiment. He called a needy woman over the telephone and asked if she would like to earn $300 in one hour. First, did she have any criminal record or DUI? The woman answered that she had only a few traffic tickets. Did she currently have a car? Yes, she did. It all sounded exciting. She was instructed to go to a certain street, enter into a given church, choose the last seat on the left side pew, and sit down. She was not to look left or right or back till someone talked to her. "Any qualms?" the journalist asked. *"Honey,"* the woman said, *"qualms with $300 calling for me? You got to be kidding."* The journalist reiterated that she was not to look back at all. She then obeyed and did as instructed. Shortly after she sat down in the church, the journalist came by and sat behind her and introduced himself simply as Jim. *"What do you want me to do, Mr. Jim?"* the woman asked. *"Go across the street,"* he told her, *"to that pawnshop; buy me item #2331 on this index card, using the check I shall give to you. It is a gun."* The woman cringed but was reassured that there was nothing to fear. *"They will give you two forms to fill,"* the journalist continued, *"one state and the other federal. Fill both very carefully with your names, your street address, telephone numbers and any other information required and hand them over to the person at the counter. He will make a phone call to ask for approval. This may take anything from twenty minutes to thirty minutes. The thing can be delayed, denied or approved. If you have no criminal record and no DUIs, you will get approved right away. Give the man this check and he will deliver you the item."* "But suppose there is a delay, say three days?" the cautious, curious woman inquired. *"Then the deal is off. You come back and take $100 for your troubles and we say good-bye"* the journalist replied. *"And the next part?"* she continued, definitely motivated to earn quick bucks. *"You come back, show me the item purchased and collect your money, go and pray and be gone"* answered the journalist. *"Are you Catholic?"* he asked as an afterthought. *"For*

*$300, mister, I am one"* the energized, exuberant woman shot back. *"O. K. go up to the front of the church and pray, come back and I will be gone"*. So the lady did as she was instructed and brought back the gun. She was handed over three $100 bills, told to return to her home and, at her convenience, but within the next seven days, to go to the local police and tell them exactly what had happened – that she had bought a gun for her self protection, gone to church, placed it among her stuff in her winter coat in the pew, and gone to pray but upon coming back someone had stolen it. And so it was.

America's gun problems cannot be so casually dismissed. As one astute observer remarked not long ago, guns do not shoot people; some NFL players do. In a rather bizarre case, Plaxico Burress, a professional athlete for the New York Giants, who had just signed a contract for $350,000,000 shot himself on the leg. That got New York's mayor, Michael Bloomberg really mad because the player had broken the law. He had run afoul of New York City's stringent gun laws.

Gun restriction laws are always very unpopular when proposed, lamented another journalist. So why were people clamoring for throwing Plaxico Burress in jail? Where was the logic in it? Where was the Second Amendment hysteria? In spite of all the noise about New York's strict gun laws, it was apparently quite easy to buy a gun in New York. All that one needed was to fill out some paperwork, pay a fee – no problem for a guy earning $7,000,000 a year – and then bring the gun to the proper bureaucrat within three days of purchase. In some counties the buyer would be required to take a safety course and learn how not to shoot himself. In Massachusetts or an anti-gun state like New York, the rules are not particularly burdensome at all. Not too long ago an eight-year-old boy accidentally shot himself in the head with an Uzi pistol (a 9mm micro submachine gun) at the Westfield Sportsman's Club. A Pelham Police Chief and owner of the COP Firearms &Training which had sponsored the gun fair and Firearms Exposition at the Westfield Sportsman's Club as well as two other persons were indicted in the boy's death and charged for involuntary manslaughter. Loopholes in the law had allowed the boy to fire that fatal shot that took his life. The court would have to determine how legal it was to give a machine gun to such a kid. An innocent kid dying by wielding his father's weapon is heart breaking indeed. A teenage boy, lured from the loving bosom of his single parent to the streets and gangs, where he succumbs to gun violence is quite demoralizing indeed. These are daily happenings in our cities but life goes on.

Slowly Americans are waking up from a long slumber and realizing how vulnerable they are to dangerous fellow citizens and their guns. The outside world must be wondering what kind of values America's presidents - first George Bush, then Barack Obama - seek to export to Iraq, Iran, Afghanistan, Pakistan, and the Far East when their own citizens are so prone to violent crime. For some persons, cognitive dissonance has become second nature – the idea of shutting one's eyes and mind and pretending that all is well around. Liberty is slowly replacing discipline at school and in the homes, so that these days the work place has seen the best and worst in people. In the long run adults cannot escape responsibility for what modern society has become since the switch was made from Common Law to the laws voted by our elected officials in Congress. Why would children kill in cold blood? What has made some American children so horrifically indifferent to the pain and death of others? Can it be indoctrination into thinking that they are superior to other human beings? Can the answer be found in the third parent - home furnishings such as the visual media - television and video games - that have virtually eclipsed the biological parents, inextricably caught in the rat race? Undoubtedly the 24/7 news cycle and all of these changes have had an impact in devaluing or blunting pain. A bullet in the head here, a knife in the chest there, have become commonplace as the entertainment industry pontificates that it is simply giving the public just what the public wants, but just why the public needs so much violence remains unanswered.

Recently released CIA report on interrogation techniques used on terror detainees contains unimaginable practices, including the notorious water boarding. The Bush Administration came up with a rationale that did not make sense at all except to suggest that the levels of violence at home here in America are aimed at conditioning the ordinary citizen and tax payer to accept violence and the lack of accountability on those who carry it out. The epidemic of violence is mostly directed at the drug trade but imperceptibly violence too is creeping into our political debates. The erosion of civil liberties and the politicization of national security issues certainly pave the way for citizens to become so numb that they don't notice any longer. In 2002, for example, during the mid-term election, citizens who challenged the war in Iraq were equated to unpatriotic cowards. Recently former Homeland Security Secretary, Tom Ridge revealed that officials tried to use the terror alert system to influence the 2004 presidential election and an unprecedented secret domestic surveillance program was also approved.

For those persons who considered such moves a sacrifice to be paid at a difficult time in the nation's history, let them consider what is now happening in the United States of America in the town hall meetings. Political discourse has completely changed hue. Citizens armed with semi-automatic weapons have been appearing in public events featuring President Barack Obama. Gun rights people praise such individuals as patriots exercising their rights in states that allow for openly carrying guns. Needless to say that this phenomenon was never seen during the Bush presidency! The Department of Homeland Security duly reported about an increase in violence by domestic right-wing militia type factions. It did not take long for an anti-abortion activist to shoot and kill a physician for providing late-term abortions and a white supremacist to shoot a guard at the National Holocaust Museum. With a four-fold increase in threats against President Barack Obama, who could predict where or when the next tragedy would strike? Inexorably America is getting a totally new label that does not augur well for the nation.

A slowly growing monster of illegal drug business is taking shape along our 700-mile southern border with Mexico and very few shoppers realize this. Those big trucks that crisscross the United States, ferrying goods for Wal-Mart, Target, McDonald and other shopping giants are a familiar sight on our highways. What is not often appreciated is the fact that some of them are carrying drugs for nameless companies to support mega businesses and on their return to Mexico, they bring back dollars and guns to the drug lords. The cartels have been methodically setting up their chains over the years, as the Drug Enforcement Administration admitted belatedly. No wonder the war raging around the Mexico/US frontier just as a burgeoning narcotic smuggling bankrolls the insurgency in Afghanistan.

As law enforcement tries to crack down on the trade, their bosses feel squeezed out and so tension builds up, leading to war as they fight back. It is estimated that every hour $4 million worth of drugs enter the US this way. That is $1 million every fifteen minutes! That is worth fighting and dying for. Rather than take on low paying jobs like selling in a convenience store, young people actually prefer this lucrative but risky business from which they can make $300 a night selling around the corner. Lives, families, and finances are built up around drugs, making it hard to take on the drug culture. Hard-working people on both sides of the border are given very little choice as thousands of people rely on this illicit trade – growers, processors, truck drivers, distributors, low level scammers, midlevel bosses, right up to the king pins. It is an enormous, violent, lawless and destructive company that has been growing for decades, building a loyal customer base.

Mexico's unbridled violence results from competition among cartels (Sinaloa in Mexico's west coast, Gulf in the border cities of Matamoros, Reynosa and Nuevo Laredo, and the Arellano-Felix or Tijuana) for American business and the competition will continue to exist as long as the US pursues the war on drugs at home. Contradictory? Not quite, even if the nexus is somewhat tenuous at first. The war does not quite make much sense since drugs have become much cheaper here in the US, are more easily accessible and have become increasingly more potent too. Civil liberties and public health have been compromised as a result of legislative obduracy. The American public is wondering why the government does not simply lower the demand for drugs by focusing on prevention instead of treating drug addiction as a legal rather than medical problem. The present approach (prohibition) seems to create a fertile market for the drug gangs. And of course the nation's lax gun laws allow huge caches of destructive weapons to be legally purchased with relative ease, and the killing machines find their way south to Mexico where they become the instruments of terror used to sustain the drug war. There is no doubt whatsoever that banning guns will help stem the tide of violence in Mexico.

At some point Secretary of State Hillary Clinton had the courage to admit that Mexico's drug wars were fuelled from failed US policies, prompting critics and American nationalists with a perverted sense of patriotism to rebuke her for daring to criticize American policy. They did so simply by ignoring or downgrading the facts and compelling evidence showing how the current Mexican crisis begins north of the border. US policy through NAFTA (North American Free Trade Agreement) contributes to this crisis. Since NAFTA went into effect, liberalizing market places allowed free entry of legal American goods into Mexico and bidirectional flow of narcotics manufacturers. The economic prosperity of small scale Mexican farmers was snuffed, leading to an increase in the number of persons willing to smuggle, sell, and manufacture drugs across the border. Hence the US is seen to be fighting a war it is instigating by some of its policies. Many persons agree that this thorny problem cannot be solved simply by looking at the supply side of the equation in Mexico and the countries south of here; the demand in the US is largely responsible for increased supply activity. It was hoped that the summit between President Barack Obama and Canadian and Mexican leaders on swine flu would address the NAFTA problem as well. Mexico would surely like to see its truck drivers ply the roads of its northern neighbor but frightened of Mexican drivers, Americans are saying 'not so fast'.

Many see a delusion of protectionism in the refusal to trade across state and national lines, declaring the practice will not make the US economically stronger; they think it will instead make the nation weaker and condemn citizens to higher prices, reduced variety, reduced purchasing power and inferior quality. Protectionism might work to the advantage of a few local producers but will do so only by depriving everyone else of economic opportunity and improved quality of life, calling into question the rationale for turning national borders into trade barriers. Seen in this perspective, protectionism is an old delusion that enriches the few at the expense of the many whereas the blessings of free trade uplift everybody.

Of course gun enthusiasts would not so soon listen to sad stories of this type and allow for some red tape in gun purchase and gun ownership. It is strange indeed that cars which are as dangerous as guns are subjected to insurance laws, regular inspections, licenses, permits, vision tests and age limits for operators. Why would a society put so much responsibility on car ownership, yet virtually none for guns? Speaking about the New York Giants' player who went into a night club with his gun for protection, one observer said that if that player needed a gun to go in there, then the night club was not the right place for him in the first place. True but that was not good enough.

Of the cases that come before the US Supreme Court, progressively fewer have been decided without dissent over the years, starting from 2005/2006 – 50%, 40%, 30%. By more comfortable margins the court decided to uphold Kentucky's method of execution by lethal injection (7-2) as well as Indiana's law requiring voters to produce photo identification at the polls (6-3). By a vote of 7 to 2, the justices of the Supreme Court upheld the use of lethal injections as a means of execution, arguing that there is nothing in the constitution that bans pain in death by lethal injection. This turned back the Constitutional challenge mounted by a certain 29-year-old law school graduate. The procedure uses three drugs, including potassium chloride, to sedate, to paralyze and then to kill the victim (inmate on death roll). As soon as the verdict was delivered, in fact just two hours after it, the Governor of Virginia lifted the moratorium he had placed on the execution of persons on the death roll. This whole thing coincided with the pope's visit. Pope Benedict XVI was making his maiden visit to the US, receiving happy birthday wishes and comforting the victims of sexual abuse perpetrated by Catholic priests.

In a 5-4 decision in the matter of *Dada vs Mukasey,* the court granted additional procedural rights to immigrants facing deportation and in a 7-2 decision the justices overturned a Louisiana court death-row inmate's conviction, giving additional teeth to cases against racial discrimination in jury selection. In cases that raised ideological questions, the court remained ideologically divided. No wonder the US News and World Report of 1995 closed as follows: Welcome to the divided states of America, dedicated to life, liberty and the pursuit of anxiety.

The Patriot Act's demand for internal security raises the question of how much freedom to yield in defense of the free society. Should Federal Intelligence Agencies have more leeway to conduct infiltration and surveillance? Available guidelines call for showing of probable cause before a group can be targeted, a practice dating far back to the anti-Vietnam War groups of the 1970s when the CIA monitored mails and the FBI spied on student groups, left-wing organizations, civil rights movements and women's liberation movements, conducting wiretappings and break-ins to get dissenters. But then Vietnam, Watergate, Irangate and other abuses served to undermine confidence that government would use its powers judiciously rather than repressively. Should Congress give carte blanche to the Feds? Justice Harry Blackmun thinks the Supreme Court should not defer too much to the Executive and Congress, because the Court is the final recourse of the people, made to protect them against arbitrary action by the other branches of government.

The matter does not quite end here. There exist also the opposing views of the originalists and non-originalists in the interpretation of the laws of the land. Originalists are usually conservative in legal outcomes, following almost an unchanging mathematical axiom. They scorn the liberal view that the Constitution is a living document whose meaning evolves with time and think the failure to use the original meaning of the text simply means the use of one's own prejudicial view. Right now our courts are filled with jurists whose dogged fundamentalism tends to undermine the true spirit of the constitution. By operating as constitutional originalists and statutory textualists, they inadvertently become allies to antidemocratic and anti-humanist policies. Justice Antonin Scalia's narrow reading of the constitutional amendment related to "cruel and unusual punishment" and due process is a good example. He has argued that "enhanced interrogation techniques" – slang for torture – do not violate the 8th amendment to our constitution, thus willfully ignoring the obvious need to link the original text to contemporary context. How will the new Supreme Court nominee, Sonia Sotomayor, interpret the constitution – as a living document to be read through the lens of empathy and critical analysis? Or will she flip the script now that she has been confirmed? President Barack Obama clearly emphasized empathy when he nominated her. Non-originalists consider everyday to be a new day; upon waking up, they ponder "I wonder what is unconstitutional today." Finding a compromise to this dichotomy is more than an academic exercise. In a world where the West and East live in mutual animosity and suspicion, compromises will go a long way to usher in a much welcome détente.

Indeed the disagreement between the originalist and non-originalist interpretation of our Constitution brings to mind the rift tearing apart Sunni and Shiite Muslims or the Purists and moderates in most of the East. Understanding Islam will determine what kind of people we are – tolerant or bigoted, enlightened or ignorant. It is most unfortunate that Islam continues to be seen largely through the press and in terms of ugly repugnant acts like hostage taking (Iran, Lebanon) death threats against and persecution of writers and thinkers (Shalman Rushdie, Dutch press), acts of extreme intolerance against women and religious minorities (Taliban), suicide bombings, sharia laws etc. More than one billion people find in Islam their spiritual and emotional sustenance and fulfillment. That is a large number of mankind. They call for introspection by true Muslims. What has gone wrong with contemporary Islam? Is the religion not still a humanistic moral force? As the scholar Khaled Abou el Fadl (*The Great theft: Wrestling Islam from the Extremists*) asks, "Who speaks for Islam?" And when are Muslims truthfully representing the true nature of their beliefs and convictions? If we are going to live with Muslims should we not make an effort to understand them? Not only is the East-West divide a reality, even here in the United States there are Muslims who are full time citizens with rights to be protected.

Whenever citizens of the West run afoul of the justice system in the East, there is popular expectation that the respective governments with American backing will come to their rescue. That is a big expectation indeed. Such missions are easy to carry out only if a consistent practice here at home recognizes the peculiarities of other nations as well. A kissing British couple easily gets one month imprisonment in Dubai for indecency in public. The flashy Muslim emirate is quite popular with sun-seeking western tourists and expatriates but vacationing in Dubai and practicing open display of affection can be painful. Throwing away conventional wisdom like *"when in Rome do what the Romans do"* simply because individual liberty trumps all else here in the west, has hurt Americans who ventured into lands under other skies.

Defending the Chinese system of jurisprudence following the execution of fifty-three year old Akmal Shaik, a British citizen, for drug trafficking and possession of four kilos of heroin in a suitcase in Xinjiang province, a spokesperson in the foreign ministry said no one had the right to comment on China's judicial sovereignty and even expressed China's dissatisfaction and opposition to the British government's unrealistic criticism of the case, urging the UK authorities to correct their mistake or else risk hurting China-UK relations.(Prime Minister Gordon Brown had earlier said he was appalled and disappointed with the execution ).

Many persons in the west have come to depend on a popular practice whereby a person can take cover under the insanity plea to get off the hook in a serious offence. Psychologists in England had said that Akmal suffered from bipolar disorder or schizophrenia and so was not accountable for his actions and Chinese authorities had refused a lawyer's request for a psychological evaluation of the mental state of the man on trial.(In China, being caught with as little as 50 grams can lead to a death penalty). Such cases cannot be conveniently handled without first bridging the gap between the legal practices in China and western countries, a thing that would require a dose of realism in view of America's current heavy indebtedness China. What debtor dares argue with their banker? Similar thorny cases are those involving the trial in Iraq of members of the Blackwater security outfit responsible for killing many civilians as they drove American diplomats through the war-torn city. With a judge in the

US throwing out the case on technicalities it was supposed to kindle a diplomatic row in Baghdad where the trial was to take place.

To understand Islam, one needs first to acknowledge the great schism between moderates and puritans. Both claim to represent the true authentic Islam, the Divine message as God intended it to be, that their convictions are rooted in the Holy Book (the Qur'an) and in the authentic traditions of the prophet Muhammad, God's final messenger and prophet to humanity. However, puritans (Bin Laden, the Taliban) accuse the moderates (the less visible and silent majority of Muslims) of having changed and reformed Islam to the point of diluting and corrupting it. Here in the US, there is a raging debate over the use of English in mosques. American-born Muslims are more comfortable with sermons and lectures in English; their parents are more at home with Arabic or other native tongue such as Urdu. English is a unifying factor that ties us together. Like Jewish immigrants who fought over English language prayer and Roman Catholics who resisted the new mass in English, Muslims too are waging their own debate over how much English they can use inside the mosque without violating Islamic law or abandoning their culture.

This places the foreign-born imams in a rather difficult position – on one hand, they are derided as modernists who use English to deliver sermons; on the other, if they continue to reinforce the notion that only Arabic is acceptable, they risk alienating the youth who fail to find a satisfying experience in the mosque, especially women who consider it a hostile environment and risk drifting away. Puritans have an impact on the religion that is largely disproportionate to their numbers. Why? Moderates accuse the puritans of miscomprehending and misapplying Islam to the point of undermining and even defiling the religion. To what extent do Islamic theology and law encourage and promote terrorism? Should acts like those of Major Nidal Malik Hassan, US army psychiatrist who went berserk and gunned down thirteen of his colleagues at the military base of Ford Hood in Texas be considered an isolated event or part of the East-West divide? Even more sobering was the recent botched attempt by youthful, innocent-looking Nigerian, Umar Farouk Abdulmutllab to blow up a North-West Airlines flight 253 over US airspace as it completed the transatlantic flight from Amsterdam to Detroit, Michigan. The twenty-three year-old had hidden in his loins thunder and brimstone as he sat on seat 19A of the aircraft ominously next to the wing and above the fuel tank. Umar had used a syringe to mix up some chemicals and powdered substances on his legs to start the fire that was to engulf the plane. Thanks to the vigilance of the crew and courageous passengers who spotted the act early and pounced on the young terrorist, the worst was averted. In retrospect it was an act of singular divine intervention that people momentarily did away with modern technological gadgets that usually adorn their sense organs and responded so promptly to the threat. Ears were able to hear the initial "pop" sound because they were free of earplugs, headphones, and other devices; some saw the glowing flames from the incendiary device, thanks to their eyes being taken off twitters, laptops, Blackberries and many of those handheld devices with keyboards the size of playing cards and unobstructed noses smelled the smoke.

Ever since 2001 when Richard Reid, the shoe bomber was subdued by passengers in his attempt to blow up a transatlantic (Paris-Miami) plane in flight using plastic explosives in his shoes, significant changes in airline security have been introduced and current practice is to screen passengers thoroughly before they get on board, jettisoning all suspicious materials of a liquid or creamy nature in hand luggages, likely to be used to detonate improvised explosives in flight. How Umar Farouk Abdulmutallab was able to avoid the screen with his deadly cargo of incendiary explosives and get on board in Amsterdam is still a mystery. What went wrong? Was it faulty airport screening, inadequate scanning equipment, non-sharing of information among federal agencies or simple human error? Any feeling of relief from the foiling of that attempt to blow up the plane was dampened by the knowledge that there was still no foolproof way to spot such dangers ahead of time.

Naturally the clamor now is for the TSA (Transportation Security Administration) to use full body scanners at airports in the US and abroad, establish a no-fly list for dangerous travelers, carry out tighter controls before issuing US visas and intercept dangerous e-mails and persons involved in exchanging them. More sobering still was the killing of seven CIA agents and their Jordanian counterpart in Afghanistan by Khalil Abu Mulal al-Balawi alias Humam Khalil Mohammed, a physician and double agent recruited by Jordanian Intelligence and entrusted with the delicate task of delivering the leaders of Al Qaida, especially its number two man, Ayman al-Zawahiri. How could elite forces of the CIA be taken in so easily? Where and when did Umar Farouk Abdulmutallab develop his anti-western sentiment and how is it possible that in England like in the US, not one person spotted the early warning signs? And should an entire nation of one hundred and fifty million be subjected to the humiliating new treatment of invasive body searches envisaged by the US, simply because of one rotten apple? Since when did one tree become a forest, Nigeria's foreign minister wondered aloud? And why target Nigeria but not the UK or Ghana or Cameroon – places the young man had visited somewhere along his path? Why would the US behave like a bull in a China shop, wondered a certain Mohammed Lagab, political science lecturer of Algerian nationality and close to the government of Algeria, which, like Iran, Iraq, Cuba, Syria, Sudan, Afghanistan, Saudi Arabia, Somalia, Libya, Pakistan, Lebanon, and Nigeria had been placed on the list of countries where US-bound passengers would be subjected to rigorous, pre-flight screening? Conspicuously missing in the list of such countries was the UK, where Umar Farouk Abdulmutallab was presumably radicalized, remarked Wole Soyinka, Nobel Laureate of Nigerian nationality. But why?

Not to worry; security checks could never be effective if only certain countries were selectively targeted. At trying moments the battle between security-minded persons (those who don't like pat downs and other invasive procedures at all but give in reluctantly provided they work) and those who shout "don't dare touch my junk" is in favor of the former. Yes, the main concern is whether such methods work to protect travelers. After all we have lived with surveillance cameras that monitor our every move, in our cities and towns and work places, making some of us uncomfortable some times, but the important thing is that they help to catch the bad guys who rob banks, convenience stores or gas stations. A small price to pay for our well being. Airline and travel industry authorities would do everything possible to forestall the wrath of those who rise up in protest each time a lone enemy is allowed to fly undetected. They have to be creative and forward looking. While some time and effort may be spent on the soft spots exposed by the foe in the past, more attention must be focused on what may come up next. Travelers want not only to arrive at their destination but to do so in one piece and so they take seriously the matter that someone cunning, committed, very patient, booked on their flight and perhaps seated on the next seat might indeed want to blow up the plane once airborne! Seen in this light, passengers find themselves caught between the Scylla of going through imaging machines that emit unhealthy doses of radiation and the Charybdis of strip searches and pat-downs involving intrusive probing of underwear, bras and skirts in full view of strangers - indeed no measure is too much to fish out the bad guys before they get on board. What is time when compared with safety? How can any sane American advocate the abrogation of the Patriot Act or consider the TSA an extension of Gestapo at these difficult times in the life of the nation? What should democracy do when faced with unprecedented assaults from enemies difficult to pinpoint? How else could authorities have fished out a 21-year-old woman who had swallowed fifty-two pellets of cocaine in the Dominican Republic to vomit and deliver them to someone on landing at Logan airport for a fee of $2000?

Whatever the case for or against the new measures, it is perhaps necessary to recall that giving up individual freedoms and privacy to defend and protect our collective freedoms has never been more pressing than now. Full body scanners may be a nuisance but they have become a necessary evil to contend with. Currently there is a war going on between established governments and all sorts of insurgencies around the world and airports have become the front line of conflict. Airplane terrorism is a type of insurgency. Jewelry or earrings that trigger alarm systems, alcohol-soaked swaps that might be used as incendiary devices and shoes that hide bomb-making stuff are all subject to scanning as passengers approach airports to take a flight. When terrorists fill handbags with innocuous-looking liquid ingredients for bombs, what else can authorities do? Limiting the amount of liquids a passenger carries on board may be painful but it is the only way to play safe. Who would have believed that an innocent-looking Nigerian boy of 23 would be laden with such incendiary materials in his underpants? To lay the matter to rest perhaps it is necessary to await the outcome of a case filed by two Harvard Law students, Jefferey Redfern and Anant Pradhan, against TSA for violating Fourth Amendment rights (against unreasonable searches and seizures) in instituting full body scanners and security pat downs at airports.

Is there in existence a reformed vision of Islam competing with a more conservative and strict version of the religion? At Umar Farouk Abdulmutallab's first appearance in court, it was quite significant to find Nigerian lawyers and all manner of Muslims, not in solidarity, but to distance themselves from someone misrepresenting their cherished religion.

At the age of twenty-three, Umar Farouk Abdulmutallab had been to school in Togo, the UK and finally in Yemen. What kind of education had he been pursuing? Was Yemen the crowning event of his Islamic pursuits? What exactly had he studied and how did that help explain his subsequent action – namely to want to bring down an aircraft with over two hundred persons on board? Was he following any commands of the prophet Mohammed? Was it the influence of the local Imam? Who had indoctrinated him and for how long?

The answers to questions like these may provide an understanding of the mindset that propels young persons like Umar Farouk Abdulmutallab along the path he had followed. Obviously jihad has been mentioned, which calls for an exploration of the meaning of the word in the Holy Qur'an. What does the Qur'an say about jihad? Did Umar Farouk's tutors tell him the true sense of jihad? Giving a young man such a heavy responsibility without the necessary basic education of the facts is analogous to placing at the hands of a neophyte a complicated analyzer or machine gun for which he has not got adequate training. That is unacceptable!

Most Americans would have loved to classify 9/11 as a rare, isolated event and hope that it never ever occurs again. But that is classical wishful thinking. The number of events perpetrated along the same lines keeps growing – Major Nidal Malik Hassan, Umar Farouk Abdulmutallab, Faisal Shahzad, Mohamed Osman Mohamud, and who knows what next? Pakistani-born US citizen, Shahzad had parked his SUV Pathfinder laden with fertilizers, propane tanks, a cheap-looking alarm clock and other incendiary explosive devices meant to cause mayhem in Times Square, a tourist haven just four miles away from Ground Zero. Thanks to a vigilant roadside hawker nearby who spotted the dangerous cargo of death and alerted the police, another monumental catastrophe was averted when the would-be terrorist was hunted and pulled out of a Dubai-bound flight EK202 at the JFK international airport in New York. 19-year –old Somali born Mohamed Osman Mohamud planned to set up and detonate a car bomb at an annual Christmas tree lighting event in Portland, Oregon where there would be tons of people to kill but was mercifully thwarted by security operatives at the nick of time.

It soon became clear that young Faisal Shahzad was connected to TTP(Tehrik-e-Taliban Pakistan), a Pakistan-based unit of the Taliban allied to al-Qaida in the Waziristan tribal areas next to Afghanistan that trains fighters and offers bomb-making training for persons interested in fighting NATO and US forces. Thus another nightmarish chapter opened in America's saga with terrorism. Why would well-to-do persons opt for such devilish undertakings? Umar Farouk Abdumutallab came from a wealthy Nigerian family and was said to have studied engineering in the UK. Major Nidal Malik Hassan was a well paid army psychiatrist. Faisal Shahzad had studied and obtained a degree in computer science and another in engineering, topped by a job, a wife and US citizenship, things for which many persons toiled night and day. Yet with such achievement the 30-year old had spent five months seeking bomb-making training in Waziristan in Pakistan. Why? What is America missing in providing opportunities to its many citizens? Curiously, it turned out that all three, together with one Zachary Adam Chesser, recently captured as he prepared to join the Somali Islamic terror group, al-

Shabab, had connections to Anwar al-Awlaki and by extension, to Osama bin Laden who is known to be extremely wealthy too!

When 9/11 took place in 2001, a Muslim cleric who had long been an imam in the US took on the role of a bridge builder linking America to the one billion Muslims around the world. Anwar al-Awlaki did his very best to explain Islam to journalists and produced very engaging lectures on CDs about the prophet Mohammed. It was a praiseworthy effort. But nine years down the road, Awlaki found himself hiding out in Yemen and declaring war on the US, adding *"America as a whole has turned into a nation of evil"* mixing scripture with plenty of vitriolic attacks on his former host country and helping lure young Muslims into every conceivable plot. Faisal Shahzad, the planner of the botched Times Square bombing told investigators that he had been inspired by Awlaki's online lectures. Such a dramatic change of heart calls for level headed reflection on what factors are responsible for homegrown terrorism. The growing number certainly warrants a closer look. Utterances like "I'm tired of being guilty of things I did not do" expressing liberal white guilt can conveniently apply to the majority of practicing Muslims painted with the same brush as criminals simply because they are Muslim Americans. On the other hand perhaps the majority of the one billion peace loving Muslims of the world can take their cue from what peace- loving citizens are doing in Egypt, Tunisia and Libya, by rising up to the extremists as well as the belligerents at the helm and winning, in this way, wiping out any lingering bad image of the orgiastic partying that took place in the streets on 9/11/2001. The remorseless Faisal Shahzad, condemned to life in prison without the possibility of a parole, was defiant even as the judgment was pronounced, telling Judge Miriam Goldman Cedarbaum that the war with Muslims had just begun and that he was just the first droplet of flood of terror against the US. Shahzad said Muslims do not abide by man-made laws because they are always corrupt. For someone who went into hiding at the time his cargo of death was discovered near Times Square, Shahzad made a remarkable reversal in becoming fearless and defiant.

At 39, Anwar al-Awlaki, a US citizen, went from mildly criticizing his country to a dramatic rise in the ranks of anti-Western Islamic extremists, prompting the Obama Administration to name him a global terrorist, thereby making him a target for assassination by US forces or CIA drones. As a mortal enemy and danger to America's national security, he has been placed on par with Osama bin Laden, the mastermind of 9/11 attacks on the WTC in New York. Like bin Laden, he is said to seek a world ruled by Islamic law, brought about violently if possible. But the two are said to differ in their approach. Former chief of CIA's Bin Laden unit and author of *Osama Bin Laden*, Michael Sheuer paints the following picture of the elusive Bin Laden: pious, brave, intelligent, generous, charismatic, patient, visionary, stubborn, egalitarian and realistic, and concludes with "I think the real danger is that we're fighting an enemy who doesn't exist." In other words, Osama Bin Laden is imaginary! While bin Laden is low key and violent, Awlaki has churned out hundreds of sermons in the Internet, thanks to his fluency in English, his familiarity with American culture and his stance as a cleric – according to the 9/11 Commission Report, he was a chief cleric in the mosque in San Diego - that has allowed him to recruit followers in the US. Using the late pop star Michael Jackson to make his point about the inevitability of death, Awlaki suggests that jihadists should not fear dying for their faith. Because of his formidable ability to recruit followers and inspire attacks through e-mails and websites, the Arab satellite network, Al Arabiya has dubbed him "bin Laden of the Internet".

What exactly is jihad really? And why does it generate so much visceral reaction on both sides of the East-West divide? The idea of a jihad held up as a banner, rallying the cause of Muslim radicals is quite common but ask the ordinary Muslim what it is and you will get answers like ...Jihad is the holy war of Islam against infidels (all non-Muslims). Is it true and does the Holy Qur'an actually advocate so? One westerner, who has explored this theme at length and provided remarkable insights, is US senator Mark Siljander (*A Deadly Misunderstanding*).

In the Qur'an Jihad is used primarily to describe the struggle or striving against negative influences in the pursuit of internal purity. It is commonly used in defensive terms —struggling against sin and vanity, avoiding contact with unbelievers and other corrupting influences very much like shunning bad company. There are various shades of meaning. In some suras of the Qur'an, jihad is used to denote avoiding unbelievers and hypocrites, striving to convince and encourage, having faith, dealing with money and self, emigration, patience and giving. Jihad covers one who struggles in the righteous path of internal purification, the rewards that await those who righteously struggle thus and righteousness itself.

Some passages in the Holy Qur'an use "jihad" to describe *defensive fighting* in the cause of Allah, passages readily taken out of context to imply armed aggression. But such views are poles apart from the genuine Qur'anic meaning! The struggle to defend family, friends, community and honor against external attack is also a jihad but this usage appears very rarely in the Qur'an, far less often and with less evocation of bloodshed than the impulse described in the Old Testament. Therefore jihad is simply an internal struggle to withstand external influences and come closer to God. Both the New Testament and the Qur'an use jihad as a struggle or fight, not against external forces or enemies but for internal peace and to get closer to God. It is this very struggle that Paul describes in his letter to the believers in Rome: *For it is not the good that I wish to do, that I do; but it is the evil that I do not wish to do, that I do. (Rom. 7:19)*

It is the same jihad when Jesus finds himself alone in the garden of Gethsemane, knowing of his betrayal and impending capture and struggling with himself to accept his fate.

So if this be the case that the idea is the same in the Bible and in the Qur'an why is it that the East and West are at daggers drawn then? Today too many Muslims don't know what the Qur'an says! And certainly the Bible did not lay down any blueprint for the pogroms of Europe that burned thousands of Jews at the stake, the Inquisition in Spain that expelled hundreds of thousands of Jews and forced conversions under torture. No, not the Bible.

During those horrendous times few people read the Bible (in any language, Semitic or otherwise) because a majority of the population was illiterate. So when their leaders told them in the name of God that they were supposed to go torture and rape and murder people, they did just that. Very unfortunately it is exactly the same situation today. Most westerners know the Bible very vaguely and consider themselves Christians because their parents were or because they occasionally go to church. Quite a few Muslims do not know the Qur'an well at all. Muslim clerics say the Qur'an can only be fully understood in its original Arabic, yet of the 1.2 billion Muslims world-wide, only 15% can read Arabic. A great many of that 15% would find the language of classical seventh century Arabic daunting.

Most Muslims today are not conversant with the actual text of the Qur'an, relying on the religious and political leaders to tell them what it says. The same is true of Christians. It is easy to see how Muslim terrorism thrives on this ignorance of the holy book and the core tenets of the faith of Islam which has now been "*dumped down*" to serve the aims of radical militancy. When unable to justify their deviant interpretation with the Qur'an, they end up manipulating jihad through the lenses of Islam's other books – the Hadith and the Sunnah.

Nothing trumps a detailed study of the holy books. Qur'an is derived from Arabic/Aramaic (*qara'a*) and simply means to recite or read. It is the sum total of the commands given by the angel Gabriel to Mohammed in A. D. 610 in the cave at Hira, north-east of Mecca. The Qur'an is divided into chapters (sura) and verses (aya) and deals with topics like Adam, Eve, Cain, Abel, Abraham, Mount Sinai, Noah, Solomon, Sheba, Moses, heaven, Satan, hell, angels, end times, Judgment day, sin, forgiveness, Zachariah, John the Baptist, Mary and of course Jesus(Isa). Lots of familiar topics.

The Qur'an speaks in very lofty terms about Jesus (Isa) – Messiah, word of Allah, supernaturally conceived but not the begotten son of God, the way the Bible puts it. For the Muslim, once this point is mentioned, the discussion comes to an abrupt end. The idea of Allah fathering a child is abhorrent. It is heresy, blasphemous and disgusting. The Majesty of Allah having carnal relations with a female? Hell, no! Allah does not, has not, and could not "beget" a child the way the Bible puts it.

Some misunderstandings are easily explained. If Muhammed speaks so nicely about Jesus, how is it that Jesus too does not speak about Mohammed? Simple. Jesus lived 500 years or more before the birth of Mohammed.

The Qur'an says Muhammad was compassionate, even in war; he prohibited the killing or mistreatment of women and children and even forbade the cutting down of trees. So where do impressionable, fanatical young men and women get the idea from to stride into public places with explosives strapped to their chests and belts and to blow apart scores of randomly chosen people, innocent civilians or jumbo jets hijacked and flown into buildings filled with thousands of people? How would Prophet Muhammad react to this? Horror perhaps?

Oh no! Not yet. That would be the Mohammed of Mecca. If one follows Mohammed from Mecca to Medina, the story is turned upside down. The humble, peaceful, devout, obedient and faithful Mohammed of Mecca moved to Medina in an effort to find support for his fledgling religion but between these two places he had the type of Saul-Paul transformation that brought him and his religion into what some have dubbed multiple personality disorder. Mohammed's political power increased when he got to Medina and his followers began raiding caravans to support the religion. Politics and religion make very weird bed partners. His enemies, like his followers, multiplied in number. A reign of terror ensued and refusal to submit to Islam was a clear invitation to death at the hands of Mohammed's followers. Unlike Jesus who forbade his disciples the use of force or violence, apparently Mohammed was content to let his followers visit terror on nonbelievers who were labeled infidels for the purpose and slaughtered. Clearly what we live today has been part and parcel of this aspect of Islam from its founding even if a large number of Muslims are peace loving and distance themselves from such carnage.

In a spirited debate, whether Islam is a religion of peace or not, Somali-born Ayaan Hirsi Ali, a former Dutch Parliamentarian and strong critic of Islam, led her team to a landslide victory over opponents Douglas Murray, director of Center for Social Cohesion in London, Pakistani-born, western educated Zeba khan, writer and advocate for Muslim American civic engagement, and Maajid Nawaz, former member of a radical Islamic party who served four years in an Egyptian prison and founder of counter-extremism Quillian Foundation. By a well selected number of examples, including Faisal Shahzad who attempted to blow up Times Square in New York City, Ayaan Hirsi Ali tore into shreds the notion that Islam is a religion of peace, increasing from 25% to 55% those who previously thought Islam was not peaceful, reducing the undecided from 34% to 9% and the supporters from 41% to 36%. Quite revealing. And indeed those riots, book burnings, world-wide ban and boycotts of publishers plus a frenzy of righteous barbarisms once directed at Salman Rushdie, author of *The Satanic Verses* made South Africa's apartheid look like an afternoon picnic. Together with her experiences in her home country, Somalia and in Holland, Ayaan Hirsi Ali knew what she was talking about. Another debate took place at Toronto's Roy Thomson Hall, pitting former British Prime Minister, Tony Blair, a new convert to Catholicism, against prominent atheist, Christopher Hitchens. This time the topic was whether religion is a force for good in the world. Both parties sparred and traded verbal blows and the winner, polemicist Hitchens, in spite of battling cancer of the upper respiratory tract, went at it with a rare flair saying, "Once you assume a creator and a plan, it makes us subjects in a cruel experiment" and comparing, to plenty of laughter, God to a "kind of divine North Korea." He beat Tony Blair at it.

And what an irony! Adolf Hitler hijacked the concept of personal purity before God (Christian purity) and distorted it into a justification for a campaign of genocide. It would appear that the promoters of Muslim militancy have similarly hijacked what in essence is the same principle – personal struggle to reach and maintain inner purity – and harnessed it to a campaign of mass murder. And so the crusaders, the Inquisitors, the Nazis, the Jihadists – all have blood-strewn agendas, claim moral superiority and a mandate direct from on high. All lies! None of this has anything to do with God, Allah, Jesus, Muhammad, or purity or jihad!

It is the invention of a bitter heart of human hatred. It is high time humanity exposed the lies for what they are instead of throwing insults, threats or bombs at them. The driving force beyond all others, behind the extremists' most fearsome and unstoppable weapon is the suicide attacker, the martyr-soldier, the promise of salvation. The idea to give up one's life in the act of destroying infidels is used by the architects of militant Muslim ideology as the only sure way to guarantee that Allah's benevolent mercy will be applied to one's individual case. Pure nonsense! At his sentencing, Faisal Shahzad actually boasted to Judge Miriam Goldman Cedarbaum that the Qu'ran allows him to kill many people! How many North American Muslims share this view? Nowhere does the Qu'ran prescribe murder or suicide as a path to salvation. The physician terrorist who blew up seven CIA agents and their Jordanian counterpart claimed he was avenging the death of a Muslim leader killed by an American UAV (unmanned aerial vehicle), popularly called a drone, remotely controlled from Nevada desert. Neither that leader nor the prophet Mohammed ever gave him such a commission!

Ayman al-Zawahiri, Osama bin Ladin's #2 and chief ideologue was a young doctor not drawn to the traditional concern of religion (relationship between man and God) but rather to religion as a political ideology. Ayman's preoccupation with injustice led him to propose a SYSTEM to give justice rather than a religion that gives inner peace (ISLAM). His highly politicized version of Islam went out to recruit in the Arab-Muslim world, especially in places with plenty of frustration, preaching Islam as the most perfect and complete expression of God's monotheistic message and Prophet Mohammed as the last and most perfect messenger of God. But the recruits, mainly youths, questioned how the Arab world could live in such less prosperous and less democratic world than the rest of the Earth's civilizations. "Why would others live so much better if ours is the superior faith, all encompassing of religion, politics and economics?" they ask. To this challenge Arab-Muslim intellectuals are now rising and in particular pointing to this backwardness with brutal honesty and demanding solutions, defying their authoritarian governments and using their media to encourage debates instead of blaming all their problems on others, especially the great Satan of the West. Clearly it is politics, not religion, at the core of the problem!

Most schools of Islam tend to treat the Qur'an as a divinely inspired text not open to any literary criticism or creative reinterpretation. Without a culture that encourages and creates space for such creative reinterpretation, critical thought and original thinking tend to wither! This explains why so few world-class scientific papers are cited by scholars coming out of Arab-Muslim universities. It has been argued that if the West had to make Shakespeare "the sole object of our study and the sole guide of our lives" it would soon enough fall into backwardness and stagnation.

And so a serious problem crops up when Muslims want stagnation and power at the same time. They want a return to the perfection of the 7th century and at the same time to dominate the 21st as they believe in the birthright of their doctrine, the last testament of God to man. Choosing to remain in a 7th century backwater, secure in a quietist philosophy poses no problem between East and the West. But then wanting the power that free inquiry confers without allowing for either the free inquiry itself or the philosophy and Institutions that guarantee it can be problematic. Faced with this dilemma there are two ways out – either abandon the cherished religion and embrace free inquiry or remain for ever at the rear of human technical advance. Neither alternative is appealing enough, hence the tension between the desire for power and success in the modern world on one hand and the desire not to abandon the cherished religion on the other.

Suicide bombs have provided some the resolution of this conflict. When faced with intractable problems some people lash out. Muslims feel humiliated and they get angry. Anger does not allow for rational thinking. This some how explains the feeling of hopelessness in Muslim countries and people, the feeling that they can do nothing right. Terrorism spreads by the poverty of dignity, not of money. When this is combined with the discrimination or alienation by those who had left home for Europe or North America, a powerful cocktail of rage is obtained. What is the better way forward? Humiliation can be overcome by modernization through learning and industries. Post-WWII Germany did it, so can the Muslim world. Spain did it too. Larger-than-life persons like Osama bin Laden or Ahmed Zaki Yamani, did achieve global notoriety by holding the whole world in their hands at some point, using oil as a weapon in one case or suicide bombers in another. They each gave the Muslim world a temporary "high', a feeling of exercising power on the world stage. Saudi Arabia's oil weapon is economic power with little productivity and bin Laden's terrorism weapon is military force without a real army, state, economy or engine of innovation to support it.

Islam is practically undergoing the same internal rift (fundamentalism) experienced by other religious organizations and perhaps this may provide the way forward for mankind. In 1910 ultra-conservative American protestants came up with a list of non-negotiable beliefs genuine Christians had to subscribe to – the virgin birth, the physical resurrection of Jesus Christ and his imminent second coming, but most important of all, the literal inerrancy of the Bible in everything. These *fundamental* beliefs were held by true believers who feared that liberal movement and openness to other faiths tended to erode the foundation of their religion. In Catholicism, the same tendency was observed beginning with Pius IX who issued the Syllabus of Errors in 1864. Most popes condemned all liberal catholic efforts. As for Muslims, they hate the word fundamentalist when it is applied to them; they think it is a foreign term. All the same scholars of the Qur'an seek to rethink their faith in the light of science and democracy even though an angry faction opposed such new ideas. With European colonial influence in the east, thinkers like Sayyed Qutb, the Egyptian scorned such reform efforts as imperialist pollution.

For each religious movement, fundamentalism expanded to accommodate the rapid changes taking place in the world and to provide certainty and assurance. Wars in Korea and Vietnam, civil rights movement in the US and youth revolts were contemporary problems in need of solutions. In Europe, highly conservative Catholic groups(integralists) gained strength in some countries. In Muslim countries oil funneled riches to the elite and drove hordes of village people into angry urban poverty. It was easy to turn to the promise of a more equal society strictly based on the Qur'an when secular solutions failed. As the twentieth century ended and the twenty-first began, fundamentalism took more formidable shapes politically and religiously, with adherents working through spiritual and educational channels as a vocal minority turned to violence that caught the attention of news media. While some seemed ready to die for faith, others were prepared to kill for it, gunning down abortionists and their clinics, hijacking aircraft, exploding bombs at weddings and much more.

But soon enough something began to happen. Thoughtful persons in the Muslim world were impatient with violent groups that killed in the name of Allah without using the same Allah to produce jobs, food, or healthcare. The jihadist wing of the Taliban has not quite addressed the real issues and is slowly losing ground in Afghanistan; the other wing owes allegiance to tribal loyalties and traditional aversion to foreigners. Al-Qaida faces a similar dilemma. In Iran clerics have resorted to the beating and imprisoning of critics. In America the religious right, once a crusade, has become just a niche with television evangelists losing audiences to more moderate preachers of the word. Pentecostals and mega churches are gaining ground once controlled by fundamentalists. Nowhere than South Korea is the growth of Christianity so palpable with an ideology tending toward moderate evangelicalism.

It seems natural to expect that fading fundamentalism will free Christians, Muslims and the Jews of the world to explore what they have in common. In retrospect, protestant fundamentalists believed in a verbally inspired Bible and Catholics, after Vatican II, in the Latin Mass (symbol of a changeless authoritative tradition). As for the Muslims, it was the short era of the "rightly guided caliphs" who led Islam immediately after the death of the Prophet Mohammed, before disunity shattered their community and outsiders warped their civilization. It smacks of defeatism when Britain's David Cameron, Germany's Angela Merkel and France's Nicolas Sarkozy say that multiculturalism –the right of different groups to live by their traditional values - has failed to promote a sense of common identity centered on values of human rights, democracy and social integration and equality before the law in their countries and go on to advocate muscular liberal western values with less of passive tolerance. Challenges like these provide opportunities to look for common ground.

## Confidentiality issues – doctor/patient, priest/penitent, lawyer/client, reporter/source?

Resolving the conflict in our interpretations of the US Constitution will certainly enhance the way we look outward to accommodate schisms in other cultures. Under President George Bush, the TSP (Terrorist Surveillance Program) authorized the NSA to listen in on suspected terrorists in the US without court-ordered warrants and there were palpable fears that such a trend could lead to an Orwellian state of affairs in future with fabricated security threats, state surveillance and anti-terrorist legislation, all endangering civil liberties. How will citizens of the future react to the drone being used to spy on them right here in the homeland? But there were problems with allegations of torture said to be necessary by some for the so-called high value detainees. Deep techniques such as sleep deprivation, water boarding (simulated drowning) were introduced, causing a lot of controversy and embarrassment for the US. These will need to be revisited in the plan to sanitize the nation and its cherished practices, to harmonize with practices prescribed by international conventions. Otherwise the US loses the moral high ground when dealing with the prosecution of warlords either in Kosovo or in the Congo. A war crime should be prosecuted wherever it occurs. Nothing is more demoralizing than a world which stands by helpless as America pontificates that these laws are made for others, not us. President Obama's unambiguous declaration that the US does not torture was a most welcome change in direction at the summit and his moves to clear the skeletons in the George Bush closet are most welcome.

During the 1995 trial of the year, Tracie Savage, a journalist of the Los Angeles station KNBC reported that DNA test showed that the blood found on a sock was that of O. J. Simpson's slain wife. Simpson's defense attorneys tried to have that journalist called and forced to reveal her source in order to demonstrate police conspiracy. But the journalist's story turned out to be wrong because the DNA test had not yet been done, hence the court ruled that a wrong source could not have been much of a source and so denied the motion to force her to testify. Had the source been right, Ms Savage would have had to face the nightmarish prospect of revealing it or possibly going to jail for contempt of court. For long most journalists opted to go to jail rather than reveal their sources, arguing that they could not and would not betray the source they had promised to protect. And so journalists kept a high ethical standard. On the other hand, in 1991, Dan Cohen, a political consultant sued the Minneapolis Star Tribune's editor for breaching the anonymity promised him, and won. In that case the Supreme Court held 5 – 4 that Cohen had a right to sue. Judge Ito who ruled in Tracie Savage's case thought she might have just listened to "elevator gossip" and so owed her source nothing.

No stone is left unturned as US citizens explore the limits of their first Amendment and other rights. In Wisconsin three men dug up a buried corpse so that one of them could have sex with it. Judges at a lower court saw nothing wrong with the act, stating that nothing in State law banned necrophilia. But public outrage and a push by state lawmakers in the direction of criminalizing such acts led to the 5 – 2 high court decision which explained the illegality simply by stating that dead bodies are incapable of giving consent. And so Wisconsin's Supreme Court made the ruling that it is illegal to have sex with a corpse.

Probable cause is a very important guide line for carrying out arrests; otherwise the idea of profiling looms large, especially in cases of racial profiling when the arresting official and the victim find themselves on opposite sides of the racial divide. At the trial of

Timothy McVeigh in Denver, highway patrolman, Trooper Charles Hanger explained that he had first pulled Timothy McVeigh over because his vehicle did not have a rear license plate, and then proceeded to arrest him for carrying a concealed weapon. It was several days later that Timothy McVeigh was linked to the more ominous Oklahoma City bombing! Imagine for one second that there had been no probable cause and that the case of that murderer had been thrown out of court! Already some persons had started stoking the xenophobic fire, alleging that some foreign power, probably Iraq, was behind the bombing instead of the native terrorism that it was. After the Oklahoma bombing Americans began to realize how heavy a price hate crimes, especially anti-government hostility, could exact if carried too far. Yet even to this day Americans stop at nothing to quote Thomas Jefferson and proclaim how the tree of democracy must be watered from time to time by the blood of patriots and martyrs. It must provide Al Qaida and Osama bin Ladin much comfort to realize that our own citizens too have joined hands with the devil to provide an internal threat as worrisome as the external one.

The thorny issue of protecting a reporter's source of information comes up from time to time and is quite sticky. In the years ahead the question of reporters' source versus national security issues will most certainly crop up again. The courts (and sometimes the public!) are disinclined to side with the press in the same way courts have done over the years with respect to recognizing doctor-patient, priest-penitent, husband-wife or lawyer-client privileges. Dr. Frederic Mailliez, the first French physician to reach the accident spot in a Paris tunnel on August 31, 1997, told the Times of London that Princess Diana had kept expressing her pain but when asked what exactly Diana had said, the French doctor cited doctor-patient confidentiality and said he could not repeat it, even after Diana's death. And nine days before his death by suicide, White House lawyer Vincent Foster consulted another lawyer, James Hamilton, a respected veteran of the Watergate investigation. For two hours Hamilton took down notes on three pages, with check marks, question marks, punctuation marks, underlined words and so on.

Two years later, independent counsel, Kenneth Starr, investigating President Bill Clinton, asked for those notes but Hamilton refused, citing lawyer-client privilege, upheld by the Federal district court. But then that was overruled by the court of Appeals, following which Hamilton took the matter to the Supreme Court. At issue was whether a client would speak freely if he thought his confidence would not survive his death.

So why shouldn't a similar consideration be accorded to confidentiality privileges between reporters and the sources of their news? And what about Miranda rights – the right to remain silent or refuse to answer for fear of self-incrimination? Does the First Amendment to the US Constitution preclude this? Are the courts and the press not seeking the truth? What to do about whistle-blowers then? Why did Judith Miller go to prison for some time before being released? It is clear that the judge who handled her matter, dug deep and came up convinced that the purpose of the leak of the CIA officer's identity appeared to be to smear someone who had cast doubt on the reasons for going to war against Iraq. How did this compare with legendary whistleblower, Daniel Ellsberg of the famous Pentagon papers, the man who fearlessly says it is better to speak up now or forever hold one's mouth? And Deep throat, America's best kept secret – CIA agent, Mark Felt who tipped off the press about President Richard Nixon's private bugging of the Watergate offices of the Democratic National Convention, leading to Nixon's forced resignation in disgrace as he faced a looming impending impeachment? Next to deep throat was "Donna" pseudonym for the Castro junior sister, Juanita Castro whose case of sibling rivalry drove her to work undercover for the CIA for over four decades against her brother Fidel and the Cuban revolution.

As far back as August 7, 1974, when law professor William Clinton was running for Congress, he was quoted as saying "*There is no question that an admission of making false statements to government officials and interfering with the CIA and FBI is an impeachable offence.*" At around that very time, freshman Trent Lott of the House judiciary Committee said "A president should be removed only for serious misconduct dangerous to the system of government, and not for general misbehavior." Since then impeachment has loomed large on two occasions – for Richard Milhous Nixon and William Jefferson Clinton. In the former both of the above criteria were met but the guy sensed danger and resigned from office before the axe fell on him. In the latter, it was debatable whether the criteria defined above were met, prompting some cynics to draw attention to the French expression *"autres temps, autres moeurs"*. It was argued that Bill Clinton's philandering with White House intern Monika Lewinksy could not carry the same weight as Richard Nixon's conduct in ordering the break-in into the Democratic National party's Watergate Headquarters, obstructing justice in its investigation and telling lies about it all. The famous Monika Lewinsky case ended up being a "one witness" affair, a battle of credibility between a woman who had admitted on tape lying all her life and a man also on tape in Little Rock, Arkansas, counseling Gennifer Flowers to "just deny everything." Clinton also benefited from the biblical lesson of John 1:8 *"He who is blameless, let him cast the first stone."*

But Americans are not so soon going to stop judging each other on matters involving their private lives. Talk show radio hosts, senators, governors and Hollywood celebrities seem to be competing for slots in the spotlight. Hardly a week goes by without some heavyweight coming under the nation's scrutiny. Even Woods, the world's billionaire athlete was not spared when he reversed his Porsche Cadillac out of his driveway at 2:00 a. m. and hit a fire hydrant and a tree, sustaining facial lacerations which required hospital intervention to put right. Well before anyone knew, there was tabloid frenzy as news media competed to publish salacious gossips about the gentleman hitherto known for his very reserved character. "Behind every great fortune is a great crime" began one commentator, who then proceeded to detail how the man's foundation, Tiger Inc., had a contract with Chevron in the guise of a philanthropy, yet Chevron was notorious for dumping wastes all over the planet – Alaska, Canada, Brazil, Angola, California - and partnering with Burma's ruling military junta on that country's Yadana gas pipe line project, a source of revenue amounting to $5 billon. The commentator then dwelt on Dubai, site of a Tiger

Woods-designed golf course, the symbol of economic excess at the southern coast of the Persian Gulf, a nation built over thirty years by slave labor and reputed to be the ground zero of the global sex trade. Tiger Woods's plea for respect of family privacy fell on deaf ears as the hounds went to work, trying to outdo the police from whom the athlete refused an interview three times in connection with his accident, citing privacy concerns. There were talks about infidelity and extramarital affairs not easily quelled by the athlete's belated apology to his family for unspecified "transgressions" on his part. The press was on high alert, ready to pillory the man for his personal problems, arguing that he had every right to keep those personal problems personal as long as there were no deals benefiting dictatorships, unaccountable corporations and others.

Speaking about the confidentiality of news sources, Special Counsel, Patrick Fitzgerald told the court "journalists are not entitled to promise complete confidentiality. No one in America is." But this is debatable. A 1972 decision of the Supreme Court held, in effect, that journalists do have a qualified First Amendment protection. The government can demand to have a source identified only after demonstrating that there is no other way to obtain the information needed in a criminal investigation. And so over the years, subpoenas for reporters have not aroused great public outcry because the public was turned off by news media symbolized by Jason Blair and Dan Rather. Fitzgerald's pursuit of Judith Miller and Matt Cooper seemed designed to discourage future leaks rather than to find out who actually leaked the identity of a CIA undercover officer. Confidential sources have played a vital role in exposing wrongdoing in government. Judith Miller was jailed for 85 days. How would this affect future journalistic investigation threatened with exposing their sources? And won't whistleblowers think twice before blowing their whistles, especially to a reporter? At the height of the financial meltdown, a whistleblower claimed that well before the crunch, he had tried unsuccessfully to draw the attention of the big boys to wrongdoing which was royally ignored. That claim should give much food for thought to those trying to sanitize the monetary market and its practices. Bradley Burkinfeld, a former employee of the Swiss banking giant, UBS became America's whistleblower of all time when he helped provide insider information to the US government concerning sanctuaries for 19,000 clients worth about $19 billion, most of them being tax evaders. But instead of gaining sympathy from the US government the whistleblower faced prosecution and imprisonment for his own role in facilitating wrongdoing, especially in helping tax evaders by hiding diamonds inside toothpaste containers.

Currently the US government is locked in a conflict with another whistleblower, WikiLeaks whose founder, Julian Assange, who claims he set up the website to expose perceived unethical behavior by government and private businesses, in a way doing what Homeland Security was supposed to have done. Among many things the website leaked were thousands of classified government documents, raising concerns that some of it might have compromised operations in the battle field as well as risked the lives of some diplomats and our men and women in uniform. It accuses US forces in Afghanistan of covering up civilian deaths (a typical war crime in need of investigation) and of using taxpayer dollars to fund Pakistani ISI(Internal Services Intelligence), a fringe of which reportedly collaborates with the Taliban, a declared enemy of the US. WiliLeaks has surely stirred a hornet's nest, exposing confidential information in such areas as the ICC judge's findings on President Al-Bashir's bloody $9 billion stashed in British banks, Saudi Arabia's insistence on cutting off the head of the snake (Iran's nuclear weapons program), and lots more. So should WikiLeaks be praised or prosecuted for exposing the classified documents? A senior Republican on the House intelligence Committee could not help lamenting over the catastrophic issue which is the breakdown in trust wondering whether many other countries –allies as well as foes- will not be asking questions like : "Can the US be trusted? Can the US keep a secret?" If Americans could turn back the clock, they would have brought WikiLeaks to the eve of George Bush's launching of the war against Iraq in search of weapons of mass destruction that never were! To support or not to support journalists like Julian Assange? That is a million dollar question, the man's action having affected politicians as well as ordinary citizens in the US, Russia, Britain, Libya, Zimbabwe and even his native Australia where the view seems to be that their citizen should not expect protection for playing outside the rules. In solidarity journalists went on the streets to demonstrate their support. It did not take long for some disenchanted former members of WikiLeaks to go open, expressing their concerns about the dangerous concentration of power in one person's hands, reminding a world short on memory that absolute power corrupts absolutely. But as the larger issue of confidentiality of news sources looms, people will have to take one step back and ask themselves whether Julian Assange should reveal or protect the source of the leaked confidential material. How can the government official who released the documents be held responsible but not Julian Assange? Is that not a typical case of joint venture in crime? In an ironic twist, the man who considered himself the purveyor of the truth, when brought before the court for alleged rape of two Swedish women, pleaded for privacy, the very commodity he denied others targeted by his reckless act.

Another citizen who tested the limits of the law was Terri Shiavo, a woman diagnosed to be in PVS (persistent vegetative state), whose lawyer fought hard to keep her alive on life support against a husband, backed by the system, who would rather end her suffering by withdrawing the support system. The attorney of the sick woman fought hard but lost, leading him to lament that we do not have justice in the US; that we have a flawed system of justice that depends on money, the magistrate and morality. He was particularly bitter that people had enough money to finance a "dream team" of the finest of lawyers from leading law firms and a parade of expert witnesses flown in to dazzle a jury. The attorney's charge was reminiscent of Robert Frost who once stated that a jury consisted of twelve persons charged to decide who had the better lawyer."

Terri Shiavo's lawyer lamented that people in America had a mistaken notion of judges as people who just uphold the law, yet there is not a fixed definition of what the "law is" since a lot depends on the background of the judge (did he have a flat tire or a fight with his wife?), his politics, varying from courtroom to courtroom and some being pro-plaintiff or pro-defendant, and the law itself. Technically the facts should speak for themselves (*res ipso loquito*) but justice is relative. Even in matters of morality, there is no longer an absolute standard of morality in US law and without such a moral foundation justice is in the eyes of the beholder. Ever since statutory law (voted by the elected representatives of the people) replaced the Common Law, there is hardly any consistency any more. When US law was based on English Law (established upon an absolute standard based on the Bible, the revered Blackstone's Commentary), knowing the bible meant having an understanding of the law because there was consistency. Since then a lot has changed.

A new school of thought – typified by Prof. Peter Singer, ethicist and self-proclaimed atheist at Princeton University's Center for Human Values - advocates that persons who are unable to work and unable to be productive are a burden to society (just like Adolf Hitler's useless eaters of the Third Reich) and so their death is justified. Progressive thinkers express pro-death ideas and feel that disabled persons tax the medical system, have no quality of life, and are in need of constant care, and therefore their medical care is futile. Thus the elderly, those suffering from dementia, Alzheimer's, epilepsy, Down's syndrome, Parkinson's and others are categorized as useless eaters and so the solution for them is to let nature take its course – passive euthanasia, assisted suicide, terminal sedation. Today it is common to overhear young persons lamenting the fact that the old have outlived their usefulness and are jeopardizing the social security of the younger generation. Targeting the elimination of the disabled will come face to face with another reality – that long life was made possible thanks to medical breakthroughs which continue to prolong life expectancy.

It is also chilling to imagine that this category of individuals – the so-called useless eaters - was targeted when bigots looked to eugenics and abortion as a means of eliminating them from the US population. Most people remember Richard Nixon only in connection with the famous Watergate tapes and scandal that brought down his presidency. Other recently released tapes of

Nixon's presidency brought to light that the man, speaking about the *Roe versus Wade* judgment, had told an aide that abortion was "necessary" in some cases such as inter-racial pregnancies. The president unequivocally mentioned when there was a black and white pregnancy or a rape. Why would Richard Milhous Nixon, an elected president of the United States and beacon of the free world, advocate such a devilish scheme or even be associated with it at a time when so many had embraced miscegenation? What could be so objectionable in pregnancies resulting from white and black love affairs? Why would any sane American, for example, consider Tiger Woods the wonder boy of golf, Oprah Winfrey, the great philanthropist, or Barack Obama now US president – all emanation of interracial procreation - less deserving of citizenship and right to life than any other? Isn't it ironic that European nationals in Ireland proudly embrace Mohammed Ali or Barack Obama as theirs whereas an American would look down on them? Isn't it ironic that the man who helped open the door to China should turn around and object to progeny born of Chinese and white Americans? Or did Nixon, in the fertile areas of his imagination consider that Chinese would accept and embrace the indignities they once suffered under Apartheid South Africa's Group Areas Act? Where on his scale of values would he place children born of Chinese and white Americans?

Even more chilling was a New York Times interview in which Justice Ruth Bader Ginsberg mentioned the straightening out of reproductive choice, referring to the Hyde Amendment which barred the use of Medicaid funds for abortions, a law that the US Supreme Court upheld in *Harris vs. McRae, 1980*. Said the judge, "Frankly, I had thought that at the time *Roe* was decided there was concern about population growth and particularly the growth in a population that we don't want to have too many of, so that Roe was going to be then set up for Medicaid funding for abortion... But when the court decided *McRae*, the case came out the other way". There it is in black and white – particularly the growth in a population that we don't want too many of. Margaret Sanger is today remembered for opening the first birth control clinic in the nation and later founding the American Birth control League which became the Planned Parenthood. But she also believed in the forced sterilization of those the state deemed unfit, notably blacks whom she considered human weeds.

Today the US is celebrating the life accomplishment of the late Eunice Kennedy Shriver who championed the cause of the disadvantaged persons in our society in ventures like the Special Olympics for which she received encomiums, yet others, including an elected president of the US, continued to scheme and think only in terms of eliminating from the US population, those they arrogated to themselves the judgment of being unwanted!

Of course everyday many persons do a commendable job to project the good side of America. Science is making giant strides and bringing happiness into many lives. One area in need of regulation is *in vitro* fertilization which has enabled many otherwise infertile families to have children. But there are a lot of gray areas to be looked into. The commendable job of sperm banks and clinics processing frozen embryos depends on anonymous donation of either sperms or eggs to help needy couples. However, lurking behind the act are a tangle of problems that can become a nightmare if left to medical science alone. Legal rights and obligations for those involved – donors, beneficiaries, the clinics, the babies – need to be well defined by legislation. In the state of Massachusetts, for example, a case appeared before Justice James McHugh where a mother sought the identity of the sperm donor in order to obtain child support and genetic information. The judge called on the legislature to pass laws to clarify such issues. Obviously such a situation with broad implications needed more than the legal luminary to untangle it. Anonymity was paramount and so it was out of the question to seek to know the identity of the sperm donor.

For a successful IVF system to operate credibly there must be guaranteed protection of the anonymity of donors. Not every person who donates sperms or eggs wishes to identify with the child at delivery or later, so contractual forms must be signed well ahead of donation to protect such concerns. In a country where a high premium is placed on privacy issues, clinics must be empowered to preserve this as well as the anonymity of the actors involved. Would-be parents must be made to sign forms that relinquish any future claims to financial support from the donors just as donors too give up any claims over the child to be born. And what about the curiosity of children who subsequently seek to know their true biological parents? That is another sticky matter the law must lay down to protect all sides.

Thanks to Robert Edwards whose work paved the way for *in vitro* fertilization (IVF), in 1978 a British woman gave birth to the world's first "test tube baby" and today many couples all over the world can have hope and the joy of getting one or more babies where they would otherwise be declared infertile. Edwards was honored with the 2010 Nobel Prize in medicine for his work. Since the inception of IVF, a new industry was born and now there are millions of cryopreserved embryos (frozen in liquid nitrogen) conceived in Petri dishes and preserved for later use due either to a failed first attempt, delay due to the delivery of twins or some intervening health and family issue. In most cases infertility treatment is so expensive that insurance coverage is the only way out, especially storage costs. Recently the fate of frozen embryos became a hot potato and Congress debated what should be done with them. Scientists need them as potential sources of cells for stem-cell research. Religious groups consider an embryo a full fledged human being with rights to be protected; prolife politicians see them as life worth protecting whereas prochoice people do not. The patients themselves display complex feelings, including emotional attachment to what they consider "children-in-waiting".

From the word go, former President George W. Bush blocked all possibility of providing federal funding for stem cell research but as soon as Barack Obama became president, he reversed that decision with an executive order of March 2009 making it possible for couples to donate their frozen embryos for stem cell research. Unfortunately a federal judge blocked such funding once more, saying it violates the law by not only destroying human embryos but also putting those other researchers working with adult stem cells at a competitive disadvantage. Now the president is looking to the

Appeal Court to allow the federal funding to continue, arguing that the ban would ruin numerous ongoing projects and cost millions of dollars.

As far as the American Society of Reproductive Medicine is concerned, three ethical options are available for spare embryos - thawing and discarding them like biohazard waste, donating them for medical research or donating them to other needy infertile couples. Laws vary from state to state. In some states it is illegal to create embryos specifically for research purposes, hence clinics must require infertile patients to sign consent forms before treatment, indicating what should be done with leftovers. The patients have sovereignty over their embryos while the doctors merely act as guardians. Some persons, who consider embryos as life, have expressed difficulty parting with them. Donating for them is hardly an option, so they prefer adoption by needy couples. The only problem here is that this reflects a first step towards defining embryos as human beings, which some find unacceptable. In the State of Louisiana, embryos are defined as "juridical persons" not to be used in medical research while Colorado went as far as putting a "Personhood Amendment" in the 2008 ballot giving constitutional rights to the embryo before it was defeated by 3 to 1. The cost of implanting an embryo is estimated at $5000 whereas undergoing IVF treatment and obtaining embryos before implanting costs $25.000.

Countries like India and China face a different kind of moral and ethical dilemma with respect to population, especially how to solve the alarming shortage of females. In India one million girls are aborted each year by parents not interested in raising girls, because of a cultural preference for boys. Modern imaging technology (ultrasound scans) makes it easy to determine the sex of children before birth. But sex selection tests are illegal in India. Some doctors circumvent the proscription of revealing a child's sex by an ingenious method of giving the parents pink candles for girls and blue for boys, thus making the law unenforceable. Some dispense with such subtleties altogether, when the doctors advise parents to consider the economics of spending just 500 rupees now for abortion and 50,000 later for bride price when daughters are given in marriage. In China, such war against girls came as a result of the one child national policy. Slowly the problem has spread to other countries in the region – South Korea, Singapore, Taiwan, the former Soviet republics of Armenia, Azerbaijan, Georgia and even to Asian-Americans on the US mainland. Modernization (more education, better living standards) has not helped as an antidote because the incidence is higher among the rich than the poor. Neither religion nor cast has anything to do with it. In virtually all of these cases, an ancient prejudice that views daughters as financial burdens to be avoided rather than a blessing to be embraced is well entrenched indeed.

One can only imagine the long term effects of such policies which tend to create an excess of males over females in a dynamic and growing population. Where marriage and children are recognized routes to society, one can foresee a looming lawlessness ahead –bride trafficking, sexual violence, suicide and so many ills on the rise.

The US Supreme Court equally waded into the quality of language spoken by Americans, especially those in the communications industry, likely to influence many. The F-word and S-word came for special scrutiny. Our declining morality can be measured by the unrestrained dropping of the F-bomb, our favorite adjective, popular among men as well as the womenfolk, at home as in the workplace, including our prestigious Academy Awards theater where Oscars are conferred on the cream of our performers. Gone are the good old days when ladies did not have dirty mouths; now most of them do and as one observer has remarked, our world is heading straight to the toilet. (Federal Communications Commission) had been used to tolerating "fleeting expletives" for some time but then decided that broadcasters should be penalized even for fleeting and figurative transgressions, adding that the F-word and S-word always reminded listeners of sex and excrement, no matter how metaphorical or meaningless the context. A Federal Appeals court had already rejected the FCC's argument, citing President Bush's and Vice President Dick Cheney's taboo utterances as having a non-literal sense. No less a personality than Vice President Dick Cheney was caught on tape using the F-word when talking to a senator. But Chief Justice John Roberts and Justice Antonin Scalia remained unpersuaded, insisting on the core meaning of the word as one of the most vulgar, graphic and most explicit for sexual activity, a coarse sexual image indeed. The Supreme Court's upholding of the FCC's crackdown on the use of profanity and expletives and all sorts of indecency on radio and television was a move in the right direction and would bring much peaceful sleep in the nation, even if leg dragging in other quarters continued to keep the anarchy in place. Radio and television are the easiest means by which such fleeting language gets passed on to the society and the twenty-four hour news cycle allows journalists and all colorations of newsmen to gather and disseminate America's many curse words to the population – cursing a malfunctioning device, an unhelpful telephone operator, slow traffic, a bounced check, a missed appointment, job loss, bad weather, taxes, the government, immigrants, everything and everybody, if that would make the cursing party any happier.

Is swearing considered a form of art or taboo? Years ago it was taboo to use expressions like "darn", "friggin", "damn" or "hell". Today they have become quite trendy. What has changed? And why does swearing still send kids to the principal's office any way? Is potty-mouth not the order of the day? Some say that certain expressions when over used become "desensitized" and so lose the original poignancy. In the US a scientific study has found swearing from day care centers right up to nursing homes. That speaks of the popularity of the art form, doesn't it? Someone backs a car into another's car and instinctively swears the s-word. It is so spontaneous. At first it was the church that policed the use of swear words but the church has since lost clout. Very few conservative groups, media watchdogs and the government try to determine what a "bad" word is and what is not bad. People have moved beyond "suck" and "ass" and are now fixated on the F-word and the S-word. Society can hardly be sanitized if adults continue to use such coarse words and expressions in daily life and in high places. It seems ridiculous to condemn bullying and coarse language in kids when they absorb these so readily from adults ever so ready to use them.

The N-word produces one of the many absurdities of our time. It is taboo for some persons and for others it has been so desensitized that people in the black community virtually address themselves freely and frequently, using it as a matter of course. But let it come out of the mouth of a white person and all hell breaks loose. Talk radio host, Dr. Laura Schlessinger tasted of this bitter pill recently when she and an African-American lady caller exchanged ideas over the phone only to be saddled with the oppressive and protest calls from people, including the Reverend Al Sharpton who took offense at her use of the word, all because she alluded to persons who were hypersensitive to the N-word and volunteered the suggestion that such persons should try not to marry out of their race. Left unanswered was "what law is there against the use of the N-word and who is authorized to police it"? Have black Americans been empowered to police the use of the N-word? Why would any society enlist the services of a police officer to track down a crime for which the officer is a habitual offender? Of course there is a big difference between callous, prejudicial and silly use of the N-word and the supposedly good natured usage in the black community. Such double standards do not make for peaceful coexistence at all. In Nigeria, supporters of the sharia law argue that it affects only Muslims; yet Muslims and non-Muslims are often partners-in-crime. In such situations, how can the law be applied to one but not the other? Nevertheless, Justice Louis Brandeis's philosophy always holds true – that freedom of speech is not free. There is a price to pay for it as Dr. Laura Schlessinger and other public figures who resigned under pressure must have found out belatedly. The job of radio talk show does take a toll after a while as the Laura Schlessingers, Don Imuses, Michael Savages, Rush Limbaughs and others will readily testify. If and when Americans begin to realize that the First Amendment was intended to protect citizens from the government rather than from each other's offensive language, the number of casualties in this category will begin to drop significantly. Until then the Dr. Lauras will most probably continue to heed Sarah Palin's prescription to reload rather than retreat.

In the political world much street talk was done behind closed doors, like the Nixon secret tapes that surfaced during the Watergate saga and were subsequently made public with the profanities deleted for the purposes of court records. In 2004 Vice President Dick Cheney blurted out the F-word at a Democratic senator from Vermont during a heated debate on the senate floor. Recently, during the signing into law of President Barack Obama's important healthcare bill, his Vice President, Joe Biden impulsively let loose the F-word. The big deal needed a qualifier and the F-word was it! Pervasive vulgarity, undignified as it may sound, has become the order of the day in America, an illustration of the growing coarseness of society, an uncontrolled expansion of the boundaries of taste. Among young people no thought is given when they toss it around in the presence of ladies or elders. Can cursing be curbed at all? Why are Americans so obsessed with cursing any way? Is it so difficult to hold one's tongue? How about expressions like *lie, fabrication, nonsense, exaggeration, bunk, baloney, drivel, hokum, hogwash,* or *balderdash* instead of *bull shit?*

Free speech and privacy laws are testing grounds for many innovations and changes and they will probably continue to be so in the years ahead. In 1884 Kodak hit the market with a comparatively small and cheap camera with which one's picture could be taken without one's permission or knowledge. Such a picture could find its way into any cheap lurid newspaper and if it contained anything compromising, that would be trouble for whoever was so pictured. Alarmed by such a prospect, two Boston lawyers went to work and wrote an article in the Harvard Law Review, an article that came to form the foundation for most of the laws that protect privacy today. Louis Brandeis and Samuel Warren made the point that people should be able to sue others for the wrong of exposing their private lives to public scrutiny. That worked fine until the age of the World Wide Web and the Internet which ushered in a power and pervasiveness not known before. The privacy regime created by the onset of the Kodak revolution is doomed if measures are not put in place to check present trends which allow for anonymous and immediate posting of information on the Internet. Worse, search engines make such information (one's address, a lewd picture or video, a written insult, one's banking information) retrievable for curious people everywhere on planet earth! Today, with the simple click of a mouse it is possible to capture such information and images round the clock.

Legal experts are still toying with this gray area, working out how to remove such damaging information from the web before harm is done. It is indeed frightfully sobering that someone we don't know or have never ever met could snap our picture and post it in the Internet or someone we know very well can elect to share our most cherished secret with the whole world! A certain Erin Anderson, beautiful, blond sports reporter and CBS stringer suffered just such a fate when a peeping Tom got naked video pictures of her through a peep hole of her hotel room and into the Internet, much to her embarrassment. This should bother lovers and soul mates who, in their intimate moments, divulge everything about their past relationships. Men of lust and perverts are at work all the time, whether "she asked for it," or "carried herself in that manner" as some have claimed, or did nothing at all. Here in America the courts seem to work on the principle that once we tell someone our secrets, unless such a person is our doctor, our priest or our lawyer, such secret is basically public and not covered by confidentiality laws. That is not good news at all!

Those suing former lovers or spouses for breach of confidentiality in telling someone else their sexual or other hang-ups are engaging in an exercise in futility. It is therefore tough luck entrusting secret values to friends who later divulge them to others. England does a better job of upholding breach of confidentiality law suits against loose-lipped ex-spouses and lovers. Taking nude pictures with readily available cell phones may appear the modern thing to do but just down the road are problems related to the practice. The sad story comes to mind of a teen girl who hanged herself in 2008 upon finding out that her ex-boyfriend had circulated her nude pictures to students at their school and the more recent case of a sophomore at Rutgers university who jumped to his death off the George Washington bridge after discovering that pictures of his love affairs with another man had found their way into the Internet. Will the US move in the direction taken by England? Probably not. Legal scholars are uncomfortable with anything that stymies free speech.

For now website administrators have some homework to do even if a 1996 federal law exempts sites from liability for user comments, especially websites that transform themselves into elevators, mutual street corners or some sort of local Trafalgar Square where everyone can gossip with relish. For now all that can be said is that people have the right to free speech but not the right to defame someone, as Matt Zimmerman, a senor staff attorney at the Electronic Frontier Foundation said recently, following online comments that sparked off a number of law suits.

The case against a blogger may soon provide the test limits of free speech. An internet radio host in Chicago who disliked how three federal judges rejected a national Rifle Association's attempt to overturn bans on handguns is awaited. Taking advantage of his free speech liberty, the blogger let loose the following: *"Let me be the first to say this plainly: These judges deserve to be killed. Their blood will replenish the tree of liberty. A small price to pay to assure freedom for millions"* he wrote on his blog, according to the FBI, who immediately arrested him. Posting the photographs of the three judges as well as a map showing the Chicago courthouse where they worked and noting the placement of "anti-truck bomb barriers" was enough to get the FBI on the move even though the man claimed that he had meant no harm and his attorney said federal authorities had over-reacted. Scholars note that the line between free speech and criminality is a very fine one. US attorney Patrick Fitzgerald and his prosecutors have their plates full as they prepare to charge the blogger admired by white supremacists, after US district Judge, Joan Lefkow's husband and mother were slain early in 2005 by a disgruntled plaintiff. Clearly, adhering to Supreme Court Justice Louis D. Brandeis's suggestion that the right to be left alone is the most important right protected by the constitution must be interpreted with lots of caution, given the interconnectedness of our citizens. No citizen can claim to be an island in our complex world.

It is an interesting argument when people express the wish to see government hands off and get out of their lives. Carried to its logical conclusion by those so obsessed with minimizing the role of government, this brings society to where it all started – with *Homo neanderthalensis*. People who spend energy and time preaching against government, especially big government, forget that in the absence of government the climate is ripe for anarchy, wild west or the world of "might makes right". Consider the case of a seventeen-year-old South Carolina boy from Florence County. Shortly after being diagnosed as HIV-positive, the young man found out that his insurance policy had been miraculously revoked by Fortis for reasons unknown to him. Thanks to the courts – an arm of government – a jury ordered the insurance company to pay the young man $15 million. If a company has an undisclosed policy of targeting and dropping policy holders with HIV or other life-threatening illnesses, who else but powerful Mr. Government can come to their rescue? For those who have forgotten the citizenship examination, government is not just the White House and all that it represents; the Supreme Court and the US Congress are also government. The size of government depends on the undertaking it is called upon to carry and this varies all the time, especially in times of emergencies like the BP oil spills on the Gulf Coast. Those clamoring for the government to take over realize the magnitude of the problem.

From the moment *"physically challenged"* replaced *"physically handicapped"* in civilized society, one would have expected the rest to follow suit. But no. The sensitivity to language may be there all right but for many Americans the will to do the right is not just there. Television celebrities, the nation's pace setters can do some good by keeping their dirty words in closets so that kids grow up in a sanitized environment. The debate continues. First Amendment rights as used in the US hardly take cognizance of the repercussions when addressing audiences beyond our borders. Most people do not give such a proposition a second thought until they are reminded that the US has embassies and business interests around the world and that people in those places can be impacted by what is said here at home. And that can be a problem.

Thirty years ago formal dressing was the norm. Swearing and cursing were relatively scarce. With time western society embraced increased casualization in smoking, dressing, speaking, studies, sex and everything as formal social behavior patterns became eroded.

In 2002 a British-trained Nigerian journalist, Isioma Daniel wrote an article in a local newspaper, *ThisDay,* in which she mentioned that Prophet Mohammed would gladly marry one of the 92 lovely contestants gathering in that African nation for the World Pageant. Almost at once Muslims went up in arms and pronounced a fatwa (death sentence) on her the way late Ayatollah Khomeini once did for the author Salman Rushdie. To Muslims, bringing those women to Nigeria to ask them to revel in vanity was bad enough; alluding to the Prophet marrying one of them was utterly provocative. The ensuing riot that took over two hundred lives and caused a lot of destruction showed how emotionally costly such cavalier journalism could be especially when practiced along latitude ten degrees or the fault line that separates Muslims from Christians. Then again in September 2005, *Jyllands-Posten,* a Danish newspaper poked fun at Mohammed the prophet by publishing a cartoon depicting him wearing a turban shaped like a bomb with a burning fuse. To the westerner, he was just satirizing the prophet Mohammed, a mere burlesque; to the extremist of Islam it was blasphemy. It is this wide gap that needs bridging. As a reaction, scores of death took place around the world. Demonstrators in Beirut set the Danish Consulate on fire. Pakistani students demonstrated. People planned to assassinate 73-year old Kurt Westergaard, the cartoonist. Violence erupted in Nigeria where demonstrators torched churches, hotels and stores. Dozens of protesters died in Afghanistan, Pakistan, Syria and Lebanon. Gasoline bombs were recovered from some Danish embassies. In Iran, Syria, Pakistan and Afghanistan, scholars said that politicians and religious leaders used the situation to further their own agendas.

Wide-spread media coverage fed the fire! Some have asked whether insulting Muslims or the Islamic religion is the right way to stand up for free speech. Angered by the representation of the Prophet Mohammed as a caricature and by various drawings and extremely sensitive and emotional topics, Pakistan, a largely Muslim nation, took steps to order the blockage of popular video-sharing websites like YouTube and the social networking site Face book. Equally troubling is the personalization of anything and everything that touches on Islam or the prophet Mohammed. The Muslim does not own Prophet Mohammed any more than the Christian owns Jesus Christ. So the pitch battle over one or the other is incomprehensible. Westergaard can take cover under the protection of Danish law and Danish police just as Molly Norris an American political cartoonist did after igniting Muslim ire with her proposal of "Everybody Draw Mohammed Day" campaign. Anwar al-Awlaki the Yemeni cleric tagged her as a prime target, unleashing the burning of her effigy. But these are only temporary expedients. Aggrieved Muslims seem to be prepared to invade the homes of those declared prime targets to kill them. That too is not the answer.

A little known priest in Gainesville, Florida with a flock of just fifty persons made head line news with his promise to commemorate the ninth anniversary of 9/11 by burning copies of the Qu'ran, a plan condemned by Americans of goodwill, troubled by the dangers such an act would pose to our troops out there in the battle fields of Iraq and Afghanistan as well as ordinary Americans around the world. Such cowardly acts could only be perpetrated by persons unable or unwilling to take up arms and fight in America's wars, taking cover under the cozy atmosphere provided by the blood and sweat of others. Pastor Terry Jones is either a neophyte totally oblivious of the game he was intending to play or delusional about his real position in society. When an individual or a group of individuals attempts to lay claim to an entity that belongs to the collectivity, there is room for circumspection. 9/11 was a national tragedy more than a personal concern of Pastor Terry Jones. If Islam's extremists are being blamed for their acts of hijacking a peaceful religion and turning it into a hostile one, how could we at the same time condone the pastor's planned act in the name of religion? Which religion any way? How is it possible to kill hate with more hate? No wonder the Bible speaks of false prophets! Such a scheme could only emanate from a mind full of pent up hatred and abhorrent imaginations. The pastor claimed that he personally did not know any Muslims, had not read the Qu'ran and did not even know the mission statement of the Dove World Outreach Center, the organization he was heading. And yet he could find two legs to stand on and propose such a scheme, a distasteful proposition that would play into the hands of our enemies. Surely America values free speech but then at what cost? According to the United States Constitution, yelling "fire" in a crowded theater is illegal if there is no fire just like uttering "fighting words" with impunity. But very strangely it allows the minister of a tiny fundamentalist church to outrage countless Muslims around the world by burning the Qu'ran. Antisocial and weird behavior surely benefit from the attention of the mass media.

What a dilemma for the Obama Administration and for many Americans for whom freedom of expression is a sort of secular religion. That a nation can allow the symbolic burning of its own flag and yet be unable to stop the burning of a book – not even when General Petraeus predicted violence by extremists erupting from images of the burning of the Qu'ran – highlights a fundamental flaw in the conception of our values. Many were of the opinion that if the government tried to stop pastor Terry Jones, it would lose. Americans, including Secretary of State Hillary Clinton, expressed frustration that a small fringe group could command such attention. Should Jones be ignored then? Certainly not! President Obama's administration would need to use public diplomacy to point out how repugnant the planned act was to Americans.

In a country where it is permissible for artists and performers to routinely ridicule established religions, Islam's sensitivity to disrespect for Allah, his word, his prophet and his book presented quite a puzzle. The saga must have presented a gold mine for Pastor Jones or at least an opportunity to rise up from relative obscurity and claim world wide attention for his congregation of 40 – 50. Mohammad Musri, a shrewd imam and president of the Islamic Society of Central Florida said he had come to have a peaceful conversation with the pastor, hear his grievances and to ask him to follow his own scripture about his enemies. America hoped and prayed that the pastor would not lead his flock down the path cult leader, Jim Jones of the People's Temple in British Guyana followed in 1978 with 918 of his 8000 flock – mass suicide by drinking poisoned Kool Aid.

A small but not insignificant contribution to resolve this state of affairs was made when the United Nations forum passed a resolution condemning "defamation of religion" as a human rights violation in spite of concerns that this could be used to justify the curb on free speech in Muslim countries. Another consisted of what took place when an Imam, a Rabbi and a Priest were seen strolling together, discussing and airing their respective views on conflicts, and trying to show the way forward in reducing tension among their flock. Approaching authorities and alerting them of his concern over a radicalized son was surely a praiseworthy effort on the part of the Nigerian father of Umar Farouk Abdulmutallab. Elsewhere other parents would bury their concerns in denial and pretend that all was fine until it was too late. Blowing an aircraft out of the skies and taking away one's life is most certainly no solution to this thorny problem.

Courting danger in the way free speech is used threatens our civilization. Taking cover under the free speech provisions of our Constitution, the New York Post recently depicted two police officers, one with a smoking gun standing over the body of a bullet-riddled chimpanzee with the caption "They'll have to find someone else to write the next stimulus bill." Such an act, coming on the eve of President Barack Obama's presentation of his economic stimulus package to the nation, left no one in doubt about the intended message. Americans did not need to be rocket scientists to see the nexus even though some supporters and apologists of such bigotry worked over time to link the cartoon instead to the shooting of Travis, a Connecticut chimpanzee that had gone berserk and assaulted and shredded the face of its owner's best friend. Some claimed it was symbolism that had backfired, arguing that former Presidents George W. Bush and Abraham Lincoln had also been portrayed as chimpanzees, a debatable proposition indeed. In what context would such a thing have taken place? They did not say. Others saw a faulty editorial process where the cartoonist had failed to get an editorial input. But the editor-in-chief of the Post, Col Allan, said the cartoon was a parody of current news in Connecticut. Yes indeed, a distraught Connecticut woman did call 911 to have the police shoot the chimpanzee she had raised from infancy but where was the connection to "someone else writing the next stimulus bill"?

Unless and until someone could come up with a better and more plausible explanation, there was no sense saying that African-Americans were over-reacting to the cartoon. Surely African-Americans had not so soon lost sight of their history where racist stereotypes painted them as monkeys and chimpanzees. Where did the concept of an 800 pound gorilla fit in? Where was the humor in comparing a newly elected President Obama to a gorilla? Even the shooting down of Travis, how humorous was that in a country where animals enjoy unprecedented protection? And some of those vying for elective office appeared not to want to be outdone by the press. An ambitious Ben Quayle carried the hyperbole one notch up by describing President Obama as the worst president ever. Not even Richard Nixon or Ulysses Grant could beat this record! Understandably, as a Republican, Ben Quayle could find no one better than a Democrat for such a distinction. I wonder where he would place Jimmy Carter or Bill Clinton on his scale of badness. The Republican hopeful prompted one cynic to remind Americans that the tomato does not fall far from the vine.

At some point, Congressman Patrick Kennedy became so incensed that he lost his cool and took the floor of the House of Representatives to lambast the press in general and the Washington D. C. media crowd in particular for focusing on trivial political matters, leaving out the heavy issues that mattered, such as a call to end the war in Afghanistan. The Rhode Island representative was mad, like many others before him, that journalism was declining as newsmen were biased, inaccurate, unfair, unhinged, and even unpatriotic. But then the news professionals, walloped by the world of advocacy programs, often pitched for the left as much as for the right, in the process taking liberty with the truth. Taking out one's anger on rivals, other public figures or the press is a calculated risk especially for those campaigning for elective office. In the very Rhode Island, candidate for gubernatorial election, Frank Caprio, reacting to the fact that President Obama had opted to remain neutral and not endorse any of the three in the race, said Obama "could take his endorsement and shove it", prompting reactions like "knucklehead", "petulant little child" and a 12 point plummeting in his ratings at the polls. The language used by public officials is obviously very sensitive and can trail them around for a long time to come. At a time when "The state of Rhode Island and Providence Plantations" was planning to vote to drop "Providence Plantations", the mouthful name that also carried the stinging reminder of its past involvement in the trans-Atlantic slave trade, nothing could be better than using refined language on the campaign trail. It is for this reason that enlightened persons try to read different view points from a variety of sources before taking a stand on major issues affecting their lives or their country.

It might not be premature to advise our New York Post cartoonist to get in touch with fellow cartoonist, 73-year-ld Kurt Westergaard of the Danish newspaper *Jyllands-Posten* to exchange notes in their messianic zeal to civilize by satirizing others across the divide, a pompous presumption of being on the higher moral ground. And the belated apology of Rupert Murdock to those offended by the cartoon would have pacified matters if it had been accompanied by firing the bad apple responsible for the furor in the first place. Why couldn't he learn from the famous Don Imus case? Wouldn't it be better to imbibe a small dose of Madeleine Albright's advice based on seasoned reasoning and many years of field work that the US is better off winning over other nations and peoples by making them see that we all share the same desire for the good things of life? At a time when the Obama administration is distancing the nation from the era of self-indulgence and beginning to put into practice the wisdom of consulting our allies rather than acting unilaterally, it seems logical to stop acting like a bull in a China shop by courting unnecessary wrath where moderation is called for.

The First Amendment may provide a level playing ground for all but there is a snag – more often than not, loud-mouthed armchair critics and talk radio drown out the voices of moderation and those of soft-spoken professionals who know what they are talking about.

The furor over the fate of Umar Farouk Abdulmutallab, author of botched Christmas day bomber is a case in point. While everyone else, including former Alaska governor, Sarah Palin clamored for trial by a military commission, professionals and those in the Justice Department opted for the Federal Court, especially so as the FBI was able to use creative methods to coax useful intelligence not only out of the suspect, but also out of family members ferried in from Nigeria. It is thus clear that psychological methods of interrogation are by far superior to the rough stuff such as water boarding that has not helped enhance America's standing in the world.

Is America Christian or a Godless nation? Should America be Christian or Godless? Aren't we constantly reminded of the Christian origins of this nation? Was it a mistake to jettison the laws based on Christianity in favor of laws voted by the people's elected representatives as a means of accommodating the expanding and diversifying population of other religions, non-religions, American Association of Atheists, agnostics and others? Has the nation crossed the Rubicon or is it still possible to revert to the Common (English) Law of earlier times derived from and based on the absolute standard of the Bible - the famous William Blackstone commentaries? Where does the blurring of the line between religion and politics stop? What exactly did the Founding Fathers say about the separation of Church and State and what is the best way to deal with the paranoia over this separation? If the Constitution actually states that "Congress shall make no law respecting an establishment of religion or prohibiting the free exercise thereof" is it not a violation preventing Bible reading or prayers in schools? If the US is not a Christian nation why are offices closed on Sundays and why are stocks not traded on Wall Street? Why do presidents take the oath of office by placing their hands on the Bible? Isn't it true that Sunday, the day of Christian worship, is the quietest day of the week in most police departments? Congressional leaders might want to revisit the First Amendment.

For some Americans, military courts would be better because they protect valuable intelligence resources and details on the methods of operation. Those who hold strongly to this view feel that civilian courts often provide propaganda forums for accused terrorists in addition to handicapping prosecutors who must also abide by Federal rules of evidence. Many persons were turned off the idea of the suspect being read his Miranda's rights or given a lawyer, but that was consistent with the change President Obama promised to bring to America, to tell the rest of the world that America is devoted to democracy, offers everyone a fair trial and the due process of law that is lacking in other countries. Anwar al-Awlaki's father, Nasser was said to be pleading for the government not to target his son and had even allowed an ACLU lawyer to file a law suit alleging that as a US citizen, Awlaki had the right to a trial and so killing him would be illegal. And the deputy director of ACLU, Jameel Jaffrey wondered aloud if the Obama administration was trying to invoke the death penalty without a charge. Countering such views is the argument that Awlaki is waging a war against the US abroad and so gets no special shield since he is outside US jurisdiction and beyond the reach of US law. How these opposing views work out for the charismatic Awlaki who seems to relate so well to disaffected Muslim Americans remains to be seen.

Can Sarah Palin deny that it is also the American way of life for every generation to have its own Atticus Finch to defend those written off by the status quo? Others have recommended sending every single prisoner to the war front in Iraq or Afghanistan, especially those on life imprisonment or the death roll. Egregious as this may sound, it has some historical antecedent. At some point in the past England sent prisoners to the wilds of Australia to go and try it out as they could. What was supposed to be a one-way ticket to doom turned out to be a blessing in disguise. Australia is today one of the most admired tourist attractions on planet earth, thanks to those early British prisoners.

Former president Jimmy Carter did not mince his words when he laid at the doorsteps of racists the unhelpful roadblocks they were making to stymie President Barack Obama's healthcare reform efforts even if the president prudently dissociated himself from those remarks, arguing that he knew some Americans did not like him because of his race, some liked him only because of his race, but that by far the overwhelming majority were concerned about what he was doing for the economy and healthcare, rejecting racism as the sole basis of the criticisms. (Curiously Americans were so obsessed with Obama's blackness that they virtually forgot or ignored to mention his mother's side, which is white. Only a little grade school kid, Cynthia Clo from Albany New York had the courage to draw attention to that anomaly). The diversion from President Obama's healthcare reform could not have come at a worse moment. As members of both Houses of Congress were intently listening to the president to learn of what innovations he had in mind to the thorny problem of healthcare, Joe Wilson, a South Carolina Republican uttered very disruptive outbursts and interrupted the president for some time. It was clear that the man was motivated by his gut feelings that Obama's plan would benefit those who were in the country illegally, the so-called undocumented immigrants.

Yet, truth be told, illegals were already benefitting from healthcare, well before President Obama came on the national scene. Everybody knew that people without status could go to the emergency rooms of our hospitals and get treated there for free. Obama did not start the practice. As far back as 1986, President Ronald Reagan signed into law the Emergency Medical Treatment Act, which made it possible for anybody, regardless of financial status, to get treated at the ER for everything from patching up simple broken bones to the really serious emergency cases requiring physician attention. The idea was to treat and stabilize the patient before anything else. To suggest that Obama's reform would initiate the practice was simply disingenuous, an undisguised attempt to foment fears that resources would be stolen for the use of illegal immigrants.

Obviously Obama's election did not quite usher in the much dreamed of post-racial America. Many on the right were quick to lambast Jimmy Carter for playing the race card, dismissing his assertion as baseless. Even Democrats who should know better, continued to argue that Obama's opponents were driven exclusively by policy. It was a difficult situation for Obama whose political success was due largely to his investment in racelessness. Yet, must America confuse political strategy with reality? Should that not have been the golden opportunity to let racism occupy center stage and receive the benefit of a full debate? Could the thorny issue be solved simply by putting it away for a more convenient time later?

From the very moment Barack Obama became the Democratic party's official nominee in May 2008, he became the victim of the most vicious racist campaign in US history – xenophobic investigation into his religious background, controversy over his real place of birth and challenge to his eligibility to run for president - and indeed the right wing political machine went into overdrive to paint the man as an untrustworthy, unprincipled outsider whose mere existence threatened the American way of life. The language of race was strenuously avoided but skillfully coated with words such as Marxist, Nazi, extremist, foreign and others, as aptly stated by Columbia University's Professor Marc Lamont, to "smuggle" racism and xenophobia into public conversation without its political consequences. Even in far away Kenya, home of the president's Luo father, unprincipled Kikuyu tribesmen, struggling with their r's and l's, allowed themselves a mirthful laughter when it looked like Obama was going to lose the 2008 US presidential election, joking "it looks like westerners too have *plobrems* with the Luo" even as they faced their own *ligged erection* (rigged election) and were *robbying* (lobbying) to do something about their country's losing 25 million shillings in *frower*(flower) exports to Europe and *emproyers*(employers) scratching their heads about what to do next.

The left remained inexplicably reticent in addressing the racist dimensions of the assault on Obama, probably as a result of the Right's masterful manipulation of America's racial anxieties. Right wingers began complaining that they could not critique him without being labeled racists, a hoax that only helped to put Democrats on the defensive. Surely there had to be ways of critiquing Obama without bringing his race into the mix. In the end, such reticence on the part of Democrats contributed to emboldening the Republicans in their racist tactics.

One could not help getting the impression that politicians invariably took Americans for stupid persons who could not reason for themselves and must therefore be spoon-fed those terrible distortions and intoxications. The all-important healthcare reform was made to appear like an entirely Obama affair or the affair of his presidency as painted with language like "his Waterloo" used as if healthcare did not concern all of us, Republicans, Democrats, Independents and indeed all Americans. Politics is supposed to be a means to an end but the way our countrymen and women went about it, it had become an end in itself. They frightened small businesses, alleging that Obama's plan would bankrupt them, stand between patients and their doctors and send seniors prematurely to their graves. Why use such despicable scare tactics to distort or conceal the truth? Why the myths? Why spend colossal sums of money ($1.4 billion per day) only to distort the facts and maintain the status quo which was manifestly hurting us all? After eight years of such tactics, didn't the American people deserve better? Perhaps it is this understanding that gave President Obama the presence of mind to appear on Dave Letterman show and feed the laughter machine with his declaration *"you know before the election I was black..."*

Truth be told, the president's vowing to provide added safeguards for people with health insurance, forbidding insurers from denying coverage for persons with preexisting conditions, introducing a new level of fairness and humanness to our healthcare financing system was a really tough sell because such reforms spelled increased costs for insurers and inevitably higher premiums for everyone. Morally and legally we might all be equal but in matters of insurance, that notion makes no financial sense given that there is not a limitless spigot to draw from. Insurance has never ever been a matter of equality. Premiums are usually higher for high risk categories, be they reckless accident-prone teenagers or aged and disabled adult car operators, persons with overweight problems or heavy smokers prone to increased medical costs. The idea of not charging more for persons with chronic debilitating conditions such as diabetes, cancer and others was financially jarring in the ears of the insurance industry. How on earth could someone with a minimum or no medical condition at all be expected to pay the same premium as someone whose condition required expensive medical and surgical intervention many times during their life times? Surely insurance must recognize higher risk categories and demand a higher premium from them. And small companies had seen the benefits of placing a premium on weight loss and cutting down smoking to help their employees shape up. Successful weight loss, reduction of BMI and reduction of heart problems for those who stopped smoking had been proven to work and so companies that had seen this work would be understandably less likely to jump on President Obama's bandwagon. We may be all equal as some are wont to argue, but when entering an aircraft, what rationale is there charging everyone a flat fee whereas some persons, by virtue of their extra girth, actually end up occupying a double seat? That is the type of dilemma insurers faced when they dragged their feet against the president's idea of not discriminating against those with preexisting conditions requiring additional costs.

With an economic crisis knocking businesses left and right, survival antics were multiplying. Summer vacations were around and airlines had their booking problems to handle, compounded by the question of whether overweight passengers should be made to buy an extra ticket, effectively paying double because of their extra mass and girth and the tendency to occupy more than their share of the allotted sitting space. It was a controversial policy pitting the commercial policy of an airline against the dignity of an overweight flier. What did anti-discrimination laws say? Some drew the parallel between a plane ticket and a real estate – one gets only the space one pays for- concluding therefore that passengers needed to buy an extra ticket if their girth prevented them from lowering the armrest that divides the seats. Of course there was the concern for adjoining passengers whose convenience too mattered and must be protected from encroaching passengers.

As America's collective girth increases, there is going to be a lot of drama in courts in the days and years ahead as lawyers fight to defend their clients' rights. Under federal law it is illegal to discriminate on the basis of age, race, color, nationality, marital status, gender, disability status, the god one believes in or does not believe in, but anything else – weight gain, tattoos, sexual orientation, unnecessary days off, bad breath, bad grooming habit – is in the air. In jobs one can get fired for just about anything, if one's employment is "at will." Here, employers weigh customer concerns heavily against the comportment of wayward employees.

In matters of careers, one cannot really plan for the future. The best bet is to prepare oneself for the changes that must come and part of that preparation should include the acquisition of basic skills needed for any job – reading, writing, mathematical skills, science, computer at high school level. A dose of Larry's proverbs – hard work pays off in the future; laziness pays off now – is in order too. The painful experience of being left out in the job market speaks volumes about the desirability to maximize those high school and college years. At college, higher education must aim to teach how to think, solve complex problems, communicate with people, and develop an open, flexible and inquiring mind. Robots and robotic science have developed so fast that they have put many people out of work, thanks to machines and other gadgets that have replaced human effort. Offices that were once full of human beings are today manned by just a couple of people. See how many doors and gates just open automatically at the approach of a human being! Today we can start our cars from a distance and open the door simply by pressing on a switch; driving is no longer the energy-consuming shifting of gears. How awesome!

Of course one cannot rule out American ingenuity, especially among the younger generation. Smart persons who failed to get regular employment on our crisis-laden job market have been known to convert themselves into headhunters, a category of people whose job is to help people get jobs. They conveniently bridge the gap between job seeking employees and employers too busy to seek out suitably qualified employees on job market. How nice! While retrograde employers still toy with the unhealthy practice of hiring unproductive blood relatives as employees, the smart ones who seek growth go after talent and skills to help them achieve their lofty goals.

Even bigger than the plight of the HIV-positive boy above are other cases in need of protection from corporate interests. The AIDS Foundation and religious activists have joined forces and are asking for protection from pornographic industries and California's

Occupational Health and Safety Standards Board is considering such requests from anti-porn activist and the nation's largest HIV/ AIDS nonprofit organization to require actors to wear condoms in sex scenes in pornographic features. Such a petition has created a division in the San Fernando Valley, Los Angeles, where America's legally distributed pornography is produced. The entertainment industry and its supporters are not taking it kindly. Statements like "hurt sales", "my body, my choice", "this is hot. It's passionate. You want to have fun" are liberally put on display even by those most vulnerable and therefore in need of such protective measures. Surely a small government will not cope with such mounting challenges that seek protection for the greater good.

Complicating this picture is a nation saddled with mothers who are barely children themselves and therefore ill-prepared for parenting. Take the humiliating incident of a mother who dragged her fifteen-year-old daughter onto CNN to demand that a yearbook photograph revealing the girl's panties be removed and further more, that all yearbooks so far distributed be confiscated, so as to destroy all evidence of the offending photographs. The fuming pair was shown on CNN together with a fuzzed over photograph thus ensuring that not thousands of her snickering High school kids on campus, but millions of strangers, witness the young woman's infamy. What could such a mother have been thinking of? How does a mother seek to protect her daughter's reputation by trying to repress embarrassing photographs already exposed by a limited print media source like a High School yearbook by going on a world-wide medium like cable television which quickly amplifies the problem world wide? And even as her daughter sat facing the CNN camera at the interview, she wore a pair of shorts and sat with one leg tugged underneath her bottom, causing the other leg to open in an unlady-like manner. How much humiliation can a mother and daughter create and still not get it? What can the law on privacy make of such gaffes? See how much of the embarrassment could have been averted by the girl simply keeping her legs closed in a posed photograph! Britney Spears can go around in a tank top without a bra but at least her father disapproves of it and has not hidden his discomfiture as he strives to encourage his daughter to put across the correct impression. If more parents would just try!

Another mother was said to be so attached to her son that she pushed her senator to introduce legislation that would enable her to be buried with her son in a cemetery specifically designated for soldiers. Won't limitless freedom breed anarchy and make nonsense of the laws that make it possible for organized society to move forward? Whose interest is served by bending the common good this way?

It has been said that when Mass Equality speaks, legislators listen. Mass Equality was founded on the heels of the ruling by the Supreme Judicial Court of Massachusetts legalizing gay marriage in the Bay State. Now the organization has gone further to fight against discrimination of gays, to protect gays and lesbian teens during school, and to fund the GLBT Youth and Safe school Programs, set anti-bullying Programs in classrooms and school playgrounds. Gay and lesbian youth are supposedly at risk populations – higher suicide rate, higher HIV rate. The organization threw its full weight behind a bill to protect gay and lesbian kids as well as senior same sex citizens. The military's top ranks noted that the 1993 "DON'T ASK, DON'T TELL" policy for gays to serve openly, came under tremendous pressures for President Obama to overturn it in view of the demands of the wars in Iraq and Afghanistan, but the president who understood the forces at play, prudently drew attention to how long it took to reverse racial discrimination. Whatever the case, it looked like President Obama was determined to scrap that 1993 policy which allowed gays to serve in the military as long as they kept their sexual orientation a secret.

Quite an easy solution but will America's cherished sexual orientation be kept a secret? People continue to wonder why it is necessary to publicize such things in the first place. There is an obsession with gays "coming out of the closet". Whose interest is served by it – the individual's or society's? The matter became so heated that a certain William Green of Americans for Legal Immigration felt compelled to call out to Senator Lindsey Graham at a Tea Party rally in these words: "Senator Graham, you need to come forward and tell people about your alternative lifestyle...I need to figure out why you're trying to sell out your own countrymen and I need to make sure you're being gay isn't it." This rant ensued from the Republican senator's crossing the isle to legislate immigration reform – in other words, perform his duty! The caller implied that the senator was only doing his duty because he was afraid of his "secret" leaking. How absurd! And why would an American purposely violate the much cherished privacy of another with such impunity?

In addition to criteria such as academics and partying, high school kids now consider also how GBLT-friendly college campuses are. It gives campuses a new kind of pride as campus organizations develop in response to new understandings. Often cited is a 1993 study by Penn State in which more than 25% of the students surveyed had been threatened with violence due to their sexual orientation. Thus a nonprofit called Campus Pride introduced websites ranking US colleges in terms of their accommodation of LGBT to enable high school and other prospective college candidates screen well before applying, especially since, for many of them, it is during college years that they actually "come out for the first time" according to a faculty advisor at the CIA (Culinary Institute of America).

Gay Rights activists alleged that the developed world leads in accommodating their movement and they gleefully cited Nepal as prepared to legalize same sex marriage as a means of attracting tourists and China as having opened its first state-sponsored gay bar in December 2009 after a dramatic rise in the spread of HIV/AIDS among gay men. The logic was offered that if people were afraid to "come out" then they would be forced into a conspiracy of silence that prevented them from receiving information that could save their lives. Citing research supposedly conducted by the UN agency on HIV/AIDS, a spokesperson of the International Gay and Human rights Commission stated that the rates of new HIV infection were higher in countries with repressible laws against homosexuality, lamenting that gay sex was still illegal in 80 countries, at least seven of them, usually under Islamic law, imposing the death penalty for homosexual acts. But then countering this view was another that gays did quite a lot of harm to an unsuspecting society. From CDC's statistics on AIDS patients, men who had sex with other men outnumbered all other demographics combined. In the emotional exchanges that were volleyed back and forth, not much was said about another sobering fact – that poverty appeared to be the sole important link in the spread of all heterosexual HIV infections, that the two Bills – Gates and Clinton – had urged AIDS activists to squeeze value out of every dollar used to fight HIV during hard times when donors insisted on careful spending. Even the very good news of a new gel containing tenofovir, an anti-HIV medication capable of reducing HIV infections by up to 39%, was not much articulated yet that was the type of information needed by loving and committed housewives, girl friends and fiancés in the countryside, whose husbands and partners were migrant workers in the cities, going from one partner to the next as they changed jobs, and in the process, spreading the infection along and eventually bringing it home to them. Nor did they point out the role ignorance and arrogance played in this painful saga, especially when one of the animators gleefully declared that he could not possibly take along his cows when it was so much more practical to obtain milk wherever he went. Being bored with his wife is understandable and a typical Anton Chekov husband would live in the country and have his wife or mistress in the city or vice versa, a spouse who, like the moon, will not appear in their sky everyday. But then with HIV all over the place, there is a stiff price to pay.

Twenty years ago when Earvin "Magic" Johnson announced to the world that he was HIV positive and accepted to become the face of AIDS, there was just one drug for treatment – AZT. Today we can count on a good number of choices in treatment, promising vaccine trials and rejoice in the fact that the diagnosis of this disease is no longer synonymous with a death sentence. Thanks to the progress realized by researchers, in Thailand the first ever proof of an HIV vaccine came following trials of AVAC (Aids Vaccine Advocacy Coalition) which produced a 31% rate of protection. South African-led microbicide trial - Caprisa 004 - based on the use of the vaginal gel tenofovir proved to be 39% effective against infection. In the US, the National Institute of Allergy and Infectious Disease discovered three human antibodies capable of neutralizing 90% of HIV-1 strains and very flattering results have been obtained with iPrEx. A combination of two antiretroviral drugs administered to HIV-positive patients resulted in 44% of them becoming less likely to contract the virus. No one is advocating going to sleep. On the contrary more is expected of every human effort, including the wonderful contribution by hairdresser Tears Wenzira of Chitungwiza, eighteen miles out of Zimbabwe's capital city, Harare. The young woman dispenses peer education on the correct use of condoms to prevent HIV-Aids to her trainees as well as her clients in a program called "Weaving Braids, not Aids."

Pope Benedict XVI, known for his implacable stand against the use of condoms appears to have softened up a little of late, telling German Catholic journalist, Peter Seewald that using condoms may some times be justified to stop the spread of AIDS in male prostitutes. Liberal Catholics, AIDS activists and health officials welcomed the change of heart which they saw as a major step forward in recognizing the vital role condoms can play in reducing the pandemic, although it was not immediately clear why the pope singled out only male prostitutes, leaving out females. Some believe there was an interpretation error which Peter Seewald's upcoming book "*Light of the World: The Pope, the Church and the Sign of the Times*" should lay to rest.

Despite Massachusetts's reputation as trailblazer in the area of marriage equality, critics still complain that the State lags behind many other states in protecting the rights of transgendered community in employment, housing, and hate crimes. Ethan St. Pierre, a security manager at Burlington received very good reviews for his work, got pay raises, enjoyed his job and then in 2003 had a gender transformation from male to female, necessitating a change of outfit and behavior. He was promptly fired by his bosses. He had no protection under the existing law and had no money to hire an attorney for a law suit. Would legislators act to protect him? The US House of Representatives did pass ENDA (Employment non-discrimination act) to ban job discrimination against gays, lesbians and bisexuals but omitted the transgender category. The late Senator Ted Kennedy said he supported ENDA despite the omission. What next? Will legislators take the bull by the horns and pass the Bathroom Law, proposed for persons born of one sex to use the public bathrooms designated for the opposite sex?

Massachusetts Senate voted 28-3 to repeal a 1913 law that said couples of any kind could not marry here in Massachusetts if such unions were not recognized in their own home states. The law was originally passed to limit interracial marriages and its repeal was expected to make the Bay State a Las Vegas for couples seeking marriage and State officials actually foresaw hordes of same sex couples coming from New York and elsewhere to tie the knot.

Occasionally when courts fail to satisfy their cry for justice, citizens must turn to their elected representatives. Law makers can force the hands of the justices although law making itself leaves a lot to be desired sometimes. Choosing the right persons for office is one thing, having them deliver the goods once in office is a different ball game altogether. Presidents, Senators and members of the House may say one thing to get elected but once on seat, other realities come intruding into their comfort zones, often at variance with what sane voters had in mind. A number of reporters got so heated up that they decided to take one senator to task on a hot button issue.

Reporter: Would you support a pledge that commits members of Congress to carefully read the bills before voting? Would you also support making the bill public by placing it online 72 hours before voting takes place?

Law Maker: *Giggles.* I find this idea of making the bill public really humorous indeed. I am laughing because…really…I don't know how long the bill is going to be… And some bills can be very long indeed.

Reporter: So?

Law Maker: *Still giggling.* If law makers had to carefully study a bill ahead of time, they would never vote for it.

Reporter: Really? Is that true and why so?

Law Maker: If every member should pledge to not vote for a bill till they read it in its entirety, well... I think we should have very few votes.

Reporter: But...I don't understand...What you are saying therefore, is that it is much more important for the US Congress to pass the bill than to understand it?

Law Maker: Not like that. I did not mean it that way...

Reporter: Let me finish, sir. Transparency is a very popular buzz word during election campaigns and in most speeches extolling good governance. Politicians are for ever promising to transact the people's business in the sunshine. Are you saying that the notion of transparency is just a joke then?

Law Maker: No, I did not say that.

Reporter: Then help me to understand this thing.

Law Maker: *silence*....

Others, like Peter Orszag, a director in President Obama's administration, told CNN's State of the Union that some senators advocate delays simply as a move of desperation to kill a bill, when asked if it was possible to pass the president's bill on healthcare reform before August recess of 2009.

More challenges lay ahead. It did not take long for Martha Coakley, the Attorney-General of the Commonwealth of Massachusetts to file a suit in US District Court over DOMA (Defense of Marriage Act), alleging that the Act unfairly excluded more than 16,000 married same-sex couples in Massachusetts and their families from critically important rights and protections based on marital status and that DOMA infringed on the state's constitutional right to determine the marital status of its residents. Under the DOMA, enacted since 1996, same sex couples are denied the ability to file joint income tax returns and to receive federal health and retirement benefits under the same plan.

People can decide to be absent from work for Gay Day Celebration and their bosses query them for not showing up at work. Such employees will certainly protest, claiming violation of their First Amendment rights. But the bosses may not know that they are gay, thanks to the other policy of "don't ask, don't tell" introduced during Bill Clinton's presidency to make it possible for gays to serve in the US armed forces. Attorneys will be called into the show. What next? How will this tie in with State law?

And in our world in which America swaggers around the globe like a cowboy gone mad, having its way whenever and wherever it wants with no regard for others, our consecration of a gay American bishop and our blessing of same-sex unions are seen as acts of North American unilateralism and defiance of the cultural sensibilities of our brothers and sisters in Christ, especially those in the Global South. Twenty years after Gene Robinson and his wife made the decision to end their marriage, an older priest in their diocese, troubled by his "coming out", approached him and for two decades he and the priest held on to each other while discussing the issues of homosexuality and faith, the older man holding steadfastly to his belief that homosexuality was incompatible with scripture and ordination. Gay issues are a minefield in which America's 44th president would have to tread with a very big dose of caution.

Transgender is another. Tracey Lagondino was pregnant but unlike most pregnancies, hers drew a lot of attention and critique, mostly of her own making because she put it up in *The Advocate*, an online gay magazine. The 34-year old who grew up in Hawaii and who participated in beauty contests and was once finalist in the Miss Hawaii Teen USA pageant, changed her name to Thomas Beatie, definitely a male name. What happened? She suffered from Gender Identity Disorder (or syndrome 302.85 in the Diagnostic and Statistical Manual of the American Psychiatric Association). It would appear that she had felt uncomfortable with her female identity since adolescence. "At age twenty," The Telegraph of London reported' "she became more masculine, began a lesbian relationship and researched what it meant to be a transgender male". There followed a breast removal surgery and testosterone injections. Thomas Beatie then grew a beard, changed her legal identity to male and married her partner, a certain Nancy.

But then it takes more than a mastectomy and testosterone hormone injections to overturn biology. In the eyes of the Law

Thomas might be a man but remained physically a woman, with a woman's reproductive system, a woman's genitals and a woman's chromosomes. The same can be said of medicine and the medical corps that will definitely have to cope with Thomas's many indispositions which will surely crop up with time. The proof is that when she and Nancy decided later to have a baby, she had little trouble getting pregnant, thanks to in vitro fertilization and artificial insemination. It was the outcome that drew attention, lots of attention – a bearded pregnant woman named Thomas who identified herself as a man and had a lawfully wedded wife! There are lots of individual rights out there but plenty of society's involvement too. Where should the line be drawn? And what is it that pushes people to these extremes? Has it always been so? The UK seemed to be a pace setter in this area. A forty-eight year old Brit named Norrie May-Welby, dissatisfied after a sex change operation to become a woman, took the decision to do away with both male and female genders. He simply became the world's first genderless person resident in Australia and had his birth certificate altered to reflect the no-gender classification given to him by the doctors. Looks can be very deceptive; gone are the days when it was possible to tell a person's gender just from external appearance, especially in African–American societies.

If ever there was a hot topic in America, this was it. Every shade of opinion is offered. The State of California played ping-ping with the gay marriage issue unlike Massachusetts which took the bull by the horns to legalize it and leave it at that. First California voted to legalize gay marriage. Then came Proposition 8 or Marriage Protection Act, a citizens' effort to ban it which successfully passed the test in 2008, prompting the state Supreme Court to reverse itself on the issue. But why? Faced with a similar scenario - mounting crime and polls showing that 80 % of whites and 49% of black South Africans wanted the death penalty to be retained - Judge President Arthur Chaskelson declared that the court could not allow itself to be diverted from its duty to act as an independent arbiter of the constitution by making choices on the basis that they would find favor with the public. The post-Apartheid court stood its ground. Why couldn't California's court do likewise? California's court decision only went to energize the proponents of gay marriage who were not about to throw in the towel so soon. Such practices have not made life easy for the men and women of the judiciary, notably the Honorable Ronald M. George, chief justice of California's Supreme Court who alluded to the revolting practices of California's voters in a speech entitled "The Perils of Direct Democracy: the California Experience". The justice lamented over the use of the ballot measures to change California law, a practice he considered unhealthy and promiscuous, rendering the state government dysfunctional during a severe economic decline. He cited the US Constitution that has undergone just 27 amendments in its 220 years of existence compared to California's 500 since 1879, the year of its ratification. Arguments were not lacking on the part of citizens seeking empowerment. Voters claimed that such initiative and referendum process provide an outlet to tackle issues that legislators will not. But the system has its thorny problems. Should the signatories of such ballot initiatives be kept secret or open? The fear of retaliation dictates the former while the need for transparency speaks for the latter.

Pressure continued to mount on President Barack Obama to sign an executive order, reversing the military's "*don't ask, don't tell*" policy for its gays and lesbians, another hot potato from the Clinton years. It would be so nice and easy if gays and lesbians could keep their act under cover. But no, not in America! The present furor is over recognition. Gays and lesbians want to "come out" in the open and be accepted and respected and given all the rights their straight heterosexual counterparts enjoy. At a California Charter school a newsletter was devoted to "*National Coming Out Day*" in spite of parental objections. Proponents claim that all the reasons concocted to keep gays out of the military have no scintilla of evidence to support them – security risks, spread of disease, unit cohesion – bogus claims which they liken to what black Americans were subjected to before racial discrimination was outlawed in the US. Many gays say they are fed up with living a life of pretense and self-denial.

The most powerful argument gay activists put forth in the drive for achieving equality, respect and all the recognition their straight counterparts enjoy is the comparison of their plight to the despicable segregation and discrimination of black Americans based on race. But the comparison is rather tenuous when seen in the light of the genetic phenotypes involved – black skin color is an immutable genetically determined trait, giving its possessor no choice in the matter. The same cannot be said of homosexuality, especially when happily married individuals switch to gay lifestyles after producing a string of kids, or those falling back on heterosexuality when the tantalizingly gay partnerships flop. Besides, a black person entering a room is quickly seen to be black but the same cannot be said of a gay person unless such a person advertised or publicized being gay. Arguments are put forth that blacks feel jealous of their sole-discrimination victim status as if they do not know that other victims of discrimination exist, citing the millions slaughtered sixty years ago in Europe for belonging to a religious minority. Pushing the comparison further, the argument holds that asking gay people to stay in the closet is like asking black people to color themselves white! Can one beat such typically American logic?

There must be some powerful force that pushes normal heterosexual humans into homosexuality. It is not heredity, so what can it be? Adolescent children in same sex educational institutions in Cameroon have been known to express an ephemeral interest in kids of their sex. In South Africa, miners separated for extended periods of time from their spouses and living in very close quarters have had to resort to homosexuality as a temporary expedient. In the Catholic Church, young vibrant priests denied the possibility of marrying have often turned to pedophilia as an outlet. But the rest of society, living in a free world with no such constraints and with sex so readily available, still push for same sex liaisons. Why?

In matters of equality virtually every American is an expert. As predicted, US District Court Chief Judge, Vaughn Walker later reversed Proposition 8 again, the voter-approved ban on same-sex marriage, stating that its opponents "demonstrated by overwhelming evidence" that the proposition violates due process as well as equal protection rights under the US Constitution, singling out gay men and lesbians for denial of marriage license. This view was vociferously denounced once again by those who considered it synonymous to stripping a majority of Californians, including blacks, of their core civil right – the right to vote! But the judge's decision left intact, at least for a while, gay men and lesbian couples in a lurch, unable to marry as this whole thing moved inexorably to the highest court in the nation. More fireworks lay ahead surely!

Supporters of Chief Judge Vaughn Walker's reversal of Proposition 8 argued that the sensible mind of one could still prevail over the irrational action of many. And yet democracy is also a dictatorship of the majority over the minority! If, as some contended, marriage equality is not about religion or traditional values but about freedom and civil rights promised by the US Constitution, then as the saga moved to the Supreme Court, only those nine luminaries would help this nation come to terms with a correct interpretation of the text. As a matter of fact Judge Vaughn Walker's ruling was quickly followed by another ruling of the Federal Appeals Court in San Francisco, blocking same-sex marriages in California till a three-man panel examined the broader questions over the constitutionality of such marriages. If doctors think they have a hard time coping with the practice of medicine and its attendant ethical and moral dilemmas, judges too face a daunting task when on the one hand they can, with a clear conscience, uphold the right of LBGT and on the other hand, slam pedophiles into prison or put electronic braces on their ankles to monitor their movements. Aren't both groups pushing individual freedom to its very limit and daring the law to punish them?

Bishop Harry Jackson Jr., senior pastor of Hope Christian Church in Beltsville, Maryland stands opposed to same sex marriage, calling the implied comparison between racism and opposition to same-sex marriage an offense to all those who remember Jim Crow laws. Thus for such persons, homosexuality is not the neurosis displayed by others but a passive activity, an expedient just like pimping or left-handedness which can be switched if the will is there. Trickier still is the definition of marriage and its implication. If marriage is simply the love between any two individuals, by what logic then can society prohibit several persons to profess love among themselves and get married polygamously, applying the logic for same-sex marriage? We might just as well usher in the two aspects of polygamy – polygyny (one man, many wives) and polyandry (one woman, many husbands). That should uphold the nondiscrimination instinct so enamored of those clamoring for all the social experiments outside of man-woman relationships.

Not to be left out, African-Americans slowly waded into the dance as well, even if the black community remained largely against gay marriage and its legalization. History tied African-Americans together – a back drop of centuries of horrific oppression under slavery and then the courage to rise and fight for liberty and equality. The civil rights brought about a community of close-knit blacks with admiration and mutual respect for one another. But the gay black male fighting for equality in the black community is a totally different ball game altogether.

Looking back at all the sacrifices of his ancestors to gain freedom and equality, today's black gay is scandalized that he is not supported by his own community. This is pure hypocrisy, he chastises. How can 57 % of the blacks in New York oppose a black man's right to same-sex marriage? Allusions are made to Rosa Parks, the brave black lady who dared to defend her civil rights, the fact that interracial marriage – a pursuit of happiness - was at one time declared illegal and denied by government, that the US Constitution clearly states that all men are created equal, that they are endowed by their Creator with certain inalienable rights…life, liberty, the pursuit of happiness, that governments are in place to secure those rights, not deny them. It just doesn't sound right!

Unfortunately African-Americans see a big difference between civil rights and gay rights, even after just celebrating the election of the first black president of the United States. If equating gay rights to civil rights was intended to gain more sympathy and empathy it was greeted instead with scorn, incredulity and lots of questioning. Drawing parallels between gay rights and civil rights is a far cry. White parents had enough problems guessing who their lovely daughters would be bringing home for dinner when the relationship was heterosexual; with same-sex relationships, it would be one heck of a tough sell.

Is homosexuality a genetic (hereditary) condition passed down from parents to offspring like hair texture and color, skin color, nasal shape and the rest of those features that formed people's opinion and shaped racial discrimination over the years? Once these thorny issues were clarified, a lot of doubts would be laid to rest and perhaps people would then be more receptive of this new fad. Until then homosexual marriage would be seen as an extension of the sexual revolution, not the civil rights struggle. But it seemed very unlikely that genetics would offer any help in that direction. Society had come too far along the road of enlightenment to let any doubts sully minds in such matters. Before Charles Darwin, Gregor Mendel and the other forefathers of genetics, it was believed that the inheritance of parental traits was simply like blending colors to obtain new colors. But that proposition did not stand the test of time. When male and female genes are brought together at conception, it is either sons or daughters that are produced as offspring, not hermaphrodites (a type of half male and half female being). Genes behave like cards in a deck – they get shuffled, not blended like paint. Homosexuality has to break this time-tested law to be put on par with the rest. Opponents argue very strongly that the failure of heterosexual marriage cannot be remedied by a homosexual one and that a restoration of the ideal, not its abandonment is called for. Proposition 8, they argue, is a step in the right direction.

Was it only black males involved in the new crusade? Absolutely not! There were black female gays too, such as Deborah Lake, a mother of four daughters produced after fifteen years of marriage. She "came out" as a lesbian and apparently married her partner or was clamoring for society to let her do so. Her society considered it an abomination. She was undaunted even though all her previous comfort, protection and security were gone as she transitioned from mother to lesbian. She lamented that being lesbian, she was exorcised from the black community as people assumed that she hated men, especially black men. Even those women who had earlier called her blessed, tended to treat her as if she had been contaminated. She even claimed that some black men made unwanted sexual advances at her, ostensibly to correct what they saw as her "lesbian waywardness". Like all gays, she too demanded respect.

In the gray area of separation of church and state, where would a lesbian turn to if thrown out of her job for breach of existing policies and regulations like using language or conduct that contravened the doctrine of the Catholic church, for that was exactly what happened to a lesbian who was given the option to choose between termination and resignation for deciding to marry her partner of twelve years. Bickering about the hypocrisy of her diocese where she had assumed that her loyalty and professionalism over the years would supersede the hypocrisy of lay persons divorcing to remarry without annulment, employees using the birth control, men having vasectomies and individuals being prochoice on natters of abortion, did not quite help her case.

From 1948 till today the revolution has come a long way even if the road ahead is still very long. In 1948 Alfred Kinsey's "Sexual Behavior in the Human Male" brought sexual preference into mainstream. In 1962 Illinois became the first state to decriminalize consensual acts of homosexuality and eleven years later, homosexuality was completely removed from the American Psychiatric Association's list of mental disorders. In 1982 Wisconsin outlawed discrimination on the basis of one's sexual orientation, followed in 1993 by the military's *"Don't Ask, Don't Tell"* policy under Bill Clinton. Vermont officially accepted civil unions between gay couples in 2000, followed in 2003 by the US Supreme Court ruling against the constitutionality of sodomy laws. In 2007 the US House of Representatives passed equal rights legislation for gays in the work force and in 2008 California's Supreme court legitimized the constitutional right for same-sex couples to get married, which was followed six months later by Proposition 8, a ballot initiative in which voters effectively banned and overturned the court's earlier ruling. Here we were in 2010; under pressure, President Obama Okayed a referendum to enable same-sex partners of federal employees to receive limited health benefits even as his reform on healthcare languished in Congress.

Any way forward? Not yet. Proposition 8 had its ardent supporters as well as those determinedly opposed to it. The cacophony was not going to end any time soon. Supporters argued that marriage is a religious union between one man and one woman and expressed concern about where contemporary society was heading since gay marriage disturbs the natural order. They insisted that marriage has a definition that does not include two men or two women, that they were Christians opposed to gay marriage but were not hateful or homophobic, merely defending their faith and tradition. But that view was not shared by Virginia A. Phillips, a federal judge in Riverside, California who, shortly afterwards, finally declared that the military's *don't ask, don't tell* policy was unconstitutional in violating the First Amendment and due process rights of lesbians and gay men. Such a position should make life easier for President Obama's administration but apparently that was not the case. The end of the ping-pong game would probably involve members of the US Congress, sitting down to pass some kind of a law to accommodate those conflicting claims even as there were forces lined up already to challenge such a move, arguing that the military is not a democracy where recruits have their say instead of simply obeying orders as it has been all along. But with the difficult times, those campaigning for elective office as well as voters were probably more concerned with putting food on the table than losing sleep over who their neighbors were sleeping with.

The arguments were often made with proponents playing ostrich, oblivious of the fact that America is not an island in the world and of what impact such novel trends might have on Americans working in other countries like diplomats, trade representatives, missionaries and others. Malawi may be a small country but when it comes to national sovereignty and the rule of law, that African nation can stand on its own two feet and defend its right to imprison all persons claiming to be gays; they violate the law and can be imprisoned for up to fourteen years. So too can Uganda and many other countries on the black continent where Christianity is dear at heart.

Are Christians using Biblical verses to support their preconceived prejudicial views? Are they merely using their Bibles the way a drunk uses the lamppost – for support rather than illumination – as Boston's Riverside Church minister, William Sloan Coffin, contends? Should contemporary society dismiss such arguments as biblical literalism? Certainly not by Leviticus 20:13 :(*Men who lay with men as they would lay with a woman are detestable. The penalty for homosexual acts is death to both partners. They have committed a detestable act and are guilty of a capital offence*). Or by Gen2:24, Matt 9:5, Mark 10:7 and indeed all biblical scriptures presuppose heterosexual marriages. Islam does not contest this. Nothing could be clearer. It was clear then that all roads were leading to the US Supreme Court where Americans hoped the dangerous social experiment would be brought to an end to save the society. How on earth could kids learn the virtues of heterosexual life at home, proceed to public or charter schools expecting to get an edifying education only to have those lessons undone by teachers preaching gay marriage and other deviant sexual behavior? The tragic death by suicide of Rutgers University's Tyler Clementi brought home this sad state of affairs. It might be old school to preach sexual activities behind closed doors but today's obsession with "coming out" is surely not helping matters when young persons prematurely take their lives because they cannot cope with the choices they make in an environment where fellow citizens, out of ignorance or cruelty, use bullying or harassment in response. Carl Paladino, GOP gubernatorial candidate for New York could not be more emphatic when he asserted that children were being "brainwashed" into believing in the acceptability of homosexuality, turning a blind eye to its consequences.

And where does procreation fit in this new order? In Medford, Massachusetts, a sign "Homosexuality is Sin" outside the church caused an uproar as people rushed to the local human rights commission to complain, arguing that the church ought to distinguish between a bad act (homosexuality) and good persons (practitioners). Bert and Bernie, two orange-yellow hand puppets – nothing exists below the waistline- from the classic children's series, *Sesame Street* have been the object of much debate, some claiming they are gay while others say they are just an odd couple. The Catholic church, seriously bruised by the clergy sex abuse cases that rocked Boston Archdiocese at the time of Cardinal Bernard law, tried the timid condemnation of saying it opposed gay marriage because if all men were gay there would hardly be any procreation, prompting a quick rebuff from a lay observer who wondered aloud: "Suppose all men were Catholic priests, prohibited from marrying and having sex, would the human race not be equally damned?" There was no reply!

For many persons, the best way to rationalize the new trends is just to deny the existence of God. God does not exist any longer. As a matter of fact, since adventurous Americans landed on the moon, walked on it, dangled in space and overcame gravity, the notion of heaven or angels has become pure phantom in some circles. And so, where the Bible speaks of Adam and Eve, it is convenient to substitute Adam and Steve. What an elegant solution to a thorny problem! Or simply pay lip service to the idea of God. Frustrated or perhaps disappointed with conventional religions some Americans are advocating turning to sports in the belief they will find spirituality, community and human connectedness, even placing sports higher on their scale of values because sports do not give false hopes and do not threaten eternal damnation for non-belief or non-adherence. The Pilgrim Fathers or Founding Fathers and the religious foundation of the nation are virtually in the recesses of our memory, in the zone of pure fantasy. Unwilling or unable to adapt religion to the Constitution or vice versa, fellow Americans simply choose the easy way out – just reject both.

In a 2009 study carried out by American Religious Identification Survey, it was found out that the number of Americans who claimed no religious affiliation had nearly doubled from 8% only a few years ago to 15%. Very significantly too, it was found that this category of Americans chiefly concentrated in the Pacific North-West was also found in the New England states of the North-East, their new stronghold! The North-East is considered the foundation or home base of American religion. Some momentous shift must be taking place and people have started talking about the post-modern, post-Christian and post-western culture in the US as Christians continue to make up a declining percentage of the population. Never had the future of the Christian church been murkier. As if these were not enough problems already, some ongoing research seemed to point to the direction that many priests did not believe what they preached any more although they had not quite come out openly to denounce it. Unbelieving priests had lost faith in the message. They were like closeted gay people, still maintaining a credible deniability. But for how long?

It should not come as a surprise to Americans. Many churches today have gained the whole world but lost their souls. One needs only see what televangelists do. They preach the gospel of health and wealth, promise of material success and prosperity for true believers. They drive flashy cars, fly private jets, put on expensive clothing and jewelry and generally rival the top rappers of modern day society as they deliver their sermons aimed more at selling self-help products than promoting righteous living.

Why not? Judged by newspaper and other press reports, this country has a monumental problem of racial segregation and discrimination in spite of all the laws. Yet, a closer look at society reveals something else. The biggest and most strident of the bigots almost always end up with a woman across the racial divide.

Take Alabama for example. While an earthshaking case was on (the famous Scottsboro Trial) involving the sentencing of nine black youths to die for allegedly raping two white women, white men, some of them reverend gentlemen of the pulpit, were regularly, secretly and routinely using their social standing to engage in sexual relationships with black women, considered lovers one minute, mistresses the next. Eating the forbidden fruit whether by white slave masters of the past or clergymen of today can have very interesting consequences, some good, others not so good, as genealogists portrayed recently in their digging and bringing to light Michelle Obama's family tree. Gay marriage does not make room for procreation but gays clamor for adoption of kids like everyone else. Will our elected representatives in Congress speak up?

Would it be all right for the courts to deny adoption rights for persons who manifestly are against procreation? Those who say yes appeal to the public to realize that the sanctity of marriage is not an invention of bigotry and cite generously from the Bible where it is stipulated that men are for women and women for men, for they are meant to find partnership and compassion in one another. Using the rule of priorities in biological taxonomy, they posit that if someone were to discover a new color today, it would be wrong to name it blue, because blue already exists. The conclusion is inescapable that a name other than marriage should be proposed for this new idea of same-sex cohabitation. Members of the Republican Party, perceived to be antigay, claim that the new GOP does not exclude anyone. But it is a catch-22 proposition, a very slippery slope indeed. Failure to back gay marriage means alienating an important voting block.

And the case for gays has awakened some singles to take a closer look at their own plight. Now they are wondering aloud if they too do not deserve recognition, especially when layoffs from jobs place them in an economic wilderness of sorts. The campaign against what is perceived as one kind of inequality has certainly highlighted what in the eyes of an affected single, is another inequality – those who by choice or by chance do not organize their lives around a romantic relationship. Singles with no offspring or parent worry about what happens to their social security savings in case of loss of employment or death. Massachusetts in general and Boston in particular continue to open up new frontiers.

The sexual revolution and its aftermath were supposed to be a global phenomenon that changed the way men and women, both heterosexual and homosexual lived their lives. The changes were not welcome by everyone and so till this day people are still fighting over the right attitude towards sex. The revolution derived partly from economic and technological developments (the birth control pill), and partly from a series of social movements led by people of all stripes - men, women, straight or gay. Its most important impact has been the decline of cultural taboos that repressed female sexual pleasure.

Human freedom was at stake, involving new possibilities and introducing new ethical and political dilemmas too. Hitherto homosexuality was grounds for expulsion from school, termination of employment, justification for harassment and violence. Then gays and lesbians determined to live on their own terms – a crucial dimension of the revolution. There followed an unavoidable backlash from sexual conservatism and neotraditionalism. The fight over sexual liberation could be quite costly and surely had a long way to go as seen from the case of an 18-year-old young man who jumped to his death from the George Washington Bridge separating New York from New Jersey. Using one of the many sleuthing devices, probably a cell phone or hidden video camera, two Rutgers University students had taken pictures of the boy's sexual encounter with another man in the dormitory and put it online at a website, presumably JustUsBoys.com, thus plunging Rutgers University and the boy's family into a period of grieving. For a young man who was cavorting with a girl just a few months earlier at his prom, the unavoidable question begging for answers was "Was this necessary?" And just what type of upbringing would throw a fragile kid into the world of such experimentation?

Beyond questions like these one cannot help wondering if the men of the west are becoming obsolete as women take on center stage in a world that was once theirs. Studies of gender changes on the work force keep indicating how superfluous men have become in some areas. In the good old days it was helpful to have them around but with mechanization of almost everything in life and the expanded use of robots and smart pets to help out, their position is visibly shaken. Men are still necessary for reproduction but here too, science is fast putting them out of business even if some women claim that they remain huggable on nice days.

Without closing the chapter on gays, another experiment in cohabitation is slowly emerging from the closet and coming out into the open, hopefully to seek recognition too, and the benefits that go with it. Its adherents say it is not quite monogamy or polygamy. They call it polyamory or simply poly – a type of loose marital arrangement which, while not quite like wife swapping, allows both partners the flexibility to continue to openly visit dating websites "and to welcome what might come along." Cameroonian author Francis Nyamnjoh captured this idea beautifully in his novel *"Married but Available,"* a stab at the loose life of seeking extramarital pleasures in spite of those solemn vows.(Nyamjoh is equally parodying leadership that professes democracy and meritocracy in governance while indeed practicing autocracy, mediocrity and totalitarianism and other repressive policies). This love's next frontier smacks of the free love of the 1960s and 1970s. While it can be quite good for men who walk away scot-free from such experiments, women and children carry the scars far into the future, especially when the women fall off the sexual radar because of menopause. In this polyamory type of marital arrangement, man and woman try their luck at dating other couples, saying nothing about *"Till death do us part"* or what accommodation, if any, is made for their children. Women seem to like it although theirs is an uphill task where labels like oversexed, slut or stud are easily thrown at them whereas "boys will be boys" continues to be the norm when men are sexually involved with more women. In a society where God-centered faithfulness in monogamy is still considered the cornerstone for stability, productivity, security and hope, there are women hailing and drinking to this as the way to go even as many others point to the depravity and disingenuous aspect underlying it.

In the years ahead, law makers will surely be given a run for the money they make. Since democracy is the dictatorship of the majority over the minority, opponents of gay marriage have held sway in many cases. In view of this, gays have turned to the courts even if litigation cannot obviously provide all the answers to this knotty problem. The argument used in a liberal state like Massachusetts to defend gay marriage is that state law protects minorities against the majority. The danger too is that freedom without limit can lead to anarchy and help to derail a people's civilization. Hopefully in the short run the homosexual (gay) fad will blow over like hippiculture or the beatnik culture before it, but it will surely leave lots of casualties along its path, judged by the number of part-time practitioners in each society. Who could have believed that those pot-smoking, free love hippies of the 1960s would transform to the yuppies of the 1980s, wearing three piece suits, Rolex watches and other paraphernalia of corporate America? South Africa, Burundi and many havens are helplessly coping with this strident call for unfettered liberty to experiment with one's sexual orientation. If conventional religion, jurisprudence or the legislature cannot resolve this matter in the short run, good old Darwinian fitness will decide, given that survival will be determined by the ability to leave offspring and viable genes in the gene pool.

And as I guessed earlier, on Saturday December 18, 2010, the United States senate voted 65 to 31 to repeal the military's *Don't Ask, Don't Tell* policy, which President Obama signed into law right away, paving the way for the Defense Department to spend the following sixty days on the modalities of implementing it. Will that end the debate? Your guess... What does the end to *Don't Ask, Don't Tell* mean to those resolutely opposed to it? Will it involve a review of all 1400 previously discharged from the military? How exactly will "coming out" affect a gay soldier rushing toward the enemy or to the aid of a straight colleague fallen on the battle field? Or is the fear mainly about what takes place in the barracks? How will this affect the rest of the military, especially those deadly opposed to serving with homosexuals, those who consider homosexuality a degradation of virtue and high moral code? Is it conceivable that this may lead to mass exodus from the military of those honorable troops who believe that active, open homosexuality destroys social values? Is it possible that some will refuse to enlist, especially persons of high caliber values who cannot fancy sharing bunk beds with perverts at Annapolis? Is it premature to speculate that another Congress will overturn this law?

One thing is certain –President Barack Obama should be returning to his native Hawaii a happy man, at least for the Christmas of 2010. The check marks for his morale boosters, especially coming out of the wreckage of the November midterm would include the $858 billion tax cut bill that went through Congress, financial regulatory overhaul, rescue of the banking and automobile sectors, repeal of *Don't Ask Don't Tell*, working overtime to close another significant political victory – Senate ratification of a new nuclear arms deal (START) with Russia and last but certainly not the least, a historic healthcare reform – quite an achievement in a crisis-scarred presidency of two years and so much of it during a lame duck Congress! Many agreed that the 111th Congress was the most productive in half a century and the most extraordinary for Obama's first two years in office. Preaching bipartisanship and pragmatism surely paid dividends even if the entire US Congress was not going to love one another and to sing *kumbaya*.

Author Susan Orback asks the interesting question "How do we get a body?" Her answer: "We get a body not from nature but from how the body is treated by those who raise us." She then supports her answer with many examples of bodies that had been treated badly and required remedy. She begins with the story of drastic remedy – a man who chose to have his legs amputated and achieved a sense of satisfaction that way in his legless body. Many people, she argues, believe themselves to inhabit false or wrong bodies. In response they seek surgery, diet, drugs. They change their sex, skin color, increase or decrease their height, enlarge or reduce their breasts or penises, refine their jaw lines, reshape their noses, all thanks to modern technology. For those with an irresistible itch to make passes, it may be prudent to make haste very slowly in approaching an individual who looks female, has earrings, and carries long hair tied into a bun or pony tail. The quest for perfection has led people to Botox, collagen, breast implants and many more of the twenty-first century's fads. Hitherto women talked in terms of how to age gracefully, to let nature take its course and to appreciate the body in every stage of getting old. Retailers like Macy's, Nordstrom, Bloomingdales, Saks and others are doing good business in spite of the economic meltdown, thanks to our womenfolk's desire for more empowerment, desire to feel good about themselves and give themselves some vanity too. Some have since thrown away or burnt the bra and embraced spanx, a body shaping girdle of the new millennium, popular among baby boomers in menopause, to achieve a number of things, including slimming, controlling weight, hiding the bra lines at the back. But then again, with the extreme pressure exerted on men and women to stay young, a lot of them go too far and end up getting the reverse effect of looking a lot older than they really are. Not so, Jennifer Aniston?

During my childhood years, the gap between the upper incisors was considered a defect to be fixed. As a matter of fact doctors gave it the name malocclusion and children in my class, especially the girls, were subjected to painful procedures, including the use of heavy metal braces to correct such defects. Today the tide has changed and gapped front teeth have been rebranded and designated the perfect imperfection. The new craze is to introduce it where it did not exist before and show it off as a symbol of beauty or sexiness (US), *les dents du Bonheur* (France) and signs of strong sex appeal (Nigeria). It all depends on what the Joneses are saying or what is written in chapter three, verse one of Alice in Wonderland. Dental surgeons and cosmetic dentists get top dollars from those who come in for the new fad.

Among several explanations offered for the late Michael Jackson's identity problems involving many nose jobs and skin color change is the idea that the megastar of pop music wanted to reflect the broad base of his fans. What a price to pay for accommodating one's fan base! Death at fifty for a wealthy man in a country where life expectancy reaches one hundred surely raises eye brows. Now the world is saddled with conspiracy theories to explain away the premature death of the man who gave the world so much entertainment in music and acting. Blacks watched with pride as Michael Jackson became the biggest entertainer during the past one quarter century, yet loving his artistic genius while looking the other way when it came to his appearance, his increasingly unrecognizable face, a living embodiment of identity crisis many blacks have faced themselves for long.

Michael Jackson moon walked through doors opened by Jackie Robinson, Nat King Cole, Harry Belafonte, Martin Luther King Jr., Sidney Poitier, Mohammed Ali and many others. He has been consistently mentioned along with Elvis Presley, Frank Sinatra, the Beatles and the other great entertainers of our time. By pushing MTV to play his videos, Michael Jackson paved the way for countless artists to be seen and heard on mainstream cable video networks. His trans-racial appeal certainly helped to open many doors and enabled contemporary prominent blacks like Oprah Winfrey and Barack Obama to enjoy universal appeal in addition to giving an entire generation a global cultural hero and citizen. It could not be otherwise after what is known to have taken place between Thomas Jefferson and slave woman Sally Hemming many moons ago.

But many unanswered questions remain. How beautiful is black and what does it mean to turn one's back to Michael Jackson's struggles with blackness, insecurity, aging? Through Oprah Winfrey the late superstar admitted in 1993 that he struggled with a skin condition called vitiligo, a condition that drained his skin of color. But then what of his face? According to USMagazine.com, some twenty-five years ago, Michael Jackson's head caught fire and a good part of his crown got burnt as he was doing a commercial for Pepsi. It would appear that that accident changed Michael Jackson's life for good and set him on the road that led to pain killers and plastic surgery. Even after the pop star's death police continued to comb every niche in his California residence to try to find out what caused his death, against a background accusation that his PCP had a hand in it. US drug enforcement agents and Los Angeles police raided a Houston clinic owned by Conrad Murray the doctor who attended to the icon before his death. They also raided his home and clinic in Las Vegas, probing into cell phone conversations, computer hard drives, medical records, and medication orders - anything that could throw light on Michael Jackson's death which was then being considered manslaughter. Dr Murray, who was apparently in deep financial troubles, was said to have been by the pop star's side at the time of his death. Speculations were that MJ had fully booked up concerts lined up in London by AEC Live promoters; hence the probe was focused on his use of drugs to keep up his marathon schedule. (*Investigations of Dr Murray brought to memory the tribulations of Elvis Presley's physician, George C. Nichopoulos, between 1980 and 1995, involving the suspension of his license and indictment for unlawful, willful and felonious prescribing of drugs for Elvis and finally being stripped of his license to practice because of overprescribing*). Michael Jackson was on a special killer routine. In his home, especially his bathroom which was likened to a pharmacy, there was a search for propofol, a strong narcotic also called Diprivan, repeatedly mentioned in connection with his last days and linked to his cardiac arrest. Meanwhile Random House was reported to have bought the rights to "moonwalk", Michael Jackson's autobiography and Kanye West was said to be anxious to become the new King of Pop. The man whose ego was said to be those of Daniel Trump, Henry Kissinger and Julius Caesar all rolled into one, was reported by one Dorothy Robinson of the Metro as dying to replace the king of pop music. Quite a lot of ego indeed.

Curiously very little was being mentioned about the pop star's mother's early obsession and prayers that her son should pass for white. More than a hundred years ago, the founder of the NAACP, the late W. E. B. Dubois wrote in *"The Souls of Black Folks"* about "this sense of always looking at oneself through the eyes of others, of measuring one's soul by the tape of a world that looks on in amused contempt and pity..." How should one merge this double self into one authentic self? This question must have troubled Michael Jackson, the quintessentially American, undeniably black and universally loved king of pop. So many plastic surgeries and an increasingly pale skin was how Michael Jackson gave expression to this longing, carrying it out to a tragic extreme perhaps. Some have argued that Michael had a troubled youth and was conditioned to loathe his African features and so his wide bulb of a nose became a precariously slender triangle, the Afro hairdo transformed into juicy Jheri curls and a chalky mask replaced his bumpy brown skin – all in an effort to graft America's white beauty myth onto the handsome youth many recall from the days of Jackson Five.

Has black compassion diminished for the late star's music, plight, talent and art? Not at all. Many African-Americans agree that Michael Jackson did make an effort to soften some of his distinct racial features, said Pearlman Hicks, a Los Angeles-based African American plastic surgeon who went on to add that throughout history it was widely shown that the lighter one's skin color and the less distinctive one's African features, the more acceptable one became in the world of whites. He even stated that patients had come to him demanding to have a "Michael Jackson nose" upon which he would discourage them saying "If you are black, you are black and no amount of surgery or creams or medication can change that. I think MJ tried to transcend that and that realization prevented him from being truly happy and at peace with himself".

Yet polls taken around the time of Michael Jackson's death showed that teens expected to die young, probably earlier than 35 - a rather bleak perception that could lead to increased rates of drug use, crime, unsafe sex, physical fights, and suicide attempts, a very sobering prospect indeed. The megastar's ever-changing face, a result of repeated plastic surgeries, reflected an inner conflict about race and sexuality. It also reflected pain as the man struggled to come to terms with a childhood lost prematurely to fame and celebrity and, by some accounts, parental parasitism. As in Elvis Presley's case, books have been written and fortunes made; similarly, telling the story of what actually killed Michael Jackson, will bring forth the same answer – that he was the author of his own demise.

What our society makes of these dramas often depends on one's political outlook. At one cultural extreme are transgender activists, radical feminists and others who argue that sex differences between men and women are patriarchal constructs, not hard wired facts of life. This category will probably applaud Thomas and Nancy as gender-bending pioneers challenging an oppressive male-female dichotomy. South Africa's gold medalist, eighteen-year-old Caster Semenya, having just experienced the greatest victory of her life, paid the stiffest price for an intractable gender issue that prompted the IAAF (International Associations of Athletics Federations) to ask for gender verification. What a humiliation! Was Caster Semenya XX, XO, XY, XXY or what? Winning the 800 meters women's final brought her a temporary glory which was quickly eclipsed by concerns about her true gender. Molatelo Malehopo, general manager of Athletics South Africa, who subsequently lost his post, was categorical in his declaration - "She is a female" - and the young woman's father came to her defense to no avail. Not even Jacob Zuma, South Africa's president's protestation of the young woman's humiliation could help matters. The IAAF was unrelenting, arguing that Athletics South Africa should have preempted this by carrying out the necessary gender testing ahead of time, especially as there were concerns from fellow competitors about her real sex. If the competition was just for females, of course it would be wrong to enroll someone who was not a female. The belated admission by South African authorities that they had concealed information from the IOC to protect the young girl's privacy came as a relief to the whole world, a vindication of IOC officials for the stand they had taken to submit Semenya to gender testing. The intersex category had not yet been defined and accommodated in Olympic sports. And nothing in the rules of the games provided for stripping down a competitor to examine his or her genitals. That would be for another time.

There are also those persons for whom gender is not a spectrum of possibilities but a matter of either one or the other. Conventional society's acceptance of these new realities will require some time. For now the idea that some persons feel ill at ease with their birth sex being incompatible with their gender and so take the courageous decision to express it, is a tough sell. Legal protection for transgender is not yet in the books, so accommodating them in public bathrooms, housing, access to healthcare and schools will take time. Until then the higher rate of suicide, unemployment and violence against this category will remain. Certainly things like these do not happen in a vacuum. For several weeks in 2008 the news focus was on the raid in a Texas compound of the Mormons where polygamists were herded out to rescue underage girls forcibly married to abusive older men. From Australia there came word of John and Jennifer Deaves, a sixty-one-year father and his thirty-nine year daughter who had had two children together, pleaded guilty to incest but said they just wanted "a little bit of respect and understanding" for their illicit relationship.

Sexual urges and appetites can be both powerful and perverse and lead to harmful consequences. Those who frown upon society for constraining sexual behavior with equally powerful taboos and moral standards can begin to decide if society has no role in the matter. Denouncing those who uphold these standards as narrow-minded bigots or hailing those who defy them as nonjudgmental and tolerant is quite common. (Ironically those who maintain this view of gender as being fluid and subjective are totally silent or argue in the opposite when it comes to matters of race).

Arrogant and defiant as California's famous "octomom" was, her action had ramifications way beyond her imagination, especially in the way her children would be brought up and catered for even if she consoled herself in the short run by marketing the so-called octomom brands of clothing and other wares. Her parents were soon on the hot seat and groping for explanations to offer a stunned society why the family had not made a timely intervention to stop such gross experimentation. A nation under the dark sky of a financial crunch was reacting with understandable awe and furor at such recklessness, knowing on whose shoulders the tab would fall and foreboding the prospects of being saddled with whatever genetic and social disorders such a mammoth delivery would portend. At delivery society would be saddled with taking the tab for all the complications that might result from Thomas' and Nancy's experiment. The octomom's bizarre experiment put Dr. Michael Kamrava at odds with the American Society of Reproductive Medicine, which threw the physician out of that prestigious organization in September, 2009 for violating ethical and group standards by implanting more eggs than stipulated into a woman's womb. The Beverly Hills doctor was thrown out and what happened to his IVF clinic was anybody's guess. Could he or could he not resist the wiles of a woman who dribbled him into facilitating her delivery of octuplets by in vitro fertilization after already being saddled with six earlier deliveries out of wedlock? What role would her supporters and advocates of such unrestrained freedoms play in the unfolding drama?

Gone are the days when it was fashionable for America to proclaim her isolationist stance in the world. After the Japanese attacked Pearl Harbor and forced the US into World War II, Michigan's Jesse Helms quickly dropped isolationism for internationalism. The logic of the Marshall Plan was clear to President Truman and so was the creation of NATO and the rest. Today we are part and parcel of the world and there is no turning back, especially when reminders like the 9/11 keep knocking at our doors. Similarly it is folly to play ostrich and claim individualism in a world where our every act has ramifications beyond the family, the community and the nation.

Reactions to these abound. Some condemn transgender phobia and question what right the society has to challenge someone else's expression of gender, regardless of their biological sex. Others claim that the decision to become a pregnant man harms nobody. Really? Is it true that the desire to match one's life with how one feels inside does not affect the society and does not harm anyone? Not even the baby? How about the doctors, nurses and lawyers called upon to play various roles arising from saddling society with such weirdoes? Even the taxpayer who will foot the bills? What of the impact on other children in schools? Surely a society may celebrate its diversity but can this be part of that diversity? What kind of respect or freedom is society being called upon to provide persons who submit to such experiments? Do the practitioners of such experiments need accolades and appearances on the Oprah show? Should society tolerate gender bending or stick to some standard of decency? It takes a special dose of chutzpah to raise the red flag on transgender issues and those who have done so do not always get applauded. God created us all male and female. It is all nice and good to propose Adam and Steve in place of Adam and Eve but the idea that a man can have a baby is preposterous; no one fools Mother Nature.

Trivializing these issues has not quite helped either. The GOP, under Michael Steel, had virtually run out of options to fight gay marriage and gone for a retooling of strategy, harping on the high cost to the tax payer. At a time when opposition to gay marriage had dropped quite low in public opinion polls, such a strategy, making financial consideration the main thrust of the argument against same sex marriage might have the unintended consequence of making marriage among straights more expensive since their number far exceeds that of gays. The inescapable conclusion would be to ban all marriages so as to save tax payers' money! The Commonwealth of Massachusetts legalized gay marriage in 2004. Since then Connecticut, Vermont, Iowa and Maine followed suit and the sky did not seem to be falling down. At least not yet. Next door in New York, the GOP candidate for governor, Carl Paladino, upon squaring off with Attorney-General, Andrew Cuomo, a Democrat, declared that children were being "brainwashed" into thinking that homosexuality is acceptable and harshly criticized his opponent for marching in a GAY PRIDE parade. There was clearly plenty of fireworks for the legislature, the judiciary and the Obama Administration as the 2010 midterm elections approached and the nation watched as politicians toyed with whether to adapt their politics to their religious views or vice versa.

A school principal ruminating the ban on hairstyles like braids, cornrows, dreadlocks and Jheri curls would need some nudging to reconsider his move in view of the storm of protests such a move would probably generate. It is true that such hairdo may not look professional, especially in the real world and the world of employment but that fact needs to be balanced against the opposing view that it limits creative expression, reinforces racist assumptions about black cultural practices and encroaches upon constitutional rights. Yet it is undeniable that some hairstyles virtually preclude the possibility of gaining employment in some establishments, the big emotional arguments notwithstanding. Ultimately the decision lies with the individual to weigh the options of dressing in a particular way against losing out on some choice opportunities. It is nice to act bold and be a trend setter, especially for a male carrying around paraphernalia like earrings, nose rings, gold teeth, cornrows and markings previously identified with females. It is a rather strange twist of events that as women fought and got the equality they asked for, more and more men are now seen adopting what was once female traits.

But there is a price to pay for such pace setting, at least by the individual harbinger, until such a time that the practice becomes main stream. Should one go to a job interview with nose rings? The answer may be yes and no at the same time. Job coaches and career counselors express reservations about body accessories and body language that speaks of defiance and rebellion against the status quo. They agree that it is important for individuals to express themselves any way they want (dreadlocks, nose rings, tattoos of all types, tongue piercings) but quickly add that out there, 50% or more of the people will not hire persons who present with such outfits. Being true to oneself can be quite nice but being aware that there are consequences is much nicer still. Hiring managers can and do raise their own objections about recruiting persons who manifest their sociopolitical beliefs in certain visible ways that may offend mainstream decorum. Obviously an enterprise involved with promoting fashion, such as a beauty saloon, will have no objection to such bodily ornamentations but in a corporate climate that places a high premium on customer tastes, such extras may pose problems for the organization. Also, in many interviews, it is not what is said that matters; often it is what was left unsaid that determines the fate of an applicant who failed to make the maximum use of those five senses, erroneously called a sixth sense. Not only hiring managers scout the Internet for inappropriate outfits put forth by young persons obsessed with their invincibility. FBI and CIA agents are constantly on the lookout too. Those weird rings, tattoos, obsession with time off, money, can all hurt one's job prospects. All the crazy things that go into Face book can hurt in later life if not immediately – threatening commentary about the president, false statements about a landlord or apartment, fake sickness turned into vacation or pornography sessions, drunken photograph of oneself - can come back to school authorities with devastating consequences. How often have constituents watched in disbelief as the favorite elected representative threw in the towel over some disreputable behavior caught in Facebook, Craigslist or similar social network site? Why risk it?

It is possible to disguise some objectionable traits during an interview but what happens when these resurface after landing the much sought after employment? How long can a chain smoker keep the practice a secret? Old habits die hard. One of such impostors was spotted out and made known to the management of an enterprise by a customer who felt very insulted that the employee arrogantly blew out his mouthful of cigarette smoke into her face. In a world where the customer is king, management did not hesitate to fire the employee on the spot! Taxi men who choke passengers with offensive cigarette smoke inside their taxis fail to realize that they are operating as public a place as restaurants, cafeterias, libraries, buses and others. Besides, some smokers believe that simply throwing away the butt of their lit cigarette before entering an interview, a bus, an office or some public facility is enough to conceal the fact of their offensive practice. How delusional! Drug and alcohol abuse have often fetched the same fate for their victims, converting the once affable Dr. Jekyll to loathsome Mr. Hyde. Body language and body traits are not so difficult to monitor; smart psychologists quickly pick them out in boardrooms, courtrooms and even bedrooms.

Of course the First Amendment to the US Constitution is quite an elegant document and one needs to doff one's hat for the foresightedness of the Founding Fathers. That a document of this nature should provide an answer for persons whose views on one issue can be so diametrically opposed speaks volumes about the wisdom of the Founders. Rick Warren, the man President-elect Barack Obama chose to give the invocation at his January 20, 2009 inaugural was a Christian who held the biblical view that homosexuality is sin. Our First Amendment allowed him that latitude to speak out his mind. And it is the very First Amendment that gays and advocates of gay rights cite when they decry intolerance or disagree freely with the Bible and ask society for tolerance of their chosen lifestyle. Why then was there such furor over Barack Obama's choice of Rick Warren? The separation of religion and state is OK until when one allows an innocent kid to die of a treatable disease with the pretext of preferring prayer instead; at that point the long arm of the law reaches out across that thin line of separation as blind practitioners have learned belatedly.

When Jesse Helms died on July 4, 2008 we all took time off singing the Star-Spangled Banner and reflected over the life of a bigot and his racist tirades and homophobic rants. What a day! The white man was remembered for utterances such as "The Negro cannot count for ever on the kind of restraints that thus far left him free to clog the streets, disrupt traffic and interfere with other men's rights. The government should spend less money on people with AIDS because they got sick as a result of deliberate, disgusting, revolting conduct." Mr. Jesse Helms used the language of cultural politics or freedom "to shrink the State and enhance the interest of ruthless corporate profit-mongering". His was a relic of the past bad old days of creative rhetorical jihadist against the New Deal. Martina Navratilova, a professional tennis star, expressed disgust at the way the corporate world treated women infected with this dreadful disease although her furor was more pronounced because of the way Mighty Johnson was embraced. She spoke very bitterly against the double standard that encouraged people and businesses to embrace Mighty Johnson after he openly acknowledged that he had contacted AIDS through profligate unprotected sexual intercourse, adding, "If it had happened to a heterosexual woman who had been with 100 or 200 men, they would call her a whore or a slut and corporations would drop her like a lead balloon."

Lurid details of New York's Governor, Eliot Spitzer's cavorting with a certain hooker named Kristen and his wife's humiliation dominated the headline news for over a week. While the ordinary American saw the hooker as having brought down the governor, her views were that the governor had brought her down instead and Playboy magazine was more than pleased to transform her from call girl to cover girl, presumably against a fat paycheck. Sex really sells. The disgraced governor would most certainly be meeting with his attorneys to seek a defense against prosecution sure to follow in view of the gargantuan amounts of money alleged to have been involved in his escapades with the prostitution ring. Like former Detroit Mayor Kwame Kilpatrick who was also involved in an affair with his chief of staff, plenty of corruption in his administration (testimony of a lawyer and police whistleblower the Detroit Free Press), and like former US President Bill Clinton, Eliot Spitzer was a Democrat and the popular press was accused of downplaying his party affiliation, quite unlike what had happened to Mark Foley or Larry Craig, whose first names were virtually synonymous with "Republican."

Democrats or Republicans, the outcome remained the same –powerful people who could virtually have any woman of their choice with a simple beck and call, often fell prey to tantalizing young women involved with prostitution. As the famous Henry Kissinger once put it, power is indeed the ultimate aphrodisiac. But more curious than the oversight of their political leanings, was the wider notion of ostracizing only the men for a game which obviously involved women as well. It surely takes two to tango. What was the logic of downplaying the role of the women in those lurid affairs? Why arrest only the buyers of contraband goods but not the sellers? Would those give peaceful sleep to Martina Navratilova? Probably not.

America may still be a nation decisively shaped by religious faith but its politics and culture are much less influenced by arguments of a Christian character the way it used to be five or more years ago. Many Christians seem to have discovered the virtues of a separation of church and state and the protection of "garden of the church" from "the wilderness of the world" as Roger William, founder of Rhode Island as a haven for religious dissenters, once put it. Conservative Christians seem to have lost the battles over issues of abortion, school prayer and same-sex marriage in this post-Christian phase of the nation. A rising number of unaffiliated Americans prefer to call themselves spiritual rather than religious. The moral teaching of Christianity has no doubt exerted great influence on western civilization; as moral teaching fades, a secular morality is bound to take its place, even if its contours are not quite clear. Could the nation be waiting for some sort of national disaster to strike to reverse this trend? The post 9/11 flag carrying by Americans has vanished the way praying vanishes after our problems are solved. Gone are the days when every roof top, dumpster, car dealership, car and other items of the American landscape were adorned with the striped US flag, when we hummed the Star-Spangled Banner at home and at work like karaoke practitioners. Does this correlate with the diminished religious zeal as people move away from tragic events?

It is clear that nationhood for Americans has certainly been shaped and influenced more by the ideals of liberty than those of religion. In this twenty-first century Americans are held together by the value of freedom and free enterprise and the propensity to lean towards libertarianism on personal morality. The foundation documents of our nation are the Declaration of Independence and the Constitution, not the bible even if there are obvious connections.

*John S. Dinga*

James Madison and Thomas Jefferson surely saw the virtue of guaranteeing liberty of conscience, hence they created a republic where religion and politics do mix but not church and state. Could this perhaps explain the trend we are witnessing?

# 5.

## The Challenges Ahead - II

To appreciate the magnitude of the problem facing America's new president outside of the US, it was instructive to take a look at the reactions to his victory in the 2008 presidential election. International reaction was ecstatic. In El Salvador, legions of jubilant supporters set off firecrackers as their counterparts danced in the streets of Liberia, Nigeria, Cameroon and Ghana, or drank shots in Obama City, Japan. Kenya declared a national holiday called Obama Day and South Africa's Desmond Tutu exulted "We have a new spring in our walk and our shoulders are straighter." The Archbishop spoke for millions of silent sufferers on the black continent. Among many things President Obama would have to do for the continent of his forebears would be to mobilize all foreign policy muscles and what Secretary of State Hillary Clinton called smart policies and restore healthy competitive democracy in Africa as well as make it possible for the International Criminal Court (ICC) to have teeth. The ICC badly needs a police force to implement its rulings. If Laurent Nkounda, the warlord of Eastern Congo slept with the ICJ's list of war crimes by his side, it shows to what extent those presiding over the continent and its many AK-47 democracies fear for their ultimate fate. The Lord's Resistance Army that started as an Acholi affair in northern Uganda has swept amoeba-like across the continent through southern Sudan to the Central African

Republic and regions beyond, spewing death and destruction and horror, presenting President Obama and his administration a special challenge. Will he or will he not work with other world leaders and put an end to this menace that has been a stain on the black continent for well over 25 years?

The visit by ICC-indicted Sudanese president Hassan Omar el-Bashir in response to an invitation from his Chadian counterpart and former foe, Idriss Deby showed the powerlessness of the court. The ICC intends to try president el-Bashir for war crimes, crimes against humanity and possible genocide in the Darfur region of his country but apparently both Sudanese and Chadian leaders considered the normalization of cross border relations between their two countries of more importance than anything else. Asked why Chad, a signatory of the Rome Statute and founding document of the ICC, should so flagrantly violate the commitment to arrest and handover for trial a man on the watch list of the court, a spokesperson for Chad said his country had done so simply because the Court unfairly targeted only third world leaders for trial, leaving similar suspects elsewhere to go scot free. Very revealing indeed! Who would he have in mind - the former flamboyant Liberian president, Charles Taylor whose impending trial for deals in blood diamond threatened to smear supermodel Naomi Campbell, an alleged beneficiary of nocturnal diamond gifts from the man accused of being the kingpin and underwriter of Sierra Leone's civil war even as he claims his role was peace broker? And then Kenya too invited the Sudanese leader! Possibly the Chadian spokesperson had in mind, not just blood diamonds, but also things like blood gold, blood timber, blood oil or blood Coltrane.

That would include the accomplices of the third world leaders such as the manufacturers of arms, cell phones, computers and all those electronic gadgets that fund the interminable war in lawless eastern Congo. Because of tin, tungsten and tantalum the people of Bukavu have been reduced to mere sub-humans to be treated as playthings by powerful and well funded militia foraging for conflict minerals. Ever since the 1994 genocide in Rwanda, the FDLR (democratic forces for the liberation of Rwanda?) moved in to form a weird alliance with Congolese militia, raping women, the backbone of what is left of that part of the world and subjugating them in the quest for wealth. And the world's top electronic manufacturers are keeping those murderous armies in business.

Nelson Mandela remains a rare breed of African leader. Here was a man who spent one quarter of his useful life in prison, came out and did not utter a single word of revenge. Quite apart from not seeking reelection the way his homologues are wont to do, President Mandela is on record as admitting that even though his country had natural resources like gold, diamond and the rest, he valued human resources by far more than the natural ones. How many of Africa's life-presidents can claim as much? How many former presidents would go out of their way to rescue their citizens trapped in foreign prisons the way Jimmy Carter and Bill Clinton did for US citizens caught in Kim Jong Il's North Korea? How many would be prepared to cut short their pleasure trips abroad to spend the time, energy and money Chile's President Sebastain Pinera spent to rescue his country's miners trapped for over two months half a mile underground? President Obama has a golden opportunity to revise the nature of bilateral ties between the US and most of these nations that have pushed their citizens to the wall, all because their leaders, pompously called stalwart allies, receive loyalty payments from the US, turn around and subject their citizens to bloody oppression and press muzzling and in the long run, become real liabilities and moral dilemmas for America. The kind of revolutionary upheavals seen on the streets of Sidi Bouzid in Tunisia yesterday, Cairo, Alexandria and Suez in Egypt today, (and who knows where next – Yemen, Libya, Gabon tomorrow?) are the translations of peaceful change denied over many decades, leaving the ordinary citizen no choice but to take to the streets. It is not far-fetched to imagine that in Morocco the monarchy sleeps with one eye wide open.

## *Cautious Optimism in the third World.*

The impending trial at the ICC would seek to connect the dots between that painful civil war in Sierra Leone, Charles Taylor and the RUF rebels, weapons, the blood diamonds and a supermodel unwittingly caught sitting next to Charles Taylor at Nelson Mandela's dining table. Could Chad's spokesperson have had in mind Rwanda's President Paul Kagame whose regime looks so attractive to the west yet is feared by nationals who dare not voice dissent within? The unanswered question remains why Rwanda refuses to let the searchlight in if things are as rosy as her foreign minister claimed to a BBC investigative reporter. The disquiet lingers on concerning the shooting of a former head of the Rwandan army in South Africa, followed by the mysterious murder of the journalist investigating that shooting. Can and should any leader of contemporary Africa live with such dark clouds? President Kagame, like Hosni Mubarak and many other homologues, may win elections by 99% but the real challenge is what a Nigerian compatriot enunciated as getting rid of Rwanda's post-genocide authoritarian complex that makes it impossible for dissident voices to be heard. Rwanda threatened to quit the peace keeping duties in Darfur if the United Nations published its findings on investigations of the Rwanda genocide. What a bind! What a hypocrisy! And what a blackmail! If it was bad for the UN to abandon Rwanda during the 1994 genocide, how good can it be for Rwanda now to threaten abandoning Southern Sudan? Monolithic rule has stymied all healthy competition from academics through economics and on to politics with the resultant stagnation that is driving hordes and hordes of citizens to seek refuge in foreign lands.

By solving one problem, both Chadian and Sudanese leaders ended up raising the specter of another more serious one, a definite challenge for the Obama team and the world as a whole. Names like Radovan Karadzic of Serbia, Manuel Noriega of Panama, Saddam Hussein and Tareq Aziz of Iraq, Mohammad Mosaddegh of Iran and Comrade Duch, the Khmer Rouge executioner probably do not yet convey any mental image for their African homologues. When umbrellas like Khmer Rouge, Revolutionary United Front, and others are lifted, only names of individual actors remain to answer before courts. But how many of today's leaders with bloodied hands ever think of this scenario?

From Sudan through Somalia, Kenya, Uganda, Rwanda, Congo, Zimbabwe, Cameroon, Nigeria, Chad, Ivory Coast, all the way to the new strongman, Moussa Camara's Guinea Conakry, leaders know what can befall them in their unrestrained use of the Kalashnikov in governance, forced labor to extract blood or conflict minerals like the three t's (tin, tungsten and tantalum which is locally known as Coltrane), so priced by cell phone manufacturers, all of which help fuel the wars. It is here that the suffering masses of the continent yearn and expect Secretary of State Hillary Clinton's smart policies (help break the supply chains, leverage the consumers of the bloody products) to be put to use to redeem them. It may sound ironic but when George W. Bush first launched his operation in 2003 to boot out Saddam Hussein, more than one African voice was raised asking the US president to come help them overthrow their local Saddam Husseins as well.

And who would these local Saddam Husseins be? Most of them are second generation leaders who came to the helm after the first crop of independence leaders had made way. Many of them had studied and acquired sound education in the west – Sorbonne, London, Ottawa, Harvard and others, sanctioned by Bachelors, Masters and sometimes Doctoral degrees in areas like education, science, religion, economics, politics, psychology and the rest, but upon returning home, fell back on the old ways of hereditary monarchy clothed in a veneer of democracy and democratic language. Some turned economics into voodoo economics while others converted their knowledge of psychology - which seeks to demystify the unknown - into magic, thereby doing the very opposite. Those with law degrees gladly accepted appointments in the judiciary where they provided useful underpinning for what happens in the executive, especially during elections when incumbency becomes a powerful tool against the opposition. The resulting alchemy has meant stagnation (officially known as stability), chronic penury, suffering, deprivation, corruption, graft, brain drain and the drift of talent to more affluent societies across the seas and deserts.

Leaders straddling two rich cultures with two worldviews can be a blessing or a curse. For most of the modern leaders it was the curse that they brought to their people. How else can one explain the succession of one Gnassingmbe by another in Togo, one Bongo by another in Gabon, and one Kabila by another in the DRC, and still in the pipeline Hosni Mubarak by Gamal Mubarak in Egypt, octogenerian Abdoulaye Wade of Senegal by his son, possibly after the third mandate he is said to be gunning for, Muamar Kadaffi of Libya by his son in the wings, ready to step in at any moment, and Paul Biya of Cameroon anxiously waiting to give his son Frank the royal nod? The list is long. Even where military force was used to oust the ruling strong man(Nigeria, Ghana, Equatorial Guinea, Uganda, Libya, Algeria, Egypt, Chad, Sudan, Rwanda, Burkina Faso, Cape Verde and more) the scenario was no different.

The imbroglio in Ivory Coast illustrates what took place in Zimbabwe, Kenya, Cameroon and elsewhere in independent Africa. Former UN Secretary-General, Kofi Anan may well formulate his wish that Southern Sudan seceding from the mother country should be an exception rather than the rule. That is only a wish. Unfortunately the realities in the field are a far cry from such wishful thinking. Judged by utterances from Southern Sudanese returning home for their long awaited referendum and the 99% result of their voting, it is clear that they were fed up with being relegated to second class status and the yearning for their own country said it all. With Houphouet Boigny's departure from the scene and the language of entrenched Laurent Gbagbo pointing to Alassane Ouattara and his supporters as lacking the quality of *Ivoirité*, who knows what will happen next? Did Somaliland not break away from the mother country? And did equally disgusted English- speaking Cameroon not file a petition in Banjul and the UN? As long as this virus exists, that some persons can, without consequence, arrogate to themselves the prerogative of calling the shots and virtually shutting out other deserving citizens from national affairs, Kofi Anan's wish will remain just that – a wish.

In Sri Lanka, former general Sarath Fonseka, hailed as hero for leading the successful military campaign that ended the prolonged Tamil tiger rebellion of over thirty years, decided to try his vast popularity at the polls by challenging incumbent president, Mahinda

Rajapaksa. Poor thing! He was court marshaled for playing politics with military uniform on and for violating a military procurement procedure, charges he claimed were politically motivated, a euphemism for tasting of the forbidden fruit of challenging the strongman at the helm. The man could very well have shot his way to the presidency like his homologues had done elsewhere. Still he could be considered lucky for still being alive; elsewhere people in a similar situation would be six feet deep in their graves. Embracing modern leadership and applying outdated methods of governance could never ever deliver the goods for a people looking to the future. Unfortunately for the opponents of these other Saddam Husseins, there was no oil in their lands to warrant George Bush sticking out his neck. The quest for cheap oil explains the presence of American troops in Saudi Arabia in support of an absolute monarchy, one of the reasons that miffed and pushed citizen Osama bin Laden to unleash his suicide bombers on New York City's WTC. As for Egypt, providing a buffer at the Gaza to enable Israel to sleep with one eye closed over the years was seen as a good investment.

Retarding the development of African nations has become quite trendy indeed as unelected officials or those who gain the presidency through dubious means lord it over their compatriots. It can be seen in Zimbabwe under Robert Mugabe's iron rule. A similar scenario was witnessed in Nigeria under the late president, Yar'Adua flown to Saudi Arabia for medical care and brought back in bad shape after three months of unsuccessful treatment, leaving Africa's most populous nation without a clear leader because nothing in the texts gave full powers to the vice president. President Omar Bongo died in a Barcelona hospital after a long illness; Houphouet Boigny of Ivory Coast was rushed home from France in a very vegetative form to die in his palace at Yamoussoukro. Over and over rumors filtered home – mercifully only rumors - to Cameroon about the death of President Paul Biya in France one day, in Geneva another day and so forth, always abroad, prompting many a citizen to wonder aloud why the leaders could not avail themselves of the resources at home. From Egypt in the north to Zimbabwe in the south and from Kenya in the east to Morocco in the west, the average age of

African presidents stands at eighty years, compared to less than fifty for their equivalents in the developed world. If age alone could guarantee development and a happy life for the population, Africa's citizens would have no cause to complain. If African leaders actually invested in their own countries and peoples the way they should, would there be any need to go out for medical treatment or to get foreign degrees conferred upon them when their home institutions could very well do the job? But alas! Politics is not a means to an end; it is virtually an end in itself as incumbents and their alliances manipulate the constitution with all sorts of arcane methods just to run again for office or to continue to stay in power even after they lose at the polls. Politics and democracy are systematically being eroded of their essence, paving the way for unavoidable anarchy.

For some reason Africa's leaders from north to south and from east to west invariably consider themselves providential rulers of the people. At the height of his reign, Alhaji Amadou Ahidjo of Cameroon said *"Après moi, c'est le deluge"* (after me there will be chaos). He left the scene without a shot being fired and Cameroon did not quite become extinct. His Excellency Hosni Mubarak of Egypt echoed a similar message –"if I quit, it would be chaos" – as pressure mounted on him to end his thirty-year oppressive rule. Asked to step down, Mubarak instead stepped aside and made room for Omar Suleiman, his appointee to take the reins of power. Unlike his Tunisian homologue who took the cue and left the scene discreetly, Egypt's strongman continued to implacably defy popular opinion, using first policemen who soon vanished into thin air, and then thugs on horse and camel back. But those were no match for the large number of determined protesters with shoe soles raised in disgust and directed at the besieged president. President Mubarak hoped to wear out the street protesters with time, prompting one observer to conclude that those the gods wish to destroy, they first make mad. Dictators hate the free press and will stop at nothing to muzzle them because the press keeps reminding them of who they really are and of basic lessons they easily forget that whoever pays the piper dictates the tunes. President Mubarak's talk of "foreign powers dictating events in his country" sounded so hollow but Egyptians understood that it is not an easy task to walk away from a yearly American subsidy of $1.5 billion. Where others use the nation's GDP or opinion polls to gauge the degree of popular support, providential rulers gag the press and use persons, able and willing to shamelessly put aside all trappings of academia and play modern day Goebbels with relish or praise singers who lavish them with encomiums *ad nauseum*. Some outwit their rivals by showing photo shots of handshakes they had made – with Bill Clinton or Nelson Mandela to validate illegitimacy! Their smart supporters quickly realize that presidential decrees, not the academic degrees against their names go many more miles along the road to the elusive nirvana.

Like all dictators President Mubarak had relied on the psychological barrier of fear to subjugate his people and like them he had committed the monumental error of blocking not only al-Jazeera but also the social network, Facebook. Overnight he had to cope with not a handful of journalists but hundreds of thousands of freelancers and twitterers who had met on the Facebook page of 30-year-old Wael Ghonim, an executive of Google Inc. That page which had been set up as a tool to expose and share photos and videos of police brutality that led to the death of Khaled Said became the tool for organizing the overthrow of Egypt's long serving dictator! Wael Ghonim thanked Facebook founder, Mark Zuckerberg on behalf of all Egyptians for making the revolution possible.

It is easy to disqualify an opposition candidate for presidential election using any number of interpretations or modifications of the country's constitution for the purpose – inadequate stay at home or lack of a national identity card (Alassane Ouattara of Ivory Coast, Muhammed El- Baradei of Egypt, Wyclef Jean of Haiti) and many others. In Kazakhstan, a former Soviet republic, the ruling strong man went as far as introducing a spelling and grammar test for opponents wishing to run against him. What a smart way of making the electoral commission to block all the Russian-speaking rivals! Blocking persons who had served not only their countries but also the international community has been particularly distressing for Alassane Ouattara and Muhammed El- Baradei. The former, using his external experience and connections, actually bailed Ivory

Coast out of difficult financial straits and even went on to serve as prime minister under the first president, Houphouet Boigny before being manipulated out of power, while the latter served honorably as director-general of IAEA, the world's nuclear watchdog. Today Alassane Ouattara has returned to Ivory Coast, run for the presidency, won but once again, the same forces are at play. As the nation held its breath for the election commission to declare the winner, a supporter of incumbent President Laurent Gbagbo is said to have snatched the results and torn them to pieces just as they were going to be announced to the nation and the world. Why did he do that? Figures don't lie; only liars figure out what to do to falsify them. The world watched in animated suspense what would happen to Ivory Coast after the independent electoral commission's Youssouf Bakayoko declared Alassane Ouattara the winner, while Professor Paul Yas Ndre, a Laurent Gbagbo appointee and president of the Constitutional Council declared Laurent Gbagbo the victor, placing that African nation in an unenviable position with two presidents and two parallel governments.

But questions were also raised about the comportment of the president of the independent electoral commission. Why, for example, did he not respect the 72 hour deadline for declaring the results and, more damaging, why did he choose to declare the results at the Golf Hotel, the headquarters of one of the candidates? And what authority did the international community of observers have in proclaiming either candidate the victor? Both were sworn in as Ivory Coast's head of state even as the international community (ECOWAS, EU, and UN) turned its back on the incumbent by recognizing Ouattara's victory. It was a gratifying stance and the continent's suffering masses saluted such unambiguous message. Shots were fired and rumors said there were deaths. It became clear why one month earlier a military officer was caught shopping for arms in California. It also became clear why so many persons resort to armed struggle in Africa; courts and their appointees are virtually at the beck and call of incumbent presidents. Just as cowardly soldiers use human shields when confronting their enemies, unpopular leaders facing sanctions often claim that sanctions hurt the ordinary citizens more. How sad!

Would former South African president, Thabo Mbeki use the famous Kofi Anan formula – African solution to an African problem – to bring about a power-sharing between loser and winner in Ivory Coast? But Raila Odinga of Kenya had warned about the dangers of obliging him to share milk with the one who stole his cow. Kenya is still not out of the woods. In view of the experience in Ivory Coast can the Independent Electoral Commission (IEC) so clamored for by opposition parties be the panacea against election fraud in the Black Continent? Surely not, if a judge of the Constitutional Court can simply toss out the IEC's report, cook up his own and declare the incumbent (his employer!) the winner. Such practices are not a rarity. In some countries the popular sport, soccer has suffered similar fates. On the field of play, a referee can declare a team winner before spectators but in the confines of offices, bureaucrats have been known to reverse such victories by use of arcane formulas, often sending out less qualified teams to represent the nation at international contests. As long as there is no separation of powers, and as long as Supreme Court or Constitutional Court judges remain at the beck and call of incumbent presidents, all that such incumbents do is wink at their appointees and the results of an election can be tossed into the waste basket and new results cooked up like magic. Not being asked is the role China may be playing in Ivory Coast's unfolding drama. And lots of Gbagbo supporters are not hard to find even as the African union pompously talked of forcing him out of office, the type of talk typical of paper tigers. Which African nation would be able to throw that first proverbial stone?

As the world waited prayerfully for Laurent Gbagbo to vacate the Ivorian presidency and let Alassane Ouattara take over peacefully so as to minimize collateral damage, the incumbent was in no mood to move and was soon overtaken by events in Tunisia. On December 17, 2010 a young unemployed Mohamed Bouazizi was selling fresh fruit and vegetables to make ends meet. Officials of his town prevented him from doing so on the streets of Sidi Bouzid without permission. That was the last straw! Young Mohamed Bouaziz set himself ablaze and died, triggering a crisis which ended with the flight of strongman Zine al-Abidine Ben Ali to exile in Saudi Arabia after France refused him landing rights. Rising food prices, a muffled press, stifled democracy and constitutional amendment to perpetuate Ben Ali's stay in power had pushed the ordinary citizens to the wall.

Next door, Egyptians were taking due note and thanking their Tunisian neighbors for showing them the light by initiating action that would send shock waves throughout the Middle East and Africa. Their turn came fast and subsequent events gave meaning to the expression "beginning of the end" as massive pressure from street protesters, western allies and the Egyptian army pushed to bring an end to Mubarak's thirty-year authoritarian rule. Ordinary Egyptians took to the streets and Tahrir Square (their own Tiananmen) in protest, asking President Mubarak to go. Thirty years at the presidency was too much, they chanted. The besieged president responded with some sort of speech, appointed Omar Suleiman, one of his close confidants as vice president and promised reforms. Unimpressed, the protesters stayed put especially as the armed forces command had declared that their demand was legitimate. Washington found itself in a most uncomfortable situation. Over the years successive US presidents made strategic coziness with dictatorships a key to stability in the Middle East, a bulwark against radical Islam and a friend to Israel, dispensing as much as $1.5 billion annually to Egypt in military and economic aid, an amount second only to the annual grant for Israel. Well before Julian Assange's whistle blowing in *WikiLeaks*, US diplomats were repulsed at government greed in the region and had no illusions about the dictatorships that wielded power for decades over the people. Heavy reliance on oil from Saudi Arabia and other Gulf States cost dearly. Thirty years ago Jimmy Carter went down in history as the American president who lost Iran, an American ally to Revolutionary Islamic Republic. Would Barack Obama go down a similar path, losing Turkey, Lebanon and Egypt? Should American support go to an old ally vomited by his people or to those on the streets enamored of America's message of democracy, human rights and freedoms?

Yemen and Sudan were also said to have joined in the dance after Egypt but not much was being said about the details, except the lone voice of Yemen's Lena Sinjap heard over the BBC after her kidnap and release, ostensibly to preempt planning a revolution. Algerian citizens too began to stir. Africa was at last on the move. Down the armpit of the continent and drawing inspiration from Ivory Coast and Tunisia, Andre Mba Obame declared himself winner of Gabon's August 2009 presidential elections, appointed a 19-member cabinet, called upon his Gabonese countrymen to rise up Tunisian style and expel Ali Bongo Ondimba who was virtually continuing his late father's 41$^{st}$ year at the helm. He immediately sought sanctuary at the United Nation's compound in Libreville. Could a tsunami sweep from Egypt across the Sahara and the Sahel down to the Kalahari and Indian Ocean?

Addressing the Obama administration some time ago, a certain Walang Abang, self-styled son of Africa was quite forthright saying, "Most of us thought and still do firmly think that you are like the Messiah who had come to wipe tears from the eyes of those who weep, give food to those who starve, medicine to those who are sick, shelter to those with no home, hope to those who fear and doubt, and correction to those who commit crimes with impunity against the common man."

*Crime against the common man*! *Impunity*! Those are words pregnant with meaning for the African from West Coast to East Coast, words that bring to mind Peter Perkins's *Confessions of an Economic Hit Man*, that behind the repeated uprisings in Ogoniland in Nigeria, the chronic penury in Cameroon, Kenya's starvation in the midst of plenty, Congo's interminable wars and many others, there were evil hands at work, using the knowledge of economic forecast and capitalist manipulation to render entire nations chronically destitute. Projects were schemed at making a few wealthy families in receiving countries and assuring long term fiscal dependence of the host country and therefore political loyalty of their governments. The larger the loans, the better. Debt burdens placed on any country would deprive its poorest citizens of health, education and social services for decades. The GNP might grow even when it profited only one person, such as the owner of a utility company, and even if a majority of the population was burdened with debt. The rich got richer and the poor poorer even as from a statistical point of view, this was recorded as economic progress. Where then do the authors of such schemes get two legs to stand on and criticize the resulting illegal immigration into the United States and elsewhere?

Good governance becomes an empty cliché when there is a climate of criminality and offenders are able to get away with impunity. Such societies are notorious for gagging the press. Under other skies the press acts as the immune system, ferreting bad elements by focusing searchlights on them and getting rid of them through court action or other means of social control. Obviously once press freedom has been compromised, the coast is clear for perpetrators of heinous crimes to go on the rampage, using hired praise singers, divide-and-rule tactics supplemented by willing and able hands of thugs where necessary. Ignorance being such a useful tool for keeping citizens in the dark, everything is done to promote it by bestowing undeserved gratifications that make the pursuit of education both an inconvenience and a waste of time. Why go for hard work that pays dividends only in the distant future whereas laziness offers immediate benefits? It is clear that those choosing the latter option end up with spouses of the same mindset whose only meaningful contribution is to serve as baby factories, often dying prematurely in the process of unplanned procreation.

It is incredible that a small triangular country like Cameroon, once known as Africa's success story, is today languishing in a hard to define type of economic lethargy. A country once proud to be the breadbasket of the sub-region is today unrecognizable as its citizens are crushed by poverty, apathy and inertia. And yet Cameroon is the very country that gave Argentina's Diego Armando Maradona a run at the 1986 World Cup competitions in soccer, the one country that came to the aid of the UK when she slaughtered all of her cattle in response to bovine encephalitis (mad cow disease), and filled the world quota for cocoa when Ivory Coast first got plunged into civil war.

The gross domestic product is usually defined as the ratio of a country's total production of goods and services to its overall population. The enlightened citizen knows that the value of such a ratio will decrease as the denominator (population and associated consumption) increases, which is usually the case, without a corresponding increase in the numerator (production). How many of the host nation's nationals are involved with drawing up such schemes? Often only a token of the ruling strongman's tribesmen, even as qualified sons and daughters undertake the hazardous journeys across deserts and oceans to go and sell their talents and knowledge elsewhere in the developed world. Everything is done to keep the US public in the dark and if possible, encourage utterances like "If they're going to burn the US flag and demonstrate against our embassy, why don't we just get out of their damn country and let them wallow in their own poverty?" Nice proposition except that *their own poverty* is artificially created by economic hit men and their local partners-in-crime. No wonder Julian Assange and his WikiLeaks saga became an African obsession!

For every $100 of crude oil taken out of a recipient country, an oil company receives $75. Of the remaining $25, 75% goes to paying off the foreign debt that initiated all the contact in the first place. Most of the remainder then goes to pay military and other government expenses, leaving about $2.5 for health, education and programs to help the poor. That is all the poor nationals get out of $100! No wonder the popular disaffection!

The big brains of corporate men, studies division of the World Bank, oblique connection to the NSA, the Peace Corps, candidate's ability to survive in hostile environments and carry out James Bond-type operations in econometrics (economic projections) all lead to the selection of a poor third world country for the purpose of "creating an economy that would soar like a bird." How? Provide loans via massive engineering and construction projects that virtually bankrupt debtor nations and make them permanently beholden to creditors and easy targets for manipulation and favors – military bases, UN votes, access to oil and more. Lord have Mercy! It is clear to see how such phantom schemes by economic hit men can work in countries dominated by one-man rule; the parliaments, if ever any existed at all, having been pocketed by a ruling oligarchy.

In spite of his very full plate, President Obama addressed the Millennium Development Goals of the UN, insisting on a change of approach in the matter of aid and development during these hard times of world-wide economic crisis. Instead of aid that breeds dependency, he proposed a change of paradigm so that help (foreign cash flow) is directed primarily to those who help themselves so as to enhance independence and facilitate the movement from poverty to prosperity. Just what did the American president mean by helping those who help themselves? Of course the fight against corruption, introduction of accountability in public life, institution of the rule of law and democracy would be top on the list. On more than one occasion the new US president emphasized that countries prosper when governments are accountable to the people. But to whom was President Mubarak accountable for the sustained US disbursement of gargantuan amounts of money over the years?

Similar words uttered following the heavy earthquake that devastated the island nation of Haiti, were very pregnant with meaning. President Obama made a commitment to stand by Haiti, a stand which had short and long term implications, given America's internal and external problems. Treading the thin line between disaster and general aid, President Obama, like other politicians aware of the long standing American tradition of reaching out to others in distress, would be acutely aware of the difficult choices once the emergency phase was over and the problem of the autonomy of the local government began to rear its ugly head, when helping began to be seen as meddling, all against a backdrop of domestic needs here in the US – unemployment, healthcare issues, immigration, and others. The same voters, who enthusiastically supported the early relief calls, would sooner or later start whining about all the money and attention going to another country just as champions of zero tax increases vilify their leaders who respond to calls for development funds by raising tax. Such ambivalence has prompted some to wonder aloud whether it is the drunken driver or the ignorant voter that is worse for American society, challenging the rationale for submitting people to a driving test but not a voting one. How would President Obama handle the thorny issue of over thirty thousand illegal immigrants already in the US from Haiti? And the new arrivals occasioned by the earthquake tragedy? Would there be a strong bipartisan reaction to back up claims of "not to be forgotten and not to be forsaken" said of those in distress?

The very way President Obama constituted his cabinet would be expected to send a powerful message to his third world homologues. Indeed it was gratifying to note that he did not draw all of his cabinet incestuously from Hawaii his birthplace or Chicago his new home, the way others in his place would do. Hardly had Obama been heard uttering things like *Chinekeee, Walahi* or similar expressions when confronted with his numerous challenges. The nearest he came to doing so was to say "we screwed up" which is quite mainstream indeed. Those were good signs.

Visiting the Black Continent on his maiden trip after becoming US president, Barack Obama landed in Ghana, next door to Ivory Coast and told the continent in clear terms that Ghana was honored above all other African countries for its example of good governance, where strong institutions were cherished over strong rulers - a powerful reminder to those providential presidents who had presided for a near eternity over the decline of once buoyant economies. Such reminders were greeted with undisguised euphoria in countries like Nigeria, whose president had virtually held the parliament hostage and paralyzed governmental machinery during his three months of absence for reasons of health, Zimbabwe where a transitional arrangement between ZANU-PF and Morgan Tsvangirai's party was teetering on the brink of collapse, or Kenya where Mzee Mwai Kibaki and Raila Odinga were having a hard time deciding on who had more powers to dismiss a minister suspected of embezzlement of public funds. The presidency had virtually become a giant patronage machine at the disposal of whoever found himself at the helm. Africa's model of governance - postulated, enunciated and popularized by the metaphor *"sharing of the national cake (pie)"*- has obviously outlived its usefulness and needs to be jettisoned for something better and more realistic to the times. Will new leaders rise to the challenge and be counted in the fight against the distribution of favors in governance?

Africa poses a special challenge for those committed to its development and growth. In a world clamoring for greater and more productive unions (European Union, ASEAN, NAFTA, Commonwealth, La Francophonie, etc.), the OAU which shed its name and became the African Union, remains a rotating venue where leaders meet to tap each other on the back for surviving a coup d'Etat, winning the continental soccer trophy or some platitude. Nothing concrete is ever realized in the way of true economic cooperation that can bring their peoples together for the prosperity and growth so advocated by President Obama. The once prosperous East African Community died long ago, ECOWAS and ECCAS remain just paper tigers, and the island nations (Madascar, Cape Verde, Equatorial Guinea, Mauritius, and Zanzibar) remain just that – islands in a world where none is supposed to be an island. I get the feeling people of Cape Verde, Mauritius, Equatorial Guinea, Madagascar and the other island neighbors of the Black Continent pay only lip service to the OAU, their leaders being the main actors known to ever get together for anything at all. Why so?

It is said that when the OAU (Organization of African Unity) was being inaugurated in Addis Ababa in 1963, President Philibert Tsiranana suggested that the organization's title should be expanded to include the words "and Malagasy" after "African" but that his homologues curtly told him that if the Malagasy didn't consider their state African, they had no place in the organization at all. And it is known that the very President Tsiranana, either expressing the detachment of his country from, or poking fun at the Black Continent's troubles, once said, "If the *Bon Dieu* proposed to me that Madagascar should be rejoined to the African continent, I would ask him to let it remain an island."

The stagnation and chronic underdevelopment of Africa is invariably blamed on the slave trade, colonialism and colonial practices, apartheid and other factors with little or no mention of the role played by the continent's own internal or innate attitudes and practices that resist change in an ever-changing world. The gullibility of persons to some absurd beliefs of ancestral worship or the tendency to swallow hook and sinker the pronouncement of one's tribesman, son of the soil, leader advocating half-baked ideas totally at odds with the reality of the times, cuts across the continent. Travel is a problem within each country either because of bad roads or man-made barriers erected by extortionists with or without uniform; traveling from one country to another is for another time. Ibos, Bakongos, Xhosas, Kikuyus, Hausas are all tied down by the powerful hands of the past. The commerce of minds will flourish once ignorance is taken away, internal road networks improved and the country itself is linked to neighboring countries in the region. It is bad enough that a citizen cannot lead; it is worse when such a citizen cannot also follow good leadership.

The colonial experience was bad but surely there was a silver lining too. In a world where it has become fashionable to beat the chest and talk in terms of cultural revival, very little is done to come up with a lingua franca that can meet the challenges of the new millennium. European languages – French, Spanish, Portuguese, German and English – came to the black continent through colonial conquest. At independence the languages did not go away with the colonizers but stayed on and were taken over and made part of the new nations' convenience and culture. That was pragmatic. The continent's writers have availed themselves of the colonial languages and made the very best use of them, earning prestigious prizes, including the Nobel Prize, in the former colonial capitals. From Kenya in the far east of the continent (Wangari Maathai) to Nigeria and Ghana in the west(Wole Soyinka, Kofi Anan), and from Egypt in the extreme north (Naguib Mahfouz, Mohamed El-Baradei) to the southern tip of Africa (Nadine Gordimer, Albert Lutuli, J. M. Coetzee, Desmond Tutu, Nelson Mandela) the continent has been well represented. Similarly, the emerging nations adopted soccer, a foreign game, played by the rules and with commitment, rising to competitions at world cup level, to the admiration of the rest of the world. But when it came to matters of politics, democracy, human rights and freedoms, there was a lamentable shift into reverse gear. The same forces that embraced the above imported models began to speak derogatively of democracy and freedom of speech even as they cruised around in imported cars.

Large chunks of the continent continue to be tied down by the powerful hands of the past. Politicians turn to witchcraft, traditional lures and voodoo economics as a matter of course in their struggle to win elections and rule their people. In the nineteenth century Nongqause, a Xhosa woman claimed to have been told in a vision that if her people gave up witchcraft, killed their cattle and razed their maize crop in sacrifice, on February 18, 1857, two blood red suns would appear, and a hurricane would sweep the whites back to the sea by which they had come, new herds and fields of maize would grow and all the Xhosa warriors that had died in wars would live again. Her people were engaged in an unwinnable war against a formidable enemy armed with modern guns against their ox hide shields and assegai, modern European technology pitted against a pastoral society's only solution – mystery and the need for a miracle. The people were led to do what Nongqause's vision had asked for. The consequence was 67000 deaths from starvation as the two suns failed to appear and whites were not swept into the ocean on the day in question. Those who managed to survive did so by finding their way to the Cape Colony to beg for food and employment from the whites (Nadine Gordimer, *Telling Times*).

That was in the nineteenth century. In the twentieth century, one of two Nigerian communities trying it out with inter-tribal war came under the spell of a witch doctor who claimed to be able to immunize warriors against death by gunshot using his craft. An entire village submitted to him. In the process of demonstrating how effective his craft had been, promising young fighters were lined up and all gunned down! A little to the east along the same Atlantic coast, albinos of villages around Mount Cameroon usually run for dear life as local tradition responds to ancestral calls, hunting them down for sacrifice during earthquakes, especially if the mountain erupts spewing lava along its slope. Each community in every country has its peculiar way of turning to the past or to witchcraft and magic in times of difficulty – famine, epidemics, droughts, floods, wars, elections and others.

And talking about epidemics the continent remains in denial as AIDS does havoc to its population. Complicating this picture is what to do with the new fad of homosexuality and persons in the GBLT community in search of recognition. While other countries are making timid efforts to accommodate GBLT communities, Africa remains implacably against it, which makes the control of the spread of HIV infections very daunting indeed. In the past healthcare providers – doctors, nurses, and pharmacists – asked persons diagnosed with sexually transmitted diseases to go and bring along their consorts for treatment. Timidly they complied and brought husbands, wives, boyfriends or girlfriends, as was the case. But today, with same sex gaining ground, the probability of bringing such a partner is zero, given the stigma and opprobrium associated with homosexuality. Persons are persecuted in any number of ways – imprisonment, public beatings, ostracism, and boycott, abandonment by family and friends and worse. Where parliamentary debate is limited to rubber stamping the budget tabled by the executive, only the judiciary is left to manage the application of whatever laws come to them by way of the decree of the ruling strong man. And so the large and ever increasing number of cases of gonorrhea, syphilis, trichomoniasis, chlamydiasis, AIDS and all the other STDs continue to take their toll against a back drop of bloated defense budgets.

Countries which refuse the democratic option do so for nebulous or selfish reasons, especially when they argue that freedom begets chaos. History teaches that it is the denial of liberty that often ends in conflicts and wars whereas democracy brings about stability. The Swiss know something about this. Supporters of third world dictatorships often hide their selfish motives behind the lame argument that the people are too poor and uneducated to vote intelligently or to abide by any laws, forgetting that persons in economic need also need a political voice. Democracy is hardly a luxury that has to await the arrival of general prosperity; it is a prerequisite to economic growth. Dictators need to be reminded of this, that democracy flourishes when minds are encouraged to explore, produce and to invent. Paul Kagame's Rwanda is a very difficult case. On the one hand, western leaders, typified by visiting French president Nicholas Sarkozy, harboring guilt over the negligence that led to the 1994 genocide, turn a blind eye to the one-party dictatorship that makes it impossible for newspapers to flourish or dissidents to voice their feelings. On the other hand, they also see the need for a modern democratic Rwanda even if its leader is on the watch list of the ICC. How this is possible remains to be seen when a journalist is declared *persona non grata* and expelled from Rwanda simply for sticking to the ethics of his profession and refusing to be dictated news by the president's henchmen instead of gathering and reporting the news the way he was taught in school.

The betrayal of African peoples by those of the World Bank and International monetary Fund, once considered allies, has been quite painful. Half-hearted measures to force the black continent's autocrats and dictators to open up to electoral plurality have failed woefully. It is true that during the cold war the main interest was a cynical practice to give loyalty payments to support autocrats and military dictators with blood on their hands as a way of keeping out communism but the Soviet Union and the Berlin wall have since collapsed, opening the gates for Perestroika and Glasnost (a breath of fresh air) for oppressed peoples all over the world. Why would the World Bank or International monetary Fund continue to turn a blind eye to *de facto* one-party rule and the bloody repressions in Africa today?

Aid giving has always suffered from some strains over the years. Donors in the past said it was necessary to stay clear of governance issues, a euphemism for graft in the receiving nations. Their logic was that raising such topics would bring up the prickly issue of interfering in the internal affairs of independent sovereign states. So soon after independence and with sharp and painful memories of colonialism still fresh, those were understandably no-go areas. And so the World Bank and IMF whose declared raison d'être was to fight poverty, not corruption, kept a respectable distance from monitoring closely the disbursal of the funds they gave out, contending their interest was economic not political, even though it was clear from the start that little, if any, of the funds would reach their targeted destination – the poor. With the passage of time came the glowing realization that financial transparency, human rights and institutional checks and balances mattered very much to the quest for prosperity than had been earlier realized. Belatedly they began to take note of the fact that Africa's big men were in danger of killing their economies and World Bank boss, James Wolfenson of Australia gathered courage and articulated the new approach of no longer tolerating tyrants presiding over failed states. There was no longer any need to blindly support bastard African regimes especially as pillaging and authorized looting with impunity began to hurt more than before. Digging their heels donors began to insist on accountability and multiparty elections and to attach detailed conditions to their money.

Wily presidents responded by playing their own games involving stopping and starting aid projects as trust came and went. It was sad to live the painfully neocolonial experience of pushing aid for Africa but failing to ask searing questions about the quality of leaderships handling the aid just because of the unstated but implied northern hemisphere chauvinism: "*It is Africa. What else can you expect?*" even as activists and protesters gathered in solidarity at Western embassies and chancelleries, expressing righteous indignation and calling for poverty and human rights abuses to end. Even isolated individuals like American actor George Clooney could gather enough chutzpah and boldly recommend that Omar El-Bashir's bank accounts be frozen as a prelude to resolving the intractable problems before the ICC, problems related to genocide in the Darfur region of Sudan as well as the potentially explosive situation facing the international community as the people of oil-rich Abyei – pro-south Ngok Dinka and pro-north Messeriya Arab pastoralists – brace themselves for a plebiscite, ostensibly to pave the way for Africa's newest country.

A condescending and pitying stance was adopted by persons who alleged that excessive enthusiasm in the fight against corruption would somehow undermine the task of fighting poverty. Yet corruption - systemic corruption - is the most efficient factor on the black continent. How sad that such unhelpful views should be held by those supposed to be the allies of the helpless poor in fighting oppressive regimes and one-party dictatorships. How unconscionable can western leaders be in continuing to accept neocolonial servitude from African leaders who are supposed to be their homologues? How comfortable can a French president be in accepting that an African homologue should reduce himself to the subservient status of "meilleur élève" (best pupil)? Wasn't this mentality of the colonized (Franz Fanon: *Black Skin White Masks*) supposed to be a thing of the past where leaders were still intellectually Lilliputians? No wonder the editor of a daily publication, *Le Temps de Genève*, had no qualms at all ridiculing African politicians and participants on the front page of his publication by including "petit nègre" along with federal French, Québécois and Belgian as the operating languages for the 2010 *Francophonie* summit.

And how can religion, the continent's forte, keep such a distressingly respectable distance from the plight of the people? No wonder their lingering skepticism! An Eritrean ambassador to the US, Girma Asmeron, once summarized this skepticism thus: "The white man brought Christianity, the Bible and prayer. He told us to read the Bible and to look up and pray. We did. When we were finished praying and looked down again, our land was gone." That was not all. While some religious missions did their best to uplift the Africans, others were simply content to use their influence to reconcile African people to white domination rather than to encourage them to demand their birthrights as free human beings, prompting Alan Paton (Cry *the Beloved Country*) to make the prophetic declaration that by the time whites turned to loving, blacks would have turned to hating, especially in apartheid South Africa. Did the colonial master promote religion or just used it? This is quite debatable in many quarters but Africans do not doubt that colonialism and religion made very strange bedfellows. Religion was surely used to keep the colonized people subservient as conquest took place, gun in one hand, the Bible in another. Belatedly when it became apparent that colonialism was a deadly scheme doomed to fail, the church washed its hands. Of course it can also be argued that some of the churchmen were hampered by the old pious condemnation they suffered at the hands of those who accused them of meddling in politics. That would be the case with the Reverend Michael Scott, Trevor Huddleston, Bishop Ambrose Reeves, the Reverend Allan Boesak and Archbishop Desmond Tutu. In the darkest of nights there are almost always some bright spots in the sky; fortunately for South Africa, Nelson Mandela and Frederic de Klerk turned out to be those bright spots.

With the rare exception of what the world witnessed recently in Ivory Coast, election monitors usually flew into African capitals on the eve of major elections when the ground work for rigging and other malpractices had been put in place and on the D-day they issued their unconvincing "*free and fair*" reports and shamelessly flew back to watch the country aflame from the safety of their countries! Yes, and most elections invariably ended in arson, looting and all sorts of mayhem, much of which was prepared months in advance – increased sales of *pangas* and *rungus*(machetes and clubs) as in Kenya, shiploads of Chinese arms as in Zimbabwe, nocturnal cash deliveries for the use of those entrusted or empowered to do the dirty job of ballot stuffing among others. Dictators and autocrats hardly lose sleep over their societies' high proportion of youngsters without jobs or prospects in towns, cities and areas perceived as opposition strongholds, deliberately pauperized by official policy, the growing pool of those aptly described by former US ambassador Harriet Isom as "Nothing to lose" people, yet these are those in need of special attention, those who spontaneously rise up and charge when election fraud smells in the air, looting, burning and doing all sorts of smash-and-grab antics in a rare vandalistic orgy of self-enrichment, reducing the city center to a sort of war zone as they empower themselves to do what their government was unwilling or unable to do – redistribute the wealth and achieve the trickle down effect so beloved of the World Bank and International monetary Fund planners.

And this distressing pattern keeps repeating itself from one country to the next and over the years in the entire sub-region. As I put down these notes, thanks to undercover agents, US federal authorities detained an Ivoirian colonel in northern California in connection with gun and ammunition purchases for the presidential elections billed for October 31, 2010. Even though the United Nations had placed an arms embargo on Ivory Coast, officials in that country apparently had no qualms sending out people to smuggle weapons in America and even defending their action. The finance minister, current and former defense minister and now adviser to President Laurent Gbagbo as well as ambassadors were quoted as arguing that government security forces were poorly equipped and outgunned by the forces of the opposition, intent on using violence to influence the outcome of the upcoming presidential election. How did they know? Clearly both sides would be considering access to power by bullets rather than ballots cast. So if this were official, why would its animators act in the shadows in trying to procure guns and ammunition worth $3.8 million using a Washington D. C. broker equally in trouble for gun smuggling and circumventing a world wide ban against the Ivory Coast?

At the very time when President Obama made his maiden African visit and addressed Ghana's national assembly, electronic mails were circulating, detailing well researched huge fortunes accumulated by one of Africa's strong men over a forty-two year rule – Omar Bongo of Gabon who died in a Paris hospital. President Bongo was among a handful of African leaders who grew larger than life and thanks to eternal rule, much larger than their countries, an aberration the West tolerated and went along with, as long as their own political ends were met. Going through that list of Omar Bongo's fortune, I could not help recalling what Nigerian military ruler, General Yakubu Gowon said on learning of the coup d'état that had overthrown him during his state visit abroad – "the world is a stage and we have our entrances and our exits".

Twenty-two million dollars in the Bank of Cyprus, fourteen in the Hellenic Bank, eighteen million Euros in Société Générale, fifteen in BNP Paribas, eight in Crédit Lyonnais, three in HSBC Paris; thirty-three million dollars in the Commercial Bank of Dubai, twenty-six in CityBank, sixteen in Emirate Bank, eleven in Standard Chartered Bank; 20% shares in AIBD, 30% in DAPORT Senegal, 80% in Dakar Dem Dikk, 30% in BIN LADEN Senegal, 30% in SATTAR, 30% in OIL LIBYA, 20% in ZAM ZAM, 10% in Jafza

Senegal, 10% in GECOM INDUSTRIES, 20% in IRIS Sénégal, 15 % in Expresso Sénégal, 5% in DELARUE Sénégal, 10% in MEDIATIQUE Afrique, 10% in AFRICA SALT, 10% in DP World Sénégal, 10% in Henan Chine Sénégal, 20% in OFFNOR Shipping Sénégal, 25% in SERM (Société d'Etude et de Realisations des Phosphates de Matam), 30% at the Cabinet CICE. Additionally, there were 90 room hotels in Casablanca, 60 rooms in Marrakesh, 48 rooms in Paris's 14th Arrondissement, 50 rooms in Switzerland. In Switzerland there were two bank accounts – Banque Migros with 43 million CHF and Banque Coop with 62 Million CHF. The string of vehicles of all makes was quite long and there was a 20 seater plane and a yacht in Nice, buildings of four storeys in Paris's 16th district, properties in Montpellier, Bordeaux, Cote d'Azur, Orleans, Lilles, Michigan, New Orleans, Wisconsin and New Jersey. With wealth like this who wants to abide by the asset declaration requirement so enamored of opposition parties?

And this was just the tip of a large iceberg for a country whose citizens barely managed to live at the fringe of penury, a country where the typewriter still has pride of place over the PC in offices and even the presidency. If that e-mail was correct, then there is absolutely no doubt that the late president virtually gained the whole world. Interestingly France's branch of Transparency International is said to have sued three African leaders for ill-gotten wealth stashed in France – Denis Sassou Nguessou of Congo, Teodoro Obiang Nguema of Equatorial Guinea and the late Omar Bongo Ondimba. This will provide the continent with something other than soccer to tune to.

These developments brought to mind a wise saying, curiously of African origin. *If you try to cleanse others, like soap, you will waste away in the process.* Whether it is the lucky few who migrated into the Diaspora to try their luck and send back home remittances to benefit those left behind or the World Bank, International Monetary Fund and its other multinational institutions trying to uplift the third world nations and their people through governmental and nongovernmental organizations, the response is invariably the same. The projects realized on the field hardly match the money disbursed.

The US is fighting the global war on terrorism and it is very tempting to want to apply the cold war practice of blindly funding Africa's dictators as natural allies while turning a blind eye to their internal disasters. But doing so today risks converting the disaffected citizens into available recruits for terrorist groups. President Obama has the difficult task of deciding whether to support grassroots or the corrupt leaders of the weak, failed or terrorist states where poverty and lack of political freedom are ingredients of instability. It is true that African leaders overwhelmingly condemned the terrorist attack of 9/11/2001 and even show some support for the current global war on terror. But almost without exception their autocratic and oppressive rule provides the ideal breeding ground for terrorism. It is very dangerous when the support for the global war on terror is predicated on US support for internal terrorism of dictators against their own people. The continent is at risk of a new breed of terrorists from those who oppose the status quo but find it impossible to change the system through peaceful means. Ivory Coast's Constitutional Court set the country on a very dangerous path by denying the winner of that country's presidential election and swearing in the incumbent who clearly lost; according to the electoral commission and the international community that monitored the elections all along. The double standards of the west date as far back as the days of Apartheid, when criminal friends were armed and assisted to stay in power in South Africa as long as western interests were served. The Omar Bongos, Idi Amins, Mobutu sese seku kuku Ngbendu wa Zabangas and the Lumumbas may be gone from the scene but their present day equivalents abound. Eastern Congo has become the rape capital of the world. Rwanda is still very fresh in the minds of the world and heavy on the conscience of the west, that under their watchful eyes, the MRDD (Mouvement Républicain pour la Démocratie et le Développement), its youth wing, the infamous Interahamwe and a colluding military of the interim government, advocated Hutu power, propagated anti-Tutsi sentiments, planned and carried out massive slaughter, beginning with the assassination of President Juvenal Hayarimani.

In condemning Bernard Madoff and his likes, Americans of African origin, especially the most recent immigrants, knew that they had to make haste very slowly down that slope, taking into consideration the fact that their continent of origin was still dominated by life presidents, providential rulers and persons surrounded by an aura of divinity, who presided over the destiny of millions of destitute citizens. How could they find two legs to stand on, given that they had not lived up to the prescriptions of President Barack Obama in rising up to the challenges back at home? With closetfuls of skeletons, they knew that, without doubt, they lived in very large glass houses. As a matter of fact, while the G8 and G20 leaders were splitting hairs over the idea of tax havens and toying with naming and shaming such places that helped to shelter ill-gotten wealth and the wealth of tax evaders, the focus was almost exclusively on the miscreants in the developed world, yet some of the main actors in the craft are heads of state of banana republics known to criss-cross the world in search of development aid and foreign investments which they quickly and quietly convert into personal fortunes lodged far away from the starvelings over whom they preside. While the most notorious cases like Sudan, Somalia, Zimbabwe, Ethiopia, Democratic Republic of Congo, Kenya and Nigeria made the head lines, lesser articulated ones which formed the majority continued to do business as usual, driving hordes upon hordes of their citizens on the perilous trans-Saharan journey to the Middle East, Europe, Canada, the United States, Australia and elsewhere in search of asylum and daily bread. No wonder authorities of Swiss banking contend that their stable and trustworthy democracy provides the kind of haven lacking in most of these countries whose fortunes find their way into Swiss bank accounts.

What Robert Mugabe was doing in Zimbabwe was being replicated elsewhere on the continent. Kenya, the pride of tourism under first independence president, Jomo Kenyatta had become a nightmare of sorts under successor Daniel arap Toroitich Moi, earning for itself the less than dignifying appellation *nchi ya kitu kidogo* (land of the small thing, a euphemism for bribe), a homeland where potbellied policemen erected roadblocks to extort bribe from road users, especially those traveling in the *matatus*. Ironically, when Moi was first installed in 1978, those who expressed concern about his ability to fit into Kenyatta's big shoes were reassured that the new president was just an interim, a mere cloud that would soon pass over the Kenyan skies. Moi tasted power and shillings and went on to rule for twenty-four years! There was a lot of ill gotten wealth and those who had it lived in fear, doing everything possible to silence whoever tried to investigate just how much had been stolen. There was the famous Robert Ouko affair, where the man called in to probe the bad guys in the Goldenberg scandal was found mysteriously murdered, necessitating an appeal to Britain's Scotland Yard to come and help. Even with the help of Scotland Yard, those arrested were still released by Kenya's police for "lack of evidence". For some, especially those in the slums, the dispossessed of Kenyan society, the unnoticed powerless and voiceless underclass, Nairobi was renamed "nairobbery" as modern day versions of Robin Hoods cropped up in an attempt to rob the rich and help the poor. It became justifiable to use criminality to fight poverty.

In December 2002 hope rose high as another presidential election took place to replace Daniel arap Moi's years of corruption and to put behind the multibillion dollar Goldenberg scandal and associated "Moi era". But then....

## *The enemy of my enemy is my friend?*

Did the west actually expect African leaders to catch one of their own and hand over for trial in the West? Incredible! That is a no-go area. That would be like asking America to arrest former Vice President Dick Cheney and hand him over to Nigeria to answer charges of corruption in connection with his chairmanship of Halliburton! Pouring vitriol on Apartheid South Africa was by far easier to do. During a recent African Union summit in Colonel Kaddafi's Libya, the continent's assembled leaders again skillfully skirted the imbroglio surrounding their many homologues guilty of war crimes, crimes against humanity, genocide and other indignities to which their hapless citizens were routinely subjected. The international court of Justice at The Hague waited prayerfully for African leaders to help arrest their indicted homologue of Sudan, Omar el-Bashir. A baffled world, including such experts on African affairs as the Goodenoughs and Toutbons that western chancelleries are wont to appoint for matters affecting the black continent, could not quite come to terms with such callous indifference. Yet, diplomats past and present failed to learn and apply one of the Black Continent's wise sayings - "*a Camel does not make fun of the hump of another,*" - a version of the glass house proverb or pot-kettle wisdom, available in little pamphlets all over. How long will the western world continue to miss this basic GIGA (garbage in, garbage out) principle that continues to place the burdens on the hapless citizens of these so-called AK-47 democracies or banana republics? It is all nice and good to place a higher premium on strong institutions over strong leaders but what is the mechanics of curbing life time presidencies and the tendency to deify those in power?

It is all good to mount the rostrum and preach against corruption, organize all sorts of workshops and seminars to x-ray and analyze it, yet the scourge cannot simply go away if the only action is wishing it away like bad weather. Corruption has become a mere cliché in many circles, even those supposed to do something about it. The buck often ends with the president himself but too often a president cannot see it even if corruption were put inside his bowl of pepper soup. The reason is simple as some visiting tourists have discovered to their chagrin, when valuables are stolen by postal staff or those at the airport. A report to the immediate boss, the most logical thing to do under other skies, has no effect because most persons who commit such brazen acts were employed not based on what they knew, but on whom they knew or how much bribe they doled out to secure their employment. The immediate boss, like the next higher boss on the chain of command is powerless to fire the culprit. Even at the top the minister or president might find it impossible to act, being helplessly entwined in the very cultural web. Camels do not normally make fun of each others' rumps!

It is also nice to send out the clarion call and advocate that Africa's youths should rise up to the challenge and do something for their countries and their futures. But sending those youths to a calling that would be better handled with Hillary Clinton's "smart policies" had resulted in the sad phenomenon of Somali-born US citizens returning home to Mogadishu from Minnesota to blow themselves up in the meaningless suicide bombings that claimed so many lives. Such a call had led the courageous 26-year old Neda Agha-Soltan, a travel agency employee, to venture out and be gunned down in the streets of Tehran following the flawed elections that pitted Mahmoud Ahmadinejad, backed by spiritual leader Khamenei, against opposition candidate, Mirhossein Mousavi and two others. Not every military is as civilized as those in Tunisia or Egypt.

And there were others. Incumbent president, Hamid Karzai won a contested election in Afghanistan, after the Electoral Complaints Commission (ECC), his country's watchdog on election fraud, ruled that the 2009 ballot was tainted with fraud and required a rerun. The murky political climate posed problems for America as well as Europeans fighting to put in place a real democracy in the war torn country. Following the withdrawal of the main opposition rival, President Karzai went ahead to form a weak government as the war raged on against the Taliban. Many of the president's nominees were rejected by the country's new parliament and even the subsequent appointments still did not meet with approval. It came as a surprise when President Karzai signed a decree giving himself the power to appoint all five members of the ECC and vowing to make sure the body never again made a similar ruling discrediting his election victory. Eye brows were raised but that was the way of things in such American-supported regimes. It had happened before and would most likely happen again. Worse, the man so supported might turn around to become America's nightmare as was the case with Saddam Hussein at one point, Osama bin Ladin who got his start as an American-backed mujahedeen in Afghanistan, at another and Ahmed Chalabi, MIT graduate and George Bush's famous Iraqi exile. Dubbed the

George Washington of Iraq, Ahmed Chalabi pushed America to war with his unproven theories of weapons of mass destruction.

A recent pronouncement to the effect that he would join the Taliban - if outside pressure continued to be mounted on him to reform and to do something about corruption - placed Hamid Karzai dangerously in the same league as the former friends-turned-foes of America. President Hamid Karzai alleged that foreigners were behind the fraud in the disputed 2009 elections in Afghanistan. Each of the above personalities brings to mind another wise adage of ancient Arab origin (the enemy of my enemy is my friend) which America adapted for home consumption (the enemy of my enemy is my friend for a little while and then he becomes my enemy also). Iraqi cleric, Muqtada al-Sadr reputed for his anti-*Amrika* rhetoric, just returned to his native Iraq from four years of self-imposed exile in Iran, the country that fought a bitter battle with his own country Iraq when Saddam Hussein was still in charge. Egypt's ousted President Hosni Mubarak was an avowed enemy of the Muslim Brotherhood which, like all such Islamic groups, is anti-American. What will happen now that pro-democracy elements in Egypt, including the Muslim Brotherhood, have united to kick out Mubarak? Will the US put aside the fear of supporting that organization now that Mubarak has bowed out as a result of his countrymen responding to America's message of democracy, freedom and human rights? Also, it will be interesting to see how this plays out in the current tug-of-war between the US and Venezuela in getting Colombia's new president Juan Manuel Santos to extradite drug lord, Walid Makled hotly wanted by both countries.

Writing on the futility of the citizen in his native Cameroon, Jean Takougang, a political analyst and specialist in social dialog wondered aloud how one should qualify a team coach who, in 27 years, lost all matches played but obdurately kept the same system of play, not being more demanding on the composition of the team and still continuing to try for each tournament, new players of exactly the same profiles who lost the competitions and scarcely did better than their predecessors. He was of course referring to the pathetic situation where, for 27 years, Cameroon's head of state locked himself up in an absurd and unfair policy of regional balance, both inoperative and sterile, promoting individuals without developing their regions. There could never be a better illustration of Einstein's notion of insanity. Football (soccer) has virtually become the cure-all cathartic of Cameroon, capable of defusing popular discontent from all quarters.

Takougang's observation was quite apt and went to support views already expressed by such nationalists as Celesten Monga of the World Bank, that the government in place in Cameroon hardly made room for individual growth, let alone the growth of the nation. Ministers had no initiative of their own, their main role being to parrot what the head of state had said and prefixing every single deed of theirs with *"sur les hautes instructions du chef de l'état"*, a situation reminiscent of Kenya under Daniel arap Moi, modern day epitome of *"L'état c'est moi"*, the ruler who instructed his ministers to sing like parrots, to sing the song he himself sang, to put a full stop if he did so, so that Kenya would move forward. It is inescapable to read resignation in Takoungang's language, a denunciation of a people who, for various reasons, had fallen into fatality and handed its destiny to its torturer or to providence. The once prosperous country of very dynamic and enterprising citizens had been turned into what Takoungang called a zombieland where citizens were still expecting a miracle from the president's 28th ministerial reshuffle as if that would be any different from the previous 27, thereby ending broken promises, disappointments, dashed hopes, disillusion, poverty and misery. How true! The very perceptive Egyptians saw through such intrigues and disdainfully rejected Mubarak's offer to step aside and appointment Omar Suleiman as vice president.

In spite the glaring flaws Cameroonian supporters of the president would urge him to take on more and more presidential mandates and run for as long as he wished - Machiavellian calculations where bread and butter issues had gained the upper hand and, according to one cynic, the stomach had virtually taken over functions originally designed for the brain. Some called it a win-win situation since by staying as long in power as possible the incumbent president would turn a blind eye to all those cases of embezzlement of public funds, bloody hands and the rest. How smart! As Kenyans chanted *"our time to eat"* their Cameroonian equivalents jubilated with *"c'est notre tour"*.

The leadership of the country continued to harp on peace as if the absence of a shooting war automatically meant the citizens enjoyed peace. Structural adjustment programs have not helped Cameroon; neither has the HIPC(highly indebted poor country) initiative parroted by the Breton Woods institutions as they dictated economic policies to African countries but failed to follow up, leading to host countries creating their own managerial carapace, a type of no-go zone called "Sovereignty Expenditures" and involving defense, international diplomacy, governmental offices and forms of conspicuous consumption by state elites in patronage governance. Nicholas Van de Walle's study of the African economies in the 1980s and 1990s is very revealing indeed and the 2005 African Economic Outlook of the OECD says it all – lack of any oversight, parliamentary or otherwise, so that sovereignty expenditures created fantastic situations such as the imbroglio over the purchase of a presidential aircraft for 70 billion CFA francs in 2003, using all sorts of arcane financial methods devoid of accountability and transparency with the result that practically all high ranking officials involved in the purchase of that "ill-fated flying coffin" aptly named "The Albatross" are today languishing in the maximum security jail in Kondengui, Cameroon, for real or imagined crimes. That is the type of challenge awaiting President Barack Obama and Secretary of State Hillary Clinton, should they decide to accept it.

By simple dictionary definition, genocide is the deliberate and systematic extermination of a national or racial group. Thus the extermination of thousands of Tutsis of Rwanda by Intrahamwes of the Hutus in 1994 or Darfurians in Sudan by the Janjaweeds were genocides. But State Department officials said, well, not necessarily or not officially. But why? The reason is that if so, the international community would be obliged to do something about it. The 1948 UN Genocide Convention which the US signed belatedly in 1989 says that signatories are obliged to prevent or punish acts intended to destroy ethnic groups. As a word, genocide carries enormous responsibility, said the New York Times, and so the only way to duck such responsibility would be to ban the word. Can President Obama collude to ban such a word pregnant with meaning for Africa?

What can one do about dictatorships and life presidencies? Obviously naming and shaming them has not worked at all. Invading and occupying their countries may pose more problems than those solved, going by recent experiences in Iraq or Afghanistan. Some have suggested the idea of credible and respectable human rights organizations getting together to brainstorm and come up with something like a citizens' Good Government Index (GGI) along the line of Transparency International's Corruption Perception Index to rank governments. GGI can then be used to rank governments and government performance in critical areas such as election fraud (Iran's Ahmadinejad 2009, America's George W. Bush, 2000, Zimbabwe's Robert Gabriel Mugabe, Socialist People's Libyan Arab Jamahiriya's Colonel Muamar Abu Minyar al-Gaddafi and others). By narrowing the dictators' reach in important forums (Human Rights Council, UN Security Council), restricting doing business with them using systematic boycotts, freezing their ill-gotten wealth, placing travel bans on them and their collaborators, lobbying media outreach and exposing their havens for terrorists, a lot of them can be cut down to their human proportions and put out of business. It is so reassuring that Swiss authorities have taken the bold step to freeze former President Mubarak's accounts in their keeping.

Such success can only be possible if developed countries stop acting in complicity with the rogues the way British banks have been shown to do in court documents recently brought to light. Barclays, NatWest, RBS, HSBC, UBS and others have been exposed as banks that accepted millions of pounds in deposits from corrupt Nigerian officials who should have been categorized as PEP (politically exposed persons) and scrutinized closely. Sadly this is hardly the first time such things have happened; as far aback as the days of late dictator Sani Abacha some of these same banks ran afoul of the UK banking regulations by helping the dictator funnel millions of pounds through the United Kingdom, helping to fuel corruption and entrenching poverty in his native Nigeria.

Nothing can trump job creation as a means of bringing stability to third world countries and retaining their talents at home. Fewer nationals will want to undertake the perilous trans-Sahara journey to Europe or the trans-Atlantic to North America in search of the good life. Investing just a fraction of the ill-gotten wealth in Swiss banks and other safe havens can do miracles in stabilizing some of the worst cases. If President Obama could extend his dragnet to sanitize also wealth belonging to some of the dictatorships that have impoverished their peoples, part of the immigration problem here in the US would be solved. Africa's plague is invariably the world's plague. Any attempt to act detached from the black continent's woes is a miscalculation, given that our world has become one big global village. That is why President Bill Clinton was hailed for taking the bold step at the World Economic Forum to pledge support for work on all serotypes of the HIV – A, B, and C. The looming crisis in governance is inescapable. As national budgets continue to favor defense over public health, it is only a matter of time before employers in the public and private sectors begin to face increased death rate, leaving them nothing but grave yards to defend with their bloated defense budgets, a typical case of shooting oneself on the foot. Corporate America has an interest to make sure this does not happen; the need for an ever expanding market for its products cannot be met when a part of the world is decimated.

The towns and cities of many third world countries are a juxtaposition of hauteur in architecture and landmarks with misery in squalor of slums, often the latter dominating the landscape as ruling elites complain of lack of budgetary provisions. Yet these are the very persons who criss-cross the world, undertaking multiple shopping sprees, staying in the Ritz and partying with the Diors, Gevenchys, Channels, Valentinos and others. It does not occur to them that with a small portion of the taxpayer monies they burn flying around the world, they could make themselves dear to their peoples simply by providing garbage collection containers along the main arteries in town. Eugene Poubelle, the *Prefet* of Paris did just that around the time of the 1884 Revolution without undertaking costly trips to anywhere. How can any town or city attract tourists with disgusting heaps of garbage and stench strewn all over the passable road ways as people just toss over their wastes? How can employment be created when elected officials fail to make the connection between the coexistence of such filth and unemployed persons roaming the streets?

With the shift in the job market, some of the new online businesses can be coaxed to find recruits overseas where labor is relatively abundant and cheap too. With the new rethinking in employment, contingent workers or free lance employees are becoming trendy where the tradition had been to have full time employees yoked to an employer at a given location over a time span. With the new system, emphasis will be placed on temporary workers, part-timers, self-employed persons and independent contractors to carry out specific functions involving fragments or chunks of bigger projects cut down to bits. With the proliferation of cell phones and ready availability of PCs, people can simply go online and do a job and even get paid right there – online. Many persons on the Indian sub-Continent earn their daily bread by performing such tasks as transcription or translation of short speeches, labeling images, making short market surveys. The last word has not yet been said about job outsourcing and as President Obama made clear during his visit to India, a win-win situation is created if a stimulated US exports more to India, a trading partner and growing economic force in south-east Asia.

At the January 1997 yearly ritual, economic movers and shakers gathering in Davos, Switzerland for the World Economic Forum that included Central Bankers of the world, ardent devotees of EMH (Efficient Market Hypothesis), placed a lot of emphasis on south-east Asia being the most dynamic part of the world economy with remarkable growth, especially the ASEAN (Association of South-East Asian Nations) along with Hong Kong and Taiwan. While ASEAN clearly benefits from American job outsourcing and off shoring, the same cannot be said of other parts of the world, especially areas that supply the world's greatest number of refugees and asylum seekers, prompting me to wonder whose interest is served by outsourcing. That is an area in need of a searchlight. While it is common to explain away job losses here in America in terms of job outsourcing, the influx of refugees, asylum seekers and other economic immigrants tells a different story.

In Cameroon there is plenty of Dole company activity around pineapple and banana cultivation but these crops are cultivated mainly as raw materials for export and that's it. Local manufacturing is for another day. Like Kenya, Cameroon too makes money from cultivation of beautiful flowers, some of which find their way to markets in Europe but a casual glance at the homes of the hardworking citizens involved with this activity does not give the impression that their economic plight is enviable at all. Here was an industry suited to tropical soil and climate. But the clientele - those love birds celebrating Valentine's Day and other occasions with flowers - is out there in Europe and North America, six to twelve hours away. Once cut the flowers need to be kept at around 35 Fahrenheit degrees in spacious storage containers for transportation. The reason is simple. The cut flowers' ability to photosynthesize food from water, light and carbon dioxide stops pretty quickly. Food stored in their stems gets quickly used up and the flowers progressively wilt and die - a process that can be slowed down by placing them in water for a short while but cold temperatures in refrigerated warehouses or trucks are better for preserving them for the long distances and times.

Ivory Coast may well be the world's number one producer of cocoa but chocolate and pharmaceutical product manufacture is for another time. In Ogoniland in south-eastern Nigeria, the locals are literally sitting on large quantities of black gold but the world knows that region only for its discontent, hot riots and kidnapping of expatriates unconcerned about the welfare and development of the local population. As a matter of fact a running joke which I would love to place in the distant past is that Nigeria is one country that exports what it does not have (democracy to troubled regional neighbors) but imports what it has in abundance (petroleum). The story is no different in the DRC where inhabitants live at the fringe of penury even as they labor with very crude tools to bring to the surface the riches of their subsoil for multimillion dollar cell phone manufacturers elsewhere. So when immigrants and refugees and asylum seekers from these places come to the US and are confronted

*John S. Dinga*

with joblessness, the explanation of outsourced jobs is very jarring to their ears. Their home countries have been courting China over the years but hardly emulate what the Asian giant is doing to stay on top – boost local production by injecting stimulus money into buying locally produced goods and services and intervening in international markets to keep the renmimbi (RMB) undervalued by 40% against the US dollar. Legendary Chinese leader Deng Xiaoping is known to have christened as Program 863 China's technological catch-up of March 1986.

The UK's reaction to Obama's election was summarized by the Sun, its most popular newspaper – One giant leap for mankind. Europe received and treated Barack Obama as a rock star! While it was understandable to be gratified by such world-wide jubilation and adulation, President-elect Barack Obama was not so naïve as to get carried away by it. As a matter of fact he needed to take it with a healthy dose of salt because it was not going to last long. Antagonism to the US is as old as the US itself. It surely didn't begin with President George Bush, unpopular though he was, nor with the American military involvement in Iraq and Afghanistan. It could not end just because Barack Obama took the Oath of Office. Current British Prime Minister, David Cameron knows that it will take some time to ease transatlantic tensions and animosities between the UK and the US, especially with the catastrophic BP oil spill over the Gulf of Mexico and its economic and social ramifications, compounded by suspicions that the very BP had played a role in liberating convicted Libyan Intelligence officer, Abdel Basset al-Megrahi from a Scottish prison. Convicted in the 1988 midair bombing of Pan Am flight 103 over Lockerbie, Scotland, the officer was released, according to Scottish officials, based on compassionate and humanitarian considerations since he was said to be in imminent danger of dying of cancer but US lawmakers suspected that BP and Libya had oil concession discussions underway for which such a gesture was deemed necessary. Would a probe help or hurt the long time special relations between the UK and the US?

In 1984 hundreds of people died and thousands got injured as a result of a chemical accident in Bhopal, central India. Under tremendous pressure, the valve in an underground storage tank had broken, releasing methyl isocyante (MIC) gas. The deadly cloud of gas floated over Bhopal, causing death and destruction. India's prime minister, Rajiv Gandhi flew over the site to see for himself one of the world's worst industrial accidents caused by Union Carbide, an American-owned factory and a subsidiary of Dow Chemicals. Fingers were pointed at Warren Anderson as the culprit for his cost cutting measures that had compromised safety and homicide charges awaited him. In 2004 India's Supreme Court stepped in and approved a compensation plan drawn up by a state welfare commission to pay $350 million to more than 570,000 victims. Looking back on that incident, there was practically little animosity against Union Carbide compared with what BP faced as a result of the accident in the Gulf of Mexico. Clearly the socioeconomic climate over the past two years contributed greatly to the corporate hate in America.

And would a quick pull out of US and UK forces from Afghanistan bring about peace in that country and guarantee security on the streets of Washington and London? President Obama had vowed to pull out our troops by August 31, 2010 in spite of the dangerous political deadlock in Baghdad and the surge in militant violence out there. The president's promise reminded Americans of his predecessor's famous *"Mission Accomplished"* announced on an aircraft carrier some time ago. Was this a realizable goal or just another election year gamble? Only time would tell. The pull out would leave behind noncombatant troops, prompting one observer to wonder what that oxymoron meant. In a world where the black box of aircraft is never quite black, Central Banks are hardly ever at the geographical centers of cities, should one expect noncombatant troops to be noncombatant or something else?

Well before George W. Bush came to the helm, anti-Americanism was strong in the Middle East and in Europe. In the 1990s, for example, the Greeks opposed US support for Kosovo's Muslims, and vented their anger at President Bill Clinton, throwing such epithets as "criminal, pervert, murderer, imposter, blood-thirsty, gangster, slayer, naïve, criminal, butcher, stupid, killer, foolish, unscrupulous, dishonest, disgraceful and rascal" at him. Before him Ronald Reagan provoked the eruption of anti-American fury in 1983 when millions of Europeans marched in protest against the installation of US ballistic and cruise missiles in West Germany in response to the Soviet Union's deployment of nuclear weapons in Eastern Europe. Daniel Patrick Moynihan, in his memoire of his tenure as ambassador of the US to the United Nations, described a 1974 World Food Conference in Rome in these words: "The scene grew orgiastic as speakers competed in their denunciations of the country that had called for the conference, mostly to discuss giving away its own wheat". It could not be otherwise for what New York Times called the number one exporter of contempt.

America is a big, rich and powerful nation. That alone is enough to provoke global resentment, no matter who lives in the White House. President Obama prudently sought to reverse some of the excesses of the past, reemphasizing diplomacy over military action, using force only when others would not, to defend its principles or protect a threatened party. How true of today's Libya! Even then, it is difficult to rationalize striking Muamar Kaddafi but not Laurent Gbagbo who has stumped his nose at the world well before the Libyan president. Is it because of the less strident calls of that nation's oppressed? Rep Scott Brown feels strongly that the world community has to step in when innocent civilians are being murdered by their so-called leaders but Rep Stephen Lynch thinks the Constitution allows for intervention only if there is a threat to US national security. And one of my coworkers thinks it is all about the money which presupposes then that oil money commands by far more clout than cocoa. There would be times when the US would play the role of the world's reluctant sheriff, said Barack Obama in his book "*The Audacity of Hope*". The new president might speak more softly than his predecessor, but he would still be carrying a very big stick and like other presidents before him, he would be loudly condemned whenever he used it. That abuse invariably goes with the job as we saw during President George Bush's press conference in Iraq when he made a last unannounced visit to see the troops.

President Barack Obama's even temper and quiet tenacity, his exceptional oratory and debating skills were used to inspire and persuade millions of American voters. As a good student with a steep learning curve, he understudied his mentor at his first job in a law firm and soon became her husband. He took useful cues from his buddy and mentor, Deval Patrick whose magnetic personality, charm and mantras *"together we can"* and *"hope over fear"* twice won him the governorship of Massachusetts. Barack Obama took office as the most admired man in the word, according to some polls. For business executives, the message was that communication tools would be more important than ever. Beyond style the new president's priorities would also influence those of business – quest for alternative energy sources, green environmental practices, climate change. Following President Obama's lead, a new openness to government working with private sector on issues like energy and healthcare, could emerge from both sides. Using the Obama pattern of inclusiveness, businesses would be more likely to shift from exclusively serving shareowners toward a broader focus on stakeholders, including customers, workers and entire communities.

Obama brought a new era of belief in government even among some of its long time cynics. In spite of popular discontent with the government, Americans can count themselves very fortunate to live under a climate of accountability, a thing that exists only in the imagination of most third world nations, some of whom are now rising up in protest. Bringing heavyweights like Toyota Motor Corporation's Akio Toyoda to explain the safety crisis involving stuck gas pedals or BP's Tony Hayward to say why US citizens and taxpayers had to endure the dangerous oil spills in the Gulf of Mexico are some of the lessons US Congressional leaders sent to parliamentarians around the world – quite a sharp contrast to what obtained in Ivory Coast where the government and its citizens received monetary compensations from *Trafigura*, a Dutch multinational company, found guilty of the 2006 dumping of toxic wastes in the capital city of Abidjan, chiefly due to the indefatigable efforts of Green Peace rather than through parliamentary or governmental action.

President Barack Obama would do well to sleep on the idea of deradicalizing terrorists instead of continuing with the policy of his predecessor. The pattern of global threat continues to change. At some point in the past the world was locked in the cold war with two great systems (Capitalism and Communism) represented in two countries (the US and the Soviet Union) in a state called a nuclear stalemate. With the collapse of the Soviet system, the early twenty-first century saw the emergence of a new kind of conflict called *radical Islam* that defied national borders. The short numerical expression 9/11 came to denote the lethal assault on America. A weird type of guerilla warfare emerged, consisting of strapping oneself with a belt of explosives and detonating where people would be gathered in large numbers – street processions, on prayer mats in mosques, inside aircraft, in pews inside churches, military convoys or convoys escorting government officials.

A novelty has been introduced in the war against terror and the fight to defuse suicide bombing. Saudi Arabia is indeed a strange venue for such an innovative venture. The Kingdom, well known for its unforgiving approach to criminal justice - amputating the hands of thieves, flogging sexual deviants, beheading drug dealers – is quietly spearheading an experiment in something new and unexpected – deradicalizing the terrorist. Over the past several years, jailed Saudi jihadists, led by therapists and motivated by the possibility of shortened sentences, started putting paint to paper (a process called Extremist Art Therapy) to work their way through. A simple, personalized version known as bibliotherapy aims at working through life's troubles with the client, using prescribed books to read that would encourage enlightenment on issues of concern, spark imagination and show that there is an alternative way out. Hopefully they would leave behind those thoughts and feelings that drove them to support violent strains of Islam. That type of therapy seems to be gaining ground also in Indonesia, Malaysia, Yemen, Jordan, Egypt, Singapore, Canada, the United Kingdom, the Netherlands and other Muslim countries or countries with large Muslim minorities.

The shifting focus on the post-9/11 war - capturing or killing terrorists - was actually launched by the US. While some continued to focus on what led people to terrorism in the first place, psychologists, political scientists and other thinkers slowly turned to the vital question of what could lead people away from it - certainly a new front worth pursuing against Al Qaeda, South-East Asia's Jemaah Islamiyah and other extremist organizations. Proponents seek a deeper grasp of terrorism's allure so as to undercut terrorist groups by peeling off supporters and turning them against the groups they once fought for. The recent experience of a Jordanian double agent infiltrating the ranks of the CIA and actually blowing himself up together with seven of the agents was surely a serious setback in this direction but loopholes in the arrangement can be remedied. Information gathered from the youthful Nigerian, Umar Farouk Abdulmutallab whose botched attempt to blow up a US plane flying from Amsterdam to Detroit will also shed light on an appeal once believed to be for persons from less privileged backgrounds. Enlisting the support of Sufi Muslims will certainly enhance the process.

The US is fighting an unwinnable war in Afghanistan, oblivious of that country's proverbial wisdom – only stretch your foot to the length of your blanket. Afghans know not to overextend themselves or their resources, so also should Americans. It is sad that so much blood should be shed over that nation's only cash crop – opium or the so-called desert rose. Anything short of obliterating those fields of opium and replacing them with something better from the USDA or perhaps repealing the law of supply and demand of the cash crop will still keep the Taliban in business. The way things are moving, it is clear that Afghanistan, Pakistan and the surrounding regions will sooner or later make the Middle East look like child's play! I wish I were wrong.

Early in 2011 Governor Salman Taseer of Punjab State in Pakistan was shot twenty-six times on his back by 26-year-old Mumtaz Qadri, his own bodyguard, outraged by the governor's opposition to a government blasphemy law. Three months earlier a Christian woman, Asia Bibi was sentenced to be executed by hanging for having defended her faith from insults by her Islamic neighbors. The law had virtually become a tool of persecution against religious minorities and the governor's opposition to it did not sit well with many, including his own security guard. Even though Pakistani government denounced the murder of the governor, a group of five hundred Muslim scholars issued an explicit statement endorsing the killing and lawyers, whose job it is to uphold the law, were reported to have even showered Qadri with flower petals as he was being brought to court. What will happen to Pakistan? Clearly it is unlikely that anything good can come of a court trial, especially as moderates and supporters of the governor were also threatened with death. What good can one expect when lawyers and Muslim scholars adulate an assassin? Extremism is slowly becoming mainstream in Pakistan and Washington is watching, powerless to do anything about it, just as in Egypt.

The eerie scenario of October 1984 when Prime Minister Indira Gandhi was assassinated by two of her Sikh bodyguards to avenge a military attack on Sikhism's holy shrine comes to mind. Some see this as Pakistani military reaping the fruits of the seeds of their demise sowed when they shifted attention from regional rival, India, to nurture and fund multiple terrorist groups now turned against them in a spectacular fashion. This state of affairs captured by Ahmed Rashid's *Descent Into Chaos* must be very troubling to Washington and Europe as the lofty goal of nation building evaporates visibly – a relatively unstable but nuclear-armed Pakistan, a renewed Al-Qaeda profiting from the booming opium trade and a Taliban resurgence even as Iraq continues to attract most western media attention and America's military might. Pakistan and Afghanistan remain the ultimate battleground. With nuclear arms in its arsenal, the last thing Pakistan needs is to descend into anarchy with extremists calling the shots.

Indonesia has contributed a lot to the process of Islam, democracy and modernity and women's rights all coexisting harmoniously, as confirmed by our own Secretary of State, Hillary Clinton during her visit to South East Asia. Indonesia is the world's most populous Islamic nation. Unlike hot spots such as Pakistan, Iran, Iraq, Morocco, Egypt, Nigeria, Somalia and others, Indonesia enjoys a rare degree of stability, thanks to a stable political system created in Jakarta without using the army to guarantee a secular rule. Militant Islamic groups which once threatened the island nation have been crushed, co-opted or are in retreat as the country adopts modern antiterrorist techniques.

Once an economic and political basket case riddled with graft under Dictator Suharto, Indonesia slowly recovered from the riots, political chaos, blocked streets and protests when its export-oriented economy collapsed with the Asian financial crisis. Hard line Islamists preyed upon the unrest, promising cleaner government against the country's traditional political parties, opened up Islamic schools called *pesantrens* similar to madrassas elsewhere, to fill the gap left by underfunded public schools. It was from such schools that Jemaah Islamiyah drew its recruits for the task of bombing touristic sites in the island of Bali, J W. Marriott hotel and the Australian embassy in Jakarta. The reelection of President Susilo Bambang Yudhoyono pinnacled the end of fear and uncertainty; the economy has recovered and political fragmentations are virtually a thing of the past.

How did this happen? For one thing Indonesia's leaders made no room for sharia (religiously derived legal system applicable to many issues, especially family laws and civil cases) to gain a foothold, except in a few isolated regions. Such laws, introduced between Muslims and non-Muslims, tend to alienate non-Muslim minorities, undermining the basic principle that democracy protects minority rights. Assuring minority rights is crucial to preventing the kind of internal violence that has rocked other Muslim nations like Pakistan (Sunni versus Shia) or the Yemen (northerners vs. southerners), and Nigeria (Christians versus. Muslims). Indonesia has also resisted the temptation to use the public treasury to promote a preferred version of Islam. President Yudhoyono, like his predecessors – Megawati Sukarnoputri and Abdurrahman Wahid – took pains to emphasize that there is no state-preferred mosque or spiritual leader, a contrast from Iran's theocracy, Saudi Arabia where the government plays a major role in overseeing clerics, Pakistan where former president Zia ul-Haq used both the power and purse of the state to institute laws consistent with sharia and packed courts with Muslim scholars considered his allies.

President Yudhoyono's massive antipoverty program as well as rice and cash subsidies to the poor certainly undercut the appeal of militancy, winning him the hearts and votes of his countrymen in addition to sparking consumer spending, a critical element at a time of lagging exports to the west. Poor families saw no need to depend on Islamic boarding schools for a decent education. Lastly, the president allowed some devolution of power to the provinces and cities, giving them greater shares of the national budget, more control over local natural resources and more money back from direct investment in their areas. It takes guts to give power to the regions, especially where the past custom favored a strong centralized government. But it pays rewards too, such as reducing separatist tendencies, giving average citizens more personal investment in the democratic process, encouraging competition in the provinces or regions and denying the Islamists another of their biggest recruiting tool – public anger at corruption. By staying out of the courts and backing the anticorruption agency, President Yudhoyono allowed justice to flow freely. He even made a public policy stating that militant groups and terrorists threatened average Indonesians, not just the west. Locals supported a policy that they saw as their own rather than one pushed on their leader by foreign powers and thanks to such collaboration it was possible for a US-trained antiterrorist squad to finally put away for good Noordin Mohammad, an accountant-turned-terrorist, Asia's most wanted Islamist militant who was responsible for the bombings at Bali's resort island and two American luxury hotels in Jakarta, Indonesia in his wild crusade to "make western nations tremble".

President Barack Obama's much applauded speech in Cairo University, Egypt was a most welcome shift in the direction the US was taking in reaching out to the world, even if, as perceived in Indonesia, there was a mixing up of religion with Arabism. The keynote speech delivered to the Muslim world by the US president did not lay to rest all fears and suspicions that exist between Muslims and the west (mutual lack of trust) but it surely paved the way for better relations in the years ahead. He spoke mainly to the educated young people, calling for new education and science partnerships between Muslim nations and the West, areas likely to have the greatest potential in moving society ahead. Wasn't this the basis of the Gamal Abdel Nasser revolution in promoting education as the engine of progress, an excellent public school education that encouraged both men and women to attend college and enabled Coptic Christians to succeed professionally? Lurking fears of the Islamization and proliferation of sleeper cells in the UK and US are not expected to disappear overnight. But surely Obama's speech was a step in the right direction of repairing America's tarnished image in the Muslim world and reawakening the stalled Middle East peace process as well as thwarting Iran's nuclear ambition. A retired Egyptian diplomat called the speech "a historic and momentous break from the past" and expressed undisguised optimism about future relations with Islamic nations.

Naturally detractors failed to give the president credit for his remarkable Cairo speech. Some picked quarrels with his inability to hit hard on the Middle East's ugly autocracies and dictatorships, the appalling subjugation of women in so many Muslim countries, especially the gender apartheid of Saudi Arabia and fanatic misogyny of the Taliban, female genital mutilation, women forced to wear the *hijab,* and radical Islam's endorsement of a global *jihad.*

Americans, ever so anxious to get results, forgot that things like mutually beneficial relationships take time and plenty of diplomacy to concretize. Only compassion for one's fellow humans is the key value in the world's many religions and cultures and only it can bring about greater understanding. The US is setting a great example by providing the social climate for diversity of religious traditions. Hopefully the heightened mutual understanding of our differences obtained through honest, respectful discussions will be able to dispel harmful stereotypes and build trust and positive relationships that allow for bonding together. In a world weary of conflicts this is the sure way to go but the new president will need time to build such bonds.

France, like a few other European countries, recently passed laws outlawing the *burqa.* Not only did such a move defy European law, it generated a lot of protests at home. It is said that Islam's face covering veil for visitors as well as residents breaks French law. How this plays out with Saudi Arabia's luxury shoppers on the glitzy

Champs-Elysees remains to be seen. In the eyes of the French, the veil is a legal and security risk, hurts the dignity of women and the equality between the sexes even though some women support the practice and defend it as offering them protection against invasive male prying. Quite apart from protecting the individual against the supposed prying eyes of the male, who can say for sure what deadly cargo is hidden under such apparel? In the US there are similar concerns of security and public safety as courts require faces to be uncovered. What will the European Court of Human Rights say to this? Will it not be classified as a violation of religion? It must be difficult adjusting to a new lifestyle of exposing one's entire body after a life time of covering everything up except the eye slits.

Critics would have wanted President Obama to use his Muslim roots, his position as the very first American president with such Muslim connections to full advantage and strike an intellectual blow against radical Islam instead of delivering the platitudes about Islamic history and teachings or western shortcomings. The president's Muslim connections which some persons had earlier cited as a repellent when they first considered him for the US presidency were now being asked to be used to diplomatic advantage! President Obama was faulted for failing to take advantage of the opportunity to openly address the pathologies and prejudices that drag Islamic societies backward, trapping so many of the world's Muslims in a culture that remains unfree and unenlightened. How times change!

There are over one billion Muslims in the world and George W. Bush's global war on terror did much to damage US-Muslim relations. Nevertheless, President Obama's opening to this world should be appreciated as a good sign. Later president Obama mustered the courage and spoke of his impatience with those in the Middle East who continued to blame the September 11, 2001 terrorist attack in New York and Washington D. C on a Jewish or American conspiracy when it was so clear that Al Qaeda had killed nearly 3000 innocent victims- men, women, children.

Conspiracy theory of course is an American pastime. Such theories abound in America – Was there ever a Pearl Harbor? Was the JFK assassination a one-man show or a team job? Did Americans really land on the moon? And the biggest of them all, even without President Mahmoud Ahmadinejad' support –wasn't 9/11 an inside job of George Bush and his men? Or the Israeli government's? And did Secretary of State Condoleezza Rice not play a prank or two on Iran's President Mahmoud Ahmadinejad, pretending to be Kim Jong-Il of North Korea? Why so many smart people believe in things so far-fetched remains a mystery. Would Israel cook up such a scheme and enlist mainly Muslim actors? The answer was blowing in the wind. And yet Occam's razor - a philosophical principle that says the simpler of two competing theories is almost always the better - has proved time and time again to be superior.

If ever an American president had his plate full, it would be Barack Obama. As if the budget deficit and unemployment at home and healthcare reform were not enough, on January 12, 2010, Haiti was hit by an earthquake estimated at 7.1 on the Richter scale. The island nation was devastated like nothing before and President Obama pledged to put all of America's goodwill to the rescue, starting with the very laudable step of putting his two predecessors – former presidents George W. Bush and William J. Clinton – to the front. Port-au-Prince was leveled as well as nearby towns and cities by an earthquake with epicenter at Lagoane, just west of the capital. Haiti's presidential palace, twice the size of the White House, was damaged and thousands of citizens in their homes, in hotels, offices or motorways were simply crushed by the rubble of falling concrete. For days stretching to weeks people were homeless as rescue missions from all over the world toiled to bring in tents, food and water. The exact death toll will never be known but estimates of between one hundred and two hundred thousand were put forward.

Life-saving potable water is a problem in Haiti. On the heels of the murderous earthquake, a cholera outbreak swept through parts of the island nation, aggravating the water shortage. 70% of our world is covered by water but of this vast quantity, more than 95% is salt water which is good only for whales, crustaceans and some species of fish. Of the remaining fresh water on which life depends, about 75% is frozen ice caps. Thus limited water resources can be one source of conflict between communities and countries. In the developed world water use is often very abusive and unconscionable. Climate change, pollution, reckless deforestation, drainage of wetlands and other inimical practices are responsible for waste; yet all of this coexists with the fact that one billion of the world's population lacks access to a steady supply of clean water!

The island nation's disaster highlighted a sad history. It is a strange saying but more than one person has said that if Haiti did not have bad luck, it would have no luck at all. As far back as 1804 Haitians mounted a successful slave revolt - the only successful one in recorded history - beat back Napoleon Bonaparte's army and formed a free black republic. Up north, Thomas Jefferson, one of the great Founding Fathers of America and prominent scribe of the Declaration of Independence, was just about entering his second term of office. As a slave owner himself he could not stomach the Haitian challenge, declaring that any country led by freed slaves should be punished to forestall inciting slaves elsewhere. He went to work right away and enlisted the help of European nations to place an embargo on Haiti, effectively cutting the new republic from the rest of the world. That was not all. For another fifteen years beginning in 1915 the US occupied Haiti and built up its military, paving the way for future dictatorship, starting with Jean-Claude Duvalier and his wife Michelle. Haitians say that when they meet people for the first time, the greeting is invariably *"Oh, Haiti! Baby Doc! Tonton Macoute!"* Terrible reminders indeed.

And so, when President Obama announced to the nation that Haiti would not be forsaken, Haitians wondered if he knew the weight of those pronouncements. Helping was the key word but it was left unsaid how soon it would turn into meddling, especially when a group of missionaries was stopped shepherding children out of the devastated country without the requisite papers. Were they child traffickers or benefactors? Haiti remains a miracle till today. Its birth as a slave nation, its diplomatic isolation, and a string of natural and man-made disasters...the list is long and the people resilient.

President Obama and Americans owe Haiti more than emergency relief indeed. Records show that the US owes its coming into nationhood and independence to her island neighbor. During the darkest days of America's revolutionary war, when it seemed unlikely to think that the mighty British Empire would allow sovereignty of 13 rogue colonies, help came from a most unusual source – Haiti, then known as French Saint Domingué. Some even called it the 14<sup>th</sup> colony. As early as 1775, America's island neighbor channeled guns, gun powder, bullets and warm clothing sent in to the Patriot cause from France, a country itself eager to chip the wings of the British lion. France needed to protect a lucrative overseas possession with a strong connection to the US and to New England in particular. Saint Domingué, with its capital at Cap Français, was the richest colony in the world. *"To be as rich as a Creole"* was a popular cliché for boasting in Paris and a substantial portion of the French economy depended on that one distant settlement – the jewel in the French Empire, furnishing coffee, sugar to sweeten it, cotton and indigo for men and women of fashion. More than one third of France's foreign trade was contributed by Saint Domingué. But the superheated economy of the island required labor in the plantations. That meant massive importation of human beings from Africa. Slaves were worked to death and Boston was linked commercially to the island.

America owed the Yorktown victory to her island neighbor. The loans, negotiated by Benjamin Franklin and John Adams in Paris, made it possible. Incredible but true. Money from one part of America (Saint Domingué) was loaned to another part (the colonies) by France. Hundreds of thousands of Haitians toiled and died for the cause of American independence. The huge loans given to America eventually weakened the French economy, leading to the outbreak of another revolution in Paris and turned the world upside down once more. Out of that emerged yet another revolution in 1804 that led to the birth of a new Haitian nation, the second American colony to do so. Haiti's path to independence was rocky, to put it very mildly, rockier by far than that of the US. It was opposed by nearly the whole world, including the United States under Thomas Jefferson!

England sought to regulate the lucrative Triangle Trade (France-Haiti-Boston) but this led to strictures. Trade between New England

and Haiti was very irritating to England and France was highly protective of Saint Dominguè which the English tried many times to seize but failed.

The French alliance allowed the US to lurch into existence. Why did France pour so much money into the American cause? Small, secretive loans channeled through clandestine agents at first, eventually became robust and open, reaching 1.3 billion pounds (equivalent to $9 billion today). The Yorktown battle that ended the war was made possible by the French, the people of Saint Dominguè enthusiastically defending the infant US, fighting alongside the Continentals. Prominent among them was a 12-year old Henri Christophe who later proclaimed himself king of Haiti after getting a taste of independence in America.

While many Americans saw similarities between Haiti's cause and that of the US, others were opposed to supporting what they saw as a rebellion led by revolutionary leader Toussaint Louverture. In 1806 Thomas Jefferson banned all trade with the newly independent nation, extinguishing its hopes for prosperity. Yet Haiti and the US are intertwined in the western hemisphere. Few people recall how Toussaint Louverture and his fellow countrymen fought for their freedom, forcing Napoleon Bonaparte to give up, especially when he learned of the death of his best general. In a world where history is made to look like the main actors were only Europeans and their descendants, most people remember only Napoleon's defeat at the hands of the Duke of Wellington, not Toussaint Louverture. Cursing "*damn sugar, damn coffee, damn colony!*" Napoleon then left Haiti alone. Many Americans have been moved by the writings of John James Audubon, W. E. B. Dubois and many other Haitian descendants, black and white and mixed who came to the US in the aftermath of Haiti's independence.

Can today's generation of Americans rise to the challenge? Is there room for bold action to save Haiti and other nations in a similar situation? Is it a realizable goal or mere wishful thinking for the United Nations to declare an International Decade for the Eradication of Poverty? What tools, if any, does the world body have at its disposal for such a lofty goal? How committed are national governments or non-governmental organizations to such a cause? Knowledge - both scientific and technical know-how – can confer the ability to do away with or turn around the consequences of non-preventable causes of poverty, yet often the tendency is to offer just charity, a palliative which serves only to satisfy the conscience. Is wealth redistribution a realizable goal? Is it feasible to place human beings at the center of development when the middle class continues to live with the misperception that it is the lack of will, initiative and commitment to work that keeps the poor in their condition? Isn't it possible to see the lack of ability and lack of skills in terms of lack of empowerment? When war or natural disasters like floods, earthquakes, and drought displace people, poverty, homelessness and hunger become unavoidable.

In the western hemisphere, the tragic earthquake of Haiti, unrelenting murders in Mexico's drug wars, Colombia's mind boggling murders and kidnappings by Marxist armies – Revolutionary Armed Forces of Colombia and the National Liberation Army (FARC) – did not give peaceful sleep to outgoing President Uribe, his successor Manuel Santos or President Barack Obama. Bogota needed a break from violence and homicides. The new Colombian president said yes to Venezuela in the matter of extraditing suspected drug lord Walid Makled for trial. Arrested in the town of Cucuta, north-east of Colombia, Walid Makled faced charges of money laundering, drug trafficking and others. Colombia is America's closest ally in South America but President Santos who wanted to improve years of strained relations with President Chavez of Venezuela, said he had given his word to President Chavez, that once the legal procedures were completed he would hand that individual over to Venezuelan authorities, adding "I have always believed that a promise must be fulfilled and I will fulfill it". Unlike his Colombian counterpart, Thailand's prime minister Abhisit Vejjajiva had only to agree with his country's parliament to hand over to the US Victor Bout, the Russian arms dealer aptly called "merchant of death" for his many baleful stories in weaponizing the civil wars in countries like Congo, Liberia, Sierra Leone, Sudan and a string of rogue nations as well as organizations such as the Taliban, al-Quaida and possibly Hezbollah.

Now that the US has got him extradited, the world holds its breadth to learn what role that Russian citizen played in procuring helicopters, Russian weapons, and transport aircraft used in rendering men, women and children of the above countries legless, armless and even faceless. Did he do business with Colombia's FARC, the Hezbollah; was he in cahoots with Venezuela's Hugo Chavez? How would Prime Minister Vladimir Putin of Russia react to the spectacular arrest masterminded by US secret agents on Thai territory? Would Victor Bout have embarrassing revelations about the US as well and how was Washington going to deal with them?

It was Chile that gave the hemisphere and indeed the entire world something to celebrate and feel good about. Away from the sad dreamy news of joblessness in the US, war in Afghanistan and flood in Pakistan, the world fixed its attention on the rescue of 33 miners trapped half a mile down Chile's copper mine for over two months. I recall being visibly frightened once when I got trapped in an elevator for twenty minutes and again when I spent ten minutes inside a claustrophobic MRI cubicle. In retrospect, those were child's play when compared to the plight of Chilean miners being trapped for two months deep inside Chile's copper mine!

Of the Chileans interviewed, 84% expressed joy and approved of the way their president, billionaire businessman Sebastian Pinera, handled the mine crisis. A meticulously planned rescue operation brought together the very best of our world and international effort. Schramm, a US company supplied the drilling technology that bored the recue hole into the mine, Japan supplied the necessary video equipment, Germany the rescue cable, NASA the high calorie liquid diet to sustain the miners and an Austrian company the capsule's winch-and-pulley system. Colorado flew in an expert in heavy drilling.

Where other leaders facing similar situations at home would opt to continue with their other preoccupations elsewhere in the world, the Chilean leader cut short all foreign engagements and visited the camp several times over the two months duration of the rescue effort and he personally oversaw the 23-hour rescue operation involving hoisting the miners up to the surface one by one, joining his fellow citizens in singing the national anthem and other hymns with plenty of hand clapping. He even organized a soccer match pitting the 33 against their rescuers! The cost of the rescue effort was estimated at $15 million, including other resources beyond Chile's national borders. That was taxpayers' money well invested. The fruit of the teamwork, inside the mine as well as above it, in short and long term will be proudly harvested through national cohesion and solidarity in the years ahead. Already San José was abuzz in book and movie deals. That was a good story and lesson for the world even if the euphoria were short lived; no one doubted that with time problems would crop up – post-traumatic stress disorders to cope with, twists of fate such as divorces, and falling out over fame and fortune.

The feel good streak continued with Myanmar's general Than Shwe freeing Opposition National League for Democracy leader and winner of the 1990 presidential election, Aung San Suu Kyi from a prolonged house arrest of over fifteen years, followed by the good news of a 50% drop in the infection rate of the HIV in Zimbabwe and Britain's Prince William and long time girl friend Kate Middleton announcing their engagement, paving the way for a royal wedding in the spring of 2011, with Kenya as a possible destination for the honeymoon. The world of 2010 deserved such morale boosters. The announcement caused a sky high rise in hotel room bookings in Central London in anticipation. The hotel industry sprang to life as the wedding fever spread. The Ritz on Piccadilly, the Dorchester, the Claridge and the other luxury ones like Royal Horse guards Hotel, within walking distance of Westminster Abbey came into high demand. Hopefully, Kenya's tourist industry was taking due note and preparing the 680, Grosvenor, and others in Nairobi for the honeymoon ahead. As America's own royalty, Oprah Winfrey did in Australia, Britain's royalty will surely bring a Midas' touch to many businesses.

The most ecstatic moments came from North Africa. Tunisian protesters using their bare hands and their determination successfully drove their president from power, followed by Egyptians sending Hosni Mubarak packing. Like a bottle of champagne the people poured on to the streets in jubilation and the world rejoiced with them.

# 6.

## You win some, you lose some

On the evening of October 3, 2009 Ashley and I wrote a letter of consolation to President Barack Obama, commiserating with him for the unsuccessful attempt at convincing the International Olympic Commission in Copenhagen to award the 2016 games to his adopted city of Chicago. Two days earlier the president had flown to Copenhagen with his lovely wife Michelle and pitched a strong case for Chicago but it would appear that the IOC did not even give the city a second thought, having settled on Rio de Janeiro on the very first round. It was quite demoralizing. Everyone had assumed that by putting the White House and all of America behind Chicago's bid to host the Olympic Games, President Obama would make things easy for the city to be launched onto the world stage. Unfortunately it was not to be. Our letter reminded him of a similar unsuccessful bid by the Big Apple with Mayor Bloomberg's promise of a multibillion dollar budget and all, examined all the negative aspects and the huge costly unpaid bills that would be left behind if Chicago had been chosen for the games – oceans of red ink in the books and headaches. We urged the president to look on the brighter side and called upon him to join us celebrate the good riddance. It could be worse.

The very next morning we tuned to the BBC to learn that the Swedish Academy had decided to award President Obama the 2009

Nobel Peace Prize! We quickly unsealed our letter and added a foot note to it, letting the president know that the Nobel Prize was adequate compensation for his efforts. And then we mailed the letter. President Obama had been singled out for recognition for his nine months in office during which he created the right international climate for world peace, especially in calling on Russia to reduce the arsenal of deadly weapons as well as reversing his predecessor's unilateralism, thereby returning multilateral diplomacy to center stage. Critics at home were quick to denounce the Swedish Academy for trivializing the Nobel Prize, forgetting that through bold action, President Obama had also halted the recession that was drifting towards a depression.

By then the idea of winning some and losing some had become a mantra worth remembering. The president had won two important battles and lost one. That's how life works. It happens to everybody. Before him did Al Gore not lose the presidency and win the Nobel Prize? Did Jimmy Carter, a one term president, not also win one? No use to brood over temporary setbacks like Chicago. The nation had to move on and so also its citizens.

After spending more than one year job hunting, I had come to the conclusion that the American dream was certainly not a piece of cake. It might have been in some remote past; not any more. In my job search, I criss-crossed metropolitan Boston, looking at job boards, sending out masses of e-mails with my resumes, tapping the brains of friends and family and their associates, convinced that some employers hardly advertised job openings in their businesses, ostensibly to save money, but aware that through personal contact such employers quickly jumped at the first compatible match that crossed their path, I had presented myself for tons of job interviews – a good number made possible through sustained elevator pitches here and there - armed with the most polished resumes reflecting the very best ideals of Leonado da Vinci – not just a listing of my past achievements but more significantly, what I intended to offer prospective employers. Faced with so many Generation Y candidates on the job market, I knew the odds were against me but I had to try my very best.

Surely in matters of dressing most of them would not score higher than I. I could never quite figure out who set American norms in matters of dressing but I was convinced that all those young persons twittering away all day long, cap worn backward, heavy pant sliding below the waistline and sometimes revealing their underpants or skins – *the derriere dilemma* - could not possibly beat me in impressing prospective employers. Should we or should we not dress to conform to some arbitrary norm? How did the culture of the three piece suit, collar and tie come about? Would a dashiki or a bou-bou not do the job? Should one put on a sombrero or a fedora; wear an agbada, a muumuu, or a gandura; put on stilettos or flip flops? Where should freedom lovers place their love for the tank top or the kimono? And the flip-flops, jeans, short shorts, skimpy sloppy attire? So far only the courts seemed to lose sleep over the way Americans dress, especially since they have the means – contempt charge - to impose some order and dignity whereas the rest of the society just shrugged it off as the fashion envelope was pushed. There are people who wear the same pajamas from the grocery store to the courtroom.

An interesting case cropped up in Indiana where parents were suing the coach of the Junior Highs School's basketball team for trying to impose a haircut rule on their son, thereby violating his constitutional right to have a shaggy haircut. Well before the actual drama in the court, there were opinions being volleyed back and forth, some claiming that in addition to health and sanitation concerns for teammates, playing basketball is a privilege not a right, others asserting that it is discriminatory to dispense coaching only to those who conform to some dress code and so on. Taking a step back, it is so much cheaper to have a haircut than hire a lawyer! But of course this is America where David must always try it out with Goliath.

Courts are known to crackdown so as to maintain decorum as well as beef up security, banning skirts shorter than four inches above the knee when standing but the very courts entertain challenges to law suits brought against indecent exposure, including saggy baggy pants in the larger society. Following repeated protest telephone calls from citizens offended by the practice, the courageous mayor Phil

Best of the municipality of Dublin, Georgia decided to amend the indecent exposure ordinance(masturbation, fornication, urination in public places) to include this new fad, indicating that the only way to uphold the law is for citizens to uphold their pants with their belts. Hopefully fines ranging from $25 to $200 for each offence should do the trick. Similar approaches had been tried in Flint, Michigan and Riviera Beach, Florida. Would this draw more supporters in the months ahead? Some complained that it sounded Catholic school-like and others cried racial profiling but that seemed to be society's last rampart. There remained the million dollar one – the Islamic veil or *burqa* that is threatening western civilization from Europe to the US. As a matter of fact, isn't it conceivable that Muslims, especially their women, are demanding to be allowed to do what other Americans are doing with relish – dress as they like? For new immigrants this is quite a challenge – dressing so as to blend in or to stand out. Those traditional garbs worn on the head, back, body, arm and other parts of the body can elicit all sorts of reactions (nervousness, anxiety, worry) from Americans and they can be a liability or an asset depending on the setting.

Does corporate America have the right to impose the ultramarine suit with matching tie or any other outfit as a dress code and, on a larger scale, should those who pay the piper always dictate the tunes? Employers too face the dilemma of choosing between the more tech-savvy youths and the more dependable baby boomers whose command of the new technologies is often wanting. But then the Generation Y is often lackadaisical and callous about work, which they consider a necessary evil, valued mainly for the pay check and whatever slow pace and vacation time it offers, the culture of entitlement notwithstanding. In the competitive work place, such a perspective would be unacceptable, especially for persons with divided loyalties, sharing the work hours between working and texting, twittering, e-mailing and doing the other odd things associated with the new technologies, often making work itself look more like an afterthought in their scheme of things. Employees sign only the back of the pay check and are supposed to earn their keep, putting in eight hours of work, not eight hours at work! Output is often inversely correlated with the professionally well done resume. When clients are given the run-around, made to spend fifteen minutes for a telephone transaction that should normally take three, it is easy to tell who is at the other end. Which employer, signing the front of the pay check, would stomach that?

Several months before the good news from the BBC, as Prime Minister Gordon Brown of the UK, Presidents Barack Obama of the US, Dmitry Medvedev of Russia, Nicolas Sarkozy of France, Angela Merkel of Germany and many other world leaders converged in London to plot a way forward, I adjusted my wake up time to 4:30 a. m. so that by 5:40 I was in the commuter train to Boston's South Station, where I spent half an hour to wait for the connection to Worcester, another one hour thirty minutes of commute, to start my first shift job at 8:30 a. m. By 5:35 p. m., I was again at Worcester's Union Station, on the return commute to south Station and then back to good old Brockton, reaching home around 9:30 p. m., all exhausted and good for nothing else than just fall on my bed and sleep.

A 161/2- hour day sounds crazy to most mortals, even me, but this became my new life as I emerged from unemployment social insurance check back on to the payroll, from hardly working to working hard, very hard. Rough as it was, I thanked my stars for making such a coveted swap that did not come to many people. What could be nobler than tackling microeconomics as our leaders burnt the midnight oil in London on the bigger picture? As an unemployed, newly minted citizen, I had a twenty-four hour stretch of boredom; now with a job in hand, I had little or no time for myself. What a world! The first few weeks I spent understudying my peers and seniors at work, putting into good use those lessons I had learned from the smart Dr. Stephen Corvey about investing in an emotional bank account, piling a reserve of trust and goodwill as well as easy communication so that with time I could draw from it. It made sense that a lot of contempt or disrespect diminishes the bank account slowly so that the slightest provocation could lead to a relationship incident and even a termination in difficult times. I learned to accumulate positive karma by depositing into my emotional account and withdrawing as sparingly as possible in anticipation of the proverbial rainy day.

But the rainy day came unexpectedly fast, much faster than I had bargained for. In spite of all the effort I put in, my immediate boss was apparently not satisfied with my contribution and just six weeks later I was asked to resign or be terminated. I chose the former and was escorted *manu militari* out of the premises of my employment by one of the heavyweights in place. It was clear to me that I was the victim of subtle discrimination clothed in other garments. Unlike *de facto* discrimination which belongs to the underclass, civilized American society does not often call it that way but it certainly is. No doubt about that. To the best of my knowledge I made neither more errors nor showed a worse learning curve than the other new hire recruited at the same time with me but given that the melanin on me did not command much indulgence in certain quarters, I took the cue and left gracefully, hoping that my subsequent encounters would prove more beneficial. It was all a question of melanin. Why make a fuss with so many other outlets around?

It was with shock and dismay that I was to learn, shortly afterwards, that next door in Manchester, Connecticut, another gentleman in a similar situation involving performance issues – he was reportedly accused of theft of drinks and other matters – opened fire and shot eight persons to death as he was being led out of the Hollander family business, a beverage distributorship where he had served as a driver for one year. Could I have done likewise? Surely I was downcast the morning they let me go but I doubt that I could go down that road.

Omar Thornton did, leaving a trail of sadness behind as he called the police and then turned the gun on himself. Grieving relatives of his victims as well as every other concerned citizen just wondered why a man would commit such a senseless act. Only a handful of psychotherapists bothered going beyond the bare facts to look closely at what could possibly have pushed a man to such extremes. Stress was blamed, as were loss of job, loss of dignity, public humiliation, victimization, alienation, rejection, lack of skills to cope with stress and finally, a desire for revenge. While these sounded plausible, no one seemed to venture into the area of defective upbringing. Given the number of children growing up in very degrading situations – lack of parental love and care, single parenthood, abusive parents, experimental parents trying themselves at the new fad of same-sex marriage – who can say how much impact is exerted on kids growing up under such experimental situations? How many kids benefitting from the love, care and support of the two-parent home ever resort to such extreme behaviors in later life?

And so as those world leaders concerted from April 3 -5, 2009 to combat the worst economic crisis since the Great Depression of 1929, it was only natural for citizens to do their part. The G-20 summit agreed on injecting about one trillion dollars into the World Bank, publishing a leaked black list of all tax havens, notably those cocooned in sanctuaries of the legendary secrecy of the 300-year Swiss banking typified by UBS, and on preparing merited sanctions for culprits (dictators, mob dealers, drug dealers, and others) who drained their respective countries' resources and evaded paying due taxes. They also agreed to impose strict oversight on large hedge funds and on credit rating agencies to sit up and make new rules for bonuses and executive pay. Lehman Bothers, AIG and many other financial goliaths had taught the tax payer a bitter lesson. Smooth as the London summit seemed to outsiders, there were blame games all over as many countries traded harsh words over the role America had played to bring about the mess. Obama's cool, gentlemanly appearance did not reflect the internal bickering at all. Why so? France's president had even threatened to walk out if his views were not accorded the pride of place they deserved and Angela Merkel was not particularly enamored of America's policies based on Keynesian economics, her country being very averse to the type of capitalism practiced in the US.

But why would all the nations line up to blame America for the world's economic woes? Was it some sort of conspiracy? How guiltless were those other Pontius Pilates? Even China openly criticized America for running a blind race for money, with little regard for consequences. Germany picked quarrels with the way we managed hedge funds. And Angela Merkel in particular was said to loathe Central banks that were so politicized as not to be able to make independent decisions at all. The pumping of so much money by our Federal Reserve Bank into the ailing economy must have frightened citizens of a country which learnt very bitter lessons at the time of the Weimer Republic and had since embarked on national savings as opposed to the spending spree on mortgages in the US and UK. But surely Germany must adapt to the times. How can one stimulate an ailing economy without encouraging some degree of consumption of goods and services? And Russia? Well…, Russia has never really been fond of the US in the first place, in spite of preposterous claims by our own Bible-thumping George W. Bush in 2001 that he was able to look into Vladimir Putin's eyes and actually see his soul -quite a claim, in view of what happened subsequently in South Ossetia and Georgia, masterminded by the former KGB spymaster who continued to call the shots even if Dmitry Medvedev was ostensibly at the helm in Russia. And Brazil, our southern neighbor? We dared not even go there!

It is quite true that America had handed out subprime mortgages like hot dogs at a ball game, turned a blind eye to the weaknesses in our regulation and felt fine undermining our nation's financial foundation as long as the dollars were flowing. But wasn't everyone else doing the same thing? And should China not be more sympathetic to our plight? What was all this business of the kettle calling the pot black any way? The climate of déjà vu was palpable. The Chinese had been lending the US government money in the billions of dollars, watching gleefully as their export sales lighted up like fireworks. They celebrated like everyone else on America's thundering locomotive of consumerism that drove it all. Now, simply because China was the largest foreign holder of American debt, the Chinese were eating some of the losses from the downturn in the markets.

Suddenly they weren't so keen on capitalism any more. On a PBOC website, Zhou Xiaochuan, the governor of the People's Bank of China, proposed replacing the dollar as the world's international currency. His reason was that the financial crisis reflected "the inherent vulnerabilities and systemic risks" of the dollar-based economy. That analysis was correct, except that he left out a very significant fact – to mention that the dollarized world economy developed huge potential instabilities (trade imbalances and massive international money flows) and that China and other nations too were implicated in the dollar system's failings. Those countries had kept their currencies artificially depressed as a means of aiding exports, thereby abetting the very imbalances they were criticizing. How could China denounce American profligacy after promoting and benefitting from it? Low priced consumer goods like shoes, toys, television sets, and computers encouraged overconsumption. Clamoring for an alternative currency was one thing; finding that currency available to do the job was another. Neither the euro nor the yen could yet rival the dollar's stability, and the renminbi (RMB), China's currency, was not freely convertible for Chinese investments, at least not yet. China was urged to raise the renminbi by 10%, reduce her exports and increase internal consumption as a way of contributing to solving the economic crisis facing the world. Economists usually agree that China's very fast growth portends trouble for the world. But Chinese Premier, Wen Jiabao said "not so fast". He thought such a move would lead to factory closures, vast unemployment and a massive return of people to the countryside, which was unacceptable. Did he take comfort in Zimbabwe's currency being equally down south?

Ahead of the G-20 summit of November 2010 in Seoul, South Korea, the need was expressed again to avoid a currency war so as to achieve strong, sustainable and balanced growth instead of debilitating currency devaluations or trade and current account imbalances such as China's vast trade surplus with the rest of the world. It was also agreed to give the developing nations more say at the IMF and to move toward a more market-determined exchange system.

With the Germans, Russians and the others, it was a different verse of the same song. Everyone was at least guilty of something, not just America. But President Obama took all the blame stoically, and in stride. I wondered why. To stand amidst all of the insults in London and act as if all was fine? That did not make much sense for the president of the most powerful nation on planet earth! How would he deal with President Medvedev? His business-like approach with smiles and hand shakes contrasted with President Bush's unnecessarily enthusiastic backslapping. Previous American leaders were rather superficial in their dealings with the Russians, preferring to gauge intentions by less invasive methods such as simply looking at the degree of baldness on their heads.

In retrospect, the phenotypic characteristic of baldness featured in a rather bizarre manner in alternate generations of leaders of Russia going back to the time of the Soviet Union. Current leader, Dmitry Anatolyevich Medvedev, has natural hair growth but his mentor and predecessor, the guy who handed over to him and who still calls the shots by some remote control mechanism, Vladimir Putin, is very bald. Boris Nikolayevich Yeltsin the first Russian president from whom Mr. Putin took over had natural hair growth even if graying, but before him there was the balding Mikhail Gorbachev who, with his foreign minister, Eduard Shevardnadze, enriched world vocabulary with *Glasnost* and *Perestroika,* made overtures to Bill Clinton and was responsible for the fall of the famous Berlin wall and those many winds of democracy that blew across the continents. Before Gorbachev there was the natural haired Andropov who took over from a bald Leonid Brezhnev and the latter in turn came after Nikita Khrushchev, the epitome of the cold war, a man with plenty of natural hair and a good dose of tantrums, America's most unlikely tourist whom the FBI estimated would likely be killed by thousands of Americans just like thousands too wanted to see him here, visiting capitalism's farmers, workers, movie stars, Disneyland and more, under guide and protection from a Boston Brahmin like Henry Cabot Lodge.

Was there a logical explanation for this alternation in the occurrence of baldness from generation to generation of Russia's leaders? What would our own Sarah Palin, the youthful governor from Alaska tell us about this phenomenon viewed from her backyard? George W. Bush, America's 43rd president who claimed to see through President Putin's soul within, did not quite impress us whatever knowledge he acquired by that act. The shrewd Vladimir Putin had carefully manipulated and made himself Prime Minister, in charge of the all-powerful ministry of foreign Affairs, convinced that Mr. Bush had thrown away all the aces dealt to him early in his presidency.

Some experts claimed that our no-drama Obama had reasons to play cool in London, considering the big political shake up over the economy here at home, the Republicans having been knocked out by the Democrats in the 2008 races. Some of the harshest criticisms came from leaders facing serious political jabs at home. Barack Obama, at that moment the most popular politician in the world, did not face a reelection for another four years down the road. Thus he could afford to let other world leader friends do a little grandstanding at his expense, especially if in return he was able to get more commitment to support his global economic recovery plans. The G-20 decision to inject trillions into the world economy was not a bad price to pay for such jabs at America. All the balderdash about his genuflecting before the Saudi monarch was moot. In a difficult world, with good and evil running neck to neck, one soon learns that just a little act can tip the balance one way or the other. By doing just a single good deed, it is possible to tip that proverbial scale for ourselves and even for the entire world on the side of good. Obama surely knew so and was working with that in mind.

Of course it would be a mistake for America's new president to conclude that all those good people were wrong. He would need to take a critical look at some of our own practices, such as taxing of savings and dividends which is like penalizing them while promoting consumption by subsidizing home equity loans with mortgage write-offs. Some level-headed, innovative thinking is that instead of taxing income, America should change course and tax expenditure, so that the more we spend, the more we pay. In this way Americans will be encouraged to save or at least curtail frivolous spending as a way of reducing the nation's huge deficit.

The Harvard-educated president even struck a compromise between angry Chinese and French leaders. Hu Jintao and Nicolas Sarkozy bickered over the wording of the final communiqué, especially the naming and shaming of tax havens, including Switzerland, Hong Kong and Macao. For decades such havens were used by corporations that used offshore operations to avoid taxes, sidestep laws or deny citizens certain rights. For decades Swiss banks such as the UBS, had acted as a haven for all sorts of ill-gotten wealth, especially money looted out of the treasuries of impoverished African and other third world countries by dictator rulers who considered themselves too important to be touched. Of late Ghana in West Africa was reportedly joining the club as well!

Now, a pleasant outcome of the London summit would be that the searchlight of the whole world would be focused on such havens and perhaps something done to retrieve the loot or at least stop the evil practice. Society had come to rely on information leaks in order to get to the bottom of hot issues like revelations about ill-gotten wealth stashed in Swiss banks, which could help fill the budget holes of the US government. Apparently Googles Inc. managed to pay less income tax by a deft shifting of revenue through Ireland, the Netherlands and on to Bermuda, taking advantage of an Irish tax law. The smart process, known to lawyers as "Double Irish" or "Dutch Sandwich" is said to be quite legal. Ever since Watergate, Americans had come to appreciate leaks of top secrets. Thanks to a whistleblower called "*tarantula*" Swiss banking authorities were reported to be on the verge of handing over to US authorities, the names of some 10,000 customers of theirs, among them some tax evaders. Smarting from a raw deal he suffered at the hands of his USB employers, the informant, a citizen of American nationality, gladly gave away the inner workings of the secrecy that enabled Swiss banking to be a haven for so many tax evaders. Having at last pierced the Swiss Bank's secrecy laws, the US treasury was set to collect a sum of $780 million fine from USB as well as cooperation to find thousands of other tax evaders among its many secret customers and people like California's real estate billionaire Igor Olenicof who came clean of their own free will were given lenient penalties as long as they paid Uncle Sam all the back taxes owed.

If such an operation could be stretched to help third world countries flush out their fiscal desiccators, wouldn't that be wonderful? But Swiss banking authorities were fighting back, especially when fingers from France pointed to Swiss fiscal complacence that had allowed huge fortunes from French immigrants resident in Switzerland (*L'Hebdo* of 07/15/2010).In view of the close ties between the French and the Swiss, no one was quite advocating an open war as yet, but the signs of conflict were there. Swiss authorities claimed that rightly or wrongly, their country had become a refuge because of its reputable democracy that was both stable and trustworthy, if annoying to and free of the disgusting atmosphere elsewhere where leaders, supposed to incarnate the dignity of the State, ended up putting roadblocks on the paths of fellow citizens, using their positions to serve themselves and their clannish interests rather than to serve their Republic.

Irked by the crackdown on the press investigating the wrong doing in Berlusconi's Italy and Sarkozy's France, the Swiss were leaving no stone unturned in letting the world know that their neighbors live in a rather large glass house, utilizing policies that tend to stymie democracy. Their allies, disaffected French nationals who had settled in Switzerland for nearly a century, were bitter and letting loose some information embarrassing to President Sarkozy and his entourage, especially with respect to what they claimed was their riches threatened by politics back in France. France has never quite produced any world class boxer but she surely knows that a good fighter does not just deliver punches but receives some as well. Such remarks from Swiss banking authorities highlight not just French fortunes stashed away in Switzerland, but also those third world fortunes from blood diamonds, swindled petroleum and other looted treasury reserves. And of course the billions of dollars America was complaining about. How the large suitcases containing such colossal sums of money did get across international borders remains unclear. Obviously the transfers could not have taken place by regular money transfer institutions which would most certainly raise red flags.

Asked if USB cooperation with US authorities would not undermine the Swiss banking system, an official of UBS said they respected the integrity of Swiss Laws. New York's Attorney-General, Andrew Cuomo had also released an investigative report indicating that giant banks like Goldman Sachs Group Inc., Morgan Stanley and JP Morgan Chase and Co. had paid out bonuses which far outweighed income, showing no clear reasons to the way the banks compensated and rewarded their employees, all of which weighed heavily on the American taxpayer.

Eventually President Obama smoothed the rough edges of the London summit with simple but smart gestures, replacing "recognizing" with "notes" the list of naughty tax havens. The very pragmatic and youthful US president used the occasion to bring home the message to Americans and to other nations who looked up to the US for leadership. He said, *"You got a sick patient and applied the right medication to stabilize the patient. There are still wounds to heal and emergencies could still arise but at least some pretty good care is being applied."* Dow–Jones, Nasdaq, S&P 500 as well as other economic indices responded favorably northward and US stocks rallied for a third day as data pointed to a stabilizing economy. For the Dow to rocket to 10,015.9, it was to reach a golden goal, the first time in a year. That was really something. The soaring of the market was good news and to be expected, coming as it did after the crack down on corruption and the many reassurances to the investing public.

Treasury Secretary, Timothy Geithner said that the national economy was showing initial signs of stability, if just a beginning, and conceded that we still had a long way to go. He was supported by other economists and professional forecasters from the National Association of Business Economists, National Association of Realtors and others who said the US recession was set to end soon in spite of continued job losses and plunging housing prices. Opinion polls showed that Americans needed much more infusion of confidence in the economy, called for a lock up of the crooks, more tax cuts and more economic stimulus. When Judge Denny Chin of the Federal Court in Manhattan, NY sentenced Bernard Madoff to 150 years for his Ponzi scheme, citizens received the news with much relief and hoped that the law would catch up to the other crooks that had brought the economy to its knees.

The early signs were quite encouraging indeed. Google searches indicated that the recession was at last waning. Queries for luxury brands like Mercedes Benz, Gucci products, champagne, Aston Martin, holidays and marriage guidance had risen while at the same time second incomes, swap shops and pawns were dwindling, reflecting the blossoming optimism here at home and in most western countries.

But skepticism still lingered, however. Was the recession really over? What the financial experts considered the waning of recession indices did not immediately touch the lay person. It was inescapable to draw the parallel with Imams who alone claim to see the moon that signals the end of fasting and beginning of feasting around the Ramadan, or seeing that elusive "green flash" at the horizon of the Grand Anse beach of Grenada sunset, a privilege claimed by the local folk, or the elusive green light at the end of a long tunnel which only Africa's providential heads of state and leaders are able to see.

Trying those novel ideas locally in Massachusetts and nationally, Governor Deval Patrick and President Barack Obama did not quite produce the earth-shaking changes hoped for. Indeed the huge inputs of economic stimulus monies had been persistently negatively correlated with rising unemployment claims, an outcome diametrically opposite of what was expected. Jobs were simply not there – white collar, blue collar, any collar at all. Ever since I found out that the color of the famous black box of aircrafts was anything but black, such job distinctions lost significance for me. Or was it too soon to expect those efforts to bear fruit? What should the ordinary citizen make of the divergent views? Some experts correlated them to the daily fluctuations of the stock market and advised investors to focus on their 401(k)s at 30 years. In other words the emphasis should be on the long term rather than the ongoing feverish reactions of the stock market. But America's life expectancy was not going to expand by 30 years! Where on earth did George W. Bush get the idea that letting Americans keep more of their money in their pockets would stimulate the economy?

What ever the case, the nation needed such good news even as citizens across the US rallied at the Boston Common and Christopher Columbus Park for Boston's second Tea Party, reminiscent of the 1773 incident when three shiploads of tea were thrown into the harbor by Americans who donned native Indian clothes to protest against British rule and the obnoxious taxation without representation. The American tax payer had simply become fed up with big government and the correspondingly heavy taxation that went with it. By railing out against President Barack Obama, Representative Frank Barney of the House Financial Service Committee and Speaker Nancy Pelosi, Americans hoped to draw attention to the pains caused by big government and big spending in bank bailouts. They hoped to apply the 1773 lessons when citizens revolted against the British rule and laid the foundation for the new nation. Even in London there were demonstrations too against the notion of unrestrained growth. Protesters asked how on earth the leaders could speak of growth without limit in a world where everyone agreed there was only so much natural resource to go round.

Meanwhile Americans were still expecting President Obama and Secretary of State, Hillary Clinton to start showing how "smart policies" were being used to do something about the flagrant abuses of human rights around the world. Historically it had been the forte of the Democrats to imprint the essence of human rights into the conscience of the world. President John F. Kennedy did it during his January1961 inaugural address when he proclaimed to friend and foe alike that America would resist the slow undoing of those human rights to which the nation had always been committed. Jimmy Carter too made the support of human rights an explicit foreign policy concern when, in his own inauguration, he declared, "Because we are free, we can never be indifferent to the fate of freedom elsewhere." Two other Democrats – Senator Henry Jackson and Representative Charles Vanik made the (Jackson-Vanik) landmark amendment that helped to win freedom for tens of thousands of Soviet dissidents.

This good record grew steadily murky over the years until it became virtually unrecognizable. Secretary of State Hillary Clinton asserted ahead of her visit to China that talking to Beijing about human rights was pointless since, according to her, "we pretty much know what they're going to say." She even went on to tell reporters that human rights must not interfere with more important issues such as the economic crisis or climate change. *Not too good, Mrs. Secretary of State!* Did Mrs. Secretary of State take a look at the note from Wei Jingsheng, imprisoned dissident to the Chinese leader, Deng Xiaoping saying, "You are at the top of one billion people and I am at the very bottom, but life isn't easy for both of us. It is just that I am not the one making your life difficult, while you're the one making it hard for me."?

Not even the belated call on Chinese officials to throw some light on the dark spot of Tiananmen massacre in China's history was enough to repair the damage already done. And on her arrival in China it was clear to the Secretary of State that Chinese authorities had virtually put dozens of democracy dissidents under house arrest. As if that was not bad enough, the proposal to name Charles Freeman to head the National Intelligence Council raised quite a few eye brows here at home. How could a man, popularly known as the Beijing sycophant, be considered for such an appointment, a man who not only defended the shocking 1989 Tiananmen Square massacres, but went ahead to publicly lament that the Chinese authorities had not cracked down soon enough? It came as no surprise that he withdrew his name from consideration. Still it was difficult to reconcile Hillary Clinton's soft stance with her husband, Bill Clinton's blasting the first President Bush for "coddling aging rulers with undisguised contempt for democracy and human rights."

On June 4, 1989 a massacre took place in China when protesters converged on Tiananmen Square in response to the death of a leading opposition figure. The Chinese military response left scores dead. Residents of Guangzhou rose in anger to protest against the government's murdering of Beijing's peaceful demonstrators. Schools and work places were shut down. People marched and occupied the main square and blocked bridges to prevent the army from moving in. Rumors of advancing tanks were rife while the local law enforcement authorities simply vanished out of sight.

One week after the massacre the Chinese government counterattacked with ruthless efficiency, imprisoning protesters, shutting down moderate newspapers, and purging the Communist party of members sympathetic to the protesters. From then on

Chinese media were forbidden to report anything related to June 4, 1989. The consequence has been that today's Chinese youth do not know anything about the Tiananmen Square massacre and the government likes it that way. Ling Chai, the lady famously called Commander-in-Chief of the 1989 Tiananmen demonstrations now lives in Massachusetts and heads a successful software company, Jenzabar Inc, only occasionally speaking out against the stifling of free speech in her native China. Safe out here in the US she occasionally remembers her fellow citizens back at home and very much under iron rule.

Western governments and governments in repressive countries around the world, more interested in promoting trade with China than democracy, have acquiesced a lot in this effort, downplaying and forsaking Tibet, Falungong, Darfur, Guinea, and human rights, all for economic convenience. The Chinese crackdown has certainly assured China's "stability," the climate our multinational corporations prefer. China's currency remains very secretive and very nonconvertible. Ask any expert why the US borrows so much from China if that country depends so much on the much larger US market and you will be drowned in legerdemain or some sort of rocket science. Good old Google, for example, like many foreign corporations wanting to maintain a presence in China, agreed to remove information about the Tiananmen massacre from its Chinese website. Today Google is practically paying the price for that naïveté as it battles with the authorities in connection with censure and hacking issues. China versus Google has got the world holding its breath. Will Google pull out of China? If so how will other companies, such as Microsoft, react? Only time will tell. Of course Iran versus Twitter and the US versus WikiLeaks are other areas of conflict riveting world attention as well.

Early in the game Google agreed to censor its Internet searches to please the Chinese and comply with their laws, a thing which greatly upset the promoters of freedom and those who valued Internet without walls. Soon some of Google's accounts were hacked into, presumably by the Chinese in their cyber spying of human rights activists. This angered Google, the Internet giant which then decided to retaliate, starting with no longer censoring content and even threatening to pull out of China if possible. It would appear that a weakness in Microsoft Internet Explorer was what the hackers exploited in the Google attack, prompting Germany and France to urge their users to stop using Internet Explorer and switch to another browser, possibly Google's Chrome or Firefox. Fingers were pointed at Microsoft for not following Google's example to teach the Chinese a lesson. Before long Washington entered the dance with the Secretary of State asking for an explanation of the whole affair and to desist from jamming the free flow of words and ideas. Hillary Clinton actually criticized the Chinese authorities for practicing cyberspace censorship. But from a position of weakness! When one is a debtor, how much leverage can one pull? A foreign ministry spokesperson, Ma Zhaoxu was unrepentant, claiming that China was actually the biggest victim of the hacking and insisting that Google needed to obey Chinese law like everyone else. He even accused the US of imposing information imperialism on China and threatened that it could hurt China-US relations. Abuses committed under the Patriot Act hung in the air. As a first step in its decision to fight back, Google decided to delay the launching with China Unicom of two Android-based mobile phones developed in cooperation with Motorola and Samsung.

In order to please the Chinese, even House speaker, Nancy Pelosi steered away from human rights and focused instead on environmental concerns during her Beijing visit in May of 2009. That contrasted sharply with the very Nancy Pelosi who had earlier unfurled a banner in Tiananmen Square to protest. Pictures beamed to China by the BBC and other world broadcasters via satellite were blacked out whenever reference was made to the massacres. Pages of the *Economist* were ripped off by Chinese authorities following orders from party officials. Massacre is systematically crossed out from Chinese history books so that the young should not know about that incident. Amnesty International estimates that about one thousand democracy advocates were killed by the Chinese army on June 4, 1989.The news blackout continues till today and outspoken critics are put under house arrest, newspapers thoroughly warned, and popular information-sharing sites like search engines and social networks and even e-mail services have been blocked so as to ensure that no sign of dissent is given a voice. And so Tiananmen Square remains China's taboo topic.

Last summer I went to Plymouth on the eastern Atlantic coast to live a dream long deferred. And so to South Station I went, boarded the 8:56 a. m. commuter train and headed for Plymouth, reaching there just short of one hour. It was freezing cold and raining but so what? I went all the same. As one of America's newly minted citizens, I had two compelling reasons to make the trip – to locate the court where I would be performing jury duty and to locate that historical monument associated with the landing of the Pilgrim Fathers from England. It was the year 1621 and the vessel was the Mayflower, carrying a cargo of one hundred and two persons (English colonists) running away from religious persecution and King George's other evils. Actually they landed first at Provincetown, a little peninsular protrusion at the tip of Cape Cod but because of the infertile (sandy) nature of the soil, they moved to Plymouth five weeks later. History has been a bit unfair to Provincetown but our gay and lesbian friends have no quarrels living out there.

And so the first contact was made with native Americans- what is popularly called American Indians – and there began the long journey that led to the New England. Slowly those early colonists spread out founding various localities and all you need do is look at any contemporary map and see how many New Yorks, New Britains, New Londons, New Hampshires, and tons of other places named after their equivalent on the British Isles. The people also held a thanksgiving to appreciate what God had done for them over the long transatlantic voyage, encounter with hostile natives, new diseases, and all sorts of obstacles. Today we celebrate thanksgiving on the last Thursday of every November in commemoration of that historic landing. I climbed into the remodeled Mayflower which is fifty years old and saw the amazing artistry and creativity of those good old folks that began it all. How exciting!

I also visited the historic Plymouth Rock as well as the plantation that houses relics of the original Native Americans (the Wampanoags) and their dresses and crafts. It was like revisiting Sapga in Cameroon and all those Fulanis and Bororos and their cattle or returning to the Masai at the Serengeti in Kenya's rift valley. That this culture has resisted European influence for so long speaks volumes about its tenacity. It made me nostalgic for our own native traditions that Christianity and education swept into the dust heap of forgotten history. We lost it all and now I experience *langa throat* for other people's preserve. I really miss those cocks and chickens roaming about freely among people and doing their own thing without fear of molestation. The last time I touched a cow and drank milk directly from its udder was long ago, well before I became a primary school pupil at Azire in Mankon. The last time I climbed a tree to harvest pears, coconuts, guavas, oranges etc was long ago. The supermarkets here have solved one problem but created more for me. I romanticize about the good old days. It was so nice to see cranberry harvest, apples hanging from branches laden with ripe fruit. City life has shielded me for too long from the real world that matters. I like to be able to return to Kenya or revisit Vogzom, Ngaoundéré and Mbai Mboum in north Cameroon, catch fish in Barombi Kotto or Barombi Mbo lakes once more. I would like to enter Muea and eat bananas like a fool. Who will bring me my spear? Who will hand me a raffia bag and a cow horn for my drinks? This visit aroused latent feelings in me that made the weeks ahead quite hard to bear.

### Welcome to Black Friday and the digital world.

The famous black Friday followed, when everyone rushed to the supermarkets to make the best possible bargain of the year, to initiate the Christmas frenzy. Coming the very next day after thanksgiving, this speaks a lot about our propensity to spending, even at these difficult moments when our economy is crawling on its stomach like a pregnant gecko. Corporate America has really gotten all of us into their pockets in an effort to go from red to black in their record keeping. The number of holidays has multiplied and every one of them is designed to encourage spending, especially the pseudo holiday called Valentine's Day, created to sell candies, flowers and greeting cards, in this way turning our wives, mothers, sisters and some of our men into shopping machines. I needed to fulfill the yearly ritual of picking up some winter stuff in preparation for the cold season. Every past winter I lost my gloves, forgetting them in buses, trains, friends' homes, cars and just about everywhere I used them to keep warm in an unforgiving freezing weather. I was determined to make a difference in the new season ahead. One month before Christmas, radio stations were known to have played Leroy Anderson's 1948 song *Sleigh Ride* at least 43,000 times, followed by *Winter Wonderland*, 38,000 times, according to ASCAP's (American Society of Composers, Authors and Publishers) survey. In a country driven by research and research findings, what could this mean? According to ASCAP's executive vice-president, Phil Crostland, music listeners are eager to get into the holiday spirit or it was just part of the Christmas creep – an incentive to get people thinking about the holidays so as to spend earlier. The fundamental principle of course is that if it does not generate advertisement revenue, no music is played on radio and so across America many radio stations were already 24/7 with holiday music. The good music was indicative of the good times – fresh signs of the economic buoying out of the doldrums, jobless benefits at a two year low, home sales experiencing an upswing and retailers experiencing a stronger than expected sales represented by shoppers flocking in large numbers for the Black Friday bonanza.

And so on black Friday Ashley and I went up to our city's shopping plaza to try our luck at bargain hunting, and later ended up at Wal-Mart, the most popular retailer in our city. (The shopping mall has been aptly described as capitalism's voting booth; every purchase made there is a "vote" in the economic sense when compared to the 50% of adults who vote politically once every year or two). Since we had different needs we decided to go on separate isles but agreed to be out of there in an hour. As we walked toward the check out line, Ashley decided to rush to the ladies' room and so I took over the shopping cart and proceeded to occupy our position on the line. By the time I reached the cash register, she had not yet returned, leaving me no option but to pay for the purchases and have her refund whatever was her due later on.

The checkout clerk worked diligently and fast, using the barcode reader and punching the prices manually where necessary. When she got to a pair of black gloves, she noticed that there was no barcode and no price tag. She asked if I knew the price. "My friend had picked the gloves but right now she is in the ladies' room" I told her. "I doubt that they would be more than $2.99" I concluded in my wise estimation. Rather than make eye contact or call for help to verify the price of the gloves, the clerk looked instead at the queue in front of her, which was getting uncomfortably long with customers waiting to check out, some held back by shopping carts whose owners had drifted back to make one last pick. She decided to bypass the computer system and ring up the gloves for $2.99. Wasn't that my lucky day?

Later, as we drove home, I proudly told Ashley how I had made a very good bargain on her behalf, talking the cashier into charging only $2.99 for the gloves which were unmarked. Surprised, Ashley looked first at the gloves in the backseat, then at me and at the gloves again before blurting out *"But those are my personal gloves which I wore into the store! You just paid Wal-Mart for gloves that I already own!"* Well, well, well, I had lost again. It was unthinkable that I would go back for a refund and be confronted with my stupidity. The corporate giant had won once more in an arena where the customer was supposed to be king.

That was the least of my problems with the way capitalism had reduced customers to playing only second fiddle in a game in which they are purported to be all kings. The things we buy in supermarkets are hardly the items of our first choice. From our shaving sticks, shaving creams and make up materials, to items of clothing like the Levi jeans, someone else decides for us. We buy mainly "redesigned" products for added comfort and value. Innovation is the key word. The sneakers we buy today can hardly compare with those good old Jack Purcell varieties which have gone out of vogue because producers improved and put them out of business. Comcast Corporation recently struck a deal with General

Electric Company to buy a majority share in NBC Universal with the aim of creating a media superpower to influence and control how TV shows and movies are made and delivered to our homes. This is an acquisition several times more powerful than when AOL bought Time Warner around 2001. As the leading cable distributor and Internet Service Provider, Comcast will soon be able to make us receive TV through our PC and vice versa, using our Internet connections to watch television shows. Entertainment, business and everything else in our lives will be rolled into one. As my neighbor aptly puts it, American consumer capitalism is at work, with its guiding ideology, the notion that a certain invisible hand of the Market is doing the trick. The market virtually takes upon itself to improve on things customers don't want or need. In the process, useful, effective products are made to disappear in the name of improvement. How I miss those open markets in Lagos, Nairobi, Accra, and Douala where goods are displayed openly on vast stretches of land for as far as the eyes can see, and where one can actually move around and haggle. This market of the west with its invisible hand is killing me! Most Americans are not even aware of the origins of the products they buy since they concentrate mostly on the cost price.

On June 12, 2009 for example, we all were in for a big surprise as digital television replaced the analogs we had become so used to. Analog signals were cut off so that customers in the Boston market (East, Center, Southern Massachusetts, the Cape, and parts of New Hampshire and Vermont) suffered this fate. Most could hardly buy and install converters to be able to receive digital TV. What had happened to the early musical devices –cassettes, cassette players, records, record players - was now also affecting television. Good bye rabbit ears! Uncle Sam's TV-transition website assured analog holdouts that "digital broadcasting allows stations to offer improved picture and sound quality". The government's converter coupons of $40 did not go far enough; so many families were left in the dark during the switch over to digital. Studies carried out by Nielson research showed that over 28,000 homes were unprepared for the switch. For most of us this was déjà vu. When New Coke was brought in to replace good old coca cola, it was quickly withdrawn following a humiliating failure. But why did the government not allow digital to compete with analog, the American way? Where on earth was the Sherman antitrust Act? Why kill the ideal of competition? And what was the $40 coupon for any way?

The old fashioned coke did not come back; customers were instead saddled with coca cola classic where a cheaper, high fructose corn syrup was used in place of cane sugar. Each day as I watched Gillette's World Shaving Headquarters on my early morning commute into Boston's South Station, and beyond it, the Boston harbor, where Americans dumped British tea into the water and switched to coffee, I regretted that my old reliable blades had been replaced by improvements that did not meet my needs. Gillette has changed it all and brought in lots of other items, sold to customers in various guises, including nudging, coaxing and coercing like *"Persons emanating foul body odor in confined spaces may be reported and cited for olfactory violation"*, used in advertising antiperspirant products that presumably turns odors into freshness. Americans still drink tea but that is nothing compared with coffee. Good old coffee. Let no one dare take away coffee from Americans! Water contamination resulting from a burst water main coupling in Boston led to Governor Deval Patrick's order to boil drinking water; nowhere was the effect more dramatic than the mad rush for coffee in Boston. Unlike Cambridge which was relatively unscathed, water scarcity was felt in Boston, making it difficult for Dunkin Donut, Starbucks and other giants to provide Bostonians their cherished and beloved morning fix of caffeine in the form of java.

Cell phones of every conceivable design are replacing good old landlines just as surely as the PC put type writers out of business and automobiles rendered buggy whips and horses virtually extinct. Cinema and television took over the novel, similar to what photography did to painting. In the twentieth century we all agreed that a picture was worth a thousand words and even more, especially as words became uselessly blunted through overuse, innovation, creativity, casualization and more. Conventional employment linking employer, employees and work premises will soon be a thing of the past as outsourcing and virtual online business take center stage. Like a dream the ATM has put many bank cashiers out of business. Capitalism surely dispenses with satisfied customers as it seeks to woo new clientele, possibly among the dissatisfied. The invisible hand of the Market is certainly not after loyal customers but those whose loyalty still needs to be negotiated on new terms.

In view of these realities, it seems prudent to try to update or else risk being left out. In the past we used the Beer-Lambert Law converting light path measurements, substance concentration and other parameters into optical density readings on our spectrophotometers as a guide to monitoring analytes that told us about diseased states like myocardial infarction, pulmonary embolism, diabetes and others. Today we must switch to the digital thing and use ultramodern analyzers interfaced with the PC. The same goes for our photography as old model cameras make way for the digitals. General Motors, Chrysler and some newspapers are paying the price for making haste too slowly along this path. Nokia, the world's biggest maker of mobile phones seems to be losing business to Apple and Google as a result of slow pace of innovation. Welcome to the digital age or consider yourself lost out in the Dark Ages of the past. The Vatican has banned American Catholics from digital confessions using the iPhone - a personalized examination of the conscience of believers – insisting that nothing of the sort could ever take the place of admitting one's sins to a priest in flesh.

The trend is changing pretty fast. Welcome aboard. Online exchanges (e-mails, Zuckerberg's Face book) are fast replacing the sounds of human voices, the presence of actual human beings. The social space is vanishing fast as the virtual world gains prominence. Libraries, like the JFK Library Digital Archive in Washington D. C., are pulling down book shelves to make room for study halls with lovely new computers as they make strides towards the digital world of the future. Only the good Lord knows what will happen to books as headmasters and college planners continue to gallop into the digital future. Computers can be found in many homes. Classes too can be there. In fact neither Socrates nor Plato ever needed brick buildings for their classes. So education leaders of today might just as well sell off all the buildings for a huge profit. My dear son works mainly from home now because his company, one of the new smart start-ups, downsized and eventually moved out of a building currently carrying a prominent "*For Lease*" sign.

Forty years ago I came to this country as a freshman, rented an apartment stacked with my belongings, prominent among which were music albums of the 45 or 78 rpm stacked in boxes, taking up space and dust. And then there was the corresponding record player with its graphite needle. I also had tape players with all sorts of music cassettes and VHS tapes which have all become obsolete. Gone also are my fountain pens and even the ballpoint ones popularized by the BIC Company. In their place came the polyvalent, all purpose cell phone. To start my car in the morning just before leaving the house for work or in the afternoon just before leaving the office, there is no need to go out of the house into a cold forbidding weather. I just use the electronic starter and start it right there in my bedroom or in the office and let it run for a while till I come out and take off.

The cell phone has shaken up life in today's society more than when machines replaced horses during the industrial revolution. Cell phones double as pens of all stripes, address books, telephone directories, newspapers, writing pads, greeting cards, maps, camera…the list is very long, mon vieux! It is amazing how many Americans are connected to the cell phone, an MP3 player or some other electronic gadget at any one moment, dancing off their heads. The new fad is quite infectious and unlike other aspects of the dominant culture new comers do not require much initiation to join in. Internet connections to an entire world, video games, calculators, and of course the telephone itself, are all possible thanks to the awesome microchip.

In those good old days, if I drove my car through a red light, the highway patrolman was sure to follow me, flag me down and issue a ticket representing a fine. Occasionally I would be smart enough to play with my foreign accent, dribble the officer with some token gesture and get away with my traffic offence especially if I acted fast enough before he issued the ticket. These days, the story is different especially if I live in modern areas under the watch of the LAPD (Los Angeles Police Department). A simple digitally-activated camera just flashes as I speed past and in the next mail there will be a ticket backed by a photo of me and my offending car at the crime scene. It won't surprise me if the next stage will involve withdrawing such a fine electronically and directly from my bank account, thanks to the next upgrades. Now that President Barack Obama has appointed Aneesh Chopra as chief technology officer to establish technologies upon which enterprises can thrive, it is hoped that in the months and years ahead, there will be more of these invasive applications, drawing inspiration from what the Internet and cell phones have done to humankind. Such ideas come in on time. Bill Aulet, professor and director of MIT's Entrepreneurship Center is said to be partnering with a former student of his, Leland Cheung, to upgrade geeks to rock star status and accord them the type of hero worship Hollywood's walk of fame bestows, this time for innovations that drive job creation, especially in recessions. Internet started as a Defense Department project. Today its application is worldwide, thanks to the government expanding access to a wireless spectrum. The focus is now on expanding broadband infrastructure to enable people start all sorts of businesses.

The reality is that our present culture, especially youth culture of conventional print-based text is in rapid decline as screen-based, multi-media enhanced text (Internet) gets firmly entrenched. A typical teenager who read eight books the past academic year did cover six hundred pages of text messages, one thousand of Face book, and three hundred of e-mail. Digital material is increasingly available in portable formats - iPads, Android 2.0 Google maps, kindle, e-readers with 3.5 inch color touch screen, MP3 players - and getting cheaper too. Smart phones are growing in number and complexity as our whims carry us, making it possible for us to make calls, take photographs, find directions to where we are going, receive and send text messages and many more. The 126-year-old Oxford English Dictionary, authoritative guide to the English language, will slim down and eventually go out of print, thanks to the Internet, says the publisher, Oxford University Press. So many people prefer to look up words using its online products such that the digital version gets two million hits a month from subscribers, a sure proof that the speed and ease of using Internet reference sites as well as their ability to be quickly updated are contributing to phase out printed reference books. Yellow pages and white pages are going out of use too, as telephone companies go paperless! A pop culture expert is of the opinion that anybody without access to the online way of looking up things is considered too old to be able to read prints in pages. Eliminating the white pages of those voluminous telephone books will reduce the environmental impact (less paper, less ink) and save tons and tons of paper; energy is conserved in printing, binding and distribution. And so another casualty falls on the way side as information is obtained through social networks.

So the fate of the library should come as no surprise as technology moves at an exponential rate into the future. In the years ahead, even digital libraries themselves will become obsolete as school children read, speak, watch, and text their school work on all sorts of hand-held devices they take to school, leaving books in the back burner. Lending will be online and there will be dramatic social and educational changes in lifestyles. Amazon's kindle is supposed to be on the verge of taking off and eventually taking on the conventional books. Libraries and librarians are in danger of becoming extinct as budgets become dangerously cash strapped. They are virtually invisible to those in power because they have their own research staff, IT support, newspaper subscriptions and therefore fail to see how dependent the rest of society is on libraries for their own economic upliftment. Can libraries rise to the challenge when political rhetoric hardly mentions libraries among economic recovery topics? The American Library Association came out with a resolution in support of WikiLeaks, likening its role to the "courageous Pentagon Papers" publication. Computing has the lofty goal of going paperless. Microsoft's founder, Bill Gates, Apple computer's guru, Steve Jobs, Face book luminary, the self-effacing 26-year-old Mark Zuckerberg and many others are all heading in the direction of cloud computing, virtualization, mobile application and other novelties. As these lines were being written, it was announced that Apple Inc. had beaten Microsoft as the biggest technology company based on market values, thanks to revolutionizing consumer electronics with stylish and easy-to-use products like iPod, iPhone, or MacBook laptops. Mark Zuckerberg, the CEO of Face book and Time magazine's man of the year thinks his behemoth is fast overtaking Google as he aims at one billion users (one seventh of the world's population) by 2011. He joins a trail that began in 1927 with Charles Lindberg, the first person to sail solo across the Atlantic and ending last year with Federal Reserve chairman, Ben Bernanke. Face book surely transforms lives, changes the way we relate to each other and, for better or for worse, has done the most to influence events in 2010 with its new technology and social engineering.

Innovation continues to drive the capitalist market, aided occasionally by copycat antics and outright plagiarism. I didn't realize the magnitude of this problem of snippets of lyrics from less well-known artists finding their way into the works of the giants until I came across the story of Cameroon's Makossa King, Manu Dibango whose *Soul Makossa* surreptitiously got into King of Pop, Michael Jackson's *Thriller(Wanna Be Startin)*, Talla Andre Marie's *Hot Koki* into James Brown's *Hustle*, Tim and Foty's *Douala By Night* into Missy Eliot Timberland's *So Addictive* and recently, Cameroon's Presidential Guard's *Zangalewa* metamorphosing from Golden Sounds into Shakira's *Zaminamina or waka waka*, poised to be 2010 World Cup's official anthem. Outright litigation, quiet diplomacy, out-of-court settlements and prodding by FIFA authorities or pressure from consumer groups were apparently instrumental in righting some of the wrongs.

The diminished demand for paper will surely benefit society in pleasantly unexpected ways, including the moderation of our climate. For a long time tropical deforestation to export wood to European and North American factories had been a problem and even today people are looking for ways to curtail it as a means of solving the thorny problem of climate change. When Congo's President Denis Sassou Nguesso put the problematic case of the world's "second lung" before the United Nations, he was using euphemism and diplomatic language to describe the naked catastrophic exploitation of Central Africa's tropical forest by the likes of Jean-Christophe Mitterand and legions of business moguls in the temperate zone. Such a diminished demand for paper should slow down deforestation. (Curiously, of recent Cameroon's Issa Tchiroma Bakary seemed to be echoing the reverse of President Sassou Nguesso's message, arguing over National Public Radio that his country must not be prevented from felling forests to develop what America did, an argument reminiscent of a former member of the same government who once spurned democracy as an imported model but was ill prepared to do the same with his fleet of luxury vehicles).

Haba! If America belatedly came to realize the folly of deforestation, should the world not learn from such realization and look for alternatives? From the 16th to the 18th centuries, the primary sources of energy for the US (still under colonial rule) were wood, wind and water. During the 1800s, a period called the Industrial Revolution or the new energy era of steam, coal and whale oil, the US was on top in energy, a type of Saudi Arabia of that period, with virtually unlimited coal reserves. On August 27, 1859 the picture changed dramatically as whale oil became virtually obsolete with the discovery of oil by drillers in underground wells at Titusville in Pennsylvania. And so to coal, wind, and water the US was able to add oil. But these being exhaustible entities, there was need for prudent, sustainable use. That did not happen, leading to the need to look elsewhere for more oil. The 1973 oil crisis taught the US a lesson and since then the need to look for alternatives is sincere and steadfast. It is in the interest of the whole world to look for alternatives, especially in view of the disastrous consequences the world faces – droughts here, floods there, extremes of temperature and others.

The great river Congo is very important to Central Africa. Along its 2900 miles length it crosses the equator two times, the only river system in the world with its main stream in both the northern and southern hemispheres, thus benefitting from two rainy seasons –April to October from the north and October to April from the south. European explorers, H. M. Stanley and Pierre Savorgnan de Brazza discovered the river and opened it up for trade and staked out rival claims on opposite banks for Belgium and France. With time

Brazzaville became the capital of one Congo and Leopoldville that of the other, thus splitting the Bakongo people in what was typical of the European scramble for Africa. Independence followed forty to fifty years of colonial exploitation.

Africa Union's representative at the UN meeting of September 2009, Congolese president Denis Sassou Nguesso sounded remarkably well informed about what is at stake and it can only be hoped that he brings his homologues on board quickly. By highlighting the fact that his country, the Congo, lies in the famous Congo Basin, an area aptly described as the second lung of the world (after the Amazon), President Nguesso made the important point that the vast tropical trees in that region absorb a good quantity of emitted carbon dioxide and give off oxygen, thus contributing to the battle against climate change. It is estimated that 20% of the world's carbon dioxide emission comes from deforestation which is as much as emissions from cars, aircraft, trucks and ships combined. Deforestation by local farmers and corporate bodies (logging) stymies this natural cycle and brings about atmospheric pollution. Rampant bush fires set by nomadic herdsmen as well as slash and burn agriculture practiced by poor farmers on vast stretches of land do the same. For too long man's job remained the killing of animals and chopping down of trees, throwing whatever leftovers into nearby streams or in the wild. From the Congo to the Serengeti to the tundra, floods and droughts are threatening elephants, camel, cattle and polar bears. That is a very powerful message for those who might be tempted to overlook third world countries and their contributions in this equation. Conservation and all efforts geared towards reforestation will help in this effort to sustain the ecosystem. In this connection, some have suggested the idea of replacing notions like demand and supply by *"requirement of equity of resource use"* and *"capacity of ecosystem to produce"*. As President Nguesso rightly says, whatever legislation the US Congress and President Obama come up with, ought to consider provisions that will help prevent the irresponsible deforestation taking place in the Congo Basin and elsewhere. By associating the indefatigable tree planting Nobel Laureate, Wangari Maathai as good will ambassador to protect the Congo Basin's

Forest Ecosystem, the African union actually placed a square peg into a square hole. The novel ideas of carbon credit market and carbon capture technology are worth exploring as an essential link between entities in the industrialized and third world. Kyoto's Clean Development Mechanism allows parties in wealthy countries to purchase emission-reduction credits in developing countries by investing in emission-reduction projects. What could be better than pursuing this to the letter?

Two top scientists, hard core academics and colleagues at MIT, one of the world's Ivory towers, are sparring over the climate change debate, making matters even more complicated for policy makers. Reputed at one point to be convivial in their relationship, both are now heading in opposite directions, one a fervent believer in climate change, the other a skeptic. Both are studying climate change and the atmosphere at MIT. From the start both actually did agree that the evidence was not just there for catastrophic man-made global warming. Not any more. The intellectual foes and dueling icons have slowly drifted apart over the years as the world's most acrimonious debate rages on. 70-year-old Richard Lindzen, a skeptic to the core, is a lead specialist in atmospheric physics and says there is little to worry about emissions from power plants, factories and automobiles. His opposite number, 55-year-old Kerry Emanuel, persuaded by evolving science, has emerged as the preeminent voice on climate change's potential dangers, following his publication in 2005 that man-made change is a real threat.

Both scientists have traded acrimonies across the divide, with views like "irresponsible, misleading, spurious hypothesis" freely tossed around. The skeptic accuses his colleague of hyping the evidence and making a play for fame and funding in the age of Obama and Al Gore. They disagree on the interpretation of data as well as how to assess the risks amidst uncertainty over global warming's future impact – prudent steps to take, costs against catastrophe on planet earth. The skeptic is noted for questioning lots of basic assumptions that most people pass around as truth. He is reputed to smoke Malboro light, for example, and doesn't worry about dying from it; he doubts that acid rain was ever much of a problem and he questions the emerging environmental issue of man-made change, casts doubt over projections of future catastrophes and instead sees opportunism in some of the loud, alarmist race to obtain federal funding for research. He is known to scoff at the idea of proposing trillion dollar solutions to a problem that is much less and to challenge the widely accepted assumption that the amount of water vapor will increase in the atmosphere as the earth heats up, amplifying global warming.

His rival disagrees. In his 2005 publication in the journal, *Nature*, Kerry Emanuel said that rising North Pacific and North Atlantic sea surface temperatures - a possible result of global warming – were linked to the fiercer hurricanes of the 30 previous years and that hurricanes were fed by warm ocean water. He projected that they would become more powerful if climate change continued heating the oceans. A few weeks after his publication, hurricane Katrina struck the Gulf Coast, unleashing death and destruction on New Orleans and catapulting Emanuel to media fame. The connection gained even wider audiences, thanks to Al Gore's *"An Inconvenient Truth"* featuring smokestack emissions fueling a hurricane. Lindzen was understandably uneasy about his colleague's stardom and did not hide it. He saw questionable motivation and took a moralistic view on the matter. Emanuel cast his vote for Obama, especially in the candidate's promise to combat climate change followed by the high profile given to the issue by the new Obama administration, all of which led to a bigger rift between the scientists. Lindzen assailed the political nature of climate science and funding. At around the same time climate skeptics sent a letter to the US Congress, prompting Emanuel to challenge Lindzen about it, followed by the great MIT "climategate" debate which involved leaked e-mails among top climate scientists, sparking questions about their data and integrity.

Yet as the two giants battled it out, floods were turning Boston's streets into canals, a phenomenon news channels were hesitant to call by its true name. Rising sea levels in the Boston harbor could spill over into city streets! Back Bay and Beacon Hill areas were quite at risk, said Vivien Li of the Boston Harbor Association. Didn't scientists say climate change causes the water in increasingly warmer oceans to expand and ice sheets and glaciers to melt, thereby exacerbating the problem? According to Maplecroft, a British consultancy, the US, Australia, the United Arab Emirates, rich nations and OPEC nations big on the emission of greenhouse gases are big on pollution and have the worst records of 183 nations surveyed. Chad, a country with limited access to electricity was understandably listed the last on that list. Such a compilation would assist investors to know those nations likely to be targeted for sanctions if current UN-led climate talks should agree on it. Unprecedented floods in Australia in early 2011 have brought about understandable serious soul searching.

While the Maldives Island is lucky to be speaking of a future event involving submersion under the sea, there is an island that has actually ceased to exist. For thirty years India and Bangladesh were at daggers drawn over ownership of the tiny rock island called New Moore Island in the Bay of Bengal. Thanks to climate change and rising sea levels the dispute has been resolved – New Moore Island is gone.

Bangladesh, like the Maldives, is one nation threatened with sea level rise and has appealed to the international community to revisit the notion of refugees and asylum seekers in view of the imminent threat that country faces as a result of climate change. Brazilian forest inhabitants are seriously turning in spears and arrows to get laptops that enable them manage their rich tropical (Amazon) forest properly. Indonesia's leaders are assuring the world of their determination to fight deforestation with local resources and whatever input the rest of the world can offer. Greek Prime minister and president of Socialist International, George Papandreou expressed the need for green investment and bonds, carbon tax applied to all the polluters and a global spread of technical knowledge to facilitate green development. Prince Charles of the UK made it clear that capitalism without nature's own capital of natural resources was a pipe dream and called for concerted efforts to embark on reforestation of wantonly deforested tropical rain forests. The wake up call is being responded to in different ways. Will this jar the leaders into a serious effort or will they continue with business as usual? Film makers are toying with the idea of a project to bring to the attention of the world the dangerous acidification (carbon pollution) of the oceans as a result of the use of nonrenewable fossil fuels like oil and coal. The world knows about pollution by cars and airplanes but very little is known about pollution by ocean-going vessels, these being out of sight and therefore virtually out of mind. A good film will surely communicate and bring home this aspect of environmental pollution to politicians and policy makers.

Climate change remains an uphill task especially as the Copenhagen summit ended without the type of outcome many had hoped for. Complicating matters was a minor error that had surfaced in the IPCC's reports which the skeptics used as their "smoking gun" to confirm their feeling that the whole thing is a hoax and claiming that the error was the final nail on the coffin of global warming. In another strange twist of the climate debate, over one thousand scientists, some former members of IPCC, came out in Geneva against climate change, especially the notion that it is man-made. They called it a fraud based on forged data. Some claimed the entire thing relied on inadequate model to blame carbon dioxide and innocent citizens for causation of global warming, a mere ploy to get funding. Before the next meeting in India, IPCC chairman, Dr. Rajenda Pachauri went out of his way to allay the fears of the world in general and the skeptics in particular, admitting that an error had slipped into their Himalaya predictions where the 2007 IPCC report spoke of glaciers disappearing by 2035 instead of 2350. He insisted that the report remained a robust scientific proof of the fast receding glaciers. Ohio State University glaciologist, Lonnie Thompson added "glaciers do not have a political agenda; they just sum up what is going on in their environment and react to that."

Fortunately for the world, committed scientists are not giving up. Following the earthquake that hit Haiti, geologists and seismologists went to work and thanks to their grist, it is becoming clear that human activity can be linked to the tragedies. The tsunami that followed the fatal earthquake was studied in detail as well as the fault lines of the quake. What emerged from the combined studies is that a massive landslide triggered the tsunami and the landslide itself was found to correlate with a stretch of deforestation where the soil had become loose along the coast of Port-au-Prince in Haiti. Those who have experienced landslides inland will readily agree that such phenomena are facilitated by denuded deforested stretch of land! Hopefully, as the dust settles over north-east Japan, the world will learn some useful lessons about the most recent murderous earthquake and tsunami that shook that island nation.

Whether such clarifications would slow down the media frenzy remains to be seen but The Sunday Mail's David Rose went after the actors, challenging them to substantiate the facts fed to the public. IPCC insisted that climate change is expected to exacerbate current stresses on water resources from population growth and economic and land use change, including urbanization. On a regional scale mountain snow pack, glaciers and small ice caps play a crucial role in fresh water availability. Wide spread massive losses from glaciers and reductions in snow cover over recent decades were projected to accelerate throughout the twenty-first century, reducing water availability, hydropower potential, and changing seasonality of flows in regions supplied by melt water from major mountain ranges such as the Hindu-Kush, Himalaya, and the Andes, where more than one-sixth of the world's population currently lives.

For most of today's generation the fuss over climate change in general and forest conservation in particular may appear abstract especially as schools do not often include environmental studies in their curricula. Natural drinking water needs to be purified and trees in our forests play a pivotal role in this process. They stop or at least curb soil erosion and protect watersheds, thanks to their roots holding the soil together. Roots also filter out nutrients and other pollutants from foul drinking water. On the leaves of plants important chemical processes take place which detoxify the surrounding air by removing carbon dioxide, nitrous oxides and other noxious entities that contribute to such chronic conditions as triggering heart attacks or worsening chronic respiratory diseases like bronchitis, asthma, and emphysema. Our forests are food for us and the animals that share our environment. Given such vital roles it seems natural to want to protect our forests.

Still, the sources of opposition to or trivialization of the facts continued to mount. No less a personality than an Iranian Shiite cleric berated women who exposed their breasts for provoking earthquakes. Ayatollah Aziz Khoshvaqt and fellow clerics alerted President Ahmadinejad of Iran about the threat and soon Tehran was abuzz with rumors of impending disaster, virtually eclipsing expert seismologists, especially when other clerics like Hojatoleslam Kazem Sedighi joined in and told worshippers in Tehran that women who do not dress modestly, lead young men astray, corrupt their chastity and spread adultery in society, leading to an increase in earthquakes. Coming on the heels of worldwide earthquakes, from remote China to Baja in California to the volcanic eruption of Eyjafjallajokull in Iceland, the prediction caused a frenzy.

As a matter of fact the allusion to God's punishment being visited on humans as a result of women exposing their curves triggered an unprecedented worldwide reaction among the women, championed by a certain Jennifer McCreight of Purdue University who sought to put the idea to test. It was called "boobquake" and calculated ostensibly to disprove the clerics. Boobquake the mother of all seismic activity would be immortalized the way those shoes thrown at former President George W. Bush turned into a huge anti-American icon. The result was an earthquake of 6.6 on the Richter scale in far away Taiwan. Did that prove the ayatollah's prediction? Did that place boobquake on the same scale as other "human activity" in the causation of climate change?

It is wrong to continue to see history only from the perspective of the halls where treaties are signed and bills debated, where the main actors are Founding Fathers, politicians, generals and the big boys, while ignoring those things that happen on the streets – rebellions of slaves and brutal suppressions, fed up farmers, labor leaders, women's liberation movements, foot soldiers refusing to obey unpopular orders and agitators. Did such disobedience in June 1999 –preventing Russia from occupying Pristina airport - not stop a WWIII? Leaders ought to listen to other voices and rethink history as it helps them with policies. Until leaders come to terms with history turned on its head as the late Howard Zinn showed (*A*

*People's History of the United States*), many mistakes will continue to be made. "Three things exercise a constant influence over the minds of men", Voltaire once said, "– climate, government and religion. Historians and the government they advise often neglect the first of these, at their peril." The British empire, the Roman Empire, the Ottoman Empire, Ming China, Russia and many more collapsed under violence; unrest and rebellions were in one way or another linked by climate and weather problems, where normal weather conditions were disrupted by extremes of temperature, occasioning droughts or torrential rains resulting in collapses in food stocks and the unavoidable invasion of neighbors with more stable conditions of land fertility and harvests.

Ever heard of mobile madness? Money transfers to bank accounts, looking up train schedules, using Google maps to get directions and so many other daily activities have tied us all to a number of wireless gadgets of the modern technological age that enable us to save time. It is not unusual to hear a seventeen year old woman in wired cities like Boston, New York or San Francisco lament that going without her *iphone* or BlackBerry or any of the new smart phones for one day was the most painful experience she had had because with these she could text, e-mail, or call any number of friends and clients. GPS devices, twitters and laptops have become miraculous time-saving devices and productivity boosters. Apple Inc. is about to add a number of mythical products, including a magic mouse to the mix so that instead of those buttons and balls for navigation, simple finger gestures can do the trick. With the *iPad* tablet, a hybrid between the laptop and smart phones, users can now browse the web, play games, check world chess standings, manage their monies, keep in touch with pals, learn a new language such as Japanese, scan shopping coupons, act as personal assistant to help with organizing how much is saved by quitting smoking, run movies, among many other applications.

The sleek tablet computer with touch screen or other accompaniment *iBooks* is expected to rival Amazon's kindle e-reader and to enable publishers like Penguin, HarperCollins or Hachette Book group do brisk business. It is quite a revolution in the direction of miniaturization and price reduction – devices that used to take up quite a large part of a bachelor's one-bedroom apartment can now be fitted into a lunch bag with lots of room to spare. On my morning commute to the South Station of Boston I run into many students busy catching up with homework assignments that must have escaped attention the evening before. Inside the train these future leaders flip page after page of their text books as they perform their assignments in mathematics, chemistry, biology and the arts. I ask myself which is easier – scrolling down these smart electronic gadgets or flipping back and forth the pages of a regular textbook. On this lies the future of our electronic readers versus regular textbooks.

Several weekends before thanksgiving, we gathered at the home of some friend for a meal. Being quite famished, I began to eat ahead of every body. The practice of saying grace before meals had not been my forte for some time. Great was my shame when I discovered that every head was bowed in prayer except mine, or so I thought. As I looked more closely, it dawned on me that those nice folks were busy, not praying, but twittering under the table. These days it is common place to see a young girl of ten crossing a busy city street, oblivious of heavy traffic as her ears are hooked on to one of the many modern gadgets with which Apple Inc. and their rivals bombard the world. It is incredible how our lives have changed! On one side of her is another youth driving under the influence of some mind changing drug with car music several decibels loud. Who can say what a split second can make in the lives of the two? Kids have taken the cultural battle right to school where they ask to be allowed to use their iPods and other gadgets because they study better that way, a proposition that is against the rules because school authorities consider them a distraction.

The above notwithstanding, the voice of moderation is sounding the alarm about these constant and costly upgrades, warning that there can be no future without a past. The attempt by some school authorities to place themselves in the future will surely face difficulties. The future is always coming and always changing. It will get here from the past, passing through the present. Our libraries hold the past and going ahead without them is hard to imagine. Didn't we all arrive here through those ancient scrolls and those monks who put words and thoughts on parchments? Cultures that survived long owed it to the written text whereas oral traditions as prevalent in most of Africa have since fallen on the wayside. One can only wait and see.

In all fairness to the new electronic craze and the geeks, designers, promoters and marketers involved with promotion, customers are not totally blameless. We derisively label "old school" the practice of making a shopping list to match our budgets before going to the market, yet it is so smart when compared with the craze to carry a credit card and swipe for every single novelty that we cast our eyes upon. Haven't we all scornfully called the regular postal mails "snail mail" as we turned our attention to e-mails? Look at what is happening to many of our post offices and the services they provide. Haven't we taken the cost of labor to such prohibitive levels that we feel more comfortable buying brand new items (TV sets, computers, automobiles) than paying for the cost of repairing the old? Did we not complain about long queues and interminable waiting times at the counters of our RMV (Registry of Motor Vehicles), prompting the government to introduce an online transaction with a price tag of $5 for license renewals, vehicle registration and others? Yet we were up in arms about the novelty! Or was it against the fee that we rebelled? Whose interest was the innovation intended to promote – the state government or the customers? Officials said the changes were meant to benefit customers by cutting down wait times. Outraged customers smelled taxation. Against a looming political backlash, it was quickly closed. Like the post offices, libraries are fighting a battle for their survival.

Big cities have a commuting dilemma to solve and it is here that their pool of brain power is greatly challenged. People need to go to work, to the cinema theater or to the shopping mall. Driving to these places and events poses the problems of accidents, traffic jams, cost of gas and the associated problem of environmental pollution and prohibitive parking fees. Mass transit by bus or trains presents an alternative solution. But this too has its down sides – long waiting times at stops, rubbing shoulders with strangers, some of whom might be carrying the dreadful swine flu or offensive body odors, sacrificing privacy, independence and convenience, walking at the end of the ride.

To address these some smart brains have proposed something called the podcar or PRT (personal rapid transit) for the future. It is revolutionary in many ways, combining the advantages of the personal car and mass transit, while at the same time jettisoning their many disadvantages. The car will be light, small, run on electricity and hold just a few passengers, probably members of one family or a very close circle of friends. It is envisaged that such a car will be driverless and run along a network of elevated tracks in such a way that passengers will select their destinations and the vehicles will go straight to them, by-passing all other stations. What could be better than easing global warming, avoiding traffic jams and the dependence on foreign oil? What could be better than freeing the hands and mouth to engage in those other activities that would otherwise attract the traffic police – texting, twittering, phoning and more? Awesome indeed!

There will be monumental skepticism to overcome, especially the feeling that this is an unrealizable goal, having lain dormant for decades, the feeling of traveling by a roller-coaster above the city, problems related to esthetics, the thought of sinking a large chunk of money into such a monster project. Prototypes at Heathrow airport in London and elsewhere in the US will probably put aside these fears. Everything has its time.

Nothing illustrates the danger of this relentless pursuit of the new and discarding of the old better than the recent volcanic eruption of Iceland that crippled air travel and lots of interconnected businesses. The eruption of the Eyjafjallajokull that led to the grounding of aircraft and closure of major European airports, especially the big three – London's Heathrow, Paris's Charles de Gaulle, and Frankfurt – was a wake up call for a world that took kangaroo steps ahead without stopping to consider fall back positions in case of trouble. Yes, the crippling effects of Eyjafjallajokull provided the impetus. For almost an entire week all aircraft were grounded because of the visibility problem created over many European countries by the massive volcanic dust that placed flying at a definite risk. Coming only a fortnight after Poland's president, wife, government ministers, parliamentarians and military top brass perished in a plane as a result of poor visibility, travelers and travel agencies did not need much nudging to take the cue. Not only were passengers unable to catch their booked flights, the delays also hurt transplant patients waiting for donated organs or doctors to be flown across the skies to carry out their surgeries.

Eurotransplant which allocates kidneys, hearts, bone marrows and other life saving tissue from Canada and North America to destinations in the UK, Austria, Belgium, Croatia, Germany, Luxembourg, Slovenia and the Netherlands, was completely handicapped to carry out its vital functions. Belatedly officials began to contemplate using sea and land travel to minimize some of the losses. While Kenya's beautiful roses were wilting away, arrangements were made for a special private jet to ferry an athlete to Spain and, hopefully, through the Channel tunnel to London for the London marathon. Stranded at the Zurich airport, my pal Zaccharias learned one heck of a lesson that going from Condom to Intercourse is not just a few minutes or a roll over on his side as he had been accustomed to thinking. It was a long Calvary involving being caught in the wrong place, doing unplanned journeys in a foreign country, running out of cash and sleeping on the floor of a hotel before reaching his destination. Before flying over to his uncle in the United States, he had nursed the hopes of spending some of his stopover time visiting friends in France or Switzerland, especially the latter where he knew missionaries who had brought the word of God from Basel to Cameroon and had done such a remarkable job educating and converting young people to Christianity. When the lady at the counter of the Zurich airport learned of his travels, she got excited and told him not to miss Condom, a name that made him raise eye brows, necessitating the explanation that it was a little picturesque village along the way, in the countryside away from city noises and pollution. Of course, why not? If Condom was along his route, that should pose no problem at all. And there was none until he got back and found himself trapped because all international travels had been cancelled as a result of the poor visibility. Not having budgeted for any extended stay in a hotel and having run out of money he found himself sleeping on the floor for several extra days until he at last got onto a transatlantic flight to JFK and from there to Intercourse, north of Philadelphia. The only good thing to come out of the Eyjaffjallajokull eruption, albeit temporarily, was a dramatic conversion of climate warming to climate cooling over those days, thanks to a 50% drop in nitrogen dioxide level as a result of reduced air and road traffic.

Over the years newspapers have chronicled the rise, reign and demise of countless institutions. It looked like the time had come for them to write their own obituaries. No matter their faults, newspapers are indispensable to the health of a democratic society. The Rocky Mountain News of Colorado folded up on the last week of February 2009, having been pressured by many forces – recession, online revolution in publishing and advertizing, changing consumer taste. After the previous year's loss of $16 million dollars, the message was clear. The Boston Globe followed a rough ride like the other giants and people began to speculate how Boston was going to look like without the Globe. It did not end with the giants. Our Patriot Ledger was in trouble too. So also was the Brockton Enterprise. Every single publication was threatened. Employees of the Boston Globe were being urged to agree to substantially reduce their compensations and benefits and to accept some layoffs, lest they end up strangling their parent company, *The New York Times Company,* in this way destroying the hand that fed them. Unemployment lines were growing long by the day as the economy slowed down; reasonable people knew it was by far preferable to remain on the payroll of a company than on unemployment insurance. But somewhere along the protracted negotiations the Boston Globe's largest union voted down by 277 votes to 265 a proposal to accept a $10 million concession (cut in benefits) prompting the paper's owners to put into effect right away a 23% wage cut as an interim measure while shopping around for a buyer. The Globe's guild felt that the parent company could do better than offer to close down the newspaper. As one of those giants too big to fail, the Globe lingered on in uncertainty.

A long list of corporations that were once prosperous and offered well paying jobs showed that some had failed to adapt quickly enough and so had faded into history. Companies like Digital Equipment Corporation, Wang Laboratories, Prime Computer, Data General, Polaroid, and GTE were history whereas IBM survived because it had tactically and strategically adapted to customer needs in an ever changing business climate. The typewriter may be resting in peace but IBM is still in business.

That was what most businesses needed to do. The newspaper is too important to fall on the way side. Thomas Jefferson, the father of our democracy is credited with saying *"And were it left for me to decide whether we should have a government without newspapers or newspapers without a government, I should not hesitate a moment to prefer the latter."* Obviously in a democracy, society needs newspapers to keep a tab on their elected representatives in the State House and in government. Like the Boston Globe, the Christian Science Monitor, the Seattle Post Intelligencer and the Rocky Mountain News were among the many others threatened with closure. Media tycoon, Rupert Murdock considered charging for online content within a year. The man whose empire runs the gamut from the Wall Street Journal, the New York Post, The Sun, the Times to the Sunday Times of the UK, was challenged by an online news celebrity, Adrianna Huffington whose editorial in the British newspaper, the Guardian, asserted that newspaper outlets would never be able to return news content behind their walled gardens.

Only time will tell which way the balance tips. The impact of social networks was recently demonstrated during the much flawed Iranian elections where the government put a tab on all conventional news outlets, pushing her citizens to fall back on cell phones and other means to tell the world how it happened. Even in less dramatic situations, most people who go on line and read a news item are reluctant to buy newspapers to read the same news published much later. As a matter of fact France has declared Internet Access a basic human right, alongside water, air and the other things because, the reasoning goes, a human being with Internet access is a full time active member of the community. Newspapers surely have an uphill task ahead and attempts to pass legislation to come to their aid with some sort of bail out (Newspaper Renewal Act) face the obstacle that government will be seen to fund the watchdog of its own actions. Some persons had suggested that the US Congress step in and create a nonprofit or limited profit tax structure similar to 501(c)(3) companies which could own and control newspapers as a way to save them. It sounded rather radical but responsible journalism is as vital to our culture and democracy as our churches. Yet churches are tax exempt whereas newspapers are not. Ultimately the saving grace for newspapers will lie in the number of readers preferring to stick it out. Preliminary studies seem to point to the direction that prolonged viewing of any screen –TV, computer – is bad for the eyes because it brings about computer vision syndrome, a condition experts think can be avoided simply by taking twenty minutes of eye rest every now and then. And prolonged keeping of the laptop on the laps is supposedly associated with secondary infertility as a result of prolonged increase in temperature around the sensitive groin region.

Walter Leland Cronkite, also known as the "most trusted man in America" received many encomiums from past collaborators, heads of state, diplomats and many citizens for his marvelous job as the anchor of the CBS news over the years. As a matter of fact it was reported in some newspapers that countries like Sweden and Holland had eponymously named their news anchors *Kronkiters* and *Cronkiters* respectively, honoring this man who showed a rare passion for the job, displayed a contagious enthusiasm and trust that earned him respect from the US and beyond. Walter Cronkite became the gold standard for objectivity and even handedness in reporting the news and passing judgment over thorny issues.

Here was a journalist who covered World War II, the Nuremberg trials, the Cold War, the Cuban missile crisis, the assassination of America's beloved president, J. F. Kennedy and charismatic civil rights leader, Reverend Martin Luther king Jr., America's space program, the first moon landing and the Watergate saga, among many other momentous events. Walter Cronkite recognized that people needed diverse and competing media outlets with resources and skills to examine issues from a variety of perspectives and to challenge entrenched power. The man stated his case very clearly that journalism's role should not be to tell Americans what they wanted to hear but what they needed to know as citizens because that is what makes democracy work. Today corporate monopolies and media are more concerned with commerce and entertainment than civics and democracy. The man sincerely believed that news outlets with multiple owners and different view points tend to encourage debate and the airing of all sides or at least most sides of any issue.

The newspaper industry's problem reflects how cruelly the failure to adapt can kill an otherwise lucrative business. Well before the Boston Globe launched a website of its own, it would appear that a young business entrepreneur had come calling and had actually offered executives of the newspaper a share in his digital world which sold help-wanted advertisements online. He was reportedly scoffed at by the financially healthy newspaper which considered it ridiculous sharing its $100 million yearly advertising business with anyone else. The entrepreneur eventually sold his idea to another undertaking that quickly expanded to Monster.com, a website that by the year 2000 was fetching more than $500 million a year! That painful pill spelled the end of monopoly of newspapers on classified advertising. Advertisers might have relied on newspapers to post job openings, sell homes and cars to a broad audience. But more and more people had begun to migrate to the Internet, making websites like Monster.com, Craigslist.com, and Cars.com equally available to the very audience. Newspapers were spectacularly slow to recognize the shift and to react to it. Changes of this type were much felt in large cities like San Francisco, Boston, and Seattle where the readership was quicker to embrace mobile technology, websites like Google, Face book and others. People with broadband access spend more time online and look to the Internet for news and advertising. The drop in print advertising has been precipitous and belated efforts to introduce online versions of newspapers came a little too late. Losses in the magnitude of $50million together with the present recession have spelled bad days for newspaper business. It is true that difficulties involving access to the electronic media still make newspapers the ideal source for news and advertisement. Businesses that do not have their own research and development (R&D) departments and are reluctant to adapt to the findings of Nielson Media Research will surely experience a rough ride ahead.

If ever there was need to show that an enterprise needs R&D as an integral component of its operations, the saga of the newspapers proved it beyond all doubts. By keeping a tab on trends – increase or decrease in sales and readership, emergence of online readership etc, policy makers are in a better position in deciding which way to go. Some persons strongly believe that the Boston Globe was suffering the loss of good will as a result of Cardinal Bernard F. Law's call for divine intervention in a Roxbury church (*"By all means we call down God's power on the media, particularly the Globe"*) two decades earlier over what was perceived as the Globe's vigor in the pursuit of the story of the church's tolerance of sexual abuse by priests, especially in the intensive coverage of James R. Porter, a serial pedophile. Others doubt it. Whichever version is correct, only a good research would throw light on the cause of the newspaper's declining sales.

This of course is a small portion of a much larger phenomenon. In the years ahead the world will surely be coming to terms with another new trend – that of giving away things in order to make money. It sounds contradictory but that seems to be the way things are moving indeed. Recently the South-West Airlines announced that it would begin flying from Logan International Airport in Boston to Baltimore and Chicago, prompting a drop of 38% and 20% of airfares respectively along the two routes. Good for competition! A new vocabulary was born – the "South-West Effect". It shook other airlines to do likewise. Dallas low fare carriers, Air Tran Airways, JetBlue Airways would have to follow the trend. Already the recession had caused a drastic cut in fares; the South-West effect would surely take this many steps further even though authorities of Delta and other Airline skeptics did not think it was going to be a cakewalk for South-West Airlines.

Still, it was inescapable that capitalism was witnessing some unusual changes in business models. Giving things away for free needs a second look. It is the harbinger of a vast and fast-growing economy which does not charge consumers for most of its products since money is made through sponsorships. The Metro newspaper is distributed free throughout Boston and its suburbs! See what Google has done to advertizing! Users pay nothing to Google whatever they want; the company makes its millions through advertizing. Advertisers pay to reach the millions of users in the company's database. Does this spell the death of price? Probably not yet but there is no doubt that the Internet has revolutionized consumption patterns, making it possible for those entities that were once consumed as physical objects (CDs, newspapers, books, videos, music) to be digitized and for professional services to be handled by software. The price of each entity drops as processing power, storage capacity and bandwidth increase exponentially, making the marginal costs of the corresponding goods and services to drop. Gross oversimplification? We can only wait and see.

The cost of doing business in the digital world – providing each additional MP3, Internet dating, electronic books – is slowly dropping to zero with a corresponding drop in what customers have to pay for them, thanks to the driving force of the explosion seen in computing capacity. What began as a mere marketing gimmick in the twentieth century is going to become the twenty-first century's bedrock business, according to Chris Anderson, editor-in-chief of Wired Magazine and author of the best seller *The Long Tail* and a forth-coming title "Free: The Future of a Radical Price". Thus in the new world one would make money simply by giving things away, torpedoing the old notion that there is no free lunch. The author thinks companies that wish to survive will have to figure out how to offer their wares for free or to contend with those competitors that do so, citing free music, free news, free movies, free video games and the gamut of software that makes it possible to do everyday tasks. How many people still go to the airlines office to buy a travel ticket or book a flight? That is not all. Today, unlike in the past, it is virtually free to look for employment, an apartment, friends, roommates, dates, romance and more. People are virtually able to dispense with the stockbroker, tax accountant, travel agents, some lawyers and other persons who charge fees to do their jobs; they have been replaced by software that do them for free! In the years ahead, journalists, more musicians, book publishers and movie makers are expected to follow suit. And the US will be making haste to catch up with places like South Korea, the Netherlands, and the Falklands in broadband provision to its citizens. ISP (Internet Service Providers) will be working hard to incorporate citizens currently out of the broadband range so as to upgrade and boost businesses. The case of the USPS is very painful. Estimates are that the postal service has suffered a drop of ten billion letters in the past twenty years as a result of people turning to new technology in communication. Will the USPS go broke?

Computer use has virtually eclipsed handwriting the way it did the typewriter. Books are slowly being replaced by handheld devices like the kindle which downloads texts for its owner to read at leisure. Gone are the days when students went about with back-breaking backpacks containing all sorts of titles. Totalitarian regimes that specialize in banning books have their jobs cut out for them. Public libraries were once justified as places to make reading affordable for everyone. With new handheld devices pushing books to the back burner, it is feared that new barriers are being created for learning and literature. If paper and digital books could coexist and compete side by side for a while instead of one replacing the other the way TV replaced the radio, automobile replaced the horse, PC the typewriter, perhaps the ordinary citizen can adjust at a slower pace.

However, there is genuine concern that Amazonification of everything is creating uncertainty for world civilization and the future. One of my friends who does not own a cell phone calls the device a nuisance and an electronic jail bracelet especially when his tech-savvy kids snub him for his ignorance of new technology, his inability to download ring tones from a play list of iTunes or to go online, his impatience with Internet Provider or customer service representatives some of whom, he claims, have very lousy accents. His twenty-year-olds accuse him of failing to download his software updates instead of blaming the ISP. A man of the older generation – the old school in popular parlance - with very little patience for new things, he refused the conventional wisdom of learning-as-you-go. Yet some times the solution to our insurmountable problem may be as simple as connecting a cable to the power supply or turning off a device and turning it back on again.

Former Alaska governor, Sarah Palin never ceased to amaze me. From the moment the construction of a certain bridge to nowhere was mooted in her campaign, I knew she was a candidate that would generate quite some fireworks and surprises. The woman who crashed out of the 2008 presidential race and went back to her post in Alaska did not stay long in office before stepping down. She kept people wondering what she had in mind. For most aspirants, the post of governor is the ideal stepping stone to the White House. Sarah Palin lost the 2008 race. Naturally one would have expected her to retain her post and lie in wait for 2012. What was she up to? The wait-and-see game did not last long. Soon the hockey mom from Wasilla was spotted in China addressing hundreds of bankers and investment managers at the Hong Kong Conference Center. Who would be financing her trip to China? With the supposedly mounting legal fees for her impending litigation in connection with ethics charges at home, underwriting such a trip and making enough money to cover her stay out there must have been the underpinning of some heavyweights here at home or out there in China. She spoke to the Chinese about free enterprise, explaining that the current financial crisis was not due to lack of government but rather to government politics. She condemned Beijing's destabilizing military build up and the one thousand Chinese missiles aimed at Taiwan. What will she be telling the Russians?

Had America written off Sarah Palin from the political landscape? Not so fast! She went on a book promotion tour and appeared on the Oprah show next. Her book, *Going Rogue* soared to the top of the best seller list well before it was published. The more I contemplated that enigmatic woman the more she reminded me of something I had come across about the late President John F. Kennedy who, according to political writer Richard Reeves, once described himself as the center of a spoked bicycle wheel, thereby posing a riddle that dogged his many biographers over the years. Kennedy's many identities were each expressible without compromising the others – a vigorous man who was deathly ill and surviving only by the grace of steroids and shooting speed to help him function; a golden child from a golden family and complex sex life; a public intellectual whose books were ghostwritten and so forth. Sarah Palin's many sides are still to be discovered, beginning with the Tea party. Like same-sex marriage, the 1773 Tea Party idea is being rebranded and marketed to the American electorate, no matter how the rest of the nation feels about conventional heterosexual marriage.